PENNSYLVANIA

RACHEL VIGODA

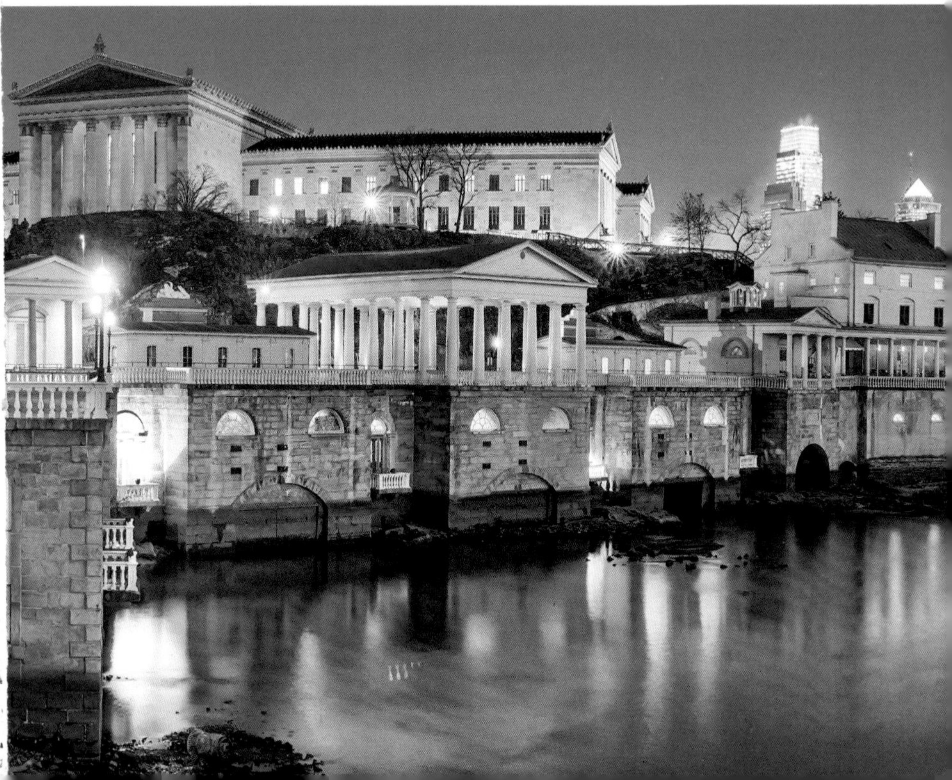

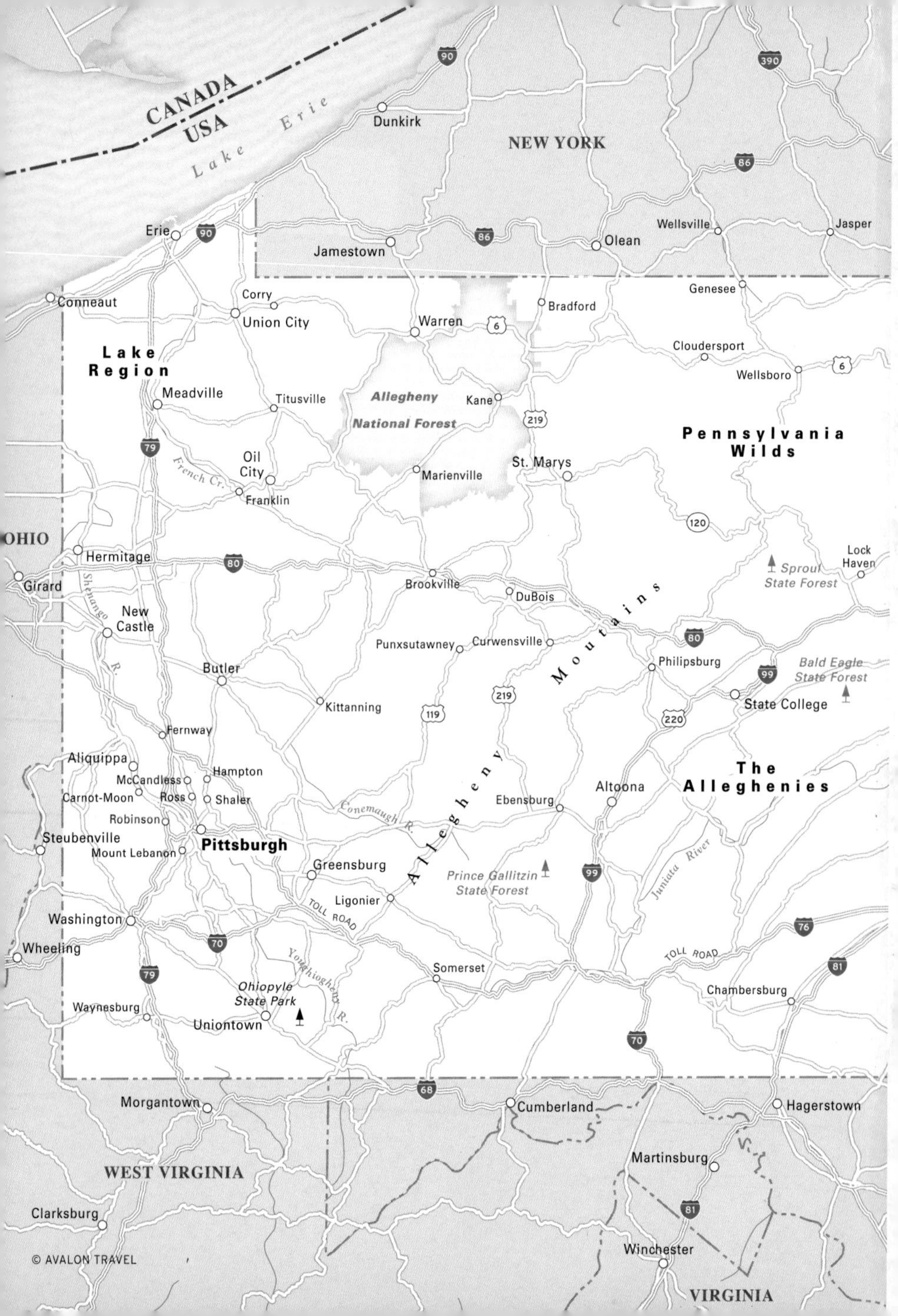
CANADA
USA
Lake Erie
90
390
Dunkirk
NEW YORK
86
Erie
90
Jamestown
86
Olean
Wellsville
Jasper
Conneaut
Corry
Union City
Warren
6
Bradford
Genesee
Cloudersport
Wellsboro
6
Lake Region
Meadville
Titusville
Allegheny National Forest
Kane
219
Pennsylvania Wilds
79
French Cr.
Oil City
Franklin
Marienville
St. Marys
120
OHIO
Hermitage
80
Lock Haven
Sproul State Forest
Girard
Shenango R.
Brookville
DuBois
New Castle
Allegheny Moutains
80
Punxsutawney
Curwensville
Philipsburg
Bald Eagle State Forest
Butler
99
219
State College
Kittanning
119
220
Fernway
Aliquippa
Hampton
McCandless
Carnot-Moon
Ross
Shaler
The Alleghenies
Altoona
Ebensburg
Conemaugh R.
Robinson
Steubenville
Pittsburgh
Mount Lebanon
Juniata River
Greensburg
Prince Gallitzin State Forest
99
Ligonier
TOLL ROAD
Washington
76
70
Wheeling
Youghiogheny R.
TOLL ROAD
81
79
Somerset
Chambersburg
Ohiopyle State Park
Waynesburg
Uniontown
70
68
Morgantown
Cumberland
Hagerstown
Martinsburg
WEST VIRGINIA
81
Clarksburg
© AVALON TRAVEL
Winchester
VIRGINIA

Pennsylvania is a wide expanse of mostly wilderness and farmlands flanked by two cosmopolitan cities. In the southeast corner: Philadelphia, the nation's birthplace and the sixth-largest city in the country. In the southwest corner: Pittsburgh, the former manufacturing powerhouse re-creating itself as a cultural hub. The places in between jockey for distinction: "The Sweetest Place on Earth" (Hershey), the "Factory Tour Capital of the World" (York County), "Antiques Capital USA" (Adamstown), and a borough made famous by a groundhog (Punxsutawney), to name a few.

Pennsylvania is a study in the art of the comeback. As the story goes, a century ago comedian W. C. Fields joked, "Last week I went to Philadelphia, but it was closed." The city today stays open late, thanks to a continually growing population, housing boom, thriving arts scene, and restaurants recognized among the nation's best. Pittsburgh, described by one 19th-century writer as "hell with the lid off," is today acknowledged as one of America's most livable cities. Forests depleted by logging have regrown. Abandoned railroad lines have morphed into multiuse trails. For visitors, too, Pennsylvania is a place of renewal.

It's safe to say that William Penn would be pleased at the shape his land has taken. Welcome.

Clockwise from top left: Roberto Clemente Bridge in Pittsburgh; elk in the Pennsylvania Wilds; Ohiopyle State Park; the Pagoda in Reading.

If there's one thing Pennsylvania's founder insisted on, it's that everyone feel welcome. Centuries before New York's Greenwich Village and San Francisco's Haight-Ashbury district gained fame as centers of counterculture, William Penn's colony was the place where people didn't have to conform. It's thanks to Billy that Pennsylvania is home to the oldest Amish community in the world. Today's visitor can, in less than 90 minutes, go from one of the largest cities in the country to a place where horse-drawn buggies share the road. "Something for everyone" may be the most tired phrase in destination marketing, but Pennsylvania really means it.

The state that goes by "PA" is a magnet for history buffs, art enthusiasts, and nature lovers. It's where the nation's founders came up with "life, liberty, and the pursuit of happiness." It's where President Abraham Lincoln delivered the timeless speech that began: "Four score and seven years ago our fathers brought forth on this continent a new nation." Pennsylvania is where Andy Warhol first touched a drawing pencil and where Andrew Wyeth painted his whole life. It's where you'll find the only U.S. museum dedicated to hiking and the largest herd of free-roaming elk in the Northeast.

Clockwise from top left: National Aviary in Pittsburgh; Independence Hall in Philadelphia; apple harvest; Pennsylvania State Capitol in Harrisburg; Gettysburg National Military Park; the Liberty Bell in Philadelphia.

DISCOVER

Pennsylvania

Contents

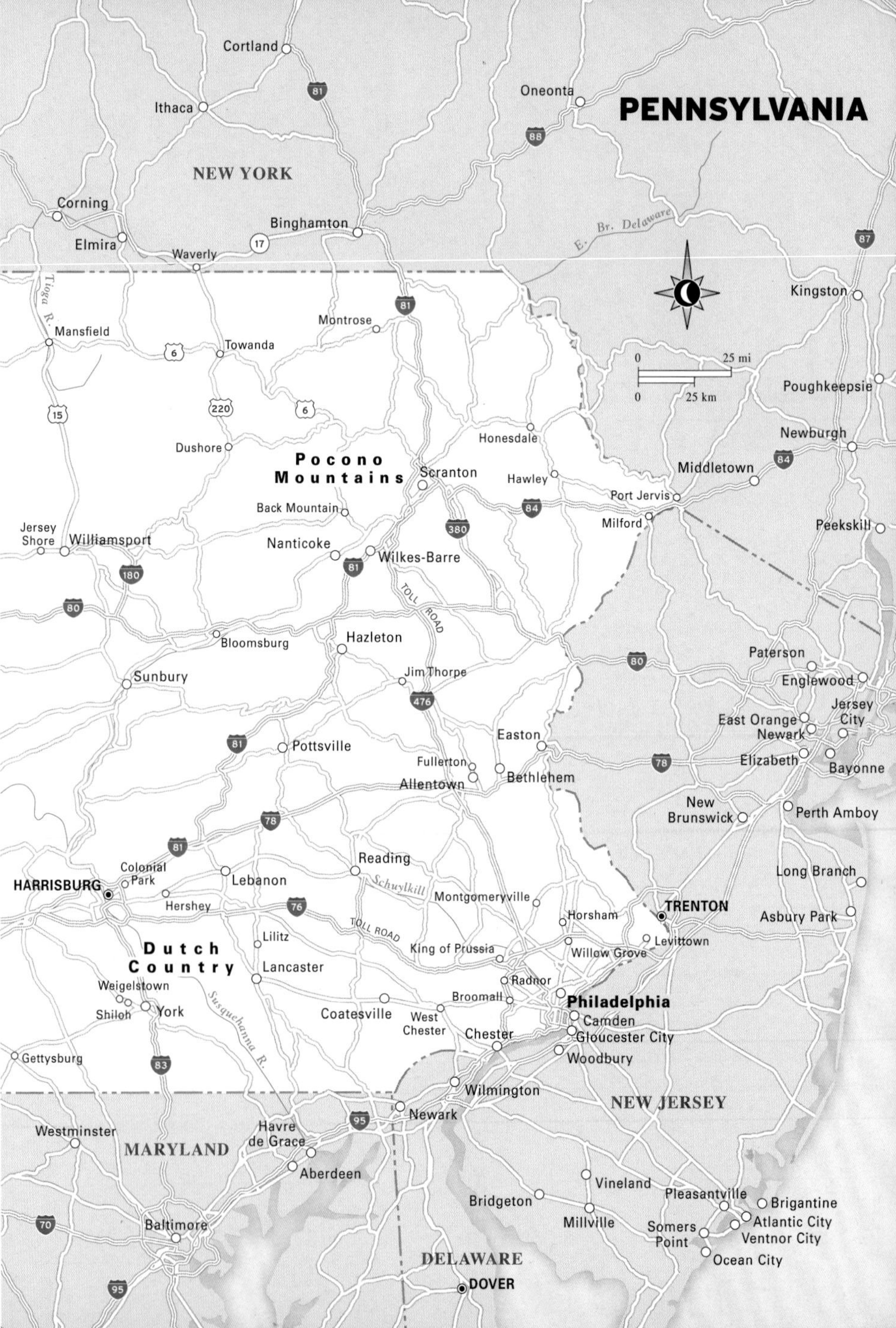
PENNSYLVANIA
NEW YORK
Cortland
Ithaca
Oneonta
Corning
Elmira
Binghamton
Waverly
E. Br. Delaware
Kingston
Tioga R.
Mansfield
Towanda
Montrose
0
25 mi
0
25 km
Poughkeepsie
Newburgh
Honesdale
Dushore
Pocono Mountains
Scranton
Hawley
Middletown
Port Jervis
Milford
Back Mountain
Peekskill
Jersey Shore
Williamsport
Nanticoke
Wilkes-Barre
TOLL ROAD
Bloomsburg
Hazleton
Paterson
Sunbury
Jim Thorpe
Englewood
Jersey City
East Orange
Newark
Easton
Pottsville
Elizabeth
Bayonne
Fullerton
Allentown
Bethlehem
New Brunswick
Perth Amboy
Colonial Park
Reading
Long Branch
HARRISBURG
Lebanon
Schuylkill
Montgomeryville
Hershey
TRENTON
Asbury Park
Horsham
Lilitz
Levittown
Dutch Country
King of Prussia
Willow Grove
Lancaster
Radnor
Weigelstown
Broomall
Philadelphia
Shiloh
York
Coatesville
West Chester
Camden
Susquehanna R.
Chester
Gloucester City
Gettysburg
Woodbury
Wilmington
NEW JERSEY
Newark
Westminster
Havre de Grace
MARYLAND
Aberdeen
Vineland
Bridgeton
Pleasantville
Brigantine
Millville
Atlantic City
Somers Point
Ventnor City
Baltimore
Ocean City
DELAWARE
DOVER
81
88
87
17
81
6
6
220
15
84
84
380
180
81
80
80
476
81
78
78
81
76
83
95
70
95

THE PAGODA
CITY OF READING

Planning Your Trip

Where to Go

Philadelphia

The state's largest city is rich in **historical and cultural attractions.** A thorough exploration of **Independence National Historical Park** is a better primer on the founding of this nation than any textbook, and the city's **art museums** are too numerous to see in a day. Known for **cheesesteaks** and **rabid sports fans,** the City of Brotherly Love has reached new heights of hipness in recent years, with galleries and eateries sprouting in the unlikeliest places. Idyllic towns such as **Kennett Square** and **New Hope** lure Philadelphians past the city limits.

Pennsylvania Dutch Country

With its **Germanic heritage,** fabled cuisine (pass the shoofly pie), and large **Amish** population, this region ranks as Pennsylvania's most unique. **Gettysburg,** site of the Civil War's bloodiest battle, reels in school groups and history buffs, while **Hershey** defends its title as "The Sweetest Place on Earth."

Pocono Mountains

Pennsylvania's **winter sports** capital holds just as much appeal during the warmer months, thanks to its **rivers, lakes, waterfalls,** and **trails.** Let's not forget its many **resorts**. Though most are geared toward families, the champagne glass whirlpool is alive and well in the Poconos.

Pittsburgh

Once known as the Smoky City, the Burgh has risen from the ashes to become a **cultural hotbed.** This sports-loving town also boasts the world's largest single-artist museum and the

a view of downtown Pittsburgh

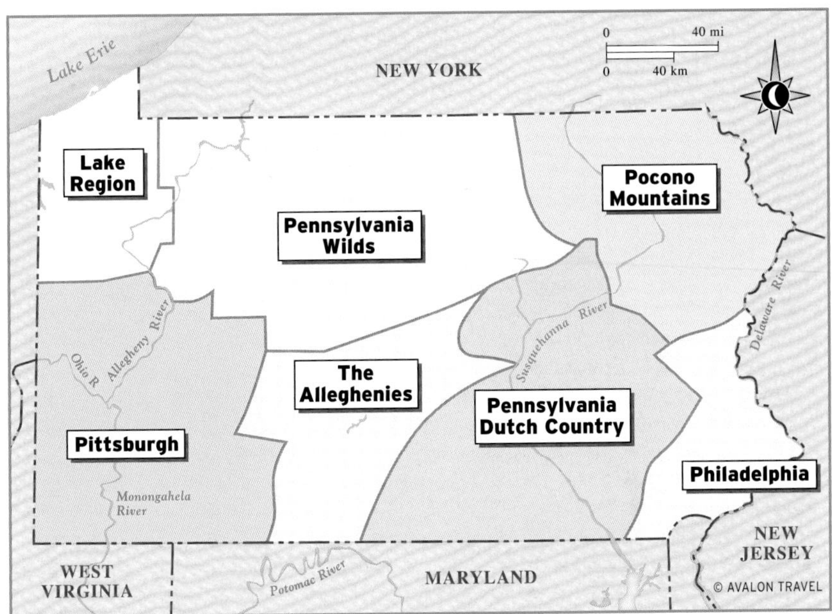

state's largest history museum. **Fallingwater,** the renowned work of architecture, is one of many reasons to explore its surrounds.

The Alleghenies

Rail fans flock to this mountainous region to drink in the famous **Horseshoe Curve** and walk through the nation's **first railroad tunnel.** Motorcyclists flood the so-called **Flood City** in June, and **football fever** strikes State College in the fall.

Lake Region

Pennsylvania's northwest corner shines in the summer months, when **Erie's natural harbor** teems with pleasure boats and the sandy beaches of **Presque Isle** are open for business. Families pack swim gear and stale bread for their pilgrimage to **Pymatuning Lake,** where fish and waterfowl compete for crumbs.

Pennsylvania Wilds

Home to the largest herd of **free-roaming elk** in the Northeast, a national forest, and the so-called **Grand Canyon of Pennsylvania,** this nature lover's wonderland is also home to a major celebrity: **Punxsutawney Phil.**

When to Go

Like the rest of the northeastern United States, Pennsylvania experiences **all four seasons.** There's no best or worst time to visit because the state has plenty to offer year-round, but some areas are better at certain times than others.

Summer is the season to take advantage of Pennsylvania's lakes: Loll on the beaches of Presque Isle, feed the ducks at Pymatuning, pilot a houseboat around Raystown Lake, or zoom across Lake Wallenpaupack. It's also a great time to visit Hershey, where a chocolate empire has given rise to an amusement park and zoo, among other family-friendly attractions.

It's not called Pennsylvania, as in "Penn's woods," for nothing. This is a tree-blanketed state, which makes **fall** a fabulous time to visit. Head to the northern half of the state—the Pocono Mountains, Allegheny National Forest, or Pine Creek Gorge—for landscapes ablaze in color. While you're there, be sure to visit Benezette, the epicenter of Pennsylvania elk country. September and October are when the elk get frisky, and their mating calls are sounds you won't soon forget.

Speaking of wildlife, fall is the best time to visit Hawk Mountain Sanctuary, which lies in the flight path of thousands of migrating raptors. It's also the season to cruise the farmlands of Pennsylvania, stopping to pick apples, stomp grapes, and take a hayride. If possible, head to Lancaster County, where Amish farmers rely on horsepower of the four-legged variety to work their fields.

Ah, **winter.** Love it or hate it, the season of snow and ice brings unique opportunities. Pennsylvania's top snow sports destinations are in opposite corners of the state: the Pocono Mountains in the northeast and the Laurel Highlands in the southwest. In early February, head to Punxsutawney to join the Groundhog Day hubbub.

Rainfall and melting snow and ice make **spring** ideal for hitting the rivers. Lehigh Gorge State Park in the Poconos and Ohiopyle State Park in the Laurel Highlands are popular for whitewater rafting and kayaking. Spring is also a swell time to visit the state's largest city, Philadelphia, which gets crowded in summer—though the Fourth of July celebrations are worth navigating the crowds.

The Best of Pennsylvania

Pennsylvania is a large state, and few visitors set out to see east, west, north, and south in one go. But you can hit many of the highlights in a week, provided you have a car and a copy of *Moon Pennsylvania* (but of course). The following itinerary assumes travel during the warmer months, when the bulk of attractions are open and the roads are more inviting.

Philadelphia

DAY 1

It only makes sense to begin in the nation's birthplace: Philadelphia. Pick up a timed ticket to **Independence Hall** at the Independence Visitor Center, loading up on maps and brochures while you're at it. Make your way to the **Liberty Bell,** and if there's still time before your Independence Hall tour, stroll down the oldest residential street in the country, **Elfreth's Alley,** or throw a penny onto Ben Franklin's grave at **Christ Church Burial Ground** (it's for good luck). After your tour, try a Supreme Court robe on for size at the **National Constitution Center.** Come sundown, head to the neon-lit, Cheez Whiz-stained intersection of 9th Street and Passyunk Avenue in South Philly, home to rival cheesesteakeries **Pat's King of Steaks** and **Geno's Steaks.**

DAY 2

Do some time at **Eastern State Penitentiary** before sprinting up the so-called **Rocky steps** and getting lost in the period rooms of the stunning **Philadelphia Museum of Art.** Then take a stroll along the picturesque Benjamin Franklin Parkway and visit your pick of museums: the **Barnes Foundation** or **Rodin Museum** for more art, or the **Franklin Institute** science museum or the **Academy of Natural Sciences.** Finally, treat your culturally enriched self to a show on the **Avenue of the Arts.**

DAY 3

Get on I-95 south for the 30-mile ride to the **Brandywine River Museum of Art,** home to

Philadelphia Museum of Art

works by three generations of Wyeths. Down the road you'll find **Chaddsford Winery,** one of Pennsylvania's largest makers of grown-up grape juice, and the stunning **Longwood Gardens,** which deserves a full afternoon. Spend the night in a B&B.

EXCURSION TO THE POCONOS

The **Pocono Mountains** are known as a ski destination, but with miles of river to kayak and trails to hike or bike, there's plenty to do on a warm summer day. From Philadelphia, pack a bathing suit and drive two hours north to the southern end of the **Delaware Water Gap National Recreation Area.** After a day tubing on the Delaware River and taking in the views at **Bushkill Falls,** pitch a tent or head to a relaxing B&B in **Shawnee on Delaware.**

Another option: Get your fill of outdoor adventure at **Lehigh Gorge State Park,** about an hour and 45 minutes northwest of Philadelphia, and stay overnight in the picturesque town of **Jim Thorpe.**

Pennsylvania Dutch Country

DAY 4

Factor in 45 minutes for the drive west to Intercourse (go ahead, snigger away), one of several Lancaster County burgs with an eyebrow-raising name. Taste your way through **Kitchen Kettle Village,** then keep going west less than two miles on Route 340 to **Plain & Fancy Farm,** where you can learn all about Amish life. After a **buggy ride** through the Amish countryside, shop your heart out at the Rockvale and Tanger **outlet malls.** Eateries close early in these parts, so come dinnertime hustle to a **smorgasbord** restaurant to eat your weight in Pennsylvania Dutch food.

DAY 5

Head west 90 minutes on Route 30 to **Gettysburg,** site of the Civil War's bloodiest battle. Take your pick of battlefield tours—horseback and Segway are two ways to go—and don't leave Gettysburg National Military Park without seeing the **cyclorama** in the visitors center. For dinner, indulge in colonial-style chow at the **Dobbin House Tavern.**

Longwood Gardens

Amish buggy in Lancaster County

Pittsburgh

DAY 6

Get an early start. Today's destination—three hours west of Gettysburg—is the **Laurel Highlands,** home to Frank Lloyd Wright's **Fallingwater** (be sure to reserve your ticket in advance). Detour on your way to the architectural masterpiece to pay your respects to victims of the 9/11 attacks at the **Flight 93 National Memorial.** From Fallingwater, drive 90 minutes on Route 381 north and I-76 west to Pittsburgh, where you'll spend the night.

DAY 7

Start your day in Pittsburgh with a visit to the **Andy Warhol Museum,** then head to the **Mattress Factory** for more jaw-dropping art or the **National Aviary** for something to tweet about. Spend the afternoon in the Oakland neighborhood, where you'll have to choose between the **Carnegie Museums of Art** and **Natural History** and **Phipps Conservatory and Botanical Gardens.** After dinner it's straight to the **South Side** to ascend Mount Washington via the **Duquesne Incline** for spectacular nighttime views.

EXCURSION TO THE LAKE REGION

Leave the steel and glass of Pittsburgh behind for a **beach vacation.** Head north on I-79 for two hours to **Presque Isle State Park,** a sandy peninsula jutting out into Lake Erie. Orient yourself at the **Tom Ridge Environmental Center** before hitting the beach or joining a **boat tour.** Spend the night in the city of **Erie.**

Start the next day by exploring the **Erie Maritime Museum and Flagship *Niagara*.** In the afternoon, taste the local vintages at one of several area **wineries.**

Outdoor Adventure

Pennsylvania is packed with mountains, forests, lakes, and rivers, so you never have to look far for outdoor adventure. The state parks alone number 121, and there's no fee for entry. Not sure where to start? Here are some ideas:

SKIING AND SNOWBOARDING

- With seven major ski areas, the **Pocono Mountains** are a popular destination for skiing, snowboarding, and tubing.
- The **Laurel Highlands** region is home to Pennsylvania's largest ski resort, Seven Springs.

HIKING

- Twenty-one waterfalls along a 7.2-mile trail? No wonder **Ricketts Glen State Park** is one of northeast Pennsylvania's main attractions. The tallest falls is an impressive 94 feet.
- Hikers are rewarded with an up-close view of migrating hawks, eagles, and falcons at **Hawk Mountain Sanctuary.** The refuge for birds of prey features eight miles of trails; the notable North Lookout is just one mile in.
- Pennsylvania is home to 230 miles of the famed **Appalachian Trail,** which passes through 14 states, and the **Appalachian Trail Museum.** The nation's first museum dedicated to hiking is located near the midpoint of the 2,180-mile footpath.
- Climb **Mount Nittany** for a bird's-eye view of Penn State, which borrowed the mountain's name for its mascot, the Nittany Lion.
- With trees as old as 450 years, **Cook Forest State Park** will have you craning your neck. Choose from 47 miles of trails.

Pocono Mountains

ON THE WATER

- Beloved by canoeists for its 40 miles of calm river, **Delaware Water Gap National Recreation Area** is one of the 10 most visited sites in the national park system.
- **Ohiopyle State Park** features the most popular section of white water east of the Mississippi. Guides are available for less experienced paddlers.
- You can rent a houseboat—complete with hot tub—at **Raystown Lake,** the largest lake entirely within Pennsylvania.
- **Presque Isle,** a peninsula jutting into Lake Erie, offers ocean-style beaches, vistas, and activities, including surfing, windsurfing, kayaking, paddleboarding, and scuba diving.

Weekend Getaways

You don't have to hit up your boss for vacation time to get to know Pennsylvania. Seeing it bit by bit is a good way to go. Here are some two-day itineraries to get you started.

From Philadelphia

While walking and public transportation are the easiest ways to get around Philly, you'll need a car for the following escapes.

BRANDYWINE VALLEY

Wake up early and drive to **Nemours Mansion & Gardens,** 30 miles southwest of Philly in Wilmington, Delaware, in time for the first tour of the day. (Reservations are strongly recommended. If you're traveling January-April, when the magnificent French-style estate is closed to the public, head to nearby **Winterthur Museum & Country Estate** instead.) After your tour, cross back into Pennsylvania and have lunch at **Talula's Table** in historic **Kennett Square,** the "Mushroom Capital of the World." Devote the afternoon to the horticultural wonderland that is **Longwood Gardens.**

The next day, visit the **Brandywine River Museum of Art,** home to a remarkable collection of works by three generations of Wyeths. If you're there April-November, take advantage of the opportunity to tour **Kuerner Farm,** which inspired nearly 1,000 works by Andrew Wyeth, one of the most celebrated artists of the 20th century. Treat yourself to a tasting at **Chaddsford Winery** before returning to the big city.

BUCKS COUNTY

Drive to Doylestown, 25 miles north of Philly, to marvel at the **Mercer Museum** and **Fonthill,** concrete castles built by one incorrigible collector. Then follow Route 202 north to **New Hope** (10 miles), stopping to browse the specialty shops of **Peddler's Village** along the way. After checking into a B&B in the New Hope area, head to **Marsha Brown** for New Orleans-style fine dining. (It's not a bad idea to book a table in advance.)

Devote the next day to exploring the boutiques and galleries of New Hope and its across-the-Delaware neighbor, **Lambertville, New Jersey.** To return to Philly, take NJ-29 South to I-95 South.

AMISH COUNTRY

Drive to the **Strasburg Rail Road,** about 60 miles west of Philly, to ride a steam train through Amish farmlands. Enjoy a light lunch, a decadent dessert, and a view of the horse-and-buggy traffic through Strasburg's main intersection at the **Strasburg Country Store & Creamery.** Then make your way to Intercourse (9 miles) via Route 896 north and Route 340 east to sample the likes of pepper jam and chow-chow at **Kitchen Kettle Village.** Check out some **quilt shops** before checking into **AmishView Inn & Suites,** midway between Intercourse and Bird-in-Hand on Route 340. For dinner, pig out at **Shady Maple Smorgasbord** (11 miles).

Devote the next day to the **Plain & Fancy Farm** complex, learning about the Amish way of life and clip-clopping through the countryside with **Aaron and Jessica's Buggy Rides.**

From Pittsburgh

Pittsburgh's surroundings are particularly appealing to outdoorsy types, and the following itineraries are weather dependent.

MORAINE AND MCCONNELLS MILL

In the heat of summer, pack the makings of a cookout, drive 40 miles north to **Moraine State Park,** rent a pontoon boat and gas grill, and while away the day on **Lake Arthur.**

After a night under the stars at **Bear Run Campground,** hit the trails of **McConnells Mill State Park** (5 miles) before heading back to the Burgh.

WRIGHT AWAY

Drive to fabulous **Fallingwater,** 60 miles southeast of Pittsburgh, and learn how much over budget architect Frank Lloyd Wright went—and how much the house leaks. In the afternoon, tour **Kentuck Knob,** one of his lesser-known creations, taking time to explore the sculpture-studded grounds. (Reservations are recommended for both Wright houses.) Rough it at a tent site in **Ohiopyle State Park** or do the opposite at **Nemacolin Woodlands Resort.**

In the morning, rent a bike in Ohiopyle and pedal part of the **Great Allegheny Passage** before finding your way to the moving **Flight 93 National Memorial** (45 miles).

COOK FOREST

Drive to **Cook Forest State Park,** 90 miles north of Pittsburgh, to size up the towering pines and hemlocks of the "Forest Cathedral." Spend the night at **Gateway Lodge** and paddle the **Clarion River** in the morning.

Ready, Aim, Fire!

A great deal of blood was shed in Pennsylvania during the 18th and 19th centuries, and military history buffs have been drawn here ever since. Because war-related sites tend to be clustered, you can see a lot in just two days.

Revolutionary War

DAY 1

Start the morning at the **Museum of the American Revolution** in Philadelphia for a crash course on the quest to end British rule in America.

Next, visit the historic sites you just learned about at **Independence National Historical Park,** where on July 4, 1776, representatives of the 13 colonies adopted the Declaration of Independence. Don't miss the **Liberty Bell.**

If you have time left, pay your respects to the Revolutionary War's fallen at the **Tomb of the Unknown Soldier** or pop by the **Betsy Ross**

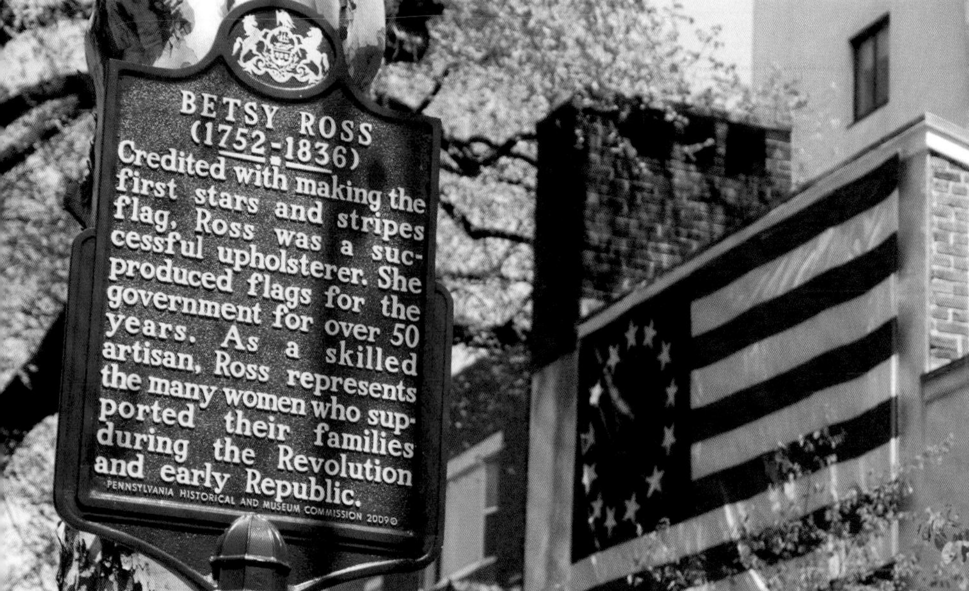

Betsy Ross House in Philadelphia

Best for Kids

Hersheypark

These weekend excursions are designed for summertime, when kids are out of school and amusement parks are open.

HERSHEY

Day 1

The so-called Sweetest Place on Earth is packed with attractions, so go easy on day 1 to avoid burnout. Start at **The Hershey Story,** which tells the story of Milton Hershey and his eponymous chocolate company and town. Children as young as four can experiment in the museum's Chocolate Lab.

Then head to **Hershey's Chocolate World,** where singing cows (of the animatronic breed) lend insights into the field-to-factory process of making chocolate. Treat yourself—and the kids, of course—to a chocolate milk shake before you leave.

In the late afternoon, stroll through the **Hershey Gardens,** which has a popular butterfly exhibit, and the **Hotel Hershey,** home to a sweets shop known for its cupcakes. Spend the night at the more affordable **Hershey Lodge,** which offers such activities as poolside movies and family bingo.

Day 2

Romp through **Hersheypark.**

LANCASTER COUNTY

Day 1

Spend the day at **Dutch Wonderland,** being sure to catch a high-dive show. Bed down at the adjacent **Old Mill Stream Campground** or at **Verdant View Farm B&B,** where the kids can give milking a go in the morning.

Day 2

Hop aboard the historic **Strasburg Rail Road,** disembarking at Groff's Grove for the Amazing Maize Maze and other activities at **Cherry Crest Adventure Farm.** Just don't miss the last train back—you still have to get to **Hershey Farm Restaurant** to try the whoopie pies.

PHILADELPHIA AND BUCKS COUNTY

Day 1

Head to Fairmount Park in Philadelphia, home to the **Philadelphia Zoo** and the **Please Touch Museum.** After a morning with the lions, tigers, and bears, bring younger kids to the museum for an afternoon of exploring. Older kids will have more fun riding the carousel and playing Philadelphia-themed mini golf at **Franklin Square** in the Historic District. Spend the night in the city.

Day 2

Wake up ready to tackle **Sesame Place,** a theme park best suited to kids still young enough to idolize Elmo. Bring swimsuits.

House before quaffing a beer based on Ben Franklin's fave recipe at **City Tavern.**

DAY 2

You'll need another early start today. Drive 35 miles north to **Washington Crossing Historic Park,** commemorating the site from which General George Washington and his men crossed the Delaware River on Christmas night 1776.

Leave plenty of daylight for **Valley Forge National Historical Park,** where Washington's army suffered through the winter of 1777-1778.

If you don't mind the cold, consider planning your trip around the annual reenactment of the Delaware crossing, held on Christmas Day.

Civil War

DAY 1

Devote today to **Gettysburg National Military Park,** site of the bloodiest battle between North and South. If time permits, visit the **Shriver House Museum** to learn about the civilian experience.

Come evening, tiptoe around town with a lantern-toting guide on a **Ghosts of Gettysburg** tour.

DAY 2

Stock up on souvenirs at the **Gettysburg Heritage Center** before heading north on Route 15 to Harrisburg to pay a visit to the singular **National Civil War Museum.**

If you don't mind crowds, consider visiting Gettysburg during the annual reenactment of the July 1-3 battle.

Philadelphia

Look for ★ to find recommended sights, activities, dining, and lodging.

HIGHLIGHTS

★ **Independence Hall:** It's here that the Founding Fathers debated and drafted the Declaration of Independence and later the Constitution. Timed tickets go fast during peak tourist periods (page 27).

★ **National Constitution Center:** Learn about the nation's supreme law and pose with life-size statues of its framers at this expansive museum (page 29).

★ **Museum of the American Revolution:** A new addition to the Historic District highlights the nation's founding with hundreds of authentic artifacts, including George Washington's wartime tent (page 30).

★ **Barnes Foundation:** This renowned art collection encompasses works by Renoir, Cézanne, van Gogh, and other Impressionist and Postimpressionist masters (page 38).

★ **Philadelphia Museum of Art:** The nation's third-largest art museum is home to more than 240,000 objects. Don't forget to sprint up the "Rocky steps" (page 39).

★ **Eastern State Penitentiary:** Opened in 1829, this sprawling prison served as a model for hundreds around the world, horrified Charles Dickens, and hosted Al "Scarface" Capone. It's a tourist attraction now, but it hasn't lost its eerie edge (page 40).

★ **City Hall:** Philadelphia's elaborately adorned seat of government is the largest municipal building in the country. The view from its observation deck is tops (page 42).

★ **Masonic Temple:** The mother ship of Pennsylvania Masonry offers a smorgasbord of architectural styles under one roof (page 44).

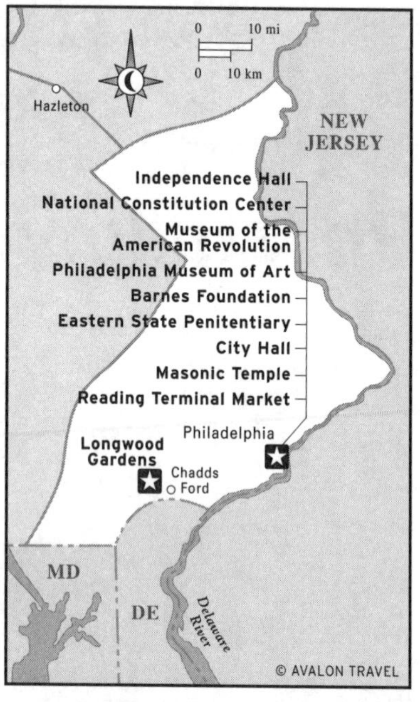

★ **Reading Terminal Market:** In business since 1893, this indoor farmers market is a great place to grab lunch and people-watch (page 46).

★ **Longwood Gardens:** This Brandywine Valley treasure, open year-round, is one of the nation's premier horticultural attractions (page 86).

Pennsylvania's largest city hardly needs introducing. It's where the Founding Fathers wrote the Declaration of Independence and the U.S. Constitution, and where Ben Franklin came up with so many bright ideas.

Philadelphia tells a vivid story of the fight for freedom from British rule: at Independence Hall, where the Founding Fathers made so many important decisions; at Valley Forge, where Washington and his troops spent the winter of 1777-1778 after Philadelphia fell to the British; at the National Constitution Center, which tells the story of the nation's supreme law; and at dozens of other historic sites and museums.

Philly is also an arts town, home to the nation's third-largest art museum, more Auguste Rodin sculptures than any place outside of Paris, an astounding number of outdoor murals and sculptures, and theaters both historic and thoroughly modern. It's a sports town, too, with teams in four major leagues (baseball, basketball, hockey, and football). And it's a food town. The cheesesteak may be its most famous dish, but Philadelphia is increasingly recognized for its profusion of innovative chefs.

Several areas around the city are also worthy of a visit. To its west is the Brandywine Valley, home to stunning Longwood Gardens and former estates of the wealthy du Pont clan. To its north is Bucks County, known for its concrete castles and boutique shopping.

PLANNING YOUR TIME

While it would take four or more full days of sightseeing to experience all of Philly's historic sites, it's possible to hit the highlights in one day. First order of business: Get a timed ticket for Independence Hall at the Independence Visitor Center.

Many of Philadelphia's art and science museums line the Benjamin Franklin Parkway, close to the Schuylkill, so visiting two or even three in one day isn't out of the question. After museum hours, soak in the scenery, boathouses, and sculptures along Kelly Drive. If you're traveling with children, set aside a day

Previous: the Barnes Foundation; Philadelphia Museum of Art. **Above:** Ben Franklin statue in The Franklin Institute.

Philadelphia

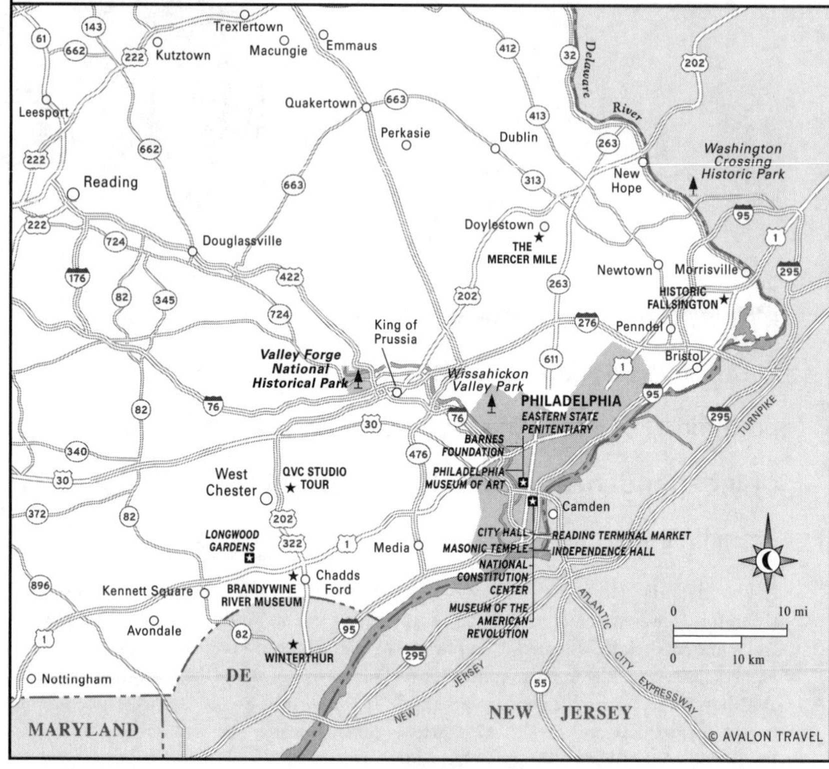

to explore the Philadelphia Zoo, across the Schuylkill.

Brandywine Valley and Bucks County can each be explored in a long weekend.

Budget Tips

Philadelphia is rich in historical and cultural attractions, some of which can be enjoyed at little or no cost. Admission to Independence Hall and the Liberty Bell Center, two major tourist draws, doesn't cost a cent. You can stroll down the nation's oldest residential street, Elfreth's Alley, for free, and, for $5, see where Betsy Ross sewed flags.

If you're an art lover on a tight budget, you're going to love this city. It's home to more than 3,600 murals and, according to the Smithsonian Institution, more outdoor sculptures than any other U.S. city. And while guided tours of the city can cost a pretty penny, an all-day pass to ride the Phlash—a purple road trolley that stops at 22 key locations—is just $5.

ORIENTATION

William Penn designed Philadelphia as a rectangular grid set between two rivers: the Delaware in the east and the Schuylkill in the west. Though the city has expanded far beyond this rectangle, most tourist attractions lie within it. The area is compact—roughly 25 blocks from river to river—and easy to navigate by foot. Most historic sites are concentrated near the Delaware.

Sights

If you plan on seeing several pricy attractions, consider investing in a CityPass or Philadelphia Pass. A **CityPass** (888/330-5008, www.citypass.com/philadelphia, $55 per person, children 2-12 $35) is a booklet of tickets good for admission to four attractions and 24 hours of hop-on, hop-off privileges with Philadelphia Trolley Works and the Big Bus Company. It's valid for nine days and cuts the cost of all that sightseeing by almost half. A **Philadelphia Pass** (877/714-1999, www.philadelphiapass.com, adults $59-103.20, children 4-12 $49-95.20) is a smart card good for admission to about 40 attractions in and around the city. The price varies based on how long it's valid: One-day, two-day, three-day, and five-day passes are available, and the more attractions you hit, the more you save. One of the best things about both passes is you get to skip the line at some attractions. They're to Philadelphia sightseeing what first-class tickets are to air travel.

HISTORIC DISTRICT

The section of Philadelphia now known as the Historic District was, for a while, the center of America. It's here that delegates from the American colonies debated and adopted the U.S. Declaration of Independence, a silver-tongued "see ya" to Great Britain, in 1776, and where the U.S. Constitution was approved in 1787. The young nation's leaders met here from 1790 to 1800 while Washington DC was taking shape. Quite a few of the buildings where the Founding Fathers conducted their business, clinked glasses, or crawled into bed are still standing, which is why the area is called "America's most historic square mile." Millions of people visit each year to walk in the founders' footsteps.

Walking is, in fact, the best way to experience the compact Historic District, which comprises two neighborhoods adjacent to the Delaware River: Old City and, moving south, Society Hill. Beyond the historic sites, Old City is also peppered with galleries and boutiques, and there's no better time to visit them than the first Friday of the month, when many stay open as late as 9pm as part of **First Fridays in Old City** (215/625-9200, www.oldcitydistrict.org). Society Hill was home to many politicians and power brokers during Philadelphia's tenure as the nation's capital but eventually went to pot. In the 1950s the city undertook a revitalization of the area, acquiring colonial houses and selling them to people on the condition that they be restored. Today it's one of the wealthiest—and most picturesque—neighborhoods in Philly.

Many of the Historic District's major attractions are part of **Independence National Historical Park** (215/965-2305, www.nps.gov/inde), and admission to most park sites is free. Guided tours are a great way to experience historic Philadelphia, but if you're visiting during summer and short on cash, look for teak benches marked "Once Upon a Nation." From Memorial Day through Labor Day, they're staffed by "storytellers" who dispense information about the area and America's birth for free.

It's best to start your visit at the **Independence Visitor Center** (6th and Market Sts., 800/537-7676, www.phlvisitorcenter.com, 8:30am-7pm daily June-Aug., 8:30am-6pm daily Sept.-May), a large modern building between the Liberty Bell Center and the National Constitution Center, two can't-miss sights. As the official visitors center for Philadelphia and its environs, it's stocked with maps and brochures, plus knowledgeable staffers. Exhibits and free films help the orientation process. Tickets for a variety of tours and area attractions are sold here. If you're visiting March-December and plan to tour Independence Hall—and you should—you'll need a free **timed-entrance ticket.** Day-of tickets are distributed at the Visitor

Historic District

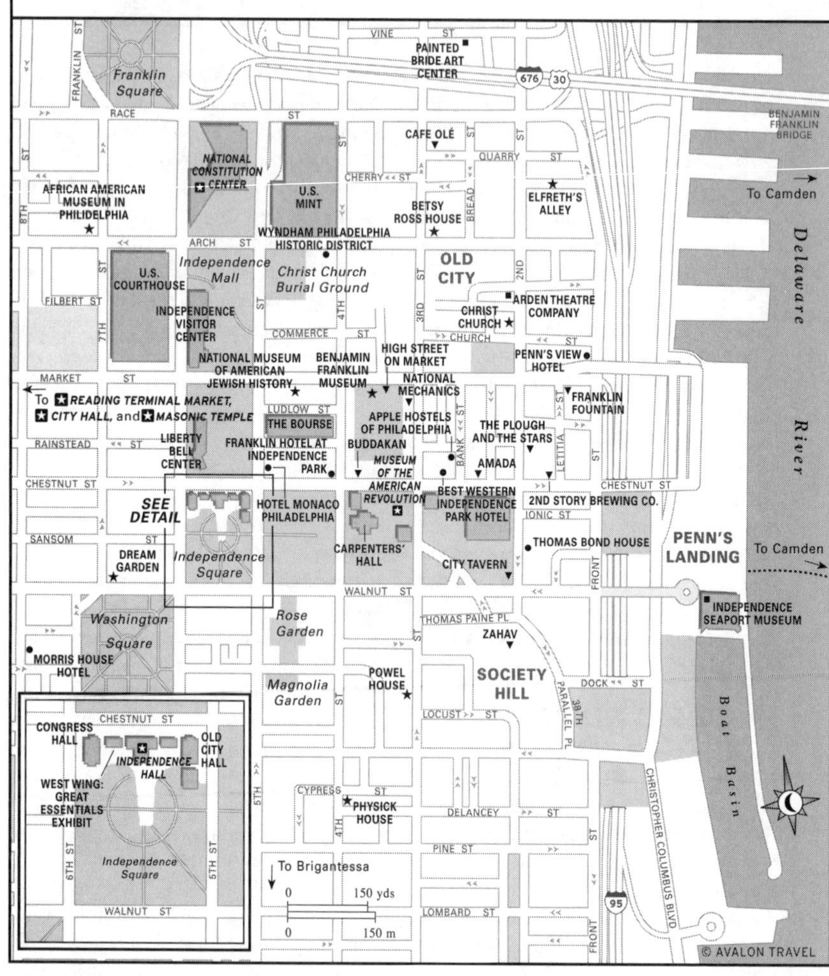

Center. It's not unusual for tickets to be gone by 1pm during peak tourist periods (summer and holidays). Reserve tickets by phone or online (877/444-6777, www.recreation.gov, $1.50 per ticket surcharge). Tickets aren't required to tour Independence Hall in January or February.

Liberty Bell Center

The much-photographed Liberty Bell is an international icon of escape from oppression. How it came to symbolize freedom is the subject of exhibits in its home since 2003, the **Liberty Bell Center** (Market St. between 5th and 6th Sts., 215/965-2305, www.nps.gov/inde, hours vary by season, generally 9am-5pm daily, free).

Its history begins in 1751, when the Pennsylvania Assembly ordered a new bell for the State House (now Independence Hall) from a London foundry. The splurge was in honor of the 50th anniversary of the

Pennsylvania Charter of Privileges, which codified William Penn's ideals of religious toleration and political rights. The speaker of the assembly chose an apt Bible quotation to be inscribed on the bell: "Proclaim liberty throughout all the land unto all the inhabitants thereof." No sooner was it hung than the bell cracked. Two local craftsmen, John Pass and John Stow, were tasked with melting and recasting it.

The bell was rung to call lawmakers together, to summon the citizenry for announcements, and to mark important occasions. It's often said that the bell tolled for the first public reading of the Declaration of Independence in 1776, but historians discount that story because the State House steeple was in shabby condition at the time.

Eventually the bell suffered a thin crack, which was purposely widened to keep the edges from vibrating against each other. When the bell tolled in celebration of the late George Washington's birthday in February 1846, the crack expanded.

By then the bell had achieved iconic status, thanks to abolitionists who had adopted it as a symbol of their cause. After the Civil War, the bell traveled the country, serving as a reminder of days when Americans were united in their quest for independence. Pass and Stow's 2,080-pound bell came home to Philadelphia in 1915, but a replica forged that year was used to promote women's suffrage. It appeared in different cities with its clapper chained to its side, a metaphor for the silencing of women, and was finally rung when women won the right to vote in 1920. To this day, oppressed groups evoke the image of the Liberty Bell. The bell itself is displayed at the southern end of the building, where Independence Hall serves as backdrop.

★ Independence Hall

Within the walls of **Independence Hall** (Chestnut St. between 5th and 6th Sts., 215/965-2305, www.nps.gov/inde, hours vary by season, generally 9am-5pm daily, free tours, timed ticket required Mar.-Dec.), the Founding Fathers debated and drafted the Declaration of Independence and later the Constitution. George Washington himself presided over the Constitutional Convention, and the mahogany armchair in which he sat is among the furnishings on display today.

There's no charge for tours of Independence Hall, but tickets are required March through December. Day-of tickets are available at **Independence Visitor Center** (6th and

Independence Visitor Center

Rose Garden, Magnolia Garden, and *Dream Garden*

There are plenty of ways to kill time while waiting for a tour of Independence Hall. The Historic District is packed with museums and other attractions. But if you only have half an hour or so, head to the **Rose Garden,** centerpiece of a landscaped area between Locust and Walnut Streets and 4th and 5th Streets. Planted by the Daughters of the American Revolution in honor of the men who penned the Declaration of Independence, the garden features around 90 rose varieties. Most flower only once a year, peaking in June. The cobblestone-paved entrance to the garden was once the courtyard of a stable. If you still have time, cross Locust Street to admire the smaller **Magnolia Garden,** a tribute to the nation's founders by the Garden Club of America. The 13 hybrid magnolias around its walled perimeter represent the original colonies. They bloom in early spring.

In the colder months, you can pass the time gazing at the ***Dream Garden*** (Curtis Center, Walnut and 6th Sts.), a dazzling glass mosaic in the lobby of a somber 19th-century office building. Measuring 15 feet high and 49 feet wide, the leafy landscape was designed by Philadelphia-born artist Maxfield Parrish and executed by stained glass guru Louis Comfort Tiffany in 1916. It's made of more than 100,000 pieces of Favrile glass in 260 colors.

Market Sts., 800/537-7676, www.phlvisitorcenter.com, 8:30am-7pm daily June-Aug., 8:30am-6pm daily Sept.-May). It's a good idea to get there early; it's not unusual for tickets to be gone by 1pm during peak tourist periods (summer and holidays). Reserve tickets by phone or online (877/444-6777, www.recreation.gov, $1.50 per ticket surcharge).

Independence Hall was built as the State House while Pennsylvania was still a British colony. Construction began in 1732 and continued for two decades. The legislature began meeting in the Assembly Room long before the ambitious building project was completed. (Even unfinished, the State House was a more dignified meeting place than private homes and taverns.) When tensions between American colonists and Great Britain erupted into war in 1775, the Second Continental Congress began meeting in the

Independence Hall

Assembly Room. Composed of delegates from the 13 colonies, including Benjamin Franklin and Thomas Jefferson, the Congress made one history-making decision after another in that room: It appointed Washington as commander in chief of the Continental Army (1775), adopted the Declaration of Independence (July 4, 1776), and settled on the design of the American flag (1777).

In September 1777 the Congress fled to York, Pennsylvania, as British forces occupied Philadelphia. During the occupation, which lasted until the following summer, the State House served as a hospital, prison, and barracks. There was much remodeling after Washington's troops regained control of the city and the Congress returned. In 1783, as the Revolutionary War drew to a close, the nation's governing body relocated from Philly. Pennsylvania's legislature reoccupied its chamber, only to surrender it to the framers of the Constitution in May 1787. The nation's supreme law was signed on September 17, and the State House reverted to its intended use until 1799, when the Pennsylvania capital was moved to Lancaster.

The building saw many alterations and uses in the 19th century. At one point it housed a museum of natural history. At another, its basement served as the city's dog pound. Since the creation of Independence National Historical Park in 1948, it has been returned to its late-18th-century appearance. Tours start in the East Wing, attached to the main building by a colonnade. Be sure to visit the West Wing, which is not part of the tour. It's home to the **Great Essentials Exhibit** (9am-5pm daily, free), which displays surviving copies of the Declaration of Independence, Articles of Confederation (the nation's first constitution), and the Constitution. There's also a silver inkstand said to have been used during the signing of the Declaration and Constitution.

Flanking Independence Hall are two park sites worth a quick peek. Constructed in the 1780s as the county courthouse, **Congress Hall** (Chestnut and 6th Sts., hours vary by season, free) is so named because the newly formed U.S. Congress met there during Philadelphia's 1790-1800 tenure as the nation's capital. Almost all the chairs on the second floor, which was occupied by the Senate, are authentic. Note the "spitting boxes" near the fireplaces. **Old City Hall** (Chestnut and 5th Sts., hours vary by season, free), so named because it was built as Philadelphia's second city hall, was home to the U.S. Supreme Court from its completion in 1791 to 1800, when the federal government moved to Washington DC.

★ National Constitution Center

The first museum dedicated to the U.S. Constitution, the **National Constitution Center** (525 Arch St., 215/409-6600, www.constitutioncenter.org, 9:30am-5pm Mon.-Sat., noon-5pm Sun., adults $14.50, seniors and students $13, children 6-18 $11, children 5 and under free) opened on July 4, 2003. It's one of the flashier sights in town. The visitor experience begins with *Freedom Rising*, a multimedia presentation in a star-shaped theater with a 360-degree screen. It's a stirring introduction to the Constitution's main themes. Anyone interested in the nitty-gritty can spend the better part of a day at the museum, which presents the story of the nation's supreme law through more than 100 exhibits. But an hour or two is enough to hit the highlights, including Signers' Hall, featuring selfie-worthy life-size bronze statues of the 39 men who signed the Constitution—and of 3 dissenters who did not.

Be sure to check the calendar of events, available on the museum's website, because the Constitution Center regularly hosts prominent lawmakers, scholars, and authors. In March 2008, then-Senator Barack Obama was there to deliver his seminal speech on race ("I am the son of a black man from Kenya and a white woman from Kansas . . ."). Hillary Clinton was awarded the Liberty Medal in a ceremony at the Constitution Center in 2013.

The building's glass-enclosed Delegates'

Café is a good place to fuel up for more sightseeing.

Carpenters' Hall

Independence Hall was the meeting place of the Second Continental Congress, the esteemed assemblage responsible for the Declaration of Independence. Nearby **Carpenters' Hall** (Chestnut St. between 3rd and 4th Sts., 215/925-0167, www.carpentershall.org, 10am-4pm Wed.-Sun. Jan.-Feb., 10am-4pm Tues.-Sun. Mar.-Dec., free) hosted the First Continental Congress, which convened in the fall of 1774 to coordinate resistance to a series of heavy-handed laws imposed by Britain. Composed of delegates from 12 of the 13 colonies, the Congress organized a boycott of British goods, petitioned King George III to redress colonists' grievances, and resolved that a second Congress would meet if the monarch turned a deaf ear.

Among the exhibits in Carpenters' Hall is a room furnished as it might have been in 1774. You'll also find a parade float built to celebrate ratification of the Constitution, a banner carried in the parade, a remarkably detailed model illustrating the hall's construction, and early carpentry tools.

The Georgian-style gem was constructed from 1770 to 1774 as a meeting hall for the Carpenters' Company, a trade guild whose members built much of colonial Philadelphia. The list of tenants includes the nation's first lending library and the American Philosophical Society, both founded by Benjamin Franklin. In 1798 the hall was leased to the Bank of Pennsylvania and later that year became the target of America's first bank robbery.

★ Museum of the American Revolution

The abundant sites in the Historic District are tied together at the **Museum of the American Revolution** (101 S. 3rd St., 215/253-6731, www.amrevmuseum.org, 9:30am-6pm daily Memorial Day-Labor Day, 10am-5pm daily Labor Day-Memorial Day, adults $19, students $17, children 6-17 $12, children 5 and under free), which opened in 2017. The museum's extensive collection paints a picture of the lead-up to the American Revolution, what life was like during the Revolutionary War and afterward, and how that's relevant today.

Along with several hundred artifacts, there are life-size tableaus, video projections, and interactive installations spread out

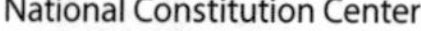
National Constitution Center

over four chronological sections that put the historical objects in context. In *The Road to Independence,* gaze up at a towering replica of Boston's Liberty Tree, where the first dissenters gathered to discuss what to do about the British. In *The Darkest Hour,* step inside the Battlefield Theater, where the sounds of battle play while the floor shakes and the smell of gunpowder fills the air. Kids can climb aboard the deck of a re-created 18th-century privateer ship, while grown-ups read letters written by soldiers and Founding Fathers.

A highlight of the impressive collection is George Washington's wartime tent, which served as the general's office and sleeping quarters during the Revolutionary War. There's a lot to see, but don't worry about packing it all into one visit: Tickets are good for two consecutive days. The on-site **Cross Keys Café** (8am-4pm daily) harkens back to the colonial era, with snapper soup and a Martha Washington-inspired chocolate cake, along with salads and sandwiches. Tickets are not required to access the café.

National Museum of American Jewish History

A striking five-story building on Independence Mall houses the **National Museum of American Jewish History** (101 S. Independence Mall E., 215/923-3811, www.nmajh.org, 10am-5pm Wed.-Fri., 10am-5:30pm Sat.-Sun., aduts $15, seniors, students, and youth 13-21 $13, children 12 and under free). The museum was originally founded in 1976 by members of the Mikveh Israel congregation, established in 1740. It moved into its current home in 2010. The collection—the largest of its kind—is unusual in that it focuses on the history and contributions of Jews in America. The first floor exhibit highlighting famous Jewish Americans, including Steven Spielberg and Albert Einstein (who became an American citizen in 1940), is always free to enter. Check the website for details on concerts, lectures, and special exhibitions, which often center on music, art, or photography. Hour-long tours included with the ticket price are usually offered at 11:30am and 2:30pm. Ask at the admissions desk to join a tour. Buy tickets online to receive a $1 discount off admission.

Franklin Square

Visitors needing a break from the hands-on history lesson that is the Historic District can head to **Franklin Square** (6th and Race Sts., 215/629-4026, www.historicphiladelphia.

Museum of the American Revolution

org, 6am-9pm daily), a kid-friendly park with a playground, an old-fashioned carousel ($3, free for children under 2), and a Philadelphia-themed mini-golf course ($7-9). On the 18th hole, players putt through a crack in the Liberty Bell. Closing hours for the attractions vary, but they're open daily at 10am from March through December.

If you're hungry, **SquareBurger** (11:30am-park closing) has hot dogs and burgers, including a veggie version, plus root beer floats and the Cake Shake: a milk shake made with vanilla ice cream, caramel sauce, and Tastykake Butterscotch Krimpets.

Franklin Square is one of five squares included in William Penn's original plan for the city. Initially known as Northeast Square, it served as a cattle pasture, burial ground, and military drill site before the city reclaimed it as a park in 1837, erecting an elegant marble fountain.

Benjamin Franklin Museum

Author and printer, politician and diplomat, scientist and inventor, Benjamin Franklin (1706-1790) gets a lot of respect in his adopted hometown of Philadelphia. A river-spanning bridge, a public square, a science museum, a scenic boulevard, and even an ice cream shop bear the name of the Boston-born Renaissance man, whose formal schooling ended when he was a preteen. Philadelphia is also home to the only museum in the world dedicated to Franklin's life and times. The **Benjamin Franklin Museum** (Franklin Ct., entrances on Market and Chestnut Sts., between 3rd and 4th Sts., 215/965-2305, www.nps.gov/inde, 9am-5pm daily, adults $5, children 4-16 $2), designed to appeal to both kids and adults, covers topics as wide-ranging as the armonica, a musical instrument Franklin invented, to his stance on slavery.

The museum is underground, beneath the site of Franklin's home during the last few years of his life. His three-story house is long gone, but it's represented by a steel "ghost structure" erected in 1976 in celebration of the nation's bicentennial. Franklin Court, as the site is called, also features the only active post office in the country that doesn't fly an American flag—because there wasn't one when Franklin became the first Postmaster General of the United States in 1775.

Franklin's death at age 84 was mourned throughout America and France. An estimated 20,000 people gathered for his funeral at **Christ Church Burial Ground** (Arch St. between 4th and 5th Sts., 215/922-1695, www.christchurchphila.org, 10am-4pm Mon.-Sat., noon-4pm Sun. Mar.-Nov., adults $2, children $1, guided tour adults $7, children $3), which is a short walk from Franklin Court and worth a visit. Established in 1719, the graveyard is peppered with 1,400 markers. Franklin is one of five Declaration of Independence signers interred here, along with a host of other colonial- and Revolutionary-era bigwigs. Some visitors believe that tossing a penny on to Franklin's gravestone brings good luck.

Betsy Ross House

Betsy Ross is famous for sewing the nation's first flag. Whether or not she actually did has long been a matter of debate. Witness the measured wording on the historical marker near the **Betsy Ross House** (239 Arch St., 215/629-4026, www.historicphiladelphia.org, 10am-5pm daily mid-Mar.-Nov., adults $5, seniors, students, and children $4, audio tour additional $2): "Credited with making the first stars and stripes flag, Ross was a successful upholsterer." And there's no debating that Ross was a gutsy patriot who produced flags for the government for half a century.

It doesn't take long to explore the little circa-1740 house, which is furnished with period antiques and some reproductions. Several items that belonged to the thrice-widowed tradeswoman are on display. The highlight of the museum is its first-floor upholstery shop, where an actress portraying Betsy welcomes visitors as if they were potential customers.

Elfreth's Alley

Touted as the nation's oldest residential street, **Elfreth's Alley** (off 2nd St., between Arch and Race Sts., www.elfrethsalley.org) makes for a charming stroll. The 30-some houses that line it were built between the 1720s and 1830s and have been so meticulously restored that the block feels like a movie set.

Like the cobblestone street itself, the houses are tiny by today's standards. In the 18th and early 19th centuries, Elfreth's Alley was the address of artisans and craftsmen, many of whom conducted business out of their homes. Immigrants from Germany, Ireland, and other parts of Europe took over the neighborhood in the 19th century. By the start of the Great Depression, it had become a blighted block. Its present prettiness—and very existence—owes much to the Elfreth's Alley Association, founded in the 1930s to rescue buildings from the wrecking ball. The organization operates the **Elfreth's Alley Museum** (Houses 124 and 126, 215/574-0560, noon-5pm Fri.-Sun. Apr.-mid-June and mid-Aug.-Dec., noon-5pm Tues.-Sun. mid-June-mid-Aug., adults $5, children 12 and under $2, private tours available by appointment), which focuses on the lives of working people. It's located in the only two houses open to the public; most of the others are private homes. Many residents throw open their doors during two annual fund-raisers for preservation programs: **Fete Day,** a celebration of colonial history usually held on the first or second Saturday in June, and **Deck the Alley** in early December. Private tours of the museum can also be arranged year-round.

African American Museum in Philadelphia

Founded in 1976, less than a decade after the assassination of Martin Luther King Jr., the **African American Museum in Philadelphia** (701 Arch St., 215/574-0380, www.aampmuseum.org, 10am-5pm Thurs.-Sat., noon-5pm Sun., adults $14, seniors, students, and children 4-12 $10) was the first institution of its kind to be funded by a major city. Its collection of art and artifacts documents the history and culture of the African diaspora. The Smithsonian affiliate's core exhibition has a high-tech twist: *Audacious Freedom: African Americans in Philadelphia 1776-1876* brings unsung heroes to life by way of video projections. When approached by a visitor, each trailblazer shares insight into life during the time period. A wide range of rotating exhibits covering art, photography, literature, film, current events, and history give museum visitors a reason to keep coming back.

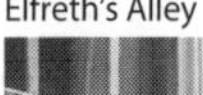

Elfreth's Alley

Take a Tour

As one of America's largest and most historic cities, Philadelphia has no shortage of tour operators. Choosing one is a matter of preference—and budget. Would you rather walk or cover more ground by bike, bus, or other vehicle? Are you hungry for history, scenery, or a good cheesesteak? Here are some tour options worth considering.

GET THE LAY OF THE LAND

As cities go, Philadelphia is supremely walkable. But the quickest way to get a feel for its main attractions is to hop on a tourist bus. **Philadelphia Trolley Works** (215/389-8687, www.phillytour.com, daily year-round, 24-hour pass adults $30, seniors $28, children 4-12 $10) offers sightseeing tours 363 days a year, weather permitting. The company operates road trolleys and double-decker buses (marked The Big Bus Company), and tickets are good for both vehicle types. They depart from the northeast corner of 5th and Market Streets in Old City, but you can hop on or off at any of their 21 stops, including Chinatown, City Hall, Eastern State Penitentiary, the Philadelphia Museum of Art, the Philadelphia Zoo, and Penn's Landing. Tickets can be purchased on board, online, at the Independence Visitor Center, and at many hotel concierge desks. Philadelphia Trolley Works offers a variety of other tours, including a **Philly by Night** bus tour. Check the website for details.

In the warmer months, Segway and bike tours are a fun way to get to know Philly. **Philly By Segway** (215/280-3746, www.phillytourhub.com, daily year-round) offers several Segway tours, including a two-hour cheesesteak tour ($85) complete with tastings. You must be at least 12 years old and weight 100-300 pounds to ride a Segway. **Philadelphia Bike Tours** (215/514-3124, www.philadelphiabiketour.com, year-round) offers three-hour river-to-river tours ($68) as well as customized tours for groups of four or more. If you prefer to explore on your own, you can have a bike, helmet, and lock delivered to your hotel ($57/day).

GET EDUCATED (AND MAYBE A LITTLE TIPSY)

A walking tour in the Historic District is a great way to learn about Philadelphia's role in American history. The 75-minute **Constitutional Walking Tour** (215/525-1776, www.theconstitutional.com, daily Apr.-Nov., adults $19, children 3-12 $12.50) stops at more than 20 sites in and around Independence National Historical Park, including the Betsy Ross House, Franklin Court, and Christ Church Burial Ground. Tours meet outside the main entrance to the National Constitution Center

Physick and Powel Houses

The narrow houses along Elfreth's Alley reflect the lifestyles of early Philadelphia's blue-collar citizens. To see how the other half lived, head south to Society Hill, where two elegant 18th-century town houses are open for **tours** (on the hour, 11am-3pm Thurs.-Sat., noon-3pm Sun. Apr.-Nov., 11am-3pm Sat., noon-3pm Sun. Mar. and Dec.). The Physick and Powel Houses, as they're known, are rented for special events, so call ahead to avoid crashing a party.

Built in 1765, the **Powel House** (244 S. 3rd St., 215/627-0364, www.philalandmarks.org, adults $8, students and seniors $6) was home to Samuel Powel, Philadelphia's last mayor under British rule and first mayor after the creation of the United States. He purchased the Georgian-style brick mansion in 1769, where he and his wife, Elizabeth, entertained frequently, welcoming the likes of George and Martha Washington, John Adams, and Benjamin Franklin. A thank-you note from the nation's first president is on display. The house museum's collection also includes a lock of Washington's hair and wood from his coffin.

The 1786 **Physick House** (321 S. 4th St., 215/925-7866, www.philalandmarks.org, adults $8, students and seniors $6) is named

(525 Arch St.). If you prefer to go at your own pace, you can download the **Constitutional Audio Tour** ($14.99).

In the summer months, volunteers for the nonprofit **Friends of Independence National Historical Park** (215/861-4971, www.friendsofindependence.org) lead free **Twilight Tours** (6pm daily mid-June-Labor Day) of the park. The tours begin at the Independence Visitor Center and last about an hour.

Historic Philadelphia Inc. (Historic Philadelphia Center, 6th and Chestnut Sts., 215/629-4026, www.historicphiladelphia.org), which operates the Betsy Ross House and other attractions in the Historic District, offers two unusual evening tours. On the **Tippler's Tour** (Thurs. Apr.-Jan., adults $50, seniors and students $45), participants visit four watering holes, where they enjoy drinks and snacks while learning about 18th-century taverns and drinking traditions. Prepare to be carded when purchasing tickets for the two-hour tour. **Independence After Hours** (select days May-Oct., adults $85, seniors and students $80, children 12 and under $55) features a three-course dinner at the famed City Tavern and an exclusive opportunity to visit Independence Hall after it's closed to the public. Actors playing a variety of 18th-century Philadelphians enhance the experience. The tour lasts about 2.5 hours and reservations are recommended.

GET SPOOKED

Philadelphia may be as haunted as it is historic, with ghosts said to inhabit Independence Hall and other Historic District sites. Created by the company behind the Constitutional Walking Tour, the **Spirits of '76 Ghost Tour** (215/525-1776, www.spiritsof76.com, nightly July-Aug. and Oct., select nights Apr.-June, Sept., and Nov., adults $19, children 3-12 $12.50) visits more than 20 sites, from paranormal hot spots to filming locations used in *The Sixth Sense* and other thrillers. The 75-minute walking tour departs from 4th and Chestnut Streets. Those who prefer to go it alone can download the **Spirits of '76 Ghost Tour Audio Adventure** ($17.50).

Ghost Tour of Philadelphia (215/413-1997, www.ghosttour.com), the city's original and much-heralded ghost tour operator, offers a few options, including a year-round **Candlelight Walking Tour** (nightly Mar.-Oct., select nights Nov.-Feb., adults $17, children 4-12 $10). The **Ghosts of the Mansion Tour** (select days, $22) includes a look inside the historic Physick House or Powel House, both said to be haunted. Electromagnetic field meters are provided for ghost-detection, and it's spooky enough that children under 13 aren't allowed. Both tours last 75-90 minutes and begin at Signers Garden at 5th and Chestnut Streets.

for Dr. Philip Syng Physick, often referred to as the "father of American surgery." Physick was one of the few doctors who remained in Philadelphia during the yellow fever epidemic of 1793, which killed several thousand people (including Samuel Powel). He moved into the 32-room house in 1815 and lived there until his death in 1837. It's notable as the only free-standing Federal-style town house remaining in Society Hill and for its unusually large city garden. Inside, you'll find excellent examples of neoclassic furnishings. The second floor serves as a museum devoted to Physick's medical career. The doctor invented a number of surgical instruments and techniques. He also created America's first carbonated beverage, which he used to treat patients with gastric disorders.

Penn's Landing and Camden Waterfront

There's plenty to see and do in the waterfront section known as Penn's Landing and across the river in Camden, New Jersey.

A mecca for maritime history buffs, Penn's Landing is home to the **Independence Seaport Museum** (211 S. Columbus Blvd. and Walnut St., 215/413-8655, www.phillyseaport.org, 10am-5pm daily, adults $16, seniors, students, and children $12) and several storied ships. The museum covers everything from the science of buoyancy to the immigrant experience to the history of undersea exploration. A boatload of interactive exhibits makes it fun for kids. They can crawl through a full-size replica of a 19th-century boat used to fish for shad. The 22-foot skiff was built in the museum's boatbuilding and restoration shop, Workshop on the Water, which offers occasional classes.

Admission includes tours of two former U.S. Navy vessels docked beside the museum. The ***Becuna,*** a 307-foot submarine launched in 1944, prowled the Pacific Ocean for Japanese ships during World War II, eavesdropped on Soviet submarines in the Atlantic during the Cold War, and served in the Korean and Vietnam Wars before she was decommissioned in 1969. Launched in 1892, the ***Olympia*** made a name for herself during the Spanish-American War. She's the sole surviving naval ship of that 1898 conflict and the oldest steel warship afloat in the world.

Penn's Landing is also home to a venerable tall ship. The ***Gazela,*** a wooden barkentine built in Portugal more than a century ago, still sails. When she's not off visiting other ports, you'll find her at the northern end of Penn's Landing, near the Market Street footbridge across I-95. She's lovingly maintained by members of the **Philadelphia Ship Preservation Guild** (215/238-0280, www.gazela.org), who will show you around if you ask nicely. The nonprofit group doesn't charge for tours of *Gazela* or ***Jupiter,*** a 1902 iron tugboat under its care, but donations are always welcome.

You can't hitch a ride on the vintage vessels, but pleasure trips from Penn's Landing are available. The three-deck ***Spirit of Philadelphia*** (401 S. Columbus Blvd., 866/455-3866, www.spiritofphiladelphia.com) cruises the Delaware year-round. With its all-you-can-eat buffets, full-service bars, dance floors, and DJs, the ship offers a taste of the Carnival Cruise life. Tickets range from $37 for a two-hour weekday lunch cruise to upwards of $100 for a dinner cruise on 4th of July weekend.

Another way to get a boat's-eye view of Philadelphia is to hop aboard the **RiverLink Ferry** (215/925-5465, www.riverlinkferry.org, daily Memorial Day-Labor Day, Sat.-Sun. May and Sept., adults $9, seniors and children 3-12 $7, children under 3 free), which shuttles between Penn's Landing and Camden's waterfront. The ferry departs from its terminal near the Seaport Museum every hour on the hour starting at 10am, arriving in New Jersey 12-15 minutes later. It makes its last run from Camden at 5:30pm weekdays and 6:30pm weekends. The RiverLink Ferry also offers specialty cruises.

With a population of roughly 80,000, the city of Camden is quite small relative to Philadelphia. But it has something its neighbor doesn't: an aquarium. The RiverLink Ferry pulls right up to **Adventure Aquarium** (1 Riverside Dr., Camden, 856/365-3300, www.adventureaquarium.com, 10am-5pm daily, adults $28, children 2-12 $21), a watery wonderland complete with 3,000-pound hippos. Tickets are steep, and there's a lot to see, so come at least three hours before closing.

A visit to Camden isn't complete without a tour of the **Battleship *New Jersey*** (100 Clinton St., Camden, 866/877-6262, www.battleshipnewjersey.org, hours vary, daily Mar.-Dec., Sat.-Sun. Feb., adults $22, seniors and children 5-11 $17), one of the biggest battleships ever built. The 45,000-ton behemoth was built in Philadelphia and launched in 1942, a year to the date after the Japanese attack on Pearl Harbor. *New Jersey* racked up so many service stars over the next five decades that she's considered America's most decorated battleship.

PARKWAY MUSEUM DISTRICT AND FAIRMOUNT PARK

Examine a Philadelphia map and you can't help but think: *One of these things is not like the others.* Per William Penn's 17th-century plan, Philly is a city of parallel lines and right angles. Bucking the trend—daring to be diagonal—is the Benjamin Franklin Parkway. Penn was long dead by the time construction of the mile-long Parkway began in 1917. Designed by landscape architect Jacques Gréber and inspired by the Champs-Élysées in his hometown of Paris, the road starts near City Hall, carves a circle through Logan Square, and ends at the magnificent Philadelphia Museum of Art, known simply as the Art Museum. Trees, sculptures, and flags representing some 90 nations line the grand boulevard. (Looking for a particular flag? With a few exceptions, they're hung alphabetically.) Like Center City's Avenue of the Arts, the Parkway is a cultural mecca. In addition to the Art Museum, it's home to the nation's oldest natural history museum, a splendid science museum, the largest collection of Auguste Rodin sculptures outside Paris, and the Barnes Foundation, renowned for its extensive holdings of works by the likes of Picasso, Matisse, Cézanne, and Renoir.

At roughly 4,200 acres, Fairmount Park is one of the largest municipal parks in the country. (For comparison's sake, New York's Central Park covers an area of 843 acres.) It stretches north from the Philadelphia Museum of Art, hugging both sides of the Schuylkill River. The portion east of the river is sometimes called East Fairmount Park and the portion west of it is—you guessed it—West Fairmount Park. Winding through East Fairmount Park is the spectacularly scenic Kelly Drive, named for a former city councilman, Olympic rower, and brother of actress-turned-princess Grace Kelly. There are so many statues along Kelly Drive that it's better experienced by foot or bicycle than by car. West Fairmount Park is home to the nation's oldest zoo, the city's children's museum, and its premier outdoor concert venue, the Mann Center for the Performing Arts.

Academy of Natural Sciences

Founded in 1812, the **Academy of Natural Sciences** (1900 Benjamin Franklin Pkwy., 215/299-1000, www.ansp.org, 10am-4:30pm Mon.-Fri., 10am-5pm Sat.-Sun., adults $18-20, seniors and students $15-17, children 3-12 $14-16) is the oldest natural history museum in the Western Hemisphere. As in most natural history museums, visitors spend a good deal of time looking at dead things. Critters from around the world strike permanent poses in 37 dioramas, most of which were created in the 1920s and '30s, before television brought the animal kingdom into people's living rooms. The skeletal remains of prehistoric beasts fill Dinosaur Hall. But living, breathing beings also have a place in this museum. Its Live Animal Center is home to more than 100 birds, reptiles, amphibians, and other animals, all of which are injured or were born in captivity and wouldn't make it in the wild. The academy also boasts a live butterfly exhibit.

The Franklin Institute

It's no surprise that Philadelphia's science museum is named for favorite son Ben Franklin, whose 18th-century discoveries are still remembered. Founded in 1824, **The Franklin Institute** (222 N. 20th St., 215/448-1200, www.fi.edu, 9:30am-5pm daily, adults $20, children 3-11 $16, additional charges for IMAX and Franklin theaters) became a venue for showcasing new technologies. In 1893 Nikola Tesla demonstrated the principle of wireless telegraphy at the institute. The first public demonstration of an all-electronic television system took place there in 1934, the same year the institute moved to its current home and opened to the public. A 20-foot-high marble statue of a seated Ben Franklin dominates its dramatic rotunda, which was modeled after Rome's Pantheon. The Founding Father's presence is also felt in an exhibit devoted to electricity, which features an electronic version of his book *Experiments and Observations on Electricity,* along with a dance floor that generates power as visitors bust a move. The museum's bioscience exhibit, with its giant walk-through model of a human heart, is a perennial favorite. (The two-story heart would fit nicely inside a 220-foot-tall person.) If you're the queasy sort, steer clear of the exhibit's full-size re-creation of a surgery room, where the "patient" is forever undergoing open-heart surgery. The aviation exhibit offers would-be pilots a chance to climb into a flight simulator and pull maneuvers like a 360-degree roll.

The museum has four theaters: a digital projection planetarium, an IMAX dome theater, a venue for live experiments and other science demonstrations, and the Franklin Theater, which specializes in 3-D films. Museum admission includes one planetarium show.

★ Barnes Foundation

The **Barnes Foundation** (2025 Benjamin Franklin Pkwy., 215/278-7000, www.barnesfoundation.org, 10am-5pm Wed.-Mon., adults $25, seniors $23, students and children 6-18 $10) is a familiar name in the art world. Founded in the 1920s by pharmaceutical magnate Albert C. Barnes, the legendary collection of Impressionist, Postimpressionist, and early Modern paintings includes more than 180 works by Pierre-Auguste Renoir, 67 by Paul Cézanne, and 59 by Henri Matisse, all arranged in an eccentric—and fascinating—configuration. In 2012, after a decade of legal wrangling, the masterpieces were moved from the suburban gallery Barnes built for them to a $150 million building on the Parkway. The exterior of the building is postmodern, but inside it's designed to mimic the rooms of original gallery, with the artwork arranged in the exact same way.

The museum hosts a themed First Friday event (first Fri. of the month) from 6pm to 9pm. The admission fee is waived on the first Sunday of the month, but the free tickets are in limited supply and can't be reserved.

Rodin Museum

The **Rodin Museum** (2151 Benjamin Franklin Pkwy., 215/763-8100, www.rodinmuseum.org, 10am-5pm Wed.-Mon., suggested admission adults $10, seniors $8, students and children 13-18 $7, garden entry free) is home to more than 120 works by its namesake sculptor, including a bronze cast of ***The Thinker,*** perhaps the most famous sculpture in the world. You'd have to go to Paris to find a larger collection of the French artist's masterpieces. The museum, which opened its Paris-made gates in 1929, was a gift to the city from movie theater magnate Jules Mastbaum. He began collecting all things Auguste Rodin

the Barnes Foundation

in 1923 and died three years later, just as his museum project was getting underway.

Bring a coat if you're visiting on a chilly day because some sculptures are displayed in the museum's formal gardens and other outdoor spaces. Among them is a bronze cast of the unfinished but incredible ***Gates of Hell,*** which the artist worked on from 1880 until his death in 1917. The museum has a "pay what you wish" admission policy. Take advantage of its free **guided tours,** offered at noon daily.

★ Philadelphia Museum of Art

It's hard to sum up what you'll discover at the **Philadelphia Museum of Art** (2600 Benjamin Franklin Pkwy., 215/763-8100, www.philamuseum.org, 10am-5pm Tues., Thurs., and Sat.-Sun., 10am-8:45pm Wed. and Fri., adults $20, seniors $18, students and children 13-18 $14), which is quite simply one of the preeminent cultural institutions in the country. Since its founding in 1876, the museum has amassed more than 240,000 objects representing 2,000 years of creative expression. It's worth a visit whether your passion is medieval armor, modern sculpture, or the movie character Rocky Balboa (more on that later). Architecture and decorative arts buffs are particularly well served. The museum, which is in itself an architectural gem, contains about 80 period rooms, including entire furnished rooms from historic houses. One can meander through a French cloister, a Chinese palace hall, a Japanese teahouse, and a stone temple straight from India. The nation's third-largest art museum has more than 200 galleries, so if you're dead set on seeing the whole thing, arrive while the neoclassical temple of art is still bathed in morning light. Better yet, come on a Wednesday or Friday, when it stays open until 8:45pm. If money is tight, visit after 5pm on a Wednesday or the first Sunday of the month, when the price of admission is up to you.

Having long outgrown the home built for it in the 1920s, the museum expanded into an art deco landmark across the way in 2007. The **Perelman Building** (2525 Pennsylvania Ave., 10am-5pm Tues.-Sun.) showcases some of the museum's more cutting-edge collections. Admission prices include two consecutive days of access to the main building, the Perelman Building, the Rodin Museum, and two historic houses in Fairmount Park. The museum offers complimentary shuttle service between the main building, the Perelman Building, and the Rodin Museum.

Philadelphia Museum of Art

It's not unusual for people to visit the main building without stepping foot inside. It sits on a granite hill, and the view from its east entranceway is one of the best in the city. Dead ahead is the plaza known as **Eakins Oval,** featuring a statue of a uniformed George Washington astride a horse, and beyond it, City Hall. The broad steps leading to the entrance are as much a tourist attraction as any in town, having appeared in an iconic scene in *Rocky,* the 1976 sleeper hit starring Sylvester Stallone as a fictional Philly boxer who takes on a heavyweight champ. Not everyone has the stamina to sprint up the steps à la Rocky, but almost every first-time visitor has an "Italian Stallion" moment at the top, posing with arms outstretched for a camera-wielding friend. A bronze statue of the movie character, commissioned by Stallone for a scene in *Rocky III,* can be found near the base of the so-called **Rocky steps.**

Al Capone's former cell at Eastern State Penitentiary

★ Eastern State Penitentiary

When **Eastern State Penitentiary** (2027 Fairmount Ave., 215/236-3300, www.easternstate.org, 10am-5pm daily, adults $16, seniors $14, students and children $12) opened in 1829, it was unlike any other prison in the world. For one thing, it was architecturally ingenious, with long cell blocks radiating from a surveillance hub like the spokes of a wheel. In an era when the White House had coal-burning stoves for heat and no running water, Philadelphia's pricey new prison had central heat and flush toilets. Its treatment of inmates was also a radical departure from the norm. Eastern State eschewed corporal punishment, adhering to a Quaker-influenced formula for reforming criminals: strict isolation plus labor. Each prisoner got a private cell complete with skylight. The prison was so serious about curbing interaction that inmates were hooded when it was necessary to move them. Left alone with their thoughts and a Bible, criminals would come to realize the error of their ways and become genuinely penitent—or so thought proponents of the "penitentiary."

Charles Dickens thought otherwise. "I hold this slow and daily tampering with the mysteries of the brain to be immeasurably worse than any torture of the body," he wrote after an 1842 visit. Some 300 prisons around the world emulated Eastern State's design and system of solitary confinement, but detractors like Dickens eventually prevailed. By the time Al "Scarface" Capone was booked into the prison in 1929, inmates lived two or three to a cell, worked alongside each other in the weaving shops and kitchens, exercised together, and ate together.

After 142 years of use, the prison closed in 1971. In 1994 the National Historic Landmark opened to the public. The *Voices of Eastern State* **audio tour** covers everything from intake procedures to escape attempts. It's narrated by actor Steve Buscemi and punctuated with firsthand accounts from former wardens, guards, and inmates. The prison isn't heated, so be sure to bundle up.

On select evenings from mid-September to early November, timed for Halloween thrills, the already eerie site moonlights as ***Terror***

Behind the Walls, one of the biggest and top-ranked haunted attractions in the country. It's truly scary. Ticket prices vary.

Philadelphia Zoo

America's oldest **zoo** (3400 W. Girard Ave., 215/243-1100, www.philadelphiazoo.org, 9:30am-5pm daily Mar.-Oct., 9:30am-4pm daily Nov.-Feb., adults $23, children 2-11 $19) packs a lot into its 42 manicured acres. It's home to more than 1,300 animals representing some 300 species and subspecies: lions, tigers, and bears, of course, but also a host of critters that only an Animal Planet addict would recognize. You won't soon forget the wrinkled mug of naked mole rats in the Rare Animal Conservation Center, the wide-eyed Coquerel's sifakas in the PECO Primate Reserve, or the aquatic acrobatics of the giant river otters in Carnivore Kingdom. Also unforgettable: hovering high above the treetops is the **Channel 6 Zooballoon** (Apr.-Nov. weather permitting, $12 per person, $40 per family of four), the region's only passenger-carrying helium balloon.

The Philadelphia Zoo received its charter in 1859 but didn't open its gates until 1874, after the Civil War. The oldest building on the grounds, **The Solitude,** predates the zoo. It was built in 1784 by John Penn, grandson of Pennsylvania founder William Penn.

Unless you're a zoo member, parking will set you back $16. It is possible to get there via SEPTA, Philly's public transit system, but an easier way to travel between Center City and the zoo is by **Phlash trolley** (800/537-7676, www.ridephillyphlash.com, single ride $2, all-day pass $5, seniors and children 4 and under free), operating May through October. Phlash trolleys (actually buses in disguise) also stop at the nearby Please Touch Museum, where parking for nonmembers is $12.

Please Touch Museum

The **Please Touch Museum** (Memorial Hall, 4231 Ave. of the Republic, 215/581-3181, www.pleasetouchmuseum.org, 9am-5pm Mon.-Sat., 11am-5pm Sun., adults $19, children under 1 free) is the answer to the question of what to do with the kids on a rainy day. Designed for the seven-and-under set, it offers several hours' worth of learning experiences disguised as fun. Kids can race sailboats, take a spin on a hamster wheel, and enter the magical world of *Alice in Wonderland.* On most days, they can also catch an original theater performance by a cast that includes puppets.

The museum has moved several times

Philadelphia Zoo

Mural, Mural on the Wall

With nearly 4,000 murals, Philadelphia has been called the world's largest outdoor art gallery. The colorful, larger-than-life artworks brighten schools, community centers, businesses, and homes from Center City to outlying neighborhoods that most tourists never see.

Philadelphia's **Mural Arts Program** (215/685-0750, www.muralarts.org) traces its roots to the mid-1980s, when the city was plastered with graffiti. Muralist and community activist Jane Golden was hired to redirect the energies of graffitists into mural painting. She still runs the program, which has not only alleviated much of the graffiti problem but also empowered thousands of at-risk youths and contributed to neighborhood revitalization in many parts of the city.

While the works of art speak for themselves, a guided tour is the best way to experience them. The Mural Arts Program offers trolley, walking, and even train tours. Most tours leave from Pennsylvania Academy of the Fine Arts (118-128 N. Broad St.) and last 1.5-2 hours. It's not unusual for tours to sell out, so advance ticket purchase is strongly advised. You can buy tickets through the Mural Arts Program website or by calling 215/925-3633.

Trolley tours (adults from $32, seniors from $30, students and children 3-12 from $28) of various neighborhoods are offered April to November. The **Mural Mile walking tour** ($22), also offered April through November, covers two miles and 15 murals in Center City. The mural program's most unique offering may be its **train tour of *Love Letter*** ($22), a public art project consisting of 50 rooftop murals in West Philadelphia. Participants take in the murals from SEPTA's elevated train and several train platforms. The tour is offered weekends April-December.

Be sure to check the website for a full schedule of tours and special events, as the Mural Arts Program is constantly adding more murals and more ways to experience them.

—Contributed by Karrie Gavin, author of Moon Philadelphia

since opening in 1976. It settled into its current home, West Fairmount Park's historic Memorial Hall, in 2008. Memorial Hall was one of about 200 buildings erected for the 1876 Centennial Exposition, the first World's Fair held in America, and it's the only major one still standing. The beaux-arts-style building served as the city's art museum until the Philadelphia Museum of Art opened in 1928. Please Touch Museum's *Centennial Exploration* exhibit gives kids a taste of the atmosphere at the World's Fair, where inventions including the telephone, the typewriter, and root beer were revealed. Its centerpiece, a 20-by-30-foot scale model of the fairgrounds, was first unveiled in 1889.

CENTER CITY

Center City is Philadelphia's downtown. It's generally regarded as the area between the Delaware and Schuylkill Rivers to the east and west, Vine Street to the north, and South Street to the south—the portion of Philadelphia that once comprised the whole city. At the center of this rectangular area is City Hall. Broad Street, the north-south thoroughfare interrupted by City Hall, divides downtown into Center City East and Center City West. It's between 13th and 15th Streets; there is no 14th Street.

In addition to being a business and governmental center, Center City is a cultural mecca. The portion of Broad Street south of City Hall is known as Avenue of the Arts because it's flanked by concert halls and theaters. The scenic Benjamin Franklin Parkway, which starts near City Hall, is lined with museums.

The Parkway Museum District and the Historic District, the easternmost part of Center City, are described in previous pages. This section deals with sights in the rest of Center City.

★ City Hall

City Hall (Broad and Market Sts., tour office room 121, 215/686-2840, www.phila.gov/virtualch, observation deck access noon-4:15pm Mon.-Fri., guided tour 12:30pm Mon.-Fri.) is

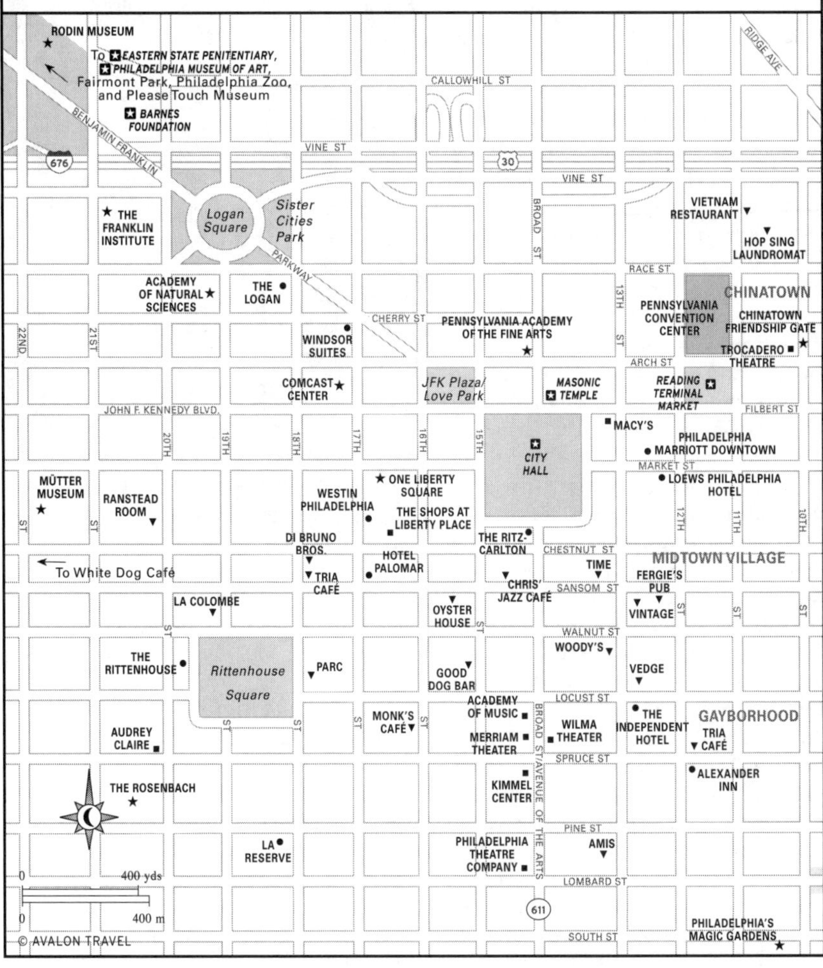

a building of many distinctions. When construction began in 1871, it was to be the tallest building in the world. The project dragged on for so long that by the time it was completed in 1901, the Washington Monument and Eiffel Tower stood higher. Still, City Hall had bragging rights as the tallest *habitable* building in the world—for a few years anyway. At 37 feet, the bronze statue of city founder William Penn that crowns its central tower is the tallest statue atop any building. Long after skyscrapers twice its height dotted the globe, City Hall remained Philadelphia's tallest thanks to a gentleman's agreement that no building would tower over Billy Penn's head. The agreement was broken in the mid-1980s, when One Liberty Place went up, and today City Hall barely makes the top 10. But it's still the world's tallest occupied masonry structure, America's largest (and most expensive) municipal building, and one of the continent's finest examples of Second Empire architecture.

There's plenty to see without stepping foot inside the building, including some 250 sculptures and motifs by Alexander Milne Calder, the Scottish-born son of a tombstone carver and grandfather of the Calder renowned for his sculptural mobiles. He devoted two decades to City Hall's ornamentation. In addition to the colossal Penn statue, Calder's crowning work (literally and figuratively), the central tower is adorned with bronze statues depicting Native American and Swedish settlers. An eagle with a wingspan of 15 feet is perched above each face of the tower's four-faced clock. The many sculptures closer to eye level include representations of continents, various arts and sciences, commerce, agriculture, and justice. Be sure to check out the courtyard's western entrance, though it's the smallest and least ornate of the four. With its carvings of thorns, thistles, and menacing serpents, it's hardly inviting. But Calder knew what he was doing: The portal was used by horse-drawn vans carrying accused criminals.

City Hall isn't nearly as ornate inside as it is outside. Its more lavish spaces are the focus of two-hour **tours** (adults $15, seniors $10, students and children $8, children 3 and under free) that depart from room 121 at 12:30pm weekdays. The tours include an elevator ride to an observation deck below the Penn statue. But you don't have to take the tour to enjoy the panoramic view: The elevator ferries visitors to the observation deck noon-4:15pm weekdays. It only fits four, and the view is fantastic, so it's not unusual for **timed tickets** (adults $8, seniors and students $6, children $4, children 3 and under free) to sell out by noon.

In front of City Hall on the west side is **Dilworth Park** (www.centercityphila.org/parks), a pleasant green space with an outdoor café and a fountain that stretches 185 feet by 60 feet—and transforms into an **ice skating rink** (noon-9pm Mon.-Thurs., noon-11pm Fri., 11am-11pm Sat., 11am-8pm Sun. mid.-Nov.-Feb., holiday hours vary, adults $5, children 10 and under $3, skate rental $10) in the winter.

City Hall

★ Masonic Temple

Philadelphia's **Masonic Temple** (1 N. Broad St., 215/988-1917, www.pamasonictemple.org, tours Tues.-Sat., adults $15, students and seniors $10, children 12 and under $5), just across the street from City Hall, is easily mistaken for a church. It's imposing, topped with turrets and spires, and clearly not of this century or the last. Divine: yes. Ecclesiastical: no. Dedicated in 1873, the temple is the mother ship of Pennsylvania Masonry. Though its origins are obscure, Masonry is considered the world's oldest fraternal organization. Some of the fraternity's practices are as shrouded in secrecy as an Apple product launch, but you don't have to whisper a password to pass through the temple's grand entrance gate. Guided tours are offered at 10am, 11am, 1pm, 2pm, and 3pm Tuesday through Saturday.

The place is an architectural wonderland, with seven resplendent meeting halls

Masonic Temple

each paying tribute to a different style. The Grecian-themed Corinthian Hall shares the second floor with Egyptian Hall, Ionic Hall, and rooms decorated in the Italian Renaissance and Rhenish Romanesque styles. Groin vaults, pointed arches, and pinnacles abound in the third-floor Gothic Hall, with its hand-carved furniture. Oriental Hall, located on the first floor, is patterned after the Alhambra, the exquisite Moorish-style palace complex in Granada, Spain.

You don't have to tour the building to visit the **Masonic Library and Museum** (9am-4pm Tues.-Fri., 9am-noon Sat., $7), which displays the Masonic apron presented to George Washington by the Marquis de Lafayette, the French aristocrat who served in Washington's Continental Army during the Revolutionary War. Washington is one of more than a dozen U.S. presidents on the Masonry's long list of "brothers."

Philly From the Top

To get a feel for the lay of the land, reading a map is no match for standing on the 57th floor of a skyscraper in the middle of the city. Ride the elevator up to **Philly From the Top at One Liberty Observation Deck** (1650 Market St., 215/561-3325, www.phillyfromthetop.com, 10am-9pm spring-summer, 10am-8pm fall-winter, adults $14, children 3-11 $9) and you'll be rewarded with 360-degree panoramic views of the city and beyond, including over the Delaware River into New Jersey. Admission includes a tour, conducted multiple times a day (check the website for an up-to-date schedule), with a guide pointing out famous sites and sharing tidbits of Philly history and lore. If you need a pit stop, there's a mall with a food court and bathrooms on the first two floors of the building. Stop by the gift shop to stock up on souvenirs like mini-Liberty Bells.

Pennsylvania Academy of the Fine Arts

In a lesser city, a museum as impressive as the **Pennsylvania Academy of the Fine Arts** (118-128 N. Broad St., 215/972-7600, www.pafa.org, 10am-5pm Tues.-Fri., 11am-5pm Sat.-Sun., adults $15, seniors and students $12, children 13-18 $8) could well top the list of cultural attractions. But Philadelphia offers art lovers a veritable buffet, and PAFA is often passed up for meatier fare like the Philadelphia Museum of Art and the Barnes Foundation. It's a shame, because its collection of 19th- and 20th-century American art is well worth a visit. Among the artists represented are Winslow Homer, John Singer Sargent, and Edward Hopper. PAFA, as the name suggests, is an art school as well as a museum—the oldest in the nation in both respects—and its collection abounds with works by its founders, faculty, and alumni, including Charles Willson Peale, Thomas Eakins, and Mary Cassatt.

Two strikingly different buildings make up the PAFA campus, and you'll find galleries in both. The older of the two is known as the Historic Landmark Building and dates to 1876. It's considered one of the premier

The Curse of Billy Penn

If you believe a broken mirror brings seven years' bad luck, rub a rabbit's foot with regularity, or stay in bed on Friday the 13th, you'll probably believe in the Curse of Billy Penn. Billy Penn—that's Philadelphia founder William Penn if you're not from these parts—has neither confirmed nor denied the existence of the curse, which may have something to do with the fact that he's been dead for almost 200 years. The story goes something like this:

For more than 80 years after its completion in 1901, City Hall stood taller than any other building in Philadelphia. It's not that developers couldn't build taller: By 1980, buildings three times its height had risen in New York and Chicago. But in Philadelphia, a gentleman's agreement dictated that the statue of Billy Penn atop City Hall remain the highest point in the city. The agreement was finally cast aside in the mid-1980s, and a 61-floor skyscraper sprouted two blocks from City Hall. Soon it was joined by other soaring towers.

As the city's skyline changed, so did the luck of its sports teams. Between the mid-1970s and early '80s, the Philadelphia Flyers had won two Stanley Cups (1974 and 1975), the Phillies had won a World Series (1980), the 76ers had won an NBA championship (1983), and the Eagles had reached the Super Bowl (1981). But the two decades starting in the mid-'80s were trying times for Philly sports fans. The four major sports teams had close-but-no-cigar seasons. It didn't escape notice that the streak of championships ended around the time that the gentleman's agreement was breached.

Had the breach unleashed a curse? When the Comcast Center marked its near-completion with a "topping out" ceremony in 2007, a statue of William Penn sat on the beam hoisted to the highest point of Philadelphia's newest tallest skyscraper, just to be safe.

The following year, the Philadelphia Phillies defeated the Tampa Bay Rays for their second World Series title. The curse—if there was one—seems to have been broken.

examples of Victorian Gothic architecture in the country. PAFA opened the adjacent Samuel M. V. Hamilton Building in 2005 as part of its 200th anniversary celebration. Built as an automobile showroom and storage facility in the early 1900s, the ingeniously repurposed building is used for traveling exhibitions.

Docent-led tours of the permanent collection are generally offered at 1pm and 2pm Thursday through Saturday.

★ Reading Terminal Market

The Reading Railroad was forced into bankruptcy several decades ago, but the indoor farmers market that bears its name still pulses with activity seven days a week. **Reading Terminal Market** (12th and Arch Sts., 215/922-2317, www.readingterminalmarket.org, 8am-6pm daily) is a regular stop for local chefs and other gastronomes foraging for fresh produce, eggs, dairy products, meats, seafood, and specialty foods. More than a third of its 80-some stands are eateries, making the market an extremely popular lunchtime destination (popular items tend to sell out early). The dizzying array of options—from spicy Cajun fare to savory crepes to caviar—can breed indecision. If you're looking to try Pennsylvania Dutch cuisine without leaving the city, you'll have plenty of vendors to choose from—but note that these will be closed on Sundays.

The market opened its doors in 1893 as part of the Reading Railroad's new train depot and company headquarters. In an age before refrigerated trucks, its location couldn't have been more ideal for shipping and receiving goods. At one point, a free service made it possible for a suburban housewife to "shop" at the market without venturing into the city. Her grocery order would be placed on a train bound for her town and held at the station until she came for it. The market's continued existence was threatened by the demise of the Reading Railroad in the 1970s and the subsequent decision to incorporate the terminal into the design of a new convention center. But Philadelphians demanded that the venerable market be preserved.

The area is well served by public transportation, but if you must drive, park in the garage at 12th and Filbert or 11th and Arch. Any merchant will validate the ticket with a purchase of $10 or more, entitling you to two hours of parking for a flat rate of $4. Regular garage rates apply after two hours.

Chinatown

Philadelphia's **Chinatown** (approximately 9th St. to 11th St. between Arch and Vine Sts.) doesn't approach New York's or San Francisco's in scale or sales of knockoff handbags and Rolexes. But if you're in the market for shark fin soup, roasted eel, dried squid, or bubble tea, the compact enclave just east of the Pennsylvania Convention Center won't disappoint. In addition to the Chinese restaurants and shops, Vietnamese, Malaysian, Thai, Korean, Burmese, and Japanese cuisines are represented. A plaque marks the Race Street site of the district's first Chinese restaurant, which opened in 1870.

The landmark most associated with Chinatown is of fairly recent vintage. **Chinatown Friendship Gate** (10th St. near Arch St.), a symbol of friendship between Philadelphia and its sister city of Tianjin, China, was dedicated in 1984 by officials from both cities. Artisans from China had a hand in the creation of the colorful portal, which stands 40 feet tall and proclaims "Philadelphia Chinatown" in large Chinese characters. The temptation to stand beneath it for a photo op is strong but, given the nature of Center City traffic, best resisted.

Mütter Museum

Best visited on an empty stomach, the **Mütter Museum** (19 S. 22nd St., 215/560-8564, www.muttermuseum.org, 10am-5pm daily, adults $18, seniors $16, students and children 6-17 $13) houses an unforgettable collection of what physicians of yore called "nature's books." We call them body parts. Its treasures include bladder stones removed from Chief Justice John Marshall, tissue from the thorax of President Abraham Lincoln's assassin, and a tumor taken from President Grover Cleveland's jaw during a secret surgery aboard a private yacht. The museum is home to the tallest skeleton on display in North America and an exhumed corpse known as "The Soap Lady." Perhaps most disturbing is the

Reading Terminal Market

preserved colon of a man so constipated that he was carrying some 40 pounds of feces when he died at the age of 29.

The Mütter is part of the College of Physicians of Philadelphia, a professional medical organization founded in 1787. Members started the museum in the mid-1800s to help educate future doctors about the human body and its myriad afflictions. Like library books, its specimens were borrowed and studied. The 1874 autopsy of conjoined twins Chang and Eng—the original "Siamese twins"—was performed in the museum. Their bodies were returned to their adopted home of North Carolina, where they'd married sisters and fathered 21 children, but the Mütter was allowed to keep their fused livers. They're on display beneath a plaster cast of the twins' torsos, which were connected by a band of skin and cartilage.

The small gift shop is guaranteed to turn exhibit-induced grimaces into smiles. Its inventory includes plush toys of deadly microbes, syringe-shaped pens, skull-shaped beads, gummy maggots, and, of course, the game Operation. Still queasy? Get some air in the college's lovely garden, which is planted with more than 50 medicinal herbs and dotted with benches.

The Rosenbach

Book lovers will be in heaven at **The Rosenbach** (2008-2010 Delancey Pl., 215/732-1600, www.rosenbach.org, by tour only, noon-5pm Tues. and Fri., noon-8pm Wed.-Thurs., noon-6pm Sat.-Sun., adults $10, seniors $8, students and children $5, children under 5 free), set in a 19th-century town house on one of the prettiest blocks in the city. The home belonged to Dr. A. S. W. Rosenbach, a prominent rare book and art dealer who worked alongside his brother Phillip. The first floor is still set up as Rosenbach's home, with art and furniture he collected from several different time periods. But it's when you get upstairs that you'll understand why people have been visiting this museum since 1954.

Every wall is lined with bookcases, including one that belonged to *Moby-Dick* author Herman Melville. Thousands of rare books and manuscripts are on display: a Gutenberg bible printed in 1455, 15th-century editions of *Canterbury Tales,* James Joyce's marked-up manuscript for *Ulysses,* Bram Stoker's notes for *Dracula,* personal letters penned by Lewis Carroll (and Carroll's own copy of *Alice's Adventures in Wonderland*), and much more. With all those fragile items, it's no surprise the museum wants to keep an eye on

Chinatown Friendship Gate

visitors—the collection is by tour only. Delve deeper into the holdings during a **Hands-On Tour** ($15, includes museum admission, check website for dates).

Philadelphia's Magic Gardens

South Street—appropriately, the southern border of Center City—is one of those rare roads with an identity all its own. Like L.A.'s Hollywood Boulevard, New York's Broadway, and New Orleans's Bourbon Street, South Street is more a destination than a route, with ecletic shops, a wide range of eateries, and sometimes-rowdy nightlife. It's also Isaiah Zagar's canvas. Since the late 1960s, the artist has been plastering the South Street area with mosaic murals that make you stop in your tracks. They're shimmering collages of mirrors, tiles, colored glass, and found objects. In a city awash with public art, Zagar's 100-plus creations are unmistakable. **Philadelphia's Magic Gardens** (1020 South St., 215/733-0390, www.philadelphiasmagicgardens.org, 11am-6pm Wed.-Mon., adults $10, seniors and students $8, children 6-12 $5) is his most ambitious creation. As colorful and textured as a coral reef, it consists of a fully mosaiced gallery and a maze-like outdoor installation covering half a block. Bent bicycle wheels, bottles, Christmas ornaments, folk art from far-flung places, pottery shards, and perseverance went into its making. When Zagar began the project in 1994, his canvas was a vacant lot. Eight years later, his work still in progress and South Street property values on the rise, the owner of the lot decided to sell. Monies were raised and a nonprofit formed to save the Magic Gardens from the bulldozer.

Tours (adults $15, seniors and students $12, children 6-12 $8, children 5 and under $5, prices include admission) are offered Friday to Sunday from April through October. During the 75-minute tour, guides take visitors on a stroll through the neighborhood, explaining Zagar's approach and the personal and community stories depicted in his murals. The site sometimes opens late or closes early for private events, so check online or call ahead before showing up.

GREATER PHILADELPHIA

Valley Forge National Historical Park

On September 26, 1777, British troops marched into Philadelphia. If Britain thought that capturing the capital of its rebellious colonies would put an end to the

Philadelphia's Magic Gardens

Revolutionary War, Britain thought wrong. That winter, George Washington and his battle-weary army set up camp in the small community of Valley Forge, 20 miles northwest of Philadelphia. The soldiers built a city of 2,000-some huts, miles of trenches, and five earthen forts. In February, a former Prussian army officer with an epic name arrived in camp. The charismatic Baron Friedrich Wilhelm Augustus von Steuben whipped the Continental Army into a finely tuned marching machine. The war for independence would continue for several years, but the six-month encampment at Valley Forge would be remembered as a turning point. In came ready-to-quit rebels. Out went warriors.

The visitors center at **Valley Forge National Historical Park** (Rte. 23 and N. Gulph Rd., Valley Forge, 610/783-1099, www.nps.gov/vafo, grounds 7am-dark daily, visitors center 9am-5pm daily winter, 9am-6pm summer, free) offers a good introduction to this chapter of history. The 18-minute film *Valley Forge: A Winter Encampment* plays every half hour, and exhibits round out the picture. A map with a suggested auto tour of historic sites is available in several languages. Among the historic sites is Washington's Headquarters, the small building that General George Washington and his military staff called home during the encampment. The soldiers' huts often seen in photos of the national park are reproductions; the hastily built originals are long gone. During the warmer months, the visitors center is the starting point for 40-minute walking tours, 90-minute trolley tours, and two-hour biking tours. Rental bikes are available.

As one of the largest open spaces in southeastern Pennsylvania, the park is as much a destination for outdoor recreation as historical edification. Almost 30 miles of hiking, biking, and horseback riding trails carve through its 3,500 acres. The Horseshoe Trail, which begins near Washington's Headquarters, connects to the legendary Appalachian Trail.

Entertainment and Events

BARS AND LOUNGES

Historic District

Beer doesn't get fresher than the pours at **2nd Story Brewing Co.** (117 Chestnut St., 267/314-5770, www.2ndstorybrewing.com, 11:30am-midnight Sun.-Thurs., 11:30am-2am Fri.-Sat.). True to its name, 2nd Story brews on the second floor of the building. The first floor is a brewpub serving the house-made suds alongside wines and cocktails. To eat, there's a menu of beer-friendly food: mussels, fish-and-chips, burgers, an "adult grilled cheese" with smoked bacon, and the like. You'll also find mussels, burgers, and fries at **Mac's Tavern** (226 Market St., 267/324-5507, www.macstavern.com, 4pm-2am Mon., 11am-2am Tues.-Sun.), where Rob McElhenney and Kaitlin Olson of *It's Always Sunny in Philadelphia* are part owners. Unlike the TV show's Paddy's Pub, Mac's Tavern is far from a dive—but it's still casual. It's decorated with images of the characters and scenes of Philly.

With its soaring ceilings, Corinthian columns, and 16-foot windows, **The Plough and the Stars** (2nd St. between Market and Chestnut Sts., 215/733-0300, www.ploughstars.com, 11:30am-2am Mon.-Fri., 10:30am-2am Sat.-Sun.) is a far cry from the typical Irish pub. And its menu ($9-27) has just a smattering of Irish specialties. But Guinness drinkers claim it pours the perfect pint, and the level of joviality reaches St. Paddy's Day proportions on a regular basis. Sunday evenings bring live Irish music.

A do-it-yourself Bloody Mary bar is a hallmark of weekend brunches at **National Mechanics** (22 S. 3rd St., 215/701-4883, www.nationalmechanics.com, 11am-2am daily), which occupies an imposing Greek Revival building that once served as a bank for the hardworking mechanics of the Industrial Revolution. Mechanical doodads, homemade lighting fixtures, and stained glass windows embellish a space far friendlier than the facade suggests. The bar features 30-odd varieties of beer, including 18 on tap. To eat, there's straightforward bar fare ($9-15), like wings, quesadillas, and crab cakes, plus a veggie burger that's landed on many a "best of" list.

With its dim lighting, flickering candles, and brick walls, *Top Chef* winner Nicholas Elmi's **Royal Boucherie** (52 S. 2nd St., 267/606-6313, www.royalboucherie.com, 5pm-2am daily) is where to go for a glass of wine and snack of oysters or house-made charcuterie.

Center City East

The half of Center City east of Broad Street is home to drinking establishments of every stripe, including most of Philadelphia's LGBTQ bars.

For the laid-back beer drinker, there's **Fergie's Pub** (1214 Sansom St., 215/928-8118, www.fergies.com, 11:30am-2am daily). Irish-born owner Fergus Carey is Philly's favorite publican, a former bartender whose beer-soaked ventures include Monk's Café in Center City West and Grace Tavern just off South Street. His namesake bar has his conviviality and good taste in beer and offers some form of entertainment most every night. Its Tuesday and Thursday Quizzo games vie for liveliest in the city. Monday night's open mic draws a talented crowd, and traditional Irish music is a Saturday afternoon staple.

Vintage (129 S. 13th St., 215/922-3095, www.vintage-philadelphia.com, 4pm-2am Mon.-Fri., 11am-2am Sat.-Sun.) is a mellow little wine bar invitingly outfitted in exposed brick, a chandelier crafted of iron and wine bottles, and flickering votive candles. It offers more than 60 wines by the glass. Beer and spirits are also available. A nearby sister establishment, **Time** (1315 Sansom St., 215/985-4800, www.timerestaurant.net, 5pm-2am daily), boasts a whiskey selection that's nearly 200 strong. It also specializes in absinthe, the storied herbal liqueur that was banned in the United States until 2007. But if you're just looking for a Miller Lite, Time has that too. There's live music seven nights a week—the downstairs leans toward jazz, while DJs spin in the second-floor lounge on Friday and Saturday nights.

It's easy to walk right past **Hop Sing Laundromat** (1029 Race St., no phone, www.hopsinglaundromat.com, 5pm-1am Tues.-Thurs., 5pm-2am Fri.-Sat.), a speakeasy-style spot in Chinatown. Once you're allowed in past the unmarked metal door, you'll be sitting pretty in a romantically gothic space drinking a superb (and strong) cocktail. You won't be capturing any of it with your camera—no photos are allowed. The owner also enforces a dress code, so leave the flip-flops, shorts, hats, and team jerseys at your hotel. You'll have better luck getting in if you're not with a big group.

The swatch of Center City approximately bounded by Chestnut, Pine, 11th, and Broad Streets is known as the "Gayborhood," with the greatest concentration of gay bars and clubs falling between Walnut and Locust Streets. (To get your bearings, note that the Gayborhood overlaps with an area known as Midtown Village.) **Woody's** (202 S. 13th St., 215/545-1893, www.woodysbar.com, 7pm-2am Mon., 5pm-2am Tues.-Sun.) is the unofficial capital of the Gayborhood. It's huge—big enough to call itself a "nightlife complex"—with several bars and two dance floors. Themed nights and special events give it broad appeal. Thursday nights feature Latin-flavored beats.

Center City West

You can't toss a beer nut without hitting a bar west of Broad Street, especially in the area around Rittenhouse Square. Among the standouts is **Tria Café** (123 S. 18th St., 215/972-8742, www.triaphilly.com, noon-late daily), which was teaching Philadelphians about fermentation in the form of wine, beer, and cheese years before it was all the rage. The menu helpfully groups the offerings under descriptors like "zippy," "extreme," and "stinky" (that's for cheese) and the knowledgeable servers can answer any question about which to pick. The concept proved so popular that three sister spots have since opened. **Tria Café** (1137 Spruce St., 215/629-9200, noon-late daily) in Center City East is similar to the original. **Tria Taproom** (2005 Walnut St., 215/557-8277, noon-late Mon.-Fri., 11am-late Sat.-Sun.) serves beer, wine, and cocktails on draft—there's not a bottle in sight.

A mecca for beer aficionados, **Monk's Café** (264 S. 16th St., 215/545-7005, www.monkscafe.com, 11:30am-2am daily) has one of the most impressive bottle selections on the East Coast and a much-ballyhooed array of Belgians on draft. But Monk's doesn't rest on its sudsy laurels. Its far-from-standard menu ($11-20) includes frog legs, lightly smoked trout, an ever-popular duck salad, and mussels.

Patrons of **Good Dog Bar** (224 S. 15th St., 215/985-9600, www.gooddogbar.com, 11:30am-2am daily) also had a hand in its decor. Framed black-and-white photos of their pooches adorn the walls of the three-level bar and restaurant, which bills itself as "a cozy alternative to the ultra-trendy" newcomers to Philly's bar scene. Good Dog's signature burger is something to bark about: Molten roquefort cheese erupts from the meat upon first bite. Head to the third floor for pool, darts, and retro arcade games.

Restaurateur Stephen Starr also excels in the bar arena. Behind his animated tacos-and-tequila joint **El Rey** (2013 Chestnut St., 215/563-3330, www.elreyrestaurant.com, 11:30am-11pm Mon.-Thurs., 11:30am-midnight Fri.-Sat., 11:30am-10pm Sun., $7-18), tucked into a quiet alley, is **Ranstead Room** (2013 Ranstead St., no phone, 6pm-2am daily). Look for the two "R"s painted on the otherwise unmarked entrance. Inside, the spiffy cocktail bar comes with dim lighting, red leather booths, and some of the most knowledgeable bartenders around. Chances are good you won't be permitted entry right away—management doesn't let the bar get crowded—so give the host your number and take a stroll around the neighborhood until you're summoned. El Rey's kitchen services Ranstead Room with a short menu of bar bites.

South Philadelphia

The neighborhoods below South Street are unpretentious and largely tourist-free—and, for the most part, so are the bars. On the divey end of the spectrum, straddling the line between Center City and South Philly, is **Tattooed Mom** (530 South St., 215/238-9880, www.tattooedmomphilly.com, noon-2am daily). You'll find graffiti-covered walls, well-worn couches, plenty of ink and piercings adorning the clientele, and an all-around affable atmosphere. Mom's serves $1 tacos (beef or vegetarian) on Tuesdays, $4 burgers, including a vegan version, on Wednesdays, and $0.50 pierogies on Thursdays. Open since 1969, **Bob & Barbara's** (1509 South St., 215/545-4511, www.bobandbarbaras.com, 3pm-2am daily) claims to be the birthplace of the ubiquitous Citywide Special: a can of Pabst Blue Ribbon and a shot of Jim Beam. It's also known for its Thursday night drag shows.

The **Royal Tavern** (937 E. Passyunk Ave., 215/389-6694, www.royaltavern.com, 11:30am-2am Mon.-Fri., 10am-2am Sat.-Sun.) is a couple of notches above a dive, leaning into the gastropub category and welcoming hipsters with open arms. It's a lively, loud, easygoing option for grabbing a beer, but most people come here with food on their minds too. The grilled cheese sandwich is a gooey marriage of smoked gouda, sharp provolone, goat cheese, and rustic French bread. The much-trumpeted burger is a choice you won't ever regret. Vegans get their own versions of Royal Tavern's comfort food, in the form of meat-free, dairy-free cheesesteaks, sloppy joes, and clubs.

In warm weather, corner spot **Stateside** (1536 E. Passyunk Ave., 215/551-2500, www.statesidephilly.com, 4:30pm-midnight Mon.-Thurs., 4:30pm-2am Fri.-Sat., 3:30pm-11pm Sun.) throws open the oversized windows that line the L-shaped bar and bartenders have merely to turn around to serve patrons sitting outside, perched on adjustable stools that jut out from the walls. Whether you choose a seat indoors or out, there are first-rate craft cocktails to be had, including excellent versions of the classics. Beer and wine drinkers are covered too, with simple but respectable lists of each.

Deciding whether to categorize **Southwark** (701 S. 4th St., 215/238-1888, www.southwarkrestaurant.com, 5pm-2am Wed.-Mon., $13-25) as a restaurant or bar is a tough call. Open since 2004, it excels as a farm-to-table eatery, but its exceptional, oddly named cocktails are arguably more beloved. If you're in a gin mood, go for an I Have To Return Some Video Tapes. Craving that smoky mescal flavor? Order a The Owls Are Not What They Seem.

NIGHTCLUBS

Silk City (435 Spring Garden St., 215/592-8838, www.silkcityphilly.com, club hours and cover vary by event) is a strange and wonderful beast: a classic diner car that's connected to a nightclub, complete with disco ball chandeliers. Once frequented by truckers, the neon-lit diner now fills with 20- and 30-somethings hungry for a good time—or just plain hungry. In the warmer months, the party spills into the 3,000-square-foot beer garden. Like owner Mark Bee's other Northern Liberties haunt, North 3rd, Silk City is known for satisfying eats. Washing them down with a cocktail or local draft brew is icing on the cake. The club hosts DJ-driven dance parties.

A block from South Street, **L'Etage** (624 S. 6th St., 215/592-0656, www.creperie-beau-monde.com, 7:30pm-1am Tues.-Thurs. and Sun., 7pm-2am Fri.-Sat., cover varies) fancies itself a French cabaret. The club upstairs from the lovely crepe café Beau Monde books DJs on Fridays and occasionally other nights. Live music, film screenings, burlesque, and other diversions round out the calendar.

In the Gayborhood, you'll have your pick of crowded clubs for dancing. Night owls can head to the multi-level **Voyeur** (1221 St. James St., 215/735-5772, www.voyeurnightclub.com, midnight-3:20am Tues.-Sun.), where the party gets going at midnight.

LIVE MUSIC

Rock, Pop, and Hip-Hop

The **Wells Fargo Center** (3601 S. Broad St., 800/298-4200, www.wellsfargocenterphilly.com) may be one of the hardest-working arenas in the country. Home to Philadelphia's professional basketball, hockey, and arena football teams, it's also the largest concert venue in the region. Acts as varied as Metallica and Barbra Streisand have brought down the house since it opened in 1996. Billy Joel and Bruce Springsteen have sold out so many concerts in the 20,000-seat arena and its predecessor that banners honoring them hang from the rafters.

Venues offering a more intimate live music experience are scattered around town. A standout is **World Cafe Live** (3025 Walnut St., 215/222-1400, www.worldcafelive.com) in the University City neighborhood, home to the University of Pennsylvania and Drexel University. Designed for major acts, Downstairs Live is a three-tiered music hall that's usually furnished with tables and chairs for 300 but can hold as many as 650 for standing-room-only events. Upstairs Live serves dinner nightly, except Sundays, with happy hour specials and live music most evenings. World Cafe Live shares a converted factory building with public radio station WXPN, which produces the nationally syndicated *World Cafe* (and licensed its name to the concert venue).

Several of Philadelphia's best-known concert halls can be found in the neighborhoods north of Old City. The largest, **Electric Factory** (421 N. 7th St., 215/627-1332, www.electricfactory.info), can pack in about 3,000 people and caters to all musical tastes. Shows are open to all ages unless otherwise specified.

Relatively new to the scene, the **Fillmore Philadelphia** (29 E. Allen St., 215/301-0150, www.thefillmorephilly.com, showtimes and ticket prices vary by performance) opened in

2015 with capacity for 2,500 in a converted foundry. The more intimate **Foundry,** a venue for up to 450 on the second floor of the Fillmore, hosts smaller acts and DJs, including regular appearances by Questlove of The Roots—the Philly-formed group that went on to become Jimmy Fallon's house band on *The Tonight Show.*

Fishtown institution **Johnny Brenda's** (1201 N. Frankford Ave., 215/739-9684, www.johnnybrendas.com, showtimes and cover vary by performance) is a triple threat: bar, restaurant, and music venue. Its owners also own gastropub Standard Tap, and they're serious about serving foods made with fresh, seasonal ingredients—check the chalkboards for daily specials. The upstairs performance space is off-limits to the underage.

A longtime presence on a street synonymous with nightlife, **Theatre of the Living Arts** (334 South St., 215/922-2599, www.tlaphilly.com, showtimes and cover vary by performance) has hosted heavyweights such as the Red Hot Chili Peppers, Dave Matthews Band, Bob Dylan, Paul Simon, Jane's Addiction, Radiohead, Norah Jones, John Mayer, and Patti Smith. Vintage concert posters and newspaper clippings decorate the onetime movie theater, known locally as TLA.

The **Trocadero Theatre** (1003 Arch St., 215/922-6888, www.thetroc.com, showtimes and cover vary by performance), located in Chinatown, was also a cinema at one point. At other points in its long life—it first opened in 1870 as the Arch Street Opera House—the Victorian theater hosted traveling minstrel shows, vaudeville, and burlesque. It did time as a dance club in the 1980s. "The Troc" can accommodate 1,200 people for shows on its main stage. **The Balcony,** an intimate venue within the venue, has a capacity of 250. It's used for screenings of recently released films and classics like *Ghostbusters* on "Movie Monday," a regular event for the 21-plus set. Most concerts are all-ages.

Center City's most unusual temple of music is an active church. Built by a large and prosperous congregation in the 1880s, the **First Unitarian Church of Philadelphia** (2125 Chestnut St.) responded to a shrinking urban population a century later not by closing its doors, as many churches did, but by opening them for non-church events. Philly-based concert promoter **R5 Productions** (www.r5productions.com) has been staging shows—including many of the punk rock variety—in the historic house of worship since the mid-1990s. Visit R5's website for a concert calendar. R5 also books some of the concerts at **Underground Arts** (1200 Callowhill St., no phone, www.undergroundarts.org, showtimes and cover vary by performance), a 12,000-square-foot subterranean venue that hosts art events in addition to a wide range of musical acts. Most shows are 21-plus and standing room only.

Standing room only is the name of the game at the midsize **Union Transfer** (1026 Spring Garden St., 215/232-2100, www.utphilly.com, showtimes and cover vary by performance), set in an 1889 building that previously housed a Spaghetti Warehouse. The soaring ceilings, big balcony, and three bars make it a fun space, with shows that tend to skew indie.

Jazz

Philly has a place in the annals of jazz. Legendary saxophonist Stan Getz was born in this city. John Coltrane, another tenor master, lived and played here. So did trumpeter John Birks Gillespie, who picked up the nickname "Dizzy" while in town. The city has few jazz clubs today, but enthusiasts are not entirely without options. **Chris' Jazz Cafe** (1421 Sansom St., 215/568-3131, www.chrisjazzcafe.com, showtimes and cover vary by performance) serves up live music every day but Sunday. The owners of the long-running Zanzibar Blue, which closed in 2007, opened **South** (600 N. Broad St., 215/600-0220, www.southrestaurant.net, showtimes and cover vary by performance), a worthy successor that's part Southern restaurant, part jazz club, with live music every night but Monday.

Founded in 1966 as a social club for

members of a black musicians union, the **Philadelphia Clef Club of Jazz & Performing Arts** (738 S. Broad St., 215/893-9912, www.clefclubofjazz.org, showtimes and cover vary by performance) counted Coltrane, Gillespie, Nina Simone, and Grover Washington Jr. among its members. Today it's a nonprofit institution dedicated to the promotion and preservation of jazz music. Its event calendar is sparse but worth keeping an eye on.

CASINOS

The **SugarHouse Casino** (1001 N. Delaware Ave., 877/477-3715, www.sugarhousecasino.com, 24 hours daily) boasts 1,800 slots, 130 table games, and waterfront dining. The city's first and only casino is located along the Delaware River in the Fishtown neighborhood.

PERFORMING ARTS

Avenue of the Arts

South Broad Street is so crowded with performing arts venues that it's known as the Avenue of the Arts. The venues are a mix of old and new. The most striking is the **Kimmel Center for the Performing Arts** (Broad and Spruce Sts., 215/893-1999, www.kimmelcenter.org), which opened in 2001. Described by architect Rafael Viñoly as "two jewels inside a glass box," the building consists of two freestanding performance halls beneath a vaulted glass ceiling. The larger Verizon Hall, which seats 2,500, features acoustics designed specifically for the illustrious **Philadelphia Orchestra** (www.philorch.org). The Kimmel Center's resident companies also include the **Philly Pops** (www.phillypops.org) and the Philadelphia Dance Company, better known as **Philadanco** (www.philadanco.org). The performing arts complex is open 10am-6pm daily, so take a look around if you're passing by. You might catch a free performance on its lobby stage, and you won't believe the views from its glass-enclosed rooftop garden.

One block closer to City Hall is the historic **Academy of Music** (Broad and Locust Sts., 215/893-1999, www.academyofmusic.org), the oldest grand opera house in the country still used for its original purpose. The long list of renowned artists who have performed at the academy since its opening in 1857 includes Pyotr Ilyich Tchaikovsky, Sergei Rachmaninoff, Anna Pavlova, Maria Callas, and Luciano Pavarotti. President Ulysses S. Grant was nominated for his second term here in 1872. The National Historic Landmark rarely gets a rest. It hosts **Opera Philadelphia** (www.operaphila.org) and the **Pennsylvania Ballet** (www.paballet.org), plus Broadway shows and other touring productions. The adjacent **Merriam Theater** (Broad and Spruce Sts., 215/893-1999, www.kimmelcenter.org), which dates to 1918, is now part of Philadelphia's University of the Arts. Students have the privilege of performing on a stage graced by John Barrymore, Katharine Hepburn, Sir Laurence Olivier, and Sammy Davis Jr.

Across from the Merriam is the **Wilma Theater** (Broad and Spruce Sts., 215/546-7824, www.wilmatheater.org), which has racked up dozens of Barrymore Awards—the local equivalent of Tony Awards—for its superbly crafted plays. "Dedicated to presenting theater as an art form," the Wilma moved into its 296-seat Avenue of the Arts digs in 1996, after packing smaller houses for 20-some seasons. Serious theater lovers seriously love the theater's tradition of postshow discussions with members of the artistic team. In 2007 the Avenue became home to **Philadelphia Theatre Company** (Suzanne Roberts Theatre, Broad and Lombard Sts., 215/985-0420, www.philadelphiatheatrecompany.org), a highly respected cradle of contemporary works. Its 365-seat theater is named for actress/benefactor Suzanne Roberts.

Other Center City Theaters

Philadelphia is home to America's oldest art museum, oldest natural history museum, oldest zoo, and oldest residential street. Perhaps not surprisingly, it's also home to America's oldest theater. The **Walnut Street Theatre**

(825 Walnut St., 215/574-3550, www.walnutstreettheatre.org) opened in 1809 as an equestrian circus, of all things. By 1812, the horses had been canned and the building converted to a bona fide theater. President Thomas Jefferson attended the first theatrical production. In 1863 the Walnut was purchased by Edwin Booth, a member of a prominent theatrical family. His actor brother would soon tarnish the family name—and etch his in the history books—by assassinating President Abraham Lincoln. The Shubert Organization snapped up the theater in the 1940s and used it as a pre-Broadway testing ground for productions including *A Streetcar Named Desire* starring Marlon Brando and *A Raisin in the Sun* featuring Sidney Poitier. In addition to a mix of popular musicals, comedies, and dramas, like *Grease, Sister Act,* and *Arsenic and Old Lace,* the Walnut also offers an annual series designed for kids in grades K-6.

Unlike the Walnut, the **Forrest Theatre** (1114 Walnut St., 800/447-7400, www.forrest-theatre.com) doesn't produce shows. It's a venue for touring companies. Owned by the Shubert Organization, Broadway's biggest bigwig, since it was built in the 1920s, the Forrest gets little use these days. The Academy of Music is the Philly venue of choice for most traveling Broadway productions.

Thanks to the **Curtis Institute of Music** (1726 Locust St., 215/893-7902, www.curtis.edu) and its "learn by doing" philosophy, Philly's classical music junkies can get a fix without paying a cent. The prestigious conservatory presents free recitals several times a week throughout the school year. Most take place in Field Concert Hall, a 240-seat auditorium in the institute's main building on Rittenhouse Square. No tickets are required, and seating is on a first-come, first-served basis. Call the student recital hotline at 215/893-5261 for the lowdown on each week's programs. Curtis has about 165 students, all of whom show such artistic promise that they get a full ride. (Leonard Bernstein is an alumnus.)

Historic District

Founded in 1969 as a cooperative art gallery on South Street, the **Painted Bride Art Center** (230 Vine St., 215/925-9914, www.paintedbride.org) relocated to Old City in 1982 and is now better known as a performance space. The Bride, as locals call the mosaic-wrapped building, showcases world and jazz music, dance, theater, and poetry. Its commitment to nurturing emerging artists is unquestioned, but it certainly doesn't discriminate against established ones. The long list of past performers includes rocker Carlos Santana, magicians Penn and Teller, and storyteller Spalding Gray.

"Dedicated to bringing to life the greatest stories by the greatest storytellers of all time," **Arden Theatre Company** (40 N. 2nd St., 215/922-1122, www.ardentheatre.org) serves up a mix of popular plays and musicals, new works, and new spins on popular works.

Fairmount Park

With covered seating for about 4,500 and space for 9,500 more on uncovered seats and the huge lawn, the **Mann Center for the Performing Arts** (52nd St. and Parkside Ave., 215/878-0400, www.manncenter.org) is one of the nation's largest outdoor amphitheaters. Named for a local businessman who championed its construction in the 1970s, the Mann hosts an incredible variety of artists, from cellist Yo-Yo Ma to folk legend Paul Simon and pop star Katy Perry. The West Fairmount Park amphitheater is also the summer home of the fabulous Philadelphia Orchestra, which frequently brings in famous special guests. Picnicking on the lawn is a Philly tradition. There are food vendors on-site.

FESTIVALS AND EVENTS

Summer

Philadelphians are treated to a host of free concerts and festivals in the summer months. They take place throughout the city, but **Penn's Landing** in particular is a hive of activity. The nonprofit **Delaware River Waterfront Corporation** (215/922-2386, www.delawareriverwaterfront.com), which oversees development of the riverfront, brings all sorts of free entertainment to the Great Plaza at Penn's Landing (Columbus Blvd. at Chestnut St.) from May through September. Movies are screened Thursday evenings in July and August. Friday evenings in August are set aside for live jazz. Festivals celebrating the diverse cultures that converge in Philly take place on weekends throughout the summer.

Beer festivals are a summer tradition in towns across the country, typically involving a couple of party tents, a cadre of craft brewers, and a day or two of mingling and tasting. **Philly Beer Week** (www.phillylovesbeer.org, June, cost varies by event) puts them to shame. Inaugurated in 2008, the 10-day celebration features hundreds of beer-soaked events throughout the city. With its list of participating venues, the Beer Week website is a great resource for beer lovers visiting the city at any time.

A Philly tradition since 1975, the **Odunde Festival** (23rd and South Sts. and surrounding area, 215/732-8510, www.odundefestival.org, second Sun. of June, free) is one of the largest African American street festivals in the country. Named for a Nigerian expression for "happy new year," it kicks off with a colorful procession to the Schuylkill River and an offering of fruits, flowers, and prayers. Back at Odunde central, musicians and dancers entertain on two stages while tens of thousands of festivalgoers browse a marketplace with vendors from various African nations, the Caribbean, and Brazil.

Volunteer organization Philly Pride Presents puts together the city's annual **PrideDay** (215/875-9288, www.phillygaypride.com, June, parade free, $15 festival admission), which draws more than 25,000 people to a parade winding from the Gayborhood down to the Historic District. The parade is followed by a waterfront festival at the Great Plaza at Penn's Landing (Columbus Blvd. at Chestnut St.). Philly Pride Presents also produces the **OutFest** block party in October.

In the city where the Declaration of Independence was signed, Independence Day warrants several days of festivities. **Wawa Welcome America** (various locations, 267/546-5424, www.welcomeamerica.com, free) traditions include outdoor movie screenings, free museum days, a Historic District block party, and more, all leading up what's billed as the largest free concert in America followed by spectacular fireworks.

Fall

Just as the weather is starting to cool, the **Fringe Festival** (various locations, 215/413-9006, www.fringearts.com, Sept., free and paid events) causes a spike in the city's cultural temperature. Performing artists from Philly and around the globe stage more than 1,000 shows over 17 days. The festival is produced by FringeArts, which offers year-round programming in its waterfront theater, also home to **La Peg** (215/375-7744, www.lapegbrasserie.com), a restaurant and seasonal beer garden. But the FringeArts venue and other traditional theaters can't contain the smorgasbord of artistic expression, which spills into galleries, bars, churches, parks, and even private homes.

Designers get a chance to show off their talents in October. Billed as the largest U.S. event of its kind, **DesignPhiladelphia** (various locations, 215/569-3186, www.designphiladelphia.org, Oct., cost varies by event) spotlights the work of hundreds of creative folks in a wide variety of disciplines, from fashion and product design to urban planning.

Winter

Philadelphia's **Thanksgiving Day Parade** (Thanksgiving Day, free) holds the distinction of being the oldest Thanksgiving parade in the country. The holiday tradition was started in 1920 by the Gimbel Brothers department store chain. When Gimbels went out of business in the 1980s, local television station 6ABC picked up the torch, and more recently, Dunkin' Donuts signed on as title sponsor. The parade starts at 20th Street and JFK Boulevard and runs along the Benjamin Franklin Parkway.

The annual **Wing Bowl** (Wells Fargo Center, 800/298-4200, http://wingbowl.cbslocal.com, $12.50) was cooked up by a local sports radio station in 1993. The early-morning wing-eating showdown packs Philadelphia's 20,000-seat indoor arena. Soused spectators and scantily clad "Wingettes" cheer on contestants vying for the title of wing king (or queen). The bacchanalia is usually held on the Friday before the Super Bowl.

Philadelphia gets a preview of springtime in early March when the largest indoor flower show in the country takes over the convention center. During the Pennsylvania Horticultural Society's **Philadelphia Flower Show** (Pennsylvania Convention Center, 1101 Arch St., 215/988-8800, www.theflowershow.com), florists and landscapers create massive, elaborate displays around a theme that changes every year.

Spring

Spring is a fertile time for festivals. Among the standouts is the **Subaru Cherry Blossom Festival** (various locations, 267/348-0250, www.subarucherryblossom.org, Apr., cost varies by event). Organized by the Japan America Society of Greater Philadelphia, the celebration of Japanese culture features drumming and dance performances, traditional tea ceremonies, Japanese movie screenings, and demonstrations of everything from sushi-making to origami. Japan's government presented Philadelphia with a gift of cherry trees on America's 150th birthday in 1926. The ephemeral blossoms can be seen along East Fairmount Park's Kelly Drive and near **Shofuso** (Lansdowne and Horticultural Drives, 215/878-5097, www.japanesehouse.org, 10am-4pm Mon.-Fri., 11am-5pm Sat.-Sun. Apr.-Oct., adults $10, seniors, students, and children 3-17 $5), a 17th-century-style Japanese house and garden in West Fairmount Park.

The **Rittenhouse Row Spring Festival** (Walnut St. between Broad and 19th Sts., www.rittenhouserow.org, May) is a classy street festival, with food and drink from several of the city's top restaurants and open-air shopping for designer duds. The **South Street Spring Festival** (South St. between Front and 8th Sts. and along Headhouse Plaza, www.southstreet.com, May) tends to be a bit rowdier, with live music and lots of beer.

Collegiate rowing teams from across North America converge on Philadelphia for the **Dad Vail Regatta** (610/246-5901, www.dadvail.org, early May), two days of racing on the Schuylkill River. Named for Harry Emerson "Dad" Vail, who coached University of Wisconsin rowers in the early 1900s, the nation's largest collegiate regatta is a beautiful sight. Grandstands in East Fairmount Park afford the best views of the finish line. Kelly Drive is closed to regular traffic during the regatta, but the grandstands can be reached by shuttle bus from the Art Museum and Boathouse Row, a set of Victorian boathouses along the southern end of Kelly Drive.

Nothing Quite Like a Philly New Year's

Mummers Parade

Few cities welcome the new year with as much pomp as Philadelphia. On New Year's Eve, revelers gather at Penn's Landing for a fireworks spectacular. The following day brings an even bigger show: the **Mummers Parade,** a ritual so unique that it landed a *National Geographic* spread in 2001. More razzle-dazzle than many people see in a lifetime, the parade is the culmination of a year's worth of planning by 40-odd clubs whose express purpose is to make the first of the year a magical day. To that end, they create costumes so fantastical that club members—Mummers, as they're called—resemble cartoon characters more than humans as they strut and twirl up Broad Street to City Hall. Such a volume of glitter, sequins, and feathers is rarely seen outside Vegas. It's worth noting that Philadelphia's Mummers are not, for the most part, performers by trade. They're notaries and nurses, postal workers and plumbers, real estate agents and retirees.

The origins of mummery are rather obscure. Some trace its roots to ancient Rome, where laborers ushered in the festival of Saturnalia by donning masks, swapping gifts, and satirizing current affairs. Some credit Swedes who settled in the area in the 1600s. We do know that Philadelphia's first official Mummers Parade was held on January 1, 1901. Like cheesesteaks, the parade has become synonymous with the City of Brotherly Love.

Dress warmly if you're planting yourself on the parade route. The pageantry lasts hours and hours. **MummersFest,** usually held at the Pennsylvania Convention Center in the days leading up to the parade, offers a temperature-controlled taste of what's in store. On New Year's Day, Mummers clubs known as Fancy Brigades put on two elaborate shows at the convention center. Tickets are required for both.

Costumes of Mummers Parades past can be seen any time of year at the **Mummers Museum** (1100 S. 2nd St., 215/336-3050, www.mummersmuseum.com, 9:30am-4pm Wed.-Sat., free), located in the South Philly neighborhood that many Mummers clubs call home.

Shopping

HISTORIC DISTRICT

Philadelphia's most historic neighborhood is peppered with chic boutiques and art galleries, most within the blocks bounded by Front and 3rd Streets and Market and Race Streets. Wandering aimlessly is as good a strategy as any for exploring the neighborhood's retail offerings. The first Friday of every month is a particularly good day for an Old City excursion: Dozens of shops and galleries stay open as late as 9pm, and many set out free wine or snacks.

Among the area's gems is **Vagabond Boutique** (37 N. 3rd St., 267/671-0737, www.vagabondboutique.com, 11am-7pm Mon.-Sat., 11am-5pm Sun.). Owners Mary Clark and Megan Murphy deal in hand-knit sweaters by Mary, hand-sewn pieces by Megan, and threads by other creative sorts, some of them local. Head to the back room for yarn, children's clothing, accessories, housewares, and art exhibitions.

Sugarcube (124 N. 3rd St., 215/238-0825, www.sugarcube.us, open daily) makes life a little sweeter with its carefully curated collection of men's and women's fashions by indie designers. Bicycles and canine friends are welcome inside. For the latest in retro, swing into **Smak Parlour** (219 Market St., 215/625-4551, www.smakparlour.com, 11am-7pm Mon.-Thurs., 11am-8pm Fri.-Sat., noon-6pm Sun.). The owners sell printed, polka-dotted, vintage-looking items from their Cut & Sew label alongside selections from similarly minded designers.

CENTER CITY

Macy's

The venerable department store chain's Center City emporium (1300 Market St., 215/241-9000, www.visitmacysphiladelphia.com, 10am-8pm Mon.-Sat., 11am-7pm Sun.) holds as much appeal for architecture and history buffs as it does for shoppers. It occupies a stately tower built more than a century ago as the flagship of Philadelphia native John Wanamaker's retailing empire. Wanamaker's was the first department store in Philadelphia and one of the first in the country. No less a dignitary than President William Howard Taft dedicated the store, which bore the Wanamaker name until a buyout in the 1990s. Tours ($12) of the National Historic Landmark leave from the first-floor visitors center at 1pm Monday through Friday.

The building's soaring atrium features a pipe organ that Wanamaker purchased in 1909 and enlarged to its current glory. With nearly 28,500 pipes and the prowess of three symphony orchestras, it's said to be the largest playable instrument in the world. Macy's shoppers are treated to 45-minute recitals twice daily Monday-Saturday. The marble-clad atrium is especially magical in March and April, when it's filled with flowers and topiaries from around the world, and during the holiday season, when a Christmas-themed light show runs every hour on the hour. Both the organ and a 2,500-pound bronze eagle statue, in the center of the ground floor, were first displayed at the St. Louis World's Fair. The store offers more than 150,000 square feet of fashion and home decor.

Midtown Village

There was no "Midtown Village" in William Penn's 17th-century plan for the city or, for that matter, a few decades ago. It's what merchants and restaurateurs in an area that overlaps with the Gayborhood have taken to calling their pocket of Center City. The heart of the hip area is the stretch of South 13th Street between Chestnut and Walnut Streets. Here you'll find **Open House** (107 S. 13th St., 215/922-1415, www.openhouseliving.com, 11am-8pm Mon.-Sat., noon-6pm Sun.), with its ever-changing collection of modern housewares. Valerie Safran and chef Marcie Turney, who opened it in 2002, have since started multiple neighboring businesses. Their empire includes five top-notch restaurants, a gourmet food market named **Grocery,** and **Verde** (108 S. 13th St., 215/546-8700, www.verdephiladelphia.com, 11am-8pm Mon.-Sat., noon-6pm Sun.), a boutique specializing in women's jewelry and accessories.

On the same block, **Duross & Langel** (117 S. 13th St., 215/592-7627, www.durossandlangel.com, 11am-7pm Tues., 11am-8pm Wed., 10am-8pm Thurs., 10am-7pm Fri.-Sat., noon-5pm Sun.) is an olfactory delight. It's stocked with its own brand of face, body, and hair care products and offers custom-blended balms for whatever ails you.

Rittenhouse Row

The area around leafy Rittenhouse Square is a destination for everything from mass-produced tees to haute couture frocks. Walnut and Chestnut Streets are especially crowded with stores.

At the corner of Broad and Walnut Streets stands **The Bellevue** (200 S. Broad St., www.bellevuephiladelphia.com, hours vary by merchant), a 1904 beaux arts building that houses a luxury hotel and stores to match, including Tiffany & Co., Nicole Miller, and Williams-Sonoma. A few blocks away, **Barneys New York** (1811 Walnut St., 215/563-5333, www.barneys.com, 11am-8pm Mon.-Sat., noon-7pm Sun.) beckons fashionistas.

Chestnut Street is home to **The Shops at Liberty Place** (1625 Chestnut St., 215/851-9055, www.shopsatliberty.com, 9:30am-7pm Mon.-Sat., noon-6pm Sun.), an indoor mall with about 20 stores, including J.Crew, Victoria's Secret, Aveda, and a Bloomingdale's outlet store.

It's not all chains in this pocket of Center City. Tucked among the nationally recognized stores are gems found nowhere else. **Boyds** (1818 Chestnut St., 215/564-9000, www.boydsphila.com, 9:30am-6pm Mon.-Tues. and Thurs.-Sat., 9:30am-8pm Wed.), family owned since its founding in 1938, stocks luxury fashions by the likes of Armani, Escada, Max Mara, and Trussini. The store also employs an army of tailors and offers free valet parking. Jewelry mavens flock to **Tselaine** (1927 Walnut St., 215/301-4752, http://shoptselaine.com, 11am-7pm Mon.-Sat., noon-5pm Sun.) for eye-catching baubles and other accessories.

SOUTH PHILADELPHIA

Fabric Row

To the Yiddish-speaking Jews who populated Philadelphia's southern outskirts a century ago, what's now called Fabric Row (S. 4th St. between South and Catharine Sts.) was known as "Der Ferder" (The Fourth). In the early 1900s it was chockablock with pushcarts and stands loaded with fabrics, produce, and other goods. Sprinkled among the fabric-related businesses still remaining are bars, eateries, and an eclectic mix of shops, including **Bus Stop** (727 S. 4th St., 215/627-2357, www.busstopboutique.com, 11am-6pm Mon.-Thurs. and Sat., 11am-7pm Fri., noon-5pm Sun.), a must-stop for those who love distinctive women's designer shoes, and **Brickbat Books** (709 S. 4th St., 215/592-1207, 11am-7pm Tues. and Thurs.-Sat., 11am-5pm Wed., noon-5pm Sun.), selling used and rare books.

Italian Market

Age hasn't slowed down South Philly's **Italian Market** (S. 9th St. between Wharton and Fitzwater Sts., www.italianmarketphilly.org, hours vary by merchant), which throbs with activity seven days a week. The outdoor food market, said to be the oldest in the country, traces its history to the 1880s, when an Italian immigrant opened a boardinghouse for his countrymen. Food stalls sprang up to serve the influx of immigrants, and then came butcher shops, cheese shops, and bakeries.

Produce purveyor **P&F Giordano** and meat-centric **Cannuli's,** where you can pick up a whole roasted pig, date to the 1920s. You'll find both along 9th Street between Washington Avenue and Christian Street, the busiest stretch of the market. Across the street from Cannuli's is the gourmet grocery

Di Bruno Bros., which opened in 1939. Di Bruno has since set up shop in additional Philadelphia neighborhoods, but the unpolished original has an inimitable old-world charm. Standout bakeries nearby include **Termini Brothers** (1523 S. 8th St.), beloved for its cannoli, and **Isgro Pastries** (1009 Christian St.), where the Italian butter cookies are out of this world. Grab a cup of coffee to go with the cannoli at **Gleaner's Cafe** (917 S. 9th St.) or at **Fante's Kitchen Shop** (1006 9th St.). The latter, in business since 1906, also sells every kitchen gadget imaginable. **Molly's Books & Records,** one of the few stores not focused on food, is next door.

More recently, casual eateries offering authentic Mexican fare have settled in alongside the Italian shops. It's as easy to find tacos *al pastor* as fresh pasta and mozzarella. The cheery **El Compadre** (1149 S. 9th St.), known for lambs tacos and torta sandwiches, is a local favorite. Another good bet is the no-frills **Prima Pizza Taqueria Mexicana** (1104 S. 9th St.)—don't let the name fool you; it's all about the tacos here.

Be aware that some merchants take Mondays off. If you're averse to crowds, it's a good day to visit. Steel yourself for thick crowds and impossibly tempting foods if you come during the **Italian Market Festival** (www.italianmarketfestival.com) in mid-May.

GREATER PHILADELPHIA

King of Prussia Mall

With 450 stores and eateries, **King of Prussia** (160 N. Gulph Rd., King of Prussia, 610/265-5727, www.kingofprussiamall.com, 10am-9pm Mon.-Sat., 11am-6pm Sun.) is the East Coast's largest shopping mall. According to mall management, its footprint could accommodate five Great Pyramids. In other words, you'd be wise to wear your comfiest shoes. If money isn't an object, toss your keys to the valets at Neiman Marcus and save yourself the trouble of walking from one of 13,000 parking spaces. What's notable about the shopping complex—besides its size—is that it's home to both garden-variety chains (Express, Forever 21, L.L. Bean) and luxury retailers (Louis Vuitton, Gucci, Hermes), food court staples and sit-down restaurants. Its anchor department stores include Nordstrom, Neiman Marcus, Lord & Taylor, Irish fast-fashion import Primark, and Bloomingdales. If you've traveled far to get your shop on, consider budgeting time for a visit to Valley Forge National Historical Park, just 10 minutes away.

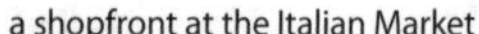

a shopfront at the Italian Market

Sports and Recreation

Philadelphia sports fans have it good: The city has the full range of professional teams. But packing stadiums and tailgating aren't the only forms of recreation in Rocky Balboa's hometown. There are parks to explore, rivers to row, and trails to hike and bike, not to mention museum steps to conquer.

SCHUYLKILL RIVER TRAIL

The Philadelphia region boasts hundreds of miles of trails that range from paved to rocky, flat to steep, and crowded to rarely trodden. None are so popular as the multiuse **Schuylkill River Trail** (484/945-0200, www.schuylkillrivertrail.com), a work in progress expected to grow to nearly 130 miles. It's already possible to travel from Center City to Valley Forge National Historical Park, a distance of about 20 miles, via the riverside trail. The Philadelphia section, which hugs the Schuylkill River's east bank, stretches north from the South Street Bridge, passes the Philadelphia Museum of Art and Boathouse Row, and continues through the charming Manayunk neighborhood. It's accessible via ramps from Market and Chestnut Streets and the South Street Bridge, stairs from Walnut Street and the South Street Bridge, and street-level crossings at Locust and Race Streets, among other places. The portion from the South Street Bridge to Locust Street is called the **Schuylkill Banks Boardwalk** (www.schuylkillbanks.org), a scenic 15-foot-wide path set over the water that was added in 2014.

The trailhead near **Lloyd Hall** (1 Boathouse Row on Kelly Dr., 215/685-3936), a community rec center just north of the Art Museum, is particularly popular because of the availability of parking, restrooms, drinking water, and **bike rentals** (215/568-6002, www.wheelfunrentals.com, 10am-sunset daily Apr.-May, 9am-sunset daily Memorial Day weekend-mid-Nov., 8am-4pm daily mid-Nov.-Mar., weather permitting).

PARKS

Philadelphia boasts more than 10,000 acres of parkland, from small urban oases like Rittenhouse Square to unmanicured areas large enough to get lost in, like Wissahickon Valley Park. If you have time for just one great outdoors activity while in town, go for a bike ride on the Schuylkill River Trail, which runs through East Fairmount Park.

Rittenhouse Square

One of five public squares included in William Penn's 1680s plan for Philadelphia, **Rittenhouse Square** (between 18th and 19th Sts. and Walnut and Locust Sts.) has been called the heart of the city. When the weather is nice, you'll find children at play, senior citizens warming the benches, office workers enjoying their lunches, and fat squirrels soliciting handouts. An address near the tree-lined park is a mark of status. Rittenhouse was known as Southwest Square until 1825, when it was renamed for 18th-century astronomer and clockmaker David Rittenhouse. The present layout, with its diagonal walkways and reflecting pool, dates to 1913, when architect Paul Philippe Cret was recruited to spruce it up. Cret would go on to design the Benjamin Franklin Bridge connecting Philadelphia and Camden, New Jersey, and the Rodin Museum, among other memorable structures.

Washington Square

Originally called Southeast Square, **Washington Square** (between 6th and 7th Sts. and Walnut and Locust Sts.) is another of Philadelphia's five original squares. It's less trafficked—and more peaceful—than Rittenhouse despite its proximity to the major historic attractions. Used as a mass graveyard for casualties of the Revolutionary

War and for victims of the yellow fever epidemics of the 1790s, it was renamed for the nation's first commander in chief and president in 1825. The **Tomb of the Unknown Soldier,** featuring a bronze sculpture of George Washington and an eternal flame, was erected in the 1950s.

Wissahickon Valley Park

Less than 30 minutes north of Center City, Wissahickon Valley Park offers more than 50 miles of trails, a stocked trout stream, and some of the region's best leaf-peeping. Stretching seven miles from Chestnut Hill in the north to Manayunk in the southwest, it's one of the largest parks in the Philly region. Wissahickon Creek, which runs through it, was once lined with water-powered mills and taverns. The only remaining example is the **Valley Green Inn** (Valley Green Rd. at Wissahickon, 215/247-1730, www.valleygreeninn.com, noon-4pm and 5pm-9pm Mon.-Thurs., noon-4pm and 5pm-10pm Fri., 11am-4pm and 5pm-10pm Sat., 10am-3pm and 5pm-9pm Sun., $15-32), built in 1850. Originally known as Edward Rinker's Temperance Tavern, it now serves new American cuisine in a cozy and romantic setting. Hitching posts are still found out front.

There are multiple entry points to the 1,800-acre park, but if you're unfamiliar with the area, you're best off parking near the restaurant. Use the public restrooms and then set out on Forbidden Drive, the wide, flat gravel road that parallels the creek. You'll find plenty of opportunities to hop on more rugged trails. The nonprofit **Friends of the Wissahickon** (8708 Germantown Ave., 215/247-0417, ww.fow.org) publishes a detailed map ($10) of the park. You can purchase it through the website and at the Valley Green Inn.

WATER ACTIVITIES

Philadelphia is known as a center for rowing, and the set of boathouses—outlined by LED lights at night—between Kelly Drive and the Schuylkill River just north of the Art Museum is one of the most recognizable sights in the city. But unless you belong to a local rowing club, boating opportunities are quite limited. Your best bet is to call or check the website of the **Schuylkill River Development Corporation** (215/222-6030, www.schuylkillbanks.org), which offers kayak and riverboat tours of the river.

SPECTATOR SPORTS

Philadelphia is one of about a dozen U.S. cities with teams in four major sports leagues: Major League Baseball, the National Hockey League, the National Football League, and the National Basketball Association. In 2010 the Philly area welcomed a Major League Soccer franchise. A discussion of the sports scene isn't complete without mention of the fierce hoops rivalries between local colleges.

Baseball

In 2007 the **Philadelphia Phillies** (Citizens Bank Park, 1 Citizens Bank Way, 215/463-1000, www.phillies.com) became the first American professional sports franchise to lose 10,000 games. So you can imagine the city's elation when the team beat the Tampa Bay Rays in the 2008 World Series. Founded in 1883, the franchise had captured baseball's highest prize only once before, in 1980. The Phillies made it back to the World Series in 2009 but fell to the New York Yankees four games to two.

Their current home, the 43,651-seat Citizens Bank Park, opened in 2004. While some die-hard fans decried the move from Veterans Stadium, demolished that same year, the new ballpark has proved a hit. The open outfield affords a scenic view of the Center City skyline, and the food is said to be the best in baseball. People for the Ethical Treatment of Animals, or PETA, has crowned it the most vegetarian-conscious ballpark.

Basketball

The **Philadelphia 76ers** (Wells Fargo Center, 3601 S. Broad St., 215/339-7676, www.nba.com/sixers) have been very good and very bad. Since moving to the city in 1963, the pro basketball franchise has won two NBA championships—one in 1967 and the other in 1983. In between, it set a league record for fewest wins in a season, finishing the 1972-1973 season with a 9-73 record. What the Sixers lack in consistency they make up for in star power. The roster has included some of the greatest players in basketball history: Wilt Chamberlain, Julius "Dr. J" Erving, Moses Malone, Charles Barkley, and Allen Iverson. The home arena, known by several names since its 1996 opening, was rechristened the Wells Fargo Center in 2010.

Local basketball fans also relish the intense rivalries between five area universities—the University of Pennsylvania, La Salle, Saint Joseph's, Temple, and Villanova—known as the **Big 5** (215/898-4747, www.philadelphiabig5.org).

Football

In a fanatical sports town, no team inspires more passion than the **Philadelphia Eagles** (www.philadelphiaeagles.com). Hundreds of thousands of people came to the victory parade in 2018 when the team won their first Super Bowl. Philadelphia fans had been waiting—and praying and obeying superstitions—for a long time. Established in 1933, the Eagles made it to playoff games, and even advanced to the Super Bowl twice before, in 1981 and 2005. But this was their first time brandishing the Vince Lombardi Trophy in front of a sea of fans singing the "Fly, Eagles, Fly" fight song. (To be fair, they did win three NFL championships before the Super Bowl was first played in 1967.) Tickets to a game at **Lincoln Financial Field** (1 Lincoln Financial Field Way, 215/463-5500, www.lincolnfinancialfield.com) were hard to come by even before the big win. The rowdy reputation of Eagles' fans is exaggerated, but if you show up at the Linc wearing the opposing team's jersey, you may get a reaction.

If you need a football fix and Eagles tickets are out of reach, you're not out of luck. Philadelphia's Arena Football League team, the **Philadelphia Soul** (215/253-4900, www.philadelphiasoul.com), plays at the Wells Fargo Center.

Hockey

The "Broad Street Bullies," as the **Philadelphia Flyers** (Wells Fargo Center, 3601 S. Broad St., 800/298-4200, www.nhl.com/flyers) were once known, are arguably the most successful of the city's pro franchises. Added to the NHL in 1967, the Flyers won back-to-back Stanley Cups in 1973-1974 and 1974-1975, along the way earning their nickname due to a rough-and-tumble style. They've since checked their violent ways. The Flyers have appeared in the playoffs almost 40 times, more than all but one other expansion team. Do home games sell out? You bet.

Soccer

In 2010 Major League Soccer awarded Philadelphia an expansion team. An 18,500-seat soccer stadium rose in the satellite city of Chester, and the **Philadelphia Union** (Talen Energy Stadium, One Stadium Dr., Chester, 877/218-6466, www.philadelphiaunion.com) began play in March 2010. By the time their riverfront stadium celebrated its grand opening that June, season tickets had sold out. The team's name alludes to the union of the 13 American colonies in the Revolutionary period, when Philadelphia was the de facto capital.

Food

Philadelphia's food scene has matured into one of the best, most talked-about in the country. Decades-old mom-and-pops share the streets with stylish destination restaurants helmed by renowned chefs. Cozy neighborhood BYOBs boast loyal followings.

It goes without saying that the food scene extends far beyond cheesesteaks—but unless you're a vegetarian, there is no excuse for not sampling Philly's signature sandwich while you're here. They're just not the same anywhere else. Philly's other culinary trademarks include soft pretzels, hoagies (elsewhere known as sub sandwiches), and water ice (the frozen dessert most Americans know as Italian ice). And no visit to Philadelphia is complete without a stop at Reading Terminal Market or the Italian Market, both of which offer a wide selection of delectable eats in a unique atmosphere.

The availability of healthy options—along with nationally lauded vegetarian and vegan eateries—has also improved in recent years, with many restaurants focusing on fresh, locally grown ingredients.

HISTORIC DISTRICT

Asian

Few people have played a bigger role in Philadelphia's culinary renaissance than Stephen Starr, who has opened more than 30 restaurants since the mid-1990s and expanded his empire to Washington DC, New York City, and Paris. Starr's **Buddakan** (325 Chestnut St., 215/574-9440, www.buddakan.com, 11:30am-2:30pm and 5pm-11pm Mon.-Thurs., 11:30am-2:30pm and 5pm-midnight Fri., 5pm-midnight Sat., 4pm-10pm Sun., $18-42) offers modern Asian cuisine in a low-lit space presided over by a massive Buddha statue. There are certainly more authentic Asian restaurants in town, but Buddakan can be counted on for a night-on-the-town vibe and undeniably tasty dishes.

Make sure there's rice and water (or beer) on the table to cut the heat of the spicy Sichuan dishes at **Han Dynasty** (123 Chestnut St., 215/922-1888, www.handynasty.net, 11:30am-10pm Sun.-Thurs., 11:30am-10:30pm Fri.-Sat., $8-21). The restaurant, set in a former bank with soaring ceilings and a long bar, is so popular it's added locations in West Philadelphia, the Philly suburbs, and New York City. Don't skip the *dan dan* noodles.

Colonial American

City Tavern (138 S. 2nd St., 215/413-1443, www.citytavern.com, 11:30am-close daily, $18-36) looks older than its years, which is exactly what its builders had in mind. Completed in time for the U.S. bicentennial in 1976, the restaurant is a historically accurate reconstruction of the original City Tavern, built in 1773 and frequented by the likes of George Washington, Benjamin Franklin, John Adams, and Thomas Jefferson. Waiters in 18th-century garb serve up medallions of venison, Martha Washington-style turkey pot pie, and other foods inspired by olden days, and there's a commendable children's menu. Don't miss the sweet potato and pecan biscuits, said to have been a favorite of Thomas Jefferson.

Southern

Across from the Museum of the American Revolution in a former bank built in 1847, **The Little Lion** (243 Chestnut St., 267/273-0688, www.thelittlelionphilly.com, 8am-midnight daily, $14-29) serves Southern-inspired comfort food. Think buttermilk fried chicken and shrimp and grits in a bright, airy dining room with oversized arched windows. It's a solid anytime option. The restaurant opens early for breakfast and goes straight through to lunch, dinner, and late night. The weekend brunch, offering everything from fried green tomatoes to cheesecake-stuffed French toast, will fill you up for a day of sightseeing.

New American

In the morning and afternoon, **High Street on Market** (308 Market St., 215/625-0988, www.highstreetonmarket.com, 7am-3:30pm Mon., 7am-10pm Tues.-Thurs., 7am-10:30pm Fri., 8am-10:30pm Sat., 9am-5pm Sun., $15-41) offers some of the best pastries and sandwiches in the city—on to-die-for house-baked bread—and then switches to an artful dinner menu with outstanding house-made pastas and unusually prepared vegetable plates. Treat yourself to one of the eminently drinkable cocktails.

Middle Eastern

The James Beard Award-winning chef Michael Solomonov wows critics and locals alike at ★ **Zahav** (237 St. James Pl., 215/625-8800, www.zahavrestaurant.com, 5pm-10pm Sun.-Thurs, 5pm-11pm Fri.-Sat., $20-28). The hummus alone is worth visiting this stylish Israeli eatery, which serves a short menu of small plates and grilled meats. The chef's tasting menu ($48 pp) is an affordable option for a fine-dining experience. If there are no reservations to be had, go for lunch in Center City at Solomonov's hummus-focused **Dizengoff** (1625 Sansom St., 215/867-8181, www.dizengoffhummus.com, 10:30am-7pm daily, $10-12) or his retro luncheonette **Rooster Soup Co.** (1526 Samson St., 215/454-6939, www.roostersoupcompany.com, 11am-8pm Mon.-Fri., 10am-8pm Sat.-Sun., $8-11), which gives all of its profits to help Philadelphians in need.

Spanish

Rivaling Stephen Starr as one of Philly's most prolific restaurateurs, Iron Chef Jose Garces has opened more than 10 restaurants in the City of Brotherly Love since 2005. ★ **Amada** (217-219 Chestnut St., 215/625-2450, www.amadarestaurant.com, 11:30am-2:30pm and 5pm-10pm Sun.-Thurs., 11:30am-2:30pm and 5pm-11pm Fri.-Sat., $24-48) was the very first and an immediate hit. It specializes in authentic Spanish tapas—from artisanal olives and aged manchego to lamb meatballs and grilled baby squid. The vibe is always stylish, fun, and energetic.

Coffee and Sweets

Opened in 2004 by brothers with a passion for history and an eye for antiques, **The Franklin Fountain** (116 Market St., 215/627-1899, www.franklinfountain.com, noon-midnight Mon.-Thurs., 11am-midnight Fri.-Sat. winter, 11am-midnight Sun.-Thurs., 11am-1am Fri.-Sat. summer, cash only) is part ice cream parlor, part time machine. Don't be surprised if "Gee whiz!" rolls off your tongue when you step inside; the place is a dead ringer for a turn-of-the-century soda fountain, complete with soda jerks in period attire. Prices for signature sundaes like the Stock Market Crunch (rocky road ice cream with peanut butter sauce and crumbled pretzels) range $10-15—and only cash is accepted.

Window shop in the galleries and boutiques along 3rd Street on your way to casual **Cafe Olé** (147 N. 3rd St., 215/627-2140, 7:30am-7pm Mon.-Sat., 8:30am-7pm Sun., $6-15) for an afternoon coffee fix or a fruit-filled smoothie. The Mediterranean-inspired salads and sandwiches on offer—like the Greek salad with feta and grape leaves or the chicken and mozzarella sandwich—make it a perfect lunch stop during a long day of sightseeing. If you're looking to grab and go, there are pastries and bagels.

CENTER CITY EAST

The half of Center City east of Broad Street is packed with restaurants, with the greatest concentrations in Chinatown and in the area known as Midtown Village, or the Gayborhood.

Vietnamese

Located in the heart of Chinatown, the warm and inviting **Vietnam Restaurant** (221 N. 11th St., 215/592-1163, www.eatatvietnam.com, 11:30am-9:30pm Sun.-Thurs., 11:30am-10:30pm Fri.-Sat., $10-16) is known for its

Cheesesteaks 101

As much as I'd love to give you a definitive answer to the question of where to get the best cheesesteak in Philly, there just isn't one. The argument will never be settled because it's truly a matter of personal preference. Some like the roll toasted and crispy, while others prefer it soft and chewy. Some like a cheesesteak dripping with grease, while others complain that too much grease makes the roll soggy. Some like the meat diced as thinly as possible, while others prefer slightly larger slices or even small chunks. Some love yellow Cheez Whiz, but American or provolone cheese are just as common. The one indisputable fact is that cheesesteaks are just not the same anywhere else. The closest I've come to a perfect cheesesteak outside of Philly is at the New Jersey shore, and not surprisingly, it turned out the chef hailed from Philly.

HOW TO ORDER

While not everyone is hardcore about ordering correctly, in South Philly or anywhere there is a long line, it's best to know what you're doing. First, don't *ever* order a "Philly cheesesteak." You're in Philly, so that part goes without saying. The basic rule of thumb is to minimize the words you need to convey what you want. "Whiz wit" means Cheez Whiz with fried onions, and "prov witout" means—yes, you guessed it—provolone cheese without fried onions. These rules are most strictly observed at **Pat's King of Steaks** (215/468-1546, www.patskingofsteaks.com, 24 hours daily) and **Geno's Steaks** (215/389-0659, www.genosteaks.com, 24 hours daily), the famous dueling spots at the intersection of 9th Street and Passyunk Avenue in South Philly. Of the two, I prefer Pat's to the neon-bedazzled Geno's. While there are certainly better cheesesteaks out there, this corner offers a worthwhile cultural experience. Perhaps best of all, it is the only place where you can find cheesesteaks (and cheese fries if you really want to go all out) 24 hours a day. Be sure to check out the autographed photos of celebs at both eateries—everyone from Justin Timberlake to Oprah has been here.

WHERE TO GO

You're never far from a great cheesesteak in Philly. They're served in every neighborhood, at diners and in bars, out of food trucks and storefront windows, and even in restaurants serving upscale twists on the classic sandwich. Here are a few of my favorites, but if you find yourself wanting a cheesesteak and not in close range of any of these spots, just ask a local to point you in the right direction. Almost as famous as Pat's and Geno's, and far superior, is **Jim's Steaks** (400 South St., 215/928-1911, www.jimssouthstreet.com, 10am-1am Mon.-Thurs., 10am-3am Fri.-Sat., 11am-1am Sun.), which has locations in West and Northeast Philly as well as on South Street.

Other great spots include **Sonny's Famous Steaks** (228 Market St., 215/629-5760, www.sonnyscheesesteaks.com, 11am-10pm Sun.-Thurs., 11am-3am Fri.-Sat.) in Old City; **Tony Luke's** (39 E. Oregon Ave., 215/892-1010, www.tonylukes.com, 6am-midnight Mon.-Thurs., 6am-2am Fri.-Sat., 11am-8pm Sun.), which has multiple locations including South Philly; and **John's Roast Pork** (14 E. Snyder Ave., 215/463-1951, www.johnsroastpork.com, 9am-7pm Mon.-Sat.), also in South Philly.

—Contributed by Karrie Gavin, author of Moon Philadelphia

crispy spring rolls and delicate rice-paper rolls. If you're unfamiliar with Vietnamese cuisine, educate yourself with any one of the clay-pot dishes or vermicelli noodle bowls. You may have to wait for a table on weekends; the bar's strong libations, including tropical tiki drinks like mai tais and the Flaming Volcano, help pass the time.

Chinese

For a quick, cheap, and tasty Chinatown meal, head to **Nan Zhou Hand Drawn Noodle House** (1022 Race St., 215/923-1550, www.nanzhounoodlehouse.com, 11am-10pm Sun.-Thurs., 11am-10:30pm Fri.-Sat., $8-11, cash only) where your hardest decision will be whether to get the long, thin, hand-spun noodles or the shaved variety (thicker, irregularly chopped) in your big bowl of flavorful broth. Then again, you also need to choose what else goes in the soup—sliced beef, shrimp, roast pork, tripe, and duck are among the fillings. Stir-fried dishes, fried rice, dumplings, and a handful of more exotic ingredients like jellyfish round out the menu. It's cash only. Another good choice for hand-drawn noodles is the similarly styled **Spice C** (131 N. 10th St., 215/923-2222, www.spicec-noodle.com, 10am-10pm daily, $7-15).

Japanese

By day **Double Knot** (120 S. 13th St., 215/631-3868, www.doubleknotphilly.com, 8am-late Mon.-Fri., 9am-late Sat.-Sun., $17-29) is a coffee shop and Vietnamese lunch spot with build-your-own rice and noodle bowls and banh mi. But it's at night when things really get interesting. The coffee shop turns into a bar, while downstairs in the basement level of the restaurant, the trendy set load their tables with sushi, grilled skewers, and other Japanese dishes in a dark, sexy space.

Italian

Simple-sounding Roman dishes—linguine with clams, rigatoni with bolognese—take on new life at **Amis** (412 S. 13th St., 215/732-2647, www.amistrattoria.com, 5pm-10pm Mon.-Thurs., 5pm-11pm Fri.-Sat., 10am-2pm and 5pm-10pm Sun., $16-28). The menu changes with the seasons, but you can always find bruschetta and the addictive *cacio e pepe* pasta. What you won't find are red-and-white checkered tablecloths in this hip trattoria, with its exposed brick walls, open kitchen, inviting bar, and sophisticated crowd. For lunch after a visit to one of the museums lining the Benjamin Franklin Parkway, try Amis's more casual sister restaurant, **Pizzeria Vetri** (1939 Callowhill St., 215/600-2629, www.pizzeriavetri.com, 11am-10pm Sun.-Tues., 11am-11pm Wed.-Sat., $12-18).

Vegetarian and Vegan

Carnivores won't miss a thing at the nationally praised ★ **Vedge** (1221 Locust St., 215/320-7500, www.vedgerestaurant.com, 5pm-10pm Mon.-Thurs., 5pm-11pm Fri.-Sat., $9-16), which serves vegan plates so good *GQ* called them "visionary." The descriptions don't do the dishes justice, so you'll just have to experience for yourself that these small plates are worth raving about. A reservation is a must. If you can't score a table, try **V Street** (126 S. 19th St., 215/278-7943, www.vstreetfood.com, 5pm-10pm Mon.-Thurs., 5pm-11pm Fri.-Sat., 5pm-9pm Sun., $14-26), the Vedge owners' trendy spot off Rittenhouse Square. It serves globally influenced small plates with a lot of heat.

Coffee and Sweets

Capogiro Gelato Artisans (119 S. 13th St., 215/351-0900, www.capogirogelato.com, 7:30am-11:30pm Mon.-Thurs., 7:30am-1am Fri., 9am-1am Sat., 10am-11:30pm Sun.) scoops out deliciously dense gelato in flavors that change with the seasons. In addition to traditional choices like chocolate and hazelnut, you'll find creations like Saigon cinnamon and pear with Wild Turkey bourbon, along with a handful of fruity dairy-free options. Ideal for a sweet ending to a date or a break in a day of shopping, Capogiro now has four other Philadelphia locations. A small cone will set you back $5, but it's worth every cent.

CENTER CITY WEST

The western half of Center City is home to many of Philly's most elegant eateries, but you can find a meal in any price range. The streets off Rittenhouse Square, especially, are lined with restaurants.

Markets

Di Bruno Bros. (1730 Chestnut St., 215/665-9220, www.dibruno.com, 7am-8:30pm Mon.-Fri., 7am-8pm Sat, 7am-7pm Sun.), Philadelphia's answer to Dean & DeLuca, began in 1939 as a small grocery store in the Italian Market. The original store (930 S. 9th St., 215/922-2876) still does a brisk business, but its selection of cheese, charcuterie, baked goods, and produce pales in comparison to that of the flagship Chestnut Street location. The two-level gourmet emporium is a popular morning coffee stop and lunch spot, with an upstairs **café** (11am-3pm Mon.-Fri., 9am-3pm Sat.-Sun.) offering salads, sandwiches, and pizza. Nearby, **Di Bruno Bros.'s Franklin Market** (834 Chestnut St., 267/519-3115) sells a similar selection of gourmet groceries and lunch options, along with beer and wine.

Seafood

An iconic Philly eatery around in various incarnations since 1947, **Oyster House** (1516 Samson St., 215/567-7683, www.oysterhousephilly.com, 11:30am-10pm Mon.-Thurs., 11:30am-11pm Fri.-Sat., $15-33) serves up its namesake mollusk along with lobster rolls, chowder, grilled fish, and other seafood delights. Stop by during happy hour (5pm-7pm Mon.-Fri. and 9pm-11pm Sat.) for buck-a-shuck oysters. The restaurant, run by the third generation of the Mink family, has been in its present location since the '70s, but it sports a sleek, modern look. In 2016 the owners opened **Mission Taqueria** (215/383-1200, www.missiontaqueria.com, 11:30am-11pm Mon.-Thurs., 11:30am-midnight Fri.-Sat., 11:30am-10pm Sun., $11-16), a bright, airy Mexican spot upstairs from Oyster House.

Mediterranean

Open since 1996, **Audrey Claire** (276 S. 20th St., 215/731-1222, www.audreyclaire.com, 5pm-10pm Sun.-Thurs., 5pm-11pm Fri.-Sat., $18-28, cash only) still holds its own amid an ever-expanding and competitive restaurant scene. The cash-only BYOB near Rittenhouse Square—a speck of a space, with seasonal outdoor seating—serves up Mediterranean-inspired fare, like grilled octopus and lamb with feta and garlic.

French

People-watching is the main draw at ★ **Parc** (227 S. 18th St., 215/545-2262, www.parc-restaurant.com, 7:30am-11pm Mon.-Thurs., 7:30am-midnight Fri., 10am-midnight Sat., 10am-10pm Sun., $15-36), a spacious corner eatery modeled after a Parisian café from award-winning restaurateur Stephen Starr. But the French fare, from ham and gruyere croissants to beef bourguignon, is nothing to scoff at. For an afternoon pick-me-up, stop in for a Kir Royale cocktail and a basket of *pommes frites*. If it's warm, ask for a sidewalk table outside, where the chairs are arranged to face

The sidewalk tables at Parc are perfect for people-watching.

Eating Well in Philly

There's no need to stray far from tourist attractions to eat well in Philadelphia. The city has undergone a restaurant boom, with local chefs bringing home national awards. Scratching the surface of all the recommendable restaurants in Center City and the Historic District would take weeks. But if you have extra time for dinner, two neighborhoods to the north and south are worth a detour.

In South Philadelphia, *Food & Wine* magazine named East Passyunk Avenue one of the 10 Best Foodie Streets in America in 2013—before it even fully hit its stride. Restaurants line the diagonal avenue from Broad Street to 10th Street. (It's pronounced "Pash-yunk.") Reservations are a good idea for **Townsend** (1623 E. Passyunk Ave., 267/639-3203, www.townsendrestaurant.com, 5pm-10pm Sun.-Mon. and Wed.-Thurs., 5pm-11pm Fri.-Sat., bar open until 2am). The romantic French restaurant is notable for its wines, which earned it a place on *Wine Enthusiast*'s list of the 100 best wine restaurants in the country in 2017.

If you didn't budget for a multicourse meal, informal options abound. Go for meat pie and mashed potatoes at British pie shop **Stargazy** (1838 E. Passyunk Ave., 215/309-2761, 11am-7pm Tues.-Fri., 11am-8pm Sat., 11am-2pm Sun., $7-11), or for seitan fajitas and a raucous crowd fueled by frozen margaritas at **Cantina Los Caballitos** (1651 E. Passyunk Ave., 215/755-3550, www.cantinaloscaballitos.com, 11am-2am daily, kitchen open until 1am, $8-20). For classic Italian-American dishes, **Marra's** (1734 E. Passyunk Ave., 215/463-9249, www.marrasone.com, 11:30am-10pm Tues.-Thurs., 11:30am-11pm Fri., noon-11pm Sat., 1pm-9pm Sun., $7-20) is an old-school charmer. At the small, colorful **Bing Bing Dim Sum** (1648 E. Passyunk Ave., 215/279-7702, www.bingbingdimsum.com, 5pm-10pm Mon.-Thurs., noon-11pm Fri.-Sat., noon-10pm Sun., $13-16), you'll find Asian-ish dishes that are anything but classic.

The owners of Bing Bing Dim Sum ventured across town to open another inventive Asian eatery, **Cheu Fishtown** (1416 Frankford Ave., 267/758-2269, www.cheufishtown.com, noon-3pm and 5pm-10pm Mon.-Thurs., noon-3pm and 5pm-11pm Fri., noon-11pm Sat., noon-10pm Sun., $12-15). It's located north of the Historic District in an evolving neighborhood often compared to Brooklyn—and not just because of the hipsters. Fishtown's current restaurant scene started with a handful of neighborhood spots but now beckons diners from all over the city.

Rittenhouse Square. In colder weather, snag a table by the oversized windows.

Coffee and Sweets

The first café of coffee roaster **La Colombe** (130 S. 19th St., 215/563-0860, www.lacolombe.com, 7am-7pm Mon.-Fri., 8am-7pm Sat.-Sun.), which has locations in several cities and supplies beans to some of the chicest restaurants and hotels in the country, is just off Rittenhouse Square. Don't be daunted by the line: Coffee and espresso drinks come in one size only and pastry offerings are few, which makes for speedy service.

Metropolitan Bakery (262 S. 19th St., 215/545-6655, www.metropolitanbakery.com, 7:30am-7pm Mon.-Fri., 8am-6pm Sat.-Sun.) is a tiny wonderland of artisanal breads, as well as croissants, muffins, brownies, and other sweets. Founded in 1993 by two alumni of White Dog Café, Metropolitan now has five locations, including a sit-down café (264 S. 19th St.) next door to the bakery, which offers sandwiches, soups, salads, pastries, and coffee.

SOUTH PHILADELPHIA

Brunch

Thoughts of ★ **Sabrina's Cafe** (910 Christian St., 215/574-1599, www.sabrinascafe.com, 8am-5pm daily, $7-12) propel many a hungover local out of bed. Quite simply the best brunch spot in Philadelphia, Sabrina's offers standard breakfast fare along with showstoppers like challah French toast stuffed with cream cheese and bananas and a constantly changing list of specials. Expect a long wait on weekends. The cozy BYOB doesn't accept reservations. Sabrina's has two other locations in the city: **Sabrina's Cafe & Spencer's Too** (1804 Callowhill St., 215/636-9061) near the Philadelphia Museum of Art and **Sabrina's Cafe @ Powelton** (227 N. 34th St., 215/222-1022), which occupies a Victorian manse in University City.

If the line at Sabrina's is simply unbearable, mosey over to **Sam's Morning Glory Diner** (10th and Fitzwater Sts., 215/413-3999, www.themorningglorydiner.com, 7am-3pm Mon.-Fri., 8am-3pm Sat.-Sun., $7-10), where the wait might be marginally shorter. Check your diet at the door and tuck into a frittata, served with a drool-worthy buttermilk biscuit and potatoes, or the French toast stuffed with caramelized bananas and mangoes. House-made ketchup adds an unusual zing to things.

Italian

A highlight of East Passyunk Avenue is ★ **Brigantessa** (1520 E. Passyunk Ave., 267/318-7341, www.brigantessaphila.com, 5pm-10pm Sun.-Thurs., 5pm-10:30pm Fri.-Sat., noon-3pm Sun., $15-36), a Southern Italian spot where Neapolitan pies with charred crust emerge from a wood-fired oven imported straight from Naples. It's hard to resist that pizza, but you won't ever regret going with the oft-changing seasonal pasta dishes.

Malaysian

Angelina Branca draws from family recipes and street food from her home country to cook up authentic Malaysian dishes over coconut shell charcoal in the open kitchen of **Saté Kampar** (1837 E. Passyunk Ave., 267/324-3860, 5pm-10pm Mon. and Wed.-Thurs., 5pm-midnight Fri., 11:30am-2:30pm and 5pm-midnight Sat., 11:30am-2:30pm and 5pm-10pm Sun., $6-20). Branca owns the lively BYOB with her husband, John, and serves juicy satay (grilled meat or tofu on sticks with peanut sauce), coconut cream rice steamed in banana leafs, and slow-cooked beef rendang. The restaurant also offers a menu of traditional coffee drinks and "pulled milk tea," which is poured back and forth between two containers to get the consistency just right.

WEST PHILADELPHIA

New American

The ★ **White Dog Café** (3420 Sansom St., 215/386-9224, www.whitedog.com, 11:30am-9:30pm Mon.-Thurs., 11:30am-10pm Fri., 9:30am-10pm Sat., 9:30am-9pm Sun., $16-34) owes its success to longtime community activist Judy Wicks, who opened it in 1983. Local farmers deliver organic produce and humanely raised meats to the restaurant, which composts in its backyard to reduce waste. The restaurant, housed in adjacent Victorian brownstones, can be counted on for inspired contemporary American cuisine.

Ethiopian

Join the locals at **Abyssinia** (229 S. 45th St., 215/387-2424, 9:30am-2am daily, $10-17) a homey, long-running Ethiopian spot serving affordable oversized platters of food, including traditional beef and lamb plates and plenty of veggie options. The stew-like dishes come with crepe-like injera bread, which is used to scoop up food in place of utensils. Choose from a regular table or one of the traditional basket tables surrounded by low seats. Service is leisurely; don't go if you're in a hurry. Up a narrow staircase you'll find **Fiume** (no phone, 6pm-2am daily), a thimble-sized bar with a very impressive whiskey list and live music.

Accommodations

Philadelphia has a wide range of lodging options, from hostels to bed-and-breakfasts to luxury hotels—but it can still be hard to get a room at the last minute. Book well in advance if you're visiting during summer or a holiday, when tourism is high.

If you're coming by car—and even if you're not—the **Visit Philly Overnight Hotel Package** may be a wise choice. The package includes free parking for one or two nights, which is no small perk in a city whose parking garages charge upwards of $25 per day. (Hotel valet parking can exceed $50 per day.) Go to www.visitphilly.com for a list of participating hotels and information on other hotel packages.

HISTORIC DISTRICT

Under $100

A short walk from the Liberty Bell Center, Independence Hall, and other marquee attractions, **Apple Hostels of Philadelphia** (32 S. Bank St., 215/922-0222, www.applehostels.com, $36-99) is as cheap as it gets in Old City—or anywhere in Philadelphia. It's not open to everyone; guests must provide a foreign passport, Canadian driver's license, college ID, or Hostelling International membership card upon check-in. College students and Hostelling International members must also show proof that they don't live within 100 miles of Philadelphia. The neighborhood's only hostel offers female-only, male-only, and couples-only dorms, plus private and semiprivate rooms. Rates include bed linens and towels, wireless Internet, and all the coffee and tea you can drink.

$100-250

Don't let "Best Western" fool you. With its grand staircase, high ceilings, and period-style furnishings, the **Best Western Plus Independence Park Hotel** (235 Chestnut St., 215/922-4443, www.independenceparkhotel.com, $110-300) is no ordinary franchise. More than 150 years old, the five-floor Italianate building was designed by an architect better known for churches, and it served as both a brewery and dry goods store before opening as a hotel in the 1980s. Book well in advance; the National Register of Historic Places property has just 36 guest rooms and a prime location.

The 364-room **Wyndham Philadelphia Historic District** (400 Arch St., 215/923-8660, www.phillydowntownhotel.com, $170-275) features a rooftop swimming pool—you couldn't ask for a better amenity on a hot summer day, especially if you're traveling with kids. Hotel parking is $36 per night.

The **Sheraton Society Hill Hotel** (2nd and Walnut Sts., 215/238-6000, www.sheratonphiladelphiasocietyhill.com, $160-320), with 364 guest rooms and suites, is a convenient option right near the sights of the Historic District and the Penn's Landing area.

Be sure to ask for a room with a river view at the **Holiday Inn Express Philadelphia Penn's Landing** (100 N. Christopher Columbus Blvd., 215/627-7900, www.hiepennslanding.com, $150-300), a stone's throw from the Ben Franklin Bridge. I-95 stands between the 184-room hotel and Old City's historic attractions, but guests needn't worry about navigating: The hotel offers free shuttle service to sights including Independence Hall, Reading Terminal Market, and the Barnes Foundation. Breakfast and wireless Internet access are also on the house. Hotel parking is $30 per night.

It's not all chains in the Historic District. Take the **Thomas Bond House** (129 S. 2nd St., 215/923-8523, www.thomasbondhousebandb.com, $140-200), a charming B&B across from the famed City Tavern restaurant. Built in 1769, the townhouse is named for its first tenant, an acclaimed surgeon and friend of Ben Franklin, with whom he founded the nation's first public hospital. Its 12 guest rooms feature period furnishings and private baths, some with whirlpool tubs. Bear in mind that the four-story house doesn't have an elevator. Rates include wireless Internet access, a continental breakfast on weekdays, a full breakfast on weekends, and a nightly wine and cheese hour.

A National Historic Landmark, the ★ **Morris House Hotel** (225 S. 8th St., 215/922-2446, www.morrishousehotel.com, $189-429) was built in 1787 as a home for one of Philadelphia's most prominent families. It boasts an idyllic private garden and 15 guest rooms and suites decorated in a variety of styles, from Victorian to contemporary. Rates include a continental breakfast, afternoon tea complete with house-baked cookies, and a glass of wine in the late afternoon. The on-site **M Restaurant** (215/625-6666, www.mrestaurantphilly.com) offers live jazz every Wednesday and Friday evening and a delightful outdoor garden to dine in during the warmer months.

Opened in 1990 in what used to be a shipping warehouse, the **Penn's View Hotel** (Front and Market Sts., 215/922-7600, www.pennsviewhotel.com, $180-280) has since expanded into two adjacent buildings on North Front Street. Its success is no surprise. The hotel is owned and operated by the Sena family, who honed their hospitality skills at nearby La Famiglia Ristorante, a local favorite since 1976. Some rooms feature balconies and others whirlpool tubs. There's no on-site parking but the lot next door is $28 per day. The on-site **Panorama** (215/922-7800) is known for its extensive selection of wines by the glass, made possible by a custom-built 120-bottle wine dispensing system. Wine flights give you the chance to taste expensive vintages without shelling out for a glass or bottle.

Over $250

Smack-dab in the heart of the Historic District, the **Franklin Hotel at Independence Park** (401 Chestnut St., 215/925-0000, www.marriott.com, $190-400) is luxurious: The smallest of the 150 guest rooms and suites is a generous 375 square feet. Don't forget to pack a swimsuit for the sauna and indoor pool, and bring your furry friend along—pets are welcome (for a $50 fee). Hotel parking is $28 a day or go with valet for $38.

Opened in 2012 in a building erected more than a century earlier, **Hotel Monaco Philadelphia** (433 Chestnut St., 215/925-2111, www.monaco-philadelphia.com, from $219) is the city's second Kimpton property. (The boutique hotel company opened Hotel Palomar in the Rittenhouse Square neighborhood three years earlier.) The 268-room hotel is distinctive in design, with a bold and modern look. The see-and-be-seen rooftop lounge, **Stratus** (215/925-2889, www.stratuslounge.com), is open year-round thanks to movable walls.

CENTER CITY

$100-250

With 1,400-plus guest rooms and suites on 23 floors, the **Philadelphia Marriott Downtown** (1201 Market St., 215/625-2900, www.marriott.com, $140-330) is one of the biggest hotels around. It's attached to the Pennsylvania Convention Center via skybridge. Another Marriott property, the **Courtyard Philadelphia Downtown** (21 N. Juniper St., 215/496-3200, www.marriott.com, $140-380), opened in 1999 in what had been the City Hall Annex. Its 498 guest rooms and suites boast 11-foot ceilings and 42-inch LCD TVs. Request a room with a view of City Hall.

Count on **Loews Philadelphia Hotel** (1200 Market St., 215/627-1200, www.loewshotels.com, $150-400) for sleek digs. Built in 1932 as the headquarters for the Philadelphia Savings Fund Society, Philly's first modern skyscraper has 581 guest rooms and suites and a 15,000-square-foot fitness center. A 27-foot-high "PSFS" sign still graces its roof. Also in the center of town is the **Westin Philadelphia** (99 S. 17th St., 215/563-1600, www.starwoodhotels.com, $150-400). Its 294 guest rooms feature the brand's signature Heavenly Beds.

If you plan to spend a lot of time exploring the museums along the Benjamin Franklin Parkway, the **Windsor Suites** (1700 Benjamin Franklin Pkwy., 215/981-5678, www.windsorsuites.com, $170-400) is a fine choice. The hotel is right on the tree-lined Parkway and features a rooftop pool. Its apartment-style accommodations add up to big savings for travelers who do their own cooking. Request an upper-floor room for the best views.

In the Rittenhouse Square neighborhood, the 230-room **Hotel Palomar Philadelphia** (117 S. 17th St., 215/563-5006, www.hotelpalomar-philadelphia.com, $199-359) was the first Kimpton property in Philly (the second, Hotel Monaco, is in the Historic District). It's true to the brand: stylish and service-oriented, with outside-the-box amenities like bikes for guests to borrow and a yoga mat in every room. Valet parking is $50 per night with in-and-out privileges.

Three blocks south of Rittenhouse Square, ★ **La Reserve** (1804-1806 Pine St., 215/735-1137, www.lareservebandb.com, $110-195) is a great value. The B&B consists of two 1850s town houses with a combined 12 guest rooms and suites. The executive suites, with their kitchenettes and separate living rooms, were designed with extended stays in mind. A few of the rooms have shared baths. Guests are welcome to tickle the ivories of the vintage Steinway in the sunny parlor, and breakfast is made to order. There's no elevator in the four-story hotel.

The "Gayborhood," aka Midtown Village, has a good number of boutique hotels. A colorful 30-foot-tall mural of Independence Hall greets guests in the lobby of **The Independent Hotel** (1234 Locust St., 215/772-1440, www.theindependenthotel.com, $160-300), which opened in 2008 in a restored Georgian Revival building. Its 24 guest rooms feature hardwood floors, 32-inch HDTVs, microwaves and refrigerators, and bathrooms with tin ceiling tiles. Breakfast is not only complimentary but delivered right to your room. Nearby, the 48-room **Alexander Inn** (12th and Spruce Sts., 215/923-3535, www.alexanderinn.com, $125-170) takes its design cues from art deco-era cruise ships. Rates include a buffet breakfast and access to an always-stocked snack bar. The hotel has a deal with a nearby parking garage—$20 for 24 hours.

Over $250

The domed lobby of ★ **The Ritz-Carlton, Philadelphia** (10 Avenue of the Arts, 215/523-8000, www.ritzcarlton.com from $330) is worth a visit even if a room at the lavish hotel is out of your price range. Modeled on Rome's Pantheon, it's one of the grandest spaces in Center City. The landmark hotel, a bank in a previous incarnation, has 300 guest rooms and suites. Housekeeping visits twice daily and room service is available around the clock. Fancy a bath strewn with rose petals? A butler will be happy to oblige. The on-site spa offers everything from haircuts to hot stone massages. The lobby restaurant, **Aqimero** (215/523-8200, www.richardsandoval.com), is international restaurateur Richard Sandoval's only Philly location.

Part of Hilton's Curio Collection, **The Logan** (1 Logan Sq., 215/963-1500, www.theloganhotel.com, $180-450) is located on the Benjamin Franklin Parkway close to Philadelphia's major museums. It offers 391 artfully decorated guest rooms, a full-service spa, and a pool. If you're visiting during the warmer months, don't miss the views from **Assembly Rooftop Lounge** (www.assemblyrooftop.com, hours vary)—and you might as well stay for a frozen cocktail. The on-site restaurant, **Urban Farmer** (215/963-2788, http://urbanfarmerphiladelphia.com, 6:30am-10pm Sun.-Thurs., 6:30am-11pm Fri.-Sat., $27-56), is a thoroughly modern steak house.

The Rittenhouse (210 W. Rittenhouse Sq., 215/546-9000, www.rittenhousehotel.com, from $350) is set right on Philadelphia's favorite public square. It's been rated the number one hotel in Pennsylvania and among the

100 best in the world, and the on-site **Lacroix** (215/790-2533, www.lacroixrestaurant.com) was hailed as the nation's best new restaurant when it opened in 2003. Make sure to stop by the elegant Library Bar for a cocktail. The independent hotel has 116 oversized guest rooms and suites, some commanding upwards of $3,000 per night. Just off Rittenhouse Square is a more intimate alternative: the 23-room **Rittenhouse 1715** (1715 Rittenhouse Square St., 215/546-6500, www.rittenhouse1715.com, from $199-669).

FAIRMOUNT PARK

Under $100

Philadelphia isn't off-limits to penny-pinching globetrotters thanks to **Chamounix Mansion** (3250 Chamounix Dr., 215/878-3676, www.philahostel.org, $22-25 per person, children 16 and under $8), which isn't nearly as opulent as its name suggests. Built in 1802 as a country retreat for a wealthy Philadelphia merchant, it was saved from demolition in the mid-1900s by community members who agitated for its conversion to a youth hostel. There are 80 beds between the mansion and carriage house, most in dorm-style rooms. The low rates include linens, as sleeping bags are prohibited. Billed as the nation's first urban youth hostel, Chamounix is actually in West Fairmount Park, across the Schuylkill and well north of Center City. But with free bikes at their disposal and public transportation nearby, guests have no excuse for staying in—in fact, they must leave the hostel by 11am each day and return no earlier than 4:30pm.

Transportation and Services

GETTING THERE

Air

Philadelphia International Airport (PHL, 215/937-6937, www.phl.org) boasts seven terminals, four runways, and daily departures to more than 120 cities. It's served by about a dozen airlines, including budget carriers JetBlue, Spirit, and Frontier. Among its amenities: free Wi-Fi, children's play areas in terminals A and D, a full-service postal facility, Travelex currency exchange booths, and more than 170 stores and eateries, including duty-free shops for international passengers.

Located seven miles southwest of Center City, the airport offers the usual array of ground transportation options, including rental cars, taxis, and shared-ride vans. Taxis charge a flat rate of $28.50 (plus $1 for each additional adult passenger; there's no extra cost for children 12 and under) from the airport and the "Center City zone," defined as the area bounded by Fairmount Avenue in the north, South Street in the south, the Delaware River in the east, and the Schuylkill River in the west, plus a portion of West Philly between the Schuylkill and 38th Street. If you're heading anywhere else, metered rates apply: $2.70 when your get in the car, $0.23 for each 0.1 mile, and $0.23 for each 37.6 seconds of wait time. Trips from the airport are subject to an $11 minimum. A tip of 15-20 percent is customary, especially if the driver handles your luggage. All taxis accept credit cards.

SEPTA offers rail service from the airport. The fare is $6.75 to Center City and $9.25 to stations beyond Center City. Trains depart every half hour from shortly after 5am to shortly after midnight.

The airport website (www.phl.org) has a directory of ground transportation providers. Call 215/937-6958 to chat with a ground transportation specialist.

Car

Philadelphia is a straightforward drive from several major cities: about 95 miles southwest of New York via I-95, 105 miles northeast of Baltimore via I-95, and 300 miles east of Pittsburgh via the Pennsylvania Turnpike. All told, about a quarter of the U.S. population lives within a half-day's drive of the City of Brotherly Love. While road trips can be fun, parking in Philly isn't. Even if you live within driving distance, consider taking public transportation.

Bus and Rail

30th Street Station (2955 Market St.), located just across the Schuylkill River from Center City, is one of the nation's busiest intercity passenger rail stations. It's a stop along several **Amtrak** (800/872-7245, www.amtrak.com) routes, including the Northeast Regional, which connects Boston, New York, Baltimore, and Washington DC, among other cities; the Pennsylvanian, which runs between New York and Pittsburgh; and the Cardinal, running between New York and Chicago. New Jersey's public transportation system, **NJ Transit** (973/275-5555, www.njtransit.com), has a commuter rail line between Atlantic City, New Jersey, and 30th Street Station. Its bus route network also extends into Philly.

The Southeastern Pennsylvania Transportation Authority, or **SEPTA** (215/580-7800, www.septa.org), provides service to Philadelphia from countless suburban towns, Philadelphia International Airport, New Jersey's capital of Trenton, and Wilmington, Delaware. It's an uncommonly versatile public transit agency, offering bus, trolley, trackless trolley, subway, and commuter rail services.

Thanks to competition among intercity bus companies, traveling to Philly can be dirt cheap. **Greyhound** (800/231-2222, www.greyhound.com) buses collect Philly-bound travelers from all over the country and deposit them at Filbert and 10th Streets in Center City. **Megabus** (877/462-6342, www.megabus.com) offers service to Philadelphia from about a dozen cities, including Pittsburgh, Boston, New York, Baltimore, Washington DC, and Toronto. Its main stop in Philadelphia is on JFK Boulevard near North 30th Street, a stone's throw from 30th Street Station. **BoltBus** (877/265-8287, www.boltbus.com) leaves from almost the same location—3131 JFK Boulevard—and travels to Boston, New York, and Newark, New Jersey.

Ferry

Philadelphia is a port city, and arriving by boat is possible in the warmer months. The **RiverLink Ferry** (215/925-5465, www.riverlinkferry.org, service daily Memorial Day-Labor Day and weekends in May and Sept., fare $9, seniors and children $7, children under 3 free) shuttles between Philly and its New Jersey neighbor, Camden. Sadly, the scenic trip across the Delaware River lasts just 12-15 minutes.

GETTING AROUND

A car is entirely unnecessary for getting around Center City. In fact, having one can be a pain. Street parking is hard to come by, the parking meter rules can get confusing, and parking garages are pricey. If you're able-bodied and not in a hurry, walking is the best way to explore the compact heart of Philly. You can always flag a cab when your feet start to hurt, or use the **Uber** (www.uber.com) or **Lyft** (www.lyft.com) ride-hailing apps. The extensive public transportation network can be intimidating, but studying it is worthwhile if you're in town for more than a couple of days.

A car is advisable if you plan to spend much time outside of Center City. Good luck getting to gorgeous Wissahickon Valley Park without one.

On Foot

Center City is eminently walkable. For one thing, it's compact. Just 25 blocks separate the rivers that serve as its eastern and western boundaries. For another, it's easy to navigate. Founder William Penn is largely to thank for that, having called for a grid street plan. Most north-south streets are numbered. If the numbers are getting lower, you're heading east, toward the Delaware River. If they're getting higher, you're on your way to the Schuylkill. (It's worth noting that there's no

1st Street or 14th Street. What would be 1st is named Front Street, and what would be 14th is Broad Street.) Many east-west streets have tree names, as in Chestnut, Walnut, Spruce, and Pine. East-west Market Street separates Center City roughly in half. Addresses with an "S" prefix, as in 99 S. 17th Street, are south of Market, and addresses with an "N" prefix are north of it.

A number of Philly outfits offer suggested walking tours. **The Constitutional Walking Tour of Philadelphia** (215/525-1776, www.theconstitutional.com), which offers guided tours of the Historic District April-November, publishes a self-guided tour brochure with information on 30-plus sites. You can print it from the website or pick it up at the Independence Visitor Center at 6th and Market Streets. The nonprofit **Preservation Alliance** (215/546-1146, www.preservationalliance.com), whose volunteers lead architectural walking tours of neighborhoods throughout the city May to October, offers several self-guided tours on its website.

Car

If you choose to drive to Center City, be prepared to spend a good amount of time looking for street parking or a good amount of money for off-street parking. It's worthwhile to look for street parking if you're only leaving your vehicle for an hour or two. Read parking regulation signs *very carefully* to make sure you don't need a permit and don't overstay your welcome. Some blocks allow parking during certain hours but prohibit it during periods of heavy traffic. The **Philadelphia Parking Authority** (888/591-3636, www.philapark.org) doesn't mess around—you will be swiftly ticketed for any violation.

Meter parking is generally $2 per hour. Some blocks have individual meters that take coins, while other blocks have pay stations that accept bills and credit cards in addition to coins.

You can eliminate the risk of getting a parking ticket—or worse yet, having your vehicle towed—by parking in a garage or lot. Be prepared to spend upwards of $20 per day. The website of the Philadelphia Parking Authority has a handy "parking locator" feature that will find and compare parking options near your destination.

Taxi

Taxis drive the streets of Center City at all hours. In less trafficked parts of town, you can call for a cab. Taxi companies include **PHL Taxi** (215/232-2000, www.phltaxi.net), **Quaker City Cab** (215/726-6000), and **All Threes** (215/333-3333, www.ridewithpride.com) Trips from the "Center City zone" to the airport are $28.50. Trips in the opposite direction, from the airport to the "Center City zone," are $28.50 plus $1 for each additional adult passenger (there's no additional cost for children 12 and under). For all other trips, metered rates apply. The meter reads $2.70 to start, and the fare climbs by $0.23 with each 0.1 mile or 37.6 seconds of wait time. Rates are regulated by the Philadelphia Parking Authority and must be posted in all cabs. It's customary to tip drivers $1 or $2 for rides within Center City and 15-20 percent of the fare for longer trips.

Public Transportation

Mastering Philadelphia's public transit system, commonly known as **SEPTA** (215/580-7800, www.septa.org), is no small thing. The multimodal system, which serves a five-county, 2,202-square-mile area, consists of almost 150 fixed routes. More than 100 of those are bus routes. SEPTA also offers trolley, trackless trolley, subway, and commuter rail (known locally as Regional Rail) services.

Trip planning is a cinch if you have Internet access. Simply enter your starting location and destination in the Trip Planner feature on SEPTA's website. The resulting itinerary spells out how to get there, how long the trip will take, and how much it will cost. The cash fare for bus, subway, and trolley service is $2.50. Exact fare must be used. Transfers are $1. Another option for the subway only is to purchase a Quick Trip ticket, good for

Getting There in a Phlash

One of the cheapest and easiest ways to travel between Philadelphia's major attractions is aboard a purple road trolley called the **Phlash** (484/881-3574, www.ridephillyphlash.com, 10am-6pm daily May-Labor Day and late Nov.-New Year's Eve, 10am-6pm Fri.-Sun. late Mar.-Apr. and Sept.-late Nov.). A single ride is just $2, and an all-day pass is $5. Passes are sold at the Independence Visitor Center at 6th and Market Streets and other visitors centers. Seniors and children four and under ride for free.

The Phlash route stretches from Penn's Landing in the east to the Philadelphia Zoo and Please Touch Museum in the west, with 22 stops in all. Service is about every 15 minutes. Stops include:

- **6th and Market Streets** (Independence Visitor Center, Liberty Bell Center, Independence Hall)
- **12th and Market Streets** (Reading Terminal Market, Chinatown, City Hall)
- **22nd Street and the Benjamin Franklin Parkway** (Barnes Foundation, Rodin Museum)
- **Philadelphia Museum of Art**

one ride, using cash or a credit or debit card at a station kiosk. Regular riders save time and money by using reloadable **SEPTA Key Cards** (855/567-3782, www.septakey.org). A ride using SEPTA Key is $2.

Regional Rail fares are a different animal. A one-way ticket can cost anywhere from $3.75 to $10 depending on where you're going, when you're traveling, and whether you pay in advance or on the train. Senior citizens ride for free on buses, subways, and trolleys and pay just $1 for Regional Rail travel within Pennsylvania. Up to two children age four and under can ride for free with a fare-paying adult. Discounts are available for riders with disabilities.

SEPTA offers two single-day options tailor-made for tourists. Both require a SEPTA Key Card, which can be acquired at a kiosk at any SEPTA station or sales location, including the SEPTA headquarters at 1234 Market Street and the Independence Visitor Center at 6th and Market Streets, as well as online at www.septakey.org. Priced at $9, the **Convenience Pass** is good for eight trips by bus, subway, or trolley taken in one day by one person. The **Independence Pass,** valid for one day of unlimited travel on all SEPTA lines and Phlash, is $13 per person or $30 for a family of up to five people.

VISITOR INFORMATION

Located in the heart of the Historic District, the **Independence Visitor Center** (6th and Market Sts., 800/537-7676, www.phlvisitorcenter.com, 8:30am-7pm Memorial Day-Labor Day, 8:30am-6pm daily early Sept.-late May) is a gold mine of information about what to do in Philadelphia and its environs. It also has one of the largest gift shops in the region. You'll also find visitors centers in **City Hall** (Broad and Market Sts., room 121, 215/686-2840, 9am-5pm Mon.-Fri.); nearby **Love Park** (16th St. and JFK Blvd., 215/683-0246, 10am-5pm Mon.-Sat.), so called because it's home to Robert Indiana's iconic *LOVE* statue; and **Sister Cities Park** (18th St. and Benjamin Franklin Pkwy., 267/514-4760, 9:30am-5:30pm Mon.-Sat., 9:30am-5pm Sun. May-Oct.), which is convenient to the museums along the Benjamin Franklin Parkway.

If you're driving to Philadelphia via I-95 north, you can load up on brochures at the state-run **welcome center** a half mile north of the Pennsylvania-Delaware line. Personalized travel counseling is available 7am-7pm daily.

The website of **Visit Philadelphia** (www.visitphilly.com) is a great source of information for visitors. In addition to descriptions of countless attractions, restaurants, hotels, and shops, it offers an events calendar and more than 30 suggested itineraries, including one that takes you to all the sites *Rocky* visited on screen.

Bucks County

Bucks County offers a blend of bucolic beauty and a bustling arts and culture scene. Popular destinations include Peddler's Village, an old-timey shopping, dining, and entertainment complex, and the lovely towns of New Hope and Doylestown. All three lie along a 10-mile stretch of Route 202, about an hour's drive from Center City Philadelphia.

SIGHTS

New Hope

The village of New Hope boasts nearly 200 independently owned shops and galleries, a relatively vibrant nightlife, and a thriving gay culture. It's the sort of place that attracts art-collecting socialites and leather-clad bikers alike. Just across the Delaware River, the New Jersey town of Lambertville tries hard to keep up with its hip neighbor, so be sure to cross the auto/pedestrian bridge that connects them. There's no need to move your car to and fro: The toll-free bridge is less than a quarter-mile long, and the sites and shops you'll want to visit are within strolling distance of the river.

If you're a first-time visitor, get your bearings at the **New Hope Visitors Center** (Main and Mechanic Sts., 215/862-5030, www.newhopevisitorscenter.org, 11:30am-5pm Sun.-Thurs., 11:30am-6pm Fri., 11:30am-7pm Sat.), built in 1839 as the first town hall. Then pop by the **Bucks County Playhouse** (70 S. Main St., 215/862-2121, www.bcptheater.org) to see what's showing. Opened in 1939 in a renovated gristmill, the theater quickly became known as a place to catch premieres of shows that would later open on Broadway. Grace Kelly, Bea Arthur, Liza Minnelli, and Merv Griffin have graced its stage.

Should you tire of exploring on foot, take a scenic cruise aboard the **Wells Ferry** (behind The Landing Restaurant, 22 N. Main St., 215/205-1140, www.newhopeboatrides.com, May-Oct., adults $12, children 2-12 $8). You'll learn a bit about the history of New Hope—which was known as Wells Ferry in the early 1700s—aboard the pontoon boats.

Alternatively, take a ride on the **New Hope & Ivyland Railroad** (32 W. Bridge St., 215/862-2332, www.newhoperailroad.com, adults $21-29, seniors $20-28, children 2-11 $19-27, children under 2 $5). The tourist railroad has an authentic steam locomotive as well as historic diesel engines, 1920s passenger coaches, and an antique bar car. Hourly excursions give you the option of disembarking near Peddler's Village, a popular shopping destination, and taking a later train back.

The Mercer Mile

The quantity and quality of museums in Doylestown, population 8,200, is remarkable for a town its size. Four are concentrated in an area known as the Mercer Mile. Get an early start if you plan to hit them all, and wear comfortable shoes so you can walk between them. You'll find charming shops and eateries along the way.

Three of the museums owe their existence to one local genius: Henry Chapman Mercer (1856-1930), a lawyer by schooling, an archaeologist and maker of architectural tiles by profession, and an artifact hoarder by passion. In his 50s, Mercer poured his talents into constructing three edifices entirely of reinforced concrete. The first was his dream home, a 44-room castle with 10 bathrooms, 18 fireplaces, 32 stairwells, and more than 200 windows of various shape and size. He named it **Fonthill**

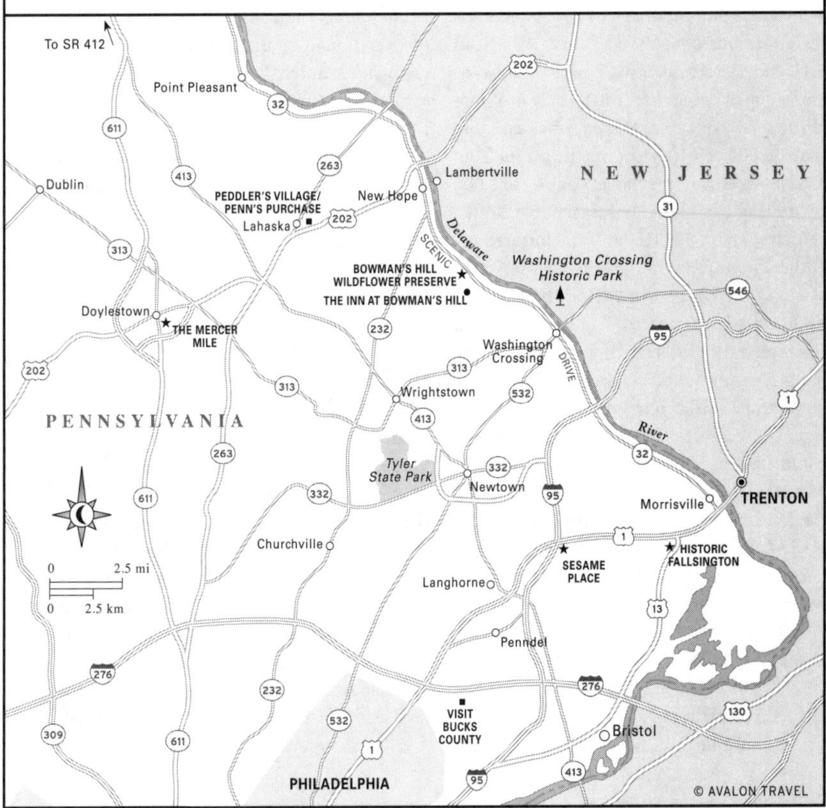

(E. Court St. and Rte. 313, 215/348-9461, www.mercermuseum.org, 10am-5pm Mon.-Sat., noon-5pm Sun., last tour at 4pm, adults $15, seniors $13, children 6-17 $8). The National Historic Landmark is elaborately adorned with Mercer's own colorful tiles as well as the Persian, Chinese, Spanish, and Dutch tiles he collected. Access is by guided tour only, and reservations are strongly advised.

Next to his home he built a tile factory. A leading figure in the Arts and Crafts movement, Mercer produced handmade tiles for thousands of private and public buildings, including the state capitol in Harrisburg and Grauman's Chinese Theatre in Hollywood. Reminiscent of a Spanish mission, his **Moravian Pottery & Tile Works** (130 Swamp Rd., 215/348-6098, www.buckscounty.org/government/moravianpotterytileworks, 10am-4:45pm daily, last tour at 4pm, adults $5, seniors $4, children 7-17 $3) is now maintained as a "working history" museum by the Bucks County Department of Parks and Recreation. Tours, offered every half hour, consist of a video—overly long at 17 minutes; feel free to get moving—and a self-guided walk through the facility, where ceramicists press and glaze tiles in a manner similar to Mercer's. The gift shop carries reissues of tiles and mosaics in the Arts and Crafts tradition.

Mercer built his final concrete masterpiece, the **Mercer Museum** (84 S. Pine St.,

215/345-0210, www.mercermuseum.org, 10am-5pm Mon.-Sat., noon-5pm Sun., adults $15, seniors $13, children 6-17 $8), to showcase his enormous collection of early American artifacts. Determined to preserve the handmade goods being discarded in favor of machine-made versions, Mercer amassed more than 30,000 objects, running the gamut from Native American implements dating to 8,000 BC to tiny clockmaking tools, horse-drawn vehicles, and a whaleboat—all cluttered together, hundreds hanging from the walls, ceiling, and beams, in the oddly designed building. Make your way up to the seventh floor to walk underneath a gallows, where hanged men would have dropped down. The collection, which has grown considerably since Mercer's death, is regarded as the most complete of its kind. The museum isn't heated or cooled, so dress accordingly. Fonthill and the Mercer Museum are administered by the Bucks County Historical Society, which offers a reduced rate ($26, children 6-17 $15) for admission to both.

A stone's throw from the Mercer Museum is the **James A. Michener Art Museum** (138 S. Pine St., 215/340-9800, www.michenerartmuseum.org, 10am-4:30pm Tues.-Fri., 10am-5pm Sat., noon-5pm Sun., adults $18, seniors $17, students $16, children 6-18 $8), known for its extensive collection of Pennsylvania Impressionist paintings. It also hosts nationally touring exhibits and showcases important regional artists. A permanent exhibit celebrates the career of its namesake, a Doylestown native who rose to fame as an author, snagging a Pulitzer Prize for 1947's *Tales of the South Pacific* and a Presidential Medal of Freedom in 1977. The museum opened in 1988, about a decade before Michener's death, in a building that served as the county jail for more than a century.

Washington Crossing Historic Park

On December 25, 1776, General George Washington and his ragged troops crossed the ice-choked Delaware River from Pennsylvania to New Jersey. **Washington Crossing Historic Park** (Rte. 32, between Rte. 532 and Aquetong Rd., 215/493-4076, www.washingtoncrossingpark.org, visitors center 10am-5pm daily, free, tours $6 per site, combination ticket for 3 tours $11), which preserves their put-in site, consists of two sections several miles apart. The lower section, near the intersection of Routes 32 and 532, features a visitors center, an 18th-century inn that

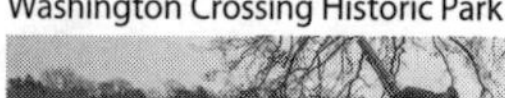
Washington Crossing Historic Park

served as a guard post during the encampment preceding the river crossing, several 19th-century structures, and a 20th-century boathouse with replicas of the type of craft used by Washington and his men. The boats are used every Christmas Day in a reenactment of the crossing that changed the course of history. Guided tours of Lower Park and the Thompson-Neely House, where wounded or sick soldiers were treated, are offered daily.

At the upper section, you'll find more historic structures, graves of soldiers who died during the winter encampment, and a 125-foot tower completed in 1931 to commemorate the Revolution. Tickets to the top of the tower, where you'll be rewarded with views of the river and surrounding countryside, are $6.

Sesame Place

Sesame Place (100 Sesame Rd., Langhorne, 215/752-7070, www.sesameplace.com, daily late May-Labor Day and select other days, admission $66, children under 2 years free) is the nation's only theme park based entirely on the enduring children's television show starring Big Bird, Elmo, and Cookie Monster. Kids can hobnob with their favorite *Sesame Street* characters in the 14-acre park, designed with the show's demographic in mind. Attractions include Cookie Mountain, a vinyl cone for pint-size mountaineers, and Ernie's Bed Bounce, a giant air mattress for aspiring moonwalkers. Bring swimwear and a towel for wet attractions such as The Count's Splash Castle, a multilevel play area featuring a 1,000-gallon tipping bucket, and the adult-friendly Big Bird's Rambling River. Admission is pricey (and parking will set you back another $17-28), but tickets are good for a second visit in the same season. The park opens at 10am and closes between 6pm and 9pm.

Historic Fallsington

Billed as "the village that time forgot," **Historic Fallsington** (4 Yardley Ave., Fallsington, 215/295-6567, www.historicfallsington.org, 10:30am-3:30pm Tues.-Sat. mid-May-mid-Oct., by appt. Tues.-Fri. mid-Oct.-mid-May, adults $7, seniors $6, children $3) consists of more than 90 buildings dating from the 1600s to early 1900s. The village formed around a Quaker meetinghouse built in 1690. Pennsylvania founder William Penn worshiped and preached there while living at Pennsbury Manor, several miles to the south. Guided walking tours, offered every half hour during the regular season, visit three preserved buildings, including a 1760s log house. You're welcome to stroll through the historic district on your own (be sure to grab a pamphlet describing about 20 structures), but don't go turning any doorknobs. Most of the buildings are privately owned.

SHOPPING

Boutique shopping is one of Bucks County's biggest draws. New Hope, Doylestown, and Newtown are great places to stroll and spend disposable income. New Hope has a particularly eclectic mix of stores. You'll find everything from antiques to motorcycle leathers to Wiccan supplies along its Main Street. About four miles west of New Hope is the popular **Peddler's Village** (Rtes. 202 and 263, Lahaska, 215/794-4000, www.peddlersvillage.com, open daily, hours vary), a 42-acre complex with about 60 specialty shops, several restaurants, a 70-room inn, and a family entertainment area featuring an antique carousel. Designed to evoke colonial America, the "village" hosts nearly a dozen annual festivals and events, including the popular **Apple Festival** (first weekend in Nov., free) and a gingerbread house display during the holiday season.

Across from Peddler's Village is an outlet center, **Penn's Purchase** (5861 York Rd., Lahaska, 215/794-2806, www.pennspurchase.com, open daily, hours vary by season), with stores including Coach, Brooks Brothers, and Gymboree.

Flea market enthusiasts can also find their bliss in the region. **Rice's Sale & Country Market** (6326 Greenhill Rd., New Hope, 215/297-5993, www.rices.com, 7am-1pm Tues. and Sat.), a 30-acre open-air market, hosts as many as 400 vendors. The indoor/outdoor **Golden Nugget Antique and Flea Market** (1850 River Rd., Lambertville, 609/397-0811, www.gnflea.com, 6am-4pm Wed. and Sat.-Sun.), across the Delaware River in New Jersey, is another gem.

FOOD

New Hope and its across-the-Delaware neighbor, Lambertville, have several top-notch restaurants. A true original, ★ **Marsha Brown** (15 S. Main St., New Hope, 215/862-7044, www.marshabrownrestaurant.com, 11:30am-4pm and 5pm-10pm Mon.-Thurs., 11:30am-4pm and 5pm-11pm Fri.-Sat., 11:30am-4pm and 4:30pm-9pm Sun., $24-49) offers New Orleans-style cuisine and Southern hospitality in a former church complete with stained glass windows. The menu features upscale versions of Creole classics like gumbo ya ya and jambalaya, a raw bar, and Maine lobster.

Housed in a restored 19th-century train station on the banks of the Delaware, **Lambertville Station** (11 Bridge St., Lambertville, 609/397-8300, www.lambertvillestation.com, 11:30am-10pm Mon.-Thurs., 11:30am-11pm Fri.-Sat., 10:30am-10pm Sun., $17-36) is a superb choice any time of year but especially in the warmer months, when its outdoor dining area is open and the on-site herb garden is in full bloom. Specialties include Chesapeake-style crab cakes and roasted rack of lamb. The Sunday brunch buffet (11am-4pm, adults $30, children 3-10 $18), served in the ballroom of the 45-room **Inn at Lambertville Station** (609/397-4400, $159-325), is a worthy splurge.

In Doylestown, try the **Pennsylvania Soup & Seafood House** (22 S. Main St., Doylestown, 215/230-9490, www.pasoupandseafood.com, 11am-3pm Mon., 11am-8pm Tues.-Thurs., 11am-9pm Fri.-Sat., $10-25). Head chef Keith Blalock is known around town as "the soup guy." His lobster bisque, Tuscan onion, and mulligatawny make it easy to stick to a liquid diet.

ACCOMMODATIONS

You'll have no trouble finding distinctive accommodations in Bucks County, especially in and around New Hope. At the top of the heap: ★ **The Inn at Bowman's Hill** (518 Lurgan Rd., New Hope, 215/862-8090, www.theinnatbowmanshill.com, $365-625), set on five idyllic acres on New Hope's outskirts. The romantic B&B is the only AAA four-diamond lodging in the county. Its eight guest rooms and suites feature king-size featherbeds, fireplaces, and bathrooms with all the bells and whistles. Can't decide if you want a massage in your room or by the pool? Book both. Hungry for breakfast in bed? Done. Want to collect your own organic eggs from the resident hens? Feel free. The 134-acre **Bowman's Hill Wildflower Preserve** (1635 River Rd., New Hope, 215/862-2924, www.bhwp.org, grounds 8:30am-dusk daily, visitors center 9am-5pm daily Apr.-June, 9am-5pm Tues.-Sun. July-Mar., adults $6, seniors and students $4, children 3-14 $3), home to 800 species of plants native to Pennsylvania, is a stone's throw away.

The **Logan Inn** (10 W. Ferry St., New Hope, 215/862-2300, www.loganinn.com, $135-300) is a lovely, and more affordable, option. Opened in the 1720s, it's the oldest continuously run inn in Bucks County and one of the oldest in the United States. It's no coincidence that lantern-lit **Ghost Tours of New Hope** (215/348-1598, www.ghosttoursofnewhope.com, 8pm Sat. June-late Nov. and Fri. and Sat. Sept.-Oct., $10 per person) begin outside its doors: the 16-room inn is said to be extremely haunted. Good luck booking the legendary Room 6 in October, when paranormal investigators flock to town. The on-site tavern serves steaks and fresh seafood. In warm weather, dine on the patio—or just sit back with a cocktail and enjoy some of the best people-watching in town.

Wedgwood Inn (111 W. Bridge St., New Hope, 215/862-2570, www.wedgwoodinn.com, $150-300) owners Nadine and Carl Glassman are so good at what they do that they run training programs for aspiring innkeepers. The couple offers 18 rooms and suites spread between three 19th-century houses a short walk from the heart of New Hope and the bridge to Lambertville. Guests enjoy a continental-plus breakfast and a tot of house-made almond liqueur when it's time to turn in.

A few miles west of New Hope and only a minute from Peddler's Village, **Ash Mill Farm Bed & Breakfast** (5358 York Rd., Holicong, 215/794-5373, www.ashmillfarm.com, $130-295) offers spacious accommodations on a working sheep farm. Feeding the sheep and pygmy goats is permitted, but unlike some farm B&Bs, Ash Mill doesn't market itself to families with young kids—no children under 13. Children of all ages are welcome at the **Golden Plough Inn** (Rte. 202 and Street Rd., Lahaska, 215/794-4004, www.goldenploughinn.com, $119-350), with 70 rooms situated throughout Peddler's Village. Many feature gas fireplaces and two-person whirlpools. Rates include a voucher toward breakfast in a Peddler's Village restaurant.

In the heart of Doylestown, the **Doylestown Inn** (18 W. State St., Doylestown, 215/345-6610, www.hatterydoylestown.com, $170-245) is set in two 1871 properties, connected in 1902 and turned into a hotel, plus a third building added in 1937—and there are still only 11 rooms. Much of the space is given over to **Hattery Stove & Still** (215/345-1527, 9am-11pm Mon.-Thurs., 9am-1am Fri., 8am-1am Sat., 8am-9pm Sun., $16-30), serving American fare in an eclectic space with a steampunk edge. In contrast, the guestrooms go for a country inn motif.

Visit the website of the **Bucks County Bed and Breakfast Association** (www.visitbucks.com) for more options.

TRANSPORTATION AND SERVICES

Central Bucks County, where New Hope, Doylestown, and Peddler's Village are found, is less than an hour north of Philadelphia and 90 minutes southwest of New York City. To reach New Hope from Philadelphia, head north on I-95, take the exit for New Hope, and then take Taylorsville Road and PA-32. From New York, head west on I-78, then south on I-278 and Route 202. The nearest major airports are **Philadelphia International Airport** (PHL, 215/937-6937, www.phl.org) and **Lehigh Valley International Airport** (ABE, 800/359-5842, www.flylvia.org). **Newark Liberty International Airport** (EWR, 973/961-6000, www.panynj.gov) isn't much farther away. **Amtrak** (800/872-7245, www.amtrak.com) can get you to Trenton, New Jersey, 17 miles southeast of New Hope. The Southeastern Pennsylvania Transportation Authority, or **SEPTA** (215/580-7800, www.septa.org), provides regional rail service between Philadelphia and Doylestown, and **Trans-Bridge Lines** (610/868-6001, www.transbridgelines.com) offers bus service between New York City and New Hope, Doylestown, and Peddler's Village.

While you can certainly make do without a car in these popular destinations, you'll want one for traveling between them and exploring the surrounding countryside. If you're not going too far, a bicycle will do. **New Hope Cyclery** (404 York Rd., New Hope, 215/862-6888, www.newhopecyclery.com, 10am-6pm Mon.-Wed. and Fri.-Sat., 10am-8pm Thurs., 10am-4pm Sun.), which rents mountain bikes, tandems, and child trailers, is near Trans-Bridge's New Hope stop.

Visit Bucks County (800/836-2825, www.visitbuckscounty.com) is a great source of information about the region. Its visitors center (3207 Street Rd., Bensalem, 215/639-0300, 9am-5pm daily) features a large gift shop and an exhibit on the region's arts heritage.

Brandywine Valley

As it winds its way from southeastern Pennsylvania to the northern Delaware city of Wilmington, Brandywine Creek crosses what geologists refer to as a fall line. In layman's terms, it takes a nosedive. That nosedive made the Brandywine Valley attractive to water-powered industries—flour mills, cotton mills, and the like—in days of yore. In 1802 a French immigrant by the name of Eleuthère Irénée (E. I.) du Pont began construction of a gunpowder works along the creek, often referred to as the Brandywine River. It wasn't long before his company was the nation's largest gunpowder producer, and the du Ponts grew wildly wealthy. The Brandywine Valley's present popularity as a tourist destination has much to do with their wealth. It was a du Pont who created Longwood Gardens, one of the nation's premier horticultural attractions. It was a du Pont who built the magnificent Nemours Mansion and its garden, one of the finest examples of a formal French garden outside of France. And it was a du Pont who turned Winterthur, another family estate, into a showplace for American decorative arts. You'll hear a lot about the du Ponts if you pay the region a visit.

You'll also hear a lot about the Wyeths, often called America's first family of art. Three generations of Wyeth artists have lived and painted in the Brandywine region, capturing its people and landscapes on canvas. The Brandywine River Museum of Art boasts a renowned collection of works by members of the talented clan, including Andrew Wyeth, one of the most celebrated and influential artists of the 20th century.

The region boasts some cute-as-a-button towns, including West Chester, which brazenly bills itself as "the perfect town," and Kennett Square, the so-called Mushroom Capital of the World. More than 60 percent of the mushrooms consumed in the United States are grown in the Kennett Square area. The annual Mushroom Festival, held the weekend after Labor Day, showcases mushrooms in every imaginable form, including ice cream. In recent years the Brandywine Valley has become associated with another crop: wine grapes. It's home to more than a dozen wineries, including one of Pennsylvania's largest.

SIGHTS

★ Longwood Gardens

Longwood Gardens (1001 Longwood Rd., Kennett Square, 610/388-1000, www.longwoodgardens.org, 9am-6pm daily winter, 9am-6pm Sun.-Wed., 9am-10pm Thurs.-Sat. summer, adults \$23-30, seniors and students \$20-27, children 5-18 \$12-16) is one of Pennsylvania's most exquisite spots. It's unusual among horticultural showplaces in the Northeast in that it's open 365 days a year. In fact, Longwood is busiest from Thanksgiving through early January, when fountains dance to holiday music and half a million holiday lights sparkle. Its 1,050 acres of gardens, woodlands, and meadows were shaped by many hands, but the greatest credit is due to Pierre S. du Pont (1870-1954), whose French-born great-grandfather founded the DuPont chemical company.

In 1906, Pierre purchased a property of about 200 acres from a Quaker family by the name of Peirce. The Peirces' 1730 farmhouse became his weekend residence, and the creation of Longwood Gardens began. Pierre drew inspiration from Italian villas and French chateaux but had a tendency to supersize. Longwood's Italian Water Garden, for example, was inspired by a garden near Florence. But where the original had only a few fountains, the Longwood version boasts 18 pools and 600 jets.

Budget at least an hour to take in the 20-plus outdoor gardens, including the otherworldly Topiary Garden and the 600-foot-long

Brandywine Valley

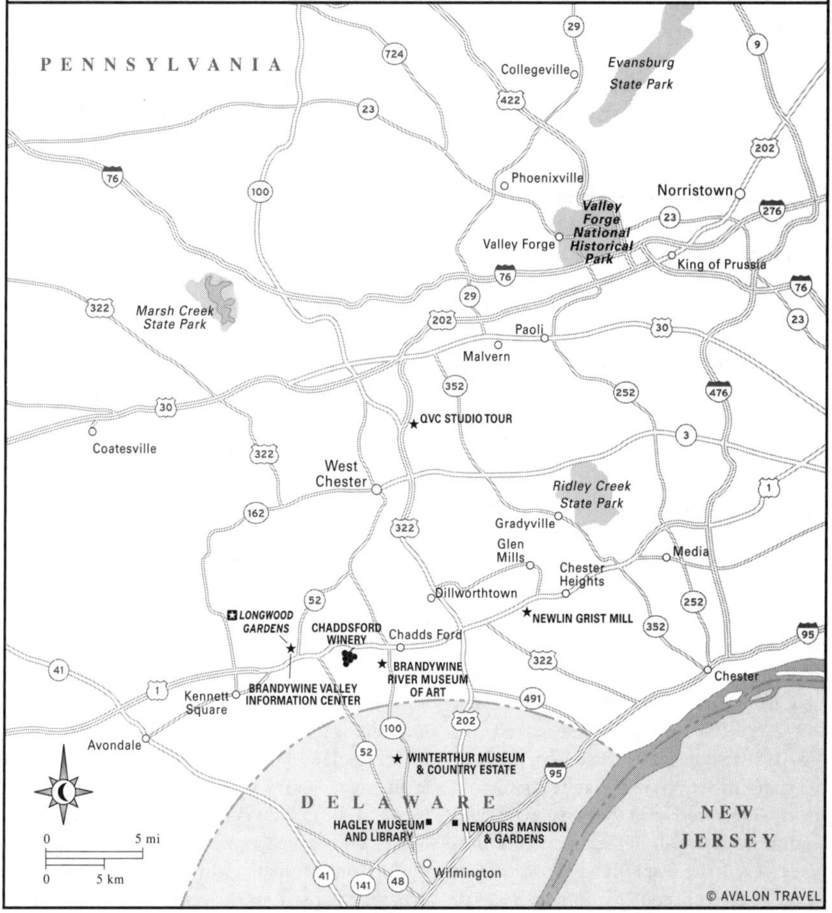

Flower Garden Walk, whose beds are replanted with more than 120,000 spring bulbs every October. You'll need at least two hours for the Longwood Conservatory, which houses everything from cacti to a colossal pipe organ. In 2017, Longwood unveiled its five-acre foundation garden. Illuminated jets of water shoot up to 175 feet in the air during the popular **nighttime fountain shows** (Thurs.-Sat. May-Oct.). It's a good idea to buy a timed ticket ahead of your visit, whether you're coming during the day or in the evening.

Longwood's **Terrace** restaurant, famous for its mushroom soup, offers both casual and fine dining. Reservations are strongly recommended for the fine-dining room, named **1906** (11:30am-3:30pm daily winter, 11:30am-7:30pm summer, $16-35) after the year Pierre purchased the grounds. Alternatively, bring a cooler of food and a bottle of wine. Longwood's picnic area, located a short drive from the main parking lot, features grills, 70 tables, and restroom facilities.

Delaware's du Pont Sights

Longwood's creator wasn't the only du Pont with lavish tastes. The Wilmington, Delaware, area boasts three du Pont estates-turned-museums. Just six miles south of Longwood on Route 52 is **Winterthur Museum & Country Estate** (5105 Kennett Pike, Winterthur, Delaware, 302/888-4600, www.winterthur.org, 10am-5pm Tues.-Sun., adults $20, seniors and students $18, children 2-11 $5), home to a vast collection of Americana and a splendid naturalistic garden. E. I. du Pont, who founded the company that made his family one of the wealthiest in America, purchased the land that would become Winterthur in the 1810s. But it wasn't until his great-grandson Henry Francis du Pont (1880-1969) got his hands on the property a century later that it evolved into the extraordinary estate it is today.

Henry doubled the size of the existing mansion and filled the rooms with his burgeoning collection of American decorative arts. By the time the mansion opened as a museum in 1951, he had created 175 period rooms. First Lady Jacqueline Kennedy was so wowed during a 1961 visit that she invited Henry to head the committee overseeing the restoration of the White House. General admission includes an introductory tour of the mansion, admittance to galleries displaying highlights from Winterthur's collection of more than 85,000 objects made or used in America from 1640 to 1860, and free rein of the Winterthur Garden. A tram tour of the 60-acre garden is offered when weather permits. The last house tour tickets are sold at 3:15pm. Winterthur (pronounced "winter-tour") also offers one- and two-hour in-depth tours that cost an additional $10 and $20, respectively. Reservations are strongly recommended for in-depth tours.

While Henry amassed all things American, another great-grandson of E. I. du Pont lived in French-style splendor a few miles away. Alfred I. du Pont (1864-1935) built **Nemours Mansion & Gardens** (Rte. 141 and Alapocas Rd., Wilmington, Delaware, 302/651-6912, www.nemoursmansion.org, 10am-5pm Tues.-Sat., noon-5pm Sun. May-Dec., adults $17, seniors and students $15, children 5-16 $7) to please his second wife, a Francophile who also happened to be his cousin. The spectacular Louis XVI-style mansion and formal French gardens, modeled after those at Versailles's Petit Trianon, offers tours that depart three times a day Tuesday through Saturday and twice on Sundays, lasting 2.5-3 hours. Reservations are strongly recommended. Nemours is closed January through April.

Wondering how the du Ponts earned all that dough? Head to **Hagley Museum and Library** (200 Hagley Rd., Wilmington, Delaware, 302/658-2400, www.hagley.org, museum 10am-5pm daily mid-Mar.-early Nov., 10am-4pm daily mid-Nov.-mid-Mar., adults $14, seniors and students $10, children 6-14 $5), located on the site of the gunpowder works E. I. du Pont established in 1802, three years after fleeing France amid the turmoil and bloodshed of the French Revolution. In time, the company established a virtual monopoly on the U.S. gunpowder industry, raking in more than $1 billion during World War I. Spanning 235 acres along the Brandywine River, Hagley features restored gunpowder mills, the remains of a workers' community, and the first du Pont home in America. Exhibits in the visitors center tell the story of the DuPont company, which evolved from America's largest explosives manufacturer into its largest chemical company.

Brandywine River Museum of Art

Museums with an emphasis on regional art rarely enjoy international renown. The **Brandywine River Museum of Art** (1 Hoffman's Mill Rd., Chadds Ford, 610/388-2700, www.brandywinemuseum.org, 9:30am-5pm daily, adults $18, seniors $15, students $6) is an exception, thanks in large part to one family with a surfeit of talent. Opened in 1971 in a converted Civil War-era gristmill, the museum on the banks of the Brandywine is home to an unparalleled collection of works by three generations of Wyeths. N. C. Wyeth (1882-1945) moved to the Brandywine region in 1902 to study with famed illustrator Howard Pyle. He became Pyle's star pupil and one of America's foremost commercial artists, painting advertisements for the likes of Coca-Cola and Cream of Wheat and illustrating such literary classics as *Treasure Island, Robin Hood, The Last of the Mohicans,* and *Robinson Crusoe.*

Three of his five children also became artists, including daughters Henriette and Carolyn, who are well represented in the museum's collection. But it was his youngest child who made the greatest mark. Realist painter Andrew Wyeth (1917-2009) was the first artist awarded the Presidential Medal of Freedom, the nation's highest civilian honor; the first living artist to have an exhibition at the White House; and the first living American artist to have an exhibition at London's Royal Academy of Arts. His 1948 painting *Christina's World,* part of the permanent collection of the Museum of Modern Art in New York, is one of the best-known images of the 20th century. Born in 1946, son Jamie Wyeth was only 20 when his first one-man show opened in New York and less than 30 at his first retrospective. He's known for portraits of larger-than-life figures such as John F. Kennedy, Rudolf Nureyev, and Andy Warhol, as well as large-scale animal portraits. Hundreds of other artists, including Pyle and many of his students, are represented in the museum's collection of more than 3,000 works.

For even more insight into America's first family of art, tour the **N. C. Wyeth House and Studio,** where N. C. raised his talented brood; the **Andrew Wyeth Studio,** where Andrew painted from 1940 to 2008; or the **Kuerner Farm,** which inspired so many of Andrew's works. The historic properties are open for tours April-November. The studio tours are $8; Kuerner Farm is $5. A complimentary shuttle bus provides transportation from the museum.

Wineries

Chaddsford Winery (632 Baltimore Pike, Chadds Ford, 610/388-6221, www.chaddsford.com, 10am-6pm Tues.-Fri. and Sun., 11am-7pm Sat., tasting fee $10) is one of the largest of Pennsylvania's 100-plus wineries. But it's hardly the impersonal operation that distinction implies. Founded in 1982 by a husband-and-wife team, the winery occupies a renovated barn along Route 1, midway between Longwood Gardens and the Brandywine River Museum of Art. It produces 30,000 cases a year of dry reds, dry whites, and sweet wines. The spiced apple wine is a hot seller in the fall. About five miles away is the vineyard and tasting room of **Penns Woods Winery** (124 Beaver Valley Rd., Chadds Ford, 610/459-0808, www.pennswoodsevents.com, 1pm-5pm Mon., noon-6pm Tues.-Thurs., 11am-7pm Fri.-Sat., 11am-5pm Sun., tasting fee $10), known for its Traminette, a hybrid white wine, and Ameritage Reserve, a blend of many grapes. Its off-site winery is not open to the public.

Paradocx Vineyard (1833 Flint Hill Rd., Landenberg, 610/255-5684, www.paradocx.com, 2pm-8pm Fri., noon-6pm Sat.-Sun., tasting fee $10) grows grapes and produces wines on a picturesque property. It's owned by two couples, all practicing physicians (hence its name, a play on "pair of docs"). The tasting room at the vineyard and winery has limited hours, but you can sample the full line of wines any day but Monday at **Paradocx's Kennett Square location** (The Market at Liberty Place, 148 W. State St., Kennett Square, noon-8pm Tues.-Thurs. and Sat.-Sun., noon-10pm Fri.). **Kreutz Creek Vineyards** (553 S. Guernsey Rd., West Grove, 610/869-4412, www.kreutzcreekvineyards.com, 11am-6pm Sat., noon-5pm Sun., tasting fee $8), which serves wine slushies at its summer concerts, is just four miles from Paradocx's Landenberg location.

Va La Vineyards (8820 Gap Newport Pike, Avondale, 610/268-2702, www.valavineyards.com, noon-5:30pm Fri.-Sun., call ahead to verify hours, tasting fee $20) is a must for oenophiles. It relies almost exclusively on its 6.73 acres of grapes to produce four distinctive wines.

QVC Studio Tour

A tour of **QVC's world headquarters** (1200 Wilson Dr., West Chester, 800/600-9900, www.qvctours.com, tours 10:30am, noon, and 2:30pm Mon.-Sat., adults $10, children 6-12 $8) is to fans of home shopping what Universal Studios Hollywood is to movie buffs: a peek behind the curtain. Guided walking tours begin with a short video introduction to the TV retailer, founded in 1986 with the goal of providing "Quality, Value, and Convenience," and culminate in a bird's-eye view of the sprawling studio from a perch within earshot of the producer's booth. QVC broadcasts live 24 hours a day, 364 days a year in the United States, so the odds of seeing a program in progress are overwhelming. In addition to the regular tour, which lasts 60-75 minutes, QVC offers a $100-per-person, three-hour "all access tour" Fridays at 8:45am, which includes lunch in the corporate cafeteria. Don't underestimate QVC's popularity; it's not unusual for the pricey tour to sell out. The QVC Studio Store (10am-5pm Mon.-Sat.) offers an ever-changing selection of beauty products, jewelry, kitchenware, home decor, and other products.

Newlin Grist Mill

Set within a 150-acre park, the **Newlin Grist Mill** (219 Cheyney Rd., Glen Mills, 610/459-2359, www.newlingristmill.org, visitors center 9am-4pm daily Mar.-Dec., 9am-4pm Mon.-Fri., 9am-3pm Sat.-Sun. Jan.-Feb., park open until dusk) is the only working 18th-century gristmill in Pennsylvania. The water-powered mill was built in 1704 and operated commercially until 1941, grinding wheat, corn, oats, buckwheat, and rye. Today it grinds corn into cornmeal that can be purchased in the visitor center, a former railroad station and post office. Adjacent to the mill is a two-story stone house built in 1739 for the miller. Admission to the park is free, but tours of the mill and miller's house are $5 per person. They're offered at 11am and 2pm daily and last about an hour. On weekends tours are also offered at 10am and 1pm. The park attracts nature lovers as well as history buffs, with eight miles of hiking trails and the West Branch of Chester Creek, a popular trout stream, running through it.

ENTERTAINMENT AND EVENTS

Festivals and Events

The Brandywine Valley is horse country, and many of its main spring and summer events fall in the equestrian category. The equestrian season opens with **Point-to-Point** (302/888-4600, www.winterthur.org, early May), a day of steeplechase racing and tailgate picnicking amid the splendor of Henry Francis du Pont's Winterthur estate in Delaware. Almost as impressive as the racehorses are the antique Rolls-Royces, Bentleys, steam autos, and horse-drawn carriages rolled out for the occasion. Proceeds from the **Radnor Hunt Races** (Malvern, 610/388-8324, www.radnorhuntraces.org, third Sat. in May), another steeplechase event, benefit the Brandywine Conservancy, the Chadds Ford-based nonprofit that operates the Brandywine River Museum of Art. Admission passes must be purchased in advance.

Started in 1896, when horses were still a primary mode of transportation, the **Devon Horse Show and Country Fair** (Devon, 610/688-2554, www.devonhorseshow.net, late May or early June) is the oldest and largest outdoor multibreed horse competition in the country. The event, which has grown from one day to 11, has raised more than $14 million for Bryn Mawr Hospital in suburban Philadelphia.

Other equine-centric traditions include **Ludwig's Corner Horse Show and Country Fair** (Glenmoore, 610/458-3344, www.ludwigshorseshow.org, Labor Day weekend) and Friday night and Sunday afternoon matches at the **Brandywine Polo Club** (232

Polo Rd., Toughkenamon, 610/268-8692, www.brandywinepolo.com).

The two-day **Chester County Balloon Festival** (Toughkenamon, 610/827-7208, www.ccballoonfest.com, June, adults $15, children 6-12 $5) is a chance to take flight or simply delight in the sight of mass balloon ascensions and fireworks. Balloon rides ($200 per person morning flight, $225 per person evening flight) must be reserved in advance.

It's not unusual for hundreds of people to run out of Phoenixville's Colonial Theatre screaming at the top of their lungs. It's tradition. Built in 1903, the theater provided the setting for a memorable scene in 1958's *The Blob,* and reenacting it is part of the town's annual homage to the sci-fi flick. Started in 2000, **BlobFest** (227 Bridge St., Phoenixville, 610/917-1228, www.thecolonialtheatre.com, July, free and ticketed events) also features a street fair and screenings of horror classics.

Nearly 200 vendors hawk everything from mushroom-shaped jewelry to mushroom ice cream during the **Mushroom Festival** (610/925-3373, www.mushroomfestival.org, weekend after Labor Day, adults $3, children under 12 free), Kennett Square's annual celebration of its number one cash crop. The fungi-themed fete features mushroom soup cook-offs, mushroom growing and cooking demos, an antique and classic car show, and a community parade.

FOOD

Chadds Ford

Two noteworthy restaurants can be found near the intersection of Route 1 (Baltimore Pike) and Creek Road, convenient to the Brandywine River Museum of Art. A humble establishment, **Hank's Place** (1410 Baltimore Pike, 610/388-7061, www.hanks-place.net, 6am-3pm Mon., 6am-7pm Tues.-Sat., 7am-3pm Sun., $6-18) is known for better-than-average diner food, including Greek specialties like gyros and spanakopita. Renowned painter Andrew Wyeth, who died in 2009, was a regular.

Chadds Ford's favorite son was also spotted at the upscale **Brandywine Prime** (1617 Baltimore Pike, 610/388-8088, www.brandywineprime.com, 5pm-10pm Mon.-Fri., noon-2pm and 5pm-10pm Sat., 10am-2pm and 4pm-9pm Sun., $19-48), a seafood and steak restaurant with a superb Sunday brunch (adults $20, children 4-12 $12).

Kennett Square

★ **Talula's Table** (102 W. State St., 610/444-8255, www.talulastable.com, market 7am-7pm daily, dinner 7pm-11pm daily) in the heart of Kennett Square accepts just one reservation a day—for that date the following year, for one party of 8-12 guests. Fortunately, you don't need foresight, or seven friends, to enjoy breakfast or lunch at Talula's, a gourmet market by day with an ever-changing mix of soups, salads, sandwiches, and other dishes ready to be heated up or packed to go. French cheeses, Italian pastas, and artisanal preserves compete for attention with house-made breads, pastries, charcuterie, sauces, spiced salts, and more. If there are macaroons in the pastry case, get at least two. Seating is sparse, so you may want to avoid the lunch rush.

West Chester

The county seat of Chester County has become something of a dining destination in recent years. More than 50 eateries representing a wide variety of cuisines can be found within its 1.8 square miles. The main intersection of Gay and High Streets is home to an **Iron Hill Brewery & Restaurant** (3 W. Gay St., 610/738-9600, www.ironhillbrewery.com/westchester, 11:30am-11pm Mon.-Wed., 11:30am-midnight Thurs., 11:30am-1am Fri., 11am-1am Sat., 11am-11pm Sun., $9-25), one of 12 and counting that have sprouted in Pennsylvania, Delaware, and New Jersey since 1996. You don't need to be into beer to enjoy the convivial atmosphere—or the seafood bisque, sweet potato fries, burgers, and hearty entrees like baby back ribs—but if you are a beer drinker you're definitely in the right place. After a meal, stroll over to **Gemelli** (12 W. Market St., 484/557-8482, www.gemelligelato.com, noon-10pm Mon.-Thurs., noon-11pm Fri.-Sat., noon-9pm Sun.) for rich, creamy gelato.

Skip the sit-down dining and head to **Carlino's** (128 W. Market St., 610/696-3788, www.carlinosmarket.com, 9am-7pm Mon.-Fri., 9am-6pm Sat., 9am-4pm Sun.), a gourmet market with a mind-blowing selection of cheeses. Belly up to the brie bar for a custom-made hunk. Load up on cured delicacies at the olive bar and fresh greens at the salad bar, order a deli sandwich or something hot—a pasta dish or hearth-fired pizza, perhaps—and take your bounty to the **Kreutz Creek Vineyards tasting room** (44 E. Gay St., 610/436-5006, www.kreutzcreekvineyards.com, 11am-8pm Tues.-Thurs., 11am-11pm Fri.-Sat., tasting fee $8), a BYOF (bring your own food) establishment that serves up live music on Friday and Saturday evenings. Add some decadence by dropping by **Eclat Chocolate** (24 S. High St., 610/692-5206, www.eclatchocolate.com, 10am-6pm Mon.-Fri., 10am-4pm Sat.) en route to pick up some single-origin mendiants (melt-in-your-mouth chocolate disks) or caramels.

A few miles south of downtown is the ★ **Dilworthtown Inn** (1390 Old Wilmington Pike, 610/399-1390, www.dilworthtown.com, 5:30pm-9pm Mon.-Fri., 5pm-9pm Sat., 5pm-8pm Sun., $24-45), offering elevated American cuisine and a stellar wine list in a colonial setting. The original section of the three-floor restaurant, which boasts 15 dining rooms and walk-in fireplaces, dates to 1754. The ruins of an old stone stable provide the setting for outdoor dining when weather permits. Candlelight and dishes like wild Burgundy escargot and chateaubriand for two—carved tableside—make the Dilworthtown a romantic choice. Its wine cellar is one of Pennsylvania's largest and a perennial winner of *Wine Spectator*'s Award of Excellence.

ACCOMMODATIONS

Bed-and-Breakfasts

As befitting a region known for mansions and gardens, wineries and horse farms, the Brandywine Valley has a healthy stock of elegant B&Bs. Fairest of them all is the ★ **Fairville Inn** (506 Kennett Pike, Chadds Ford, 610/388-5900, www.fairvilleinn.com, $185-320), with 15 rooms and suites spread between three buildings on five bucolic acres. It's conveniently located between Longwood Gardens and Winterthur on Route 52, but guests have been known to forgo sightseeing in favor of an afternoon on their private deck, by their in-room fire, or in their canopied bed. Breakfast features a buffet of fresh fruit, yogurt, cereal, and house-baked breads and muffins, plus your choice of three hot entrées.

Just minutes from Longwood Gardens, **Inn at Whitewing Farm** (370 Valley Rd., West Chester, 610/388-2013, www.innatwhitewingfarm.com, $159-296) offers plenty of privacy with guest rooms and suites set in three buildings—all separate from the main house. Breakfast (served 8:30am-9:30am) is enjoyed in what was once the hay barn, built in 1796. The grounds also include a tennis court and a tranquil pond.

For closer-to-town digs, **Faunbrook Bed & Breakfast** (699 W. Rosedale Ave., West Chester, 610/436-5788, www.faunbrook.com, $141-209) is an excellent choice. Less than two miles from the heart of West Chester, the 1860 manse has seven antique-filled guest rooms and grand common areas. Once home to a U.S. congressman, it still has a dignified air about it. Breakfast is served by candlelight.

Hotels

Bed-and-breakfasts aren't for everyone, and the Brandywine Valley is not without recommendable hotels. The 80-room **Hotel Warner** (120 N. High St., West Chester, 610/692-6920, www.hotelwarner.com, $144-194) is the only hotel in downtown West Chester. It's a great choice if you want to be within easy walking distance of restaurants, shops, and galleries. Amenities include free Wi-Fi, an indoor pool, and a complimentary continental breakfast.

The **Inn at Mendenhall** (323 Kennett Pike, Mendenhall, 610/388-2100, www.

choicehotels.com, $129-189) has an old-world charm, even though it only dates to 1990. It's on Route 52, just minutes from Longwood Gardens to its north and Winterthur to its south. Each spacious room and suite is equipped with a microwave, refrigerator, coffeemaker, safe, and flat-screen TV. The hotel's sundry shop, fitness center, and business center are accessible 24/7. Rates include wireless Internet access and a breakfast buffet. Fine dining is available in the on-site **Mendenhall Inn,** which also offers a Sunday champagne brunch (10am-2pm, $36).

TRANSPORTATION AND SERVICES

Longwood Gardens, the Brandywine River Museum of Art, and Chaddsford Winery, located within a few miles of each other along Route 1, are about 30 miles west from the heart of Philadelphia. They're even closer to **Philadelphia International Airport** (PHL, 215/937-6937, www.phl.org), which is about seven miles southwest of Center City. Although the Southeastern Pennsylvania Transportation Authority, or **SEPTA** (215/580-7800, www.septa.org), connects Philadelphia to West Chester, Phoenixville, and other Brandywine towns, exploring the region without a vehicle of your own is tough. If you're dead set against driving, familiarize yourself with the services of the **Transportation Management Association of Chester County** (TMACC, 610/993-0911, www.tmacc.org) and **DART First State** (302/652-3278, www.dartfirststate.com), Delaware's public transportation system.

You'll find hundreds of free brochures at the **Brandywine Valley Information Center** (300 Greenwood Rd., Kennett Square, 484/770-8550, www.brandywinevalley.com, 9am-5pm daily), adjacent to Longwood Gardens's main entrance. The **Greater Wilmington Convention & Visitors Bureau** (100 W. 10th St., Ste. 20, Wilmington, 800/489-6664, www.visitwilmingtonde.com, 9am-5pm Mon.-Thurs., 8:30am-4:30pm Fri.) represents Delaware's largest city and its surrounds, where the Nemours Mansion and Winterthur Museum are found.

Pennsylvania Dutch Country

This part of the state lacks blockbuster cities, yet tourism is a multibillion-dollar industry here. Part of the reason is the public's fascination with the Amish, whose way of life stands in contrast to the average American's.

Lancaster County, the most popular destination in the region, has the largest concentration of Amish in the world. Their use of horse-drawn buggies, adherence to strict dress codes, and rejection of technologies including television and computers inspires curiosity and awe in the many visitors to the region.

Those unfamiliar with the term Pennsylvania Dutch may wonder what the state has to do with the Netherlands. The answer: nothing. "Dutch," in this case, is a corruption of the word Deutsch, the German word for "German." Many German-speaking Europeans immigrated to Pennsylvania in the 18th century. They, their descendants, and their English-influenced dialect came to be called Pennsylvania German, or Pennsylvania Dutch. A common misconception is that "Pennsylvania Dutch" is synonymous with "Amish." In fact, the Amish made up a small percentage of the settlers. But the Amish and a handful of related "plain" groups have emerged as the guardians of the Pennsylvania Dutch dialect.

Less than 40 miles from the heart of Amish Country is the town of Hershey, the product of one chocolatier's expansive vision. Few places offer as high a concentration of family-friendly attractions as "The Sweetest Place on Earth." To the south is the town of Gettysburg, site of the Civil War's bloodiest battle and President Abraham Lincoln's most memorable speech. The region is also home to the state capital, Harrisburg, and York County, the self-proclaimed "Factory Tour Capital of the World."

Note: While Amish Country may feel made for Instagram, resist the urge to snap a picture, as the Amish take offense at being photographed.

Previous: Gettysburg National Military Park; Amish Country farm. **Above:** Aaron and Jessica's Buggy Rides.

Look for ★ to find recommended sights, activities, dining, and lodging.

HIGHLIGHTS

★ **Amish Attractions:** If everything you know about the Amish is from the movie *Witness,* you've got a lot to learn. Get schooled at Plain & Fancy Farm, the Amish Farm and House, or the Mennonite Information Center (page 98).

★ **Strasburg Rail Road:** Take a trip to Paradise on the nation's oldest operating short-line railroad (page 104).

★ **Air Museums:** Take to the skies in an antique plane or take a trip back in time during World War II Weekend (page 123).

★ **Hawk Mountain Sanctuary:** Some 20,000 hawks, eagles, and falcons soar past this raptor sanctuary on their southward journey. The sight is awe-inspiring and the hiking terrific (page 124).

★ **The Hershey Story:** If only every history museum included a hands-on Chocolate Lab (page 130).

★ **Hersheypark:** Hershey's century-old, chocolate-scented amusement park has more than 70 rides, from waterslides to dizzying roller coasters (page 130).

★ **Gettysburg National Military Park:** Site of the Civil War's most hellish battle, this national park is heaven for history buffs (page 147).

Pennsylvania Dutch Country

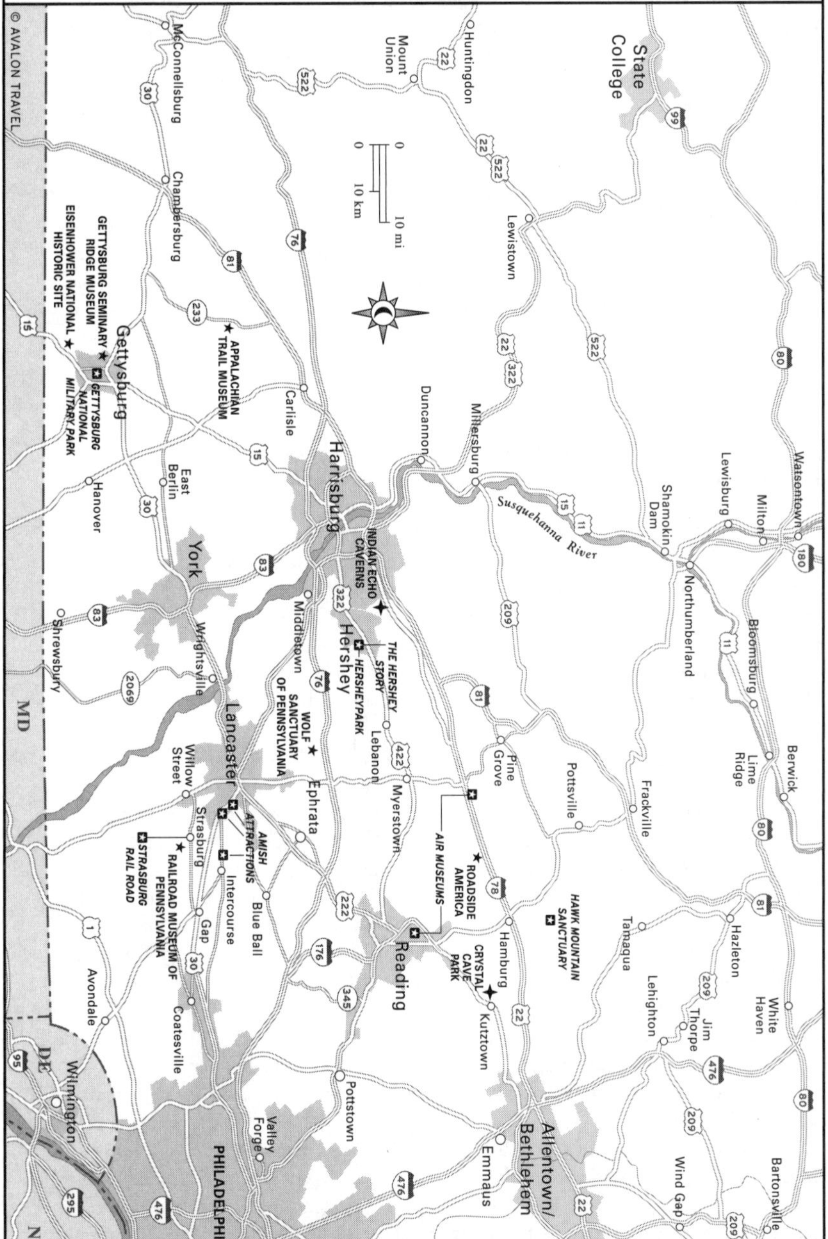

McConnellsburg
Chambersburg
Gettysburg
GETTYSBURG SEMINARY RIDGE MUSEUM
EISENHOWER NATIONAL HISTORIC SITE
GETTYSBURG NATIONAL MILITARY PARK
Hanover
APPALACHIAN TRAIL MUSEUM
East Berlin
York
Shrewsbury
Wrightsville
MD
Mount Union
Huntingdon
Carlisle
Harrisburg
INDIAN ECHO CAVERNS
Middletown
Hershey
THE HERSHEY STORY
HERSHEYPARK
WOLF SANCTUARY OF PENNSYLVANIA
Lancaster
Willow Street
Strasburg
AMISH ATTRACTIONS
RAILROAD MUSEUM OF PENNSYLVANIA
STRASBURG RAIL ROAD
Intercourse
Blue Ball
Gap
Ephrata
Lebanon
Myerstown
Avondale
Coatesville
DE
Wilmington
PHILADELPHIA
NJ
State College
Lewistown
Duncannon
Millersburg
Susquehanna River
Pine Grove
AIR MUSEUMS
ROADSIDE AMERICA
Reading
Pottstown
Valley Forge
CRYSTAL CAVE PARK
Hamburg
Kutztown
Allentown/ Bethlehem
Emmaus
Pottsville
HAWK MOUNTAIN SANCTUARY
Tamaqua
Lehighton
Frackville
Shamokin Dam
Northumberland
Lewisburg
Milton
Watsontown
Bloomsburg
Lime Ridge
Berwick
Hazleton
Jim Thorpe
White Haven
Wind Gap
Bartonsville
0 10 mi
0 10 km

PLANNING YOUR TIME

You could spend weeks exploring the small towns of Pennsylvania Dutch Country, but 3-4 days is sufficient to hit the highlights. Plan to spend at least a day driving around Lancaster County's Amish countryside, sharing the roads with horse-drawn buggies and buying direct from farmers, bakers, quilters, and furniture makers. Keep in mind that the Amish don't do business on Sundays. Eat at a restaurant serving Pennsylvania Dutch fare.

If your agenda includes outlet shopping, save it for the evening. The Rockvale and Tanger outlets, minutes apart along Lancaster County's main east-west thoroughfare, are open until 9pm every day but Sunday. Anyone into antiques should plan to spend Sunday in Adamstown, aka "Antiques Capital USA," about 20 miles northeast of Lancaster city.

Boasting more than 150 B&Bs, the Lancaster area is a good base of operations for exploring other parts of Pennsylvania Dutch Country. Reading is about 30 miles to Lancaster's northeast, Hershey and Harrisburg are 30-40 miles to its northwest, and Gettysburg is 55 miles to its southwest.

If you have kids, a visit to Hershey is non-negotiable. You'll run yourself ragged trying to hit all the attractions in one day, so set aside two. A day is generally enough for Gettysburg, but ardent history buffs and ghost hunters can keep busy for several.

Lancaster County

After the 1955 Broadway production of *Plain and Fancy,* the story of two New Yorkers who travel to Lancaster County, the region found itself inundated by tourists. The fervor never really died down. Today, Lancaster County now welcomes around 8 million visitors annually. It's flush with information centers, attractions, and tour operators offering an Amish 101 curriculum.

About 308,000 Amish live in North America. Lancaster County is home to about 33,000 Amish—roughly half of Pennsylvania's Amish. As you explore the region, keep in mind that not all traditionally dressed people are Amish. Some conservative Mennonite and Brethren groups also practice "plain" dress, with slight variations you'll likely learn about during your visit. Amish men, for example, use hook-and-eye closures on their shirts, while Mennonite men use buttons. But, of course, it would be rude to stare too closely to spot the differences.

There's more to Lancaster County than its Amish population. The county seat, Lancaster city, boasts a thriving arts scene. Rail fans will find an abundance of train-related attractions in and around the town of Strasburg. Antiques enthusiasts will fall in love with Adamstown, aka "Antiques Capital USA." Bargain hunters can get their fix at a pair of outlet malls along Route 30. Other Lancaster County communities are noteworthy for their names: Intercourse, Paradise, Blue Ball, Fertility, and, of course, Bird-in-Hand.

★ AMISH ATTRACTIONS

If you're visiting Lancaster County to see the Amish, you may be at a loss as to where to start. Unlike a museum or historic site, the Amish are people living their lives—people who don't necessarily appreciate being the focus of tourists' attention. And while it's not hard to catch sight of them, you'll shortchange yourself if you don't garner some understanding of why they live the way they do.

Plain & Fancy Farm, the Amish Farm and House, and the Mennonite Information Center are great places to acquaint yourself with the ways of the Amish. There's no need to visit more than one. Plain & Fancy is in the heart of Amish Country, while the other two are located along Route 30, a major east-west thoroughfare. Plain & Fancy is the only one that offers buggy rides through Amish

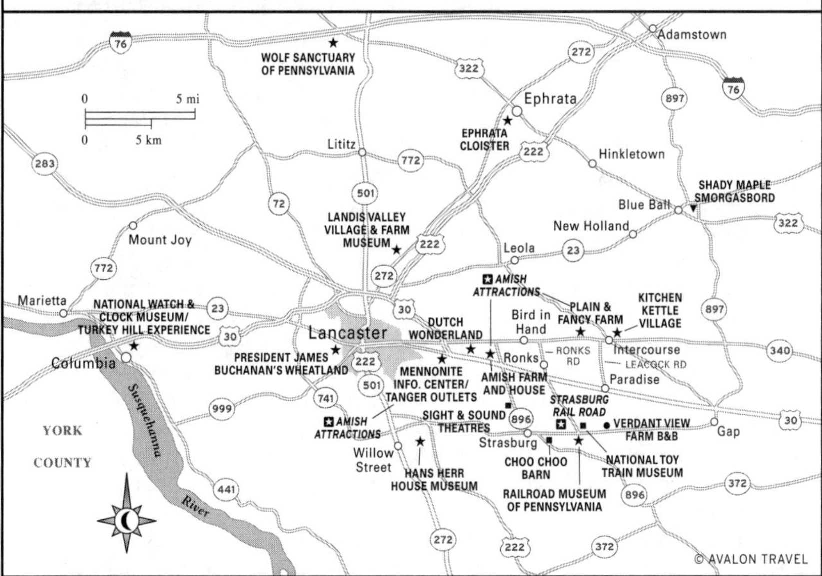

countryside and the opportunity to visit an Amish family in their home, but it's also the priciest of the three. Packed with animals and offering child-friendly activities, the Amish Farm and House is your best bet if you're traveling with kids. While all three offer driving tours of the countryside, the Mennonite Information Center is unique in that it doesn't operate tour buses. Instead, a guide will climb into your car and lead you on a personal tour. It's the way to go if you tend to ask loads of questions. It's also a great value: $53 for a vehicle carrying as many as seven people. On the downside, the Mennonite Information Center is closed on Sundays.

Plain & Fancy Farm

In 1958, a few years after *Plain and Fancy* hit the Broadway stage, a man named Walter Smith built an Amish-style house and barn along Route 340, midway between the villages of Bird-in-Hand and Intercourse, with the intent of giving house tours and holding barn dances. Shrewdly, he named the property after the Broadway musical that had ignited so much interest in Amish Country. Half a century later, **Plain & Fancy Farm** (3121 Old Philadelphia Pike, Bird-in-Hand, www.plainandfancyfarm.com) offers everything a tourist could want: food, lodging, souvenirs, and an excellent orientation to the Amish way of life.

Begin your orientation at the **Amish Experience Theater** (717/768-8400, ext. 210, http://amishexperience.com, daily Apr.-Oct. and select days Nov.-Mar., shows on the hour 10am-5pm, adults $13, children 4-12 $9). Designed to look like a barn, the theater features five screens, a fog machine, and other bells and whistles that produce three-dimensional effects. *Jacob's Choice*, the film for which the theater was built, packs some 400 years of history into 40 minutes. It's the contemporary story of an Old Order Amish family and the teenage son torn between joining the church and leaving the fold for a modern life. As the title character learns about the persecution his religious ancestors faced in

Europe and their journey to the New World, so does the audience. Filmed locally in 1995, *Jacob's Choice* doesn't dwell on the blood and gore, but some loud noises and a burning-at-the-stake scene could rattle children.

The Amish-style house Mr. Smith built back in 1958 is still open for tours. Tickets can be purchased at the Amish Experience Theater box office. Now known as the **Amish Country Homestead** (http://amishexperience.com, daily Apr.-Oct. and select days Nov.-Mar., adults $13, children 4-12 $9), the nine-room house is continually updated to reflect changes in the Amish lifestyle. (Contrary to popular belief, the Amish don't live just as they did centuries ago.) Guides explain such head-scratchers as why the Amish eschew electricity but use refrigerators and other appliances powered by propane gas. The tour takes about 45 minutes. Combo tickets for the theater and house tour are available.

Several minibus tours depart from the theater. The most popular is the **Amish Farmlands Tour** (daily Apr.-Oct. and select days Nov.-Mar., adults $30, children 12 and under $17), a 90-minute cruise through the surrounding countryside. Guides are well versed in the Amish way of life. A "SuperSaver Package" is available for those who wish to experience *Jacob's Choice*, the house tour, and the Farmlands Tour.

Other tours include the evening **Visit-in-Person Tour** (Mon.-Sat. Apr.-Oct., Sat. Nov., adults $60, children 6-16 $40), which gives visitors the opportunity to interact with Amish locals at a dairy farm during milking time, a place of business (such as a canning kitchen or wooden toy shop), and an Amish home. The three-hour excursion often sells out, so it's a good idea to purchase tickets in advance.

If you're short on time or traveling with antsy kids, a buggy ride is a better option than a bus tour. **Aaron and Jessica's Buggy Rides** (717/768-8828, www.amishbuggyrides.com, 9am-6pm daily Apr.-Oct., 9am-4:30pm daily Nov.-Mar., adults from $10, children 3-12 from $6) depart from Plain & Fancy Farm on a regular basis. Trips range from 20 minutes to an hour. Aaron and Jessica's—named for owner Jack Meyer's oldest daughter and her first horse—bills itself as Lancaster County's only buggy tour operator staffed entirely by "plain" people (except on Sundays, which they set aside for worship).

Plain & Fancy Farm's other attraction is its restaurant, **Smokehouse BBQ & Brews** (3121 Old Philadelphia Pike, Bird-in-Hand, 717/768-4400, www.plainandfancyfarm.com,

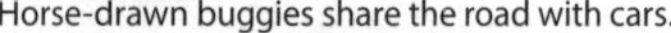

Horse-drawn buggies share the road with cars.

11:30am-close daily, $9-17), famous for its family-style meals. The on-site **AmishView Inn & Suites** (3125 Old Philadelphia Pike, 866/735-1600, www.amishviewinn.com, $150-220) makes Plain & Fancy Farm a 24-hour attraction.

The Amish Farm and House

The easiest way to find the **Amish Farm and House** (2395 Covered Bridge Dr., Lancaster, 717/394-6185, www.amishfarmandhouse.com, hours vary but generally 9am-5pm or 6pm daily Apr.-Oct., 10am-4pm Nov.-Mar., adults $9.50, seniors $8.50, children 5-11 $6.50) is to look for its neighbor, a Target. The store opened in 2005 on property carved from the hundreds-year-old farm, and its bull's-eye logo is easier to spot than the barn, silo, and windmill that once dominated the skyline.

Opened to the public in July 1955, the Amish Farm and House bills itself as the first tourist attraction in Lancaster County and the first Amish attraction in the United States. The operating farm has since shrunk from 25 acres to 15, but there's more to see than ever. Start with a guided tour of the farmhouse, included in general admission. Built in 1805 of limestone quarried on the property, the house has counted Quakers, Mennonites, and Amish as residents. The front room features wooden benches arranged in preparation for a church service, opening the door for a discussion of why the Amish worship in their homes and other aspects of their religion. Their manner of dress is explained in the bedrooms. After the 45-minute tour, explore the farm at your own pace. Children love the chicken house and the barn with its cows, horses, and pigs. The farm also has an original tobacco shed, one of the few remaining limekilns in Lancaster County, a working waterwheel, a circa 1855 covered bridge, and a one-room Amish schoolhouse built specifically for tourists in 2006.

The Amish Farm and House offers 90-minute **Countryside Tours** (adults $22, seniors $21, children 5-11 $15, children 4 and under $5) year-round. Reservations are recommended, especially in the warmer months. The minibus tours usually stop at an Amish roadside stand or two (except on Sundays, when the Amish don't conduct business). Combo tickets for the house, farm, and bus tour are available.

Mennonite Information Center

Don't be put off by its name. You *will* learn about the Amish at the **Mennonite Information Center** (2209 Millstream Rd., Lancaster, 717/299-0954, www.mennoniteinfoctr.com, 9am-5pm Mon.-Sat. Apr.-Oct., 9am-4pm Mon.-Sat. Nov.-Mar.), located next to Tanger Outlets. Start by watching the three-screen feature *Who Are the Amish?* (on the hour 9am-4pm Apr.-Oct., 9am-3pm Nov.-Mar., adults $6, children 6-16 $4). The images are beautiful and the narration interesting, but at 30 minutes long the movie won't necessarily hold the attention of young children. Also showing: *We Believe,* which elucidates the similarities and differences between the Amish and Mennonites, both of whom trace their roots to the Anabaptist movement in 16th-century Europe. There's no charge to see the 17-minute film, shown on the half hour. Admission to the center's exhibits on Anabaptist life is also free.

What sets the Mennonite Information Center apart are its **personal tours** (vehicle with 1-7 people $53 for 2 hours, $17 each additional hour) of Amish Country. For about the cost of two seats on other countryside tours, a guide will hop in your vehicle and point the way to Amish farms, one-room schoolhouses, quilt shops, covered bridges, and more. All guides have a Mennonite or Amish heritage. Call ahead to arrange for a tour at a specific time or just show up and request one. The wait for a guide is rarely longer than 30 minutes. Another great service from the Mennonite Information Center is its list of **Mennonite guest homes,** available on its website and in pamphlet form at the center.

The center is home to a life-size reproduction of the portable place of worship described in the biblical book of Exodus. A wax figure of the high priest sports a breastplate of gold and precious stones. The **Biblical Tabernacle Reproduction** (adults $8.50, children 6-16 $6) can only be seen via a 45-minute guided tour, offered at regular intervals year-round. The reproduction has no real connection to Lancaster County's Anabaptist communities. It was constructed in the 1940s by a Baptist minister in St. Petersburg, Florida, purchased by Mennonites in the 1950s, and installed in its current home in the 1970s.

Next door to the center is the headquarters of the **Lancaster Mennonite Historical Society** (2215 Millstream Rd., 717/393-9745, www.lmhs.org, 8:30am-4:30pm Tues.-Sat.), which has a fantastic bookstore. Its **museum** ($5) showcases Pennsylvania German artifacts.

DOWNTOWN LANCASTER

It's not unusual for tourists to come and go from Lancaster County without stepping foot in downtown Lancaster. Many are entirely unaware that the county has an urban center. It's hard to blame them. Lancaster County's countryside and quaint towns have gotten all the press for decades and its major east-west thoroughfare, Route 30, bypasses the city altogether. But revitalization efforts in recent years have given downtown a fresh look and it's worth stopping in to check out the new restaurants, stores, and galleries—along with the oldest continuously operated farmers market and one of the oldest theaters in the United States. Plan your visit for a Tuesday, Friday, or Saturday, when the farmers market is open. Ideally, make it the first or third Friday of any month, when many galleries, boutiques, and other businesses extend their hours. **First Fridays** (5pm-9pm first Fri. of the month, 717/291-4758, www.visitlancastercity.com) feature special exhibitions, artist receptions, and other arts-related events. Live music wafts from one doorway after another on third Fridays, known as **Music Fridays** (third Fri. of the month, 717/291-4758, www.visitlancastercity.com).

Walking Tour

The city of Lancaster is so steeped in history—it was capital of the 13 colonies for one day during the American Revolution and capital of Pennsylvania for 13 years—that a guided tour is a good idea. Led by a volunteer guide in 18th- or 19th-century garb, the **Historic Lancaster Walking Tour** (Lancaster City Visitors Center, 38 Penn Sq., 717/392-1776, www.historiclancasterwalkingtour.org, adults $8, seniors $7, students $6, children under 6 $1) visits dozens of sites. Allow about 90 minutes for the tour. It's offered at 1pm daily April-October. On Tuesdays, Fridays, and Saturdays, when nearby Central Market is open, tours depart at 10am as well as 1pm.

Central Market

Central Market (23 N. Market St., 717/735-6890, www.centralmarketlancaster.com, 6am-4pm Tues. and Fri., 6am-2pm Sat.) is the pulsing heart of the city. Granted, the indoor farmers market pulses just three days a week, but given its advanced age, it's incredible that it pulses at all. Central Market is the oldest continually operated farmers market in the country. When Lancaster was laid out in the 1730s, a lot adjacent to the town square was designated as a public marketplace in perpetuity. In its early years, the market was simply an open space where farmers and others could sell their wares. The current market house, an eye-catching Romanesque Revival structure with two towers and ornate brick and stone work, was built in 1889. Many of the 60-some market stalls have been operated by multiple generations of the same family. The Stoner's vegetable stall, famous for its arugula, has been around for more than a century. Fresh produce isn't the half of it. Central Market is one-stop shopping for beef, poultry, and fish; milk and cheeses; breads and pastries; coffees and teas; candies; and preserves and prepared foods. There's even a stall devoted to horseradish. Come on the early side for the best selection. On Tuesdays and Fridays, some vendors call it quits at 3pm, an hour before the market closes.

Art Museums and Galleries

Lancaster has a thriving arts scene, with galleries, artist studios, fine craft stores, and art museums. It has an art college and even an art-themed hotel. Start at **Gallery Row,** roughly defined as the section of Prince Street between Walnut Street and King Street to its south. Notable tenants include the **Red Raven Art Company** (138 N. Prince St., 717/299-4400, www.redravenartcompany.com, 10am-5pm Tues. and Thurs.-Sat., 10am-8:30pm first Fri. of the month), which showcases a diverse array of fine art. If you're partial to folk art, you'll dig **CityFolk** (146 N. Prince St., 717/393-8807, www.cityfolkonprince.com, 10am-5pm Tues.-Sat., 10am-9pm first Fri. of the month) with its ever-changing display of furniture, paintings, carvings, pottery, and other works.

A couple of blocks east of Gallery Row is the onetime home of Lancaster's most acclaimed artist, the Modernist painter Charles Demuth. It's now open to the public as the **Demuth Museum** (120 E. King St., 717/299-9940, www.demuth.org, 10am-4pm Tues.-Sat., 1pm-4pm Sun. Feb.-Dec., free). Demuth was born in Lancaster in 1883 and died there in 1935 but in between moved in avant-garde circles in Paris, New York, and Bermuda. He was very much appreciated during his lifetime, earning a place in the permanent collection of New York's Metropolitan Museum of Art by his 40s. Rotating exhibits showcase works by Demuth's contemporaries or artists with a thematic or stylistic connection to him.

The **Lancaster Museum of Art** (135 N. Lime St., 717/394-3497, www.lmapa.org, 10am-4pm Tues.-Sat., noon-4pm Sun., free) is home to an extensive collection of works by contemporary regional artists. The museum building is a remarkably intact example of Greek Revival-style domestic architecture. The Grubb Mansion, as it's called, was built in the 1840s for an ironmaster with an eye for art.

Lancaster Science Factory

Geared toward children 7-13, the **Lancaster Science Factory** (454 New Holland Ave., 717/509-6363, www.lancastersciencefactory.org, 10am-5pm Mon.-Sat., noon-5pm Sun. May-Aug., 10am-5pm Tues.-Sat., noon-5pm Sun. Sept.-Apr., $9) features dozens of interactive exhibits that help visitors—even those well over 13—wrap their heads around electricity, magnetism, acoustics, and fluid dynamics. If your kids like blowing bubbles, they'll love the *Minimal Surfaces* exhibit.

Central Market in downtown Lancaster

Budding Beethovens can experiment with the "bongophone," a bongo/xylophone. The Factory isn't the only science museum in Lancaster. Less than two miles away is the **North Museum of Nature and Science** (400 College Ave., 717/291-3941, www.northmuseum.org, 10am-5pm Mon.-Sat., noon-5pm Sun. Jun.-Aug., 10am-5pm Tues.-Sat., noon-5pm Sept.-May, adults $9, seniors and children 3-17 $8, museum and SciDome admission $13, seniors and children $12), which includes a dinosaur gallery, a live animal room, and a planetarium.

TRAIN TOWN USA

The town of **Strasburg,** some nine miles southwest of downtown Lancaster, bills itself as "the real Lancaster County." Which is to say that it has changed little in the last couple of centuries. Buggies clip-clop through the town square at the intersection of Routes 741 and 896. Families stream in and out of the old-timey **Strasburg Country Store & Creamery** (1 W. Main St., Strasburg, 717/687-0766, www.strasburg.com, hours vary, open daily), where scoops of homemade ice cream are pressed into just-made waffle cones. Much of *Witness,* the 1985 romantic thriller that did more for tourism to Amish Country than any marketing campaign, was filmed on a farm nearby.

But what brings tourists here by the busload is train mania. There are half a dozen train-related attractions within two miles of the square, including the **Red Caboose Motel and Restaurant** (312 Paradise Ln., Ronks, 717/687-5000, www.redcaboosemotel.com, accommodations $70-160, food $4-17), where rail fans bed down and chow down in refurbished train cars. The Strasburg area is such a magnet for rail fans that it's sometimes called "Train Town USA" (not to be confused with "Railroad City," aka Altoona, three hours away). The oldest of the attractions and a good place to start is the Strasburg Rail Road. Don't leave town without a visit to the Choo Choo Barn, where you can see the historic railroad and much more in miniature.

From the town square, head east on Route 741 (Main Street). You'll see the Choo Choo Barn on your right after half a mile. Half a mile after that, you'll arrive at the Strasburg Rail Road and the Railroad Museum of Pennsylvania, located on opposite sides of Route 741. Continue to the next intersection and turn left onto Paradise Lane to check out the Red Caboose or the National Toy Train Museum.

★ Strasburg Rail Road

Incorporated in 1832, the **Strasburg Rail Road** (300 Gap Rd., Ronks, 866/725-9666, www.strasburgrailroad.com) is America's oldest operating short-line railroad. It was almost abandoned in the late 1950s, after an upsurge in the use of highways for freight transportation and a series of storms that destroyed parts of its 4.5-mile track. But rail fans came to its rescue, turning it into a tourist attraction and time capsule of early-1900s railroading. Steam locomotives pull painstakingly restored passenger cars past farm fields plowed by horses and mules on their way to the town of Paradise and back.

Trains run every month but January, with limited dates in December and February. Ticket prices vary widely, depending on the type of excursion and your choice of passenger car. In addition to standard rides, which depart hourly on most operating days, the Strasburg Rail Road offers themed trips like "The Great Train Robbery" and "Santa's Paradise Express." On select days each June, September, and November, fans of Thomas the Tank Engine can ride behind a steam locomotive based on the storybook character. **Day Out With Thomas** and the other themed trips sometimes sell out, so it's a good idea to purchase tickets in advance.

The round-trip takes just 45 minutes, but train buffs and families with young children should plan to spend a couple of hours at the home station. A guided tour of the railroad's mechanical shop ($18) is offered at noon on most operating days. It's limited to 25 people and often sells out. Kids can operate a vintage pump car along a short track or ride in a circa 1920 miniature steam train. A train-themed play area was added in 2013. The station also features gift shops geared toward train lovers, a toy store with a large selection of Thomas the Tank Engine merchandise, and a café. Consider packing a picnic basket or buying a box lunch at the station and disembarking the train at one of two picnic groves. Groff's Grove is popular with families because it has vintage playground equipment and is convenient to **Cherry Crest Adventure Farm** (150 Cherry Hill Rd., 866/546-1799, www.cherrycrestfarm.com, hours vary by season, from $12). Leaman Place Grove, at the end of the line, appeals to rail fans because it's adjacent to active Amtrak lines. Just don't miss the last train back.

Combo passes good for a train ride and admission to the nearby Railroad Museum of Pennsylvania are available. The Strasburg Rail Road also sells discounted Cherry Crest tickets.

Railroad Museum of Pennsylvania

Directly across the street from the Strasburg Rail Road, the **Railroad Museum of Pennsylvania** (300 Gap Rd., Ronks, 717/687-8628, www.rrmuseumpa.org, 9am-5pm Mon.-Sat., noon-5pm Sun. Apr.-Oct., 9am-5pm Tues.-Sat., noon-5pm Sun. Nov.-Mar., adults $10, seniors $9, children 3-11 $8) displays a world-class collection of railroad artifacts, including many last-of-their-kind locomotives. Its 100,000-square-foot exhibit hall holds some 50 locomotives and railcars. Dozens of others reside in the restoration yard, which is open to visitors when weather and staffing permit. The museum offers daily tours of its restoration shop, normally closed to the public for safety reasons. The additional $10 tour fee goes to the museum's efforts to rescue historic railroad equipment from extinction.

Rail fans hoping to find a rare "Big Boy" steam locomotive will be disappointed. The museum, which opened in 1975, is owned and operated by the Pennsylvania Historical and Museum Commission and endeavors to preserve objects relating to the history of railroading in Pennsylvania. The legendary Big Boys didn't ply Pennsylvania's rails. With its 195-ton engine, Pennsylvania Railroad "Mountain" No. 6755 is the largest and heaviest steam locomotive in the museum's collection.

Strasburg Rail Road

National Toy Train Museum

Real trains are well and good, but there's something enchanting about their miniature kin—which makes the **National Toy Train Museum** (300 Paradise Ln., Strasburg, 717/687-8976, www.nttmuseum.org, hours vary by season, adults $7, seniors $6, children 6-12 $4) an exceptionally enchanting place. It houses one of the most extensive collections of toy trains in the world. More than 100 different manufacturers are represented in the museum's collection, which includes some of the earliest and rarest toy trains. It also includes some model trains. The museum, which aspires to look like a Victorian-era station, has five large train layouts.

The museum is operated by the Train Collectors Association, which has its national headquarters there. Those new to "the world's greatest hobby," as the TCA calls it, can learn the ropes via video presentations in the museum. Seasoned collectors can bury their noses in repair guides, trade catalogs, and other materials in the reference library.

Choo Choo Barn

Model train enthusiasts should chug on over to the **Choo Choo Barn** (226 Gap Rd., Strasburg, 717/687-7911, www.choochoobarn.com, 10am-5pm daily early Mar.-Dec. and select days in Jan., adults $7.50, children 3-12 $4.50), which predates the National Toy Train Museum. The family-owned attraction has just one layout: a massive, marvelous display featuring 22 operating trains and more than 150 tiny animated figures and vehicles. Local landmarks including the Strasburg Rail Road and Dutch Wonderland amusement park are represented.

Located next to the Choo Choo Barn, the **Strasburg Train Shop** (717/687-0464, www.etrainshop.com, 10am-5pm daily) caters to the layout builder. It's known as the place to go for uncommon things such as garbage cans.

PRESIDENT JAMES BUCHANAN'S WHEATLAND

The only U.S. president from Pennsylvania lived—and died—on a handsome estate west of downtown Lancaster. James Buchanan, the only bachelor to lead the nation, was secretary of state when he moved to **Wheatland** (230 N. President Ave., Lancaster, 717/392-4633, www.lancasterhistory.org, 9:30am-5pm Mon.-Sat. with tours on the hour 10am-3pm Apr.-Oct., hours vary Nov.-Mar., adults $10, seniors $8, children 10 and under free) in 1848. He

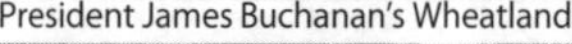
President James Buchanan's Wheatland

announced his 1856 presidential campaign on the front porch of the Federal-style mansion. Reviled for his cowardly stance on slavery and his handling of the secession crisis, the 15th president penned a defensive memoir after retiring to Wheatland in 1861. His writing desk is among the many artifacts displayed. The collection includes everything from his White House china to his bathing tub and even a bottle of 1827 Madeira, now half evaporated, from his wine cellar. Buchanan died at his beloved Wheatland in 1868 and is buried at Woodward Hill Cemetery in Lancaster.

DUTCH WONDERLAND

Dutch Wonderland (2249 Lincoln Hwy. E., Lancaster, 717/291-1888, www.dutchwonderland.com) doesn't boast of adrenaline-pumping, gravity-defying rides like many amusement parks. The 48-acre park, fronted by a castle facade visible from Route 30, bills itself as "A Kingdom for Kids." In addition to 30-some rides, it offers a variety of live shows daily. They're all quite delightful but none so much as the high-dive shows at Aqua Stadium. Performers twist, somersault, and splash their way through Disneyesque storylines. Bring swimsuits for Duke's Lagoon, the park's water play area.

Dutch Wonderland is open daily from late May through Labor Day and some weekends before and after that period. Gates open at 10am. A variety of admission plans are available. One-day admission is $37 for ages 3-59, $32 for ages 60-69, and $24 for those 70 and older. Hang on to your ticket stub in case you decide to come back the next day; consecutive-day admission is $29. A two-day flex pass, good for visits on any two days during the season, is $52. If your summer plans also include Hersheypark in nearby Hershey, ask about combo tickets; Hershey Entertainment & Resorts owns Dutch Wonderland.

KITCHEN KETTLE VILLAGE

What started as a home-based jelly-making business has grown into **Kitchen Kettle Village** (3529 Old Philadelphia Pike, Intercourse, 717/768-8261, www.kitchenkettle.com, 9am-6pm Mon.-Sat. May-Oct., 9am-5pm Mon.-Sat. Nov.-Dec. and Mar.-Apr., hours vary by shop Jan.-Feb.), home to about 40 specialty shops, a pair of restaurants, and a handful of kid-centric attractions. To call it a mall would fail to convey its quaintness. The canning kitchen is still the heart of it all. Its repertoire has grown to include not just jellies, jams, and preserves but also relishes, pickles, mustards, salad dressings, grilling sauces, and salsas. All products are made by hand in small batches and visitors get a front-seat view. (Because the kitchen is staffed by Amish women, photos aren't permitted.) Plenty of visitors have discovered a taste for pickled beets or pepper jam in the **Jam & Relish Kitchen,** which abounds with samples. An attached bakery fills the air with the smells of shoofly pie, whoopie pies, snickerdoodle cookies, and other local favorites.

Many of the village shops feature locally made foods or goods, including ice cream from a dairy farm just a few miles away, fudge and kettle corn made on-site, fabric bags, quilts, and pottery. The popular **Kling House Restaurant** (8am-3pm Mon.-Thurs., 8am-4pm Fri.-Sat., $8-15) serves breakfast and lunch, plus a killer coconut cream pie. There's also a cafeteria-style restaurant.

The village is home base to **AAA Buggy Rides** (717/989-2829, www.aaabuggyrides.com, 9am-6pm Mon.-Sat. May-Oct., 9am-5pm Mon.-Sat. Apr. and Nov.), which offers a 35-minute ride (adults $15, children 3-7 $7) through Amish countryside and a 55-minute ride (adults $19, children 3-7 $9) that passes over a covered bridge. Other village attractions include a petting zoo and a playground.

Want to stick around after dark? Scattered throughout the village are guest rooms and suites collectively known as **The Inn at Kitchen Kettle Village** ($110-190). Rates include breakfast at the Kling House Restaurant every day except Sunday. Book well in advance if you're coming for the **Rhubarb Festival** (third weekend in May) or another of the village's annual events.

LANDIS VALLEY VILLAGE & FARM MUSEUM

Born two years apart in the 1860s, brothers Henry and George Landis were the kind of people who never threw anything away. By 1925 the brothers had amassed so many objects reflective of Pennsylvania German rural life that they opened a small museum on their homestead a few miles north of downtown Lancaster, charging visitors 25 cents apiece. They died a year apart in the 1950s, but the **Landis Valley Village & Farm Museum** (2451 Kissel Hill Rd., Lancaster, 717/569-0401, www.landisvalleymuseum.org, 9am-5pm Wed.-Sat. Jan.-mid-Mar., 9am-5pm Tues.-Sat., noon-5pm Sun. mid-Mar.-Dec., adults $12, seniors $10, children 3-11 $8) lives on. Owned by the state since 1953, it has grown into an assemblage of 30-plus historic and re-created buildings housing a collection of more than 100,000 farm, trade, and household artifacts. While some buildings are original to the site, including the Landis brothers' 1870s house, many were relocated here over the years. Rather than a time capsule of a particular era, Landis Valley is a repository for all things illustrative of Pennsylvania German village and farm life from the mid-1700s to mid-1900s. Costumed interpreters are often on hand to demonstrate skills such as open-hearth cooking and horse-drawn plowing. Heirloom gardens and heritage breed farm animals help bring the past to life. Be sure to stop by the museum store, which features traditional handicrafts.

Landis Valley shares a parking lot with **Hands-on House** (721 Landis Valley Rd., Lancaster, 717/569-5437, www.handsonhouse.org, 10am-5pm Mon.-Thurs. and Sat., 10am-8pm Fri., noon-5pm Sun. Memorial Day-Labor Day, 11am-4pm Tues.-Thurs., 11am-8pm Fri., 10am-5pm Sat., noon-5pm Sun. Labor Day-Memorial Day, $9.50), a museum designed for children 2-10.

HANS HERR HOUSE MUSEUM

Built in 1719, the **Hans Herr House** (1849 Hans Herr Dr., Willow Street, 717/464-4438, www.hansherr.org, 9am-4pm Mon.-Sat. Apr.-Nov., by guided tour only) is the oldest structure in Lancaster County and the oldest Mennonite meetinghouse in the Western Hemisphere. Though named for the Mennonite bishop whose flock established the first permanent European settlement in present-day Lancaster County, the stone house was actually built by his son Christian. Today it's the centerpiece of a museum complex that also includes two 19th-century Pennsylvania German farmhouses, several barns and other outbuildings, a collection of farm equipment spanning three centuries, and a replica of a Native American longhouse—a multifamily home made of logs, saplings, and tree bark.

You can explore the grounds at your own pace for free but the Herr House and longhouse can only be seen by a **guided tour** (one structure adults $8, children 7-12 $4, both structures adults $15, children 7-12 $7). Tours begin on the hour. Aficionados of 20th-century American art may recognize the 1719 house. The great Andrew Wyeth, a descendant of Hans Herr, captured it on canvas before its restoration.

NATIONAL WATCH & CLOCK MUSEUM

The largest and most comprehensive horological collection in North America can be found in the river town of Columbia, about 10 miles west of Lancaster. Horology is the science of measuring time. Sounds like staid stuff, but a visit to the **National Watch & Clock Museum** (514 Poplar St., Columbia, 717/684-8261, www.nawcc.org, 10am-5pm Tues.-Sat., noon-4pm Sun. Apr.-late May and early Sept.-Nov., 10am-5pm Mon.-Sat., noon-4pm Sun. Memorial Day-Labor Day, 10am-4pm Tues.-Sat. Dec.-Mar., adults $9, seniors $8, children 5-16 $5) will convince you otherwise. Located in the headquarters of the National

Association of Watch and Clock Collectors, the museum traces the history of timekeeping from the ancient world to present day. Here you can learn how bowls of water, candles, oil lamps, and incense were used to measure the passage of time.

Perhaps its most impressive holding is a "monumental clock" made in Hazleton, Pennsylvania by Stephen Engle. Designed to awe and amuse audiences, monumental clocks had their heyday in the late 19th century, touring the United States and Europe like rock stars. Engle spent more than 20 years crafting his 11-foot-tall clock, which has 48 moving figurines and displays the month, day of the week, and moon phase along with time. Finishing it around 1878, he entrusted it to promoters who touted it as "The Eighth Wonder of the World" as they hauled it around the eastern United States, charging people to see it. In 1951, after an appearance at the Ohio State Fair, the clock vanished. Members of the National Association of Watch and Clock Collectors spent years hunting for it, finally discovering it in a barn in 1988.

TURKEY HILL EXPERIENCE

Like the Hershey Story in Hershey, the **Turkey Hill Experience** (301 Linden St., Columbia, 888/986-8784, www.turkeyhillexperience.com, adults $10, seniors and children 5-12 $9.50) is a family attraction centered on a consumer brand. Opened in 2011, it tells the story of Turkey Hill Dairy, a Lancaster County-based producer of ice cream and iced tea. Kids get a kick out of milking the mechanical cows and creating their own virtual ice cream flavor. The Taste Lab exhibit gives visitors the opportunity to turn their virtual recipe into actual ice cream. The Taste Lab costs an additional $5.45 per person, and reservations are required.

There's no actual production at the Turkey Hill Experience, which occupies a former silk mill in the borough of Columbia, a few blocks from the National Watch & Clock Museum.

EPHRATA CLOISTER

The town of Ephrata, about 15 miles north of downtown Lancaster, is best known as the onetime home of a religious community whose faithful ate meager rations and slept on wooden benches with blocks of wood for pillows. The **Ephrata Cloister** (632 W. Main St., Ephrata, 717/733-6600, www.ephratacloister.org, 9am-5pm Wed.-Sat. and noon-5pm Sun. Jan.-Feb., 9am-5pm Mon.-Sat. and noon-5pm Sun. Mar.-Dec., adults $10, seniors $9, children 3-11 $6) was the hub of their community and home to members who chose a celibate life. The buildings where white-robed Brothers and Sisters lived, worked, and prayed in the 1700s are now open to the public. At its zenith in the mid-1800s, the community consisted of about 80 celibate members and 200 "householders" who lived on farms around the cloister. The community became known for its Germanic calligraphy, publishing center, and original a cappella music. Their leader, Conrad Beissel, prescribed a special diet for members of the choir, who sang at an otherworldly high pitch. Today the music composed by Beissel and crew is performed by the Ephrata Cloister Chorus at occasional concerts.

Beissel died in 1768 and was buried in a graveyard on the cloister grounds. His successor wasn't married to the idea of monastic life. After the death of the last celibate member in 1813, householders formed the German Seventh Day Baptist Church. The congregation disbanded in 1934, and several years later the state purchased the cloister property, now a National Historic Landmark. Some of the original buildings can only be viewed during guided tours, which are offered daily. You can explore other structures on your own.

ENTERTAINMENT AND EVENTS

Performing Arts

Downtown Lancaster is home to one of the oldest theaters in the country. Built in 1852 on the foundation of a pre-Revolutionary prison, the **Fulton Theatre** (12 N. Prince St.,

Lancaster, 717/397-7425, www.thefulton.org) hosted lectures by Mark Twain and Horace Greeley, performances by Sarah Bernhardt and W. C. Fields, a production of *Ben-Hur* featuring live horses in a spectacular chariot-racing scene (fistfights broke out at the box office when tickets went on sale), and burlesque in its first 100 years. In the 1950s and '60s it served primarily as a movie house. Since then the Fulton has reinvented itself as a producer of professional theater. The auditorium, which seats about 700, was restored to its original Victorian splendor in 1995. Named for a Lancaster County native credited with developing the first commercially successful steamboat, the Fulton is the primary venue of the **Lancaster Symphony Orchestra** (717/397-7425, www.lancastersymphony.org). The orchestra occasionally plays at the **Ware Center** (42 N. Prince St., 717/871-7018, www.artsmu.com) of Millersville University. The downtown venue hosts a wide range of arts events, including theater, gallery shows, dance performances, classical and contemporary concerts, and film screenings.

Lancaster County has not one but two dinner theaters. In business since 1984, **Rainbow's Comedy Playhouse** (3065 Lincoln Hwy. E., Paradise, 717/687-4300, www.rainbowdinnertheatre.com) produces several knee-slappers per year, including a Christmas show. The **Dutch Apple Dinner Theatre** (510 Centerville Rd., Lancaster, 717/898-1900, www.dutchapple.com) serves up mainly musicals, including well-known shows like *Wizard of Oz* and *Rent.* Both theaters are set back from the road and easily missed. Rainbow is behind the Best Western Plus Revere Inn & Suites on Route 30, about three miles east of the Rockvale Outlets. The Dutch Apple shares a driveway with the Heritage Hotel Lancaster, just off the Centerville exit of Route 30.

With a theater in Lancaster County and a second in Branson, Missouri, **Sight & Sound Theatres** (800/377-1277, www.sight-sound.com) is the nation's largest Christian theatrical company. Founded in the 1970s by a Lancaster County native, it pulls out all the stops to dramatize biblical stories such as Noah's animal adventures, Joseph's journey from slavery to power, and the birth of Jesus. Expect elaborate sets, special effects, professional actors, and live animals. The Lancaster County **theater** (300 Hartman Bridge Rd., Strasburg) is a vision inside and out. The sprawling, pastel-hued palace features three exterior domes (representing the

the Fulton Theatre

Trinity), a wraparound stage double the size of Radio City Music Hall's, and one of the largest moving light systems on the East Coast. Four-legged cast members amble to their spots—and "dressing rooms"—via specially designed passageways under the theater floor.

Festivals and Events

What started in 1980 as a jousting demo to draw attention to a new winery has grown into one of Pennsylvania Dutch Country's marquee attractions. Jousting is just the tip of the lance at the **Pennsylvania Renaissance Faire** (Mount Hope Estate, 2775 Lebanon Rd., Manheim, 717/665-7021, www.parenfaire.com, adults $27-32, children 5-11 $12), held weekends August-October. Transported to Elizabethan England, fairgoers party like it's 1589 alongside sword swallowers and firebreathers, magicians and musicians, jugglers and jesters. The Ren Faire features more than 70 shows per day, including performances of Shakespeare's plays in a three-story replica of London's Globe Theatre. Human pawns, knights, and bishops battle it out on a massive chessboard. Merchants in period costumes demonstrate glassblowing, pottery throwing, leatherworking, bow and arrow making, and more. Even the food vendors wear the clothes and talk the talk of Shakespeare's day as they serve up everything from gelato to giant turkey legs. Mount Hope Estate hosts a variety of other events throughout the year, including murder mystery dinners, a beer festival, and a Celtic festival. Located 15 miles north of Lancaster, the National Register-listed property was home to a prominent iron-making family in the 19th century.

Lancaster's **Long's Park** (Rte. 30 and Harrisburg Pike, Lancaster, 717/735-8883, www.longspark.org) is another site of merrymaking. On the third Saturday of May, the Sertoma Club of Lancaster holds its annual fund-raiser for the city park, with members of the civic organization serving almost 25,000 chicken dinners over the course of eight hours. The **Sertoma Chicken BBQ** (717/354-7259, www.lancastersertomabbq.com, $10-12), a tradition since 1953, held the Guinness World Record for most meat consumed at an outdoor event for more than a decade, losing it to a Paraguayan shindig in 2008 (it's still the largest chicken barbecue). June marks the start of the **Long's Park Summer Music Series** (7:30pm Sun. June-Aug.), another decades-old tradition. Bring blankets, lawn chairs, and a picnic for the free concerts. Alcohol isn't permitted in the 80-acre park. The music series is funded in part by proceeds from the **Long's Park Art & Craft Festival** (Labor Day weekend), which showcases 200 artists from across the country.

SHOPPING

Outlet Malls

Lancaster County's two outlet malls are just a couple of minutes apart on Route 30. **Rockvale Outlets** (35 S. Willowdale Dr., Lancaster, 717/293-9292, www.rockvaleoutletslancaster.com, 9:30am-9pm Mon.-Sat., 11am-5pm Sun.) features about 80 brands, including Lane Bryant, Levi's, Casual Male XL, Gymboree, and Disney Store. It's a great place to shop for the home, counting Pottery Barn, Lenox, and West Elm among its tenants.

Tanger Outlets (311 Stanley K. Tanger Blvd., Lancaster, 717/392-7260, www.tangeroutlet.com, 9am-9pm Mon.-Sat., 10am-7pm Sun.), located across Route 30 from Dutch Wonderland amusement park, has nearly 90 stores in its lineup of designer outlets. Shop Michael Kors, The North Face, J.Crew, OshKosh B'gosh, Coach, Nike, Rockport, Bath & Body Works, Yankee Candle, and more.

Antiques

Located just off exit 286 of the Pennsylvania Turnpike, little Adamstown has made a big name for itself in antiquing circles. It's crowded with antiques shops, malls, and markets, most of which can be found along North Reading Road (Route 272). Sundays are a big day in "Antiques Capital USA." That's when **Renninger's Antiques Market** and the **Black Angus Antiques Mall** are open. The former (2500 N. Reading Rd., Denver,

717/336-2177, www.renningers.net, indoor market 7:30am-4pm Sun., outdoor market 5am-4pm Sun.) features 375 dealers indoors and, weather permitting, hundreds more outdoors. Bring a flashlight to get in on the early-morning action.

The 70,000-square-foot **Black Angus Antiques Mall** (2800 N. Reading Rd., Adamstown, 717/484-4386, www.stoudts.com, mall 7:30am-4pm Sun., outdoor pavilions 5:30am-noon seasonally) is part of a sprawling complex of attractions operated by husband and wife Ed and Carol Stoudt. More than 300 dealers set up shop inside the mall, selling everything from fine art and early American furniture to tools and small collectibles. About 100 more can be found outside. The Stoudts, with Carol taking the lead as the first female brewmaster in America since Prohibition, established microbrewery **Stoudt's Brewing Company** in 1987 with the goal of making an authentic German-style beer. And they succeeded: Gold Lager and Pils, the brewery's flagship beers, have racked up awards and accolades. Brewery tours, offered Saturday and Sunday afternoons, meet in the lobby of the adjacent **Black Angus Restaurant & Pub,** which specializes in steaks. Its breads are made in the **Wonderful Good Market** (9am-3pm Thurs., 9am-4pm Fri.-Sun.), the Stoudts' bakery, creamery, and specialty foods store.

Also a Sunday-only outing, **The Country French Collection** (2887 N. Reading Rd., Adamstown, 717/484-0200, www.country-frenchantiques.com, 11am-3pm Sun. and by appointment) imports 18th- and 19th-century antiques from France and England and restores them to pristine condition.

The area offers plenty of antiquing on other days. **Heritage Antique Center** (2750 N. Reading Rd., Adamstown, 717/484-4646, www.heritageantiquecenter.com), one of the area's oldest antiques stores, and the **Antiques Showcase & German Trading Post** (2152 N. Reading Rd., Denver, 717/336-8847, www.blackhorselodge.com), with nearly 300 showcases full of fine antiques and collectibles, are open seven days a week.

Adamstown's antiquing scene goes into overdrive during **Antique Extravaganza** (www.antiquescapital.com), held each April, June, and September. Outside markets mushroom and inside markets keep longer hours during the four-day event, which attracts dealers from across the country.

an Amish quilt

Mud Sales

Held at fire companies throughout Lancaster County, "mud sales" are a chance to get dirt-cheap prices on everything from antiques to aluminum siding, lawn equipment to livestock, homemade food to horse carriages. Teeming as they are with Amish and Mennonite buyers and sellers, these fund-raising sales/auctions are also a cultural immersion experience. Why are they called mud sales? Because many take place in the spring, when the ground is thawing—though it's not unusual for fire companies to hold mud sales in summer or fall. Visit www.discoverlancaster.com or call 717/299-8901 for a schedule of mud sales.

Quilts and Fabrics

Mud sales are great places to buy locally crafted quilts, but if your visit to Lancaster County doesn't coincide with one, you're not out of luck. Quilt shops are more common than stoplights in the Amish countryside. Most sell a variety of handicrafts and many are home-based businesses, allowing shoppers a glimpse into the everyday lives of locals. Just about all quilt shops are closed on Sundays. The **Quilt Shop at Miller's** (2811 Lincoln Hwy. E., Ronks, 717/687-8439, www.quiltshopatmillers.com, 10am-5pm Wed.-Sun. Jan.-Feb., 10am-7pm Mon.-Fri., 10am-8pm Sat., and 10am-6pm Sun. Mar.-Dec.) is an exception. It's right next to the popular Miller's Smorgasbord on Route 30, about 1.5 miles east of Route 896.

Intercourse is a good place to start a quilt shopping spree. The village along Route 340 (Old Philadelphia Pike) is home to **The Old Country Store** (800/828-8218, www.theoldcountrystore.com, 9am-6:30pm Mon.-Sat. June-Oct., 9am-5pm Mon.-Sat. Nov.-May), stocked with thousands of items made by local craftspeople, most of them Amish or Mennonite. In addition to hundreds of quilts, it carries potholders and pottery, Christmas ornaments and cornhusk bunnies, faceless Amish dolls and darling stuffed bears, pillows of various sizes, and paper cuttings known as *scherenschnitte.* With its selection of more than 6,000 bolts of fabric, the store is as much a starting point for needlecraft projects as a showplace for finished products. There's a quilt museum on the second floor of the store.

In the complex of shops known as Kitchen Kettle Village is the airy **Village Quilts** (3529 Old Philadelphia Pike, Intercourse, 717/768-2787, www.kitchenkettle.com/quilts, 10am-5pm Mon.-Fri., 9am-5pm Sat. Jan.-Feb., 9am-5pm Mon.-Sat. Mar.-Apr. and Nov.-Dec., 9am-6pm Mon.-Sat. May-Oct.), which commissions works from home quilters. Each masterpiece is signed and dated and comes with a certificate for insurance purposes.

A few minutes east of Intercourse along Route 340 is **Esh's Handmade Quilts** (3829 Old Philadelphia Pike, Gordonville, 717/768-8435, hours vary Mon.-Sat.), an Amish-owned shop on an operating dairy farm. And a few minutes west of Intercourse is **The Quilt & Fabric Shack** (3137 Old Philadelphia Pike, Bird-In-Hand, 717/768-0338, hours vary Mon.-Sat.), with four rooms of fabrics, including a "bargain room." Just northwest of Intercourse along Route 772, **Family Farm Quilts** (3511 W. Newport Rd., 717/768-8375, www.familyfarmquilts.com, 10am-5pm Mon.-Sat. Jan.-Feb., 9am-5pm Mon.-Sat. Mar.-Dec.) counts more than 200 local women among its quilt suppliers. Its selection of handicrafts includes purses made of antique quilts, place mats, chair pads, children's toys, and baskets.

Witmer Quilt Shop (1076 W. Main St., New Holland, 717/656-9526, hours vary Mon.-Sat.), located five miles north of Intercourse along Route 23, is remarkable for its selection of lovingly restored antique quilts. Emma Witmer's shop/home is also stocked with more than 100 new quilts, many in patterns she herself designed. Give her a few months and she'll give you a custom quilt.

FOOD

Leave your diet at the Lancaster County line. Visiting this corner of the globe without indulging in a Pennsylvania Dutch-style meal

Side Trip to Lititz

In a county studded with lovely little towns, Lititz is generally regarded as the loveliest one of all. The clip-clop of Amish buggies that contributes so much to the appeal of Bird-in-Hand, Intercourse, Strasburg, and other communities west of Lancaster is rarely heard in Lititz. What draws visitors to the borough nine miles north of downtown Lancaster is a combination of historical ambience, boutique shopping, and a busy calendar of events. It doesn't hurt that the smell of chocolate wafts through the streets.

Most of the shops, galleries, eateries, and landmarks lie along East Main Street (Route 772) or Broad Street (Route 501), which meet in the center of town. Be aware that many are closed on Sundays. On **Second Fridays** (717/626-6332, www.lititzpa.com, 5pm-9pm second Fri. of the month) every month, merchants pull out all the stops with free entertainment and free parking throughout town. First held in 1818, the **4th of July Celebration** (717/626-8981, www.lititz4thofjuly.com, $15) in Lititz Springs Park is the oldest continuous observance of the national holiday. The daylong festivities conclude with the lighting of thousands of candles and a fireworks show.

SIGHTS

Lititz was founded in 1756 by members of the Moravian Church, an evangelical Protestant denomination that originated in what's now the Czech Republic. For almost 100 years, only Moravians were permitted to live in the village. After opening its doors to outsiders in the 1850s, Lititz became a stop on the Reading and Columbia Railroad and a summer resort area. Lititz Springs Park and the limestone springs that give it its name were the main attraction. A replica of the passenger depot that stood at the entrance to the park from 1884 to 1957 houses the **Lititz Welcome Center** (18 N. Broad St., 717/626-8981, www.lititzspringspark.org, 10am-4pm Mon.-Sat., 10am-8pm second Fri. of the month). On the opposite side of the train tracks is **Wilbur Chocolate** (48 N. Broad St., 717/626-3249, www.wilburbuds.com, store and museum 10am-5pm Mon.-Sat., free), founded in 1884 in Philadelphia and based in Lititz since the 1930s. The factory store sells chocolate and other sweets, while the attached Candy Americana Museum showcases antique candy machinery and more than 150 porcelain chocolate pots from around the world.

The Darlington family began taking in wolves and wolf hybrids in the 1980s after the state forbade keeping them as house pets. Today more than 40 former pets—who can't be released into the wild because they rely on humans for food—roam the **Wolf Sanctuary** (465 Speedwell Forge Rd., Lititz, 717/626-4617, www.wolfsancpa.com). Tours are available, and so are overnight

is like visiting Disney World and not riding the rides. The cuisine is anything but light—after all, this is the food of hardworking farm families—and chances are good you'll find yourself immersed in more than one all-you-can-eat experience. Approach it with the abandon you bring to Thanksgiving dinner.

Lancaster County also has some excellent non-Pennsylvania Dutch eateries, particularly in the city of Lancaster.

Pennsylvania Dutch Fare

If you're new to Pennsylvania Dutch cuisine, you should know a few things. Around here, **chicken potpie** isn't a pie at all. It's a stew with square-cut egg noodles. A **whoopie pie** isn't a pie either. Think of it as a dessert burger: creamy icing pressed between two bun-shaped cakes. Chocolate cake with white icing is most common, but you'll also encounter variations such as pumpkin cake with cream cheese icing. The annual **Whoopie Pie Festival** (Hershey Farm Restaurant & Inn, Rte. 896, Strasburg, 717/687-8635, www.whoopiepiefestival.com, early Sept., free) features more than 100 varieties. Pennsylvania Dutch Country's most iconic dessert, the **shoofly pie,** is, in fact, a pie with a crumb crust. But it's nothing like the fruit or cream pies served at diners throughout the country. Packed with molasses and brown sugar, the joltingly sweet treat comes in "wet bottom" and "dry bottom" stays. The Darlingtons operate a B&B on their 120-acre property, which was the site of an iron forge from the 1760s.

FOOD

Head to **Café Chocolate of Lititz** (40 E. Main St., 717/626-0123, www.chocolatelititz.com, 10:30am-5pm Mon.-Thurs., 9am-9pm Fri.-Sat., 9am-5pm Sun., $6-14) for sweet and savory dishes made with dark chocolate, including a signature fondue. Nearby is the **Julius Sturgis Pretzel Bakery** (219 E. Main St., 717/626-4354, www.juliussturgis.com, 9am-5pm Mon.-Sat., tour adults $3.50, children 4-12 $2.50). Established in 1861, it's regarded as America's first pretzel bakery. Tours include a hands-on lesson in pretzel twisting. The sturdy stone house that Julius turned into the bakery was built in 1784. It's one of more than a dozen 18th-century buildings still in use on East Main Street.

ACCOMMODATIONS

The charming town of Lititz has several recommendable accommodations. Chief among them is the **General Sutter Inn** (14 E. Main St., Lititz, 717/626-2115, www.generalsutterinn.com, $120-240), which offers 16 rooms and suites, ten of which are decorated in a Victorian style. The rest are on the third floor, known as the Rockblock Penthouse. The decor is rock-and-roll inspired: Picture curtain rods fashioned from microphone stands and a signed poster from Roger Daltrey of The Who. More than 200 years old, the inn took its present name in the 1930s to honor John Augustus Sutter, who established a settlement in California in the 1840s, saw it overrun by gold-seekers, and lived his final years in Lititz. The inn also houses the much-lauded **Bulls Head Public House.** The **Alden House Bed & Breakfast** (62 E. Main St., Lititz, 717/627-3363, www.aldenhouse.com, $129-179), with seven guest rooms and suites, is another fine choice in the center of town. Its breakfast is a multicourse affair.

Speedwell Forge B&B (717/626-1760, www.speedwellforge.com, $150-350) offers three guest rooms in what used to be the ironmaster's mansion and three private cottages. The Paymaster's Office cottage, so named because it's where forge employees were paid, is a honeymoon-worthy retreat complete with vaulted ceiling, massive brick fireplace, king-size bed, and in-room whirlpool tub.

varieties. A wet-bottomed shoofly pie is more gooey and molasses-y than its dry-bottomed cousin. Other regional specialties include egg noodles with browned butter, **chow-chow** (a pickled vegetable relish), **scrapple** (a breakfast food made with pork scraps), and **schnitz un knepp** (a dish consisting of dried apples, dumplings, and ham).

With seating for 1,200 and a seemingly endless array of dishes, ★ **Shady Maple Smorgasbord** (129 Toddy Dr., East Earl, 717/354-8222, www.shady-maple.com/smorgasbord, 6am-8pm Mon.-Sat., $20-24) is the behemoth of the bunch. Don't be surprised to find a waiting line. On Saturday evenings it can take upwards of an hour to get seated. You really need to see this place to appreciate its enormity. Lunch and dinner buffets feature everything from Pennsylvania Dutch dishes to pizza to fajitas. Save room for dozens of dessert options. Seniors enjoy a 10 percent discount, and children 4-10 eat for half price. (Anyone who has recently undergone a gastric bypass operation also gets a discount.) Shady Maple's breakfast buffet ($10 Mon.-Fri., $12 Sat.) gets high marks from scrapple fans. A breakfast menu is available on weekdays.

Bird-in-Hand Family Restaurant & Smorgasbord (2760 Old Philadelphia Pike, Bird-in-Hand, 717/768-1500, www.bird-in-hand.com, 6am-8pm Mon.-Sat., $9-21, age-based pricing for children 4-12) offers both menu and smorgasbord dining for breakfast, lunch, and dinner. Its kids buffet is designed to look like Noah's Ark, complete with stuffed animals peering through the portholes. If you enjoy the baked goods, stop by the **Bird-in-Hand Bakery** (2715 Old Philadelphia Pike, Bird-in-Hand, 800/524-3429, www.bird-in-hand.com, 6am-6pm Mon.-Sat.) and take some home. It's just down the road. Specialties include soft potato rolls, red velvet cake, and apple dumplings.

Hershey Farm Restaurant (240 Hartman Bridge Rd., Ronks, 717/687-8635, www.hersheyfarm.com, 8am-8pm Tues.-Sat., 8am-3pm Sun. Mar.-Apr. and Nov.-Dec., 8am-8pm Tues.-Sun. May and Oct., 8am-10am Mon., 8am-8pm Tues.-Fri., 7am-8pm Sat.-Sun. June-Sept., adults $9-27, children $9-11) also offers a choice of menu or smorgasbord dining. The on-site bakery is known for its whoopie pies (Hershey Farm hosts the Whoopie Pie Festival) and triple-layer chocolate cake. Check the website for the most up-to-date hours, which vary throughout the year. **Miller's Smorgasbord** (2811 Lincoln Hwy. E., Ronks, 717/687-6621, www.millerssmorgasbord.com, breakfast 7:30am-10:30am Sat.-Sun. year-round, lunch/dinner from 11:30am daily early Mar.-Dec., dinner from 4pm Mon.-Thurs. and lunch/dinner from 11:30am Fri.-Sun. Jan.-early Mar., $24, age-based pricing for children 4-12) is unusual in that it serves alcohol, including cocktails made with its own shoofly liqueur. Menu dining is available during lunch and dinner.

Smokehouse BBQ and Brews (3121 Old Philadelphia Pike, Bird-in-Hand, 717/768-4400, www.plainandfancyfarm.com, 11:30am-close daily, $9-17) at Plain & Fancy Farm offers what its name promises: pit-smoked meats and beers to wash them down. The build-your-own-feast option is a great deal, with a starter, two meats, two sides, a nonalcoholic beverage, and dessert for $22. Get a dessert even if you order al la carte—the sour cream apple crumb pie is not to be missed.

Lancaster

With a wide variety of cuisines represented under one roof, **Central Market** (23 N. Market St., 717/735-6890, www.centralmarketlancaster.com, 6am-4pm Tues. and Fri., 6am-2pm Sat.) is one of downtown Lancaster's most popular lunch spots. You'll find vendors selling everything from made-to-order salads to homemade rice pudding. Ethnic options include Narai Thai & Asian Cuisine (get there early for the hot-selling fresh spring rolls) and Saife's Middle Eastern Food. The downsides: Central Market is open just three days a week and seating is limited.

More upscale dining options abound. Lancaster County native Tim Carr lent his culinary talents to area country clubs before putting his name to a restaurant. Right outside Central Market, **Carr's Restaurant** (50 W. Grant St., 717/299-7090, www.carrsrestaurant.com, 11:30am-2:30pm and 5:30pm-9:30pm Tues.-Thurs., 11:30am-2:30pm and 5:30pm-10pm Fri.-Sat., 11:30am-2:30pm Sun., $14-32) serves up a sophisticated American menu, with cheaper entrées like the BLT&C (the "C" is for cheddar) and more intricate plates like a surf and turf of filet mignon and crab cake. The wine selection is one of the best in town.

A short stroll away, German-born chef Gunter Backhaus presides over **The Loft** (201 W. Orange St., 717/299-0661, www.theloftlancaster.com, 11:30am-1:45pm and 5:30pm-close Tues.-Fri., 5:30pm-close Sat., $17-36), locally famous for its jumbo shrimp cocktail. Backhaus doesn't shy away from the likes of frog legs and snails, but timid palates needn't fear. The menu also features chicken, rack of lamb, filet mignon, and lobster. Cozy and unpretentious, the restaurant gets its name from the open-beam ceiling in one of two dining rooms.

The convivial vibe at ★ **Horse Inn** (540 E. Fulton St., 717/392-5528, www.horseinnlancaster.com, 5pm-midnight Tues.-Thurs, 5pm-1am Fri.-Sat., $9-26) may come from the long list of craft cocktails or the oft-changing gastropub menu. Or maybe it stems from the live music, games, and speakeasy vibe (appropriate, given that Horse Inn, in business since the 1920s, was at one point a bona fide speakeasy). Either way, this bar/restaurant about a mile east of Central Market is worth a stop for a full meal or just a Manhattan with an order of "horse fries" topped with sausage, cheese, and garlic cream.

It's not just dieters who sup on salad at the **Belvedere Inn** (402 N. Queen St., 717/394-2422, www.belvederelancaster.com, 11am-2pm and 5pm-11pm Mon.-Thurs., 11am-2pm and 5pm-midnight Fri., 5pm-midnight Sat., 5pm-11pm Sun., bar open until 2am daily, $16-36). The dressing-drenched grilled Caesar, a signature dish at this chic spot, can be topped with tenderloin tips, chicken, scallops, shrimp or salmon. **Crazy Shirley's** (7pm-2am Wed.-Thurs., 5pm-2am Fri.-Sat.), a piano bar and lounge on the second floor of the Belvedere, hosts karaoke every Wednesday and DJs Thursday-Saturday.

The classic cocktails at **Checkers Bistro** (300 W. James St., 717/509-1069, www.checkersbistro.com, 5pm-10pm Mon.-Fri., noon-10pm Sat., 5pm-9pm Sun., bar open until 11pm Fri.-Sat., $18-30) bode well for the meal ahead. "Classic" can describe the food menu too, with its French onion soup, steak frites, and grilled swordfish, Like Checkers, ★ **FENZ Restaurant & Latenight** (398 Harrisburg Ave., Ste. 100, 717/735-6999, www.fenzrestaurant.com, 5pm-close Mon.-Sat., lounge 4pm-close, $11-34) excels in cocktails. Housed in a 19th-century foundry, it has two levels with a bar on each. The upstairs has a livelier, younger vibe. Take a seat at the downstairs bar to watch the chefs at work. No need to hunt for street parking: There's a lot behind the building accessible from Charlotte Street.

A discussion of Lancaster's fine-dining scene wouldn't be complete without words of praise for **Gibraltar** (488 Royer Dr., 717/397-2790, www.gibraltargrille.com, 11:30am-2pm and 5pm-9:30pm Mon.-Thurs., 11:30am-2pm and 5pm-10:30pm Fri., 5pm-10:30pm Sat., 10:30am-3pm Sun., bar open as late as 2am, $18-38), with its Mediterranean-influenced cuisine, *Wine Spectator*-lauded wine list, and gracious service.

Strasburg

Strasburg, with its train-related attractions and proximity to the Sight & Sound theater, sees large numbers of tourists. But its restaurants feel refreshingly un-touristy. In the center of town, the **Strasburg Shoppes at Center Square** (1 W. Main St., 717/687-0766, www.strasburg.com, hours vary, open daily) is a country store, creamery, candy shop, and deli all rolled into one. It's best known as a destination for dessert and a dose of nostalgia but it also offers Reuben sandwiches, cheeseburgers, and hot dogs, all served with locally made potato chips. Cross your fingers that the day's specials include a bread bowl filled with Pennsylvania Dutch-style chicken corn soup. For dessert, choose from 20-plus flavors of ice cream. A wide variety of chocolate-covered goodies vie for attention with fudge, peanut brittle, and caramel corn. Sit inside to soak in the old-timey touches, from vintage Cream of Wheat posters to a 19th-century marble soda fountain, or take a seat outside to watch horse-drawn buggies negotiating the intersection of Routes 741 and 896.

Just east of town on Route 741 is an outpost of regional chain **Isaac's Restaurant & Deli** (226 Gap Rd., 717/687-7699, www.isaacsdeli.com, 10am-9pm Mon.-Sat., 11am-8pm Sun. summer, winter hours vary, $6-12). The Strasburg location, which shares an address with the Choo Choo Barn, features a dining area decked out like a train car. Its repertoire of made-from-scratch soups is 200 strong, but only the delicious creamy pepper jack tomato is available every day. The long list of sandwiches includes half a dozen veggie options. Pretzel sandwiches like the Salty Eagle (grilled ham, Swiss cheese, mustard) are particularly popular. You'll also find Isaac's in downtown Lancaster (25 N. Queen St., 717/394-5544), Lititz (4 Crosswinds Rd., 717/625-1181), and Ephrata (120 N. Reading Rd., 717/733-7777), among other places.

Mount Joy

Bube's Brewery (102 N. Market St., 717/653-2056, www.bubesbrewery.com) is reason enough to visit the town of Mount Joy, which at 14 miles northwest of Lancaster isn't particularly close to major tourist attractions. Listed in the National Register of Historic Places, Bube's looks much as it did in the late 1800s, when German immigrant Alois Bube produced lager beers there. The brewer died in 1908 and the brewery's adjoining buildings were largely untouched until 1968, when restoration work began. Today they house a microbrewery, a casual brewpub, a romantic underground restaurant, a tree-filled beer garden, and a bar that looks like it time traveled from the '20s. Occupying the original bottling plant is the **Bottling Works** (11am-close Mon.-Sat., noon-close Sun., $8-26), which has a tiny stage for bands and open mic nights. Its menu is typical of brewpubs: beer-friendly bar snacks, burgers and sandwiches, mussels served with fries. Open-air dining is available in the adjacent **Biergarten,** where you'll find the huge boiler that created steam to power Mr. Bube's brewery.

Make a reservation if you prefer to eat more than 40 feet belowground in the candlelit **Catacombs** (5:30pm-close Mon.-Fri., 4:45pm-close Sat.-Sun., $22-40). Leave the high heels behind. It's a long flight of stairs down to the fine-dining restaurant, which is set in the original brewery's stone-walled cellars, and the stone floor is uneven. A few times a month it serves a themed feast with a heaping side of theatrics. Bawdy medieval-themed evenings are most common, but the repertoire also includes Roman, pirate, Halloween, and Christmas feasts. Tickets must be purchased in advance.

Bube's also offers murder mystery dinners ($50) set in different time periods—including during Mr. Bube's day—in **Alois,** a bar/event space in the brewery's original Victorian-style tavern, and ghost tours ($10, restaurant guests $5).

ACCOMMODATIONS

Lodging options in Lancaster County run the gamut from major brands, like Best Western and DoubleTree, to unique independents. Travelers who prefer bed-and-breakfasts can take their pick of more than 150. If you travel with young children, a B&B might not be the right fit, but a farm stay is a different animal. It's lodging, education, and entertainment rolled into one—assuming you find gathering eggs and bottle-feeding calves entertaining. A

Bube's Brewery

list of Lancaster County farms that offer overnight accommodations is available at www.afarmstay.com.

Tourism board **Discover Lancaster** (717/299-8901, www.discoverlancaster.com) is a good source of information about lodging options. Its website allows for searches by lodging type and price range. The **Mennonite Information Center** (2209 Millstream Rd., Lancaster, 717/299-0954, www.mennoniteinfoctr.com) maintains a list of Mennonite-owned guesthouses, available at the center and on its website.

Under $100

A unique lodging is the **Red Caboose Motel and Restaurant** (312 Paradise Ln., Ronks, 717/687-5000, www.redcaboosemotel.com, from $85), which is made out of several historic train cars—mostly cabooses, plus baggage cars. The 97-room **Fulton Steamboat Inn** (Rtes. 30 and 896, Lancaster, 717/299-9999, www.fultonsteamboatinn.com, $80-190) also fits the "unique" bill. It was built to resemble a steamboat and named for a Lancaster County native who pioneered steam-powered shipping.

Located next to Dutch Wonderland amusement park, **Old Mill Stream Campground** (2249 Lincoln Hwy. E., Lancaster, 717/299-2314, www.oldmillstreamcampground.com, campsite $36-66, mobile home rental $136-195, Apr.-Dec.) makes a great home base for families with young children. The 15-acre campground has more than 160 tent and RV sites, a game room, a country store, laundry rooms, and free wireless Internet access.

The **Carriage House Motor Inn** (144 E. Main St., Strasburg, 717/687-7651, www.carriagehousemotorinn.net, $59-109) is a good non-camping option in this price range. It's walking distance from the Railroad Museum of Pennsylvania and the Strasburg Rail Road, which makes it appealing to rail fans. Families will appreciate its three-room suite. Rates include a continental breakfast. For not too much more, you can spend the night at nearby **Rayba Acres Farm** (183 Black Horse Rd., Paradise, 717/687-6729, www.raybaacres.com, $90-95) or **Neffdale Farm** (604 Strasburg Rd., Paradise, 717/687-7837, www.neffdalefarm.com, $90), both Mennonite-owned.

$100-250

Located just off Route 30 west of Lancaster city, the **Heritage Hotel Lancaster** (500 Centerville Rd., Lancaster, 800/223-8963, www.heritagelancaster.com, $110-200) is a

Red Caboose Motel and Restaurant

great choice for nightlife-loving travelers. **Loxley's** (717/898-2431), its restaurant and bar, attracts locals and hotel guests alike. Named for Robin of Loxley, the archer and outlaw better known as Robin Hood, it boasts a two-level deck that looks like a giant tree house. The hotel has guest rooms, a business center, a fitness room, and an outdoor pool. The Dutch Apple Dinner Theatre is right next door.

Sleep under handmade quilts at **The Inn at Kitchen Kettle Village** (3529 Old Philadelphia Pike, Intercourse, 717/768-8261, www.kitchenkettle.com, $120-210). Scattered throughout the quaint village, accommodations range from standard rooms to two-bedroom suites that sleep up to six. Guests enjoy a free breakfast at the on-site Kling House Restaurant Monday through Saturday.

It's not unusual for two, three, or even four generations of the Ranck family to join guests around the breakfast table at ★ **Verdant View Farm B&B** (429 Strasburg Rd., Paradise, 717/687-7353, www.verdantview.com, $79-199). The Rancks have operated the 118-acre dairy and crop farm, located one mile east of Strasburg on Route 741, for over a century. But breakfast—with its pitchers of raw milk, platters of farm-fresh meat and eggs, and homemade pies—isn't the first thing on the menu at Verdant View. Guests can begin the day with a farm tour, complete with opportunities to milk a cow, frolic with kittens, and feed calves, goats, and bunnies. Wear boots or sneakers you don't mind getting dirty. Verdant View also offers "farmer's apprentice" workshops. (Breakfast and some farm experiences aren't offered on Sundays, when the Rancks attend their Mennonite church.) The nine guest rooms, spread between an 1896 farmhouse and the "little white house" down the lane, are nothing fancy. But what it lacks in frills the B&B more than makes up for in hospitality. Two of the rooms share a bathroom.

Visitors to downtown Lancaster may find it hard to believe that the **Lancaster Marriott at Penn Square** (25 S. Queen St., Lancaster, 717/239-1600, www.lancastermarriott.com, $150-280) and adjoining Lancaster County Convention Center opened in 2009. The 19-floor hotel in the center of town looks historical. That's because developers incorporated the beaux arts facade of a shuttered century-old department store into its design. A contemporary aesthetic takes over in the soaring lobby and spacious rooms. The hotel has an indoor pool and a spa (717/207-4076, www.mandarinrosespa.com). Central Market, the Fulton Theatre, the Demuth Museum, and other downtown attractions are close by. On the downside: On-site parking is $19 per day ($35 for valet), and in-room Internet access will set you back $12 per day.

Over $250

With its brick walls and wood beams, locally crafted furnishings, and first-floor art gallery, the ★ **Lancaster Arts Hotel** (300 Harrisburg Ave., 717/299-3000, www.lancasterartshotel.com, $180-360) is the city's hippest lodging property. "Hip" implies new, but the building itself dates to the late 1800s. Built as a tobacco warehouse, it found a new life as a boutique hotel in 2006. Original works by area artists adorn the 63 eclectically decorated guest rooms and suites, some of which tempt with in-room whirlpools. Amenities include 24-hour business and fitness centers, bicycle rentals, and free parking. **John J. Jeffries** (717/431-3307, www.johnjjeffries.com), the on-site restaurant and lounge, bills itself as the leading consumer of local organic meats and vegetables in central Pennsylvania. The **Cork Factory Hotel** (480 New Holland Ave., Ste. 3000, 717/735-2075, www.corkfactoryhotel.com, $150-220) set in a 19th-century cork factory, goes for a similar vibe. Opened in 2009, it's part of a complex that includes apartments, **Cork & Cap Restaurant** (717/735-2025, www.corkandcaprestaurant.com), and café **The Bakers Table** (717/735-1150, www.thebakerstable.com).

Located midway between the villages of Intercourse and Bird-in-Hand on Route 340, ★ **AmishView Inn & Suites** (3125 Old Philadelphia Pike, Bird-in-Hand,

866/735-1600, www.amishviewinn.com, $125-315) is right in the heart of Amish Country. Rooms on the back side of the hotel boast farmland views, and it's not unusual to see a farmer working his fields with horse-drawn equipment. The bucolic views aren't the only perk. AmishView has an indoor pool and whirlpool, a fitness center, an arcade room, and a guest laundry. The well-appointed guest rooms feature mahogany furniture, kitchenettes, and free high-speed Internet access. Suites come with fireplaces and/or whirlpools. Traveling without the kids? There's a five-story adults-only building. The complimentary breakfast rivals—and beats—expensive morning meals at many hotels. Fill up on eggs, sausage, potatoes, sticky buns, yogurt, baked oatmeal, fresh fruit, made-to-order omelets and Belgian waffles, and more.

TRANSPORTATION AND SERVICES

The city of Lancaster is about 70 miles west of Philadelphia via Route 30 and 80 miles northeast of Baltimore via I-83 north and Route 30 east. The Pennsylvania Turnpike (I-76) passes through the northern part of Lancaster County, but many of the main attractions lie along or near Route 30, which traverses the central part.

Lancaster Airport (LNS, 717/569-1221, www.lancasterairport.com) is served by just one airline, Southern Airways Express. The larger **Harrisburg International Airport** (MDT, 888/235-9442, www.flyhia.com) is about 30 miles from Lancaster city. **Amtrak** (800/872-7245, www.amtrak.com) provides rail service to the city. Lancaster's Amtrak station (53 E. McGovern Ave.) was built in 1929 by the Pennsylvania Railroad.

For getting around Lancaster County, it's best to have your own wheels, but public transportation is available. **Red Rose Transit Authority** (717/397-5613, www.redrose-transit.com) operates 17 bus routes throughout the county. It also has a tourist trolley in Lancaster city on weekdays.

Discover Lancaster (717/299-8901, www.discoverlancaster.com) is an excellent source of information about Lancaster County. Visit the website to request a free "getaway guide" or flip through a digital version. At the Discover Lancaster visitors center (501 Greenfield Rd., Lancaster, 9am-5pm Mon.-Sat. and 10am-4pm Sun. Memorial Day weekend-Oct., 10am-4pm daily Nov.-Memorial Day weekend), located just off Route 30 at the Greenfield Road exit, you can load up on maps and brochures and chat with travel consultants. Ninety-minute tours of the Amish countryside depart from the visitors center from May through October.

Reading and Vicinity

With a population of 88,000, Reading is the largest city in Pennsylvania Dutch Country. The construction of the Reading Railroad in the 19th century ushered in the region's economic heyday. The original line stretched south from the coal-mining town of Pottsville to Reading and then on to Philadelphia, a distance of less than 100 miles. Over the next century, the Reading grew to consist of more than 1,000 miles of track. The railroad filed for bankruptcy and was absorbed by Conrail in the 1970s. But it lives on in the form of a property in the board game Monopoly. One of Berks County's 30-plus historical museums and sites is dedicated to the railroad.

Historical attractions notwithstanding, the county is best known as a shopping destination. It's home to an outlet mall and the only Cabela's outdoor megastore in Pennsylvania. It also has much to offer antiques lovers.

By the way, it's pronounced "RED-ing," not "REED-ing."

SIGHTS

The Pagoda

Reading's most prominent landmark is not what you'd expect. Perched atop Mount Penn, 886 feet above downtown, the **Pagoda** (98 Duryea Dr., 610/655-6271, www.readingpagoda.com, 2pm-6pm Thurs., noon-6pm Fri.-Sun. summer, winter hours vary, suggested donation $1) has become a symbol of the city, seen in the logos of businesses and civic organizations and on a shoulder patch worn by the men and women of the Reading Police Department. More than a century old, it's believed to be one of only three pagodas of its scale in the country and the only one in the world with a fireplace and chimney. The reason a headline in the August 10, 1906, issue of the *Reading Eagle* announced "Reading to Have Japanese Pagoda" starts with William Abbott Witman. The local businessman had made himself very unpopular by starting a stone quarrying operation on the western slope of Mount Penn. The Pagoda would cover the mess he'd left on the mountainside. Moreover, it would serve as a luxury resort.

The building was completed in 1908, but Witman's plan to operate it as a mountain retreat was dealt a fatal blow: His application for a liquor license was denied. By 1910, the property was in foreclosure. To save the bank from a loss, local merchant and bank director Jonathan Mould purchased the Pagoda and presented it to the city as a gift. Before radios came into common use, the seven-story structure served as a sort of public announcement system. Lights installed on its roof flashed Morse code to direct firemen and relay baseball scores, political outcomes, and other information. Today it's a tourist stop. Visitors can climb 87 solid oak steps to a lookout offering a view across 30 miles. There's a small café and gift shop on the first floor.

Reading Railroad Heritage Museum

Opened in 2008 in a former Pennsylvania Steel foundry complex, the **Reading Railroad Heritage Museum** (500 S. 3rd St., Hamburg, 610/562-5513, www.readingrailroad.org, 10am-4pm Sat., noon-4pm Sun., adults $7, seniors $5, children 5-12 $3) tells the story of the profound impact the railroad had on the communities it served. It's operated by the Reading Company Technical & Historical Society, which began rounding up locomotives and freight and passenger cars several years after the railroad's 1971 bankruptcy filing. The all-volunteer nonprofit is now the

the Pagoda in Reading

proud owner of the nation's largest collection of rolling stock dedicated to a single railroad.

Reading Public Museum

The **Reading Public Museum** (500 Museum Rd., Reading, 610/371-5850, www.readingpublicmuseum.org, 11am-5pm daily, adults $10, seniors, students, and children 4-17 $6, planetarium show adults $8, seniors, students, and children 4-17 $6) is an art museum, natural history museum, and anthropology museum all rolled into one. Founded in 1904 by a local teacher, the museum even has a gallery devoted to its own history. Its fine art collection is particularly strong in oil paintings and includes works by John Singer Sargent, Edgar Degas, Winslow Homer, N. C. Wyeth, and Berks County native Keith Haring. Among the highlights of the natural history collection are the fossilized footprints of reptiles that roamed the immediate area some 200 million years ago. They were found just a few miles away. The collections include everything from an Egyptian mummy to 16th-century samurai armor to Pennsylvania German folk art. A 25-acre arboretum and a domed planetarium round out the offerings.

GoggleWorks Center for the Arts

Like other cities wrestling with the erosion of their industrial base, Reading has rolled out the red carpet for artists and cultural organizations. In 2005 an abandoned factory in Reading's urban core was transformed into the **GoggleWorks Center for the Arts** (201 Washington St., Reading, 610/374-4600, www.goggleworks.org, 9am-9pm daily, free). So named because the factory manufactured safety goggles, the arts center boasts multiple galleries, a film theater, a café, dozens of artist studios, and teaching studios for ceramics, woodworking, glassblowing, photography, and more.

The **GoggleWorks Store** (11am-7pm Mon.-Fri., 11am-5pm Sat.-Sun.) offers unique handcrafted items. GoggleWorks is also home to the **Greater Reading Visitors Center** (610/375-4085, www.gogreaterreading.com), where you can load up on maps and brochures.

★ Air Museums

Berks County is home to not one but two museums dedicated to the history of aviation. Both offer thrilling rides in antique planes. Larger and older, the **Mid-Atlantic Air Museum (MAAM)** (11 Museum Dr., Reading, 610/372-7333, www.maam.org, 9:30am-4pm daily, adults $8, seniors $6, children 6-12 $3) at Reading Regional Airport is home to more than 60 aircraft built from 1928 to the early 1980s. Among them is a Northrop P-61 Black Widow—one of only four in existence. In January 1945, the night fighter crashed into a mountainside on the South Pacific island of New Guinea. World War II veteran Eugene "Pappy" Strine and his son established the air museum in 1980 for the purpose of recovering the rare aircraft, which had logged only 10 flight hours before stalling and crashing during a proficiency check. Green-lighted by the Indonesian government in 1984, the recovery project took seven years. Other highlights of the collection include a North American B-25 Mitchell, a World War II bomber that appeared in half a dozen movies before she was donated to the museum in 1981, and a Douglas R4D-6 Skytrain, which delivered supplies and specialist personnel to combat zones during the war. MAAM's impressive holding of vintage military aircraft and annual **World War II Weekend,** held the first weekend in June, have given it a reputation as a "warbird" museum, but in fact about two-thirds of its flying machines were built for civilians.

The **Golden Age Air Museum** (Grimes Airfield, 371 Airport Rd., Bethel, 717/933-9566, www.goldenageair.org, 10am-4pm Sat., 11am-4pm Sun. May-Oct., self-guided tour adults $5, children 6-12 $3, guided tour adults $8, children 6-12 $3), about 20 miles away, was established in 1997. True to its name, it concentrates on what's called the golden age of aviation: the years between the two World

Wars. More than 20 of its 30-some aircraft were built in the late 1910s, '20s, and '30s. The museum is also home to a handful of antique automobiles, including a 1930 Ford Model A roadster. Its **"Flying Circus" air shows,** held twice yearly, pay tribute to barnstorming, a popular form of entertainment in the 1920s.

MAAM offers rides in a pair of 1940s aircraft, including an open-cockpit biplane trainer, on the second weekend of May and July-October, as well as during the WWII-themed extravaganza in June. The cost of the flight, which lasts about 20-25 minutes, is $313. Reservations are required. Golden Age Air Museum offers rides in an open-cockpit 1929 biplane year-round by appointment. A 15-minute flight costs $115 for one person, $135 for two. One or two people can fly for 30 minutes for $229.

Roadside America

Billed as "the world's greatest indoor miniature village," **Roadside America** (109 Roadside Dr., Shartlesville, 610/488-6241, www.roadsideamerica.co, 10am-6pm Mon.-Fri., 10am-5pm Sat.-Sun., adults $8, children 6-11 $5) ranks among the most unique attractions in Pennsylvania. The massive display features more than 300 miniature structures, 4,000 miniature people, and 10,000 miniature trees. There are horse-drawn carriages and muscle cars, trollies and trains, construction crews and a coal mine. There's even an animated circus. Started in the 1930s by a local carpenter, the masterpiece depicts rural life from pioneer days to the present. In addition to Roadside America, the small town of Shartlesville offers Pennsylvania Dutch food and quaint shops. It's in northern Berks County, about 20 miles northwest of Reading.

★ Hawk Mountain Sanctuary

Located 25 miles north of Reading, **Hawk Mountain Sanctuary** (1700 Hawk Mountain Rd., Kempton, 610/756-6000, www.hawkmountain.org, trails dawn-dusk daily except during deer hunting season in Nov. or Dec., visitors center 8am-5pm daily Sept.-Nov., 9am-5pm Dec.-Aug., trail use fee $10 adults, $7 seniors, $5 children 6-12) is one of the best places in the country to watch migrating hawks, eagles, falcons, and other winged predators. During the fall migration, counters may record upwards of 1,000 birds in one day. That's because of the sanctuary's location on the Blue Mountain (aka Kittatinny) ridge, part of the Appalachian range. Lookouts at Hawk Mountain allow for eye-level views of the

Mid-Atlantic Air Museum

I'll Have a Lager

If Pennsylvania had an official state beer, it would have to be **Yuengling Traditional Lager.** It's so ubiquitous that asking for it by name is often unnecessary. Bartenders translate "I'll have a lager" as "Pour me a Yuengling." Pronounced properly (YING-ling), the brand sounds like an Asian import. But D. G. Yuengling & Son brewing company has been based in Pottsville, Pennsylvania, since its 1829 founding—making it America's oldest brewery, a fact stamped on every bottle. It survived Prohibition by producing "near beers"—now known as nonalcoholic beers—and celebrated the 1933 repeal of the 18th Amendment by shipping a truckload of real beer to the White House. We don't know how then-president Franklin Roosevelt felt about the suds, but Barack Obama is a fan. When he lost a friendly wager on the outcome of the U.S.-Canada battle for ice hockey gold at the 2010 Winter Olympics, he sent a case of "lager" (as in Yuengling) to the Canadian prime minister.

About 35 miles north of Reading, Pottsville lies in Pennsylvania's coal region, home to the largest fields of anthracite in the country. The city is still recovering from the demise of the anthracite industry after World War II. Yuengling also had it rough in the postwar decades, as the full-flavored products of regional breweries lost favor to lighter national brands. But the company has more than recovered since Richard L. Yuengling Jr. became its fifth-generation owner in 1985. According to a 2017 report by the Boulder, Colorado-based Brewers Association, Yuengling is the fourth-largest brewing company in the country, and the largest craft brewing company. Only Anheuser-Busch, MillerCoors, and Pabst sell more beer.

Free tours of the Pottsville **brewery** (5th and Mahantongo Sts., 570/622-4141, www.yuengling.com, gift shop open 9am-4pm Mon.-Fri. year-round and 10am-3pm Sat. Apr.-Dec.) are offered at 10am, 11am, noon, 1pm, and 1:30pm weekdays year-round and 10:30am-1pm on Saturdays April through December. They include a visit to the "caves" where beer was fermented in years past and end with free samples. You don't have to be of drinking age to take a tour (just to sample the brews), but you do have to wear closed shoes. Built in 1831, the facility isn't handicapped accessible.

While in Pottsville, you may want to pay a visit to **Jerry's Classic Cars and Collectibles Museum** (394 S. Center St., 570/628-2266, www.jerrysmuseum.com, noon-5pm Fri.-Sun. May-Oct., adults $8, seniors $6, children 6 and under free), a tribute to the 1950s and '60s.

majestic birds. Some fly so close you can't help but duck. The southbound migration begins in mid-August and continues into December, peaking September through November. The very best time to visit is two or three days after a cold front passes. Sightings are considerably less frequent during the northbound migration, when prevailing easterlies push raptors west of the sanctuary. Still, it's possible to spot as many as 300 on a day in April or early May.

Founded in 1934 to stop hunters from shooting the migrating birds, Hawk Mountain is the world's oldest refuge for birds of prey. The nonprofit charges a fee for use of its eight-mile trail system, which connects to the epic Appalachian Trail. The most popular path winds past a series of lookouts and is known, appropriately enough, as the Lookout Trail. The first lookout is only a couple hundred yards from the trailhead and is accessible by all-terrain wheelchair, available at the visitors center. The trail becomes rocky and uneven after the first few overlooks, and you could find yourself scrambling over bigger rocks. Hiking boots aren't a bad idea. At the end of the mile-long trail is the famed **North Lookout,** site of the sanctuary's official hawk count. It's hard to tear yourself away from the panoramic view from 1,490 feet above sea level, so consider bringing a cushion and something to eat or drink. Definitely pack food and water if you plan to tackle longer trails like the four-mile River of Rocks loop, which drops into a valley and skirts an ice-age boulder field. Trail maps are available on the sanctuary's website and in the visitors center.

If you're new to bird-watching, browse the visitors center's educational displays before starting your hike. A bit of time in the **Wings of Wonder Gallery,** featuring life-size wood carvings of each migrating raptor, will do wonders for your ability to identify the real deal. Educators are stationed at some lookouts during busy periods.

Crystal Cave Park

Discovered in 1871, **Crystal Cave** (963 Crystal Cave Rd., Kutztown, 610/683-6765, www.crystalcavepa.com, 9am-5pm daily Mar.-Nov., open later in summer, tour adults $14.50, children 4-11 $10.50) is the oldest operating show cave in Pennsylvania. Guides who know their stalagmites from their stalactites lead visitors along concrete pathways, pointing out the "prairie dogs," "giant's tooth," "crystal ballroom," and other formations. Tours last 55 minutes and include a short video presentation on cave geology. It's a constant 54 degrees inside, so dress accordingly.

There's quite a bit to keep visitors entertained outside the cave, including an 18-hole miniature golf course ($3.25), a panning-for-gemstones attraction, and an ice cream parlor and café open daily in July and August and weekends in June and September. Amish buggy rides and use of the picnic facilities are included in the price of admission.

ENTERTAINMENT AND EVENTS

Concert Venues

Home to Reading's professional ice hockey team, **Santander Arena** (700 Penn St., Reading, 610/898-7469, www.santander-arena.com) also hosts concerts, professional wrestling, conventions, and other events. Opened in 2001, the arena seats 7,100. It's sometimes converted into a smaller, more intimate venue known as the **Reading Eagle Theater.**

Performing Arts

In 2000 the Berks County Convention Center Authority purchased Reading's only surviving movie palace and spent $7 million on renovations. Now known as the **Santander Performing Arts Center** (136 N. 6th St., Reading, 610/898-7469, www.santander-arena.com), the 1,700-seat theater is home to the **Reading Symphony Orchestra** (www.readingsymphony.org). It also hosts touring

Hawk Mountain Sanctuary

Broadway productions, music concerts, and other events.

The **Miller Center for the Arts** (4 N. 2nd St., Reading, 610/607-6270, www.millercenter.racc.edu) welcomes a wide array of touring acts: modern dance, musicals, Berks Opera Company performances. The glass-walled theater on the campus of Reading Area Community College seats about 500.

Festivals and Events

First held in 1991, **Berks Jazz Fest** (various venues, tickets 800/745-3000, www.berksjazzfest.com, Apr.) has grown bigger and bigger over the years. Famed trumpeter Wynton Marsalis, who played at the inaugural fest, returned in 2010 with his Jazz at Lincoln Center Orchestra. Other past performers include Béla Fleck and the Flecktones, the Count Basie Orchestra, and Kurt Elling. The 10-day festival is presented by the Berks Arts Council, which is also to thank for a series of free concerts held on Friday evenings in July. These **Bandshell Concerts** (City Park, 1281 Hill Rd., Reading, 610/898-1930, www.berksarts.org) showcase various musical genres, including blues, alt-rock, and bluegrass.

Berks County's premier event is the **Kutztown Folk Festival** (Kutztown Fairgrounds, 450 Wentz St., Kutztown, 888/674-6136, www.kutztownfestival.com, late June/early July, adults $14, seniors $13, children 13-17 $5, children 12 and under free, weekly passes available), a nine-day celebration of Pennsylvania Dutch culture. Founded in 1950, it's said to be the oldest continuously operated folklife festival in the country. To call it a unique event is an understatement. Where else can you see a reenactment of a 19th-century hanging, watch a Mennonite wedding, take a seminar on the Pennsylvania Dutch dialect, *and* buy bread baked in an early 1800s oven? The festival also features one of the largest quilt sales in the country with more than 2,500 locally handmade quilts are available for purchase. Demonstrations of quilting and other traditional crafts are a hallmark of the event. Family-style all-you-can-eat Pennsylvania Dutch dinners are a festival tradition. The borough of Kutztown is about 20 miles northeast of Reading.

Winter's main event is a Christmas display on steroids located about 15 miles northwest of Reading. **Koziar's Christmas Village** (782 Christmas Village Rd., Bernville, 610/488-1110, www.koziarschristmasvillage.com, first weekend of Nov. to Jan. 1, adults $10, senior $9, children 4-10 $8) traces its history to 1948, when William M. Koziar strung lights around his house and barn in rural Berks County to the delight of his wife and four children. Each year, he stepped up his game, decorating more and more of his property. The increasingly elaborate display began attracting people from nearby, and then people from not so nearby. These days a million Christmas lights go into the creation of the winter wonderland. A reflective lake doubles the wow factor. Koziar's also offers large dioramas of scenes such as "Christmas Beneath the Sea" and "Santa's Post Office," extensive model train layouts, and shops selling ornaments, souvenirs, toys, and other gifts. Santa's on-site, of course.

SHOPPING

VF Outlet Center

One of greater Reading's most popular tourist destinations, the **VF Outlet Center** (801 Hill Ave., Wyomissing, 610/378-0408, www.vfoutletcenter.com, 9:30am-9pm Mon.-Sat., 10am-6pm Sun., winter hours vary) has a rich history. For most of the 20th century, its buildings comprised the Berkshire Knitting Mills. The Berkie, as locals called it, was the world's largest manufacturer of hosiery in the early decades of the century, before seamless nylons became all the rage. In 1969 it was purchased by VF Corporation, which opened a factory store in one end of a manufacturing building. A drop cloth separated the retail and manufacturing areas. The mill ceased operations several years later, but the store remained. Today the VF Outlet store sells brands including Wrangler, Lee, Nautica, Timberland, Samsonite, and Dooney & Bourke.

Cabela's

The 2003 opening of a **Cabela's** (100 Cabela Dr., Hamburg, 610/929-7000, www.cabelas.com, 8am-9pm Mon.-Sat., 9am-8pm Sun., winter hours vary) store less than 20 miles north of Reading warranted a story in the *New York Times* travel section. After all, it was the first Cabela's outpost on the East Coast. The revered retailer of outdoor gear has since expanded up and down the coast, but the Pennsylvania store still reels in millions of hunting and fishing enthusiasts a year. The 250,000-square-foot showplace just off I-78 features shooting and archery ranges, massive aquariums, life-size wildlife dioramas that put many natural history museums to shame, and a restaurant offering sandwiches stuffed with your choice of meats—the choices including elk, wild boar, and bison. And then there's the merchandise. The dizzying selection includes everything from guns to outdoor-inspired home decor. Live bait is available for anglers heading to nearby waters. Also available: kennels for shoppers who bring their canine friends, a corral for those who bring their equine friends, and a dump station for those arriving by RV.

Antiques

Antiques lovers can find plenty of what they're looking for in the Reading area. Just 10 miles southwest of Reading, straddling Berks and Lancaster Counties, is the borough of Adamstown, also known as "Antiques Capital USA." See the *Lancaster County* section for the lowdown on Adamstown. Twenty miles northeast of Reading is another antiquing destination: Kutztown's **Renninger's** (740 Noble St., Kutztown, 610/683-6848, www.renningers.com, antique market 8am-4pm Sat., flea market 7:30am-4pm Sat., farmers market 10am-7pm Fri. and 8am-4pm Sat.). With locations in Adamstown and Florida as well, Renninger's is a big name in antiquing circles. The Kutztown location is open Saturdays and the Adamstown location Sundays, so it's not unusual for treasure hunters to hit both in one weekend. What's for sale? Everything from Indian artifacts and early farm tools to neon beer signs and Pez dispensers. There's also a farmers market with produce, fresh and smoked meats, baked goods, handmade candies, and coffees and teas.

FOOD

Reading

Most of Reading's recommendable restaurants are concentrated in the gritty downtown area. The most famous, thanks to its longevity and a 2008 visit from the Travel Channel, is **Jimmie Kramer's Peanut Bar** (332 Penn St., 610/376-8500, www.peanutbar.com, 11am-11pm Mon.-Thurs., 11am-midnight Fri., noon-midnight Sat., $9-26). At the "bar food paradise," as the Travel Channel dubbed it, patrons are welcomed with a bowl of peanuts and encouraged to toss the shells on the floor. The casual joint is also known for its hot wings, seafood, and house-made desserts. Opened in 1933 as Jimmie Kramer's Olde Central Cafe, the bar and restaurant originally plied patrons with pretzels. When the pretzels ran out one day in 1935, Jimmie sent someone to a peanut roaster across the street, and the shell-tossing tradition was born. Renamed for the humble legume in 1958, the restaurant is now run by Jimmie's grandson.

One block south of the Peanut Bar is a cluster of three eateries owned by Reading native Judy Henry. **Judy's on Cherry** (332 Cherry St., 610/374-8511, www.judysoncherry.com, lunch and dinner Tues.-Fri., dinner Sat., $11-39) offers Mediterranean-influenced fare, most of it cooked in a 6,000-pound hearthstone oven, in a brightly decorated former farmers market. For the adjoining **Speckled Hen Cottage Pub & Alehouse** (30 S. 4th St., 610/685-8511, www.speckledhenpub.com, 4:30pm-midnight Wed.-Sat., $10-21), Henry transformed downtown Reading's oldest building—a log house built in the 1780s—into the sort of pub you'd find in the countryside of England or Ireland. With its working fireplaces and comfort cuisine (chicken potpie, fish-and-chips, baked mac and cheese) the Speckled Hen hits the spot on a wintry day.

On a warm day, make a beeline for **Plein Air** (610/374-8511, open for lunch Wed.-Fri. and dinner Wed.-Sat. mid-May-Sept., $8-18), an outdoor café accessible from either Judy's or the Speckled Hen.

Just outside the downtown area is the lovely **Abigail's Victorian Tea Room** (1441 Perkiomen Ave., 610/376-6050, www.abigailstearoom.com, 11am-2pm Wed.-Sat.), which offers a simple lunch menu ($13) as well as high tea experiences ($15-27). Private parties occasionally take over the space, so be sure to call ahead. Abigail's is Victorian through and through, from its setting—an 1883 manse outfitted with period furnishings and crystal chandeliers—to its delicate floral china. Lady Gaga has been photographed with exquisite teacups purchased from the owner's website.

Set in a 200-year-old inn a few miles south of town, ★ **Dans at Green Hills** (2444 Morgantown Rd., 610/777-9611, www.dansatgreenhills.com, 4pm-8pm Sun.-Mon., 4pm-9pm Tues.-Sat., $19-37) is no longer owned by the two Dans who opened it in 1989 but carries on their mission of providing "a contemporary alternative to the traditional Berks County dining scene." If it's fine dining you seek, look no further.

ACCOMMODATIONS

Reading

Though it's the cultural, governmental, and business capital of Berks County, downtown Reading has few lodging options. Its only hotel is a gleaming **DoubleTree** (701 Penn St., 610/375-8000, www.doubletree3.hilton.com, $140-220) opened at the end of 2015 directly across from the Santander Arena and a few blocks from the Santander Performing Arts Center. The hotel's 209 well-appointed rooms come with 42-inch TVs and minifridges. Shuttle service to area attractions, on-site parking, and Wi-Fi are all included, as is the warm chocolate chip cookie you'll be handed upon check-in. Suites are available. Off the lobby, **Cheers American Bistro** serves standard American fare.

The great stone mansion now known as the **Stirling Guest Hotel** (1120 Centre Ave., 610/373-1522, www.stirlingguesthotel.net, $175-275) was built in the early 1890s in what was then considered a far suburb of Reading. It's a mere mile north of the city center. Designed in the Châteauesque style for a local iron and steel magnate and named for a castle in Scotland, the mansion has nine sumptuously decorated guest suites. A large Tudor-style carriage house offers six more.

Less than a mile north of the VF Outlet Center, **The Inn at Reading** (1040 N. Park Rd., Wyomissing, 610/372-7811, www.innatreading.com, $72-102) has 170 traditionally furnished rooms and suites. Amenities include a large outdoor pool open May-September, a half-court basketball court, an exercise facility, and a restaurant modeled on a traditional English pub.

Northern Berks County

A short drive from the Hawk Mountain Sanctuary and the Appalachian Trail, ★ **Pamela's Forget Me Not B&B** (33 Hawk Mountain Rd., Kempton, 610/756-3398, www.pamelasforgetmenot.com, $115-160) is as charming as its name. It offers just four rooms, including the romantic Cottage Suite with handcrafted four-poster bed, gas fireplace, and private deck. The comfy Carriage House Suite, which sleeps up to six people, is perfect for families. The remaining suite and guest room are in the main house, dating to 1879 and Victorian in decor.

TRANSPORTATION

Located about 60 miles northwest of Philadelphia via I-76 west and I-176 north and 30 miles northeast of Lancaster, Reading is primarily a drive-to destination. There's no scheduled service to Reading Regional Airport, home to the Mid-Atlantic Air Museum. **Lehigh Valley International Airport** (ABE, 800/359-5842, www.flyvia.com), served by airlines including Delta, American, and United, is 40 miles from Reading. **Harrisburg International Airport** (MDT, 888/235-9442, www.flyhia.com)

and **Philadelphia International Airport** (PHL, 215/937-6937, www.phl.org) are about 60 miles away.

Intercity bus service to Reading is available through **Greyhound** (20 N. 3rd St., 800/231-2222, www.greyhound.com) and its interline partners. Local bus service is provided by the Berks Area Reading Transportation Authority, or **BARTA** (610/921-0601, www.bartabus.com). Call **Reading Metro Taxi** (610/374-5111) if you need a lift.

Hershey and Vicinity

Hershey owes its name and existence to Milton S. Hershey, founder of the largest chocolate company in North America. The Hershey Company, as it's now named, does business all over the world. But the company is still based in the town built by Milton Hershey—a town with streetlights shaped like Hershey's Kisses. It still makes chocolate there. You can smell it in the air. "The Sweetest Place on Earth," as Hershey is called, attracts several million visitors a year. Start at the Hershey Story for an excellent overview. If you have kids in tow, they'll probably insist on starting at Hersheypark, which boasts more than 60 rides and attractions, including more than a dozen roller coasters.

SIGHTS

★ The Hershey Story

The Hershey Story (63 W. Chocolate Ave., Hershey, 717/534-3439, www.hersheystory.org, hours vary but generally open 9am-5pm daily) opened in 2009, the first new landmark building on Chocolate Avenue in 75 years. It delivers exactly what its name promises: the story of the man, the company, and the town named Hershey. Visitors learn about Milton Hershey's childhood and rocky road to success, his chocolate-making innovations and creative promotion strategies, his model town, and his philanthropies. Among the artifacts displayed are a chocolate-mixing machine from the 1920s and a Hershey's Kisses-wrapping machine, both in working order. Admission to the exhibit area is $12.50 for adults, $11.50 for seniors, and $9 for children 3-12.

The main floor features the Chocolate Lab, where visitors get hands-on experience in chocolate-making. Arrive early if you're interested. Classes can only be booked on the day of and they fill quickly. They're $10 for adults, $9 for seniors, $7.50 for children 4-12. Children under 4 aren't permitted in the lab. Combo tickets are available for visitors who want to take in the exhibits and take part in a class: $20 for adults, $19 for seniors, $15 for children 4-12 (kids under 4 can't participate in the Chocolate Lab).

Fuel up at the on-site café, serving coffee, breakfast fare, salads, sandwiches, and, of course, plenty of chocolate desserts.

★ Hersheypark

Even before his chocolate factory was built, Milton Hershey had laid out the plans for a town. He set aside 150 acres along Spring Creek for a park where his employees could picnic and paddle the day away. The park opened in the spring of 1907 and soon became a tourist attraction, with excursion trains and trolleys delivering day-trippers from surrounding communities. Today **Hersheypark** (100 W. Hersheypark Dr., Hershey, 717/534-3900, www.hersheypark.com) lures people from across the state and beyond with more than 60 rides and attractions, including a baker's dozen roller coasters. Bring bathing suits to enjoy Hersheypark's water attractions, which include Tidal Force, one of the tallest splash-down rides in the world, and a 378,000-gallon wave pool. For those who prefer to stay dry and firmly planted on the

Milton Hershey's Story

Born in 1857 in a small central Pennsylvania community, young Milton Hershey moved frequently while his father pursued a series of get-rich schemes, and as a consequence, he never advanced past the fourth grade. At 14, he began a four-year apprenticeship with a Lancaster confectioner. His first candy business, in Philadelphia, collapsed after six years. In 1883 he opened a candy shop in New York. It failed. Penniless, he returned to Lancaster and gave it a third try, making caramels by day and selling them from a pushcart in the evenings. A large order from a British candy importer and a loan from a local bank marked a turning point for the persistent entrepreneur. His Lancaster Caramel Company soon became one of the leading caramel manufacturers in the country.

At the Chicago World's Fair in 1893, Hershey was transfixed by an exhibit of German chocolate-making equipment. He purchased the machinery and had it installed in the east wing of his caramel factory. The Hershey Chocolate Company was born.

Back then, milk chocolate was a Swiss luxury product. Hershey was determined to develop a formula for affordable milk chocolate. By the dawn of the new century, he had succeeded. He sold the Lancaster Caramel Company for $1 million, retaining his chocolate-making machinery, and in 1903 broke ground on a new, larger factory on a cornfield in Derry Township, Pennsylvania, about a mile from his birthplace. It wasn't simply nostalgia that brought him back. Hershey needed fresh milk for his milk chocolate and the area was rich in dairy farms. There was a railroad line and turnpike nearby. The absence of housing and other infrastructure for future employees didn't faze him. He was bent on building not only a manufacturing plant but also a model town.

The intersection of two dirt roads a short distance from the factory became the center of his town. He named one Chocolate Avenue and the other Cocoa Avenue. A trolley system was up and running even before the factory was completed. As Americans fell in love with his chocolate, homes for workers and executives were built on streets named after cocoa-growing regions: Trinidad, Java, Ceylon, and such. Builders used a variety of designs so the community wouldn't look like a company town. Before long, the town had a fire company, barber shop, blacksmith shop, gas station, service garage, and weekly newspaper. A park sprung up, and by 1910 it boasted a band shell, swimming pool, zoo, and bowling alley. Today it's known as Hersheypark, and is a full-blown amusement park.

ground, Hersheypark offers shopping and a busy schedule of live entertainment.

The park is open daily from Memorial Day weekend through Labor Day and some weekends before and after that period. Gates open at 10am during the summer and close between 6pm and 11pm. One-day admission is $65 for guests ages 9-54, $42 for children 3-8 and adults 55-69, and $27 for those 70 and older. Hang on to your ticket stub in case you decide to come back the next day; consecutive-day admission is $39. The park also offers special "sunset" rates for those showing up later in the day, as well as a variety of season passes. Hersheypark tickets are good for same-day admission to the on-site ZooAmerica, which is open year-round. Parking costs $15.

The park opens several times outside its regular season. **Springtime in the Park** is a chance to preview what's in store for summer over several days in April. **Hersheypark in the Dark** offers Halloween-themed fun. The park is also open part of November and throughout December for **Hersheypark Christmas Candylane.** The Christmastime drive-through spectacular **Hershey Sweet Lights** is located a few minutes from the amusement park.

Hershey's Chocolate World

When the Hershey Company ceased factory tours in the 1970s, it gave the public **Hershey's Chocolate World** (101 Chocolate World Way, Hershey, 717/534-4900, www.hersheys.com/chocolateworld, hours vary, open year-round). Adjacent to Hersheypark,

Chocolate World is part mall, part interactive museum. Its shops sell anything and everything Hershey's, including pillows shaped like packets of Reese's Peanut Butter Cups, Twizzlers-shaped pens, and personalized chocolate bars. A primer on the chocolate-making process is available in the form of a slow-moving amusement ride. The ride is free; other Chocolate World attractions have an admission fee. The interactive *4D Chocolate Mystery* show (adults $8, children 3-12 $7) features animated characters controlled by professional puppeteers. For $15, visitors can create their own candy bar and design the package. And since it's just not right to gaze at all that chocolate without eating any, Chocolate World also has a chocolate-tasting attraction (adults $11, children 3-12 $8).

To fill up on something other than candy, head to the food court for sandwiches, soups, pizzas, chocolate milk, ice cream, and milk shakes. And then, what the hell—you might as well stop by The Bakery.

Complimentary shuttle service is available between Chocolate World and Hersheypark. You can also hop aboard an old-fashioned trolley car for a fascinating tour of the town. **Hershey Trolley Works** (717/533-3000, www.hersheytrolleyworks.com, adults $16, seniors $15.50, children 3-12 $13) tours depart Chocolate World daily rain or shine (but not in heavy snow).

Hershey Gardens

When Milton Hershey was asked to sponsor a national rose garden in Washington DC, he decided to create one in his eponymous town instead. "A nice garden of roses," as he called it, opened to the public in 1937. It's now a 23-acre horticultural haven. Roses are still the specialty at **Hershey Gardens** (170 Hotel Rd., Hershey, 717/534-3492, www.hersheygardens.org, 9am-5pm daily winter, 9am-6pm daily summer, adults $12.50, seniors $11.50, children 3-12 $9), located across from the Hotel Hershey. More than 3,500 roses of 275 varieties bloom during the summer months. In the spring, 20,000 tulips blanket the Seasonal Display Garden. Bold-colored chrysanthemums steal the show in fall. Hundreds of butterflies flit around the tropical Butterfly Atrium year-round. The atrium is within a lovely light-filled conservatory opened in 2016. Also popular is the Children's Garden, filled with not only flora but also engaging activities.

roller coaster at Hersheypark

Antique Auto Museum at Hershey

Home to the Lakeland bus used in the movie *Forrest Gump* and a green Cadillac Seville once owned by actress Betty White, the **Antique Auto Museum at Hershey** (161 Museum Dr., Hershey, 717/566-7100, www.aacamuseum.org, 9am-5pm daily, adults $12, seniors $11, children 4-12 $9) is one of the few attractions in town that have nothing to do with chocolate. An affiliate of the Smithsonian Institution, the museum has more than 150 cars, motorcycles, and buses, with as many as 100 on display at any given time. You don't have to be an auto enthusiast to appreciate the elaborate dioramas depicting scenes such as a 1940s gas station and 1950s drive-in.

Indian Echo Caverns

Geological forces make for family entertainment at **Indian Echo Caverns** (368 Middletown Rd., Hummelstown, 717/566-8131, www.indianechocaverns.com, 9am-5pm daily Memorial Day-Labor Day, 10am-4pm early Sept.-late May, adults $18, seniors $16, children 2-11 $10), located four miles west of Hershey off Route 322. The first visitors to the limestone caverns were likely Susquehannock people seeking shelter from inclement weather. The caverns still do a brisk business on rainy days, when Hersheypark holds less than its usual appeal. Guides point out spectacular formations and share cavern lore during 45-minute walking tours. It's always a cool 52 degrees inside, so dress accordingly. In summer, allot an extra hour if you're bringing kids. The grounds include a playground, a petting zoo, and Gem Mill Junction, where budding prospectors can search for amethysts, agates, and other treasures.

ENTERTAINMENT AND EVENTS

Performance Venues

Best known as the home arena of the Hershey Bears hockey team, **Giant Center** (550 W. Hersheypark Dr., Hershey, 717/534-3911, www.hersheyentertainment.com) hosts some of the biggest-name performers to pass through Hershey. It opened in 2002 with a Cher concert. The arena seats 10,000-12,500 depending on the nature of the event.

Hersheypark Stadium (100 W. Hersheypark Dr., Hershey, 717/534-3911, www.hersheyentertainment.com) can accommodate 30,000 fans for concerts. The outdoor stadium has hosted the likes of The Who and U2. Built as part of Milton Hershey's Depression-era building campaign, the stadium at one point served as the summer home of the Philadelphia Eagles. The **Star Pavilion** opened at Hersheypark Stadium in 1996. It's a more intimate open-air venue with reserved and lawn seating for 8,000.

The spectacular **Hershey Theatre** (15 E. Caracas Ave., Hershey, 717/534-3405, www.hersheyentertainment.com) went up during Mr. Hershey's "Great Building Campaign," which created jobs for an estimated 600 skilled workers. The lobby boasts a floor laid with polished Italian lava rock, soaring marble arches, and a ceiling adorned with bas-relief images of swans, war chariots, and more. An intricate lighting system creates the illusion of twinkling stars and floating clouds overhead. The 1,904-seat theater hosts touring Broadway shows, concerts, dance performances, and classic films.

If you catch a summer concert at any of these venues, you can visit Hersheypark the day before, day of, or day after the concert for a discounted admission price of $44.95. Present your ticket or ticket stub at Hersheypark's front gate to receive the discount.

Festivals and Events

There's no shortage of entertainment in Hershey during the summer months. February, on the other hand, with Hersheypark closed and temps that dip below freezing, doesn't seem like the best time to visit. But if you love both chocolate and a bargain, **Chocolate-Covered February** (800/437-7439, www.chocolatecoveredfebruary.com) will appeal with its discounts on everything from museum tickets to spa treatments. The monthlong celebration of Hershey's signature foodstuff features chocolate-inspired meals, chef demonstrations, and classes in topics such as truffle-making, chocolate martini mixology, and wine and chocolate pairing.

Hershey draws thousands of antique automobile enthusiasts during the first full week of October. The **Antique Automobile Club of America's Eastern Division Fall Meet** (717/566-7720, www.hersheyaaca.org), held in Hershey since 1955, is one of the largest antique automobile shows and flea markets in the country.

SPORTS AND RECREATION

Spectator Sports

The **Hershey Bears** (Giant Center, 550 W. Hersheypark Dr., Hershey, 717/508-2327, www.hersheybears.com) have competed in the professional American Hockey League since 1938. Amateur hockey came to Hershey even earlier, in 1931. The popularity of matches between college teams convinced Milton S. Hershey and his longtime chief of entertainment to sponsor a permanent team the following year. They called it the Hershey B'ars. Renamed the Hershey Bears in 1936, the team has brought home at least one Calder Cup, the AHL's ultimate prize, every decade since the 1940s. The Bears "draw more fans and inspire more passion than just about any team in minor league hockey," the *Washington Post* wrote of the Washington Capitals affiliate in 2009. Later that year, the Bears became the first team in league history to win 10 championships.

FOOD

Some of Hershey's best restaurants are within the Hotel Hershey (100 Hotel Rd., Hershey). The most elegant is ★ **The Circular** (717/534-8800, www.thecircular.com, 7am-10:30am and 5pm-9:30pm Mon.-Thurs., 7am-10:30am, noon-2pm, and 5pm-9:30pm Fri.-Sat., 7am-10:30am, noon-2:30pm, and 6pm-9:30pm Sun., $15-45), which dates to the 1930s. Milton Hershey insisted the restaurant have no pillars or corners, noting that other restaurants seated single diners at tables with obstructed views and poor tippers in corners. A large central bar serves up multiple varieties of chocolate martini. There's a dress code, but it's not too strict: no hats, graphic tees, ripped jeans, or tank tops for men. "Appropriate footwear" is required, so make sure to upgrade from flip-flops before dinner. Jackets and ties are optional. Circular puts a sophisticated spin on all-you-can-eat dining, offering a daily breakfast buffet ($22.50, children 3-11 $10.50), a lunch buffet ($28, children 3-11 $12.50) on Fridays and Saturdays, and an elaborate Sunday brunch buffet ($42.50, children 3-11 $20.50). Breakfast is also available a la carte. Dinner showcases the restaurant's highly trained servers and ends with a salted caramel, a tribute to Mr. Hershey's first successful candy business. Make a reservation if you're coming for lunch, Sunday brunch, or dinner.

The Hotel Hershey's other restaurants include **Harvest** (717/534-8800, www.thehotelhershey.com, 11:30am-10pm Mon.-Sat., 10am-10pm Sun., $13-43), which prides itself on using ingredients from nearby farms and purveyors. It's also rightly proud of its burgers and steaks. **Trevi 5** (717/534-8800, www.thehotelhershey.com, 11:30am-10pm daily, $12-36) is an Italian grill. Delicious antipastos and meat and cheese platters threaten to sate your appetite before your main course.

Fenicci's of Hershey (102 W. Chocolate Ave., Hershey, 717/533-7159, www.fenicci s.com, 11am-1am Sun.-Thurs., 11am-2am Fri.-Sat., $12-33) is just outside Hersheypark, but don't mistake it for a tourist trap. The casual Italian eatery, which dates to 1935, is beloved by generations of locals. It's famous for its upside-down pizza—cheese on bottom, sauce on top—and its homemade meat, marinara, and mushroom sauces. The Italian wedding soup, made daily, is also a hit. The menu is extensive, with several risottos, six parms, and scores of variations on pasta. There's a kids menu, too. Grown-ups have the benefit of a full bar and late-night hours.

A newer addition to the Hershey food scene is **The Mill** (810 Old W. Chocolate Ave., Hershey, 717/256-9965, www.themillinhershey.com, $12-36), set in a former mill dating back to the early 1900s just over a mile from Hersheypark. The three-floor restaurant draws from local farmers and East Coast fishers to create American fare like smoked brisket, crab cakes, and burgers. Kids can choose an entrée, side, beverage, and ice cream for $8. Stop in during happy hour (4:30pm-6:30pm Mon.-Fri., 1pm-3pm Sat.) for discounted beers, cocktails, and snacks. There's live music a couple of nights a week.

The curiously named **What If...** (845 E. Chocolate Ave., Hershey, 717/533-5858, www.whatifdining.com, 11am-10pm Mon.-Thurs., 11am-11pm Fri.-Sat., 4pm-10pm Sun., $15-36) is in an off-putting location: below street level in the Howard Johnson Inn Hershey. But if you can overlook the lack of natural light, you'll be glad you came. Start with the crab martini and end with the profiterole du jour, made in-house along with every other dessert. In between, tuck into an entrée from the menu of continental cuisine.

ACCOMMODATIONS

Hershey Entertainment & Resorts (www.hersheypa.com), the company founded when Milton Hershey decided to separate his non-chocolate ventures from the business that made them all possible, controls not only most of the tourist attractions in town but also three lodging properties: the ritzy Hotel Hershey, the somewhat more affordable Hershey Lodge, and Hersheypark Camping Resort. There are plenty of other places to bed down, but guests of the Hotel Hershey and Hershey Lodge get free admission to the Hershey Gardens and the Hershey Story, while campground guests get discounted admission. Other perks include discounted admission to Hersheypark and access to some rides before the gates officially open.

Most Hershey hotels charge a lot more in summer, when the kids are out of school and families are in vacation mode.

Under $100

Open year-round, **Hersheypark Camping Resort** (1200 Sweet St., Hummelstown, 717/534-8999, www.hersheyparkcampingresort.com, campsites $39-109, cabins $99-179) offers more than 300 tent and RV sites and cabins ranging from rustic to deluxe. The 55-acre campground is minutes from Hersheypark. Amenities include two swimming pools, a game room, basketball and volleyball courts, horseshoe pits, and a country store. There's free Wi-Fi. Organized activities add to the fun in summer. Another good budget option is **White Rose Motel** (1060 E. Chocolate Ave., Hershey, 717/533-9876, www.whiterosemotel.com, $89-185, from $55 in winter), a few miles east of Hersheypark. Rooms come with refrigerators, microwaves, and Wi-Fi. There's an outdoor pool. If you need space for more people, two cottages are available. Each is $270 a night with a full kitchen and living room. They look like little suburban homes.

$100-250

Owned and operated by a lifelong Hershey resident, the **Days Inn Hershey** (350 W. Chocolate Ave., Hershey, 717/534-2162, www.daysinnhershey.com, $100-260) has more to recommend it than convenience. The rooms are spacious and the staff gracious. Guests get hotel-wide wireless Internet access, a hot breakfast, 24-hour coffee and tea service, and shuttle service to Hersheypark.

For homier digs, head to the **1825 Inn Bed & Breakfast** (409 S. Lingle Ave., Palmyra, 717/838-8282, www.1825inn.com, $150-300). The main house has six country-style guest rooms with private baths. A pair of cottages with a more contemporary aesthetic, king-size beds, two-person whirlpool tubs, and private decks seem to have been designed with honeymooners in mind.

Some of the area's most elegant accommodations can be found on a picturesque horse farm. ★ **The Inn at Westwynd Farm** (1620 Sand Beach Rd., Hummelstown, 717/533-6764, www.westwyndfarminn.com, $120-270) is just 10 minutes north of Hershey but, as owners Carolyn and Frank Troxell are fond of saying, "a world apart." They pamper guests with refreshments upon arrival, a bottomless cookie jar, and gourmet breakfasts that reflect the season, often flavored with herbs from their own garden. Bringing your family? Ask for the carriage house with its full bath, living room, and space enough for six. The main house has nine charming en suite guest rooms.

Over $250

With 665 guest rooms and suites and 100,000 square feet of function space, ★ **Hershey Lodge** (325 University Dr., Hershey, 844/330-1802, www.hersheylodge.com, $150-400) is Pennsylvania's largest convention resort. Not surprisingly, it's quite often crawling with conventioneers. But it's also wildly popular with families won over by amenities like the arcade, fitness center, and Hershey's Water Works, a 30,000-square-foot indoor pool complex opened in 2016 with waterslides (named the Twizzlers Twists) and other pool activities. The outdoor pool is open seasonally. Don't be surprised to see a giant Hershey's Kiss or other product characters strolling the grounds. The chocolate theme extends to the decor of the guest rooms, which feature complimentary Wi-Fi, refrigerators, and flat-screen TVs.

At **SpringHill Suites Hershey** (115 Museum Dr., Hershey, 717/583-2222, www.springhillsuiteshershey.com, summer $120-400), Internet access and breakfast are free. It's next door to the Antique Auto Museum. All guest rooms are studio-suites with a pull-out sofa in addition to one or two beds. The hotel has an indoor pool, a fitness center, and guest laundry facilities.

Milton Hershey poured $2 million into his plan for a luxury hotel. **The Hotel Hershey** (100 Hotel Rd., Hershey, 717/533-2171, www.thehotelhershey.com, summer traditional room from $380, cottage room from $600, off-season traditional room from $240, cottage room from $360) opened on May 26, 1933, and is even more luxurious now, having treated itself to a $67 million facelift and expansion on the occasion of its 75th anniversary. Among the new facilities is an outdoor swimming complex with an infinity-edge pool, a family pool with two large slides, and swanky cabanas. Also added as part of the expansion: 10 luxury cottages. Guests can reserve

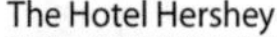
The Hotel Hershey

individual bedrooms or an entire cottage. The hotel's main building has 228 guest rooms and suites, including the 2,100-square-foot, two-bedroom Milton Hershey Suite with its veranda overlooking the town of Hershey.

TRANSPORTATION

Hershey is about 30 miles northwest of Lancaster via Routes 283 west and 743 north, and 15 miles east of Harrisburg via Route 322. Major airlines fly into, and out of, **Harrisburg International Airport** (MDT, 888/235-9442, www.flyhia.com), about a 20-minute drive from Hershey. Note that while locals refer to the airport as HIA, its Federal Aviation Administration booking code is MDT. That's because of its physical location in the borough of Middletown, about eight miles south of Harrisburg.

Harrisburg is served by **Amtrak** (800/872-7245, www.amtrak.com) and intercity bus companies. Once there, rent a car to get to Hershey. You can also travel to Hershey from Harrisburg by **Capital Area Transit** (717/238-8304, www.cattransit.com) bus, which stops at Hersheypark and the Hotel Hershey.

Harrisburg

Like many state capitals Harrisburg isn't much of a vacation destination, though it's awfully close to one. Hershey, aka Chocolate Town, USA, is just 15 miles to its east. Most people come to Harrisburg because they have business there and, more often than not, it's government business. That's not to say there's nothing to see or do in the city, which lies on the east bank of the Susquehanna River. Harrisburg has some worthwhile museums, including the State Museum of Pennsylvania and the National Civil War Museum. It has a charming park along the river and another *on* the river, and more minor league sports teams than you'd think could fit in one small city.

The dining and nightlife scenes are established enough that it's not unusual for innkeepers in the Hershey area to point guests toward Harrisburg for dinner. It's best to visit Harrisburg during the warmer months, when the Susquehanna calls to boaters and anglers and the riverfront hosts one festival after another.

SIGHTS

Whitaker Center for Science and the Arts

A science museum, performing arts center, and movie theater rolled into one, the **Whitaker Center** (222 Market St., Harrisburg, 717/214-2787, www.whitakercenter.org, 9:30am-5pm Tues.-Sat., 11:30am-5pm Sun., science center adults $16, children 3-17 $12.50) is downtown Harrisburg's cultural hub. The $53 million center, which opened in 1999, houses the Sunoco Performance Theater and a digital theater with an 80-foot-wide screen. Hands-on exhibits in the Harsco Science Center cover everything from weather systems to the physics of dance. KidsPlace, a gallery for children five and under, features a miniature version of Harrisburg's Broad Street Market, the oldest continuously operated market house in the United States. Combo tickets for science center visitors who want to catch a big-screen documentary are $20 for adults and $17 for children 3-17. Hollywood movies shown on the giant screen are $14 for adults and $12 for children.

State Museum of Pennsylvania

The four-story **State Museum of Pennsylvania** (300 North St., Harrisburg, 717/787-4980, www.statemuseumpa.org, 9am-5pm Wed.-Sat., noon-5pm Sun., adults $7, seniors $6, children 1-11 $5) next to the State

Capitol offers a well-rounded perspective on Pennsylvania's story. The Hall of Paleontology and Geology introduces visitors to earlier life forms, including a massive armored fish that prowled the seas of Pennsylvania and Ohio some 367 million years ago. Also popular is the Hall of Mammals, a set of 13 life-size dioramas of native animals in their natural environments. The Civil War gallery features Peter Rothermel's famous painting of Pickett's Charge at the Battle of Gettysburg. Unveiled in 1870, the massive masterpiece (32 feet long and almost 17 feet high) toured the country, appearing at the World's Fair in Philadelphia in 1876.

Access to Curiosity Connection, a play area designed for children ages 1-5, is included in general admission. Planetarium shows are $3 apiece.

National Civil War Museum

Harrisburg's premier Civil War attraction, the **National Civil War Museum** (1 Lincoln Circle at Reservoir Park, Harrisburg, 717/260-1861, www.nationalcivilwarmuseum.org, 10am-5pm Mon.-Tues. and Thurs.-Sun., 10am-8pm Wed., adults $12, seniors $11, students $10) bills itself as a bias-free presentation of the Union and Confederate causes: "The only museum in the United States that portrays the entire story of the American Civil War." Its focus isn't on famous figures like President Lincoln and General Robert E. Lee, but on the common soldier and the men and women on the homefront. Particular attention is paid to the African American experience. Lifelike mannequins star in depictions of a slave auction, soldier life at the city's Camp Curtin training facility, the amputation of a soldier's leg, and other facts of 19th-century life.

Pennsylvania State Capitol

Completed in 1906, the current **Capitol** (N. 3rd St. between North and Walnut Sts., 800/868-7672, www.pacapitol.com) was the tallest structure between Philadelphia and Pittsburgh for 80 years. It's still among the most ornate. The seat of state power features a spectacular vaulted dome inspired by Michelangelo's design for St. Peter's Basilica in Rome. Architect Joseph Huston incorporated elements of Greek, Roman, Renaissance, and Victorian design into the building, envisioning a "palace of arts." His vision cost a pretty penny and Huston was sentenced to prison for overcharging the state. Look down to admire the colorful mosaic tile floor depicting

Harrisburg is on the Susquehanna River.

scenes of Pennsylvania history, industry, and animals. There's no charge for guided tours of the capitol, part of a large complex of government buildings. They're offered every half hour 8:30am-4pm Monday-Friday and at 9am, 11am, 1pm, and 3pm on weekends and most holidays. Reservations are required for groups of 10 or more and recommended for smaller parties. A welcome center in the East Wing is open 8:30am-4:30pm weekdays. Its interactive exhibits explain how laws are made.

ENTERTAINMENT AND EVENTS

Performing Arts

The 600-plus-seat **Sunoco Performance Theater** within the Whitaker Center for Science and the Arts (222 Market St., Harrisburg, 717/214-2787, www.whitaker-center.org) hosts live theater, music, and dance by touring and local performers. Resident companies include **Theatre Harrisburg** (717/232-5501, www.theatreharrisburg.com), a community theater that dates to 1926.

Part of the Capitol Complex, **The Forum** (N. 5th and Walnut Streets, Harrisburg, 717/783-9100) is a 1,763-seat concert hall where "star-studded" refers to the architecture: Its ceiling is studded with hundreds of lights arranged to depict constellations. Dedicated in 1931, the Forum is home to the **Harrisburg Symphony Orchestra** (717/545-5527, www.harrisburgsymphony.org).

Festivals and Events

Harrisburg kicks off each year with the largest indoor agricultural event in the nation, the **Pennsylvania Farm Show** (717/787-5373, www.farmshow.state.pa.us, Jan., free). Some 6,000 animals and hundreds of thousands of people pass through the **Pennsylvania Farm Show Complex & Expo Center** (N. Cameron and Maclay Sts., Harrisburg, 717/787-5373, www.pafarmshowcomplex.com) during the weeklong event. Farmers show off everything from produce to pigs and horses in the hopes of taking home prize money and bragging rights. Come for an education in the state's number one industry, and come hungry. The Farm Show's best feature could very well be its food court, where proceeds go to nonprofit commodity associations like the Pennsylvania Co-Operative Potato Growers and Pennsylvania Maple Syrup Producers Council. Though admission to the Farm Show is free, parking is $15.

Harrisburg's largest arts event, **Artsfest** (717/238-1887, www.jumpstreet.org), brings

the National Civil War Museum

artists and craftspeople from around the country to Harrisburg's Riverfront Park over Memorial Day weekend. Riverfront Park also provides the setting for the city's annual Independence Day and Labor Day celebrations. **Taste of Independence** (717/255-3040, www.harrisburgpa.gov, free) on July 4th is a food truck festival with a fireworks show to boot. Live music and activities for the kids round out the celebration. **Kipona** (717/255-3040, www.harrisburgpa.gov, free), held over Labor Day weekend, pays homage to the Susquehanna River. (*Kipona* means "sparkling water" in the Delaware Indian tongue.) The riverside fest includes live entertainment on multiple stages, children's activities, arts and crafts vendors, food, and fireworks. It's also the occasion for a Native American powwow with demonstrations of traditional dance, drumming, and arts and crafts.

SPORTS AND RECREATION

Spectator Sports

The Hershey-Harrisburg region doesn't have any major league franchises, but baseball and hockey fans still have plenty to cheer about. The **Harrisburg Senators** (FNB Field, City Island, Harrisburg, 717/231-4444, www.senatorsbaseball.com) baseball team is the Class AA minor league affiliate of the Washington Nationals. Formed in 1987, the team won the Eastern League championship in its first season. It captured four consecutive championships from 1996 to 1999, becoming the first team in league history to do so. More than 200 of its players have been called up to the majors.

Hockey fans have the **Hershey Bears** (Giant Center, 550 W. Hersheypark Dr., Hershey, 717/508-2327, www.hersheybears.com). Originally named the Hershey B'ars, the team has competed in the professional American Hockey League without interruption since 1938. In 2010 the Washington Capitals affiliate became the first team in league history to win 11 championships.

City Island

Harrisburg's recreational hub is **City Island** (www.visitcityisland.com), a mile-long island on the Susquehanna River. It's home to the Harrisburg Senators minor league baseball team and the **Harrisburg City Islanders** (717/441-4625, www.cityislanders.com) USL Pro soccer team. Beyond spectator sports, the island offers **batting cages** (717/461-3223, www.cityislandfun.com), an

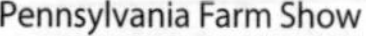

Pennsylvania Farm Show

arcade, a playground, a scaled-down version of a Civil War-era steam train, a **miniature golf course** (717/232-8533, www.h2ogolf.com), and a marina. If you didn't pack your boat, board the ***Pride of the Susquehanna*** (717/234-6500, www.harrisburgriverboat.com), an old-fashioned paddle-wheeler that plies the river May-November. Or set off in a kayak or canoe from **Susquehanna Outfitters** (717/503-0066, www.susquehannaoutfitters.com).

You can walk or bike to the island from downtown Harrisburg via the Walnut Street Bridge, which was closed to cars after Hurricane Agnes in 1972. Cars access the island via the Market Street Bridge.

FOOD AND ACCOMMODATIONS

Politicos don't have to venture far from the Capitol Complex to strategize over a meal that receives bipartisan approval. Second Street in downtown Harrisburg is home to enough restaurants and bars to be dubbed Restaurant Row. One you won't regret: ★ **Café Fresco** (215 N. 2nd St., Harrisburg, 717/236-2599, www.cafefresco.com, 6:30am-1am Mon.-Fri., 10am-1am Sat., $10-36). By day, it's a low-key spot with sandwiches, wraps, salads, and pizza. It glams up in the evening, becoming a destination for fancy cocktails and Asian-influenced cuisine, though pizzas are still on the menu if you're not in the mood for lobster fried rice or tea-smoked duck breast. Dance off dinner upstairs at **Level 2** (717/236-6600, www.level2.us, 8pm-2am Fri.-Sat.).

Also on Restaurant Row, **Federal Taphouse** (234 N. 2nd St., Harrisburg, 717/525-8077, www.federaltaphousehbg.com, 11:30am-2am Mon.-Fri., 11am-2am Sat., 10:30am-2am Sun., $12-28) pours 100 draft beers. Customers nosh on soft pretzels or crab mac and cheese while waiting for smoked beef brisket, swordfish tacos, bison burgers, and other hearty fare. A wood-fired oven turns out crispy pizzas. There's also pizza to be had at **Cork and Fork** (2nd and State Sts., 717/234-8100, www.corkandfork.us, $10-16), along with pastas made in-house and locally sourced cheeses and charcuterie. Start with one of the classic cocktails and end with the Nutella pizza with marshmallows and powdered sugar.

Not every noteworthy restaurant has a 2nd Street address. On 3rd Street, owners Juan and Lisa Garcia serve up tacos, enchiladas, fajitas, and more at **El Sol Mexican Restaurant** (18 S. 3rd St., Harrisburg, 717/901-5050, www.

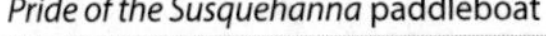
Pride of the Susquehanna paddleboat

elsolmexicanrestaurant.com, 11am-10pm Mon.-Thurs., 11am-11pm Fri., 4pm-11pm Sat., 10am-3pm Sun., $12-20). House specialties include the molcajete mixto: steak, chicken, shrimp, mushrooms, cactus, and cheese served in a hot volcanic rock bowl.

Across the street, ★ **Bricco** (31 S. 3rd St., Harrisburg, 717/724-0222, www.briccopa.com, 4:30pm-10pm Mon.-Sat., 4:30pm-9pm Sun., $14-32) creates masterly Mediterranean dishes with the help of students from the Olewine School of Culinary Arts at Harrisburg Area Community College. Though inspired by Tuscan cuisine, Bricco sources Pennsylvania products whenever possible. Particularly popular are its raw-bar offerings and pizzas, baked in a stone oven and topped with delicacies such as fig jam, white truffle oil, and local feta. The restaurant has an extensive wine list.

If you're looking for a central location to lay your head, look no further than the ★ **Hilton Harrisburg** (1 N. 2nd St., Harrisburg, 717/233-6000, www.hilton.com, $145-250). It's connected by an enclosed walkway to the Whitaker Center for Science and the Arts and a shopping center called Strawberry Square. The State Capitol Complex and City Island are a short walk away. The hotel is at the end of Harrisburg's Restaurant Row, but there are meals to be had on-site. The Hilton is home to the steakhouse **1700 Degrees** (717/237-6400, www.1700restaurant.com, 5:30pm-10pm Mon.-Sat., $32-56) and the more casual **Ad Lib Craft Kitchen & Bar** (717/237-6419, www.adlibrestaurants.com, 6:30am-2pm and 4pm-midnight Mon.-Fri., 7am-midnight Sat.-Sun.). The hotel's 300-plus guest rooms feature flat-screen TVs, refrigerators, and free wireless Internet access.

For cozier lodgings, a 15-minute stroll up the Susquehanna banks will land you at **City House B&B** (915 N. Front St., Harrisburg, 717/903-2489, www.cityhousebb.com, $125-165), set across the street from the river. The largest of the four en suite guest rooms boasts a fireplace and an oversized shower built for two.

TRANSPORTATION

Harrisburg is about 15 miles west of Hershey via Route 322 and 40 miles northwest of Lancaster via Route 283. **Harrisburg International Airport** (MDT, 888/235-9442, www.flyhia.com) is served by several major airlines. Note that while locals refer to the airport as HIA, its Federal Aviation Administration booking code is MDT. That's because of its physical location in the borough of Middletown, about eight miles south of Harrisburg.

Amtrak (800/872-7245, www.amtrak.com) provides rail service to the Harrisburg Transportation Center, located at 4th and Chestnut Streets. **Greyhound** (800/231-2222, www.greyhound.com) and other intercity bus operators also deliver travelers to the station.

Local bus service is provided by **Capital Area Transit** (717/238-8304, www.cattransit.com), or CAT. Call **Keystone Cab** (717/395-5732) for door-to-door service.

York County

Just west of Lancaster County, York County touts itself as the "Factory Tour Capital of the World." More than a dozen factories open their doors to visitors and admission is free in almost every case. So many of the factories are dedicated to guilty pleasures that York County also claims the title of "Snack Food Capital of the World." One of the biggest draws here is the Harley-Davidson factory, which attracts bikers from across the United States and around the world.

Long before the county became the Factory Tour Capital, its only city, also named York, served as the capital of what would soon be known as the United States of America. The Continental Congress, that body of delegates who spoke for the colonies during the Revolutionary period, met in York for nine months in 1777 and 1778, adopting the Articles of Confederation. Murals throughout downtown York serve as a record of local history.

Gettysburg and its Civil War battlefield are 30 miles west of York. Lancaster's Amish farmlands are about that distance to its east. The state capital, Harrisburg, is 25 miles north of the city, and Hershey, aka "The Sweetest Place on Earth," is just 10 miles farther.

FACTORY TOURS

The "Factory Tour Capital of the World" has more factories than you can visit in a day. You'll find a comprehensive list at www.yorkpa.org, the website of the York County Convention & Visitors Bureau. Bear in mind that most factories don't offer tours on weekends. Photos are usually not allowed. Open-toe shoes and heels are prohibited in some areas, so be sure to wear closed-toe, flat-heeled shoes.

The most famous name on the list is Harley-Davidson. The company has been producing its legendary motorcycles in York since 1973. Free tours of the **Harley-Davidson factory** (1425 Eden Rd., York, 877/883-1450, www.harley-davidson.com, tour center and gift shop open 8am-4pm Mon.-Fri.) start at regular intervals between 9am and 2pm Monday-Friday. They offer a limited view of the assembly line and last about an hour.

Harley-Davidson factory

Friday isn't the best day to visit because production may not be scheduled. For $38, you can have a two-hour tour that's more personalized and includes access to some "employee-only" areas. The in-depth "Steel Toe Tour" is offered at 9:30am and noon Monday-Friday. It sells out quickly, so it's a good idea to book tickets ahead by phone or online. Children under 12 aren't allowed on the factory floor, but they're welcome in the tour center, which has exhibits on assembly processes and motorcycles for the straddling.

If you're traveling with kids, put **Perrydell Farm Dairy** (90 Indian Rock Dam Rd., York, 717/741-3485, www.perrydellfarm.com, 7am-9pm Mon.-Sat., 11am-6pm Sun., self-guided tours free) on your itinerary. Depending when you visit the family-owned farm, you might see cows being milked, calves being fed, or milk being bottled. The fresh milk is sold onsite, along with ice cream, locally grown produce, and locally baked goods.

To see why York County bills itself as the "Snack Food Capital of the World," head to the borough of Hanover, 20 miles southwest of York. Best known for its pretzels, **Snyder's of Hanover** (1350 York St., Hanover, 800/233-7125, ext. 28592, www.snydersofhanover.com, store open 9am-6pm Mon.-Sat., noon-5pm Sun.) offers free tours at 10am, 11am, and 1pm Tuesday-Thursday. Reservations are required. Snyder's snacks are sold around the world, so the half-hour tours are an education in large-scale manufacturing. You'll get to see the raw material warehouse, finished goods warehouse, packing room, and oven room. Tours start and end at the factory store, where you'll get a free bag of pretzels and bargains on everything from Old Tyme Pretzels, first made in 1909, to the popular flavored pretzel pieces, introduced some 80 years later.

Hanover is also home to **Utz Quality Foods** (900 High St., Hanover, 800/367-7629, www.utzsnacks.com), where you can watch raw spuds become crunchy chips from an observation gallery. The gallery is open 8am-4pm Monday-Thursday. Though famous for its potato chips—Rachael Ray talked up Utz Kettle Classics on her eponymous TV show—the company also makes pretzels, cheese curls, pork rinds, and more. Stock up at its outlet store (861 Carlisle St., Hanover, 9am-7pm Mon.-Sat., 11am-5pm Sun.), a half mile from the plant.

Far smaller than Snyder's or Utz, **Revonah Pretzels** (507 Baltimore St., Hanover, 717/630-2883, www.revonahpretzel.com) takes its name from the town—Revonah is Hanover spelled backward—and its cues from the past. Pretzels are rolled and twisted by hand, hearth-baked, and slowly hardened in a kiln. Word has it that the Pittsburgh Steelers munch on these when they're on the road. Revonah offers free 20-minute tours 9am-noon Tuesday-Thursday. Reservations are required. Visitors can sample a "greenie": a pretzel that's crunchy on the outside but still warm and soft on the inside.

HERITAGE RAIL TRAIL

The 21-mile **Heritage Rail Trail** (717/840-7440, www.yorkcountyparks.org) stretches from York City to the Mason-Dixon Line, where it connects to Maryland's 20-mile Northern Central Railroad Trail. It's open for hiking, bicycling, horseback riding, cross-country skiing, and snowshoeing. The parking lot for the York City trailhead is on Pershing Avenue near the Colonial Courthouse. Traversing the trail is part exercise, part history lesson. About six miles south of the reconstructed courthouse is the 370-foot Howard Tunnel, one of the oldest railroad tunnels in the country. The rail line adjacent to the Heritage Rail Trail was a vital link between Washington DC and points north in the 19th century. As such, it was a prime target for Confederate troops during the Civil War. After the Battle of Gettysburg in 1863, President Lincoln traveled via these rails to deliver the Gettysburg Address, stretching his legs at York County's **Hanover Junction Station** (Rte. 616, Hanover Junction). The station at the midpoint of the Heritage Rail Trail has been restored to its 1863 appearance and houses a small Civil War museum.

York's Central Market

There's another historic station near the southern end of the trail. The **New Freedom Station** (Front and Franklin Sts., New Freedom) has been restored to its 1940s appearance and houses a railroad museum. The **New Freedom Rail Trail Café** (117 N. Front St., 717/227-0299, www.nfrailtrailcafe.com, 10am-6pm Wed.-Fri., 8am-6pm Sat.-Sun.) at the station serves sandwiches and coffee.

The museums are open on select days May-October. Check the York County Parks & Recreation website (www.yorkcountypa.gov/parks-recreation) for dates and times.

Four Springs Winery (50 Main St., Seven Valleys, 717/428-2610, www.fourspringswinerypa.com, 1pm-6pm Fri. and Sun., 11am-6pm Sat.) is also adjacent to the rail-trail. It's not unusual to see spandex-clad cyclists in the tasting room.

FOOD AND ACCOMMODATIONS

York's **Central Market** (34 W. Philadelphia St., York, 717/848-2243, www.centralmarketyork.com, 7am-2pm Tues. and Thurs., 6am-2pm Sat.) is a hopping lunch spot. It's perfect for dining companions with different tastes, offering everything from soups and salads to gyros, burritos, and pasta dishes. On the downside, it's closed four days of the week.

Located across the street from Central Market, **White Rose Bar and Grill** (48 N. Beaver St., York, 717/848-5369, www.whiterosebarandgrill.com, 7am-10pm Sun.-Thurs., 7am-11pm Fri.-Sat., bar open until 2am Mon.-Sat. and midnight Sun., $8-30) dates to the 1930s. Extensive renovations in recent years have given it a thoroughly modern feel. Entrées range from a classic turkey club to a Cajun-spiced salmon fillet with a side of sweet potato fries.

York's most impressive martini list can be found at ★ **The Left Bank** (120 N. George St., York, 717/843-8010, www.leftbankyork.com, 4pm-close Mon., 11am-close Tues.-Fri., 5pm-close Sat., $23-40), a chef-owned fine-dining restaurant with a big-city feel. This is where Yorkers come on special occasions. The seafood entrées are outstanding, as is the service. Your filet mignon can come with a coffee crust rub, if you wish, or topped with crab scampi. Don't hesitate to ask for wine recommendations.

Most hotels in and around York are chains—Comfort Inn, Days Inn, Courtyard by Marriott, Best Western, Motel 6, and so on. For something more personal, try the **Lady Linden Bed and Breakfast** (505 Linden Ave., York, 717/850-6166843-2929, www.ladylindenbedandbreakfast.com, $139), a meticulously restored 1887 Queen Anne Victorian with just two guest suites. Breakfast is a four-course affair. At **Grace Manor Bed and Breakfast** (258 W. Market St., 717/542-0787, www.gracemanorbandb.com, $149-189), each of the four guests rooms is decorated in the style of a different country. Choose the expansive French suite to lounge in the "Parisian parlor" or sip a cup of coffee in the Provencal-themed kitchenette.

TRANSPORTATION

York County shares its southern border with Maryland. Its county seat and largest municipality, York, is about 50 miles north of Baltimore and 25 miles south of Harrisburg via I-83. Route 30 provides east-west access to the city, which is about 30 miles from Gettysburg to its west and Lancaster to its east.

Harrisburg International Airport (MDT, 888/235-9442, www.flyhia.com), about a 30-minute drive from York, is served by several major airlines. **Baltimore-Washington International Thurgood Marshall Airport** (BWI, 800/435-9294, www.bwiairport.com) is farther—about an hour from York assuming minimal traffic—but considerably larger.

Intercity bus service to York is available through **Greyhound** (53 E. North St., 717/699-0343, www.greyhound.com) and its interline partners. York County's public bus system is **Rabbittransit** (800/632-9063, www.rabbittransit.org).

Gettysburg and Vicinity

Few towns in America have the name recognition of Gettysburg, which has fewer than 8,000 residents. It earned its place in the history books in 1863 when it was the setting for the Civil War's bloodiest battle and President Abraham Lincoln's most famous speech. The former took place July 1-3, with more than 165,000 soldiers converging on the crossroads town. Under the command of General George G. Meade, the Union army desperately and successfully defended its home territory from General Robert E. Lee's Confederate army. The war would continue for almost two years, but the Confederacy's hopes for independence effectively died on the Gettysburg battlefield. The hellish battle's human toll was astronomical: 51,000 soldiers were dead, wounded, or missing. Interestingly, only one of Gettysburg's 2,400 citizens was killed during the biggest battle ever fought on this continent. The casualty was a young woman named Jennie Wade, and the bullet-riddled house in which she died is now a museum.

living history in downtown Gettysburg

In the aftermath of the battle, the townspeople dedicated themselves to caring for the wounded and burying the dead. A group of prominent residents convinced the state to help fund the purchase of a portion of the battlefield to serve as a final resting place for the Union's defenders. Gettysburg attorney David Wills was appointed to coordinate the establishment of the Soldiers' National Cemetery (now Gettysburg National Cemetery) and he invited President Lincoln to deliver "a few appropriate remarks" at the dedication ceremony on November 19, 1863. The commander in chief arrived by train a day prior and strolled down Carlisle Street to Wills's stately home on the town square. There, in a second-floor bedroom, he polished his talk. The National Park Service acquired the house in 2004 and opened it as a museum in 2009. Lincoln's two-minute Gettysburg Address—so succinct that a photographer on the scene failed to snap a picture—is regarded as the rhetorical zenith of his career and one of the greatest speeches in history.

PLANNING YOUR TIME

Two days is sufficient to explore Gettysburg. When to visit depends on your interests and tolerance for crowds. The area is busiest in early July, during the annual battle reenactment, which is held not on the battlefield but on private land. The town swarms with tourists and reenactors and the weather tends toward hot and humid. Visitation tapers off at the end of summer and then picks up in October, leading up to Halloween, when paranormal enthusiasts flock to what they believe is one of the most haunted places in the country. Mid-November brings scores of Lincoln scholars and admirers for a symposium and celebration of his famous address. Winter is the slow season. Some Gettysburg attractions are closed during the coldest months, but the battlefield is open daily year-round. April and May see the arrival of busload after busload of schoolchildren. By June, tourism is in full swing again.

★ GETTYSBURG NATIONAL MILITARY PARK

Expect to spend the better part of a day at **Gettysburg National Military Park** (717/334-1124, www.nps.gov/gett, 6am-10pm daily Apr.-Oct., 6am-7pm daily Nov.-Mar., free admission), site of the Civil War's biggest and bloodiest battle. The 6,000-acre park is not only one of the nation's most popular historical attractions but also one of the world's most extraordinary sculpture gardens. The more than 1,300 monuments, markers, and memorials include equestrian bronzes of the battle's commanders, tributes to common soldiers, a statue of a civilian hero, and another of a priest who gave absolution to Irish soldiers as they prepared for battle.

Begin your visit at the **Museum and Visitor Center** (1195 Baltimore Pike/Rte. 97, Gettysburg, 717/338-1243, tickets 717/334-2436, www.gettysburgfoundation.org, 8am-6pm daily Apr.-Oct., 8am-5pm daily Nov.-Mar., adults $15, seniors $14, children 6-12 $10), operated by the nonprofit Gettysburg Foundation. There you can orient yourself to the park and learn about the nightmarish clash of armies. Be sure to ask for a schedule of lectures, guided walks, and other special programs, which are especially frequent in the summer months. If you plan on touring the battlefield on your own, pick up the National Park Service map and guide (also available at www.nps.gov/gett). It outlines a 24-mile auto tour and briefly describes what transpired at each tour stop. For detailed descriptions of the three-day battle, you can buy an audio tour CD in the museum bookstore or hire a licensed guide, who will get behind the wheel of your car and take you on a two-hour personalized tour ($75 per vehicle with 1-6 people). The highly knowledgeable guides are available on a first-come, first-served basis as soon as the visitors center opens, but reservations are recommended. Bus tours with a licensed guide ($35, children 6-12 $21) are also offered.

The visitors center, which opened in 2008,

Gettysburg Guides

It's easy to explore Gettysburg on your own but a tour can make for a richer experience. Which tour operator to pick depends on your preferred mode of transport and whether you want to interact with a guide or go with recorded narration.

Many Gettysburg tours are led by members of the **Association of Licensed Battlefield Guides** (717/337-1709, www.gettysburgtourguides.org), who have spent years studying the Battle of Gettysburg. Licensure applicants first take a rigorous written exam; the highest scorers prove themselves further by passing an oral test. If you appreciate a lot of detail and ask a lot of questions, hire a licensed guide who will take the wheel of your car and show you around. Guides are available on a first-come, first-served basis at the **Gettysburg National Military Park Museum and Visitor Center** (1195 Baltimore Pike/Rte. 97, Gettysburg, 717/338-1243, tickets 717/334-2436, www.gettysburgfoundation.org, 8am-6pm daily Apr.-Oct., 8am-5pm daily Nov.-Mar.), but reservations are strongly recommended. A two-hour tour costs $75 per vehicle with 1-6 people, $100 per vehicle with 7-15. It's customary to tip your guide. Bus tours with a licensed guide (adults $35, children 6-12 $21) also leave from the Museum and Visitor Center. Allow 2.5 hours for the bus tour.

Gettysburg Tours (778 Baltimore St., Gettysburg, 717/334-6296, www.gettysburgbattlefieldtours.com) provides two-hour tours in open-air double-decker buses or air-conditioned buses. The former offers a choice of licensed guide (adults $35, children 6-12 $21) or recorded narration complete with cannon booms and rifle cracks (adults $27, children 6-12 $16). The enclosed bus comes with a licensed guide (adults $35, children 6-12 $21). Gettysburg Tours operates several area attractions, including the Jennie Wade House. Combo packages are available.

National Riding Stables (610 Taneytown Rd., Gettysburg, 717/334-5100, www.nationalridingstables.com), just across the street from the battlefield, offers one- to four-hour horseback tours with licensed guides, starting at $65. Riding experience isn't necessary but you must be older than 6 and under 240 pounds. Instead of a horse, you can ride a Segway. **SegTours** (22 Springs Ave., Gettysburg, 717/253-7987, www.segtours.com) offers a three-hour tour ($70) of the most famous battlefield sites and a two-hour tour ($50) to a lesser-known part of the battlefield, both with recorded narration. Live guides are available for an additional fee. Reservations are recommended for recorded tours and required for live guides.

Located in the bus parking lot at the Gettysburg National Military Park Museum and Visitor Center, **GettysBike** (1195 Baltimore Pike/Rte. 97, Gettysburg, 717/752-7752, www.gettysbike.com) offers bicycle tours of the battlefield and the town of Gettysburg. Led by licensed guides, the tours range from $49 to $75 per person. Bike rental is $5 extra, or you can bring your own. GettysBike also offers bike rentals for those who want to explore on their own.

Paranormal enthusiasts consider Gettysburg one of the most haunted places in the country. The original and most reputable operator is **Ghosts of Gettysburg** (271 Baltimore St., Gettysburg, 717/337-0445, www.ghostsofgettysburg.com, adults $10.45-11, children 7 and under free). Its walking tours, led by guides in period attire with candle lanterns in hand, are based on the books of historian, ghost hunter, licensed guide, and former National Park Service ranger Mark Nesbitt.

is home to a colossal cyclorama depicting Pickett's Charge, a futile infantry assault ordered by Confederate general Robert E. Lee on the final day of battle. It's said that veterans wept at the sight of the 360-degree painting when it was unveiled in 1884. Measuring 42 feet high and 377 feet in circumference, the **Gettysburg Cyclorama** is the largest painting in the country. It's displayed with a diorama that gives the masterpiece a 3-D quality. A sound and light show amps up the drama. The cyclorama experience is preceded by a 22-minute film, *A New Birth of Freedom*, narrated by Morgan Freeman. Timed tickets are issued for the film and cyclorama. They include admission to the on-site **Gettysburg Museum of the American Civil War,** which explores the causes and consequences of the deadliest war in American history. Museum-only tickets are available.

Gettysburg National Cemetery, where President Lincoln delivered his famous Gettysburg Address, is a short walk from the visitors center. It's open from dawn to sunset and closed to vehicular traffic. Walking tour brochures are available at the visitors center and online at www.nps.gov/gett. Work on the cemetery began soon after the bloodshed ended. Thousands of Union and Confederate dead had been hastily buried on or near the battlefield, many of them in shallow graves. Heavy rains would expose decaying bodies, a grisly sight that helped convince Pennsylvania governor Andrew Curtin to appropriate state funds for the cemetery project. About 3,500 Union soldiers were interred there. The Confederate dead remained in scattered graves until the 1870s, when they were relocated to cemeteries in the south. Today Gettysburg National Cemetery is the final resting place for veterans from all of America's wars through the present day. It's the setting for several annual events, including a Memorial Day service and a commemoration of the Gettysburg Address held each November.

GETTYSBURG SEMINARY RIDGE MUSEUM

The **Seminary Ridge Museum** (111 Seminary Ridge, Gettysburg, 717/339-1300, www.seminaryridgemuseum.org, 10am-5pm daily Mar.-Oct., 10am-5pm Fri.-Mon. Nov.-Feb, adults $9, seniors and children 6-12 $7) opened July 1, 2013, exactly 150 years after the Battle of Gettysburg erupted. That first day of battle is one of the museum's main focuses. Built in 1832 for the Lutheran Theological Seminary at Gettysburg, the museum building was used as a field hospital during the 1863 battle. The museum also places special emphasis on Civil War medicine and the moral and spiritual debates of that tumultuous era. It features four floors of exhibits, large-scale reproductions of 10 commissioned paintings by renowned historical artist Dale Gallon, interactive stations for children, and an outdoor interpretive trail. The building's cupola, which was used by Union general John Buford to survey the battlefield, is accessible by guided tour. You must be at least 13 years old and able to climb stairs to take the **cupola tour** (adults $29, seniors $27, includes museum admission).

cyclists at Gettysburg National Military Park

EISENHOWER NATIONAL HISTORIC SITE

Adjacent to the Gettysburg battlefield, **Eisenhower National Historic Site** (717/338-9114, www.nps.gov/eise, adults $9, children 6-12 $5) preserves the onetime home and farm of President Dwight D. Eisenhower. The Texas-born army general and 34th president first visited Gettysburg as a cadet at the U.S. Military Academy at West Point and returned during World War I to run a training camp. After commanding the Allied forces during World War II, "Ike" came to Gettysburg with his wife, Mamie, in search of a weekend retreat. It later became their permanent residence. Furnishings include a coffee table given to the Eisenhowers by the first lady of South Korea, a rug from the shah of Iran, and a desk fashioned from old floorboards removed from the White House during a 1948 renovation. Visitors can also explore the grounds, which include a putting green, rose gardens, and a garage that still houses the Eisenhowers' jeep, golf carts, and station wagon. Due to limited on-site parking and space in the home, visitors must arrive by shuttle bus from the Museum and Visitor Center at Gettysburg National Military Park (1195 Baltimore Pike/Rte. 97, Gettysburg, 717/338-1243, tickets 717/334-2436, www.gettysburgfoundation.org).

SHRIVER AND JENNIE WADE HOUSES

Two house museums explore the civilian experience during the Civil War. Both feature tour guides in period attire.

The **Shriver House Museum** (309 Baltimore St., Gettysburg, 717/337-2800, www.shriverhouse.org, 10am-5pm Sun.-Thurs., 10am-6pm Fri.-Sat. Apr.-Oct., select days Nov.-Dec. and Mar., adults $9, children 7-12 $7) tells the story of George Washington Shriver and his family. In 1860, Shriver paid $290 for what was then considered a double lot on the edge of town. He built a home for his family, opening a saloon in the cellar and a 10-pin bowling alley in an adjacent building. When the Civil War erupted in 1861, Shriver answered President Lincoln's call for troops. He was still away when the war came to Gettysburg in July 1863. While his wife and two young daughters hunkered down at her parents' farm, Confederate soldiers occupied their home. Today visitors learn about life during the Civil War as they tour all four floors of the house, including the attic used by Confederate sharpshooters. Live Civil War bullets and period medical supplies were discovered underneath floorboards when the house was under restoration in 1996. They're among the artifacts displayed in the museum shop next door.

The nearby **Jennie Wade House** (548 Baltimore St., Gettysburg, 717/334-4100, www.gettysburgbattlefieldtours.com, hours vary by season, Mar.-Dec., adults $8.75, children 6-12 $6) is a shrine to the only civilian casualty of the Battle of Gettysburg. Jennie Wade was baking bread for Union soldiers when bullets ripped through the door of the house, taking her life. She was 20 years old and engaged to a childhood friend who'd been mustered into the service two years earlier. He died just nine days later of wounds sustained in a Virginia battle, never knowing of his sweetheart's fate.

GETTYSBURG HERITAGE CENTER

Visitors learn about what life was like in Gettysburg before, during, and after the battle at the **Gettysburg Heritage Center** (297 Steinwehr Ave., Gettysburg, 717/334-6245, www.gettysburgmuseum.com, 9am-8pm Sun.-Wed., 9am-9pm Thurs.-Sat. summer, 9am-5pm daily spring and fall, 9am-5pm Sat.-Sun. Jan.-Feb., adults $9, children 6-17 $7). Along with historical artifacts and interactive displays, the educational museum features a 20-minute video that gives an overview of the battle. But the real draw here is the gift shop. It's one of the largest and best in town.

APPALACHIAN TRAIL MUSEUM

Housed in a former gristmill in Pine Grove Furnace State Park, the **Appalachian Trail Museum** (1120 Pine Grove Rd., Gardners, 717/486-8126, www.atmuseum.org, May-Oct., hours vary by season, free) pays tribute to pioneer hikers such as Earl Shaffer, the first person to thru-hike the trail, and "Grandma" Gatewood, who was 67 when she became the first female to complete the journey alone. There's even an exhibit on Ziggy, the first feline to conquer the Georgia-to-Maine trail. (To be fair, the cat spent most of the journey riding in the backpack of hiker Jim "the Geek" Adams, but he contributed much in the way of mice patrol at trail shelters.) Highlights of the collection include a trail shelter that Shaffer, a native of nearby York County, built about a decade after his 1948 history-making hike.

Visitors stand a good chance of rubbing shoulders with modern-day thru-hikers because the museum is located just off the Appalachian Trail in **Pine Grove Furnace State Park** (1100 Pine Grove Rd., Gardners, 717/486-7174, www.dcnr.pa.gov/stateparks). The state park is a few miles north of the 2,180-mile trail's midpoint. Tradition dictates that thru-hikers stop at the park's general store—located across from the museum—to face a test of mettle known as the "half-gallon challenge." Those who succeed (i.e., eat half a gallon of ice cream in one sitting) are rewarded with a commemorative wooden spoon.

The 696-acre park also features a campground and two small lakes with beaches and boat rental. Pine Grove allows overnight parking for anyone who wants to hit the AT, but registration at the park office is required. The park is about 20 miles north of Gettysburg.

ENTERTAINMENT AND EVENTS

Performing Arts

The **Majestic Theater** (25 Carlisle St., Gettysburg, 717/337-8200, www.gettysburgmajestic.org) was the largest vaudeville and silent movie theater in south-central Pennsylvania when it opened in 1925. President Dwight D. Eisenhower and First Lady Mamie Eisenhower attended performances in the 1950s, often with world leaders in tow. In 1993 the Majestic hosted the world premiere of *Gettysburg*, one of the longest films ever released by a Hollywood studio. Today it hosts live performances along with new-release movies.

Festivals and Events

Held the first two full weekends in October, the **National Apple Harvest Festival** (717/677-9413, www.appleharvest.com, adults $10, seniors $9, children under 12 free) features orchard tours, a petting zoo, antique cars, arts and crafts vendors, live entertainment, and appearances by the reigning Pennsylvania Apple Queen. It's held at the South Mountain Fairgrounds, 10 miles northwest of Gettysburg on Route 234. Admission includes parking.

Thousands of reenactors take part in the annual **Gettysburg Civil War Battle Reenactment** (800/514-3849, www.gettysburgreenactment.com, early July, adults from $35, children 6-12 from $16), firing period weapons and feigning death on farm fields just a few miles from the original battlefield. Several clashes are staged over three days. Spectators can stroll through the soldiers' camps, listen to live Civil War music and speakers, watch period demonstrations, and shop for wares. Arrive early to claim a spot near the front of battle viewing areas. It's a good idea to bring folding chairs, binoculars, and sunscreen. Limited bleacher seating is available but usually sells out before the event.

A host of events commemorate President Abraham Lincoln's Gettysburg Address, delivered at the dedication of the Soldiers' National Cemetery less than five months after the Battle of Gettysburg. Held on the speech's anniversary, **Dedication Day** (717/338-1243, www.lincolnfellowship.org, Nov. 19) begins with a wreath-laying ceremony at the cemetery. Past speakers have included director Steven Spielberg and Justice Sandra Day O'Connor. Held within a few days of Dedication Day, **Remembrance Day** (www.destinationgettysburg.com) features a parade of Civil War reenactors—from drummer boys to generals on horseback—that winds through Gettysburg and ends at the battlefield. As the day draws to a close, a luminary candle is placed on each Civil War grave in Gettysburg National Cemetery. The cost to sponsor a candle for the **Remembrance Illumination** (717/339-2148, www.friendsofgettysburg.org) is, appropriately enough, $18.63.

SHOPPING

Downtown Gettysburg

Most downtown Gettysburg shops are of the independent variety, and many offer things you'd be hard-pressed to find in a big city: Civil War collectibles, military artifacts from the American Revolutionary War and onward, and anything a reenactor could want, from candle lanterns to cavalry swords. Dale Gallon, one of the nation's premier historical artists, has a gallery in town, the **Gallon Historical Art Gallery** (9 Steinwehr Ave., 717/334-8666, www.gallon.com, hours vary).

Greater Gettysburg

Pennsylvania's sales tax exemption on clothing lures many a Marylander to the **Outlet Shoppes at Gettysburg** (1863 Gettysburg Village Dr., Gettysburg, 717/337-9705, www.theoutletshoppesatgettysburg.com, 10am-9pm Mon.-Sat., 10am-6pm Sun.) at Route 15 and Baltimore Street (Route 97). Stores include Brooks Brothers, Old Navy, Tommy Hilfiger, Adidas, and Coach. There's a 10-screen movie theater (717/338-0101) on-site.

The quiet, tree-lined borough of **New Oxford,** 10 miles east of Gettysburg on Route 30, is an antiquing mecca. A partial list of dealers can be found at www.newoxfordantiques.com, website of the New Oxford Antique Dealers Association.

FOOD

Gettysburg is no dining mecca but it does offer an opportunity for culinary time travel, with a number of restaurants specializing in period fare.

The **Dobbin House Tavern** (89 Steinwehr Ave., Gettysburg, 717/334-2100, www.dobbinhouse.com) serves colonial and continental cuisine in Gettysburg's oldest building. The Dobbin House was built in 1776—the same year the American colonies declared their

the annual Gettysburg Civil War Battle Reenactment

independence from Great Britain—as a home for an Irish-born minister and his large brood. It served as a station on the Underground Railroad in the mid-1800s and as a hospital in the immediate aftermath of the Battle of Gettysburg. Great pains have been taken to restore the house-turned-restaurant to its 18th-century appearance. The china and flatware match fragments unearthed during an excavation of the cellar. For casual dining, head to the basement **Springhouse Tavern** (from 11:30am daily, $8-25). With three natural springs and two fireplaces, it's a cozy spot (that can get clammy in winter and humid in summer). Specials include spit-roasted chicken, chargrilled strip steak, and Maryland crab cakes. Deli sandwiches are also available. For fine dining, there are six candlelit rooms known as the **Alexander Dobbin Dining Rooms** (5pm-close daily, $24-43). The "bedroom" features a table beneath a lace bed canopy. Servers in period attire help satisfy the craving for history that brings most visitors to Gettysburg. Reservations are accepted for the dining rooms but not the tavern, where you can expect a considerable wait on summer weekends.

The **Meade and Lee Dining Rooms** at the **Farnsworth House Inn** (401 Baltimore St., Gettysburg, 717/334-8838, www.farnsworthhouseinn.com, 5pm-9pm daily, winter hours vary, $17-30) is a popular destination for period dining complete with costumed servers. Game pie, the house specialty, is a stew of turkey, pheasant, and duck topped with a golden egg crust. Built in the early 1800s, the house sheltered Confederate sharpshooters during the Battle of Gettysburg. It's believed that one of them accidentally shot Jennie Wade, the only civilian killed during the three-day struggle. Oil paintings of the commanding officers at Gettysburg and photos by famed Civil War photographer Mathew Brady decorate the bullet-scarred house, which has been restored to its 1863 appearance. Its pub, **Sweney's Tavern** (11am-9pm daily, winter hours vary, $9-24), popular with reenactors, offers hot and cold sandwiches, pork and sauerkraut, meatloaf, and more. Garden dining is available in the warmer months.

Eight miles west of Gettysburg on Route 116, the **Fairfield Inn** (15 W. Main St., Fairfield, 717/642-5410, www.thefairfieldinn.com, 5pm-9pm Thurs.-Fri., 11am-2pm and 5pm-9pm Sat., 10:30am-2pm Sun., $19-32) has hosted such VIPs as Thaddeus Stevens and President Dwight D. Eisenhower since opening in 1757. The day

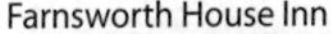
Farnsworth House Inn

after the Battle of Gettysburg, as the weary Confederate army retreated west through Fairfield, the inn hosted their generals. Today's guests can sup on hearty ham and bean soup and chicken and biscuits, just as General Robert E. Lee did.

If you're not into period dining, you're not out of luck. **Gettysburg Eddie's** (217 Steinwehr Ave., Gettysburg, 717/334-1100, www.gettysburgeddies.com, 11am-10pm Mon.-Thurs., 11am-10:30pm Fri.-Sat., 11am-9pm Sun., bar open until 11pm Mon.-Thurs., midnight Fri.-Sat., and 10pm Sun., winter hours vary, $6-27), across the street from Gettysburg National Cemetery, is a casual, welcoming spot. Named for Baseball Hall of Fame pitcher Eddie Plank, born in 1875 on a farm north of Gettysburg, the restaurant has an expansive menu of burgers, steaks, sizzling fajitas, and pasta dishes. The house-made peanut butter pie is a home run. Big TVs and a full-service bar make Eddie's a popular place to watch college and pro sports.

With its "vegetable powerhouse" sandwich, wild mushroom pizza, and truffle parmesan fries, modern diner **Food 101** (101 Chambersburg St., Gettysburg, 717/334-6080, www.food101gettysburg.com, 11am-8pm Sun.-Thurs., 11am-9pm Fri.-Sat., $8-17) is a great lunch choice, especially if you have vegetarians in your party. The veggie options are available during dinner, too, when the kitchen also adds rack of lamb, steak, and other carnivorous entrees to the menu. It's BYOB; pick up a bottle before dinner at the **Adams County Winery shop** (25 Chambersburg St., 717/334-1381).

Wine is definitely on the menu at **The Inn at Herr Ridge** (900 Chambersburg Rd., Gettysburg, 717/334-4332, www.innatherrridge.com, 5pm-9pm Tues.-Sat., $27-36), which features an award-winning 4,000-bottle cellar. The fine-dining restaurant, located just west of downtown Gettysburg on Route 30, was built in 1815 and turned into a Confederate hospital in 1863. It's said that amputated limbs were thrown out of a window into a waiting wagon—no wonder the staff have some ghost stories to share. A few miles farther west is another historic and reportedly haunted dining destination. The ★ **Cashtown Inn** (1325 Old Rte. 30, Cashtown, 717/334-9722, www.cashtowninn.com, 11:30am-2pm and 5pm-close Tues.-Sat., winter hours vary, $26-32) was also overrun by Confederates during the battle. The general who assumed command of the defeated army's retreat made it his headquarters. Its current owners have resisted the temptation to lure history-hungry tourists with period fare, offering New American cuisine instead.

ACCOMMODATIONS

Gettysburg has loads of lodging properties, many of which have a story to tell. There are B&Bs scarred by bullets and rooms once occupied by generals. If you visit when the town is crawling with tourists, expect two- or three-night minimums at many properties. Rates are at their lowest from December through March.

Under $100

Camping is a popular and inexpensive way to stay near the battlefield during the high season. Gettysburg has half a dozen campgrounds. If your idea of camping is quietly communing with nature, you may be in for a shock. These campgrounds are fairly bustling places. Some have cottages so luxurious they make hotel rooms look rustic, and all offer a host of modern amenities. **Drummer Boy Camping Resort** (1300 Hanover St., Gettysburg, 800/293-2808, www.drummerboycampresort.com, tent site $44-69, hookup site $59-95, cabin or cottage $89-360, weekly rates available) has, in addition to more than 400 campsites and about 50 cabins and cottages, two heated pools, a 250-foot waterslide, a mini-golf course, a game room, basketball and volleyball courts, and a fishing pond. Add to that a full schedule of activities and it's a wonder that campers ever leave the 95-acre resort. Drummer Boy is a few minutes east of downtown on Route 116.

A few minutes west of downtown on Route 116 is the 260-site **Gettysburg Campground** (2030 Fairfield Rd./Rte. 116 W., Gettysburg, 717/334-3304, www.gettysburgcampground.com, tent site $35-48, hookup site $43-72, cabin or cottage $70-170, weekly rates available). It too has amenities up the wazoo. Try to snag a campsite along Marsh Creek.

$100-250

In the center of town, the iconic ★ **Gettysburg Hotel** (1 Lincoln Square, Gettysburg, 717/337-2000, www.hotelgettysburg.com, $100-300) is just steps from the house where President Lincoln polished his Gettysburg Address. It's steeped in history, beginning in 1797 when a tavern opened its doors on the site. It withstood the bloody and pivotal battle of 1863 but was replaced in the 1890s by the current structure, which was christened the Hotel Gettysburg. In 1955 the hotel served as President Eisenhower's national operations center while he recuperated from a heart attack at his Gettysburg home. Eisenhower and his wife were the hotel's last guests before it closed its doors in 1964, rendered unprofitable by changes in travel habits. The building reopened as a Best Western in 1991, though the Best Western brand no longer runs it. The hotel has 119 guest accommodations, almost half of which are suites; a rooftop swimming pool; and on-site restaurant **One Lincoln** (717/338-5455, www.onelincoln.net).

Also historic but considerably smaller, the **James Gettys Hotel** (27 Chambersburg St., Gettysburg, 717/337-1334, www.jamesgettyshotel.com, $110-250) is half a block from the town square. Named for the founder of Gettysburg, it dates to 1804 and looks much as it did in the 1920s. Like the Gettysburg Hotel, it closed in the 1960s and reopened as an emulation of its former self in the 1990s. The James Gettys has a dozen suites, each with a bedroom, sitting room, kitchenette, and private bath. A complimentary continental breakfast is delivered to guests daily.

A few blocks west of the James Gettys, the **Federal Pointe Inn** (75 Springs Ave., Gettysburg, 717/334-7800, www.federalpointeinn.com, $150-250) is set in an 1897 property originally built as a school. Peter

Gettysburg Hotel

and Liz Monahan turned it into a hotel in 2012. The 23 elegant guest rooms and suites have high ceilings and some feature four-poster beds. It's part of Choice Hotel's upscale Ascend brand.

Just outside Gettysburg National Military Park, the **Best Western Gettysburg** (301 Steinwehr Ave., Gettysburg, 717/334-1188, www.gettysburgbestwestern.com, $85-180) is within walking distance to Gettysburg National Cemetery, where President Lincoln gave his famous speech. Opened in 2017, the hotel might not have the history of other lodgings, but it does offer a convenient location, a fitness center, and an indoor pool. Wi-Fi and breakfast are included.

B&B options include the impeccable ★ **Brickhouse Inn Bed & Breakfast** (452 Baltimore St., Gettysburg, 717/338-9337, www.brickhouseinn.com, $120-220) in downtown Gettysburg. The oldest of its buildings dates to the 1830s and was occupied by Confederate sharpshooters during the Battle of Gettysburg. Its south wall still bears the scars of Union bullets. The main house is an 1898 Victorian with original wood floors and chestnut trim. Between them they have 14 guest rooms and suites, each named for a state represented in the bloody battle. Behind the main house is a modern carriage house, with one guest room on the second floor. Breakfast always includes a hot entrée and the B&B's signature shoofly pie.

A few miles south of town is a countryside oasis, the **Lightner Farmhouse Bed & Breakfast** (2350 Baltimore Pike, Gettysburg, 717/337-9508, www.lightnerfarmhouse.com, $145-199). Built shortly before the Battle of Gettysburg, the Federal-style farmhouse was used as a hospital for three weeks after the bloodshed. If you want to see if any Civil War soldiers are still lingering about, innkeepers Dennis and Eileen Hoover have paranormal investigation equipment ready to rent out. The B&B has five en suite rooms, a suite that sleeps up to four, and a two-story cottage with a private wraparound deck. Quilt designs inspired the décor and nature trails wind through the 19-acre property.

TRANSPORTATION

Gettysburg is in the center of Adams County, which hugs the Pennsylvania-Maryland line just west of York County. It's about 45 miles southwest of **Harrisburg International Airport** (MDT, 888/235-9442, www.flyhia.

Federal Pointe Inn

com) via I-76 west and Route 15 south and 60 miles northwest of the larger **Baltimore-Washington International Thurgood Marshall Airport** (BWI, 800/435-9294, www.bwiairport.com). Private aircraft can fly into **Gettysburg Regional Airport** (888/235-9442, www.flyhia.com) just west of town.

There's no passenger train or commercial bus service to Gettysburg. It's very much a driving destination.

Pocono Mountains

Like New York's Catskill Mountains and the Berkshires of Massachusetts and Connecticut, Pennsylvania's Poconos are synonymous with R&R.

Less than two hours by car from New York City or Philadelphia, the highlands of northeast Pennsylvania have provided respite from the rigors of urban life since the early 1800s. For decades, the big draw was the dramatic Delaware Water Gap, a pass through the mountains carved by the Delaware River. In a 1908 New York Times ad, one hotel promised "commanding views for 30 miles in every direction of the grandest scenery east of the Rockies."

In the mid-1920s, an energy company dammed a creek near the town of Hawley, 20 miles north of the gap. The hydroelectric project created a recreational gem with 52 miles of shoreline: Lake Wallenpaupack. During World War II, many young GIs whisked their new brides to the Pocono Mountains before shipping overseas or while on leave, inviting the region's reputation as "Honeymoon Capital of the World." Pennsylvania's first commercial ski area opened in the Poconos in the 1940s. Today there are seven major ski areas.

The water gap that captivated Victorian-era urbanites is now the centerpiece of a large national park beloved by canoeists for its 40 miles of calm river. To its west is Lehigh Gorge State Park, which offers white-water paddling. The Lackawaxen River, which flows through the quaint towns of Honesdale and Hawley on its way to the Delaware, is a magnet for fly fishers. And then there are the lakes—more than 150 in all. Still the largest in northeast Pennsylvania, Lake Wallenpaupack teems with powerboats, Jet Skis, pontoon boats, and sailboats.

Pocono Raceway is the only NASCAR track in Pennsylvania and one of only four in the northeastern United States, which helps explain why its marquee events attract tens of thousands of fans.

PLANNING YOUR TIME

How you organize your time depends on what brought you to this corner of Pennsylvania. If it's an outdoor activity such as skiing, snowboarding, or white-water rafting, a day trip

Previous: shops lining Broadway in Jim Thorpe; Lehigh Gorge Scenic Railway train in Lehigh Gorge State Park. **Above:** Bushkill Falls.

Look for ★ to find recommended sights, activities, dining, and lodging.

HIGHLIGHTS

★ **Delaware Water Gap National Recreation Area:** Canoeists flock to this park, which features 40 miles of calm river (page 162).

★ **Bushkill Falls:** This privately owned piece of nature's artwork is hyped as "the Niagara of Pennsylvania" (page 164).

★ **Lake Wallenpaupack:** Boaters who feel the need for speed can satisfy it on this 13-mile-long lake, one of the few places in Pennsylvania where you can give parasailing a try (page 170).

★ **Ski Areas:** Though not terribly tall, the Pocono Mountains are an appealing destination for skiing, snowboarding, and snow tubing. In warmer months, water parks are the main attraction (page 176).

★ **Lehigh Gorge State Park:** Roiling white water and a 26-mile rail-trail make this park a must-visit for active sorts. Prefer to take it easy? Hop on the train that chugs through the river gorge (page 184).

★ **Ricketts Glen State Park:** Home to the 94-foot Ganoga Falls—and 21 other named waterfalls—this exceptionally scenic park is a must-visit for hikers (page 186).

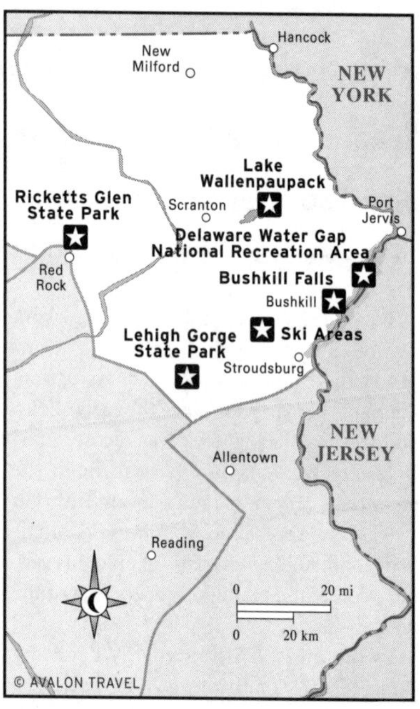

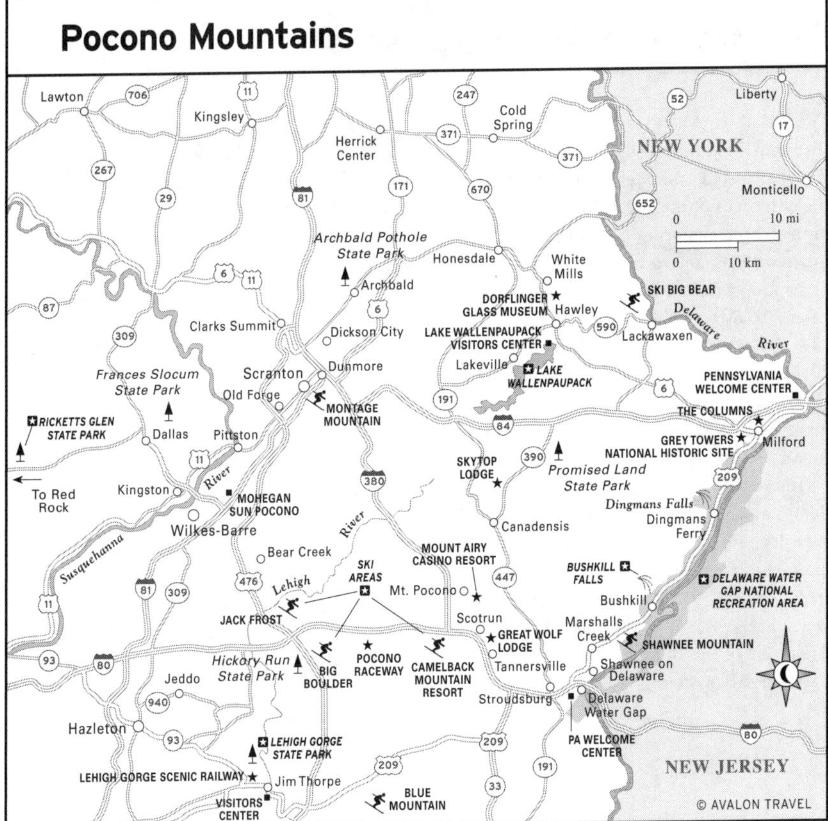

could suffice. If it's a combination of hanging out with your honey or family at an amenity-rich resort, dining out and shopping the outlet stores, and throwing in an easy, scenic hike, plan for a few days.

Because of the concentration of ski slopes, some people think of this region as a winter destination. But winter is actually the off-season for many hotels and other tourism-reliant businesses in northeast Pennsylvania. There's plenty to do in the warmer months, thanks largely to the region's rivers and lakes.

Delaware Water Gap Area

The Delaware Water Gap, a wide chasm cut through Kittatinny Ridge by the Delaware River, attracted urbanites by the trainload in the latter half of the 1800s. Why? "From the mountain peaks on every hand open magnificent vistas, and from the river both below and above the chasm views are of marvelous extent," crowed the *New York Times* in June 1897. Its popularity persisted into the early 20th century. Theodore Roosevelt paid a visit to the palatial Water Gap House, one of many hotels in the area, in 1910. A young Fred Astaire returned repeatedly with his family.

Today the Gap is enjoying another heyday—not as a resort area but as a recreation area. Its core constituency is outdoorsy people rather than society people. The chasm in Kittatinny Ridge is the centerpiece of Delaware Water Gap National Recreation Area, one of the 10 most visited sites in the national park system.

★ DELAWARE WATER GAP NATIONAL RECREATION AREA

Established in 1965 under President Lyndon Johnson, **Delaware Water Gap National Recreation Area** (www.nps.gov/dewa) encompasses nearly 40 miles of the Delaware River and 67,000 acres of river valley in Pennsylvania on one side and New Jersey on the other.

Getting your bearings is job one. The park is about five miles wide and 35 miles long, with the Delaware Water Gap and the Pennsylvania village named for it at its south end and the pretty town of Milford, Pennsylvania, at its north end. Route 209 is the major north-south artery on the Pennsylvania side. The exceptionally scenic Old Mine Road runs the length of the park on the New Jersey side. There are only three bridges spanning the Delaware within the park: the I-80 bridge at the south end of the park; the privately owned Dingmans Bridge linking Pennsylvania Route 739 and New Jersey Route 560; and the Route 206 bridge at the north end of the park. Maps

Delaware Water Gap

and brochures are available on the park website or you can pick them up at the ranger-staffed **Dingmans Falls Visitor Center** (Johnny Bee Rd. off Rte. 209, Dingmans Ferry, 570/828-6125, 9am-5pm Wed.-Thurs., 9am-6pm Fri.-Sun. Memorial Day weekend-Labor Day weekend) or **park headquarters** (River Rd. off Rte. 209, Bushkill, 570/426-2452, 8:30am-4:30pm Mon.-Fri.). Information is also available at the Pennsylvania **welcome centers** at I-80 exit 310 and I-84 exit 53.

Paddling

If you've come to paddle the river—be it for a few hours or a few days—you can get all the information and gear you need from one of the dozen or so boat liveries that operate within Delaware Water Gap National Recreation Area. They generally open in April and close at the end of October. More than 400 miles long, the Delaware is the longest undammed river east of the Mississippi. The Middle Delaware River, which flows through the park, is calm enough for even novice paddlers to navigate without a guide. On hot days it's not unusual for people to jump ship and float in their life jackets. Liveries near I-80 and the south end of the park include **Adventure Sports** (Rte. 209, Marshalls Creek, 570/223-0505, www.adventuresport.com) and **Chamberlain Canoes** (River Rd., Minisink Hills, 800/422-6631, www.chamberlaincanoes.com). Both rent canoes, kayaks, and rafts. Chamberlain also offers inner tubes. Most liveries near the north end of the park facilitate trips on the Upper Delaware, with its abundant white water, as well as the placid Middle Delaware. **Kittatinny Canoes** (800/356-2852, www.kittatinny.com) has multiple bases on the Upper and Middle Delaware and a huge fleet of canoes, kayaks, rafts, and tubes. It also boasts two riverfront campgrounds, a **paintball operation,** and a pair of 3,000-foot **zip lines.**

If you have your own kayak or canoe, you can take advantage of free bus service through the Pennsylvania side of the park. The Monroe County Transit Authority's **River Runner** (570/839-6282, www.gomcta.com) operates weekends from Memorial Day weekend through Labor Day. Buses are equipped with a trailer that carries boats and bikes.

Swimming

The Middle Delaware is an exceptionally clean river, so don't hesitate to take a dip. There are two lifeguarded beaches on the Pennsylvania side of the park: **Smithfield Beach** (River Rd., 3.2 miles north of the village of Shawnee on Delaware, part of East Stroudsburg) and **Milford Beach** (off Rte. 209 near Milford). The entrance fee is $7 per vehicle on weekdays and $10 on weekends and holidays. If you arrive by foot or bicycle, the fee is just $1. The beaches have restrooms and picnic tables. If you plan to cook, bring your own grill. Alcohol and pets aren't allowed at the beaches.

The Park Service cautions against swimming elsewhere, but plenty of folks do. Be sure to wear a life jacket. Trying to swim across the river is a terrible idea. It's a leading cause of death on the Delaware. Swimming in and around waterfalls—and jumping into waterfalls—is not allowed anywhere in the park.

Fishing

Prefer catching fish to swimming with them? Smallmouth bass, muskellunge, walleye, catfish, and panfish are found in the Delaware River. Schools of shad, which live in the ocean but migrate upstream to spawn, reach the park around May. A license from either Pennsylvania or New Jersey will do for fishing on the Delaware or from its banks. To fish in its trout-laden tributaries, you'll need the appropriate state license.

Trails

The Delaware River may be its main attraction, but Delaware Water Gap National Recreation Area has plenty to offer landlubbers, starting with 100 miles of **hiking trails.** It contains more than 25 miles of the famed **Appalachian Trail,** which crosses the Delaware River at the Water Gap (via a walkway on the I-80 bridge). Climbing the Gap's gateposts—Mount Tammany in New Jersey and Mount Minsi in Pennsylvania—is popular with day hikers. But you don't have to climb more than 1,000 vertical feet for a visual feast. Several short trails on the Pennsylvania side of the park lead to striking waterfalls. Near the village of Dingmans Ferry, a Delaware River tributary named Dingmans Creek dives 130 feet. Dingmans Falls was privately owned from 1888 to 1975, when the federal government snapped it up, and tourists used to pay for the privilege of seeing it. Less than half a mile long, the **Dingmans Falls Trail** is a flat, wheelchair-accessible boardwalk leading to the base of the falls. You can climb to the upper falls via some 240 steps. The trailhead is at Dingmans Falls Visitor Center (Johnny Bee Rd. off Rte. 209, Dingmans Ferry). The eponymous falls of Raymondskill Creek, which empties into the Delaware a few miles farther upstream, are only a little harder to get to. A short hike through hemlock forest puts you at the upper falls; steep, uneven stairs descend to the middle falls. Look for Raymondskill Road near milepost 18 of Route 209.

The 32-mile **McDade Trail,** which parallels the Delaware on the Pennsylvania side of the park, also deserves mention. Don't be put off by its length. With more than 15 trailheads, the McDade is a choose-your-own-adventure path. Most of the trailheads are along Route 209. The unpaved trail is open to **biking** as well as hiking. In the winter, it makes for scenic **cross-country skiing** and **snowshoeing.**

Guided hiking tours are available through **Edge of the Woods Outfitters** (110 Main St., Delaware Water Gap, 570/421-6681, www.edgeofthewoodsoutfitters.com). Located two blocks from the Appalachian Trail, the outdoor gear store is a popular resupply point for backpackers. It also offers shuttle service to points on the AT, mountain bike rentals, river trips, and a pedal-and-paddle package.

OTHER SIGHTS

★ Bushkill Falls

A place that bills itself as "the Niagara of Pennsylvania" had better deliver, and **Bushkill Falls** (Bushkill Falls Rd., off Rte. 209, Bushkill, 570/588-6682, www.visitbushkillfalls.com, daily Apr.-Nov. weather permitting, adults $14.50-16.50, seniors $13.50-15.50, children 4-10 $8.50) does not disappoint. No, you can't don a plastic raincoat and ride a steamship into a waterfall basin. But you can get close enough to a towering waterfall for a mist bath—and load up on souvenirs.

Bushkill Falls is a privately owned attraction. When Charles E. Peters opened it to the public in 1904, charging 10 cents for admission, a single path and a swinging bridge brought visitors to the head of a 100-foot waterfall now known as the Main Falls. Today a series of mostly easy trails connects eight waterfalls. The original is still the best. A 15-minute walk yields a good view of it. For even better vantage points and access to a second waterfall, follow the popular yellow-marked trail, which takes about 45 minutes and crosses several wooden bridges strung across roaring waters. Avid hikers can take in all eight waterfalls via the two-mile **Bridal Veil Falls Trail.**

Still owned by the Peters family, Bushkill Falls has added a host of kid-friendly amenities over the years. Visitors can play a round of miniature golf ($5), ride a paddleboat ($5), race through a maze ($5 for first run, $2 for subsequent runs), fish in a pair of lakes (permit $5), mine for gemstones ($10), and view free exhibits on Bushkill Falls, local wildlife, and Native Americans. The park also has a playground and picnic areas with charcoal grills.

Shawnee Mountain

Shawnee Mountain Ski Area (401 Hollow Rd., East Stroudsburg, 570/421-7231, www.shawneemt.com, all-day lift ticket adults $35-62, seniors and college students $35-40, children 18 and under $35-45, children under 46 inches and seniors 70 and older free, all-day ski equipment rental $35, snow tubing 2-hour session $22-27) offers 700 feet of vertical, 23 slopes and trails, two terrain parks, and a snow tubing park. If you've never tried skiing, it's a good place to get your feet (and butt) wet. It's an even better place to introduce kids to the sport. The ski area has an excellent reputation for its children's programs, which include ski lessons for children as young as three, snowboarding lessons for children as young as four, and mommy-and-me ski lessons. Multiday lift tickets can add up to big savings for families. Children too young or too timid to hit the slopes can chill at Shawnee's childcare facility ($5/hour, $40/day), open to children 18 months and older.

Grey Towers National Historic Site

The onetime home of Gifford Pinchot, first chief of the U.S. Forest Service, is open to the public as **Grey Towers National Historic Site** (151 Grey Towers Dr., Milford, 570/296-9630, www.greytowers.org, tours adults $8, seniors $7, children 12-17 $5). Under Pinchot's watch, the number of national forests climbed from 32 in 1898 to 149 in 1910. He later served two terms as Pennsylvania governor.

His son donated Grey Towers, the family's Milford estate, to the Forest Service in 1964. The mansion, which resembles a medieval French castle, can only be seen by guided tour. Built in the 1880s, the house originally had 43 rooms. Gifford Pinchot's wife found it rather dreary and had dividing walls knocked down to create larger rooms. She also oversaw the construction of a playhouse for their son and a moat. The moat might have been her crowning achievement were it not for the Finger Bowl, a unique outdoor dining table consisting of a pool of water surrounded by a stone ledge wide enough for place settings. Food floated on the water in wooden bowls.

The regular tour season runs from Memorial Day weekend through October. Tours of the first floor and several outdoor areas begin on the hour 11am-4pm Thursdays to Mondays. Special three-floor tours are offered at 4pm on Saturdays and Sundays. The mansion is reopened for about two weeks in December, when it's decorated for the holidays. Call or check the website for a schedule of holiday tours.

The Columns

A bloodstained American flag is the draw at the museum of the Pike County Historical Society, called **The Columns** (608 Broad St., Milford, 570/296-8126, www.pikehistorical.org, 1pm-4pm Wed.-Sun. July-Aug., 1pm-4pm Wed. and Sat.-Sun. Apr.-June and Sept.-Nov., adults $5, students $3, children 12 and under free). The large 36-star flag was draped over a balustrade in Ford's Theatre on the night of April 14, 1865, when John Wilkes Booth shot Abraham Lincoln in the back of the head. Thomas Gourlay, an actor and stage manager at the Washington DC theater, placed the flag under the mortally wounded president's head. Gourlay kept the flag and gave it to his actress daughter, Jeannie Gourlay Struthers, who also had a role in the play Lincoln was watching when he was assassinated. She moved to Pennsylvania's Pike County in 1888. Her son later donated the flag to the historical society, along with some of her clothing and other artifacts from the Civil War era.

The Columns, a 1904 Neoclassical mansion, also houses Native American artifacts, historical photographs, and an 1800s stagecoach. One of its exhibit rooms is dedicated to the brilliant logician and scientist Charles Sanders Peirce, who moved to Milford in the late 1800s.

ENTERTAINMENT AND EVENTS

Concert Venues

Jazz aficionados have been finding their way to the **Deer Head Inn** (5 Main St., Delaware Water Gap, 570/424-2000, www.deerheadinn.com) for more than 50 years. Built as a hotel in the mid-1800s, the four-story Victorian in the heart of Delaware Water Gap still offers lodging, and its proximity to the Appalachian Trail and Delaware Water Gap National Recreation Area makes it a good choice for those in search of outdoor adventure. But jazz is its raison d'être. Maestros such as saxophonists Stan Getz and Phil Woods, pianist Keith Jarrett, and guitarist Pat Metheny have played the Deer Head, which offers dinner and live music Thursday through Sunday.

The **Sherman Theater** (524 Main St., Stroudsburg, 570/420-2808, www.shermantheater.com) in downtown Stroudsburg opened on January 7, 1929, with a live performance by Stan Laurel and Oliver Hardy. Today it's best known as a rock venue, but other music genres, theater, and dance also find their way onto the calendar.

Performing Arts

In 1985 arson claimed a playhouse that had stood since 1904. Thanks in part to donations from its many fans, the **Shawnee Playhouse** (552 River Rd., Shawnee on Delaware, 570/421-5093, www.theshawneeplayhouse.com) rose again. Located on the grounds of the Shawnee Inn and Golf Resort, the playhouse auditions actors in New York City for its main stage season, which runs from May through December. The theater's resident troupe performs in the off-season.

Festivals and Events

The **Delaware River Sojourn** (646/205-2724, www.delawareriversojourn.org, June, registration fees charged) is a weeklong paddling trip designed to heighten awareness of the ecological and recreational significance of the river that flows through New York, New Jersey, Pennsylvania, and Delaware. It's open to both novice and experienced paddlers, who can sign up for the entire event or a portion of it. Participants catch their winks at campgrounds near the scenic river.

Other notable happenings include three events at **Shawnee Mountain Ski Area** (East Stroudsburg, 570/421-7231, www.shawneemt.com). The **Poconos' Wurst Festival** (July, $9-12.50) is a tribute to both Polish and German cultures. Joining wursts on the menu are kielbasa, pierogies, stuffed cabbage, sauerkraut, and more. The festival also features craft brews, crafts, and plenty of polka music. Keep vampires at bay during the **Pocono Garlic Festival** (www.poconogarlic.com, Labor Day weekend, $12.50). Expect such unexpected foods as roasted garlic ice cream and garlic funnel cake. Lumberjacks show their stuff during the **Autumn Timber Festival** (early Oct., $12-15), held during the peak of fall foliage season. Festivalgoers can board a chairlift for a bird's-eye view of hills ablaze with color. Tickets to Shawnee events are cheaper when purchased in advance.

FOOD

Shawnee on Delaware and East Stroudsburg

Located on the grounds of the Shawnee Inn and Golf Resort, the multilevel ★ **Gem and Keystone Brewpub** (526 River Rd., 570/424-0990, www.gemandkeystone.com, 11:30am-10pm Sun.-Thurs., 11:30am-11pm Fri.-Sat., $9-26) speaks to locavores with its slogan of "Beer from here. Food from near." Dishes are designed to pair with ShawneeCraft beers, brewed a short walk away. The food is hearty pub fare with beer cooked in wherever possible—beer-braised sausage, beer-battered fish-and-chips, a cheesesteak with cheddar ale sauce—along with several vegetarian options and a kids menu. Rest assured that the meats are all-natural, the seafood sustainable, and the doggie bags biodegradable. Want to know more about the beer? **Brewery tours** (570/213-5151, www.shawneeinn.com, 4pm Wed.-Fri., noon and 4pm Sat., noon Sun.) leave from the lobby of the resort.

Fresh food, full-bodied flavors, and fair prices can add up to a line out the door of **Saen Thai Cuisine** (1 Buttermilk Falls Rd., 570/476-4911, www.saenthai.com, 11:30am-2pm and 5:30pm-9pm Tues.-Fri., noon-2pm and 5:30pm-9pm Sat.-Sun., $9-20), which doesn't take reservations. It's not a bad idea to arrive about 20 minutes before the place opens for dinner on a weekend. Everything is superb, from the spring rolls to the curries to the exquisitely presented specials.

Just down River Road from Shawnee on Delaware, locals gather at **Minisink Hotel** (110 Post Office Rd., Minisink Hills,

570/421-9787, 11am-2am daily, $6-20), a divey pub on the banks of Marshalls Creek in a building the Minisink claims dates back to the 1740s. A covered walking bridge spans the creek right outside the restaurant. The burgers, nachos, chicken parmesan, fried shrimp, and similar fare pair well with beers, of which there are several to choose from.

Milford

The reputation of the **Hotel Fauchère** (401 Broad St., 570/409-1212, www.hotelfauchere.com) as a culinary destination dates to the 1860s, when a Swiss-born chef named Louis Fauchère took over the hotel. An 1888 portrait of Fauchère presides over its fine-dining restaurant, **The Delmonico Room** (6pm-close Fri., 10am-3pm and 6pm-close Sat.-Sun., $26-40), open only three nights a week. The service is superlative and the setting romantic. Though it's decorated with vintage menus from famed European restaurants, The Delmonico Room is actually named for the New York City restaurant that created the Delmonico steak. Fauchère served as master chef there before moving to Milford. **Bar Louis** (5pm-close Mon.-Fri., 10am-3pm and 5pm-close Sat.-Sun. Jan.-Mar., 11am-close Mon.-Fri., 10am-close Sat.-Sun. Apr.-Dec., $14-29) is named for Fauchère himself. The sleek, sexy bistro on the hotel's ground level is famous for its specialty cocktails and sushi "pizza." Also notable: the house-cured meats and the signature burger with parmesan fries. An enormous framed photo of Andy Warhol planting a smooch on John Lennon's cheek sits behind the minimalist bar. It's all so very cool that you're liable to feel disoriented upon emerging onto Milford's sleepy main drag.

Something you'll never see in a New York City eatery: a working 19th-century waterwheel. Milford's ★ **Waterwheel Café, Bakery and Bar** (150 Water St., 570/296-2383, www.waterwheelcafe.com, 8am-3:30pm Sun.-Wed., 8am-3:30pm and 5:15pm-9:30pm Thurs.-Sat., bar menu available until 10pm, $18-29) offers diners a view of water rushing over a three-story waterwheel built in the early 1800s to power grain-grinding equipment. You can power up for your day with a house-baked scone or challah French toast. The Waterwheel spans the globe for its lunchtime options, which include a long list of sandwiches ranging from a fried tofu banh mi (a Vietnamese sandwich) to duck liver mousse on brick oven-baked Italian bread. Dinner in the café is a fine-dining affair featuring Mediterranean and Vietnamese cuisine.

The Gem and Keystone Brewpub is at the Shawnee Inn and Golf Resort.

If a picnic is in your plans, fill your basket at **Fretta's Italian Food Specialties** (223 Broad St., 570/296-7863, www.frettas.com, 8am-6pm Tues.-Sat., 9am-2pm Sun). Established in 1906 in New York City's Little Italy neighborhood, the *salumeria* relocated to picturesque Milford in 1998. Run by fourth-generation proprietor Joseph Fretta and his wife, Denice, the shop carries all sorts of imported goodies, plus house-made cheeses, charcuterie, and cannoli. The takeout menu features soups, sandwiches, wraps, and pasta dishes.

ACCOMMODATIONS

Camping

There are plenty of camping options in and around **Delaware Water Gap National Recreation Area** (570/426-2452, www.nps.gov/dewa), including free campsites right on the river. (Those sites, however, are reserved for boaters and paddlers on overnight trips and cannot be reserved.) A list of campgrounds is available on the park's website. They include Dingmans Campground and River Beach Campsites, which boast riverfront sites and canoe and kayak rentals. **Dingmans Campground** (1006 Rte. 209, Dingmans Ferry, 570/828-1551, www.dingmanscampground.com, open seasonally, $40-52) has about 20 riverfront tent sites and more than 100 tent and RV sites in wooded areas. The rustic campground is on federal property, and alcohol is prohibited. **River Beach** (378 Rte. 6/209, Milford, 800/356-2852, www.kittatinny.com, $11-18 per site, adults $16, children 6-11 $9) is one of two campgrounds owned by Kittatinny Canoes, one of the oldest and most reputable outfitters in the region. Located just north of Delaware Water Gap National Recreation Area, the campground has about 160 tent and RV sites, two modern bathhouses, laundry facilities, an arcade, and a store where you can buy everything from matches to kayaks. The store also has Wi-Fi.

Hotels and B&Bs

When weighing lodging options near the southern end of Delaware Water Gap National Recreation Area, note that the more mellifluous Shawnee on Delaware is a town within East Stroudsburg. Some accommodations use Shawnee on Delaware on their websites; don't be confused if the same hotel pops up with an East Stroudsburg address in Internet search engines and maps.

"Santosha" is Sanskrit for "contentment," which is easy to achieve when you're lazing in a hammock on a deck overlooking the Delaware River Valley at **Santosha on the Ridge** (121 Santosha Ln., Shawnee on Delaware, 570/476-0203, www.santoshaontheridge.com, $180-240). Run by husband-and-wife innkeepers, the secluded four-room bed-and-breakfast feels more like a home than a hotel. Start the morning with a gourmet breakfast at the communal table. After a day of kayaking or hiking, kick back on the deck and spot the campfires far below. For a livelier evening, book a stay at **Deer Head Inn** (5 Main St., Delaware Water Gap, 570/424-2000, www.deerheadinn.com, $120-180), which is best known for its long-running jazz club. Indeed, there's no check-in desk; just find the bartender. The eight en suite guest rooms and suites are simple but sufficient.

Milford's charming downtown is home to one of only two Relais & Châteaux properties in Pennsylvania: the eminently chic ★ **Hotel Fauchère** (401 Broad St., Milford, 570/409-1212, www.hotelfauchere.com, $160-450). The 19th-century Italianate hotel reopened in 2006 after a three-decade hibernation and five-year restoration. Today's guests walk through the same marble entryway and run their hands along the same mahogany banisters as Henry Ford, Charlie Chaplin, Mae West, Babe Ruth, Franklin D. Roosevelt, and John F. Kennedy. Among the newer features in the 16 guest rooms: flat-screen TVs, Nespresso machines, free Wi-Fi, and marble bathrooms with heated towel racks and floors. Room rates include a continental breakfast, taken in the hotel's famed restaurant, the Delmonico Room.

TRANSPORTATION AND SERVICES

Getting There and Around

Delaware Water Gap National Recreation Area is about 5 miles wide and 35 miles long, with the Gap at its south end and the pretty town of Milford, Pennsylvania, at its north end. It's about 70 miles northwest of New York City via I-80 and 100 miles north of Philadelphia via I-476 north, Route 22 east, and Route 33 north. Passenger airlines won't get you terribly close to the park. The nearest airports—**Lehigh Valley International Airport** (ABE, 800/359-5842, www.flylvia.com), **Wilkes-Barre/Scranton International Airport** (AVP, 570/602-2000, www.flyavp.com), and **Newark Liberty International Airport** (EWR, 973/961-6000, www.panynj.gov)—are 60-70 miles away.

While the park is primarily a driving destination, you can get by without a car. **Martz Trailways** (570/421-3040, www.martztrailways.com) offers intercity bus service to Delaware Water Gap, the Pennsylvania town alongside the geologic gap. From the bus station, you can walk to the Appalachian Trail or **Edge of the Woods Outfitters** (110 Main St., Delaware Water Gap, 570/421-6681, www.watergapadventure.com), which offers guided hiking tours, river trips, and mountain bike rentals. You can also catch the **River Runner** (570/839-6282, www.gomcta.com), a free bus that runs through the Pennsylvania side of Delaware Water Gap National Recreation Area. It operates weekends from Memorial Day weekend through Labor Day.

Car-less New Yorkers have another option: arrive in Port Jervis, New York, by bus (201/529-3666, www.shortlinebus.com) or rail (973/275-5555, www.njtransit.com) and get a lift from the station from **Kittatinny Canoes** (800/356-2852, www.kittatinny.com), which offers river trips, camping, and more.

Visitor Information

Maps, trail guides, and brochures on every sort of attraction can be found at area **Lehigh Valley International Airport.** There are Pennsylvania **welcome centers** at I-80 exit 310, near the south end of Delaware Water Gap National Recreation Area, and at I-84 exit 53, near the north end. The National Park Service operates the **Dingmans Falls Visitor Center** (Johnny Bee Rd. off Rte. 209, 570/828-6125, 9am-5pm Wed.-Thurs., 9am-6pm Fri.-Sun. Memorial Day weekend-Labor Day weekend) in Dingmans Ferry, Pennsylvania, a popular starting point for river trips.

The **Pocono Mountains Visitors Bureau** (1004 W. Main St., Stroudsburg, 570/421-5791, www.poconomountains.com, 8:30am-5pm Mon.-Thurs., 8:30am-4pm Fri.) is a good source of information about things to see and do in the region. You can request free brochures through its website.

Lake Region

Pennsylvania's northeast corner is home to more than 100 lakes. At 5,700 acres, Lake Wallenpaupack is the largest. Created in the 1920s by Pennsylvania Power & Light, the lake is a popular destination for powerboating, sailing, fishing, and camping. The residential and vacation homes that ring the lake are testament to its recreational appeal. The tiny town of Hawley, just north of Lake Wallenpaupack, is popular with New Yorkers escaping the city for a weekend.

The largest town in the lake region is charming Honesdale, about 15 minutes from Hawley. With its Victorian architecture, tall church steeples, and quaint shops, the Wayne County seat is worth a stroll.

Flowing through the region is the Lackawaxen River, a 25-mile tributary of the Delaware that's beloved by fly fishers. Bald eagles seem to love it too, which brings out the birders.

The **Lake Wallenpaupack Visitors Center** (2512 Rte. 6, Hawley, 570/226-2141, 9am-5pm daily) is a good first stop for anyone new to the region. You'll find maps, brochures, exhibits, and people who know the area like the back of their hands.

★ LAKE WALLENPAUPACK

Boating

Lake Wallenpaupack, its islands, and most of its 52-mile shoreline are now property of Brookfield Renewable Energy Partners. Boat ramps and slips can be found at four Brookfield-owned recreation areas: **Wilsonville** (113 Ammon Dr., Hawley, 570/226-4382, www.wilsonvillecampground.com), located near the Lake Wallenpaupack Visitors Center and the only public beach on the lake; **Caffrey** (431 Lakeshore Dr., Lakeville, 570/226-4608); **Ironwood Point** (155 Burns Hill Rd., Greentown, 570/857-0880, www.ironwoodpoint.com); and **Ledgedale** (153 Ledgedale Rd., Greentown, 570/689-2181, www.ledgedalerecarea.com). Boat slip rates and reservation policies vary from one to the other. All charge a fee for boat launching. For no-fee boat launching, head to the **Pennsylvania Fish & Boat Commission access area** at Mangan Cove, located off Route 590 about a mile west of its junction with Route 6.

If you don't have your own boat, you're not out of luck. Located at Lighthouse Harbor Marina, **Pocono Action Sports** (969 Rte. 507, Greentown, 570/857-0779, www.poconoactionsports.com) offers rental ski boats, fishing boats, pontoon boats, and sailboats. Full-day rates range from $210 for a 19-foot sailboat to $495 for a high-end pontoon boat. Kneeboards and inner tubes are $30 with boat rental. Pocono Action Sports also offers Jet Skis for $120 per hour and **parasailing rides** for $70 per person. Kayak rentals are $35 for two hours. Find a similar lineup—powerboats, Jet Skis, watersports equipment—at **Rubber Duckie Boat Rentals** (Rte. 507 and Rte. 390, Tafton, 570/226-3930, www.rubberduckieboatrentals.com).

Perfect for anyone who wants to get on the water but leave the navigating to pros, the **Wallenpaupack Scenic Boat Tour** (2487 Rte. 6, Hawley, 570/226-3293, www.wallenpaupackboattour.com, mid-May-early Oct., adults $15, seniors $14, children 2-12 $11) is a 50-minute cruise aboard a patio boat. (Not

Lake Wallenpaupack

to be confused with a party boat. There's no food, booze, or DJ on this ride.) The tour company also offers rental pontoon boats, kayaks, and stand-up paddleboards.

Fishing

Lake Wallenpaupack is considered one of the best fishing spots in the state. The Pennsylvania Fish & Boat Commission has gone so far as to install artificial habitat structures in the lake to make it more inviting to fish—and anglers. It's home to smallmouth bass, largemouth bass, walleye, muskellunge, pickerel, yellow perch, and trout, to name a few. Call **Bill's Guide Service** (570/698-6035, www.billsguideservice.com) or **Ray's Fishing Guide Service** (570/654-5436 or 570/510-9219, www.raysguideservice.com) for a helping hand.

Wallenpaupack Creek and the Lackawaxen River, which the lake drains into, offer mountain stream fishing. Both are stocked by the Fish & Boat Commission. Anglers on the Lackawaxen should watch for sudden rises in water level, which occur when water is released from the hydroelectric plant. Call 877/775-5253 or visit www.lakewallenpaupackhydro.com for information on lake elevation and discharge to the river.

Fishing licenses can be purchased in advance on the Fish & Boat Commission website (www.fishandboat.com) or at local bait shops. Handicap-accessible fishing piers are located at the commission-run Mangan Cove and Brookfield's Ironwood Point.

Swimming

Lake Wallenpaupack has 52 miles of shoreline but only one **public beach** (570/226-9290, 9am-6pm daily Memorial Day weekend-Labor Day weekend). It's located near the Lake Wallenpaupack Visitors Center on Route 6, about half a mile west of the Route 6 and Route 507 junction. Operated by Palmyra Township, the beach has lifeguards, picnic tables, charcoal grills, bathrooms, and a snack bar. Admission is $5 for adults, $3 for kids. Seniors and infants get in free.

Swimming is not permitted at Brookfield's recreation areas.

SIGHTS

Dorflinger Glass Museum

The village of White Mills lies halfway between Hawley and Honesdale on Route 6. Blink and you could miss it. There's little to suggest that White Mills was once a bustling industrial center, but that's exactly what it became after Christian Dorflinger came to town in the 1860s. Only in his 30s, the French-born glassmaker had already opened three factories in Brooklyn, New York. Sleepy little White Mills offered an escape from the rigors of city life, but Dorflinger wasn't ready to retire. He built a glass factory in the hamlet, which became home to so many workmen and craftsmen that it could no longer be called a hamlet. The White Mills plant produced some of the most exquisite cut lead crystal in the country.

In 1980 Dorflinger's White Mills estate opened to the public as the **Dorflinger-Suydam Wildlife Sanctuary** (Elizabeth St., White Mills, 570/253-1185, www.dorflinger.org, dawn-dusk daily, free admission). Several miles of trails traverse the 600-acre sanctuary, which is home to the **Dorflinger Glass Museum** (10am-4pm Wed.-Sat. and 1pm-4pm Sun. May-Oct., Sat.-Sun. only in Nov., adults $5, seniors $4, children 6-18 $2). Opened in 1989, the museum boasts the largest collection of Dorflinger glass in the country—more than 900 pieces strong. The gift shop demands as much time as the galleries. It's filled with glass treasures, including Christmas ornaments, vases, paperweights, jewelry, and kaleidoscopes.

The wildlife sanctuary hosts the **Wildflower Music Festival,** a summer concert series that attracts touring performers. Dates, times, and ticket prices are available on the sanctuary's website. Bring lawn chairs or a blanket for the outdoor concerts.

If your GPS doesn't seem inclined to locate White Mills, use this address to reach Dorflinger: 55 Suydam Drive, Honesdale.

ENTERTAINMENT AND EVENTS

Festivals and Events

An end-of-summer tradition started in 2010, **Wally Lake Fest** (multiple locations, 570/226-2141, www.wallylakefest.com, late Aug., cost varies by event) is three days of events and activities celebrating the lake region's recreational and cultural amenities. Past fests have featured everything from fly-casting and paddleboarding demos to group bicycle and motorcycle rides to live music on a floating stage. The annual boat parade—with prizes for the best "dressed" boats—is open to the public.

The lake region's most unusual event takes place when the lake is frozen over. In 2007 professional ice carver Mark Crouthamel used a post-holidays lull in business to create life-size sculptures of a log cabin and some critters and invited the public to come have a look. Thousands turned out for **Crystal Cabin Fever** (Sculpted Ice Works, Rte. 590, Lakeville, 570/226-6246, www.crystalcabinfever.com, Feb., $15), now an annual event. Playing on a different theme each year, Crouthamel and team carve an interactive display out of more than 100 tons of ice. There's always a dual-run ice slide, so wear snow pants. Ice-carving competitions are among the highlights of the event, which lasts more than two weeks.

SPORTS AND RECREATION

Winter Sports

Located about 10 miles east of Hawley, near the Pennsylvania-New York border, **Ski Big Bear** (192 Karl Hope Blvd., Lackawaxen, 570/226-8585, www.ski-bigbear.com, Jan.-Mar., all-day lift ticket adults $45-59, seniors and children 6-12 $36-53, all-day equipment rental $35, snow tubing 2-hour session $25) is the northernmost ski area in the Poconos. It's relatively small, with 650 feet of vertical, 18 trails, and six lifts, which makes it a good place to learn to ski or snowboard. Group lessons for beginners age six and up are $32. Private lessons are available for children as young as four. Ski Big Bear also offers snow tubing on weekends and select weekdays during holiday periods.

FOOD

Hawley

Organic farmers and producers within an hour's drive provide a great deal of what's served at **The Settlers Inn** (4 Main Ave., 570/226-2993, www.thesettlersinn.com, 7:30am-10am and 5:30pm-8:30pm Mon.-Thurs., 7:30am-10am and 5:30pm-9:30pm Fri., 8am-10:30am, 11am-2:30pm, and 5:30pm-9:30pm Sat., 8am-10:30am, 11am-2:30pm, and 5:30pm-8:30pm Sun., $24-40), a small hotel and immensely popular restaurant on the banks of the Lackawaxen River. Portions are on the small side, so don't shy away from the soups and other starters. If the dinner menu doesn't fit your budget, consider dining in the inn's cozy tavern, where you can order a cheeseburger as well as more refined fare. In the warmer months, snag a table on the river-facing terrace.

Honesdale

"From farm to forks—keeping the distance short" is the motto at **Dyberry Forks** (939 Main St., 570/253-2266, www.dyberryforks.com, 5pm-close Wed.-Sat., closed winter, $15-30), set in a former general supply store and farmers' meeting spot. The rustic-chic eatery serves artful cocktails and meals from a short, oft-changing menu. Cheeses come from Calkins Creamery and the produce is straight from Lackawaxen Farm Co., both in Honesdale. The restaurant takes its name from the area's old moniker, describing where Dyberry Creek meets the Lackawaxen River.

The ★ **Trackside Grill** (734 Main St., 570/253-2462, www.tracksidegrill.net, 6am-3pm Mon.-Wed., 6am-7pm Thurs. and Sat., 6am-8pm Fri., 7am-2pm Sun., $6-16) is the kind of place seasoned travelers love to stumble upon. The atmosphere is welcoming, the food is satisfying, and the staff is as happy to point you to favorite spots as they are to pour you more coffee. The diner pays tribute to Honesdale's legacy as the "birthplace of the American railroad." It's decorated with train memorabilia and photos of local landscapes and landmarks taken by owner Jeff Hiller. Servers wearing engineer caps and red bandanas take orders for plate-size pancakes, omelets, and sandwiches like the Choo Choo and the Caboose Melt. Be sure to leave room for a Conductor Sundae or the Orange Blossom Special, a Creamsicle-flavored milk shake. Its children's menu and sensible prices ($2.50 for a breakfast sandwich!) make it ideal for families.

Another great option for breakfast or lunch is **Branko's Patisserie du Jour** (501 Main St., 570/253-0311, www.brankos-patisserie.com, 7am-3pm Tues.-Sat., $6-17). Chef Branko Bozic, originally from Germany, worked in high-end restaurants in Europe and Las Vegas and served as personal chef to Pennsylvania governor Bob Casey before opening the café in 2005 with his wife, Lyn. The vibe is casual, but the soups, salads, and sandwiches are très sophisticated. Seared duck breast rests on organic greens. Salami from Barcelona meets French brie on house-baked bread. Bozic is also a skilled pastry chef, and his fruit tarts and Parisian chocolate domes are divine. On select Saturdays October through May, Branko's offers a prix fixe dinner in a candlelit setting. Reservations go quickly.

ACCOMMODATIONS

Accommodations in the lake region run the gamut from walk-in campsites and basic motels to romantic inns and a destination spa resort. Being that boating is a main attraction, prices are generally highest in the hottest months.

Camping

Brookfield Energy, the company that owns Lake Wallenpaupack, maintains four public campgrounds on the lake. They're open from late April to late October. All have RV sites, boat ramps and slips, restrooms and showers, laundry facilities, and a general store. Nightly rates range from $30 to $44. With 29 sites, **Caffrey** (431 Lakeshore Dr., Lakeville, 570/226-4608, no website) is the smallest of the four. Good prevailing westerlies make it popular with sailboaters. **Ironwood Point** (155 Burns Hill Rd., Greentown, 570/857-0880, www.ironwoodpoint.com) is situated on a wooded hill overlooking the lake. It has about 60 sites, including 13 lakefront sites for walk-in camping. Located at the southern tip of the 13-mile lake, **Ledgedale** (153 Ledgedale Rd., Greentown, 570/689-2181, www.ironwoodpoint.com) offers 70 sites, kayak rentals, a playground, and a game room. It's adjacent to **Ledgedale Natural Area** (Kuhn Hill Rd., Greentown, open dawn to dusk), 80 forested acres with two miles of hiking trails. **Wilsonville** (113 Ammon Dr., Hawley, 570/226-4382, www.wilsonville-campground.com) is the largest of the four campgrounds with 160 sites. It's just off Route 6, adjacent to the only public beach on Lake Wallenpaupack and not far from the dam.

Lake Wallenpaupack is just one of many lakes in these parts. Located off Route 6 about seven miles west of Honesdale, the 300-site **Keen Lake Camping & Cottage Resort** (155 Keen Lake Rd., Waymart, 570/488-6161, www.keenlake.com, campsites $39-63) features a privately owned lake teeming with bass, bluegill, perch, and pickerel, to name a few. It's easiest to buy a fishing license through the Pennsylvania Fish & Boat Commission's website (www.fishandboat.com) in advance. Campers can rent a rowboat, paddleboat, canoe, or kayak for a spin around the 90-acre lake or take a dip in the designated swim area. The pet-friendly campground also has a pool, several playgrounds, a game room with pool tables, and a movie lounge. A dozen unique cottages and a couple of RVs are available for rent for $80-320 per day or $895-1,825 per week. Some are available year-round. If privacy is paramount, reserve Hermit Island, a rustic three-bedroom cottage on an island accessible only by boat.

Couples Only

The region once known as the "Honeymoon Capital of the World" has lost most of its couples resorts, but the species isn't extinct. Each year, some 65,000 couples vacation at the three remaining couples resorts in the Pocono Mountains. They uncork more than 20,000 bottles of champagne, empty twice as many bottles of bubble bath, splish-splash in heart-shaped hot tubs, canoodle in private pools, and slumber on round beds under mirrored ceilings.

Run by **Cove Haven Entertainment Resorts** (800/432-9932, www.covepoconoresorts.com, packages $225-500), the all-inclusive resorts have much in common. Each offers several suite types, all-you-can-eat breakfast and dinner (and breakfast in bed at no additional charge), a variety of indoor and outdoor activities, and live entertainment nightly. Located on the shores of Lake Wallenpaupack, **Cove Haven Resort** (194 Lakeview Dr., Lakeville, 570/226-4506) tends to draw the biggest entertainers. **Paradise Stream Resort** (6213 Carlton Rd., Mount Pocono, 570/839-8881) has the fewest amenities, but a $20 million renovation in recent years turned it into the hippest of the three. The poshest digs can be found at **Pocono Palace Resort** (206 Marquis Rd., East Stroudsburg, 570/588-6692), located just minutes from Delaware Water Gap National Recreation Area. Its multilevel Roman Tower Suites feature a king-size round bed, heart-shaped pool, dry sauna, log-burning fireplace, and seven-foot-tall champagne glass whirlpool. (All three resorts have suites with the enduringly popular champagne glass whirlpool, created in 1984 by Cove Haven founder Morris B. Wilkins.)

Guests get unlimited access to amenities at all three resorts. So couples staying at Cove Haven or Paradise Stream, which don't have a golf course, can play to their heart's content on Pocono Palace's nine-hole course. Paradise Stream and Pocono Palace guests can journey to Cove Haven for snow tubing or ice-skating. All three offer fishing, tennis, indoor and outdoor pools, mini golf, archery, and snowmobiling, among other activities.

Hotels and B&Bs

The all-inclusive ★ **Woodloch Resort** (731 Welcome Lake Rd., Hawley, 570/685-8000, www.woodloch.com, $265-368 per person all-inclusive) has been owned by the same family since 1958. The resort on Lake Teedyuskung has 1,000-plus acres with accommodations for more than 900. Lodging options range from endearingly outdated rooms with accordion dividers to modern trilevel houses with cathedral ceilings and fireplaces. Guests can lounge on a sandy beach; fish for bass, bluegill, and catfish; swim in the shimmering lake or the pool along its shore; or take to the water in a canoe, kayak, paddleboat, rowboat, or Sunfish sailboat. Winter activities include ice fishing, ice-skating, snowshoeing, and snow tubing. Woodloch is as famous for its lavish Broadway-style revue as its array of activities. The pyrotechnics-enhanced performance is held in the sizable nightclub. Entertainment is offered every night of the week. Rates include two or three meals a day, almost all activities, and entertainment. Not included: golfing at **Woodloch Springs** (732 Woodloch Dr., Hawley, 570/685-8102, www.woodloch.com/golf, greens fees $45-79), an 18-hole par-72 course. Don't confuse kid-friendly Woodloch Resort with the Lodge at Woodloch, an adults-only spa resort.

East Shore Lodging (2487 Rte. 6, Hawley, 570/226-3293, www.eastshorelodging.com, $75-200) offers reasonably priced and majorly comfy accommodations right across Route 6 from Lake Wallenpaupack's only public beach. The motel is run by the same family behind Wallenpaupack Scenic Boat Tour—also across the street—which offers hour-long boat cruises, boat slips, and boat rentals. Most of its rooms are roomy enough for four. If you really want to feel at home, reserve the second-floor king suite, which features a spacious living room and private deck. All rooms have a microwave, refrigerator, flat-screen TV, and wireless Internet. Rates include a continental breakfast.

Since 1980, ★ **The Settlers Inn** (4 Main Ave., Hawley, 570/226-2993, www.thesettlersinn.com, $166-306) has been in the hands of the Genzlinger family, whose mastery of the art of hospitality earned the inn membership in Select Registry and its farm-to-table restaurant a Wine Spectator Award of Excellence. A handsome example of the arts and crafts style both inside and out, the bed-and-breakfast is ideal for travelers who find hotels too impersonal and many B&Bs too frilly. It's also ideal for anglers: The trout-filled Lackawaxen River runs through the property. The inn has 23 guest rooms including a two-bedroom suite perfect for a family. Many feature fireplaces and hot tubs. Rates include a way-above-average breakfast. The inn's nearby sister property, **Ledges Hotel** (119 Falls Ave., Hawley, 570/226-1337, www.ledgeshotel.com, $130-375), occupies a former glass factory perched over Wallenpaupack Creek. The building isn't the only example of adaptive reuse. Guest rooms feature furnishings custom-built with wood from a nearby 19th-century silk mill. In addition to regular rooms, the boutique hotel offers two-story suites with 12-foot ceilings and spiral staircases. Stunning views come standard.

"Luxury" is a word used liberally in descriptions of **The Lodge at Woodloch** (109 River Birch Ln., Hawley, 570/685-8500, www.thelodgeatwoodloch.com, from $329/person). It's been named to *National Geographic Traveler*'s "Stay List" and *Condé Nast Traveler*'s "Hot List" and voted one of the world's best spas by readers of *Travel + Leisure*. The adults-only resort on 75 sylvan acres has 58 guest rooms and suites. Even the smallest of them have private verandas and marble bathrooms with oversized showers. But the resort's showpiece is its spa. Soaking tubs with hydro-massaging waterfalls, an outdoor whirlpool with a radiant-heated deck, and woodland views ensure that guests slip into a blissed-out state even before setting foot in one of the 27 treatment rooms. Guests can unwind in other ways: kayaking on the private 15-acre lake or golfing at **Woodloch Springs** (732 Woodloch Dr., Hawley, 570/685-8102, www.woodloch.com/golf, greens fees $45-79), an 18-hole championship course across the street from the resort. Overnight rates include three gourmet meals daily and nonalcoholic beverages. The many and various group

Woodloch Resort is on Lake Teedyuskung.

fitness classes—from meditation to cardio kickboxing—are included.

TRANSPORTATION AND SERVICES

The lake region is a driving destination. The town of Hawley, at the north end of 13-mile-long Lake Wallenpaupack, is about 90 miles northwest of New York City and 140 miles north of Philadelphia. From New York, head west on I-280 and I-80, north on Routes 15 and 206, and finally west on Route 6. From Philadelphia, head north on I-476, east on Route 22, north on Routes 33 and 402, and finally west on Route 6. **Wilkes-Barre/Scranton International Airport** (AVP, 570/602-2000, www.flyavp.com), the nearest commercial airport, is served by United Airlines, American Airlines, Delta, and the low-cost carrier Allegiant. Hawley and Honesdale can be reached by bus (845/610-2600, www.shortlinebus.com) from New York City.

If you're new to the lake region, make the **Lake Wallenpaupack Visitors Center** (2512 Rte. 6, Hawley, 570/226-2141, 9am-5pm) your first stop. Operated by the **Pocono Mountains Visitors Bureau** (www.pocono-mountains.com), the center is stocked with maps and brochures about area activities, attractions, restaurants, and lodging options. Pocono Mountains "brand ambassadors" are on hand to offer personal assistance.

The website of the **Chamber of the Northern Poconos** (570/253-1960, www.northernpoconoschamber.com)—the local chamber of commerce—is also a good resource.

Ski Region

With seven major ski areas, the Pocono Mountains are Pennsylvania's number one destination for snow sports. Most of the ski areas are in the southern part of the four-county region, in Monroe and Carbon Counties. They're not the only attraction in this swath of the state. It's home to a casino, a NASCAR track, and an outlet mall. It has resorts both historic and new. Water parks are the latest rage around here. If you're looking for a winter getaway that doesn't involve snow, a resort with an indoor water park may be just the thing.

★ SKI AREAS

First off, it's worth noting that the ski mountains of northeast Pennsylvania are modest relative to those out west. Even Blue Mountain Ski Area, which boasts the greatest vertical drop in Pennsylvania (1,082 feet), is Smurf-size compared with Colorado's slopes, where verticals of more than 4,000 feet are not uncommon. Avid athletes used to carving turns in places such as Colorado, Montana, and Utah won't have the thrill of their lives in Pennsylvania. That's not to say that the Pocono Mountains don't attract plenty of experienced skiers and snowboarders—after all, it's a lot easier and cheaper for Philadelphians with a passion for powder to get to Blue Mountain than to Telluride.

If you're new to skiing or snowboarding, the modest mountains of northeast Pennsylvania will do just fine. All of the major ski areas offer lessons. They also offer snow tubing, which means you can chicken out of skiing and still say you hit the slopes.

Blue Mountain Ski Area

Blue Mountain (1660 Blue Mountain Dr., Palmerton, 610/826-7700, www.skibluemt.com, all-day lift ticket adults $55-70, youth 6-21 $45-55, seniors 70 and older ski for free, all-day equipment rental $40, snow tubing $30 per 3-hour session) is closest to the population centers of Philadelphia and Allentown. Partly for that reason, it can get very busy on weekends and holidays. It features 39 trails on 164 skiable acres, 21 tubing lanes, and 14 lifts. Six terrain parks of varying degrees of trickiness make it popular with the young and the restless. If the kids are young and the parents are restless, babysitting is available weekends and holidays for $10 per hour.

The Slopeside Pub & Grill serves up burgers, sandwiches, salads, alcohol, and mountain vistas year-round. In warmer months, Blue Mountain switches from winter sports to disc golf, mountain biking, zip lines, and laser tag.

Camelback Mountain

Camelback (301 Resort Dr., Tannersville, 570/629-1661, www.skicamelback.com, all-day lift ticket adults $53-67, seniors and children 6-18 $45-49, all-day equipment rental $97, snow tubing $25 per weekday, $30 per 3-hour session on weekends) has the second-greatest vertical drop in the Poconos at 800 feet. It has 34 trails on 166 skiable acres, 16 lifts, and a terrain park with five trails. With 42 lanes, its snow tubing park is billed as the largest in the country. On weekends and holidays, tickets for three-hour sessions are sold on the hour starting at 9am and often sell out. It's a good idea to arrive before 9am if you have your heart set on snow tubing.

Camelback can get crowded. Location is one of its selling points: It's about three miles from exit 299 of I-80, a major east-west artery. The Crossings Premium Outlets are also at that exit, which makes Camelback a great choice if members of your party prefer shopping to snow sports.

Come spring, waterslides replace ski slopes as Camelback transforms into **Camelbeach** (www.camelbeach.com, day passes $42, seniors and children under 48 inches $32, free for children 2 and under), an outdoor water park billed as the largest in Pennsylvania. They offer discounted twilight tickets ($29, seniors and children under 48 inches $24) for entry after 3pm.

The resort has a host of other between-ski-seasons attractions, including an expansive **ropes course,** a pair of 1,000-foot **zip lines,** and two 4,000-foot zip lines stretching from the summit of Camelback Mountain to its base. The resort also tempts the adventurous with a year-round **mountain coaster,** featuring 4,500 feet of track and two 360-degree turns. Riders can control the speed of their two-person car on their way down the mountain. Left to gravity, the cars can reach speeds of 25-30 miles per hour.

The 125,000-square-foot **Aquatopia**

Blue Mountain

(10am-9pm or later daily, $59) indoor water park is also open year-round. It's at the base of the mountain and part of the hotel **Camelback Lodge** (193 Resort Dr., Tannersville, 855/515-1283, www.camelback-resort.com). Unlike Camelbeach, Aquatopia is exclusively for hotel guests. The eight-story hotel includes an adults spa, a kids spa, shops, mini golf, an arcade, and multiple restaurants.

Jack Frost Big Boulder

If you're a bargain hunter, you're going to like **Jack Frost Big Boulder** (570/443-8425, www.jfbb.com, all-day lift ticket adults $48-58, seniors and children 7-17 $35-45, children 6 and under $10, all-day equipment rental $35, snow tubing $25-47 per day, $25-27 per 3-hour session on weekends, $10 with ski lift ticket). It's actually two ski areas for the price of one. In fact, skiing both mountains is cheaper than skiing either Blue Mountain or Camelback. Dating to the 1940s, Big Boulder (357 Big Boulder Dr., Lake Harmony) is the oldest commercial ski area in Pennsylvania. Its builders played a hand in the invention of snowmaking machines. Today it's best known for its terrain parks. Jack Frost (434 Jack Frost Mountain Rd., White Haven), which opened in 1972, offers a greater vertical drop (600 feet), more slopes (20), and more lifts (12) than its older sibling, but it's not equipped for night skiing and closes at 4pm. Big Boulder stays open as late as 10pm. To get the biggest bang for your buck, hit the Jack Frost slopes in the morning and migrate to Big Boulder in the afternoon. The drive takes about 20 minutes.

WATER PARKS

The region long known for its ski mountains has in recent years emerged as a major destination for splashing good times. Lest you think that water parks are a summertime attraction, the tide has turned toward massive indoor versions.

Every spring, Camelback Mountain undergoes an extreme makeover, transforming from a ski destination to **Camelbeach Mountain Waterpark** (309 Resort Dr., Tannersville, 570/629-1662, www.camelbeach.com, adults $42, seniors and children under 48 inches tall $32, children 2 and under free). Billed as the largest outdoor water park in Pennsylvania, Camelbeach has nearly 40 rides, slides, and other attractions, from play zones for pint-size guests to the Titan, an eight-story tubing slide. The water park is open daily from mid-June through Labor Day and several weekends before that period. It opens at 10am and closes

hitting the slopes on Camelback Mountain

at 6pm or 7pm depending on the day. Come in the late afternoon for discounted admission (adults $29, seniors and children under 48 inches tall $24). But splish-splashing isn't limited to summertime. Opened in 2015, **Camelback Lodge & Aquatopia Indoor Waterpark** (193 Resort Dr., Tannersville, 855/515-1283, www.camelbackresort.com, 10am-9pm or later daily, $59) is an eight-story hotel complete with a colossal indoor water park. Seven pools and 13 slides are set under a transparent roof. It's maintained at 84 degrees year-round. The catch? You have to be a hotel guest to gain admission into Aquatopia. Out of the water, the hotel features a family entertainment center with games, a rock climbing wall, a ropes course, mini golf, laser tag, and even a kids spa.

Just minutes from Camelbeach, **Great Wolf Lodge** (1 Great Wolf Dr., Scotrun, 800/768-9653, www.greatwolf.com) features a massive indoor water park. The resort, part of a nationwide chain, became the first new Poconos resort in three decades when it opened in 2005. Alas, its water park is also reserved for registered guests. Recognizing a good thing, Split Rock Resort & Golf Club opened its own indoor water park in 2008. **H2Oooohh!** (100 Moseywood Rd., Lake Harmony, 570/722-9111, www.splitrockresort.com, adults $38, seniors $18, children under 42 inches tall $33, children 2 and under free, observer passes available) is open to the general public. It has slides, a surfing simulator, a wave pool, and play areas for little kids. Hot tubs and a tiki bar keep the grown-ups happy.

Opened in 2015 and expanded to double its original size, **Kalahari Resorts** (250 Kalahari Blvd., Pocono Manor, 877/525-2427, www.kalahariresorts.com, water park day pass $79, children under 2 free) now boasts a 220,000-square-foot indoor water park billed as the biggest in the country. Admission is included for hotel guests, who get to glide along the lazy river and slide down the looping Screaming Hyena starting at 9am, an hour before those with day passes. The water park closes at 9pm weekdays and 10pm on weekends. The African-themed resort also features a seasonal outdoor water park, a family entertainment center, shops, a spa, restaurants, and almost 1,000 guest rooms and suites.

OTHER SIGHTS

Mount Airy Casino Resort

Feeling lucky? **Mount Airy Casino Resort** (312 Woodland Rd., Mount Pocono, 877/682-4791, www.mountairycasino.com, casino 24 hours daily) has more than 1,800 slot machines and 70 table games, along with a championship golf course, a full-service spa, several restaurants, a nightclub, and 188 guest rooms. The resort is luxe enough to have earned the prestigious AAA four diamond rating. Dining options range from the 24-hour Guy Fieri's Mt. Pocono Kitchen to an upscale steak house to a classic casino buffet. The buffet is best known for its Sunday brunch ($26), which features an elaborate seafood station.

Mount Airy is one of two casinos in northeast Pennsylvania. The other, Mohegan Sun Pocono, is about an hour away in Wilkes-Barre.

Pocono Raceway

NASCAR fans flock to **Pocono Raceway** (1234 Long Pond Rd., Long Pond, 800/722-3929, www.poconoraceway.com) for two 400-mile Monster Energy Cup Series races: the Pocono 400 in June and the Overton's 400 in July. The 2.5-mile track is triangular in shape with straights of varying lengths and severe turns, each with a different degree of banking. Nicknamed "the Tricky Triangle," it's unlike any other track used for NASCAR's top racing series. In 2013 IndyCar racing returned to Pocono Raceway after a hiatus of 20-plus years. The ABC Supply 500, part of the Verizon IndyCar Series, is held in August.

Family owned since its inception in 1968, Pocono prides itself on its fair-like atmosphere. Grandstand seating starts at $45 for the NASCAR races and $25 for the IndyCar race. Premium seating options range from an open-air hospitality area ($150 for race day) to air-conditioned skyboxes ($500 for entire race weekend). Fans can pitch a tent or park an RV on the grounds for the duration of a race weekend.

Wannabe car racers can get their training wheels at Pocono. **StockCar Racing Experience** (570/643-6921, www.877stockcar.com) is a chance to suit up, strap in, and see the track from the inside of a 600-horsepower vehicle. Brave souls can either ride shotgun with an instructor or get behind the wheel. A ride-along is $139-149 for three laps, $278-298 for six laps. Four laps in the driver's seat will set you back $349-399. For drivers who can't get enough, there are 8-lap, 16-lap, 24-lap, and 32-lap options, plus opportunities for more advanced training. You must be at least 18 and have experience in operating a manual transmission to drive. Riders can be as young as 14, but both parents must be present for those under 18. StockCar Racing Experience, in business since 1998, also offers a team pro kart racing program. Pocono Raceway is also used by the locally based **Bertil Roos Racing School** (570/646-7227, www.racenow.com), the place to go for seat time in a Formula 2000 race car.

FESTIVALS AND EVENTS

Split Rock Resort & Golf Club (Lake Harmony, 570/722-9111, www.splitrockresort.com) hosts two popular tasting events: the **Great Tastes of Pennsylvania Wine & Food Festival** in June and the **Great Brews Classic Beer Festival** in November. The former is held outdoors and, true to its name, focuses on Pennsylvania wineries. The latter is an indoor festival that showcases breweries from around the country. Both feature live music, food and craft vendors, and a pairing dinner.

SHOPPING

The Crossings Premium Outlets

With 100 stores, **The Crossings Premium Outlets** (1000 Premium Outlets Dr., Tannersville, 570/629-4650, www.premiumoutlets.com, 10am-7pm Sun.-Thurs., 10am-9pm Fri.-Sat. Jan.-Mar., 10am-9pm Mon.-Sat., 10am-8pm Sun. Apr.-Dec.) are good reason for people who aren't fond of outdoor recreation to head to the Poconos. Pennsylvania's sales tax exemption on clothes and shoes lures many New Yorkers and New Jerseyans to the outlet mall, located off exit 299 of I-80. Stores

Pocono Raceway

include Banana Republic, J.Crew, Coach, and Michael Kors.

Specialty Shops

Got a sweet tooth? Swing by **Callie's Candy Kitchen** (Rte. 390, Mountainhome, 570/595-2280, www.calliescandy.com, 11am-5pm Sat.-Sun. Jan.-early Feb., 10am-5pm daily mid-Feb.-Dec.) and **Callie's Pretzel Factory** (Rte. 390, Cresco, 570/595-3257, 11am-5pm Sat.-Sun. Jan.-early Feb., 10am-5pm Sat.-Sun. mid-Feb.-Apr., 10am-5pm daily May-Dec.). Local legend Harry Callie was 19 when he began selling handmade candy in 1952. He died in 2013 but the shop, which sells gummies, licorice, fudge, and chocolate-covered everything, is still in the family. The Pretzel Factory, which opened in the 1980s, makes hard and soft pretzels as well as flavored popcorn. A window-lined wall gives customers the opportunity to observe the pretzel-making process.

ACCOMMODATIONS

Resorts

The **Aquatopia Indoor Waterpark** at **Camelback Lodge** (193 Resort Dr., Tannersville, 855/515-1283, www.camelbackresort.com, from $170) is for hotel guests only. Away from the looping slides and lagoons, the resort offers 453 guest rooms and suites, spas, restaurants, and a family entertainment center. Camelback is a ski destination in the winter. The outdoor water park **Camelbeach** is open seasonally.

The African-themed **Kalahari Resorts** (250 Kalahari Blvd., Pocono Manor, 877/525-2427, www.kalahariresorts.com, $200-400) is a lodging option where all of your needs—from sleeping to food to activities—can be met on-site. The hotel has a whopping 977 guest rooms. Its indoor water park is billed as the biggest in the country. You don't need to be staying at the resort to access it.

The **Mount Airy Casino Resort** (312 Woodland Rd., Mount Pocono, 877/682-4791, www.mountairycasino.com, from $170) offers 188 rooms and suites with modern furnishings, spacious bathrooms, pillow-top beds, and LCD TVs. The resort's central location—just minutes from the Crossings Premium Outlets and Camelback Mountain Resort and within half an hour of Delaware Water Gap National Recreation Area and Pocono Raceway—is a major selling point. That being said, it's entirely possible to while away a day without leaving Mount Airy, even if you're not a gambler. In addition to a 24-hour casino, the resort has an 18-hole golf course, a first-rate spa, and a tradition of booking well-known entertainers. Its restaurants are well above average for the region but on the pricey side.

GREAT WOLF LODGE

Opened in 2005, **Great Wolf Lodge** (1 Great Wolf Dr., Scotrun, 800/768-9653, www.greatwolf.com, from $240) kicked off the trend of indoor water parks in the Pocono Mountains. Its water park is for hotel guests only—which means shorter lines. The family-friendly resort's amenities include a bowling alley with half-length lanes, a large arcade, a 4-D theater, and a glow-in-the-dark mini-golf course. Great Wolf has two spas: the tranquil Elements Spa Salon and an ice-cream-themed kids spa.

On-site eateries include a Starbucks coffee shop and the Loose Moose, where breakfast and dinner are buffet-style. Food isn't included in room rates—and it isn't cheap—so plan to dine off-site if you're on a budget. Great Wolf's 401 suites come in a dozen styles. A real hit with pup-size guests: themed suites with bunk beds in a walled-off space resembling a cave, tent, or log cabin.

SKYTOP LODGE

If the stately stone manor at the heart of **Skytop Lodge** (1 Skytop Lodge Rd., Skytop, 855/345-7759, www.skytop.com, from $240) strikes you as an exclusive retreat for the exceptionally wealthy, that's because it used to be. Built in the 1920s, it welcomed the likes of Lucille Ball. Celebs still check in from time to time, but these days Skytop specializes in giving regular folks the star treatment. At 5,500 acres, the resort is larger than many towns in northeast Pennsylvania. And it offers more recreational opportunities. Among its amenities: a spa, a championship golf course, a private trout stream, a 75-acre lake, 30 miles of hiking trails, horseback rides, a climbing wall, and paintball fields. Skytop even has its own ski hill. With a vertical drop of 295 feet and four gentle slopes, it won't knock anyone's wool socks off. But for novices, it's an appealing alternative to crowded ski mountains. Ski lessons for children as young as two are available. Other wintertime activities include ice-skating, tobogganing, snowshoeing, and even dogsledding. (Dogsledding is a year-round option. When there's no snow on the ground, Skytop's huskies pull a golf cart or off-road vehicle instead of a sled.)

The resort offers a variety of accommodations and booking options, from room-only rates to packages that include meals and activities. Perched on a high plateau, the historic Main Lodge has 125 guest rooms and suites, heavy wooden furniture and plaid accents, and a buttoned-up ambience. Golfers gravitate toward the more intimate Inn at Skytop, located on the course designed more than 80 years ago by the first president of the PGA of America. With its two-story atrium, exposed beams, and cozy cocktail lounge, the 20-room inn recalls a European ski chalet. Its 135-seat restaurant offers great views and a relatively casual dining experience. Families may prefer to stay in one of Skytop's four-bedroom cottages, which have conveniences such as washers, dryers, and small refrigerators but no common areas. The interconnecting bedrooms can be rented individually.

B&Bs

Its hilltop setting is reason enough to splurge on a stay at ★ **The French Manor Inn and Spa** (50 Huntingdon Dr., South Sterling, 570/676-3244, www.thefrenchmanor.com, from $250). Need more reasons? How about the fine-dining restaurant, named one of Pennsylvania's best by *Gourmet* magazine? Or the green spa, where couples can enjoy side-by-side massages by a crackling fire? **Le Spa Forêt** also beckons with an indoor saltwater pool and hot tub. The B&B is set in four buildings: a stone chateau built in the 1930s, a remodeled carriage house with country-style furnishings, La Maisonneuve (French for "the new house") with its private balconies and in-room whirlpool tubs, and the even newer spa building. Its location north of the Poconos'

Great Wolf Lodge

major ski areas is also convenient to the lake region.

TRANSPORTATION AND SERVICES

The ski region is very much a driving destination. Blue Mountain, the southernmost ski area, is about 90 minutes north of Philadelphia via I-476 and only 30 minutes north of Allentown via Route 145. New Yorkers can also arrive in about two hours via I-78 west. Most of the ski region's major attractions can be found along I-80, a major east-west artery.

If you're driving to the ski region from New Jersey or New York, stop at a Pennsylvania **welcome center,** where you'll be up to your eyeballs in information. The I-80 welcome center is a half mile west of the Pennsylvania-New Jersey border at exit 310, the I-84 welcome center is a mile west of the Pennsylvania-New York border at exit 53, and the I-81 welcome center is a half mile south of the Pennsylvania-New York border. Personalized travel counseling is available 7am-7pm daily.

The website of the **Pocono Mountains Visitors Bureau** (www.poconomountains.com) is a good source of information.

Jim Thorpe and Vicinity

Tucked into the hills and dotted with charming Victorian buildings, the town of Jim Thorpe was known to 19th-century rail excursionists as the "Switzerland of America." Today it's better known as a gateway to outdoor adventure. Rafters, canoeists, and kayakers come for the Lehigh River, which flows through town. South of town, the river snakes languidly toward its confluence with the Delaware River. To the north, the Lehigh Gorge offers some of the most exciting white water in the East. Bikers, hikers, and even cross-country skiers come for the river-hugging 26-mile trail between Jim Thorpe and White Haven to its north. Blue Mountain Ski Area and Jack Frost Big Boulder are just 20-30 minutes from Jim Thorpe, making it a good base of operations for alpine skiing enthusiasts. The waterfalls of Ricketts Glen State Park are a little over an hour northwest. It's

a view of Jim Thorpe

okay if you show up unprepared for adventure. Finding an outfitter in Jim Thorpe is easier than finding a Starbucks in Seattle.

Prior to 1954, Jim Thorpe was called Mauch Chunk (pronounced mock-CHUNK). In the 19th century, Mauch Chunk thrived as a transportation hub for the anthracite coal so plentiful in the hills around it. Fortunes were made and mansions and grand hotels were built. It's said that half of America's millionaires lived in Mauch Chunk at one time. By the 1950s, however, the town was in sorry condition. The decline of the coal and railroad industries and the Great Depression had sapped its wealth. In the hopes that a new name would give it new life as a tourist destination, Mauch Chunk officials struck a deal with the widow of Jim Thorpe, former Olympian and pro football and basketball player. Thorpe, subject of a 1951 biopic starring Burt Lancaster, had been born in Oklahoma and died in California and had no ties to Mauch Chunk whatsoever. No matter. In exchange for his remains, Mauch Chunk and its neighbor across the Lehigh, East Mauch Chunk, merged under the name Jim Thorpe and erected a 20-ton mausoleum for the Native American sports star.

The town's turnaround wasn't immediate, but turn around it did—though it's still a ways from the era of anthracite fortunes.

SIGHTS

Most visitors to Jim Thorpe are more interested in outdoor adventure than local history, but the town formerly known as Mauch Chunk has a past as colorful as the Lehigh Gorge in fall. The **Mauch Chunk Museum** (41 W. Broadway, Jim Thorpe, 570/325-9190, www.mauchchunkmuseum.com, 11am-5pm daily summer, Sat.-Sun. winter, adults $5, children under 8 $2) does a fine job of telling its story, which is also the story of 19th-century coal mining and transportation innovations. Housed in a former church, the museum chronicles not just the town's industrial golden age but also its decline in the early 20th century, its peculiar decision to trade its name for the body and name of a sports icon, and its revitalization as Jim Thorpe.

The **Old Jail Museum** (128 W. Broadway, Jim Thorpe, 570/325-5259, www.theoldjail-museum.com, noon-4:30pm Thurs.-Tues. Memorial Day-Labor Day, noon-4:30pm Sat.-Sun. Sept.-Oct., adults $10, seniors and students $8, children 6-12 $5) zeroes in on a grim chapter in local history. In the late 1870s, seven Irish coal miners known as "Molly Maguires" were hanged there for terrorizing and murdering mine bosses. A tour of the museum, a fortress-like structure that served as the county jail from 1871 until 1995, is a walk on the macabre side, complete with a dungeon and gallows. Its most irresistible selling point is a dash of the supernatural. Legend has it that on the day of his execution, one of the condemned coal miners pressed a dirty hand against the wall of his cell and swore that his handprint would remain forever as proof of his innocence. Wardens tried to remove the mark, washing, painting, and even re-plastering the wall. But the handprint always returned, or so it's said. See for yourself in cell 17.

For insight into the coal miner's life, head to **No. 9 Coal Mine & Museum** (9 Dock St., Lansford, 570/645-7074, www.no9mine-museum.wixsite.com/museum, 11am-4pm Wed.-Sun. May-Oct., adults $10, children 5-10 $6.50, children under 4 free), about 10 miles southwest of Jim Thorpe. A train carries visitors into the belly of an anthracite mine, active from 1855 to 1972 and a tourist attraction since 2002. The guided tour continues on foot to areas including a miner's hospital and a passageway originally used by coal-hauling mules. The mine's temperature is cool, so dress appropriately. The museum, displaying tools and a tableau of a coal miner's kitchen, is aboveground in a former "wash shanty," where miners tidied themselves up after their shift.

★ Lehigh Gorge State Park

Lehigh Gorge State Park (570/443-0400, www.dcnr.pa.gov/stateparks, sunrise-sunset daily, free) features some of the best white water in Pennsylvania. It contains about 30 miles of the Lehigh River, from the Francis E. Walter Dam in the north to Jim Thorpe in the south. This section offers Class II and III rapids in a season that stretches from March through October and sometimes into November. Left in the hands of Mother Nature, the white-water season would have been woefully short. But the U.S. Army Corps of Engineers, which manages the dam, releases loads of water on select weekends, providing for rollicking rides even during the hot months of July and August.

Inexperienced paddlers should engage the services of a guide, and there's no shortage of them in or near Jim Thorpe. **Pocono Whitewater** (1519 Rte. 903, 800/944-8392, www.whitewaterrafting.com), **Jim Thorpe River Adventures** (1 Adventure Ln., 570/325-2570, www.jtraft.com), and **Whitewater Rafting Adventures** (Rte. 209 and Hunter St./Rte. 93, Nesquehoning, 570/669-9127, www.adventurerafting.com), all within 10 minutes of each other, offer **white-water rafting** through the park as well as float trips on the milder waters south of Jim Thorpe. There's also a rafting outfitter near the midsection of the park, **Whitewater Challengers** (288 N. Stagecoach Rd., Weatherly, 570/443-9532, www.whitewater-challengers.com).

The 26-mile **Lehigh Gorge Trail,** which follows an abandoned railroad corridor along the river, has been called one of "America's sweetest rides" by *Outside* magazine. The **biking** is especially sweet in October, at the peak of fall foliage. Start at the park's northern access area, White Haven, for an all-downhill ride to Jim Thorpe. (It's a very slight downhill grade, so you'll still break a sweat.) All of the above-mentioned outfitters offer bike rentals and shuttle service. In winter the trail is open for **cross-country skiing.** The 15-mile section from White Haven to Penn Haven Junction is also open for **snowmobiling.** To reach the park's northern access area from I-80, take exit 273 and follow Route 940 east to the White Haven Shopping Center. Turn right on Main Street and bear right.

Experienced **hikers** may find the rail-trail too tame. A never-boring alternative is the **Glen Onoko Falls Trail** (1.5 miles) located on state game lands adjacent to the park. The terrain is steep and sometimes treacherous—"we're always in there rescuing people," confides one park ranger—but the payoff is rich. Come in spring to see the cascading falls at

Lehigh Gorge State Park

their most ferocious. The trail begins at the park's southern access area, Glen Onoko, reached from Coalport Road in Jim Thorpe.

If you have a mind to raft, bike, and hike all in one day, you may be a little bit crazy, but you're not alone. Pocono Whitewater's "Big Day Out" is a chance to do just that. It starts with a hearty breakfast and ends with dinner around a bonfire. In between, participants bike the rail-trail, hike to an abandoned railroad tunnel, and raft the Lehigh. The $110 price tag includes all the necessary gear, shuttle service, and meals.

LEHIGH GORGE SCENIC RAILWAY

Paddling the river is one way to see Lehigh Gorge State Park. Biking the rail-trail alongside the river is another. The deliciously lazy way: riding a train through the deep gorge. **Lehigh Gorge Scenic Railway** (1 Susquehanna St., Jim Thorpe, 570/325-8485, www.lgsry.com, Sat.-Sun. May, Sept., and Nov., Fri.-Sun. June, daily July-Aug., Wed.-Sun. Oct., select days Dec.) began offering train excursions in 2006, more than 40 years after railroads in the region put the brakes on passenger service. The 70-minute trip begins in Jim Thorpe's historic district at a restored train station that now houses a visitors center. The train follows the curves of the Lehigh River for eight miles before returning the way it came. If it's a beautiful day, make a beeline for the open-air car or the caboose platform. The excursion is so popular in October that rides are cut to 45 minutes to squeeze more in.

★ Ricketts Glen State Park

Exceptionally scenic hiking trails make **Ricketts Glen State Park** (570/477-5675, www.dcnr.pa.gov/stateparks) one of northeast Pennsylvania's main attractions. The park is 75 minutes from Jim Thorpe heading north on Interstate 476 to the industrial city of Wilkes-Barre and then west on Route 188 to Route 487. If you're coming from the Poconos ski region instead, it's about the same distance.

Backpacker magazine has for years heaped accolades on the 13,050-acre park, which includes 22 named waterfalls. The highest of them, **Ganoga Falls,** is 94 feet tall. The waterfalls lie in a section of the park known as the **Glens Natural Area,** a registered National Natural Landmark with giant pines, hemlocks, and oaks. Many of the wide trees are more than 500 years old and dizzyingly tall. Twenty-six miles of trails crisscross the park. The one-mile **Evergreen Trail** is an

Ricketts Glen State Park

The Story of Jim Thorpe, the Man

Loads of towns in Pennsylvania are eponyms for a long-buried historical figure. The town of Jim Thorpe is unusual in that it's named for a man who made his mark in the 20th century.

James Francis Thorpe was born in 1887 in a single-room cabin in what is now Oklahoma and was then known as Indian Territory. His birth name, Wa-Tho-Huk, meant "Bright Path." In 1904 he began attending Carlisle Indian School, a boarding school in Carlisle, Pennsylvania. It was there that Thorpe found his calling: athletics. In addition to playing football under legendary coach Glenn "Pop" Warner, he competed in track and field, baseball, lacrosse, and even ballroom dancing. In 1912 the 24-year-old sailed to Europe for the Stockholm Olympics. He won the pentathlon and the decathlon by wide margins, setting records that stood for decades. He was celebrated with a ticker-tape parade in New York.

The following year, things took an ugly turn. After a newspaper reported that Thorpe had played two seasons of semiprofessional baseball in North Carolina, he was stripped of his gold medals. His records were struck from the books. But the ordeal didn't sour Thorpe on athletics. The six-foot-one phenom played six seasons of professional baseball for teams including the New York Giants (now the San Francisco Giants). Professional football also came calling. He played both sports for several years before retiring from baseball in 1919. His career in pro football continued for another decade and included a stint with the Chicago Cardinals (now the Arizona Cardinals). Thorpe was 41 when he finally hung up his cleats.

Over the next two decades, the father of seven struggled to make a living. He held a string of menial jobs, including as a ditchdigger and a bouncer. In 1950 Thorpe was voted greatest athlete of the first half of the century in an Associated Press poll, beating out baseball great Babe Ruth. The following year, the Associated Press reported that he was "flat broke." He died on March 28, 1953, after suffering a heart attack in his trailer home in Lomita, California.

The posthumous honors were many. In 1954 the Pennsylvania towns of Mauch Chunk and East Mauch Chunk merged and took the name of the multisport star. President Richard Nixon proclaimed April 16, 1973, as "Jim Thorpe Day," noting that "millions of young people who aspire to achievements transcending a disadvantaged background continue to take heart from Jim Thorpe's example." In 1982 his supporters won a hard-fought battle to have his Olympic titles reinstated.

Visitors to Jim Thorpe, the town, can learn about Jim Thorpe, the man, at the **Jim Thorpe Memorial,** his final resting place (though he never set foot in the town when alive). Located along Route 903 on the northeast fringe of town, the memorial features a bronze statue of a football-toting Thorpe and an abstract sculpture, *The Spirit of Thunder and Lightning.* Flags representing America, Pennsylvania, and the Olympics stand behind his gravestone, inscribed with the words of King Gustav V of Sweden. The town pays tribute to its namesake on the third weekend of May. The **Jim Thorpe Birthday Celebration** (888/546-8467, www.jimthorpe.org, free) kicks off with a Native American ritual at the memorial, but most festivities, including a torch-lighting ceremony, take place at Josiah White Park in the heart of town.

easy hike through one of the oldest forest stands in Pennsylvania. The most talked-about trek is 7.2 miles long and passes by 21 waterfalls. It's called the **Falls Trail,** for obvious reasons, and it's accessible from several parking areas. The Lake Rose parking lot, at the end of a dirt road across from the park's campground, provides the closest access but fills up quickly. The less convenient options are the beach parking lots and a lot on Route 118 about two miles east of the town of Red Rock. It's a challenging trail: often rocky, sometimes slippery, and very steep in places. You can skip the lower section, trimming the trek to 3.2 miles, and still see most of the waterfalls.

Hiking isn't the only draw. The 245-acre **Lake Jean** allows for swimming and boating (electric motors only) in the warmer months and year-round fishing. Boat rentals are available in the summer. Hunting and trapping are allowed on more than 10,000 acres of the park, which abuts some 83,000 acres of state game lands. Horseback riding is permitted on certain trails and roads within the park. **Braces Stables** (62 Jamison City Rd., Benton, 570/925-5253, www.bracesstables.com), just outside the park, offers one- to two-hour trail rides for a reasonable $35-50 per person. In winter Ricketts Glen attracts cross-country skiers, snowshoers, snowmobilers, and ice climbers.

The park has a modern **campground** (reservations 888/727-2757, http://pennsylvaniastateparks.reserveamerica.com) with 120 tent and trailer sites, some of which are available year-round. More than half are on a peninsula extending into Lake Jean. Ten modern cabins can be rented year-round.

ENTERTAINMENT AND EVENTS

Concert Venues

The Beach Boys, Cheap Trick, and Kenny Rogers are among the many varied acts that have played **Penn's Peak** (325 Maury Rd., Jim Thorpe, 866/605-7325, www.pennspeak.com), a mountaintop venue with lofty ceilings and a capacity of 1,800. Its luncheon and dinner shows often sell out weeks in advance. The picturesque views from the open-air decks and patios are alone worth the price of a ticket.

Ten minutes away is the **Mauch Chunk Opera House** (14 W. Broadway, Jim Thorpe, 570/325-0249, www.mauchchunkoperahouse.com), built in 1881 as a combo farmers market and concert hall. Once a regular stop on the vaudeville circuit, the opera house became a movie theater in the 1920s and later a warehouse for a pocketbook manufacturer. Today it's once again a venue for live entertainment. Operated by the Mauch Chunk Historical Society, the acoustically superior opera house seats 370. It's a favorite venue of Canadian folk trio the Wailin' Jennys, who recorded a live album there in 2008.

Festivals and Events

The white-water season may be winding down in October, but Jim Thorpe bustles more than ever. People pour into town on the first three weekends of the month, known as **Fall Foliage Weekends** (throughout Jim Thorpe, 888/546-8467, www.jimthorpe.org, free and paid events). The leaf peeping is superb, but it's not even the main draw. The festival features free music events at four stages, ticketed shows at the Mauch Chunk Opera House, train rides through the gorgeous Lehigh Gorge, and vendors selling everything from cheesesteaks and corn dogs to quilts and mittens. Organizers recommend arriving bright and early to avoid heavy traffic into town. If you're planning to spend the night, book well in advance—and brace yourself for peak rates.

FOOD

For a small town with big appeal to outdoorsy types, Jim Thorpe has a surprisingly diverse food landscape—from hoagies and pizza to handmade pasta and escargot.

With its full-service bar and laid-back atmosphere, **Molly Maguires Pub & Steakhouse** (5 Hazard Sq., Jim Thorpe, 570/325-4563, www.jimthorpedining.com, 11am-10pm Sun.-Thurs., 11am-11pm Fri.-Sat., $8-25) is often the most happening spot in town. Its proprietors hail from Dublin and the kitchen dishes out Irish classics along with plenty of American pub grub. The half-pound burger topped with caramelized Guinness onions is a local favorite. Despite the flat-screen TVs, there's an old-timey feel to the place. It occupies the circa 1830 Hotel Switzerland, one of the oldest commercial buildings in Jim Thorpe. A large deck is an appealing alternative to the bar area.

Owned by a husband-and-wife team, ★ **Moya** (24 Race St., Jim Thorpe,

570/325-8530, www.jimthorpemoya.com, 5pm-9pm Mon.-Tues. and Thurs., 5pm-10pm Fri.-Sat., 5pm-8pm Sun., $20-30) showcases his culinary skills and her artistic talents. Chef Heriberto Yunda got his start cooking for American oil company executives in his native Ecuador and lent his talents to restaurants in New York City and Istanbul before moving to Pennsylvania in 2002. Named for his hometown, Moya is decorated with colorful, energetic abstract paintings by Yunda's wife, Stephanie Verme. The menu changes frequently. Expect dishes like braised lamb shank, polenta with gorgonzola sauce, red curry shrimp, and roasted quail. Moya draws a lot of locals and is always packed on weekends; a reservation will spare you the disappointment of being turned away. The service can be hit-or-miss, especially when the house is full, but the food is unassailable.

ACCOMMODATIONS

Camping

If the purpose of your visit is outdoor adventure, pitch a tent at **Adventure Campground** (288 N. Stagecoach Rd., Weatherly, 570/443-9532, www.whitewaterchallengers.com, Apr.-Oct., campsite $7.50/person). It's operated by Whitewater Challengers, a rafting, kayaking, and biking outfitter whose headquarters is a short walk from the campground. Whitewater Challengers also offers zip-lining, paintball programs, boxed lunches, and breakfast and dinner buffets, taking the hassle out of planning action-packed days. The campground has bathrooms, hot showers, and volleyball and basketball courts. Don't have a tent? Tent rentals ($35/night for the tent plus $7.50/person) and rustic bunkhouses ($48/night plus $7.50/person) are available. Reserve either well in advance. The campground occasionally admits RVs; call for clearance.

A better choice for RV vacationers is the immaculate **StoneyBrook Estates Campground** (1435 Germans Rd., Lehighton, 570/386-4088, www.stoneybrookestates.com, campsite $49-59 for up to 4 people, $314/week). It's about 12 miles south of Jim Thorpe.

Hotels and B&Bs

During its heyday in the late 1800s, the town now known as Jim Thorpe was a tourist destination on par with Niagara Falls—so scenic that it was called the "Switzerland of

Shops line Broadway in Jim Thorpe

America." More than half a dozen grand hotels sprang up including ★ **The Inn at Jim Thorpe** (24 Broadway, Jim Thorpe, 800/329-2599, www.innjt.com, $110-390), built in 1849 and originally called the New American Hotel. Set in the heart of the small historic district, the 44-room hotel has floral carpets, tin ceilings, period furnishings, and a friendly staff. Accommodations range from generously sized standard rooms to suites with whirlpools and gas fireplaces. Cast-iron balconies dotted with wicker rockers overlook Broadway's shops, restaurants, and galleries. The on-site restaurant has live music nightly. In the warmer months, The Inn at Jim Thorpe is a popular base camp for adventures in nearby Lehigh Gorge State Park, so reserve well in advance. No luck? The hotel also books rooms at two sister properties with comparable rates: **55** (55 Broadway), a restored Victorian building across the street from the inn with six rooms, and the more basic **Broadway House** (44-46 W. Broadway), a 13-room guesthouse a few blocks away. Check-in for both properties is at the main inn. All three properties have free Wi-Fi, but note that 55 and Broadway House lack elevators and do not have telephones in the guest rooms.

The three spacious suites at **Suites on Broadway** (97 Broadway, 570/325-3540, www.suitesonbroadway.com, $160-245) are as private as can be. It's like having a little apartment for the night. The complimentary breakfast is stocked in the in-room refrigerator—no communal table to face first thing in the morning. Owners Marianne and Darryl Monteleone are accessible but not in the way. Find them downstairs at women's clothing shop Marianne Monteleone Design.

For a homier experience with a hot breakfast, look no farther than **The Parsonage Bed & Breakfast** (61 W. Broadway, 570/325-4462, www.theparsonagebandb.com, $110-265). Built in 1844, the building was the home of Reverend Richard Webster. The B&B is bursting with bright artwork, etchings, antiques, and cozy spots to put your feet up. Gourmet breakfasts are cooked by owners Michael Rivkin and Jeffri Coleman, who met in culinary school in the 1970s. The four en-suite rooms each have their own design.

The Inn at Jim Thorpe

TRANSPORTATION AND SERVICES

Jim Thorpe is about 30 miles northwest of Allentown and 80 miles northwest of Philadelphia via I-476. The nearest commercial airport is **Lehigh Valley International Airport** (ABE, 800/359-5842, www.flyvia.com) in Allentown. **Wilkes-Barre/Scranton International Airport** (AVP, 570/602-2000, www.flyavp.com) is also within an hour's drive.

The **Pocono Mountains Visitors Bureau** (www.poconomountains.com) operates a visitors center in Jim Thorpe's historic train station (2 Lehigh Ave., 570/325-3673, 9:30am-5:30pm daily).

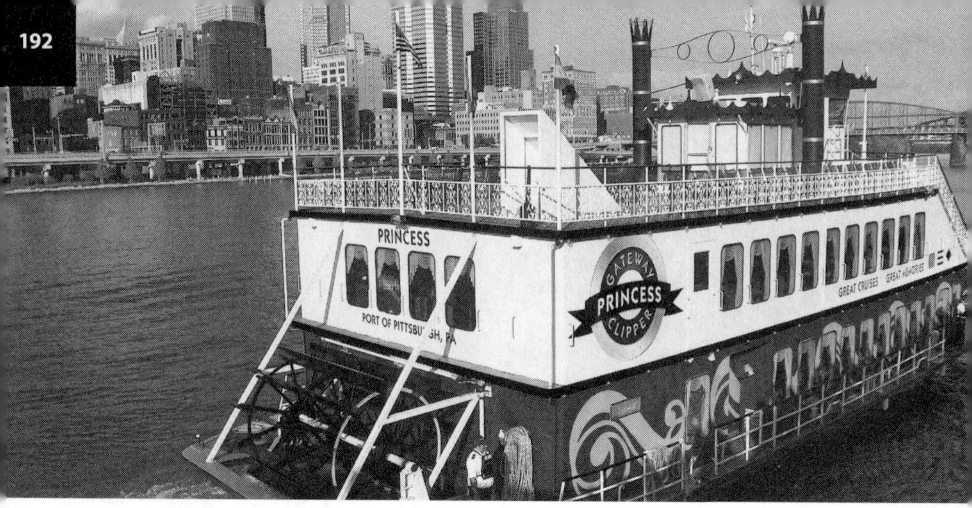

Pittsburgh

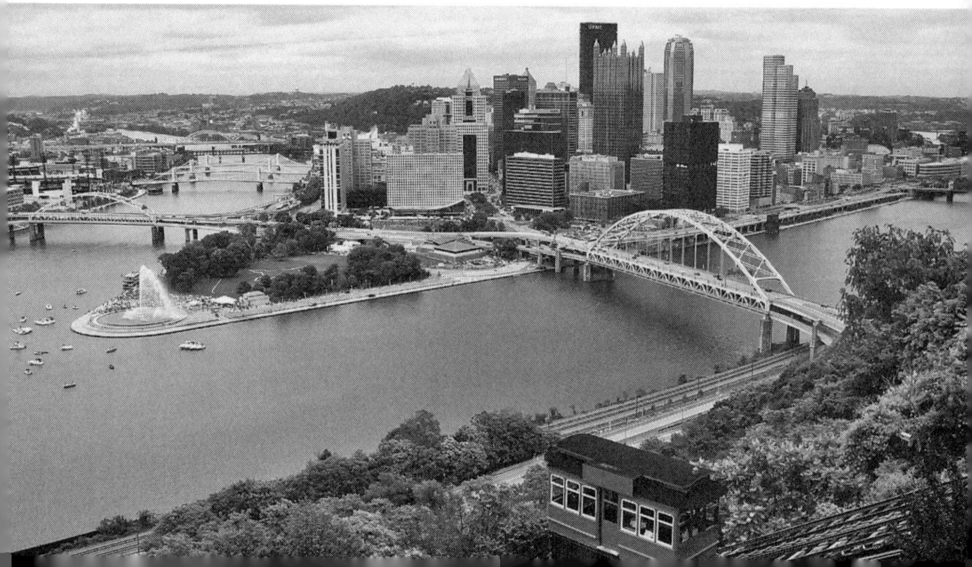

Ask people what they think when they hear "Pittsburgh," and they're liable to answer "steel." What they're picturing is the Pittsburgh of old, a place nicknamed "Smoky City" and described in an 1868 magazine article as "hell with the lid off." That image is as current as petticoats. The 260-year-old city is no longer an industrial powerhouse. In steel's place: lush parks, world-class museums, and a skyline that inspires accolades from even the most cosmopolitan of visitors. A writer for the *New Yorker* who visited in 1990 called it one of the three most beautiful cities in the world, along with Paris and St. Petersburg, Russia. "If Pittsburgh were situated somewhere in the heart of Europe," he wrote, "tourists would eagerly journey hundreds of miles out of their way to visit it."

Pittsburgh is a work in progress. Something is always being knocked down. Something bigger is always rising. Shuttered factories, abandoned warehouses, obsolete railyards, and even churches have been repurposed. The Cork Factory doesn't cut corks these days. It's a luxury apartment complex. The opulent Grand Concourse at Station Square isn't a railroad terminal. It's a seafood restaurant. The "Burgh" will make you a believer in reincarnation.

If you're coming from the international airport, your tour begins when you emerge from the tunnels bored through Mount Washington. The visual feast laid out before you—rivers, bridges, and uncommonly shaped buildings—has placed Pittsburgh near the top of best-skyline lists. The city is famous for its hills, too. You need only scan the names of its 90 neighborhoods to understand the topography: Brighton Heights, Highland Park, Southside Slopes, Squirrel Hill. Exploring them is both anthropology and exercise.

Leave time for the countryside. Southeast of the city in the Laurel Highlands region, you'll find the state's largest ski resort, highest mountain, largest cave, and most decorated restaurant. You'll also find three houses by Frank Lloyd Wright, America's favorite architect.

Pittsburgh is working overtime to shake its outdated image. It may one day succeed

Previous: Gateway Clipper riverboat; one of Pittsburgh's inclines on Mount Washington. **Above:** Giant Heinz ketchup bottle at Senator John Heinz History Center.

Look for ★ to find recommended sights, activities, dining, and lodging.

HIGHLIGHTS

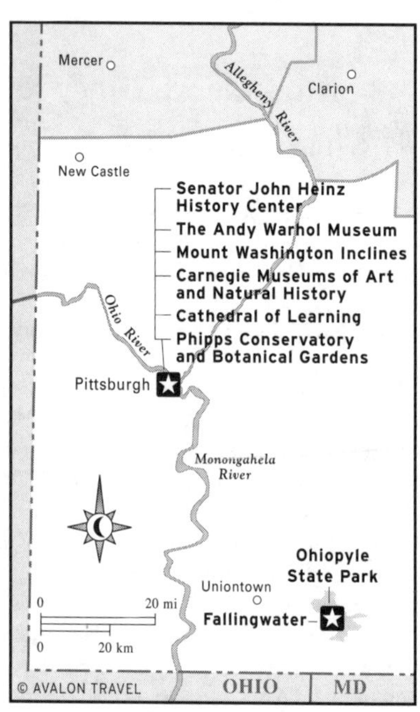

★ **Senator John Heinz History Center:** Gain a new appreciation for southwestern Pennsylvania at the state's largest history museum (page 201).

★ **The Andy Warhol Museum:** One of the country's best-known and most provocative artists gets a multilevel museum all to himself (page 202).

★ **Mount Washington Inclines:** The sweeping city and river views from the top of the Monongahela and Duquesne Inclines are especially captivating at night (page 207).

★ **Carnegie Museums of Art and Natural History:** Born of industrialist Andrew Carnegie's largess, the conjoined museums have grown into international sensations (pages 209 and 210).

★ **Cathedral of Learning:** The facade of this architectural paean to higher education is impressive, but it's the inside you don't want to miss (page 211).

★ **Phipps Conservatory and Botanical Gardens:** Wander through the floral displays in Pittsburgh's "crystal palace" and you'll forget you're anywhere near a bustling city (page 213).

★ **Ohiopyle State Park:** This gorgeous expanse offers some of the best white-water boating in the eastern United States, plus access to the Great Allegheny Passage rail-trail (page 240).

★ **Fallingwater:** Sure, it's a 90-minute drive from the city, but Frank Lloyd Wright's masterpiece is worth crossing an ocean to see. Lots of people do (page 242).

Pittsburgh

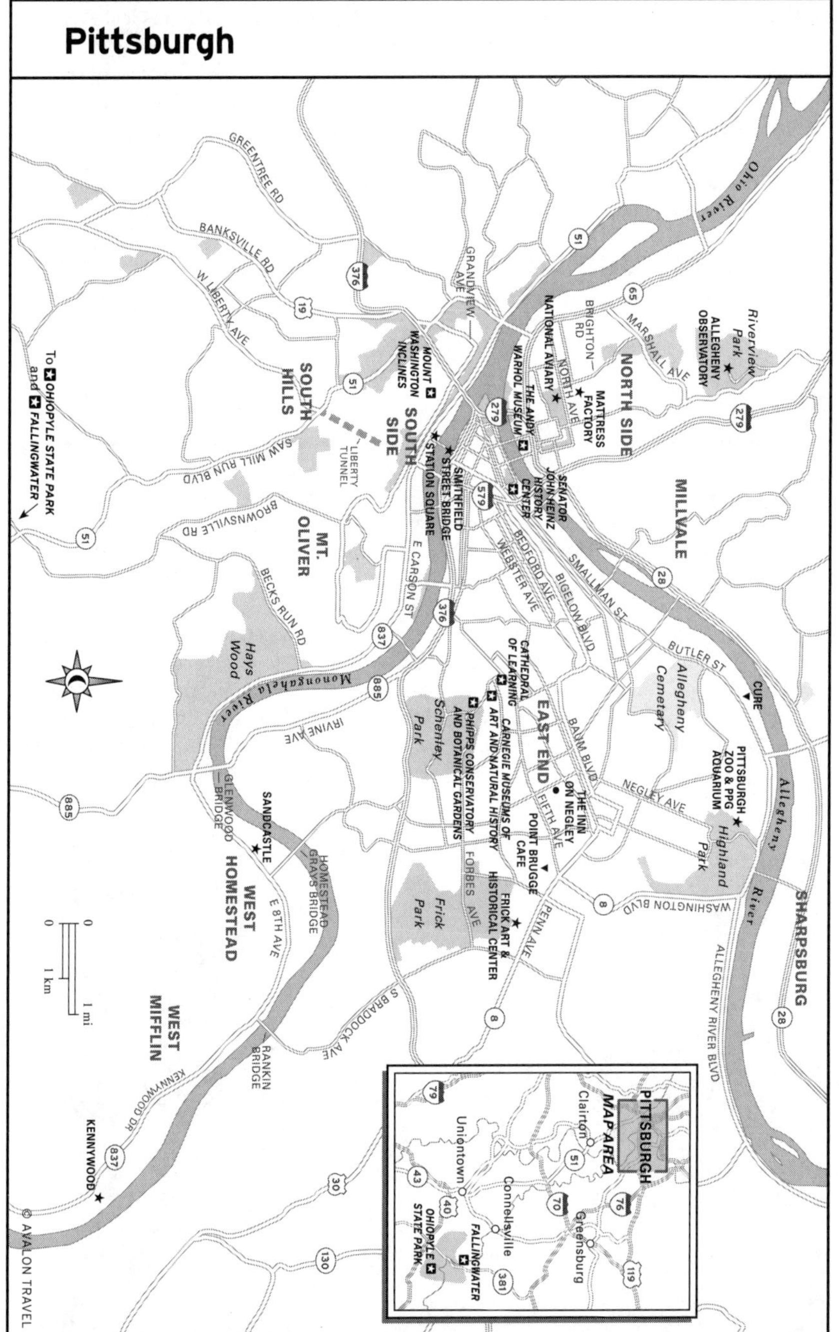

Ohio River
Allegheny River
Monongahela River
NORTH SIDE
MILLVALE
SHARPSBURG
SOUTH SIDE
SOUTH HILLS
MT. OLIVER
EAST END
WEST HOMESTEAD
WEST MIFFLIN
Riverview Park
ALLEGHENY OBSERVATORY
MATTRESS FACTORY
NATIONAL AVIARY
THE ANDY WARHOL MUSEUM
SENATOR JOHN HEINZ HISTORY CENTER
MOUNT WASHINGTON INCLINES
STATION SQUARE
SMITHFIELD STREET BRIDGE
LIBERTY TUNNEL
CATHEDRAL OF LEARNING
CARNEGIE MUSEUMS OF ART AND NATURAL HISTORY
PHIPPS CONSERVATORY AND BOTANICAL GARDENS
Schenley Park
Allegheny Cemetery
CURE
PITTSBURGH ZOO & PPG AQUARIUM
Highland Park
THE INN ON NEGLEY
POINT BRUGGE CAFE
FRICK ART & HISTORICAL CENTER
Frick Park
Hays Wood
SANDCASTLE
KENNYWOOD
GLENWOOD BRIDGE
HOMESTEAD GRAYS BRIDGE
RANKIN BRIDGE
GREENTREE RD
BANKSVILLE RD
W LIBERTY AVE
GRANDVIEW AVE
SAW MILL RUN BLVD
BROWNSVILLE RD
BECKS RUN RD
E CARSON ST
BRIGHTON RD
NORTH AVE
MARSHALL AVE
SMALLMAN ST
BIGELOW BLVD
BEDFORD AVE
WEBSTER AVE
BUTLER ST
BAUM BLVD
NEGLEY AVE
FIFTH AVE
FORBES AVE
PENN AVE
WASHINGTON BLVD
ALLEGHENY RIVER BLVD
IRVINE AVE
E 8TH AVE
S BRADDOCK AVE
KENNYWOOD DR
To OHIOPYLE STATE PARK and FALLINGWATER
0 1 mi
0 1 km
PITTSBURGH MAP AREA
Clairton
Uniontown
Connellsville
Greensburg
FALLINGWATER
OHIOPYLE STATE PARK
© AVALON TRAVEL

in attracting large numbers of new residents and droves of tourists. In the meantime, be glad it's underrated. You can have your run of the place: Squeeze into any hot spot save for Heinz Field, where the winningest team in Super Bowl history plays, and dine without a reservation at just about any restaurant. But hurry. This offer may not last for long.

PLANNING YOUR TIME

The city has enough cultural and historical attractions to keep intensely curious types busy for a week, but it's possible to hit the highlights in two or three days. If you can devote more time than that, get off dry land for a spell. Take a cruise on a Gateway Clipper riverboat or, during the warmer months, set off from Kayak Pittsburgh's base on the North Shore.

Skip town for a day or two to explore its surrounds, including Frank Lloyd Wright's Fallingwater.

Sights

DOWNTOWN AND THE STRIP DISTRICT

Downtown Pittsburgh, aka the Golden Triangle, sits at the confluence of the Allegheny and Monongahela Rivers, which join to form the Ohio River. The arrowhead-shaped neighborhood has a storied past, which visitors can explore at the Fort Pitt Museum and Senator John Heinz History Center. Today it's the city's financial center. Like many business districts, it's sleepy weekday nights. But it comes alive on weekends, when Pittsburghers and visitors flock to its performance venues and upscale eateries.

The Strip District extends from 11th Street to 33rd Street, hugging the Allegheny River the whole way. Its name implies commerce of the red-light variety, but "the Strip" was and remains a center of sanctioned trade. In the 19th century, mills and factories mushroomed along the river. In the early part of the 20th, the Strip became the hub of Pittsburgh's wholesale produce industry. These days the mile-long neighborhood is famous for its

fountain in Point State Park

specialty foods markets. It's also home to restaurants and bars.

Point State Park

It's hard to believe that the green oasis at the tip of the Pittsburgh peninsula was once a brownfield site. Completed in the mid-1970s, as the local steel industry was beginning to implode, **Point State Park** (601 Commonwealth Place, 412/565-2850, www.dcnr.pa.gov/stateparks) is a symbol of the city's renaissance. As the only large public park in downtown, it's a frequent site of festivals and concerts and a great place to picnic or sunbathe on a summer day. The central column of water in its iconic fountain soars to a height of more than 100 feet, making it visible from main entry points to the city.

The Point, as locals call it, is steeped in history. In 1753, Lieutenant George Washington of the Virginia militia advised that the British establish an outpost there to gain command of the rivers. Alas, the French also had their eye on the strategic spot. In 1754 they chased away a force of Virginians who'd built a weak stockade and proceeded to erect a fort they called Duquesne. Britain's attempts to retake control failed until November 1758, when the French burned their fort and fled two days before the arrival of a massive army led by General John Forbes. Upon his arrival, Forbes ordered the construction of a new fort, naming it after British secretary of state William Pitt. The settlement around Fort Pitt became "Pittsbourgh." (The current spelling appeared in the 1816 city charter.)

A re-created bastion houses the **Fort Pitt Museum** (101 Commonwealth Pl., 412/281-9284, www.heinzhistorycenter.org, 10am-5pm daily, adults $8, seniors $7, students and children 6-17 $4.50), which tells the story of the French and Indian War. Exhibits also speak to the ensuing hostilities between the British victors and Native Americans. Kids tend to gravitate toward the trader's cabin and its assortment of animal pelts. A costumed guide explains how Native Americans purchased everything from mirrors to muskets with buckskins and other furry currency.

The nearby **Fort Pitt Block House** (412/471-1764, www.fortpittblockhouse.com, 10:30am-4:30pm Wed.-Sun. Apr.-Oct., 10:30am-4:30pm Fri.-Sun. Nov.-Mar., free) is the only original fort structure and the oldest building in Pittsburgh. It was constructed in 1764 to help protect the fort from possible attacks by Native Americans. Eventually it was repurposed as a dwelling. Neville Craig, Pittsburgh's first historian, was born there in 1787. In 1894 the property was transferred to the Daughters of the American Revolution, who blocked it from destruction by the Pennsylvania Railroad and maintain it to this day. Its stone foundation, brick walls, ceiling beams, and roof rafters are original, as are the gun loops through which soldiers aimed their muskets.

Mellon Square and Vicinity

Downtown boasts a number of distinctive buildings, ranging from the old and ornate to the modern and sleek. Architecture buffs should contact the **Pittsburgh History & Landmarks Foundation** (412/471-5808, www.phlf.org), which organizes free walking tours led by guides who know their Flemish Gothic from their Georgian Classical. One good place to begin a self-guided tour is Mellon Square on Smithfield Street between Oliver and 6th Avenues. When the weather is good, downtown workers crowd the plaza's terrazzo walks and granite benches. There's no bad seat in the house, but the best face the 1916 **Omni William Penn Hotel** (530 William Penn Pl., 412/281-7100, www.omnihotels.com). The oldest hotel in the city underwent a renovation in 2004 to the tune of $22 million, and many of its original features were restored. Its grand facade whispers of crystal chandeliers and leather armchairs. (You'll find both in the main lobby, along with a grand piano.)

Walk northwest on 6th Avenue for a gander at the **Duquesne Club** (325 6th Ave.), the Romanesque home of Pittsburgh's oldest

Downtown, Strip District, and North Side

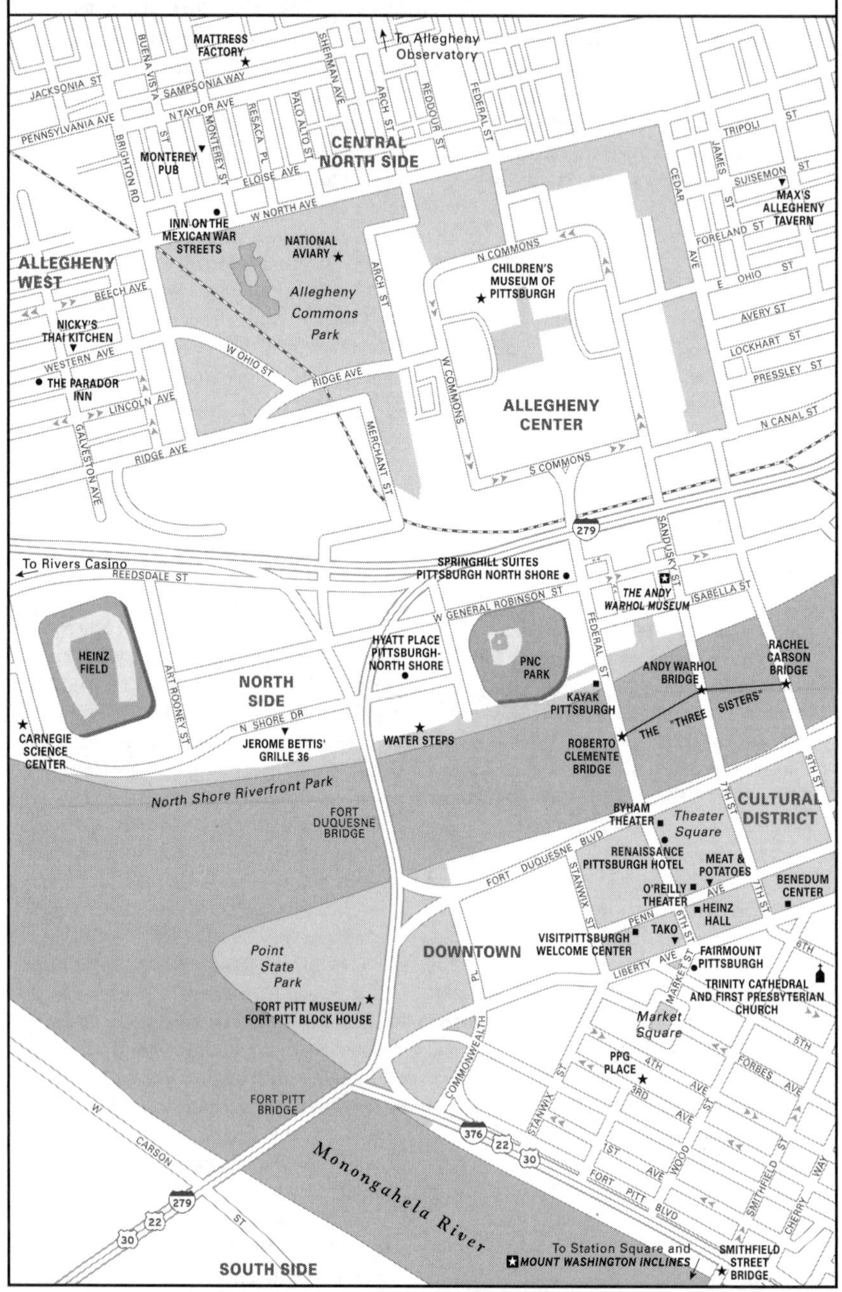

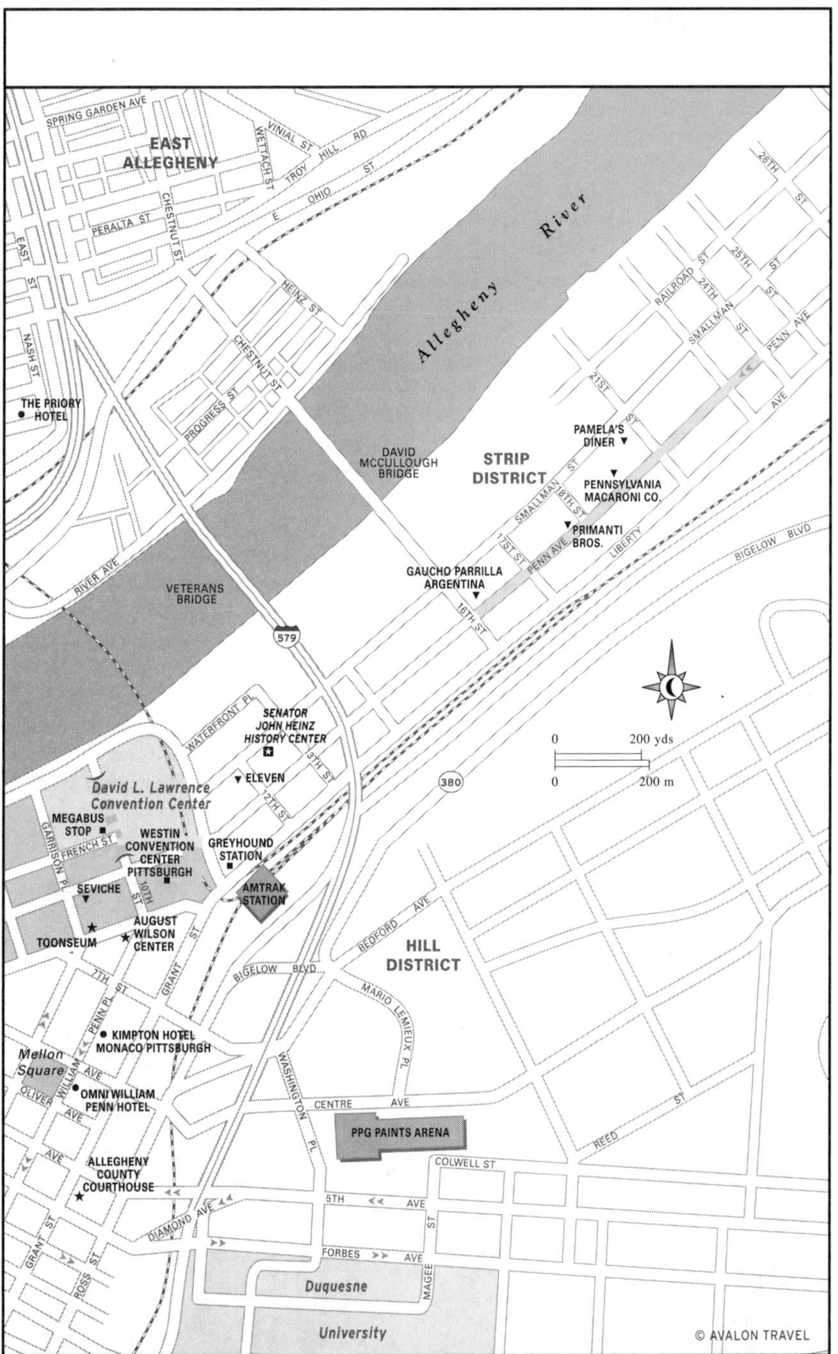
EAST ALLEGHENY
SPRING GARDEN AVE
VINIAL ST
TROY HILL RD
WETTACH ST
E OHIO ST
PERALTA ST
CHESTNUT ST
EAST ST
NASH ST
HEINZ ST
Allegheny River
THE PRIORY HOTEL
PROGRESS ST
DAVID MCCULLOUGH BRIDGE
STRIP DISTRICT
PAMELA'S DINER
PENNSYLVANIA MACARONI CO.
PRIMANTI BROS.
SMALLMAN ST
RAILROAD ST
PENN AVE
LIBERTY AVE
BIGELOW BLVD
GAUCHO PARRILLA ARGENTINA
RIVER AVE
VETERANS BRIDGE
579
380
WATERFRONT PL
SENATOR JOHN HEINZ HISTORY CENTER
ELEVEN
0 200 yds
0 200 m
David L. Lawrence Convention Center
MEGABUS STOP
WESTIN CONVENTION CENTER PITTSBURGH
GREYHOUND STATION
AMTRAK STATION
FRENCH ST
GARRISON PL
SEVICHE
AUGUST WILSON CENTER
TOONSEUM
BEDFORD AVE
HILL DISTRICT
BIGELOW BLVD
7TH ST
GRANT ST
MARIO LEMIEUX PL
KIMPTON HOTEL MONACO PITTSBURGH
Mellon Square
WILLIAM PENN PL
OLIVER AVE
OMNI WILLIAM PENN HOTEL
WASHINGTON PL
CENTRE AVE
PPG PAINTS ARENA
REED ST
COLWELL ST
ALLEGHENY COUNTY COURTHOUSE
5TH AVE
DIAMOND AVE
FORBES AVE
MAGEE ST
ROSS ST
Duquesne University
© AVALON TRAVEL

private club. Founded in 1873, it welcomed the captains of industry whose names still grace so many Pittsburgh buildings. The current clubhouse, which opened in 1890 and didn't admit women until 1980, was dubbed "the citadel of Pittsburgh tycoonery" by *Time* magazine in 1940.

Across the street are two churches designed in the English Gothic style. **Trinity Cathedral** (328 6th Ave., 412/232-6404, www.trinitycathedralpgh.org), with its striking steeple, was dedicated in 1872. Its neighbor, the twin-towered **First Presbyterian Church** (320 6th Ave., 412/471-3436, www.fpcp.org), is three decades younger and the third church to be built on this site. All but one of its nave windows were designed and produced by the Tiffany Studios in New York. The graveyard between the churches dates back to the 1700s.

In the late 1800s, before skyscrapers started sprouting in Pittsburgh, the skyline was dominated by the **Allegheny County Courthouse** (436 Grant St.), located on Grant Street between 5th and Forbes Avenues. It's still one of the city's most impressive buildings. The courthouse and adjacent jail were designed by Boston architect Henry Hobson Richardson, whose style was so distinctive that it got its own name: Richardsonian Romanesque. He died in 1886, two years before the courthouse was finished, and reportedly had this to say on his deathbed: "If they honor me for the pygmy things I have already done, what will they say when they see Pittsburgh finished?" The jail was closed in 1995 and later repurposed as a court building. A portion of a cellblock was preserved, and you can learn about prison life with a carefully timed visit. The **Jail Museum** (440 Ross St.) is open 11:30am-1pm Mondays from February through October.

PPG Place

Downtown's most impressive buildings form a shimmering glass complex known as **PPG Place** (4th Ave. between Stanwix and Wood Sts., www.ppgplace.com). The centerpiece is the headquarters of PPG Industries (formerly the Pittsburgh Plate Glass Company), a 40-story glass castle complete with 231 neo-Gothic spires.

Walking between the PPG Place buildings is an otherworldly experience. Images dance across the glass panes, making for a unique photo with every click. Nearly one million square feet of PPG-made reflective glass went into the facades. The purpose of all that glass

PPG Place

is not only aesthetic; it helps keep the buildings cool in summer and cozy in winter. You'll also find glass paneling in the lobbies and cracked-glass mirrors in the elevators.

From spring through fall, the one-acre plaza between the buildings features a granite fountain with 140 columns of water. Come winter, the plaza transforms into an outdoor ice-skating rink—part of the reason why PPG Place has been likened to New York's Rockefeller Center. **The Rink at PPG Place** (412/394-3641, adults $8, seniors and children 12 and under $7, skate rental $4) is open from mid-November through February. If you're visiting between mid-November and early January, pop into the glass-enclosed **Wintergarden** (1 PPG Pl.) for a look at the holiday exhibits.

ToonSeum

One of only a handful of museums dedicated to the cartoon arts, the **ToonSeum** (945 Liberty Ave., 412/232-0199, www.toonseum.org, 11am-5pm Wed.-Sun., adults $8, seniors and students $7, children 6-12 $4) relocated from its original home in the Children's Museum of Pittsburgh in 2009. The move opened the door for exhibits of more provocative works. But fear not, Mickey Mouse fans: America's favorite rodent and other beloved characters such as Snoopy, Superman, and SpongeBob SquarePants still have places of honor at the ToonSeum, which changes exhibits often. Jean Schulz, widow of Snoopy creator Charles M. Schulz, was one of its earliest supporters.

★ Senator John Heinz History Center

The **Senator John Heinz History Center** (1212 Smallman St., 412/454-6000, www.heinzhistorycenter.org, 10am-5pm daily, adults $16, seniors $14, students and children 6-17 $6.50), a six-floor former icehouse that stretches a city block in the Strip District, is the largest history museum in Pennsylvania. It tackles 250 years of Pittsburgh history, from the pre-Revolutionary period to present day. The Smithsonian-affiliated museum is a kid-friendly medley of artifacts, artwork, audio-visual programs, and interactive exhibits. Long-term exhibits include *Clash of Empires,* which examines the French and Indian War; *From Slavery to Freedom,* which examines the history of slavery and abolitionism; and *Heinz,* a tribute to the king of condiments.

Sports junkies can get a fix at the **Western Pennsylvania Sports Museum,** a museum

Senator John Heinz History Center

within the museum that celebrates the home runs, touchdowns, goals, and other proud moments of the region's athletes. If "Immaculate Reception" means nothing to you, this is the place to go for a primer in Pittsburgh sports lore.

NORTH SIDE

Many of Pittsburgh's main attractions are located north of downtown in an area known, appropriately enough, as the North Side. The area closest to the riverfront is known as the North Shore. It's where many of the attractions are found, including the Pittsburgh Steelers' Heinz Field and the Pirates' PNC Park.

The North Side was once an independent municipality named Allegheny. In 1907, when it was forcibly annexed by Pittsburgh, Allegheny was a sooty city of industry with a charming park, Allegheny Commons, at its center. The residential area east of the park had become known as Deutschtown for its large population of German immigrants. Many well-to-do citizens lived north of the park in the Mexican War Streets section, where streets had been named for the battles (Buena Vista, Monterey, Resaca, Palo Alto) and leaders (Taylor, Sherman, Jackson) of the Mexican-American War. Today, both neighborhoods are national historic districts well worth a stroll on a pleasant day.

The Three Sisters

Four vehicular bridges connect downtown and the North Side, and all of them can be crossed on foot. The busiest is Fort Duquesne Bridge, a double-decker that feeds into an interstate. Its lower-deck walkway makes for a less-than-scenic stroll. For fantastic views, go for one of the "Three Sisters." There's no Cinderella here—the bridges are all but identical. The yellow triplets were built between 1924 and 1928 on orders of the U.S. War Department, which feared that certain vessels wouldn't be able to pass under the bridges they replaced. The Sisters were the first self-anchored suspension bridges in the United States and remain the only trio of neighboring, nearly indistinguishable large bridges.

The bridges were originally named for the downtown streets they adjoin: 6th Street, 7th Street, and 9th Street. Starting in 1999, they were renamed to honor local luminaries. Closest to the tip of downtown is the **Roberto Clemente Bridge** (6th Street Bridge). Clemente, a National Baseball Hall of Famer, was drafted by the Pittsburgh Pirates in 1954. He remained with the team until 1972, when he died in a plane crash during a relief mission to earthquake-torn Nicaragua. PNC Park, where the Pirates have played since 2001, is a stone's throw from the span's northern end. The bridge is closed to vehicular traffic during Pirates home games, when it's flooded with fans, vendors, and scalpers.

The Andy Warhol Museum sits near the northern end of the **Andy Warhol Bridge** (7th Street Bridge). The bridge was renamed in 2005 as part of the museum's 10th anniversary celebration. The **Rachel Carson Bridge** (9th Street Bridge) got its new name on Earth Day in 2006. Carson, who ignited the environmental movement with the publication of *Silent Spring*, was born in 1907 in Springdale, about 18 miles north of Pittsburgh along the Allegheny River.

★ The Andy Warhol Museum

Andy Warhol was born and buried in Pittsburgh, which might have remained a little-known fact were it not for **The Andy Warhol Museum** (117 Sandusky St., 412/237-8300, www.warhol.org, 10am-5pm Tues.-Thurs. and Sat.-Sun., 10am-10pm Fri., adults $20, students and children 3-18 $10). It opened in 1994 to celebrate the work of the influential artist whose career unfolded in New York City. The Warhol is one of the four Carnegie Museums of Pittsburgh. (As a child, Andy Warhol took free Saturday art classes at the Carnegie in Oakland, a neighborhood east of downtown.) It's also the largest U.S. museum dedicated to a single artist. The collection includes about 900 paintings and 2,000 drawings, along with sculptures, prints, photographs, films, videos, books, and even wallpaper designed by the artist. About 500 works from the permanent collection are exhibited at any one time.

The "pope of pop" was born in 1928 to working-class immigrants from what is now Slovakia. There's another museum devoted to his work in the Slovakian town of Medzilaborce, not far from his parents' birthplace. After graduating with an art degree from the Carnegie Institute of Technology (now Carnegie Mellon University), Warhol moved to New York and gained recognition as a commercial illustrator. In the early 1960s, he shot to fame as a pop artist with paintings of consumer products such as Campbell's Soup and celebrities including Marilyn Monroe. He is buried at St. John the Baptist Cemetery in the Pittsburgh suburb of Bethel Park. Admirers still leave soup cans at the gravesite.

If possible, visit on a Friday evening, when the museum stays open until 10pm and a cash bar adds a twist to the Warhol experience. Tickets are half price after 5pm on Fridays.

Water Steps in North Shore Riverfront Park

The North Side has no shortage of kid-friendly attractions, including the Carnegie Science Center, Children's Museum of Pittsburgh, and National Aviary. Admission, however, can be pricey. If you're looking for a cost-free way to entertain kids on a hot day, you can't do better than the **Water Steps** (North Shore Trail, between Mazeroski Way and Fort Duquesne Bridge, www.pgh-sea.com), a terraced wading pool with knockout views of downtown. The creative display of water landscaping is a short walk from PNC Park by way of the paved trail that runs along the Allegheny River. If you're driving, park near the Hyatt Place Pittsburgh-North Shore (260 N. Shore Dr.). The steps are across North Shore Drive from the hotel.

Carnegie Science Center

Like the Andy Warhol Museum about a mile away, the **Carnegie Science Center** (1 Allegheny Ave., 412/237-3400, www.carnegiesciencecenter.org, 10am-5pm Sun.-Fri., 10am-7pm Sat., adults $20, children 3-12 $12, with laser show adults $25, children $17) is one of the four Carnegie Museums of Pittsburgh. It's the most kid-friendly and interactive of the four, and its store, Xplor, is shopping nirvana for the nerdy set. Astronaut food? Check. Submarine models? Check.

The science center's permanent exhibits include *Exploration Station*—a godsend to

The Andy Warhol Museum

Extreme Makeovers

Demolitions make good spectacles, but many Pittsburgh developers choose instead to adapt old buildings for new purposes. What looks like a church could very well be a brewpub, nightclub, or hookah bar. The building that resembles a warehouse could be gallery space. Examples of adaptive reuse can be found throughout the city.

Church Brew Works

THE ANDY WARHOL MUSEUM

The museum, which opened in 1994, occupies a former warehouse built in 1911. It was known as the Frick & Lindsay building when it housed mining supplies, and Volkwein Music & Instruments Co. after it became a music store in the 1960s.

CHILDREN'S MUSEUM OF PITTSBURGH

This kid-centric museum occupies the former post office of Allegheny City, the municipality annexed by Pittsburgh in 1907 and now known as the North Side.

CHURCH BREW WORKS

St. John the Baptist Church closed in 1993 due to a decline in parishioners. The brewery and restaurant that took its place fills with revelers on weekends. Brewing kettles occupy the former altar.

PENN BREWERY

This brewery and restaurant opened in the 1980s in the onetime home of the Eberhardt & Ober Brewery, which operated from the 1840s to the early 1900s. A fruits and vegetables wholesaler used the building as a warehouse in the interim.

THE PRIORY HOTEL

A Catholic church called St. Mary's was built on the North Shore in 1852. A priory for the Benedictine priests and brothers who served the parish was added several decades later. Today the priory is a boutique hotel and the church a banquet hall.

SENATOR JOHN HEINZ HISTORY CENTER

The 19th-century building that houses Pennsylvania's largest history museum was once a warehouse for an ice company.

STATION SQUARE

The riverfront dining and entertainment complex was at one time the headquarters of the Pittsburgh & Lake Erie Railroad, which carried materials to and from the steel mills starting in the 1870s.

parents stumped by their progeny's never-ending "why" questions. Aerodynamics, embryology, magnetic forces, and dozens of other concepts and processes are explained. *SpacePlace* features a two-story replica of the International Space Station and a climbing wall designed to simulate weightlessness. The *Miniature Railroad & Village* offers a bird's-eye view of western Pennsylvania at the turn of the 20th century. Among the 2,000 hand-built replicas is Forbes Field, Pittsburgh's beloved, bygone ballpark. *Highmark SportsWorks*

National Aviary

explores the science of sports and the mechanics of the human body, while *Roboworld* explores the mechanics of the robot body.

Regular shows at the full-dome digital planetarium and tours of the World War II submarine moored alongside the science center are included in the price of admission. There is an additional charge for laser shows in the planetarium and movies in the Rangos Giant Cinema.

Rivers Casino

Carnegie had nothing to do with the adjacent **Rivers Casino** (777 Casino Dr., 412/231-7777, www.theriverscasino.com, open 24 hours), which opened in 2009 to the tune of $780 million. It boasts almost 3,000 slot machines, more than 100 table games, and five restaurants including that casino staple: the buffet. Parking in the immense garage is usually free. When the Steelers or Pirates are playing at home, there's a $30-60 fee to park starting four hours before game time.

Children's Museum of Pittsburgh

The fabulous **Children's Museum of Pittsburgh** (10 Children's Way, 412/322-5058, www.pittsburghkids.org, 10am-5pm daily, adults $16, seniors and children 2-18 $14) is housed in two historic landmarks. The older of the two, notable for its copper dome, served as the post office for Allegheny City before its annexation by Pittsburgh in 1907. The younger opened in 1939 as a planetarium. They're linked by a polycarbonate and glass structure.

Inside, it's back-to-back playgrounds. There's an art studio, where budding Picassos can paint and sculpt; a Makeshop for building and learning how tools work; a play area designed for infants and toddlers; a water exhibit with opportunities to get wet from head to toe; and more. It's a good idea to bring a towel and change of clothes for your wee ones. In Pittsburgh, no major children's attraction would be complete without a tribute to the homegrown public television series *Mister Rogers' Neighborhood.* Some of the puppets make their home at the museum, along with Mister Rogers' sweater and sneakers.

If you're visiting in summer, be sure to check out ***Cloud Arbor,*** a mist-emitting metal sculpture that serves as the centerpiece of a community park in front of the museum.

National Aviary

Just west of the Children's Museum is the **National Aviary** (700 Arch St., 412/323-7235, www.aviary.org, 10am-5pm daily, adults $15, seniors and children 2-12 $14), home to some 500 birds. Free-flight rooms and public feedings allow for close encounters of the bird kind. Visitors can toss fish to the pelicans, hand-feed nectar to the rainbow lorikeets, or watch the bird zoo's chefs prepare vittles for condors, macaws, and other residents. Don't skip Penguin Point. The open-air exhibit features 20 African penguins, also known as jackass penguins because of their donkey-like bray. An acrylic-fronted pool and

Step Aerobics

Pittsburgh has over 700 outdoor staircases comprising 45,000 steps. No city in the country has more, and no neighborhood in Pittsburgh has more than the South Side Slopes. Rising from the Monongahela River, the area rewards those who conquer its steps with knockout views.

Driving through the Slopes is almost as challenging as hoofing it. The streets are narrow and winding and in some spots so steep that you can't see the road for the car hood. If you're working your way down and see an oncoming car, it's customary to pull to the side so the climber can have the right of way. Complicating driving is the matter of "paper" streets, so called because they appear to be streets on maps but are actually staircases. Pittsburgh has 334 of them.

During Pittsburgh's industrial heyday, the staircases linked hilltop communities with the steel mills and other workplaces on the riverbanks. The Slopes were home to Poles, Germans, and other immigrants. Their faith left an indelible mark on the neighborhood. It's dotted with churches and a larger number of former churches, rectories, and convents. Yard Way, the longest of the paper streets, climbs from a street named Pius toward a street named St. Paul, which curves to an avenue named Monastery.

Good to have if you're interested in exploring the staircases is Bob Regan's *Pittsburgh Steps: The Story of the City's Public Stairways* ($16.95, www.globepequot.com). Or mark your calendar for the South Side Slopes Neighborhood Association's StepTrek (412/246-9090, www.southsideslopes.org, Oct., adults $13, children under 12 free). Armed with maps and course descriptions, participants in the noncompetitive event climb about half of the Slopes' 5,447 steps.

crawlspaces make it possible to observe their underwater antics.

Mattress Factory

The historic Mexican War Streets neighborhood is home to one of the nation's top museums for installation art. The **Mattress Factory** (500 Sampsonia Way, 412/231-3169, www.mattress.org, 10am-5pm Tues.-Sat., 1pm-5pm Sun., adults $20, seniors and students $15, children under 6 free) presents room-size works created on-site. Its permanent installations include pieces by James Turrell, Bill Woodrow, and Yayoi Kusama. Each year, 8-10 new works are exhibited for several months at a time. The museum's expansion has made it an engine for community development as well as artistic expression. It has purchased nine properties since 1975, turning them into galleries, artist residences, and even an artist-created garden. The first acquisition was a former mattress warehouse built at the turn of the 20th century.

SOUTH SIDE AND MOUNT WASHINGTON

It's been said that the South Side has both types of "blue-hairs." One type is fond of studded collars and punk rock; the other favors sensible shoes and Dean Martin. That diversity is part of what makes the area so interesting. What's referred to as the South Side is actually several neighborhoods near the southern bank of the Monongahela River. The smallest of these is the South Shore, dominated by a dining and entertainment complex called Station Square. Overlooking it is Mount Washington, once called Coal Hill for its abundant coal seams, which supplied fuel to Pittsburgh's settlers and riverbank industries. The growth of these industries in the mid-19th century created more and more jobs—and a shortage of housing in the flatlands. So workers built houses on Pittsburgh's hillsides. For a while, they commuted on foot, trudging up steep paths after a hard day's work in the plants. The first people-moving incline opened in 1870. In the 25 years that followed, more than 15 others were built. Two remain, a mile apart on Mount Washington.

The hilltop is now accessible by car, but some of its residents still use the inclines to commute to jobs in downtown or the South Side. They're also popular among tourists for the vista from up top.

The main drag is East Carson Street in the South Side Flats. The low-lying neighborhood was once crowded with glassmaking factories and, later, iron and steel operations. Today it's crowded with bars, bars, and more bars, plus restaurants and quirky shops. If you need to stroll off a few beers, press on toward the South Side Slopes. The neighborhood's steep streets rival a treadmill at its highest setting.

Smithfield Street Bridge

Some years ago, the Pennsylvania Department of Transportation decided to demolish the **Smithfield Street Bridge,** which connects downtown and the South Side, and replace it with a modern bridge. Preservationists lobbied to save it and won. Instead of being torn down, the oldest steel bridge in the United States got a new deck, a paint job, and an extra traffic lane.

Constructed in the early 1880s, the Smithfield Street Bridge is a National Historic Landmark. But what really distinguishes it from so many bridges in Pittsburgh and across the country is the foot traffic. Downtown workers who live south of the Monongahela River stream across the bridge in the morning and again come quitting time. For visitors staying in downtown hotels, the bridge's pedestrian walkways are a great way to reach the famous Mount Washington inclines.

Station Square

A railroad facility turned dining and entertainment complex, **Station Square** (Carson St. at Smithfield Street Bridge, 800/859-8959, www.stationsquare.com) is the gateway to America's oldest and steepest incline, the **Monongahela Incline,** and home to the **Gateway Clipper Fleet,** which offers popular river cruises. Station Square itself isn't as robust as it could be. But it does feature a Sheraton hotel, a dozen eateries (almost all chains, including a Hard Rock Cafe), and a soccer stadium. **Highmark Stadium** (510 W. Station Square Dr., 412/224-4900, www.highmarkstadium.com) is home to the Pittsburgh Riverhounds, which play in the USL Professional Division, and the Pittsburgh Passion women's football team.

Station Square hasn't shed all traces of its history as the headquarters of the Pittsburgh & Lake Erie Railroad. Its signature restaurant, **Grand Concourse,** looks much as it did when it served as a passenger terminal, with its stained glass cathedral ceiling and brass accents. A 1930s Bessemer converter, which was used to convert molten iron to steel, is on display in the outdoor **Bessemer Court.** The 10-ton artifact is easy to miss if you arrive when the Fountain at Bessemer Court is putting on an illuminated water show. Shows begin every 20 minutes 9am-midnight from April through early November.

★ Mount Washington Inclines

Three 19th-century inclines remain in Pennsylvania, and two of those climb Mount Washington. (The third is in Johnstown, about 65 miles east of Pittsburgh.) They've been around for so long that you might think twice about boarding the cable cars. Board. The views more than compensate for the fear factor. The scene at night is especially enchanting.

The **Monongahela Incline** (lower station Carson St. near Smithfield Street Bridge, 412/442-2000, www.portauthority.org, 5:30am-12:45am Mon.-Sat., 8:45am-midnight Sun., one-way fare adults $2.75, seniors free, children 6-11 $1.35) is the oldest and steepest incline in America. It's also the oldest cable car operation—three years older than San Francisco's famous counterparts. The incline began operating in 1870. Its cars, which were replaced in the 1980s, ply two parallel tracks at about six miles per hour. The creaks and groans of the machinery recall a wooden roller coaster. Rest easy; there's no plunge after the "Mon Incline" summits. The lower station is a short walk from the Smithfield Street Bridge

Sightseeing Tours

Many of the city's tour operators are based at Station Square, the dining and entertainment complex on the southern bank of the Monongahela River. Busiest of those is the **Gateway Clipper Fleet** (412/355-7980, gatewayclipper.com, prices vary), which offers a wide variety of cruises, from the kid-centric Superhero and School of Wizardry cruises to sunset dinners to beer tastings. Its five riverboats explore the Monongahela, Allegheny, and Ohio Rivers year-round. They also shuttle sports fans to PNC Park and Heinz Field on game days. If the boats look up in years, it's because they're reproductions of vessels of yore.

Station Square is also home to **Just Ducky Tours** (412/402-3825, www.justduckytours.com, daily Apr.-Nov., adults $25, children 3-12 $15, infants $5), offering Pittsburgh's only land-and-water tours. Designed for use in WWII, its amphibious vehicles ferry passengers across the Monongahela River and through downtown. Tours are approximately one hour.

Other Station Square-based tour operators include **Molly's Trolleys** (412/391-7433, www.mollystrolleyspittsburgh.com, adults $27, children 3-12 $15, infants $5), which offers two-hour sightseeing tours in a vehicle reminiscent of a 1920s-style trolley, and **Segway Pittsburgh** (412/515-3333, www.segwaypittsburgh.com, $39-53), which offers 90-minute and 2-hour tours of downtown and the North Shore as well as 2.5-hour Destination tours that include a museum visit. Riders under 14 aren't allowed.

The Pittsburgh Tour Company (445 S. 27th St., 412/381-8687, www.pghtours.com, daily Apr.-Dec., adults $25-30, children 3-10 $15-25) makes its home at the SouthSide Works, a shopping and dining complex about 2.5 miles upriver from Station Square, but you can catch a ride on one of its hop-on/hop-off double-decker buses at about 20 stops, including Station Square, Heinz Field, the Children's Museum of Pittsburgh, and Phipps Conservatory.

Whether you're hungry for local history or just plain hungry, a **'Burgh Bits and Bites Food Tour** (412/901-7150, www.burghfoodtour.com, $43) is sure to satisfy. The food-centric walking tours offer a taste of neighborhoods including the Strip District, Bloomfield, and Lawrenceville. Tickets must be purchased in advance.

and across the street from Station Square, where you can park for a modest fee.

The **Duquesne Incline** (lower station 1197 W. Carson St., 412/381-1665, www.duquesneincline.org, 5:30am-12:30am Mon.-Sat., 7am-12:30am Sun., one-way fare adults $2.50, seniors free, children 6-11 $1.25), one mile west, opened in 1877. It joined three other Mount Washington inclines but didn't lack for passengers. In 1880, *Scientific American* magazine wrote of the Duquesne Incline: "On Sundays during the summer, 6,000 passengers are carried during the day and evening, the cars ascending and descending as rapidly as filled and emptied." Ridership shrank after the advent of the automobile, and in 1962, the company that owned the incline decided not to invest in sorely needed repairs. The incline was shut down. A group of Mount Washington residents took up its cause, raising $15,000 in six months through the sale of souvenir tickets, baked goods, and shares in the incline company. Repairs were made, and the incline reopened. There's an inexpensive parking lot across the street from the lower station, between West Carson Street and the Ohio River. Follow the red pedestrian bridge that crosses West Carson to reach the station. You'll board one of two original Victorian cable cars and gain 400 feet of elevation in less than three minutes. At the upper station, find a small, free museum, gift shop, and observation deck with binocular telescopes.

Grandview Avenue

Both inclines deposit passengers on Mount Washington's **Grandview Avenue.** George Washington is said to have spotted the forks of the Ohio River from this bluff. He saw a highly strategic site for a fort; what we see today is an acclaimed cityscape—a grand view indeed. Pittsburghers rarely fail to bring out-of-town guests here.

The historic inclines aren't the only way to reach Grandview Avenue, which clings to the rim of the hill for about 1.5 miles. PJ McArdle Roadway and Sycamore Street also climb to the penthouse of Pittsburgh. Street parking is plentiful unless you arrive on the Fourth of July or another occasion for fireworks. Once on foot, make your way to one of the observation decks that jut over the hillside. You may have to bypass a wedding party or gaggle of prom-goers, as this is the mother of Pittsburgh photo ops. The western (Duquesne Incline) end of Grandview is crowded with restaurants of the special-occasion variety, many of which are open only for dinner. The views from their dining rooms are so romantic, they could serve gruel and still be packed on Valentine's Day.

OAKLAND AND POINTS EAST

In the 19th century, pollution and overcrowding drove some Pittsburghers to the city's outskirts. Oakland, about three miles east of downtown, started as an elite enclave. By the 1920s, thanks in no small part to its moneyed residents, Oakland had blossomed into an academic and cultural powerhouse with two major universities, a pair of world-class museums, and outstanding hospitals.

First stop for many visitors are three connected buildings that house the Carnegie Museum of Art, the Carnegie Museum of Natural History, Carnegie Music Hall, and the main branch of the Carnegie Library of Pittsburgh. Schenley Park fans out behind them, offering relaxation, recreation, and, frequently, free entertainment. Oakland's most arresting building, the 42-story Cathedral of Learning, can be seen from points near and far, guiding home coeds who wander too far from the campuses of the University of Pittsburgh or Carnegie Mellon University. Central Oakland is awash in the sort of restaurants, bars, and coffee shops favored by students.

The neighborhoods east of Oakland include Squirrel Hill, Shadyside, and Bloomfield. To the north is Lawrenceville. Dotted with synagogues, Squirrel Hill is the center of Jewish culture in the city—when a Dunkin' Donuts opened on one of the neighborhood's main thoroughfares in 2009, it resolved to adhere to Jewish dietary laws. Shadyside is among the most affluent neighborhoods in Pittsburgh. Its Walnut Street shopping district is home to high-end chains such as Williams-Sonoma and Lululemon. (Skip the workout gear and go a couple of doors down to Prantl's Bakery for a local favorite: the burnt almond torte.) The parallel Ellsworth Avenue is known for its nightlife offerings. Bloomfield, centered on Liberty Avenue, is Pittsburgh's Little Italy. In the revitalized riverfront district of Lawrenceville, Butler Street is lined with hip restaurants and galleries. These and other neighborhoods are collectively known as the East End.

★ Carnegie Museum of Art

Don't have the budget to visit the Parthenon in Greece? Head to the **Carnegie Museum of Art** (4400 Forbes Ave., 412/622-3131, www.cmoa.org, 10am-5pm Sun.-Mon., Wed., and Fri.-Sat., 10am-8pm Thurs. Labor Day-Memorial Day, 10am-5pm Sun.-Wed. and Fri.-Sat., 10am-8pm Thurs. late May-early Sept., adults $20, seniors $15, students and children 3-18 $12, includes same-day admission to Carnegie Museum of Natural History), where you'll find the Hall of Sculpture, a replica of the ancient temple's heavily columned inner sanctuary. It's made of white marble from the same quarries that provided stones for the 5th century BC Parthenon. Decorative arts objects from more recent centuries are displayed on the balcony of the hall, along with several works from the museum's celebrated architectural cast collection. Only the Victoria and Albert Museum in London and Musée National des Monuments Français in

Paris have architectural cast collections that rival the Carnegie's.

The Carnegie, of course, isn't just about architecture. It has a dozen galleries devoted to art from ancient times to the 20th century and several more filled with contemporary works. In fact, the Carnegie has been called the first museum of modern art. The industrialist and philanthropist Andrew Carnegie, who founded the museum in 1895, wished that it be filled not with the works of long-dead artists but rather with the art of "tomorrow's old masters." Early acquisitions included paintings by Winslow Homer, James A. McNeill Whistler, and other Carnegie contemporaries.

Every three to five years, the museum presents the Carnegie International, an exhibition of contemporary art from around the world. The exhibition draws the art world to Pittsburgh, which is exactly what Andrew Carnegie had in mind when he established the tradition in 1896. Featured artists have included Mary Cassatt, Henri Matisse, Edward Hopper, Andy Warhol, and Willem de Kooning. The museum's permanent collection includes more than 300 works purchased from its Carnegie Internationals.

★ Carnegie Museum of Natural History

Three years after opening his eponymous museums, Andrew Carnegie set his sights on bagging a dinosaur. In 1899, a bone-digging crew bankrolled by Carnegie discovered the skeleton of an 84-foot sauropod in southeastern Wyoming. A longer dinosaur had never been found. Exhibiting the colossal fossil—named *Diplodocus carnegii* in recognition of its benefactor—required a $5 million expansion of the **Carnegie Museum of Natural History** (4400 Forbes Ave., 412/622-3131, www.carnegiemnh.org, 10am-5pm Sun.-Mon., Wed., and Fri.-Sat., 10am-8pm Thurs. Labor Day-Memorial Day, 10am-5pm Sun.-Wed. and Fri.-Sat., 10am-8pm Thurs. late May-early Sept., adults $20, seniors $15, students and children 3-18 $12, includes same-day admission to Carnegie Museum of Art). "Dippy" was soon joined by other dinosaur skeletons. The Carnegie boasts the third-largest display of real mounted dinosaurs in the United States, after the National Museum of Natural History in Washington DC and the American Museum of Natural History in New York City. You'll find them in dramatic poses in historically accurate environments.

Hall of Architecture at the Carnegie Museum of Art

Carnegie Museum of Natural History

The exhibit of two sparring *T. rex* specimens is particularly striking.

Dinosaurs may be its main draw, but the Carnegie has other distinguished displays. It has been building its collection of ancient Egyptian artifacts ever since Andrew Carnegie donated a mummy and its sarcophagus. The collection now includes more than 2,500 artifacts dating back to 3100 BC, about 600 of which are displayed in the Walton Hall of Ancient Egypt.

The life-size dinosaur sculpture near the museum's entrance on Forbes Avenue depicts Dippy as he would have looked with skin and flesh. It was erected in 1999 to commemorate the 100th anniversary of the museum's first dinosaur discovery. Few visitors pass up the photo op.

★ Cathedral of Learning

The 42-story **Cathedral of Learning** (4200 5th Ave., 412/624-4141, www.pitt.edu) is the second-tallest university building in the world. (It was robbed of the number one spot by a Moscow building with fewer stories and an oversized spire.) The geographic and symbolic heart of the University of Pittsburgh was designed in the early 1920s by one of the foremost neo-Gothic architects of the time and was to be the tallest building in Pittsburgh. By the time the limestone skyscraper was dedicated in 1937, the 44-story Gulf Tower had risen in downtown. But the Cathedral didn't fail to make its point that scholarliness is next to godliness. Its three-story foyer, known as the Commons Room, is so churchlike that you half expect to find kneeling parishioners beneath the soaring arches. Instead, you find students hunched over books and laptops. Any prayers are silent.

The Cathedral houses classrooms, administrative offices, libraries, and several departments. But the main attraction is a set of classrooms gifted to the university by the city's ethnic communities. Each of the **Nationality Rooms** (412/624-6000, www.nationalityrooms.pitt.edu, 9am-4pm Mon.-Sat., 11am-4pm Sun., audio tour adults $4, children 6-18 $2) depicts a culture in a period prior to the 19th century. The first four rooms were dedicated in 1938 and the 29th in 2012. Several others are in the works. The Chinese Classroom, inspired by a palace hall in Beijing's Forbidden City, features a round teakwood table and a slate portrait of Confucius. The Armenian Classroom, with its domed ceiling, emulates a 10th- to 12th-century monastery, and the Greek Classroom represents 5th-century BC Athens. Classrooms are off-limits when they're in use, so it's a good idea to visit on a weekend or during the summer break (mid-April through mid-August). Audio tours are available when school is out, with the last tour dispatched at 2:30pm. From mid-November to mid-January, the classrooms are dressed in holiday finery. Check the website for holiday hours.

Philadelphia-born architect Charles Klauder designed two buildings to accompany his Cathedral. The university's interdenominational **Heinz Memorial Chapel** (4200 5th Ave., 412/624-4157, www.heinzchapel.

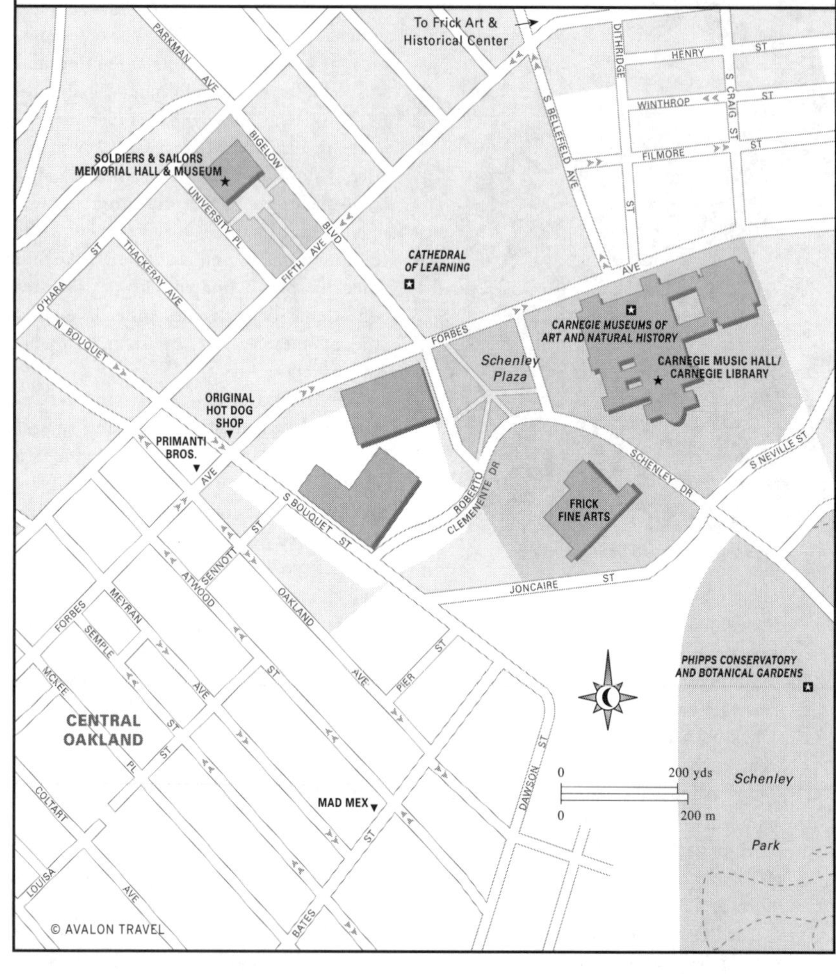

pitt.edu), on the Bellefield Avenue side of the Cathedral, hosts about 1,000 events a year. A lot of those are weddings, but choral and organ concerts are held occasionally, and many of them are free. At 73 feet, the stained glass transept windows are among the tallest in the world.

The **Stephen Foster Memorial** (4301 Forbes Ave., 412/624-4100) is just outside the Forbes Avenue doors of the Cathedral. It houses two theaters, a library with one of the nation's top collections of 19th-century American music, and a museum (9am-4pm Mon.-Fri.) dedicated to the Pittsburgh-born composer for whom it is named.

Schenley Plaza

Not so long ago, the verdant public park across from the Cathedral of Learning was a parking lot. Today **Schenley Plaza** (4100 Forbes Ave., 412/682-7275, www.pittsburghparks.org/schenleyplaza) is a popular sunbathing and picnicking spot and a frequent venue for free concerts. New Yorkers may experience a touch of déjà vu: The Schenley Plaza design team drew on the Big Apple's Bryant Park for inspiration, borrowing elements such as a carousel, a great lawn, flower gardens, and food kiosks. There's also a full-service restaurant, **The Porch at Schenley** (221 Schenley Dr., 412/687-6724, www.theporchatschenley.com).

Stroll across Schenley Drive for a peek inside the **Frick Fine Arts** building, home to the University of Pittsburgh's History of Art and Architecture Department and Studio Arts Department. What makes it of interest to nonstudents is the collection of art copies displayed in the cloister. The scale reproductions of 15th-century Italian Renaissance paintings are masterpieces in their own right. They're the work of Russian artist Nicholas Lochoff, commissioned in 1911 by the Moscow Museum of Fine Arts. If you can't make it to Italy to see Botticelli's *Birth of Venus,* make it to the Frick Fine Arts building.

For many years, Schenley Plaza had a neighbor nicknamed the "House of Thrills." Officially known as Forbes Field, it was the third home of the Pittsburgh Pirates and the first home of the Pittsburgh Steelers. The 1909 stadium where Babe Ruth hit his last three home runs closed in 1970, but its remnants still attract sports fans. Look for the stadium's flagpole and part of the outfield wall to the right of the Frick Fine Arts building. Baseball fans gather here every October 13 to celebrate Bill Mazeroski's ninth-inning home run in the final game of the 1960 World Series, which gave the Pirates a 10-9 win over the New York Yankees.

Schenley Park

Schenley Plaza is a gateway to a much larger oasis, **Schenley Park** (412/682-7275, www.pittsburghparks.org/schenley). The 456-acre park is home to an ice-skating rink, an outdoor swimming pool, the only golf course within city limits, and a sports complex, among other facilities. A good place to start is the lovely **Schenley Park Café** (Panther Hollow Rd. and Schenley Dr., 412/802-8511, 10am-4pm Tues.-Sun.), which doubles as a visitors center. You'll find light lunch fare, desserts, coffee and espresso drinks, free wireless Internet access, restrooms, and trail maps. There are trailheads behind the café.

Grassy **Flagstaff Hill,** across from Phipps Conservatory and Botanical Gardens, is awash with sunbathers on summer days. On Wednesday nights, it's packed with movie buffs and their picnic baskets. Flagstaff Hill is one of several **Cinema in the Park** (www.pittsburghparks.org, 412-682-7275) sites in the city. Family-friendly flicks are screened at Schenley Plaza on summer Sundays.

In winter, the action shifts to the **Schenley Park Skating Rink** (Overlook Dr., 412/422-6523, www.pittsburghpa.gov/citiparks, adults $5, seniors $4, children 17 and under $3, skate rental $3). The outdoor rink generally opens in early November and closes in late March. Public skating times vary from day to day.

The 18-hole **Bob O'Connor Golf Course** (5370 Schenley Dr., 412/622-6959, www.thebobgc.com) is open year-round. So is the **Schenley Oval Sportsplex** (Schenley Park Oval, 412/422-6523, www.pittsburghpa.gov/citiparks), which boasts a 400-meter running track, tennis courts, and a turf soccer field.

★ Phipps Conservatory and Botanical Gardens

The crown jewel of Schenley Park is **Phipps Conservatory and Botanical Gardens** (1 Schenley Park, 412/622-6914, www.phipps.conservatory.org, 9:30am-5pm daily and until 10pm Fri., adults $17.95, seniors and students $16.95, children 2-18 $11.95). The "crystal palace," as the steel-and-glass structure has been called, opened in 1893, stocked with tropical plants from that year's Chicago World's Fair. Today the Victorian greenhouse has a series of indoor and outdoor gardens whose oxygen-producing inhabitants range from towering palm trees to rare miniature orchids. A good mix of permanent and changing displays make repeat visits a must for the horticulturally inclined. In spring and summer you can watch butterflies emerge from chrysalises. On weekends throughout the year, Phipps offers educational programs on everything from origami to moss gardening. They're free with admission. On your GPS, enter "700 Frank Curto Drive."

Soldiers & Sailors Memorial Hall & Museum

A grand Greco-Roman structure, **Soldiers & Sailors Memorial Hall & Museum** (4141 5th Ave., 412/621-4253, www.soldiersand-sailorshall.org, museum 10am-4pm Mon.-Sat., adults $10, seniors and children 5-17 $5) opened in 1910 as a tribute to local Civil War veterans. Since then, the museum has broadened its scope to include all men and women who have served the United States in its military endeavors. Bronze plaques on the outer walls of four exhibit-filled corridors are engraved with the names of 25,000 men from the Pittsburgh area who served in the Union Army during the Civil War. The *Slave to Soldier* exhibit in the Gettysburg Room explores the experiences of African Americans in the military.

Frick Art & Historical Center

In December 1881, industrialist Henry Clay Frick married Adelaide Howard Childs. After their wedding trip, the couple purchased an Italianate-style house on the corner of Penn and South Homewood Avenues, about two miles east of Oakland. They named it **Clayton,** and it served as the family's primary residence until 1905, when they moved to New York. Today Clayton is one of three museums on the grounds of the **Frick Art & Historical Center** (7227 Reynolds St., 412/371-0600, www.frickart.org, 10am-5pm Tues.-Thurs. and Sat.-Sun., 10am-9pm Fri.). More than 90 percent of the furniture and artifacts in the restored home, which opened to the public in 1990, are original. The only way to see them is via docent-led tour (adults $12, seniors and students $10, children 16 and under $6). Tour times vary and reservations are strongly recommended. There's no charge for admission to the intimate **Frick Art Museum,** which houses the personal collection of Helen Clay Frick, Henry and Adelaide's younger daughter. Helen, who inherited Clayton and its contents at her father's death in 1919, was particularly fond of early Renaissance paintings and 18th-century French paintings and decorative arts.

Henry Clay Frick's 1914 Rolls Royce Silver Ghost and an 1898 Panhard believed to be the

Phipps Conservatory and Botanical Gardens in Schenley Park

The Incorrigible Heiress

The woman for whom Schenley Park and Schenley Plaza are named started life as Mary Elizabeth Croghan. She gained the Schenley name—and created an international scandal—at the age of 15, when she eloped with a 43-year-old captain in the British Army. The 1842 elopement made headlines not just because of their age difference but because Mary Croghan Schenley stood to inherit large tracts of land amassed by her maternal grandfather, one of Pittsburgh's earliest captains of industry.

In 1889, Pittsburgh's director of public works learned that a real estate developer's agent planned to travel to London to persuade Mary to sell a swath of land then known as the Mount Airy Tract. The city official had another idea for the property: a grand park. He dispatched a Pittsburgh lawyer, who beat the agent to England by two days. The quick-footedness paid off. Mary gave the city 300 acres of the Mount Airy Tract, stipulating that the park be named after her and never sold. Over the next few years, the city purchased an additional 120 acres of her property and some adjoining land to complete Schenley Park.

first car in Pittsburgh are among 20-some vintage automobiles on view in the **Car and Carriage Museum.** Admission is free, as is a cell phone tour.

What used to be the Frick children's playhouse is now a visitors center and museum shop. No ordinary museum commissary, the **Café at the Frick** (11am-3pm Tues.-Thurs., 11am-3pm and 5:30pm-8pm Fri., 11am-4pm Sat.-Sun., $11-16, reservations recommended) offers one of the loveliest lunches in Pittsburgh. The vegetables and herbs couldn't be fresher; they're grown in the on-site garden and greenhouse. Tea service is available 2pm-4pm weekends.

Pittsburgh Zoo & PPG Aquarium

More than a century old but not the least bit timeworn, the 77-acre **Pittsburgh Zoo & PPG Aquarium** (7340 Butler St., 412/665-3640, www.pittsburghzoo.org, summer 9:30am-6pm daily, gates close at 4:30pm, fall and spring 9am-5pm daily, gates close at 4pm, winter 9am-4pm daily, gates close at 3pm, adults $16, seniors $15, children 2-13 $14 Apr.-Nov., discounted rates Dec.-Mar.) is home to thousands of animals representing more than 400 species. Thanks to extensive renovations that began in 1980, they reside in naturalistic habitats. Highlights include the African Savanna, populated by elephants, rhinos, and giraffes, among other beasts, and the indoor Tropical Forest, which teems with primates. But nothing wows the little ones like Kids Kingdom, featuring playful sea lions, playgrounds, and a petting zoo. No wonder *Parents* magazine named this one of the top 10 children's zoos in the country.

Completed in 2000, the state-of-the-art PPG Aquarium is home to all sorts of swimmers, from ethereal seahorses to menacing sharks. Don't miss the chance to pet a stingray. Adjacent to the aquarium is Water's Edge, home to polar bears, sea otters, and more sharks. Thanks to underwater viewing tunnels, you can practically rub snouts with them.

GREATER PITTSBURGH

Allegheny County has 130 municipalities, more than any other county in the state. None match Pittsburgh, the county seat, in size or sophistication. When Pittsburghers leave the city limits, it's often to shop at sprawling suburban malls. In summer, they stream across the Monongahela River to ride coasters at Kennywood and cool off at its sister water park.

Kennywood

It rarely makes headlines when the National

Amusement Park Historical Association names **Kennywood** (4800 Kennywood Blvd., West Mifflin, 412/461-0500, www.kennywood.com, adults $45, seniors 55-70 $22, seniors over 70 $10, children under 46 inches tall $29) among its favorite traditional parks. The National Historic Landmark has earned that accolade many times. About 10 miles southeast of downtown, Kennywood is virtually synonymous with summer fun for generations of Pittsburghers. Founded in 1898 as a small trolley park, Kennywood has weathered everything from World War II to competition from Disneyland by enhancing its portfolio of rides. Today it's a well-balanced mix of classic and cutting-edge thrills. Its six roller coasters include two wooden beauties erected in the 1920s—Jack Rabbit and Racer—as well as Phantom's Revenge, a 21st-century steel machine. Also on tap: water rides, dark rides, and upside-down action for serious adrenaline junkies. Kiddieland caters to tots with rides such as Lil' Phantom, a pint-size coaster that maxes out at 15 mph. Famous for its fresh-cut Potato Patch fries, Kennywood is one of the few amusement parks that still permit guests to bring their own food. Alcohol isn't allowed.

The park is open daily from mid-May to late August and some weekends before and after that period. Gates usually open at 10:30am. Quittin' time is based on weather and crowd size but usually around 10pm. The park marks the end of each season with two weeks of nightly parades. It reopens weekends in October for Halloween-themed daytime Happy Hauntings and evening Phantom Fright Nights—the latter isn't recommended for children under 13—and again on select days in late November and December for holiday festivities.

Sandcastle

Opened in 1989 on a former railroad yard, **Sandcastle** (1000 Sandcastle Dr., 412/462-6666, www.sandcastlewaterpark.com, adults $33-36, seniors and children under 48 inches tall $23-26) quickly became Pittsburghers' favorite place to cool off on sweltering days. The water park on the bank of the Monongahela River has more than a dozen waterslides and a 300,000-gallon wave pool. Tykes get a pool and play area of their own.

Arrive by boat and dock at Sandcastle for free; drive and it's $7 for parking. The water park is open daily from mid-June to late August and some weekends before and after that period. Gates generally open at 11am and close at 6pm or 7pm.

Entertainment and Events

BARS AND LOUNGES

It shouldn't come as a surprise that a sports-obsessed city with several colleges would support numerous bars. Pittsburgh's watering holes are a diverse bunch, with sticky-floored, student-packed, Bud-and-wings joints only a slim majority. This is a town that's coming around to five-ingredient cocktails and microbrews. Generally speaking, head downtown for bars filled with smartly dressed professionals and theatergoers. To barhop with herds of 20-somethings, hightail it to East Carson Street on the South Side. When the Steelers or Pirates are playing, bob in a sea of black and gold on the North Side.

Downtown and the Strip District

The house drinks at **Seviche** (930 Penn Ave., 412/697-3120, www.seviche.com, 4pm-10pm Tues.-Thurs., 4pm-11pm Fri.-Sat., tapas $5-16) are the caipirinha and pisco sour, but who can resist the mojito list? The high-ceilinged, multihued bar, offspring of its French proprietor's love affair with Latin culture, also has a sweet selection of South American and Spanish wines and beers. Food-wise, Seviche specializes in—what else?—ceviche, offering an assortment of fresh seafood in different preparations. Be sure to sample the Fire and Ice version, made spicy with habanero peppers and cooled with prickly pear granita. On Tuesday nights, tables are moved aside for salsa dancing.

You could go to **Olive or Twist** (140 6th St., 412/255-0525, www.olive-twist.com, 3:30pm-close Mon.-Sat., food $10-31) every night for two weeks and never order the same martini twice. Options at the brick-lined, romantically lit bar range from the classic gin and vermouth to liquid desserts like the Chocolate Covered Pretzel Martini. Above-average appetizers, sandwiches, and entrées make Olive or Twist a fine choice for a meal.

Small-production wines and craft cocktails are the star attractions at **Bar Marco** (2216 Penn Ave., 412/471-1900, www.barmarcopgh.com, 5pm-11pm Tues.-Sat., brunch 10am-3pm Sat.-Sun., food $15-27), an in-vogue wine bar in the Strip District with subway tile walls and bottle-lined shelves. The short menu skews Mediterranean. On weekends the former firehouse opens early for brunch. Note that if prices seem a dollar or two more than they should, it's because you won't be adding on 15-20 percent at the end: Bar Marco doesn't accept tips.

North Side

You can't swing a bat without hitting a sports bar outside PNC Park, home of the Pittsburgh Pirates. **Mullen's Bar and Grill** (200 Federal St., 412/231-1112, www.mullensbarandgrill.com, 11am-1am Sun.-Thurs., 11am-2am Fri.-Sat., food $9-15), part of a Chicago-area chain, and **McFadden's** (211 N. Shore Dr., 412/322-3470, www.mcfaddenspitt.com, 11am-2am Mon.-Sat., open for Sun. stadium events, food $9-14), which has its roots in New York City, are both packed when the Pirates or Steelers are playing but rather cheerless otherwise. The salad section of the McFadden's menu includes the Yinzer Diet, which is a house salad "smothered" in steak, cheese, and fries and should give you an idea of what to expect here. (A yinzer is a person from Pittsburgh.)

Plan to spend awhile choosing a beer at another Illinois export, **Beerhead Bar** (110 Federal St., 412/322-2337, www.beerheadbar.com, 3pm-12:30am Mon.-Fri, noon-2am Sat., noon-12:30am Sun., extended hours on game days). The draft and bottle lists are never-ending, but the bartenders know their stuff and are ready with advice and suggestions. Beerhead doesn't serve food, but the bar encourages patrons to bring takeout or have a bite delivered from a local eatery. The staff will even help you pick a beer that pairs well with your food delivery.

There are good reasons to leave the orbit of the stadiums. The **Monterey Pub** (1227 Monterey St., 412/322-6535, www.montereypub.com, 3pm-midnight Mon.-Sat., kitchen 5pm-10pm, food $10-16) is tucked into a residential street in the historic Mexican War Streets neighborhood, but you'll know it by its paint job: forest green with orange and white trim. If you haven't guessed already, this is an Irish-style establishment. Inside, it's cozy as can be. Slip into a mahogany booth, order a pint, and ponder the menu's unorthodox selection of nachos. If you prefer a little piece of Germany to a little piece of Ireland, head to **Max's Allegheny Tavern** (537 Suismon St., Pittsburgh, 412/231-1899, www.maxsalleghenytavern.com, 11am-10pm Mon.-Thurs., 11am-11pm Fri.-Sat., 9:30am-9pm Sun., food $7-18) in the heart of the Deutschtown neighborhood. The bar and restaurant dates to the turn of the last century. Wash down the *kielbasa and scnitzel* with a Hacker-Pschorr, Spaten, or other German brew.

South Side

The South Side's East Carson Street is party central. There's a bar—or two or three—on nearly every block in the business and entertainment district, roughly defined as the section between 9th and 28th Streets. Shot-n-beer joints predominate, but there's sleek sprinkled into the mix and even the occasional velvet rope. Word of caution: If you're over 25, you might feel downright geriatric as you navigate this swiftly flowing river of youth.

When it comes to beer selection and bar food, **Fat Head's Saloon** (1805 E. Carson St., 412/431-7433, www.fatheads.com, 11am-midnight Sun.-Thurs., 11am-1am Fri.-Sat., food $9-14) is head and shoulders above the rest. Its 30-plus draft beers are mainly of the craft variety. Munchies include a dozen different varieties of wings. Consider splitting one of the ginormous "headwiches." The Southside Slopes Headwich, an incomparable combo of kielbasa, fried pierogies, American cheese, and grilled onions, weighed in at number five when men's mag *Maxim* scoured the United States for the best "meat hog" sandwiches.

Speaking of gargantuan vittles, the specialty drinks at **Carson City Saloon** (1401 E. Carson St., 412/481-3203, www.carsoncitysaloon.com, 5pm-1:45am Mon.-Fri., 11:30am-1:45am Sat.-Sun., food $8-11) include the prophetically named Call A Cab, a 64-ounce bowl of rums and fruity liqueurs that's meant to be shared. Balance the alcohol with an order of 50 wings for $32. Yes, 50. There are nightly drink deals, including $2 Miller Lites on Tuesdays and $1 32-ounce Yuengling Lager drafts on Thursdays. Check out the wheelchair-accessible bathroom; it was a vault when the building was a bank.

If craft cocktails are more your thing than cheap beers and novelty bowls, go to **Acacia** (2108 E. Carson St., 412/488-1800, www.acaciacocktails.com, 5pm-2am Mon.-Sat.)—if you can find it. From the outside, the Prohibition-themed bar looks boarded up. But inside, knowledgeable bartenders mix up delectable drinks in a small, unflashy space that usually has a hushed vibe, especially compared to other East Carson Street establishments.

Spandex never goes out of style at **OTB (Over The Bar) Bicycle Café** (2518 E. Carson St., 412/381-3698, www.otbbicyclecafe.com, 11am-2am Mon.-Sat., noon-2am Sun., food $7-11). The watering hole is a tribute to two-wheeled travel, with bicycles hanging from the ceiling, gears decorating the walls, and sconces made of spokes. Even the toilet paper holders are made from bike parts.

Two blocks north of East Carson in the SouthSide Works development, you can't miss the humongous **Hofbräuhaus Pittsburgh** (2705 S. Water St., 412/224-2328, www.hofbrauhauspittsburgh.com, 11am-11pm Mon.-Wed., 11am-midnight Thurs., 11am-2am Fri.-Sat., noon-11pm Sun., closes earlier in winter, food $9-26). The Bavarian-style *bier* hall couldn't be more cartoonish if Walt Disney himself had designed it. Picture female servers clad in dirndls and men in lederhosen playing oompah music. Modeled after Munich's famous Hofbräuhaus, the Pittsburgh bar employs a brewmaster who supervises the production of four year-round beers and a seasonal concoction unveiled on the first Wednesday of every month. Try the soft pretzels, imported from Germany and served with homemade beer-infused cheese. Revelers spill from the *bier* hall into a riverside *biergarten* in summertime.

East End

It's not hard to find a bar in East End neighborhoods. Standouts include Friendship's **Sharp Edge Beer Emporium** (302 S. Saint Clair St., 412/661-3537, www.sharpedgebeer.com, 11am-midnight Mon.-Thurs., 11am-1am Fri.-Sat., noon-9pm Sun., food $12-17), which may well have the largest beer selection in the Burgh, with 70 taps and more than 150 bottles. It's nationally recognized for its Belgians but doesn't discriminate against brews of other provenance. Sharp Edge has four sister establishments, including one in downtown, but the beer list at the Friendship location is unparalleled.

Squirrel Hill may be nowhere near a beach, but you can pretend you're on a tropical isle at the neighborhood's resident tiki bar, **Hidden Harbor** (1708 Shady Ave., 412/422-5040, www.hiddenharborpgh.com, 5pm-midnight Tues.-Thurs., 5pm-1am Fri.-Sat.). Cocktails garnished with orchids, over 250 rums to choose from, and jungle décor create a vacation vibe. Next door, sister spot

Independent Brewing Company (1704-1706 Shady Ave., 212/422-5040, 5pm-11pm Mon.-Wed., 5pm-midnight Thurs., 4pm-midnight Fri-Sat., 4pm-9pm Sun.) skips the Zombies and planter's punch in favor of craft brews.

For a quintessential dingy dive bar experience, you can't beat **Gooski's** (3117 Brereton St., 412/681-1658, no website, 11am-2am Mon.-Sun.) in the Polish Hill neighborhood. Graffiti-covered walls, punk rock regulars, a jukebox and pool table, cheap beer and pierogies—this place has all the angles covered. Bands play on the weekends. Be forewarned that it's not uncommon to find a bar in Pittsburgh where smoking is allowed, and Gooski's is on that list. The fog of smoke didn't stop *Esquire* from adding Gooski's to its list of the best bars in America in 2017.

The art deco **Kelly's Bar & Lounge** (6012 Penn Circle S., 412/363-6012, no website, 11:30am-2am Mon.-Sat.) in East Liberty evokes an era when gents called dames "doll" and *Double Indemnity* was in theaters. Contrived? Hardly. This place has been around since the 1940s. Order a classic cocktail—a sidecar, perhaps—for maximum effect. The beer selection is quite good, and the mac and cheese worth every calorie. Kelly's is more authentic than polished, and there's a no-frills patio out back.

NIGHTCLUBS

Nightclubs tend to come and go with a rapidity that's maddening to guidebook writers. If you're in the mood to dance, check the event listings in the weekly *Pittsburgh City Paper* (www.pghcitypaper.com) to see where the DJs are. At least one of them will be at **Diesel Club Lounge** (1601 E. Carson St., 412/431-8800, www.dieselclublounge.com, 9pm-2am Fri.-Sat.). Lighting maestros from Miami had a hand in its design, which helps explain why the slick multilevel nightclub looks more South Beach than South Side.

The Strip District also has its share of nightlife options, including **Room 16** (1650 Smallman St., 412/315-7330, www.room16pgh.com, 10pm-2am Sat., open some Fridays), notable for its devotion to electronic music. Its neighbor, **Club Zoo** (1630 Smallman St., 412/201-1100, no website, 7:30pm-1am Sat.), caters to the under-21 crowd.

LIVE MUSIC

The **PPG Paints Arena** (1001 5th Ave., general information 412/642-1800, tickets 800/745-3000, www.ppgpaintsarena.com), home to the Pittsburgh Penguins, is also equipped for elaborate stage shows, which attracts big-name artists like Lady Gaga and Katy Perry. Paul McCartney christened the $321 million venue in 2010.

The region's largest concert venue, **KeyBank Pavilion** (665 Route 18, Burgettstown, 724/947-7400, www.livenation.com), boasts pavilion and lawn seating for more than 20,000. It's about 25 miles west of downtown.

Outdoor concerts are also held at **Stage AE** (400 North Shore Dr., 412/229-5483, www.promowestlive.com), located on the North Shore next to Heinz Field. The amphitheater has room for 5,550 and the indoor concert hall seats 2,400. Both stages attract a wide variety of musical acts, from the Pixies to Megadeth.

Just north of the city, **Mr. Smalls** (400 Lincoln Ave., Millvale, 412/821-4447, www.mrsmalls.com) is housed in a former Catholic church. Most concerts are standing room only. The Mr. Smalls complex also includes recording studios that count the Black Eyed Peas, 50 Cent, and Ryan Adams among their clients.

The South Side's most revered music venue is **Club Cafe** (56-58 S. 12th St., 412/431-4950, www.clubcafelive.com), an intimate nightclub that books biggish singer-songwriters. Norah Jones made an appearance not long before collecting multiple Grammys for her debut album. The nearby **Rex Theater** (1602 E. Carson St., 412/381-6811, www.rextheater.net) dates to 1905. Vaudeville is out, but you can still count on an eclectic lineup.

Artsy types head to **Brillobox** (4104 Penn

Ave., 412/621-4900, www.brilloboxpgh.com) in the Bloomfield neighborhood to see local and touring indie bands. The venue is perhaps better known for DJ dance parties.

PERFORMING ARTS

Cultural District

Bordered by the Allegheny River on the north, 10th Street on the east, Stanwix Street on the west, and Liberty Avenue on the south, the Cultural District fits in seven theaters. Think of it as a miniature version of New York's Broadway theater district. Not unlike Times Square, it's the stardust-sprinkled reincarnation of a seedy section of town. The transformation can be traced to the mid-1960s, when H. J. Heinz Company chairman Jack Heinz resolved to turn a shuttered movie palace into a new home for the Pittsburgh Symphony Orchestra. In 1971, the former Loew's Penn Theater was dedicated as **Heinz Hall** (600 Penn Ave., 412/392-4900, www.trustarts.org), a vision in red velvet, Italian marble, crystal, and 24-karat gold leaf. It's enough to give you goose bumps even before the renowned **Pittsburgh Symphony Orchestra** (www.pittsburghsymphony.org) starts playing. For extra goose bumps, come on a night when the 115-voice **Mendelssohn Choir of Pittsburgh** (www.themendelssohn.org) is also under the spell of the conductor's baton. Heinz Hall also hosts free concerts by the **Pittsburgh Youth Symphony Orchestra** (www.pittsburghyouthsymphony.org), touring Broadway shows, and other guest performances.

Jack Heinz's recycling of a 1927 theater scheduled for demolition inspired further development. In the mid-1980s, the newly formed Pittsburgh Cultural Trust undertook a $43 million restoration of another former movie house a block away. Billed as "Pittsburgh's Palace of Amusement" when it opened in 1928, the resplendent Stanley Theater had fallen into disrepair and into the hands of a rock concert promoter by the late 1970s. (Bob Marley played his final concert there in 1980.) It reopened in 1987 as the **Benedum Center** (237 7th St., 412/456-6666, www.benedumpittsburgh.com), a dead ringer for the Stanley on opening night in 1928, right down to the original 4,700-pound chandelier. The largest theater in the Cultural District, the Benedum hosts performances by the **Pittsburgh Opera** (www.pittsburghopera.org) and **Pittsburgh Ballet Theatre** (www.pbt.org), along with musical theater productions by **Pittsburgh CLO** (www.pittsburghclo.org). Touring acts also take the stage.

The Cultural Trust's next project was the **Byham Theater** (101 6th St., 412/456-6666, www.trustarts.org), which opened in 1904 as a vaudeville house named the Gayety and became the Fulton movie theater in the 1930s. Look for its original name in the salvaged mosaic tile floor in the entry vestibule. Less ornate than Heinz Hall or the Benedum, the 1,300-seat Byham draws a more casual crowd with dance and theater performances, live music, films, and lectures. The mural on the Fort Duquesne Boulevard facade of the Byham is a tribute to Pittsburgh's steel heritage.

The Cultural Trust's first from-scratch theater project, the **O'Reilly Theater** (621 Penn Ave., 412/316-1600, www.trustarts.org), cost less than renovating the Benedum, even with hotshot architect Michael Graves on the job. The 650-seat theater opened in December 1999 with the world premiere of playwright August Wilson's *King Hedly II*. It's the only downtown venue with a thrust stage, surrounded by seats on three sides. As the permanent home of the professional **Pittsburgh Public Theater** (www.ppt.org), good for more than 200 performances a year, the O'Reilly rarely gets a rest.

Wilson, one of the 20th century's most celebrated playwrights, grew up in the Hill District just east of downtown. He's best known for a 10-play series often referred to as the Pittsburgh Cycle. Each play depicts African American life in a different decade of the 1900s, and all but one are set in the Hill District, once known as a hotbed of jazz. Wilson won Pulitzer Prizes for *Fences* (later made into a movie starring Denzel Washington and Viola Davis) and *The Piano Lesson* and was the first African American to have two plays running on Broadway at the same time. Owned by the nonprofit African American Cultural Center, the performing arts venue **August Wilson Center** (980 Liberty Ave., 412/471-6070, www.culturaldistrict.org) is named in his honor. It hosts exhibits, talks, dance performances, and concerts.

Carnegie Music Hall

Arrive early if you're coming to the 1,950-seat **Carnegie Music Hall** (4400 Forbes Ave.), part of the complex that includes the Carnegie Museums of Art and Natural History. Its most magnificent feature is its gilded foyer with 45-foot ceilings and green marble columns. The hall itself, humble by comparison, is the setting for concerts presented by the **Pittsburgh Chamber Music Society** (412/624-4129, www.pittsburghchambermusic.org), which imports the world's most celebrated ensembles. It's also one of the stomping grounds of the **River City Brass Band** (412/434-7222, www.rivercitybrass.org), 28 brass players and percussionists with a repertoire that ranges from traditional marches to Hollywood tunes.

City Theatre

Not content to recycle tried-and-true theatrical works, **City Theatre** (1300 Bingham St., 412/431-2489, www.citytheatrecompany.org) embraces the edgy and new. Expect a good number of world premieres in a typical season. The 254-seat main stage and a second smaller theater are a block from the South Side's carousing corridor, East Carson Street.

FESTIVALS AND EVENTS

Summer

Pittsburghers elevate picnicking to an art form during **Summer Fridays** concerts (412/371-0600, www.thefrickpittsburgh.org, first Friday June-Sept., free), which signal the start and end of summer in this city. Regulars begin laying claim to sections of lawn at the Frick Art & Historical Center 90 minutes before showtime.

What started in 1960 as an effort by museum types to bring the arts to non-museum types has blossomed into the **Three Rivers Arts Festival** (412/456-6666, www.3riversartsfest.org, June, free). The 10-day festival draws hundreds of thousands of people to Point State Park and other downtown sites. There are public art installations, gallery exhibits, theater and dance performances, and activities for the kids, plus plenty of food and craft vendors.

Machines capable of speeds of 130 mph ply local waterways during the **Three Rivers Regatta** (www.yougottaregatta.org, Aug., free). But the spectacle-packed weekend isn't just about powerboat racing. Past regattas have treated the crowds to water-ski stunt shows, skydiving displays, Red Bull Flugtag competitions, waterfront concerts, fireworks, and lighted boat parades.

If you find yourself driving alongside a "gullwing" Mercedes-Benz or a 1959 Ferrari, chances are it's **Pittsburgh Vintage Grand Prix** (412/299-2273, www.pvgp.org, July, free) time. The 10-day tribute to classic and exotic cars started as a one-day race in 1983 and has grown to include shows, cruises, and races in half a dozen locations. It culminates the third weekend in July with a show of some 2,000 vehicles and a series of vintage sports car races at Schenley Park. Nowhere else in the nation can you see such races on city streets.

Fall

The **Pittsburgh Irish Festival** (412/422-1113, www.pghirishfest.org, weekend after Labor Day, adults $12-15, seniors and students $10, children 12 and under free) could make you fall in love with the Emerald Isle—maybe even enough to fork over 15 bucks for a bag of soil presumably gathered there. The three-day festival is heavy on music and dance but dutifully showcases other aspects of Celtic culture, including sports, crafts, cuisine, and even native dog breeds. It's set at the appropriately emerald Riverplex, a large picnic grounds adjacent to Sandcastle water park.

Winter

An estimated 200,000 people turn out to see buildings and trees decked out for the holiday season during **Light Up Night** (412/566-4190, www.downtownpittsburghholidays.com, Nov., free). Highlights include the unveiling of holiday window displays at Macy's, the lighting of towering Christmas trees, and, of course, the arrival of Santa.

First of all, **First Night Pittsburgh** (412/456-6666, www.firstnightpgh.com, Dec. 31) takes place on the last night of the year, not the first. Second of all, it's not the bacchanalia you may have come to expect from New Year celebrations. First Night is family friendly and, like all projects of the Pittsburgh Cultural Trust, arts-focused. You can take in a comedy show or concert, watch fire dancers or a magic act, pick up puppetry, get your face painted, check out an art exhibit, and settle in for story time—all before counting down to midnight. The grand finale: fireworks, of course. The Cultural Trust squeezes more than a hundred programs into the six-hour party, which spans dozens of downtown locations. A First Night button (adults $10, children 5 and under free) is required.

Spring

Performing arts groups from all over the world entertain at the **Pittsburgh International Children's Festival** (412/456-6666, www.pghkids.org, May). The four-day event takes places in and around Oakland's Schenley Plaza. All featured performances require tickets, which can be purchased in advance online or at the on-site box office. Kids under two get in free.

Three Rivers Regatta

Shopping

THE STRIP DISTRICT

The narrow strip of a neighborhood just northeast of downtown is bordered by the Allegheny River on the north, 11th Street on the east, and 33rd Street on the west. It's home to block after block of specialty foods purveyors. If you're up for navigating a crowd, go on a Saturday morning, when the air is permeated with the smells of street foods and the Strip is more of an experience than a shopping trip.

Most stores are clustered along **Penn Avenue** between 17th and 22nd Streets. For chocoholics, there's **Mon Aimee Chocolat** (2101 Penn Ave., 412/395-0022, www.monaimeechocolat.com, 8:30am-5pm Mon.-Fri., 7:30am-5pm Sat., 10am-3:30pm Sun.) at Penn and 21st. Across the street is **La Prima Espresso** (205 21st St., 412/281-1922, www.laprima.com, 6am-4pm Mon.-Wed., 6am-7pm Thurs., 6am-5pm Fri.-Sat., 7am-4pm Sun.), run by the first certified organic coffee roaster in Pittsburgh. A few blocks away, **Prestogeorge** (1719 Penn Ave., 412/471-0133, www.prestogeorge.com, 8am-4pm Mon.-Thurs., 8am-5pm Fri., 7am-5pm Sat.) offers 400-plus varieties of coffee and loose-leaf tea.

The legendary selection of cheeses at **Pennsylvania Macaroni Co.** (2010-2012 Penn Ave., 412/471-8330, www.pennmac.com, 6:30am-4:30pm Mon.-Sat., 9am-2:30pm Sun.) can be downright overwhelming. Penn Mac, as locals call it, was founded in 1902 by three Sicilian brothers and the same family is still at the wheel. Pasta manufacturing was its first business. Today it offers more than 5,000 items, including all things Italian. Five Greek brothers who landed in America in 1907 opened **Stamoolis Brothers Co.** (2020 Penn Ave., 412/471-7676, www.stamoolis.com, 7am-4pm Mon.-Fri., 7:30am-4pm Sat.). Olives in every shade, size, and flavor can be found here, along with cheeses, olive oils, spices, and Mediterranean specialties like stuffed grape leaves, spanakopita, and baklava.

For even more spices, put **Penzeys Spices** (1729 Penn Ave., 412/434-0570, www.penzeys.com, 9am-5pm Mon.-Sat., 9am-3pm Sun.) on your list. Penzeys carries everything from salt and pepper to ajwain seeds from Pakistan and

shopping in the Strip District

whole Turkish mahlab. With locations across the country, Penzeys is one of the few Strip merchants that's not locally based.

SOUTH SIDE

It's easy to while away an afternoon shopping in the **East Carson Street business district,** roughly bounded by 9th and 28th Streets, especially if you factor in time for admiring the Victorian architecture.

The retail/dining/entertainment/residential/office complex **SouthSide Works** (riverfront between 26th and Hot Metal Sts., 412/481-8800, www.southsideworks.com) was once a massive steelmaking enterprise. Now it features a 10-screen movie theater and a collection of chain stores, including Urban Outfitters and H&M. Heading west on East Carson Street from SouthSide Works, you'll find small boutiques, thrift shops, and record stores interspersed with bars and eateries, tattoo parlors, and live music venues.

SQUIRREL HILL

Just east of Oakland, Squirrel Hill is best known for its large Jewish population. It's home to **Pinsker's Judaica Center** (2028 Murray Ave., 412/421-3033, www.judaica.com, closed Sat.), which has been a source for Jewish books and gifts since 1954, and more recently added a kosher café and wine bar called Eighteen. But the shopping on the neighborhood's main thoroughfares, **Forbes and Murray Avenues,** is mostly of the secular variety. Just a block from Pinskers is **Jerry's Records** (2136 Murray Ave., 412/421-4533, www.jerrysrecords.com, 10am-6pm Tues.-Sat., noon-5pm Sun.), a magnet for vinyl enthusiasts from near and far. Like its albums, which number well over a million, the expansive store is a relic of another era. *Paste* magazine crowned it the "best place to spot world-renowned crate diggers—and nab a bargain at the same time."

LAWRENCEVILLE

Lawrenceville is a study in arts-driven urban revitalization. Boutiques, artist studios, and galleries line the neighborhood's **Butler Street.** Shoppers should focus their energies on the stretch of Butler between 36th and 47th Streets, home to fashion boutiques such as **Pavement** (3629 Butler St., 412/621-6400, www.pavementpittsburgh.com, 11am-6pm Tues.-Sat., 11am-4pm Sun.) and **Pageboy** (3613 Butler St., 412/224-2294, www.pageboypgh.com, noon-8pm Tues.-Thurs., noon-7pm Fri., 9am-3pm Sat.-Sun.), which doubles as a salon. Work your way toward the other end of the corridor, where you'd be wise to treat yourself to a croissant or a chocolate éclair from French bakery **La Gourmandine** (4605 Butler St., 412/682-2210, www.lagourmandinebakery.com, 7:30am-4:30pm Mon.-Fri., 9am-2:30pm Sat.-Sun.). If you're not worn out from shopping yet, keep going to **Von Walter & Funk** (5210 Butler St., 412/784-0800, www.vonwalterandfunk.com, 11am-7pm Tues.-Fri., 11am-6pm Sat., 11am-4pm Sun.) for vintage martini glasses, whimsical throw pillows, and other uncommon home goods.

Sports and Recreation

Pittsburgh has a well-earned reputation as a sports town. It became known as the "City of Champions" for a time in the 1970s and early '80s, when the Pirates won two of their five World Series titles and the Steelers claimed four Super Bowl wins. In 2009, the Steelers became the first team in the National Football League to win six championships. The Pittsburgh Penguins captured the nation's attention in the early 1990s, bringing home the Stanley Cup twice in two years. They repeated the feat in 2016 and 2017 with back-to-back wins.

"Enthusiastic" doesn't begin to describe Pittsburgh sports fans. "Rabid" comes close. A wardrobe without a black and gold sports jersey is something of an anomaly. (Pittsburgh is unique in that all of its major pro sports teams wear the same colors.) The citizenry's accessory is the black and gold Terrible Towel, an emblem of Steelers devotion waved by fans at every game. According to Steelers.com: "When babies are born, they are wrapped in the Terrible Towel in the hospital. Couples have waved Terrible Towels at their wedding."

Of course, cheering on the teams isn't the only pastime in a city of three rivers. Boating and fishing are among the ways to unwind. The city and its environs also afford opportunities for hiking, biking, cross-country skiing, snowshoeing, and more. If you're new to any of these activities or unfamiliar with the area, consider a **Venture Outdoors** (412/255-0564, www.ventureoutdoors.org) outing. The nonprofit recreation company offers a year-round calendar of group activities, from early-morning paddles to sunset hikes to overnight bike tours. Fees vary.

PARKS

Frick Park

Schenley Park may be Pittsburgh's most beloved green expanse, but it's not the largest. That distinction goes to **Frick Park** (412/682-7275, www.pittsburghparks.org/frick), a 561-acre sanctuary that straddles several East End neighborhoods. It's woodsier and less manicured than Schenley. Most mountain bikers will tell you Frick has the best trails in the city. It's also popular with hikers, though the sound of vehicles on the nearby Parkway East (I-376) can really break one's reverie. Another recreational option: the medieval sport of lawn bowling. The **Frick Park Bowling Green** (7300 Reynolds St., 412/402-8211, www.lawnbowlingpittsburgh.org) is the only public lawn bowling green in Pennsylvania. You'll also find off-leash exercise areas for dogs, off-leash exercise areas for kids (aka playgrounds), and red clay tennis courts dating to 1930. Frick has a number of entrances, some marked by distinctive stone gatehouses. Families with young children flock to the playgrounds near the intersection of Forbes and South Braddock Avenues and at Beechwood Boulevard and English Lane. Both are good starting points for a walk in the woods, as is the Frick Environmental Center at 2005 Beechwood Boulevard.

Highland Park

The award for grandest entrance goes to **Highland Park** (412/682-7275, www.pittsburghparks.org/highland), located in the East End neighborhood of the same name. Follow North Highland Avenue to its northernmost point and you'll pass between sculptures atop tall pedestals, arriving at a Victorian-style entry garden complete with fountain, reflecting pool, and neatly arranged benches. Steps at the far end of the garden lead to the park's iconic feature: a 19th-century municipal reservoir circled by a three-quarter-mile promenade. You'll find walkers and joggers and, sometimes, waterfowl. Road cyclists adore Highland Park for its half-mile velodrome, formerly a driver's training course. The park is also home to the Pittsburgh Zoo & PPG

Aquarium, a summer jazz series, several playgrounds, a pair of sand volleyball courts, and the city's only long-course **swimming pool** (151 Lake Dr., 412/665-3637, 1pm-7:45pm Mon.-Fri., 1pm-5:45pm Sat.-Sun. summer, adults $5, children 3-15 $3).

Riverview Park

The North Side's **Riverview Park** (Riverview Ave., 412/682-7275, www.pittsburghparks.org/riverview) is popular for its wooded trails, space-themed playground, and **swimming pool** (400 Riverview Ave., 412/323-7223, 1pm-7:45pm Mon.-Fri., 1pm-5:45pm Sat.-Sun. summer, adults $5, children 3-15 $3). It's particularly packed on Saturday evenings in summer, when it hosts a jazz concert followed by an outdoor movie—both free.

BICYCLING

Pittsburgh's steep hills and tangled streets can be intimidating to novice and new-in-town cyclists. Here to help: **Bike Pittsburgh** (188 43rd St., Suite 1, 412/325-4334, www.bikepgh.org). The advocacy group publishes the free *Pittsburgh Bike Map,* available at its office in Lawrenceville and at like-minded businesses. The map identifies car-free trails, on-street bike routes, and very steep hills. The online version allows cyclists to explore routes in terrain and satellite modes.

If you're interested in a scenic excursion, hit the 24-mile **Three Rivers Heritage Trail.** Rather than a continuous route, it's a set of trails along the Allegheny, Monongahela, and Ohio Rivers with names to match the areas they traverse. Maps are available from Friends of the Riverfront (2345 Preble Ave., 301/491-1733, www.friendsoftheriverfront.org), which spearheads development of the trail. If a days-long journey is on the agenda, there's the **Great Allegheny Passage** (www.gaptrail.org), a 150-mile trail stretching from Point State Park in downtown to Cumberland, Maryland. There it meets the 184.5-mile C&O Canal towpath, which traces the Potomac River to Washington DC. Biking to the nation's capital has become a rite of passage for Pittsburgh cyclists.

Need wheels? **Golden Triangle Bike Rental** (600 1st Ave., 412/600-0675, www.bikepittsburgh.com, 8:30am-7pm Mon.-Tues., Thurs., and Sat.-Sun., 8:30am-4pm Wed. and Fri. Apr.-mid-Oct.) is conveniently located along the Eliza Furnace Trail in downtown, part of the Three Rivers Heritage Trail and Great Allegheny Passage. It offers a wide variety of bikes, including children's bikes and tandems, plus child trailers and tag-a-longs that essentially transform an adult bike into a tandem. Adult bikes start at $8 per hour or $32 per day. Reserve at least a day in advance for a discounted day rate.

Bike enthusiasts should mark their calendars for **BikeFest** (412/325-4334, www.bikepgh.org, Aug.), Bike Pittsburgh's 18-day celebration of all things cycling. Mountain bikers will appreciate **Trail Fest** (www.ptagtrails.org), a series of organized rides, runs, and hikes showcasing Allegheny County's parks.

HIKING

If a heart-pumping walk is what you're after, this famously hilly city is happy to oblige. Test your mettle on Canton Avenue in the neighborhood of Beechview, southeast of downtown. With a grade of 37 percent, it's the steepest street in these parts and, possibly, the world. (*Guinness World Records* tips its hat to New Zealand's Baldwin Street, with a grade of 35 percent.) Of course, hiking isn't quite hiking without soil under your feet. Excellent trails can be found in many city and county parks. A standout: the 35.7-mile **Rachel Carson Trail,** which has its western terminus in North Park and its eastern terminus in Harrison Hills Park. Between the county parks, it visits woods and fields, creeks and steep bluffs, suburbia and farm country. A hiker's guide is available through the Rachel Carson Trails Conservancy (412/475-8881, www.rachelcarsontrails.org), the volunteer-based organization that maintains the trail. There are no shelters along the trail, which is intended for day hiking. It's not impossible to do the whole trail in one day—in fact, it's encouraged. Scads of brave souls attempt it every summer during the Rachel Carson Trail Challenge, a 34-mile, sunrise-to-sunset endurance hike.

BOATING

Crisscrossed as it is by three rivers, Pittsburgh offers plenty of opportunities to get off dry land. In fact, the city boasts the second-largest number of registered pleasure boats in the country. About 20 marinas dot Allegheny County's shorelines. Go to the Pennsylvania Fish & Boat Commission website (www.fishandboat.com) for locations. Boaters can moor at Station Square, the South Side's dining and entertainment complex, or along the North Shore, home to the Steelers and Pirates, for free. Other attractions accessible by boat include Point State Park and Sandcastle water park.

If you're not in possession of a yacht or humbler vessel, you're not out of luck. The Station Square-based **Gateway Clipper Fleet** (412/355-7980, www.gatewayclipper.com) boasts five riverboats and an array of cruises, from the kid-centric Superhero cruise to sunset dinners to beer tastings. A smaller operation, **Pittsburgh Water Limo** (412/221-5466, www.pittsburghwaterlimo.com), operates the 110-passenger *Fantasy* and the 39-passenger *Miss Pittsburgh.* The latter hosts "Sailgate" parties before Steelers games.

Get closer to the water by renting a kayak. **Kayak Pittsburgh** (www.ventureoutdoors.org/kayakpittsburgh) offers flat-water kayaks, which require no experience, at three locations. Most convenient to downtown is Kayak Pittsburgh North Shore (412/337-1519, daily Memorial Day-Sept., Sat.-Sun. May and Oct.), located under the north side of the Roberto Clemente Bridge, aka the 6th Street Bridge, a stone's throw from PNC Park. Solo kayaks are $16-19 for the first hour and $8-9.50 per additional half hour; tandems are $21.50-24.50 for the first hour and $10.75-12.25 per additional half hour.

The **Three Rivers Rowing Association** (300 Waterfront Dr., 412/231-8772, www.threeriversrowing.org) offers rowing, kayaking, and dragon boating programs for all skill levels. It also hosts the **Head of the Ohio Regatta** (www.headoftheohio.org, fall), a 2.8-mile race that attracts about 2,000 rowers and thousands of spectators.

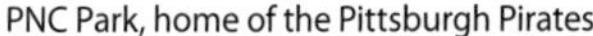

PNC Park, home of the Pittsburgh Pirates

SPECTATOR SPORTS

"Sixburgh," as the city dubbed itself when the Steelers captured their sixth National Football League championship, is a sports town through and through. On game days, it seems like half the populace is clad in black and gold, colors shared by the city's professional football, hockey, and baseball teams. When the Penguins brought home the Stanley Cup, hockey's holy grail, in 2017, an estimated 650,000 people turned out for the victory parade in the middle of a Wednesday—this at a time when the city's population stood at 303,000.

Football

Founded by Art Rooney in 1933, Pittsburgh's football franchise is the fifth oldest in the National Football League. Originally called the Pittsburgh Pirates in deference to the city's much older ball club, the **Steelers** (www.steelers.com) are still property of the Rooney family. Since 2001, they've played at 65,050-seat **Heinz Field** (100 Art Rooney Ave., 412/323-1200, www.heinzfield.com) on the North Side. Tickets were hard to come by even before the team captured its sixth Super Bowl title in 2009. The University of Pittsburgh football team also calls the stadium home. Tickets to its games are considerably easier to come by. Stadium **tours** (adults $8, seniors and children 5-17 $7) are offered select weekdays from April through October. Call or check the website for details.

Catch the Steelers in action—for free!—at their summer training camp on the campus of **Saint Vincent College** (300 Fraser Purchase Rd., Latrobe, 724/532-6600, www.stvincent.edu) in Latrobe, about 40 miles east of the city. The annual training camp has been held at Saint Vincent since 1966. The Steelers arrive in late July and leave about a month later. Check the team's website for training camp dates and times. Often the schedule isn't confirmed until sometime in June or early July. The afternoon practices are open to the public. After practice, fans jostle for autographs in designated areas.

Hockey

Art Rooney's huge clout in the sports world proved invaluable in the mid-1960s, during Pittsburgh's successful bid for a National Hockey League franchise. When it came time to name the expansion team, inspiration came from the downtown arena that would serve as its home, nicknamed "the Igloo" for reasons apparent to anyone who saw it. The **Penguins** (PPG Paints Arena, 1001 5th Ave., 412/642-1842, www.nhl.com/penguins) played their first game in the arena in October 1967 and their last in April 2010. The five-time Stanley Cup winners moved to a new home across the street—the $321 million PPG Paints Arena—in time for the 2010-2011 season. There's a waiting list for season tickets, but individual game tickets can be purchased at the arena box office, at Ticketmaster outlets, online at ticketmaster.com, or by phone at 800/642-7367.

Baseball

Pittsburgh's Major League Baseball club is its oldest professional sports franchise, dating to the late 1800s. The **Pirates** (tickets 877/893-2827, www.pirates.com) play at **PNC Park** (115 Federal St., 412/321-2827), located on the Allegheny River. The team captured two World Series titles while the Steelers were still a twinkle in Art Rooney's eye and three more in the 1960s and '70s. Then, in the 1990s, their fortunes soured, which is a polite way of saying they sucked. In 2012 the "Bucs" posted their 20th consecutive losing season—a first in the history of U.S. professional sports. They finally turned things around in 2013, posting a winning season and advancing to the playoffs for the first time since 1992. Pittsburgh fell back in love with its ball team.

Walking tours (adults $10, seniors and children 6-14 $8) of PNC Park are conducted weekdays from mid-April through late September and select Saturdays. They last about 90 minutes and include the Pirates dugout, batting cages, and press box. Tour tickets are available at the main ticket window on the corner of Federal and General Robinson Streets.

Food

Unlike Philadelphia, which is practically synonymous with the cheesesteak, Pittsburgh doesn't have a famous dish. Pierogies—semicircular dumplings traditionally filled with the likes of mashed potatoes and sauerkraut—may be the closest thing, thanks to an influx of Polish immigrants during the city's industrial heyday. French fries also figure prominently in local cuisine. A "Pittsburgh-style" sandwich is stuffed with fries. A "Pittsburgh-style" salad is topped with them. If you haven't figured it out already, this is a meat-and-potatoes kind of town.

If you're not a fan of meat and potatoes, don't despair. While the Burgh has a long way to go before it's considered a dining destination, vegetarians, vegans, and those just looking to eat a little lighter have options, too.

DOWNTOWN AND THE STRIP DISTRICT

New American

Downtown has no shortage of restaurants catering to professionals, theatergoers, and anyone who expects a dining *experience* as much as a meal. Its name may suggest otherwise, but ★ **Meat & Potatoes** (649 Penn Ave., 412/325-7007, www.meatandpotatoespgh.com, 5pm-11pm Mon.-Tues., 5pm-midnight Fri., 10:30am-2pm and 5pm-midnight Sat., 10:30am-2pm and 5pm-10pm Sun., $11-35) delivers. With its large central bar, chicly rugged decor, and high decibel level, the restaurant has been a hit since it opened in 2011. Its self-billing as Pittsburgh's first gastropub is disputable, but with menu items like bone marrow, pâté, and wild mushroom risotto, there's no disputing that chef-owner Richard DeShantz raises the bar on bar food. The weekend brunch features a do-it-yourself Bloody Mary bar.

Highly regarded for its wine selection, **Eleven** (1150 Smallman St., 412/201-5656, www.elevenck.com, 11:30am-2pm and 5pm-10pm Mon.-Thurs., 11:30am-2pm and 5pm-11pm Fri., 5pm-11pm Sat., 11am-2pm Sun., $24-65) has been luring diners to the Strip District since 2004. It's part of Pittsburgh's Big Burrito Restaurant Group, which owns eateries more stylish than the name implies. A tavern menu ($12-24) available in Eleven's first-floor lounge and inviting second-floor patio lets budget-minded sophisticates enjoy the modern space.

Mexican

Diners might be surprised to learn Richard DeShantz of Meat & Potatoes is also chef-owner at **Täkō** (214 6th St., 412/471-8256, www.takopgh.com, 11am-2pm and 5pm-11pm Mon.-Thurs., 11am-2pm and 5pm-midnight Fri., 5pm-midnight Sat., 3pm-9pm Sun., $12-18). Those expecting another upscale gastropub will instead find Asian-infused south-of-the-border street food served in a lively, colorful setting while a DJ provides the evening's soundtrack. (This is not the place to go for a quiet meal.) Tacos range from the traditional to a Korean version with wagyu short rib, peanuts, and cucumber. The food pairs well with a selection from the lengthy margarita list.

Italian

It's often said that if you can make it in New York, you can make it anywhere. TV chef and cookbook author Lidia Bastianich already had two successful restaurants in Manhattan, Felidia and Becco, when she opened **Lidia's Pittsburgh** (1400 Smallman St., 412/552-0150, www.lidias-pittsburgh.com, 11:30am-2pm and 5pm-9pm Mon.-Thurs., 11:30am-2pm and 5pm-10pm Fri., 11am-2:30pm and 4:30pm-10pm Sat., 11am-2:30pm and 4:30pm-9pm Sun., $18-42) in the Strip District, so it stands to reason that Pittsburghers have embraced her brand of Italian cooking. Borrowing a page from

Eat Your Way Through Pittsburgh

Thanks to TV shows such as *Food Paradise* and *Man v. Food,* Primanti's sandwiches are as synonymous with Pittsburgh as steel and the Steelers. And Primanti's isn't the only eatery offering an authentic Pittsburgh dining experience.

BREAKFAST

On weekend mornings, there's often a line out the door at **Pamela's Diner** (www.pamelasdiner.com, under $10). Fortunately, the line moves quickly—Pamela's is a fast-paced place. The food comes sooner than you can say "eggs Benedict." That's because the local chain doesn't do eggs Benedict, or anything else in the chichi category of breakfast foods. Pamela's does scrambled eggs and cheese omelets, corned beef hash and home fries. It does what most greasy spoons do. But there's one thing it does differently: pancakes. No light and fluffy flapjacks here. Pamela's pancakes are crepe-like in their thinness, with crispy edges. Then-candidate Barack Obama flipped for them during a 2008 swing through the Keystone State. The following year he invited co-owners Pamela Cohen and Gail Klingensmith to the White House, where they cooked their famous pancakes for the Obamas and 80 veterans. Head to the Strip District location (60 21st St., 412/281-6366, 7am-3pm Mon.-Sat., 8am-3pm Sun.) to walk in the president's footsteps. Pamela's also has locations in Oakland (3703 Forbes Ave., 412/683-4066, 7:30am-4pm daily), Shadyside (5527 Walnut St., 412/683-1003, 8am-4pm Mon.-Sat., 8am-3pm Sun.), Squirrel Hill (1711 Murray Ave., 412/422-9457, 7:30am-3:30pm Mon.-Sat., 8am-3pm Sun.), Millvale (232 North Ave., 412/821-4655, 8am-4pm Mon.-Fri., 8am-3pm Sat., 8am-2pm Sun.), and the South Hills suburb of Mt. Lebanon (427 Washington Rd., 412/343-3344, 7:30am-3pm Mon.-Sat., 8am-3pm Sun.).

LUNCH

Fries are deli staples, but few delis do what **Primanti Bros.** (www.primantibros.com, under $10) does, which is place the traditional side *inside* the sandwich. For 50 cents, it will throw a fried egg into the mix. Primanti's, which had 27 locations in Pennsylvania at last count, dates to the 1930s, when Joe Primanti began selling sandwiches in the Strip District, then crowded with wholesale produce merchants. Many of Joe's customers were truckers on the go and needed a meal they could eat with one hand. The rest, as they say, is history.

If possible, visit the original location (46 18th St., 412/263-2142, 24 hours daily) in the Strip. You'll also find Primanti's in downtown (2 S. Market Sq., 412/261-1599, 10am-midnight Sun.-Thurs., 10am-2am Fri.-Sat.), Oakland (3803 Forbes Ave., 412/621-4444, 10am-midnight Sun.-Wed., 10am-3am Thurs.-Sat.), and the South Side (1832 E. Carson St., 412/381-2583, 11am-2am Mon.-Thurs., 11am-3am Fri., 10am-3am Sat., 10am-2am Sun.).

DINNER

Pamela's and Primanti's are easy on the wallet, if not the arteries. Come dinnertime, consider

Becco's playbook, Lidia's offers unlimited servings of three pasta preparations for a fixed price (lunch $17, dinner $22). The weekend brunch is a popular gut-buster: one entrée and unlimited helpings from the antipasti and sweets tables for $32 per person.

South American

Lines are always out the door at ★ **Gaucho Parrilla Argentina** (1601 Penn Ave., 412/709-6622, www.eatgaucho.com, 11am-9pm Tues.-Thurs., 11am-10pm Fri.-Sat., $9-26). Sniff the air as you walk by this BYOB at the edge of the Strip District and you'll understand why: The grilled meats Gaucho puts out are worth the wait. The different cuts of steak earn most of the raves, but you won't be disappointed with the cast iron-seared shrimp or veggie sides. Gaucho offers counter service

LeMont

splurging on a meal on Mount Washington's "Restaurant Row." The eateries along Grandview Avenue aren't necessarily the best in town, and you're more likely to be sitting next to out-of-towners than locals. But the skyline views they serve up are so incredible that you can forgive the forgettable food.

LeMont (1114 Grandview Ave., 412/431-3100, www.lemontpittsburgh.com, dinner 5pm-9pm Tues-Thurs., 5pm-10pm Fri.-Sat., 4pm-8pm Sun., $30-56), which celebrated its 57th anniversary in 2017, bills itself as "the place for special occasions." It's the picture of fancy schmancy, right down to the bow-tied servers. You can soak up the ambience without breaking the bank in the lounge, featuring nightly entertainment. Seafood lovers favor **Monterey Bay Fish Grotto** (1411 Grandview Ave., 412/481-4414, www.montereybayfishgrotto.com, 11am-3pm and 5pm-10pm Mon.-Thurs., 11am-3pm and 5pm-11pm Fri., 5pm-11pm Sat., 5pm-9pm Sun., $28-50), located well above sea level at the top of a luxury apartment building. It offers several varieties of fresh fish on any given day. The more casual **Grandview Saloon** (1212 Grandview Ave., 412/431-1400, www.thegrandviewsaloon.com, 11:30am-9pm Sun.-Thurs., 11:30am-10pm Fri.-Sat., $12-45) is notable for its outdoor seating. The menu covers all cravings with burgers, sandwiches, pasta, grilled seafood, and steak. It's not exactly cheap, but it's the best choice if you're on a budget but can't pass up that view.

only and doesn't take reservations; your best bet for dinner is to show up by 5pm.

Seafood

The **Original Oyster House** (20 Market Sq., 412/566-7925, www.originaloysterhousepittsburgh.com, 10am-10pm Mon.-Sat., 11am-7pm Sun., $10) holds the distinction of being Pittsburgh's oldest bar and restaurant. Oysters sold for a penny when it opened in 1870. Today a breaded oyster will set you back $2.75, and the size of the fish sandwich will blow your mind. Quench your thirst with a cold draft or a glass of buttermilk, which sold quite well during Prohibition. If the frozen-in-time joint looks familiar, it's probably because you've seen it in one of 20-plus movies, including *Night of the Living Dead*.

NORTH SIDE

Classic American

One of the Burgh's most beloved sports figures got into the restaurant game in 2007. **Jerome Bettis' Grille 36** (393 N. Shore Dr., 412/224-6287, www.jeromebettisgrille36.com, 11am-midnight Sun.-Thurs., 11am-2am Fri.-Sat., $10-59) boasts an astonishing 50 televisions and a large patio with views of the Pittsburgh skyline and Heinz Field, where Jerome "the Bus" Bettis wore the number 36 jersey for a decade. This place is so dedicated to game time that the bathroom mirrors are designed to let you see out to the TVs. (Don't worry, other patrons can't see in.) Famished? Start with the Hall of Fame nachos, proceed to the deep-fried cheeseburger, and finish with the one-pound carrot cake. Wash it all down with a made-in-Pennsylvania beer.

Asian

★ **Nicky's Thai Kitchen** (856 Western Ave., 412/321-8424, www.nickysthaikitchen.com, 11:30am-3pm and 5pm-9pm Mon.-Thurs., 11:30am-3pm and 5pm-10pm Fri.-Sat., 4pm-9pm Sun., $10-21) offers outstanding takes on familiar dishes like *tom yum* soup and pad thai, chef's specials that threaten to ruin you for other Thai eateries, and a delightful plant-filled patio. The Thai iced tea is terrific, but if you prefer something stronger, bring your own bottle. The corkage fee is $5.

SOUTH SIDE

Classic American

The 500-seat **Grand Concourse** (100 W. Station Square Dr., 412/261-1717, www.grandconcourserestaurant.com, 11am-10pm Mon.-Thurs., 11am-11pm Fri.-Sat., 9am-9pm Sun., $22-59) is the largest restaurant in the city and one of its, well, grandest. Set in a former train terminal, it's awash in marble, mahogany, brass, and stained glass. Seafood is its stock-in-trade, but those averse can turn to the beef and fowl section of the menu. The Sunday brunch (9am-3pm, adults $29, children under 12 $18) features everything from made-to-order omelets to chicken penne alfredo. Its attached sister restaurant, **Gandy Dancer Saloon** (4pm-11pm Mon.-Thurs., 4pm-midnight Fri., 11:30am-midnight Sat., 10am-10pm Sun., $11-19), offers a more casual atmosphere and menu prices to match.

Asian

For a steaming curry with a side of sexual innuendo, head to **Thai Me Up** (118 S. 23rd St., 412/488-8893, www.thaimeuppittsburgh.com, 11am-2:30pm and 4pm-9:30pm Mon.-Fri., noon-9:30pm Sat., $11-13), a BYOB that does a brisk takeout business. The steamed dumplings and lemongrass soup will have you begging for more.

Vegetarian

No two tables are the same at **The Zenith** (86 S. 26th St., 412/481-4833, www.zenithpgh.com, 11:30am-8:30pm Thurs.-Sat., 11am-2:30pm Sun., $7-11.50), where your seat could literally be sold out from under you. The vegetarian eatery doubles as an antiques shop, and everything from the glassware to the lamps can be yours for a price. You won't find a better deal than the $11.50 Sunday brunch. An entirely vegan buffet groans with more than a dozen dishes (cross your fingers for crunchy mayo-less slaw and noodles in peanut sauce), breads, pies, and so many Bundt cakes that veganism could easily be confused with hedonism. The cost includes an entrée from the menu, which isn't strictly vegan, and coffee or tea. Thursdays through Saturdays, the Zenith offers a modest variety of salads, sandwiches, and entrées.

OAKLAND AND POINTS EAST

Classic American

The neon-lit **Original Hot Dog Shop** (3901 Forbes Ave., 412/621-7388, 10am-10pm Sun.-Wed., 10am-2am Thurs.-Sat., $10) is to Oakland what Pink's is to Hollywood: a landmark where hazy memories are made. The O, as it's known, has been feeding the inebriated masses since 1960. It's justly famous for its fries, cooked twice for good measure and doused with cheese if you so choose, and also serves subs, burgers, and a few other items. So what if your feet stick to the floor? If you need another hot dog fix, **Franktuary** (3810 Butler St., 412/586-7224, www.franktuary.com, 11am-10:30pm Tues.-Thurs., 11am-11:30pm Fri.-Sat., 11am-8pm Sun., $3-12) in Lawrenceville is a classier joint than the O. Standard franks share the menu with a vegan version and the Locavore, made with Pennsylvania grass-fed beef. Gluten-free and vegan buns are available. Toppings range from classics like chili and sauerkraut to grilled pineapple and Thai peanut sauce. The menu also features cheesy poutines, an impressive cocktail list, and craft beers.

In Pittsburgh's Little Italy, **Tessaro's** (4601 Liberty Ave., 412/682-6809, 11am-11pm Mon.-Sat., $9-32) has been serving what many consider to be the city's best burger for more than 30 years. Its flame-grilled patties, made with house-ground meat, weigh in at half a pound. Be prepared to wait: The Bloomfield institution has a legion of regulars.

Shadyside's **Harris Grill** (5747 Ellsworth Ave., 412/362-5273, www.harrisgrill.com, 11:30am-2am Mon.-Fri., 11am-2am Sat., 10am-2am Sun., kitchen open until 1am, $9-22) inspires similar devotion, due in part to its signature frozen cosmos. Choose from a vegetarian-friendly selection of salads, sandwiches, and entrees, including a mac and cheese prepared with lobster tail and lump crab meat. The Pittsburgh-famous burnt almond torte from Prantl's Bakery makes a cameo on the dessert menu. On Tuesdays baskets of bacon are $1. In the warmer months, Harris's outdoor tables are among the most coveted in town.

Brewpubs

Some call it sacrilegious. Others call it a shining example of adaptive reuse. The **Church Brew Works** (3525 Liberty Ave., 412/688-8200, www.churchbrewworks.com, 11:30am-9:30pm Mon.-Thurs., 11:30am-11pm Fri.-Sat., noon-9pm Sun., bar open later, $8-34), a microbrewery and restaurant in a restored 1902 church building, has been called many things but never "typical." Stainless steel and copper brew vessels occupy the main altar of the former St. John the Baptist Church, which closed its doors in 1993. The oak planks of the pews were used to build both the long, curving bar and the seating in the dining section. There are separate pub and dinner menus with sandwiches on the former and hearty entrees on the latter, but both feature pierogies. A courtyard between the church building and onetime rectory provides for outdoor seating in the warmer months. Service can be sluggish, so flag down a waiter before your glass is half empty.

Mediterranean

Charcuterie is the star at ★ **Cure** (5336 Butler St., 412/252-2595, www.curepittsburgh.com, 5pm-close Mon. and Wed.-Fri., 4pm-close Sat.-Sun., $12-44), a buzzing Lawrenceville restaurant that's earned a spot on many a "best of" list. Chef-owner Justin Severino is serious about butchery, coming up with creative ways to make use of the whole animal for his Mediterranean-ish plates. With the pig-themed décor vegetarians might shy away, but there are excellent meat-free pastas and salads. Meat-eaters shouldn't skip the salumi board for the duck speck alone. The salumi skews Spanish at Severino's nearby **Morcilla** (3519 Butler St., 412/652-9924, www.morcillapittsburgh.com, 5pm-9pm Mon. and Wed.-Thurs., 5pm-10pm Fri., 4pm-10pm Sat., 4pm-9pm Sun., $10-35).

Casbah (229 S. Highland Ave., 412/661-5656, www.casbahpgh.com, 11:30am-2:30pm and 5pm-10pm Mon.-Thurs., 11:30am-2:30pm and 5pm-11pm Fri., 11am-2pm and 5pm-11pm Sat., 11am-2pm and 5pm-9pm Sun., $23-39) doesn't look like much from the outside. But inside it's a chic dining destination that pays homage to Mediterranean cuisines while showcasing Pennsylvania lamb, poultry, and produce. Its wine cellar is one of the best in town and the enclosed front patio is open year-round. The prix fixe weekend brunch (adults $28, children 12 and under $12) eschews waffles for lamb and eggs, Scottish salmon, a wild mushroom and goat cheese omelet, and other savory treats.

Mexican

With offerings like buttermilk fried chicken tacos and a Thai curry burrito, **Mad Mex** (370 Atwood St., 412/681-5656, www.madmex.com, 11am-1am daily, bar open until 2am, $8-12) is a far cry from traditional Mexican. Just about every burrito, enchilada, and taco can be made with portobellos or marinated tofu as well as chicken, steak, or shrimp. During happy *hora* (4:30pm-6:30pm Mon.-Fri.), the small Oakland restaurant is as crowded with coeds as Cancun during spring break. Mad Mex, part of the restaurant group that includes Eleven and Casbah, has half a dozen other locations in the Pittsburgh area. The Shadyside outpost is across the street from Casbah—a meal at either should be followed with a cone from neighboring ice cream shop **Millie's** (232 S. Highland Ave., 412/404-8853, www.millieshomemade.com, noon-10pm Sun.-Thurs., noon-11pm Fri.-Sat.).

Vegetarian and Vegan

Apteka (4606 Penn Ave., no phone, www.aptekapgh.com, 5pm-late Wed.-Sun., late-night menu served until midnight, $8-12) cooks up the best vegan Central and Eastern European food you've ever had. OK, so maybe it's the only vegan Central and Eastern European food you've ever had. It's excellent either way. Get in line, order at the bar, and find a table. The cafeteria-style ordering belies the complexity of the food and drink. Delicate potato dumplings rest in a spicy carrot broth and pierogies come stuffed with mushrooms and sauerkraut or celery root, apples, and horseradish. The tartines change daily. To drink, try the cocktail with Slivovitz, a plum brandy.

Chinese

If you prefer your Chinese food bland and Americanized, steer clear of **Chendu Gourmet** (5840 Forward Ave., 412/521-2088, www.chengdugourmet.net, 11am-9:30pm Mon.-Sat., 11:30am-9pm Sun., $10-21). The traditional Sichuan cuisine will make you flush from the heat, but power through. Chef Wei Zhu's menu is enormous, with everything from dan dan noodles to braised sea cucumber and sizzling cumin lamb to tea-smoked duck soup. When you start to feel overwhelmed, ask your server for guidance. There is also an American Chinese menu, if someone in your party can't go without General Tso's chicken. The restaurant is simply decorated and gently run-down.

Belgian

It's a shame that ★ **Point Brugge Café** (401 Hastings St., 412/441-3334, www.pointbrugge.com, 11am-10pm Tues.-Thurs., 11am-11pm Fri.-Sat., 11am-9pm Sun., $9-32) doesn't take reservations. Waiting for a table as servers whiz by with steamed mussels, steak frites, and hot-out-of-the-oven macaroni gratin is downright torturous. But trust that the Belgian-style fries with basil mayo are worth it. Tucked away in residential Point Breeze, the cozy neighborhood bistro is also known for its Belgian beer list. Golden waffles with notes of caramelized sugar make for particularly long waits during Sunday brunch (11am-3pm, $6-20).

Accommodations

Pittsburgh proper has a pleasant mix of chain hotels and independently owned establishments, and capacity is rarely an issue. It lacks budget accommodations, though. Budget travelers can bunk down in chain motels on the city's outskirts.

DOWNTOWN

$100-250

Downtown is home to the city's grandest hotels, and the ★ **Omni William Penn** (530 William Penn Place, 412/281-7100, www.omnihotels.com, from $160) is the grandest of them all. With nearly 600 guest rooms and suites—beautifully appointed with cherrywood furnishings and windows that actually open—it's also one of the largest hotels in the Burgh. You don't have to be a guest to soak up the grandeur. The massive lobby has crystal chandeliers, soaring archways, and plenty of inviting couches and armchairs.

Opened in 2015 in a beaux-arts building erected in 1903, the ★ **Kimpton Hotel Monaco Pittsburgh** (620 William Penn Pl., 412/471-1170, www.monaco-pittsburgh.com, from $160) is a chic addition to the city's hotel scene. The rooms aren't especially large, but they have the Kimpton brand's signature eclectic style with playful decor (including birdcage light fixtures), comfortable beds, and sparkling bathrooms. The closets come stocked with plush robes and yoga mats. Amenities at the pet-friendly hotel include a 24-hour fitness center, in-room spa services, and bicycles guests can borrow for free. Its hopping on-site restaurant, **The Commoner,** is open from early morning through late night. In warmer weather, the rooftop beer garden is open every night except Monday.

The **Westin Convention Center Pittsburgh** (1000 Penn Ave., 412/281-3700, www.westinpittsburgh.com, from $190) is a great choice for anyone with business at the David L. Lawrence Convention Center because the two are connected by a skywalk. But leisure travelers needn't shy away from the massive hotel. Its location near the intersection of downtown and the Strip District makes it convenient to numerous attractions and restaurants. The rooms are spacious, the service superb, and the rates quite reasonable for the area. The Westin also boasts an indoor pool and hot tub.

Despite having 300 guest rooms and suites and Marriott as its overlord, the **Renaissance Pittsburgh Hotel** (107 6th St., 412/562-1200, www.renaissancepittsburghpa.com, from $200) pulls off the feel of a boutique lodging. Set in the heart of the Cultural District, the Renaissance is a short stroll to several theaters. It's also so close to the Allegheny River that guests on the uppermost floors can take in a Pirates game on the opposite shore without leaving their plush rooms.

Over $250

The **Fairmont Pittsburgh** (510 Market St., 412/773-8800, www.fairmont.com/pittsburgh, from $250) opened in 2010 in a new skyscraper named Three PNC Plaza. Its guest rooms boast floor-to-ceiling windows that make for spectacular views. The hotel is justifiably proud of its commitment to sustainability. It was the first hotel in Pittsburgh to receive LEED certification. The Fairmont Pittsburgh is also notable for its 6,000-square-foot health club and day spa.

NORTH SHORE

$100-250

The North Shore has a smattering of unique, independently owned accommodations. Perhaps the most unusual is **The Parador Inn** (939 Western Ave., 412/231-4800, www.theparadorinn.com, $160), a slice of the Caribbean in the heart of Steeler Country. Owner Ed Menzer, whose long career in the hospitality industry included a stint at an oceanfront hotel in Florida, decorated the B&B in turquoise and other bright colors and filled the enclosed courtyard with tropical plants. Built in the 1870s, the manse boasts three porches, a formal parlor, and multiple dining rooms. Each of its eight large guest rooms has a private bathroom and working fireplace. The beds could stand to be upgraded.

One of the finest B&Bs in the Pittsburgh area, the **Inn on the Mexican War Streets** (604 W. North Ave., 412/231-6544, www.innonthemexicanwarstreets.com, $139-219) has eight guest rooms and suites of varying sizes, each with a private bathroom. Guests are more than welcome to tickle the ivories of the baby grand piano in the parlor. Breakfast is continental-style.

Built in 1888 as a home for Benedictine priests, ★ **The Priory Hotel** (614 Pressley St., 412/231-3338, www.thepriory.com, $99-250) is a 42-room beaut. The boutique hotel is decorated with antiques and oil paintings, equipped with cable and Wi-Fi, and filled with charm. The rooms are far from cookie-cutter and rates range considerably. A suite that takes up the whole fourth floor boasts a full kitchen and a view of the Pittsburgh skyline. On the other end of the spectrum are two single-person rooms, available for as little as $99 per night.

It's not all boutique lodging in this neighborhood. Two recommendable chain hotels are **SpringHill Suites Pittsburgh North Shore** (223 Federal St., 412/323-9005, www.marriott.com, from $130) and **Hyatt Place Pittsburgh-North Shore** (260 North Shore Dr., 412/321-3000, www.pittsburghnorthshore.place.hyatt.com, from $130). Both offer guest rooms with divided living and sleeping areas, contemporary decor, complimentary breakfast and Wi-Fi, an exercise room, and an indoor pool.

SOUTH SIDE
$100-250

Just one block from the South Side's hard-partying main drag, the **Morning Glory Inn** (2119 Sarah St., 412/431-1707, www.gloryinn.com, $155-220) is the picture of tranquility. Many a bride's fantasy wedding has come to pass in its brick-paved, gorgeously landscaped Savannah-style courtyard. The B&B also caters to the business traveler with high-speed Internet and shuttle service to downtown.

The **Sheraton Station Square Hotel** (300 W. Station Square Dr., 412/261-2000, www.starwoodhotels.com, from $150) is the

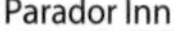

Parador Inn

linchpin in the redevelopment of the city's South Shore, once the site of a massive railway complex. Its best amenity is its skyline-and-rivers view; try to get a room facing the water. The guest rooms are well sized but have dated bathrooms. The 399-room hotel is also convenient: It's within walking distance of downtown, thanks to the pedestrian-friendly Smithfield Street Bridge. You can also stroll to the Gateway Clipper Fleet of riverboats and the famous Monongahela Incline.

OAKLAND AND POINTS EAST

Oakland, dominated by universities and hospitals, is peppered with chain hotels. For digs with more character, head to other East End neighborhoods.

$100-250

Pittsburgh's only Select Registry property, ★ **The Inn on Negley** (703 S. Negley Ave., 412/661-0631, www.innonnegley.com, $190-360), is a short walk from Shadyside's Walnut Street and Ellsworth Avenue, both lined with shops and eateries. The restored Victorian has eight exquisitely decorated guest rooms and suites. A full-menu breakfast is prepared by a professional chef and served on fine china.

It took six years and 200 union craftsmen to restore a pair of mansions to their 20th-century grandeur for **Mansions on Fifth** (5105 5th Ave., 412/381-5105, www.mansionsonfifth.com, $159-499). They're filled with antique and reproduction furnishings, fine European art, and the sort of architectural features that make preservationists weak in the knees. Guests also enjoy a host of modern amenities, including a fitness room and flat-screen TVs. You don't have to be a guest to enjoy a cognac or wine in the oak-paneled bar, which opens at 4pm daily.

The Burgh's hippest visitors head straight to the **Ace Hotel Pittsburgh** (120 Whitfield St., 412/361-3300, www.acehotel.com, from $149), set in a 100-year-old former YMCA in East Liberty. It's a chain hotel that feels unique. Guest rooms, designated as Small, Medium, Large, and Suite, have an industrial feel with big windows, window seats, wood furniture, and flat-screen TVs. The lobby bar is a good spot for a nightcap or late-night snack.

The Inn on Negley

Transportation and Services

GETTING THERE

Pittsburgh is about 130 miles southeast of Cleveland via I-80 and I-76, 250 miles northwest of Baltimore via I-70, and 300 miles west of Philadelphia via the Pennsylvania Turnpike.

Roughly 18 miles from downtown, **Pittsburgh International Airport** (PIT, 412/472-3525, www.flypittsburgh.com) is served by about a dozen carriers, including budget airlines JetBlue, Frontier, and Spirit.

At $2.75, the **Port Authority of Allegheny County** (412/442-2000, www.portauthority.org) bus **28X Airport Flyer** is the cheapest ride into town (unless, of course, you have a pal in Pittsburgh). You'll find the bus stop outside door 6 of the ground transportation area. The 28X operates seven days a week, including holidays, departing from the airport about every 30 minutes from 5:30am to midnight. It takes about 40 minutes to get downtown. The bus then makes its way to Duquesne University, Carlow University, and the University of Pittsburgh before reaching the end of its route at Carnegie Mellon University. You can transfer between the 28X and most other Port Authority buses in downtown. If you get a **ConnectCard** smart card (www.connectcard.org), a transfer costs $1 and is good for three hours. Be sure to request a transfer before paying your fare. If you're paying cash, your second ride is full fare ($2.75). Drivers do not carry change. **SuperShuttle** (800/258-3826, www.supershuttle.com) provides shared-van service to downtown, Shadyside, Oakland, the North Shore, and other neighborhoods. You can book online or by phone or simply stop by the SuperShuttle counter in the airport's ground transportation area. If you're bound for downtown, you'll pay $18-30. The same trip by cab will set you back $40-45. Ride-hailing services Uber and Lyft are also available. The pickup location is outside baggage claim door 4.

It's also possible to travel to Pittsburgh by rail or intercity bus. **Amtrak** trains (local 412/471-6170, general 800/872-7245, www.amtrak.com) pull into a historic station at 1100 Liberty Avenue in downtown, just shy of the Strip District. Constructed at the turn of the 20th century, the station building featured a spectacular waiting room that's since been converted into a lobby for well-heeled residential and office tenants. Amtrak's Pennsylvanian, which travels daily between New York City and Pittsburgh, rolls through Amish farmlands and the famous Horseshoe Curve near Altoona. The Capitol Limited route linking Washington DC and Chicago also serves Pittsburgh.

Greyhound (local 412/392-6526, general 800/231-2222, www.greyhound.com) and **Megabus** (877/462-6342, www.megabus.com) provide bus service to Pittsburgh. The Greyhound terminal is across from the Amtrak station, at the intersection of Liberty Avenue and 11th Street. The Megabus stop is beneath the David L. Lawrence Convention Center, just north of the intersection of 10th Street and Penn Avenue. When it's not possible for buses to stop beneath the convention center, you'll find them on Penn Avenue between 10th and 11th Streets. Megabus runs between Pittsburgh and a handful of cities, including Philadelphia, New York, and Washington DC.

GETTING AROUND

With its rivers, hills, and uncommon street grids, Pittsburgh is notoriously hard to navigate. ("Undoubtedly the cockeyedest city in the United States," marveled newspaper columnist Ernie Pyle in 1937. "It must have been laid out by a mountain goat. It's up and down, and around and around, and in betwixt.") If you're renting a car, spring for a GPS device. Fortunately, a car isn't necessary if you're not straying far from the heart of the city.

Neighborhoods including downtown, the Strip District, the North Shore, the South Side Flats, and Oakland are fairly walkable, and public buses (or ride-hailing services Uber and Lyft) can get you from one to the other.

Port Authority of Allegheny County (412/442-2000, www.portauthority.org) operates some 700 buses, a light-rail system known as the T, and the Monongahela Incline. Its website has a handy "trip planner" feature that spells out how to get from point A to point B. You can also call the authority and speak to a live trip planner. The fare is $2.75 if you're paying with cash or $2.50 if you have a **ConnectCard** smart card (www.connectcard.org). Transfers are $1 with a ConnectCard. Transfers are not available with cash—riders paying with cash must pay another full fare. Seniors with proper ID and children five and under ride for free. Children 6-11 are eligible for half-price fares with a Kids ConnectCard, but you have to apply in person at Port Authority's Downtown Service Center at 534 Smithfield Street.

Drivers do not carry change. It's free to ride the T within downtown or between downtown and the North Shore.

If your visit is short, getting acquainted with the public transportation system probably isn't a priority. Cabbing it is always an option. Call **Yellow Cab Co.** at 412/321-8100. Ride-hailing services Uber and Lyft are also available.

VISITOR INFORMATION

Visit Pittsburgh (800/359-0758, www.visitpittsburgh.com), the official tourism promotion agency for Pittsburgh and the rest of Allegheny County, operates several welcome centers stocked with brochures and maps and staffed by knowledgeable folk. If you're flying into Pittsburgh International Airport, look for the welcome center near baggage claim (9am-4pm Mon., 10am-5pm Tues.-Fri., 10am-4pm Sat., noon-5pm Sun.). Visit Pittsburgh's main welcome center is downtown (120 5th Ave., 1st level, 10am-6pm Mon.-Fri., 10am-5pm Sat., seasonal Sun. hours), in a skyscraper topped with the logo of health insurer Highmark. It carries postcards, magnets, and other souvenirs, plus products from local attractions such as the Carnegie Science Center.

Laurel Highlands

The Laurel Highlands are to Pittsburghers what the Hamptons are to New Yorkers: respite from urban bustle. As early as the 1800s, Pittsburghers of certain means fled to this mountainous region southeast of the "Smoky City" to escape industrial pollution and summer heat. Captains of industry built second homes; the less affluent filled boardinghouses. Today the region's forests, peaks, and rivers attract not only Pittsburghers but also outdoor enthusiasts from Baltimore, Washington DC, and other cities within a half-day's drive. Its most renowned attraction, Fallingwater, draws visitors from around the world. Don't be surprised to hear a medley of languages if you visit the architectural masterpiece, which *Smithsonian* magazine named to its Life List—28 places to see before you die—along with India's Taj Mahal and Peru's Machu Picchu. What few people know is that Fallingwater is just one of *three* Frank Lloyd Wright houses in the Laurel Highlands.

"Laurel Highlands" is a label applied to the adjacent counties of Westmoreland, Fayette, and Somerset. "Laurel" is for the flowering shrubs that typically bloom in June. "Highlands" is for the terrain. The region is home to Mount Davis, the highest peak in Pennsylvania, and the state's largest ski resort. It's a region that lends itself to travel budgets big and small. Accommodations range from trailside shelters to the five-star

Laurel Highlands

Falling Rock, where guests enjoy 24-hour butler service. Eateries include the Big Mac Museum Restaurant, which pays homage to the McDonald's burger, and Lautrec, named to both the Forbes Travel Guide five-star list and the AAA five-diamond list.

OHIOPYLE AND VICINITY

★ Ohiopyle State Park

Ohiopyle State Park (124 Main St., Ohiopyle, 724/329-8591, www.dcnr.pa.gov/stateparks) is the Laurel Highlands' biggest tourist draw and one of Pennsylvania's most visited parks. Its star attraction is the curiously spelled **Youghiogheny River**. The full name is pronounced "yaw-ki-GAY-nee". But it's better known as the "Yough," said "yawk." The north-flowing river is a mecca for white-water enthusiasts. The Lower Yough, which starts at the heart of the 20,500-acre park, is the busiest section of white water east of the Mississippi. Its Class III and IV rapids aren't for the faint of heart. Unless you're an experienced paddler, find yourself a guide. You don't have to look far. There's an outfitter around every bend in the wee town of Ohiopyle ("ohio-pile"), nestled within the park. The tamer Middle Yough is appropriate for beginning kayakers, rafters with young children, and anglers.

You don't need a boat to experience the rushing waters of Ohiopyle. One of the park's most popular summertime attractions is a **natural waterslide** in Meadow Run, a Yough tributary. If you're up for the bumpy ride, look for the parking lot adjacent to the Route 381 bridge crossing Meadow Run, just south of Ohiopyle Borough. There's a path from the parking lot to the waterslide.

Cyclists also flock to Ohiopyle. The park is home to 27 miles of the **Great Allegheny Passage** (www.atatrail.org), a nearly level trail stretching from Pittsburgh to Cumberland, Maryland. The Ohiopyle trailhead, near the intersection of Sheridan and Sherman Streets in Ohiopyle Borough, is the most popular trailhead for the 150-mile GAP.

Ohiopyle State Park also boasts a whopping 79 miles of hiking trails (including those 27 miles of the Great Allegheny Passage). They range from short and flat to long and rocky. The 70-mile **Laurel Highlands Hiking Trail,** one of the finest rugged paths in Pennsylvania, has its southern terminus in Ohiopyle. (Contact Laurel Ridge State Park at 724/455-3744 for more information and to reserve overnight shelters, located every 8-10 miles along the trail.) Portions of Ohiopyle's trail system are open to mountain biking, horseback riding, cross-country skiing, and snowmobiling.

The park also offers fishing, hunting, rock climbing, and camping.

The itty-bitty Borough of Ohiopyle has four major outfitters: **Wilderness Voyageurs** (103 Garrett St., 800/272-4141, www.wilderness-voyageurs.com), **Laurel Highlands River Tours** (4 Sherman St., 800/472-3846, www.laurelhighlands.com), **White Water Adventurers** (6 Negley St., 724/329-8850, www.wwaraft.com), and **Ohiopyle Trading Post** (4 Negley St., 888/644-6795, www.ohiopyletradingpost.com). All offer guided rafting trips and boat and bike rentals. Between them, they provide a host of other services, including kayaking and canoeing instruction, fly-fishing clinics, guided mountain biking, guided rock climbing, and even lodging. Wilderness Voyageurs is highly regarded for its fully supported bike tours. Laurel

Ohiopyle State Park

Highlands River Tours broke from the pack in 2012 by opening a zip-lining park.

★ Fallingwater

What do you get Brad Pitt for his birthday? If you're Angelina Jolie (pre-split), you spring for a private tour of **Fallingwater** (1491 Mill Run Rd., Mill Run, 724/329-8501, www.fallingwater.org, Thurs.-Tues., tours adults from $30, children 6-12 from $18, children under 6 not permitted), Frank Lloyd Wright's architectural masterpiece. Wright designed the house in 1935 for the Kaufmann family of Pittsburgh, owners of the now-defunct Kaufmann's department store chain. The Kaufmanns wanted a vacation home with a view of their favorite waterfall. Wright decided instead to cantilever the house directly over the 30-foot falls—killing the view, but creating an enchanting illusion the house sprung from nature. Concrete terraces and a glass-walled living room project over the water, which provides a constant soundtrack. Fallingwater made such a splash when it was featured on the cover of *Time* magazine in 1938 that Wright, who was believed by many to be retired or dead, never wanted for work again. His last major project was Manhattan's Guggenheim Museum, which opened six months after his death in 1959. The Kaufmanns used Fallingwater until 1963, when Edgar Kaufmann Jr. entrusted it to the Western Pennsylvania Conservancy. The family's artworks and furnishings, many of which were designed by Wright, still fill the house.

Tours of the National Historic Landmark are offered the first two weekends of March, every day but Wednesday from mid-March through November, and Friday-Sunday in December, plus several days around Christmas. Purchase tickets in advance; it's not unusual for tours to sell out. In addition to regular tours, which last about an hour, there are a variety of specialty tours, including an in-depth tour ($80), a sunset tour ($130), and a brunch tour ($140). The house is closed in January and February. You can see the outside and explore the grounds any day of the year, weather permitting, for $10.

The visitors center has a café and a museum store that carries everything from postcards to jewelry to reproductions of Wright-designed furnishings.

Kentuck Knob

Six miles south of Fallingwater is a less famous but most impressive Frank Lloyd Wright creation. **Kentuck Knob** (723 Kentuck Rd.,

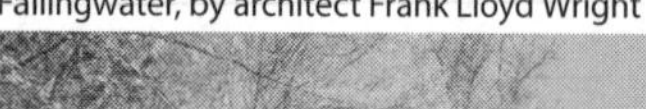

Fallingwater, by architect Frank Lloyd Wright

Wright Overnight

If Fallingwater and Kentuck Knob whet your appetite for all things Frank Lloyd Wright, don't leave the Laurel Highlands without visiting—or staying in—the architect's **Duncan House** at **Polymath Park Resort** (187 Evergreen Ln., Acme, 877/833-7829, www.franklloydwrightovernight.net).

The Duncan House was built in 1957 in Lisle, Illinois. How it got to this wooded resort five miles from the Donegal exit (#91) of the Pennsylvania Turnpike is a long story. To hear it, book a tour of the resort, which also boasts two houses designed by Wright apprentice Peter Berndtson. Tours (adults from $24, children 6-12 from $17) are offered daily except Saturday. Children under six aren't permitted.

By Wright standards, the Duncan House is a modest structure. The architect envisioned mass production of such prefab homes. But even his least expensive design was too expensive to take off. No matter—rarity magnifies their appeal. The Duncan House has all the Wright stuff: built-in cabinetry, an oversized fireplace, clerestory windows, exposed rooflines. You'll also find stuff that belonged to its original owners, including a pastel-hued hair dryer and bathroom scale. The house, which sleeps as many six people, rents for $399-550 per night. You can also bunk at Berndtson's **Blum House** or **Balter House,** which offer less cachet but more comforts.

Chalk Hill, 724/329-8501, www.kentuckknob.com, tours adults from $25, children 6-18 from $18, children under 6 not permitted) sits high above the Youghiogheny River Gorge, wedged into the brow of a hill. Like Fallingwater, it's entwined with the terrain. Wright was 86 when ice cream magnate I. N. Hagan and his artist wife beseeched him to design a house for their 80-acre mountain property. The Uniontown couple had visited the Kaufmanns at Fallingwater and fallen in love with the architect's work. Wright was overbooked—at work on the Guggenheim in New York, Beth Sholom Synagogue in the suburbs of Philadelphia, and about a dozen residences—but took on the project anyway. He never saw the completed home, a symphony of native sandstone, tidewater red cypress, glass, and flagstone. In fact, he set foot on the site only once, when local builders were laying the foundation.

The Hagans lived in the house for 30 years, then sold it in 1986 to Peter Palumbo, a British baron, property developer, and art collector. He and his family vacationed at Kentuck Knob for a decade before opening it to the public. They still entertain there on occasion, and the house is still filled with their furniture, family photos, and artwork. A shuttle ferries guests from the visitors center to the house, about a third of a mile away. Don't pass up the opportunity to walk back. Drink in the view from the crest of the hill before meandering through fields and woods dotted with sculptures.

Tours are offered daily from March through November and Saturday-Sunday in December, plus several days after Christmas. Regular tours last about 30 minutes. In-depth tours ($65), brunch tours ($85), and sculpture garden tours ($15) are also available.

Fort Necessity National Battlefield

Fort Necessity National Battlefield (1 Washington Pkwy., Farmington, 724/329-5512, www.nps.gov/fone, sunrise-sunset daily, free) is a must-stop for military history buffs. It was here that a young George Washington fought his first battle—on the side of the British. It was the only time in his military career that he surrendered.

Start in the Interpretive and Education Center, where a film and exhibits tell the story of the July 3, 1754, battle that ignited the French and Indian War. A short path leads from the visitors center to a reconstruction of the fort built by Washington's men. The

French burned the fort after their victory here, leaving few clues for historians and archaeologists. Debate over its shape raged for decades. Some experts claimed the fort was triangular, while others believed it to be diamond-shaped. The diamond camp triumphed in 1932, when the fort was first reconstructed. But both sides ate crow in the 1950s, when archaeologists unearthed evidence of a circular fort. That's what you'll find today.

Five miles of hiking trails meander through the meadow and woods around the fort. Some trails lead to a picnic area and another to **Mount Washington Tavern,** which served as a stagecoach stop in the mid-1800s. It no longer offers food, drink, and lodging to weary travelers; instead, it's a museum focusing on life along the National Road, the first federally funded highway. It's open May through October. The picnic area and tavern can also be reached by car.

Jumonville Glen, the wooded hollow where Washington confronted a band of French soldiers several weeks before the battle at Fort Necessity, is a few miles away. From the fort or tavern, follow Route 40 (aka the National Road) west for about four miles, hang a left at Jumonville Road, and continue until you reach the glen. On Route 40, you'll pass **Braddock's Grave,** a granite monument to the British commander in chief killed in 1755 during a disastrous advance on the French-held Fort Duquesne in present-day Pittsburgh. Jumonville Glen is open May through October. The parking area by Braddock's Grave is only open during summer.

Laurel Caverns

With ceilings as high as 50 feet and an average width of more than 12 feet, **Laurel Caverns** (Skyline Dr., off Rte. 40 between Chalk Hill and Hopwood, 724/438-3003, www.laurelcaverns.com, 9am-5pm daily May-Oct., tours adults $12, seniors $11, children grades 6-12 $10, children grades K-5 $9) is Pennsylvania's deepest cave. It's also the state's largest natural bat hibernaculum. As soon as the bats clear out—around the end of April—the cave is opened to people. Guided tours are offered every day until the cave closes in late October. They last about an hour and require quite a bit of walking, so be sure to wear comfortable shoes. A sweater or jacket is also recommended; the cave temperature is 52 degrees year-round. In addition to the regular tour, Laurel Caverns offers spelunking trips ($20-25) and cave rappelling ($35). Call or check the website for caving and rappelling schedules. Leave time for a round of mini golf ($7) in Kavernputt, a large faux cave on the grounds of the real deal.

SKI REGION

Seven Springs Mountain Resort

The state's largest ski resort boasts 33 slopes and trails, seven terrain parks, and consistently high marks from readers of *Ski* magazine. But snow is seasonal inventory. The average ski season lasts just four months, ending with a whimper near the end of March. That's why **Seven Springs** (777 Waterwheel Dr., Seven Springs, 800/452-2223, www.7springs.com, all-day lift ticket adults $65-89, children 6-11 $53-69, all-day equipment rental $46-51, snow tubing $20-30 per 2-hour session) works hard to position itself as a year-round destination. There's fly-fishing. There's golf. There's paintball, bowling, horseback riding, and swimming. There's a full-service spa, a sporting clays complex, a downhill bike park, two zip-line courses, a 24-foot climbing wall, and an alpine slide. In fact, Seven Springs hosts more visitors between ski seasons than during the winter months, due in large part to its conference facilities.

The resort also plays host to concerts, festivals, and other special events. Its food and booze festivals, in particular, are among the highlights of the region's social calendar. The springtime **Brewski Festival** features specialty beers from dozens of breweries and a buffet groaning with beer-basted chicken, mussels and shrimp broiled in beer, beer bread, chocolate stout cake, and more. The summertime **Wine & Food Festival** is a celebration of fine cuisine and Pennsylvania wines, complete with grape-stomping contests.

During ski season, a Highlands Ticket will get you access to the slopes, trails, and terrain parks at Seven Springs, **Hidden Valley Resorts** (1 Craighead Dr., Hidden Valley, 814/443-8000, www.hiddenvalleyresort.com), and **Laurel Mountain Ski Resort** (374 Summit Ski Rd., Boswell, 724/238-2801, www.laurelmountainski.com). A weekend Highlands Ticket is $209 for adults and $158 for children 6-11.

SOMERSET AREA

Flight 93 National Memorial

On September 11, 2001, United Airlines Flight 93 crashed into a field near Shanksville, Pennsylvania, at 563 miles per hour. There were no survivors. Soon after, a grieving public began journeying to the remote site to pay respects to the 40 passengers and crew who perished while trying to wrest back control of the hijacked plane. They created temporary memorials: homespun collages of flowers, flags, scrawled tributes, and all manner of personal effects. In 2009, ground was broken on a permanent memorial. The **Flight 93 National Memorial** (6424 Lincoln Hwy., Stoystown, 814/893-6322, www.nps.gov/flni, visitors center 9am-5pm daily, grounds sunrise-sunset daily, free) is a powerful tribute to the men and women who thwarted a planned attack on the nation's capital. It is also their final resting place; while investigators recovered most of the Boeing 757, including the cockpit voice recorder, less than 10 percent of the human remains were found. This is where the victims' families come to pay their respects.

Visitors walk along a low black wall that marks the edge of the crash site to a tall white wall composed of 40 marble panels, each inscribed with the name of a passenger or crew member. The Wall of Names is aligned with the plane's flight path. A boulder marks the impact point.

A concrete-and-glass visitors center with exhibits and a bookstore overlooks the memorial. Connecting the two is a walking path set at the edge of 40 groves planted in tribute to the victims. The memorial site also houses a 93-foot-tower containing 40 wind chimes.

LIGONIER

Fort Ligonier

Like Fort Necessity to its south, the

Flight 93 National Memorial

reconstructed **Fort Ligonier** (200 S. Market St., Ligonier, 724/238-9701, www.fortligonier.org, 9:30am-5pm Mon.-Sat., 11am-5pm Sun. Apr.-May and Sept.-Nov., 9:30am-5pm Mon.-Wed. and Sat., 9:30am-7pm Thurs.-Fri., 11am-5pm Sun. June-Aug., adults $10, children 6-16 $6) tells the story of the French and Indian War, the mid-1700s power struggle between Great Britain and France. The original Fort Ligonier was built in 1758 as a supply depot and staging area for British-American troops bent on ousting the French from present-day Pittsburgh. After the war ended in 1763, it served the British during the Native American uprising known as Pontiac's War.

Even more impressive than the reconstructed fort is the **museum** (11am-5pm Sun. Apr.-May and Sept.-Nov., 9:30am-5pm Mon.-Wed. and Sat., 9:30am-7pm Thurs.-Fri., 11am-5pm Sun. June-Aug., 9:30am-4pm Fri.-Sat., 11am-4pm Sun. Dec.-Mar.) near its entrance, where relics vastly outnumber reproductions. They include the mundane—canteens, coins, chamber pots, cannon balls, and gin bottles—as well as showstoppers such as a pair of pistols that belonged to George Washington.

Fort Ligonier is closed in winter, though the museum is open. The best time to visit is mid-October, during **Fort Ligonier Days** (724/238-4200, www.ligonier.com). The three-day festival commemorates the successful defense of the fort from a French attack on October 12, 1758. Reenactors flood the town of Ligonier, setting up camp on the grounds of the fort. Food and craft booths pop up all over town and the community puts on a parade.

Idlewild & SoakZone

You can tell that **Idlewild & SoakZone** (Rte. 30 E., Ligonier, 724/238-3666, www.idlewild.com, adults $45, seniors $35, children 2 and under free) is no ordinary amusement park by the sheer number of baby strollers. This place is as kid friendly as kid friendly gets. Its seven theme areas include Raccoon Lagoon, one of the largest kiddie-ride areas in the country. Mister Rogers' Neighborhood of Make-Believe, another tyke-suitable area, was designed by Fred Rogers himself. (The creator and host of *Mister Rogers' Neighborhood* was born in nearby Latrobe.)

Idlewild also holds the distinction of being the oldest amusement park in Pennsylvania and one of the oldest in the country. It opened in 1878 as a picnic and camping area for city dwellers seeking a country escape. By the 1950s, Idlewild had grown into a bona fide amusement park, complete with a three-row carousel. Today that carousel is the centerpiece of Olde Idlewild, home to the park's two roller coasters and other major rides.

Kids can splash the day away at Idlewild's water park. SoakZone features a 280,600-gallon wave pool, a lazy river, and a 50-foot Pipeline Plunge raft ride.

The park is open daily from early June to late August and some days before and after that period. Gates usually open at 10:30am, with rides and SoakZone opening at 11:30am. The park remains open until at least 8pm, but most of its theme areas close earlier. Idlewild reopens on October weekends for **HallowBoo,** an all-ages Halloween celebration. Come in costume if you like, but steer clear of racy or gory getups. They're an Idlewild no-no, along with masks on adults.

GREENSBURG AND VICINITY

Westmoreland Museum of American Art

It comes as a bit of a surprise to discover a first-rate museum in the foothills of southwestern Pennsylvania. The **Westmoreland Museum of American Art** (221 N. Main St., Greensburg, 724/837-1500, http://thewestmoreland.org, 11am-5pm Tues. and Thurs.-Sun., 11am-7pm Wed., suggested donation adults $15, seniors $10, free for students and children) is home to works by Winslow Homer, Mary Cassatt, John Singer Sargent, and other nationally recognized names. Even more impressive is its trove of art inspired by southwestern Pennsylvania.

"Won't You Be My Neighbor?"

Before Dora the Explorer, before Teletubbies, and even before Big Bird, there was **Mister Rogers.** *Mister Rogers' Neighborhood* began airing in 1968 and continued to captivate kids for more than 30 years. Creator and host Fred McFeely Rogers was an unlikely television personality. Born in Latrobe, about 40 miles southeast of Pittsburgh, Rogers was more interested in spirituality than celebrity. Several years before the public television program debuted, he graduated from Pittsburgh Theological Seminary and was ordained a Presbyterian minister. "I went into television because I hated it so," he once told CNN, "and I thought there was some way of using this fabulous instrument to be of nurture to those who would watch and listen."

Rogers taped almost 900 episodes of his eponymous show. They began the same way, with Rogers entering his home, changing out of his outdoor shoes, and pulling on a sweater, while singing: "Would you be mine, could you be mine, won't you be my neighbor?" (For many years, his mother knitted the cardigan sweaters that were his signature.) He took viewers on field trips, showing them how things are made. And he took them to the Neighborhood of Make-Believe, a kingdom of puppets. Rogers tackled any topic that might weigh on a child, be it war or the first day of school. He even explained, in song, that you can't be pulled down the bathroom drain. Produced in Pittsburgh, *Mister Rogers' Neighborhood* remained in syndication until September 2008, five years after its creator's death at the age of 74.

Colonial Sites

The Greensburg area serves up two slices of colonial history. **Bushy Run Battlefield** (1253 Bushy Run Rd., Jeannette, 724/527-5584, www.bushyrunbattlefield.com, visitors center 9am-5pm Wed.-Sun. May-Oct., adults $5, seniors $4.50, children 3-12 $3) was the site of a pivotal clash in the Native American uprising known as Pontiac's War. The August 1763 battle ended in a victory for the British, opening western Pennsylvania to settlement. The site is open 8am-dusk year-round, but it's best to visit April-October, when the visitors center is open. Certified tour guides are on hand during the regular season.

Less than 10 miles away, **Historic Hanna's Town** (809 Forbes Trail Rd., Greensburg, 724/532-1935, www.westmorelandhistory.org, 10am-4pm Sat., 1pm-4pm Sun. May and Sept.-Oct., 10am-4pm Wed.-Sat., 1pm-4pm Sun. June-Aug., adults $5, seniors and students $4) offers a glimpse of 1770s frontier life. Founded in 1773, the original Hanna's Town was a hub of political and military activity during the Revolutionary War. At the tail end of the war, it was attacked and burned by a party of Native Americans and their British allies. Today's Hanna's Town features a reconstructed Revolutionary-era fort, a reconstructed tavern/courthouse, and three 18th-century log houses.

ENTERTAINMENT AND EVENTS

Festivals and Events

More than 100 locals make up the cast of *The Legend of the Magic Water,* a song-filled account of the discovery of maple syrup. The pageant has been a **Pennsylvania Maple Festival** (Meyersdale, 814/634-0213, www.pamaplefestival.com, Mar.) tradition since 1971. First held in 1948, the folksy celebration of Pennsylvania's sweetest commodity put Meyersdale on the map and gave the town its nickname: "Maple City, USA." Highlights include sugaring demonstrations, a parade, auto shows, a Maple Queen contest, and spotza making. What's spotza, you say? It's a taffy-like treat made by pouring boiled maple syrup over crushed ice. (Native Americans, who shared the recipe with settlers, used snow.) Events take place throughout Meyersdale, but the hub of activity is Festival Park. Admission to the park is $5 for adults, $1 for children 6-12.

The **Westmoreland Arts & Heritage**

Big Mac Museum

Not long after meeting McDonald's founder Ray Kroc at a Chicago restaurant show, Jim Delligatti bought into the Golden Arches dream and began opening franchises in the Pittsburgh area. In 1967, the entrepreneur added a new hamburger to the menu of his Uniontown McDonald's. Delligatti's invention, the Big Mac, was rolled out nationally the following year, becoming such a fixture on the fast-food landscape that Pittsburgh was temporarily renamed Big Mac, USA, on the sandwich's 25th anniversary. Its 40th was celebrated with the opening of the **Big Mac Museum Restaurant** (9061 Rte. 30, North Huntingdon, 724/863-9837, 5am-midnight), a McDonald's restaurant filled with exhibits about the two-patty burger. The collection includes the world's largest Big Mac statue (the pickles alone measure two feet across), a bronze bust of the burger's inventor, and Big Mac Christmas ornaments. Located off the Irwin exit (#67) of the Pennsylvania turnpike, the museum-restaurant also has an indoor playground.

Festival (Twin Lakes Park, Latrobe, 724/834-7474, www.artsandheritage.com, July, free), an arts-infused Fourth of July celebration, showcases the work of 200-plus craftspeople and artisans from across the country. The four-day festival also features a juried exhibition of fine art, live performances, and food.

Squeeze as many as you can into the family van. Admission to **Overly's Country Christmas** (Westmoreland Fairgrounds, Greensburg, 724/423-1400, www.overlys.com, late Nov.-Jan. 1) is $15-18 per carful. The holiday light display had its beginnings more than 50 years ago, when Harry Overly first decorated his rural home with a few strands of lights. Encouraged by his children's delight, he stepped up his game. Year after year, the lights got brighter and the crowds got bigger. After 35 years, the spectacle outgrew its creator's seven-acre property and, in 1993, found a home at the Westmoreland Fairgrounds. These days it features more than two million lights, a walk-through Christmas Village, and a life-size nativity scene complete with live animals. Visitors can roast marshmallows around the bonfire, hop in a horse-drawn wagon or sleigh (for an additional fee), and, of course, meet Santa. It's cash only.

FOOD

Ohiopyle and Vicinity

Order a burger and a milk shake, pick up last-minute supplies, and pick out a few postcards at **Falls Market Restaurant & General Store** (69 Main St., Ohiopyle, 724/329-4973, www.fallsmarketrestaurant.com, 7am-7pm daily, $5-12) in the heart of Ohiopyle Borough. The menu is all-American: grilled cheese, hot dogs, chicken fingers, chili-topped burgers, onion rings, and the like. The amount of ice cream they manage to pile into a cone is impressive. Whatever you get, make sure to add a side of the fresh-cut fries. If you want a beer with your fries, just up the road, **Ohiopyle House Cafe** (144 Grant St., Ohiopyle, 724/329-1122, www.ohiopylehousecafe.com, 11am-midnight Mon.-Fri., 7am-midnight Sat.-Sun. Memorial Day-Labor Day, hours vary Apr.-May and Sept.-Nov., $9-16) boasts a full bar, tasty salads and sandwiches, several pasta options on the after-5pm dinner menu, and strawberry rhubarb pie for dessert. Both eateries offer outdoor seating—Ohiopyle House Cafe has a fantastic deck—but an even better idea is to get your food to go and have a picnic on one of the benches by the river.

Dining at Nemacolin Woodlands Resort's **Lautrec** (1001 LaFayette Dr., Farmington, 866/344-6957, www.nemacolin.com, 6pm-9pm Tues.-Thurs., 6pm-10pm Fri.-Sat.) is an hours-long culinary adventure. Guests can choose between a four-course prix fixe menu ($110 per person, $200 with wine pairings), seven-course chef's tasting menu ($145 per person, $270 with wine pairings), and the "ultimate experience" ($250 per person,

$360 with wine pairings). Vegetarian and vegan tasting menus are also available. The service is impeccable. Waitstaff are not only well versed in the food and the placement of forks but are also friendly and unpretentious. While men are urged to wear jackets, the atmosphere in the richly hued dining room is entirely unstuffy.

Just minutes down the historic National Road from Nemacolin, the ★ **Stone House** (3023 National Pike, Farmington, 724/329-8876, www.stonehouseinn.com, 4pm-9pm Mon.-Thurs., 11am-10pm Fri.-Sat., 11am-9pm Sun., $13-35) first opened its doors in 1822. The inn has attracted renewed interest since 2012, when Jeremy Critchfield took over its kitchen. Critchfield's resume reads like a list of luxury resorts. He joined the Stone House as co-owner and chef after stints as executive chef at Nemacolin and vice president of food and beverage at the Greenbrier in West Virginia. Don't let his high-end credentials scare you off from the Stone House: The atmosphere is historic-casual, the prices reasonable, and the food approachable, highlighted by Critchfield's fondness for barbecue. He even opened a butcher shop next door to the restaurant. During the warmer months, the chef fires up a smoker and serves ribs, brisket, pulled pork, and other barbecue classics from a tent in the parking lot.

Ski Region

Out of the Fire Café (3784 State Rte. 31, Donegal, 724/593-4200, www.outofthefirecafe.com, 11am-9pm Tues.-Sun., $26-40) opened in 2007, but its roots go back to 1974, when owner Jeff Fryer got his first taste of smoked salmon. It was love at first bite, and in the years that followed, Fryer perfected his own recipe. Out of the Fire makes ample use of that recipe, offering smoked salmon as an appetizer, salad, and sandwich. But the stylish BYOB isn't a one-note operation. Its seafood entrées and steaks are also top-notch, and its dessert menu deserves attention. The roasted mushroom soup has such a following that it's available to go (as is the signature smoked salmon). Out of the Fire is just off the Donegal exit (#91) of the Pennsylvania Turnpike, western gateway to the Laurel Highlands' ski resorts.

Seven Springs Mountain Resort has a diverse portfolio of eateries. One, **Helen's** (777 Waterwheel Dr., Seven Springs, 800/452-2223 ext. 7827, www.7springs.com, 5pm-9pm Tues.-Thurs., 5pm-10pm Fri.-Sat., 11am-3pm Sun., $26-50), is worth going out of your way for. Formerly the home of Seven Springs' founders, the upscale restaurant favors locally sourced and sustainably raised ingredients, showcasing them in dishes like puree of corn soup, rainbow trout, and duck prepared two ways. The restaurant is known for its warm service and sylvan views. Helen's is particularly romantic when there's snow piled outside and frosting the trees.

Somerset

In business since 1941, **Pine Grill** (800 N. Center Ave., Somerset, 814/445-2102, www.pinegrill.com, 11am-1pm Mon.-Sat., 10:30am-9pm Sun., $5-22) is a good place to fuel up with a filling lunch en route to the Flight 93 National Memorial, about 20 minutes away. A quarter-pound burger on a house-baked roll will set you back less than 5 bucks. Dinner entrees, like the New York strip steak or grilled crab cakes, are also reasonably priced.

Ligonier

Built for the town's first mayor, the large Victorian now known as the **Ligonier Tavern** (139 W. Main St., Ligonier, 724/238-7788, www.ligoniertavern.com, 11am-9pm Sun.-Thurs., 11am-10pm Fri.-Sat., $10-25) was the first home in Ligonier with indoor plumbing. Today it's many locals' first choice for a casual, high-quality meal. Homemade is the name of the game here, from the meatloaf to the focaccia pizza.

The Kitchen on Main (136 E. Main St., Ligonier, 724/238-4199, www.thekitchenonmain.com, 9am-3pm Tues., 9am-3pm and 5pm-8pm Wed.-Thurs., 9am-3pm and 5pm-9pm Fri., 8am-3pm and 5pm-9pm Sat.,

8am-3pm Sun., $29-36) opened in 2012 to high expectations. Chef-owner Josh Fryer is the son of Jeff Fryer, owner of Donegal's acclaimed Out of the Fire Café. The younger Fryer didn't disappoint. Offerings like pepper-crusted rib-eye steak sandwich, crispy shrimp and corn fritters, and sweet potato risotto quickly earned him a following. His father's famed smoked salmon shows up at breakfast. Like Out of the Fire, the Kitchen is a BYOB establishment. Bloody Mary fans need only bring vodka; the restaurant supplies the rest.

Don't leave Ligonier without a visit to **Joe's Bar** (202 W. Main St., Ligonier, 724/238-4877, 11am-2am Mon.-Sat., noon-2am Sun.). To the naked eye, Joe's is a smoky beer-and-shot joint. But walk beyond the bar and you'll enter a taxidermy museum that's at once ghastly and impressive. If you've never seen a rhinoceros, red lechwe, or blue wildebeest up close, here's your chance. Globetrotting hunter Joe Snyder couldn't keep all his trophies at home, so he displayed them in his bar. They take up four rooms on two floors. A massive elephant head, trunk raised and ears flared, hangs from the ceiling.

Nearby Laughlintown is so small that it makes Ligonier look like a metropolis, but it has a huge reputation among dessert lovers thanks to **The Original Pie Shoppe** (1379 Rte. 30, Laughlintown, 724/238-6621, www.theoriginalpieshoppe.com, 6am-6pm daily spring-summer, 6am-5pm daily fall-winter). Established in 1947, the bakery is best known for its cinnamon rolls. In addition to sweets, sweets, and more sweets, it offers dough-dependent savory foods like pizza and sandwiches.

Greensburg

Chef-owner William Csikesz offers a mix of French and Italian dishes at **Brasserie du Soleil** (5274 Rte. 30, Greensburg, 724/691-0006, www.brasseriedusoleil.net, 5pm-9pm Tues.-Wed., 11am-4pm and 5pm-9pm Thurs., 11am-10pm Fri.-Sat., 11am-4pm Sun., $10-31). Save room for a dessert crepe with chocolate and cognac-infused strawberries. The restaurant is BYOB.

ACCOMMODATIONS

Ohiopyle and Vicinity

Accommodations in the Ohiopyle area range from campgrounds to world-class hotels. Book early if you're coming in summer, when visitation is highest.

Camping in **Ohiopyle State Park** (124 Main St., Ohiopyle, 724/329-8591, www.dcnr.pa.gov/stateparks, campsite $15-42) is a great option for budget-conscious nature lovers. Open from April to mid-December, Ohiopyle's Kentuck Campground has about 200 campsites, flush toilets, and showers. Many of the sites have electrical hookups. The campground also has a handful of yurts and rustic cottages, all of which sleep five people in bunk beds. Reserve online at http://pennsylvaniastateparks.reserveamerica.com or by calling 888/727-2757.

The area also has some excellent private campgrounds loaded with amenities. Kids go cuckoo for ★ **Yogi Bear's Jellystone Park** (839 Mill Run Rd., Mill Run, 724/455-2929, www.jellystonemillrun.com, campsite $55-92, cabin $125-300, campsites half price in off-season), where they can hobnob with Yogi Bear, his sidekick Boo Boo, and other costumed Hanna-Barbera characters. The "camp-resort" boasts a mini-golf course, mining sluice, paintball field, game room, playgrounds, train and wagon rides, and more. Its portfolio of pools and waterslides is especially impressive. That's part of the reason why campsites cost twice as much in summer as the rest of the year. Yogi Bear's has an array of adorable cabins in addition to tent and RV sites. Other family-friendly campgrounds include **Benner's Meadow Run** (315 Nelson Rd., Farmington, 724/329-4097, www.bennersmeadowrun.com, campsite $29-50, cabin $59-194-189), which is convenient to Fort Necessity National Battlefield and Ohiopyle State Park. It's open from mid-April to mid-October. Winter stays are available by reservation.

Camping isn't the only option for budget travelers. The tiny Borough of Ohiopyle, which is entirely surrounded by Ohiopyle

State Park, has a motel and basic guesthouses. Built and operated by the family behind rafting company White Water Adventurers, the **Yough Plaza Motel** (28 Sherman St., Ohiopyle, 800/992-7238, www.youghplaza.com, $110) has 10 rooms that sleep up to four and five suites ($200 for four people) that sleep up to six. Another family-owned rafting company, Laurel Highlands River Tours, owns three centrally located **guesthouses** (Grant St., Ohiopyle, 800/472-3846, www.laurelhighlands.com, $47.50 per person based on double occupancy). You can rent a room or an entire house.

If the idea of renting an entire house appeals, another option is **Ohiopyle Vacation Rentals** (877/574-7829, www.ohiopylevacationrentals.com, $185-885). Its scattered properties sleep from 6 to 22. No two are alike, but they're all quite lovely.

NEMACOLIN WOODLANDS RESORT

The area's most luxurious accommodations can be found at ★ **Nemacolin Woodlands Resort** (1001 LaFayette Dr., Farmington, 866/344-6957, www.nemacolin.com). Amenities at the sprawling resort include a standard spa, a kids spa, a pet spa, several restaurants, golf courses, tennis courts, a bowling alley, pools, a Jeep Off-Road Driving Academy, a casino, and even its own ski mountain, **Mystic Mountain.** About $45 million in art, rare automobiles, and antique planes collected by Nemacolin founder Joseph Hardy III are scattered around the property. The resort's Woodlands Wine Cellar is the largest private cellar in Pennsylvania. More than 100 animals, including lions, tigers, and bears, are housed on the property.

Guest room rates vary considerably based on time of year and room type. The humblest of Nemacolin's three hotels is the Tudor-style **Lodge** ($99-739; average $419), built in 1968 when the property was a Pittsburgh industrialist's private game reserve and later expanded by Hardy. Room decor evokes an English country inn. **Chateau Lafayette** ($209-809; average $509) is Hardy's tribute to the grand hotels of Europe. With its vaulted ceilings, crystal chandeliers, and two-story Palladian windows, the hotel built in 1997 aptly emulates the famed Ritz Paris, a century older. It's home to a cigar bar, a high-end jewelry store, and Lautrec, Nemacolin's most celebrated restaurant. Round-the-clock butler service is available to guests of the fifth-floor club level. Butler service is available to every guest of **Falling Rock** ($229-869; average

Nemacolin Woodlands Resort

$549), Nemacolin's most acclaimed lodging. It's as understated as the Chateau is ornate, a reverent nod to architect Frank Lloyd Wright, whose masterpiece Fallingwater is less than 20 minutes away. The hotel sits on the 18th green of one of two Pete Dye-designed golf courses at Nemacolin, a good distance from the hub of activity at the resort. It features 42 guest rooms and suites, an infinity pool reserved for hotel guests, and an upscale steak house. Guests can take their pick of 10 pillow types, including air pillows, buckwheat pillows, and even anti-snore pillows. Families and groups should inquire about Nemacolin's two-bedroom townhomes ($249-819, average $534) and luxury homes that sleep as many as 20 people.

Ski Region

If skiing is what brings you to the Laurel Highlands, there's little reason to look beyond **Seven Springs Mountain Resort** (777 Waterwheel Dr., Seven Springs, 866/437-1300, www.7springs.com, from $179) for lodging. The resort's hotel has more than 400 guest rooms and suites, making it the largest hotel in the region. Its decor is nothing remarkable, but what does that matter? There's too much to do on the 5,500-acre resort to be hanging in your room. Located at the base of the mountain, the 10-floor hotel is attached to the main lodge, which houses eateries and bars, specialty shops, a heated pool and hot tubs, a game room, and more. Families and small groups may be better off renting one of the resort's condos, townhouses, cottages, or chalets. Call for rates.

A pair of nearby state parks offer alternatives to the resort scene. **Kooser State Park** (943 Glades Pike, Somerset, 814/445-8673, www.dcnr.pa.gov/stateparks, campsite $15-24, cabin from $32) has a small campground, eight rustic cabins, and one modern cabin. The campground closes in mid-October, but the cabins can be rented year-round. They sleep up to eight people. **Laurel Hill State Park** (1454 Laurel Hill Park Rd., Somerset, 814/445-7725, www.dcnr.pa.gov/stateparks, campsite $15-24, lodge from $194) boasts a five-bedroom, three-bathroom lodge that sleeps 14. It's specially equipped for winter recreation, with ski and snowboard racks, glove and boot dryers, and a large fireplace. Laurel Hill also has a campground open from early April to mid-October. State park reservations can be made online at http://pennsylvaniastateparks.reserveamerica.com or by calling 888/727-2757.

Somerset

An expansive marble foyer and gold leaf chandeliers greet guests at **The Georgian Inn of Somerset** (800 Georgian Inn Dr., Somerset, 814/443-1043, www.thegeorgianinnofsomerset.com, $125-150), a 22-room Georgian mansion built in 1915 for a local coal and cattle baron. Its 12 guest rooms and suites range from quaint to dignified. Guests are treated to a gourmet breakfast.

Ligonier and Vicinity

Drenched in pink and delightfully frilly, **Campbell House Bed & Breakfast** (305 E. Main St., Ligonier, 724/238-9812, www.campbellhousebnb.com, $90-165) is a stone's throw from historic Fort Ligonier. Patti Campbell calls her eponymous B&B "an adult getaway," recognizing that tots could easily mistake whimsical collectibles and heirlooms for toys. Part innkeeper and part romance facilitator, Campbell offers a couples massage package and an elopement package complete with marriage ceremony and wedding cake. In addition to the B&B's six rooms and suites, she offers four efficiency motel rooms for extended stays. They're a bargain at $368 per week, but you'll have to pay extra for her delectable breakfasts.

Ligonier Country Inn (1376 Rte. 30 E., Laughlintown, 724/238-3651, www.ligoniercountryinn.com, $90-165) is actually in Laughlintown, a wee little town about three miles east of Ligonier. The main house has 18 guest rooms, a restaurant known for its Sunday breakfast and brunch buffets, a pub, a charming courtyard pool, and a country feel. The adjacent Shafer House has six guest rooms with a more Victorian vibe. Innkeepers Maggie and PJ Nied also own a handful of rental cottages.

TRANSPORTATION AND SERVICES

Most visitors to the three-county Laurel Highlands region arrive by car. Donegal, its approximate center, is about 50 miles southeast of Pittsburgh via the Pennsylvania Turnpike (I-76).

Arriving by plane, train, or bus isn't out of the question. Latrobe's **Arnold Palmer Regional Airport** (LBE, 724/539-8100, www.palmerairport.com), named for the golf legend who grew up less than a mile from its runway, is served by Spirit Airlines. **Amtrak** (800/872-7245, www.amtrak.com) provides train service to Latrobe, Greensburg, and Connellsville. You can also get to Latrobe and Greensburg via **Greyhound** (800/231-2222, www.greyhound.com) bus. However you get there, you'll want a car to get around.

Before you arrive, visit the website of the **Laurel Highlands Visitors Bureau** (800/333-5661, www.laurelhighlands.org) to request a free destination guide or view a digital version. The visitors bureau has its headquarters in Ligonier Town Hall (120 E. Main St., Ligonier), but it's only open weekdays. It also has a visitors center in Ohiopyle's former train station (7 Sheridan St., Ohiopyle), adjacent to the Great Allegheny Passage. The center is open from dawn to dusk year-round. Information specialists are on hand 10am-4:30pm daily from late May to mid-October. On Fridays, Saturdays, and Sundays from Memorial Day to Labor Day, they stick around until 6pm.

Butler County and Lawrence County

The counties to Pittsburgh's north and northwest beckon with spectacular state parks. Recreational opportunities run the gamut, from barbecuing on a pontoon boat to rappelling down a rock face.

MORAINE STATE PARK

Dedicated in 1970, **Moraine State Park** (park office 225 Pleasant Valley Rd., Portersville, 724/368-8811, www.dcnr.pa.gov/stateparks, sunrise-sunset daily, free), which offers year-round recreation, is Butler County's biggest attraction. Its greatest asset is the sprawling Lake Arthur, the 3,225-acre product of a dam built on Muddy Creek. Here's a recipe for summertime fun: Pack a cooler with your favorite cookout foods, rent a pontoon boat and gas grill from **Crescent Bay Marina** (south shore, 724/368-9955, www.moraineboatrentals.com, 7am-8pm daily Memorial Day-Labor Day), and spend the day on the lake. The boat rental also offers kayaks, canoes, and motorboats.

Another way to cruise the lake is aboard ***Nautical Nature*** (McDanel's Launch, north shore, 724/368-9185, www.morainepreservationfund.org), a 37-passenger enclosed pontoon boat operated by the Moraine Preservation Fund. Boat tours (adults $14, seniors $12, children 2-12 $7) are offered on Saturday and Sunday afternoons Memorial Day weekend through October. The Fall Foliage cruises in early autumn are especially popular.

Boating isn't the only way to enjoy the lake. There's also swimming, sunbathing, and picnicking at one of two **beaches,** which are open from Memorial Day weekend to Labor Day. Pleasant Valley Beach on the south shore of Lake Arthur is a better choice if you have small children because it has a playground. It also has sand volleyball courts. Both beaches have bathrooms, shower facilities, and snack shops. Watch your step when taking a stroll because the shores serve as bathrooms for waterfowl.

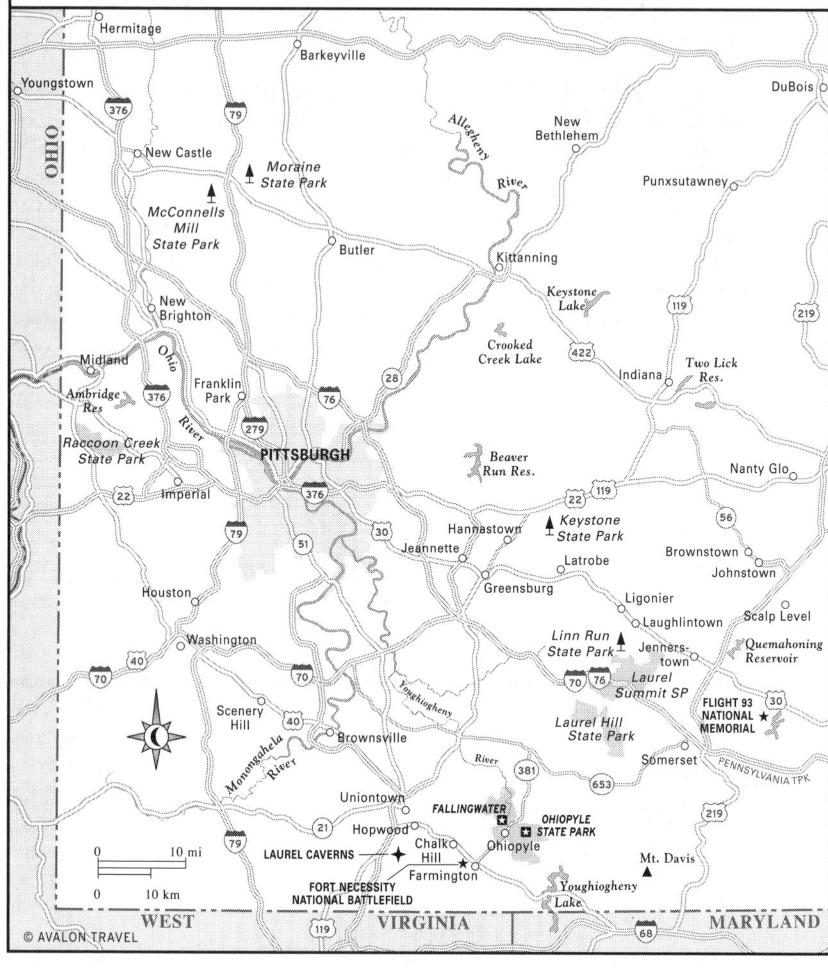

Other popular warm-weather activities include hiking and biking. The park's 28 miles of hiking trails run the gamut from short and easy to rough and rocky. Stop at the park office near the entrance to the south shore for trail maps. Cyclists have a choice between seven miles of paved trail or six miles of rugged off-roading. The bike trails are on the north shore, where you'll also find a **bike rental** (North Shore Dr., about 1.5 miles from Rte. 422, 724/368-9011 or 724/510-5195, hours vary, daily Memorial Day weekend-Labor Day, Sat.-Sun. Apr.-May and Sept.-Oct.) with a wide selection, including tandem bikes and children's bikes.

Cold weather brings other recreational opportunities: cross-country skiing, snowmobiling, sledding, iceboating, ice fishing, and ice-skating.

What Moraine State Park lacks are overnight facilities. There are 11 modern cabins on its 16,725 acres, which can be reserved online at http://pennsylvaniastateparks.reserveamerica.com or by calling 888/727-2757. An overnight shelter is available to backpackers, and tent camping areas are available to organized groups, but anyone else with a yen to sleep under the stars should head to a nearby private campground. **Bear Run Campground** (184 Badger Hill Rd., Portersville, 724/368-3564, www.bearruncampground.com, mid-Apr.-late Oct., tent sites $29-41, RV sites $46-564, cabins $85-169) has more than 300 tent and RV sites, a variety of cabins, Wi-Fi, a heated swimming pool, a game room, laundry facilities, and more. Rates cover up to two adults and two children; additional people are $10 per night. Bring a roll of quarters for the coin-operated hot showers.

MCCONNELLS MILL STATE PARK

Just five miles west of Moraine State Park, the much smaller **McConnells Mill State Park** (2697 McConnells Mill Rd., Portersville, 724/368-8811, www.dcnr.pa.gov/stateparks, sunrise-sunset daily) is the adrenaline junkie's first choice. Its central feature is a steep-sided gorge created by the draining of glacial lakes thousands of years ago. Rocky outcrops, huge boulders, and the swift-flowing Slippery Rock Creek make for challenging hiking, climbing, and white-water paddling. The park has nine miles of hiking trails and two climbing and rappelling areas. One climbing spot is across the creek from the 1800s gristmill that gave the park its name. The other, near Breakneck Bridge, is for more advanced climbers. Rafters, canoeists, and kayakers generally start near a Route 422 bridge upstream of the park. (There's no boat rental facility in the park.) Depending on water level, Slippery Rock Creek can provide a mild to wild ride; helmets are strongly recommended. Don't even think about going for a swim; more than a few people have drowned in the creek. Fishing is fine.

Guided tours of the gristmill, which was retired in 1928, are offered Memorial Day through late September. The mill is feted every year during the **McConnells Mill Heritage Festival,** held the last full weekend in September. Festivalgoers can try their hand at old-timey games and crafts and enjoy a Civil War encampment. Best of all, they get to see the forested park in its fall splendor.

INFORMATION

You'll find the latest visitors guides to Butler and Lawrence Counties on the websites of their tourism bureaus: the **Butler County Tourism and Convention Bureau** (310 E. Grandview Ave., Zelienople, 724/234-4619, www.visitbutlercounty.com) and the **Lawrence County Tourist Promotion Agency** (229 S. Jefferson St., New Castle, 724/654-8408, www.visitlawrencecounty.com).

The Alleghenies

These mountains we call the Alleghenies used to be a real headache. They didn't make it easy on settlers traveling west, where land and opportunity awaited them.

Traversing the mountains by wagon took ages and not a little bit of gumption. They stymied canal systems. They baffled railroad builders. In time, of course, engineers tamed this section of the Appalachian range. They threaded a rail line right through the Alleghenies and, later, highways. What made the region so challenging two centuries ago—peaks and valleys, wide rivers and dense woods—is what makes it appealing today. It calls to hikers, cyclists, boaters, anglers, and wildlife-watchers. The scenery makes getting from point A to point B so pleasant that the region's image-makers promote motor touring more zealously than they do most destinations.

That's not to say that the destinations are ho-hum. They include towns rich in history, the state's largest inland lake, and a premier mountain biking trail. Towns like Johnstown, Altoona, and Bedford are so diligent about preserving their heritage that visitors can virtually taste life as a steelmaker, railroader, or frontiersman. State College is home to Pennsylvania State University and the mega parties that are Nittany Lions football games. Countless villages offer quaint bed-and-breakfasts and quietude. The region is especially quiet in winter, when amusement parks, show caverns, and even some museums are closed, boats are in storage, and the open road is less welcoming.

PLANNING YOUR TIME

It's possible to digest Johnstown's heritage sights in a day. Plan on catching the sunset and a nightcap at the top of the famous inclined plane. Altoona is also doable in a day—unless you're a diehard rail fan. If that's the case, book a room at a B&B where you can watch the choo-choos go by and take a few days to explore the various railroad-related sights. Be aware that most of them, including the Railroaders Memorial Museum and Horseshoe Curve National Historic Landmark, are closed during the coldest months.

If you're visiting State College, chances are

Previous: the town of Bellefonte; Pennsylvania State University (Penn State). **Above:** covered bridge in Bedford County.

Look for ★ to find recommended sights, activities, dining, and lodging.

HIGHLIGHTS

★ **Johnstown Inclined Plane:** The world's steepest vehicular funicular carried people to safety during two deadly floods in the 20th century. Hop on for killer views of "Flood City" (page 261).

★ **Horseshoe Curve:** The 1854 feat of engineering that allowed trains to traverse the Alleghenies is still awe-inspiring after all these years (page 266).

★ **Berkey Creamery:** Best. Ice cream. Ever (page 271).

★ **Seven Points Recreation Area:** Take a dip, hit the trails, or rent a houseboat for a few days of peaceful, easy living (page 281).

★ **Omni Bedford Springs Resort:** The mineral-rich springs at this luxury resort were believed by Native Americans to have curative powers. "Take the waters" and decide for yourself (page 288).

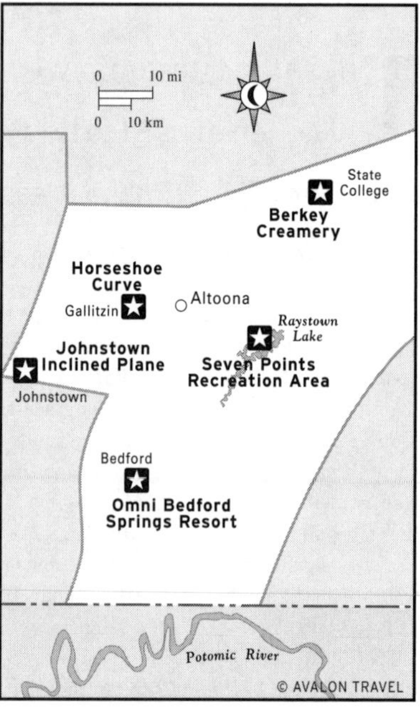

The Alleghenies

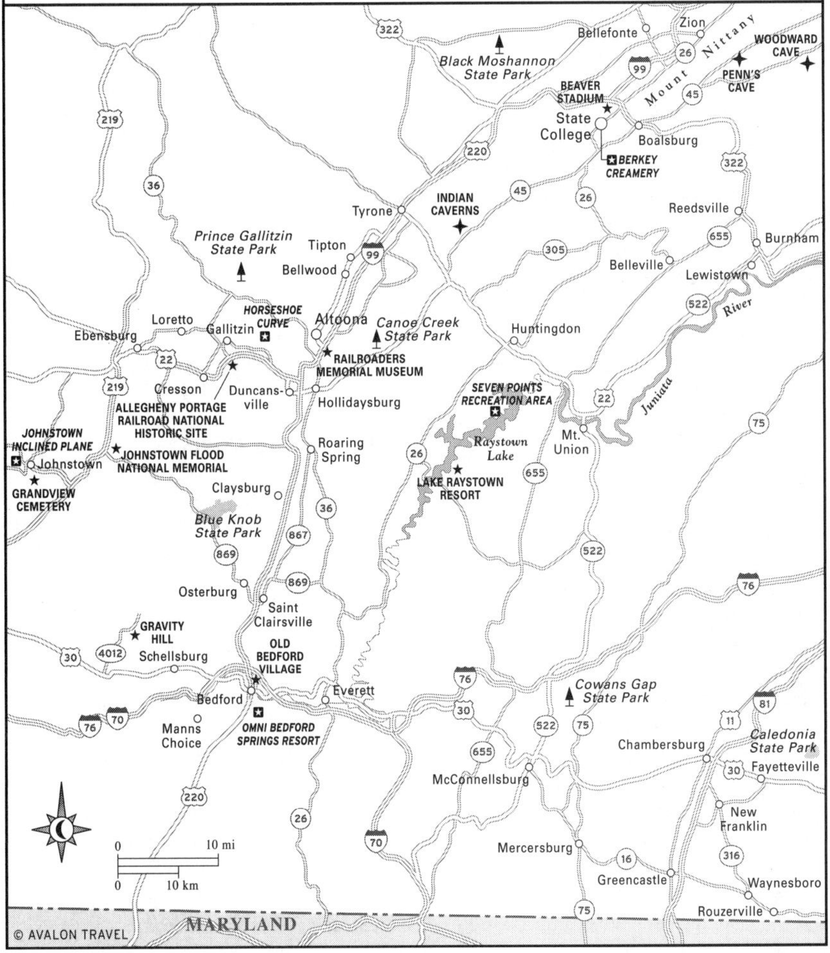

you're the parent of a Penn Stater, a prospective student, or a nostalgic alumnus, and you don't need a guidebook to tell you how long to stay (if you're a Penn State parent, your offspring will take care of that). Raystown Lake and the Bedford area are vacation destinations. The former attracts boaters, mountain bikers, and other outdoorsy types. The latter, with its historic "springs resort," attracts a well-heeled crowd. Suggested stay length: as long as possible.

Johnstown and Vicinity

Johnstown was once an unrivaled steel producer and a magnet for the industry's innovators and working-class immigrants. Today, Johnstown's rivers are still lined with former mills. Its cityscape is still ornamented with ethnic churches, though many no longer house parishes. This is only part of its story. The better-known part is the Great Flood of 1889, which razed large swaths of the city and killed about 2,200 people.

There are two museums dedicated to the tragedy: one in the downtown area and another about 10 miles northeast of Johnstown, at the site of the dam break that caused the flood. Before you visit, pick up Pittsburgh native David McCullough's *The Johnstown Flood.* The page-turning account of America's worst inland flood was published in 1968. The Pulitzer Prize-winning historian researched the disaster while the last survivors were still alive.

Flood City, as Johnstown was dubbed after two more deadly floods, has more recently become known as a motorcycle town. Bikers are fond of the scenic routes on all sides of the valley that cradles the town. Every June, they descend upon the city in great numbers for a motorcycle rally that may be the largest in the state. Johnstown holds another distinction, one recognized by *Guinness World Records:* The Johnstown Inclined Plane, which climbs 900 feet from the river valley, is the world's steepest vehicular inclined plane. No visit is complete without a trip to the top.

SIGHTS

Johnstown Flood Museum

The 26-minute documentary shown hourly at the **Johnstown Flood Museum** (304 Washington St., Johnstown, 814/539-1889, www.jaha.org, 10am-5pm Tues.-Sat., noon-5pm Sun. Apr.-Oct., 10am-5pm Wed.-Sat., noon-5pm Sun. Nov.-Mar., adults $9, seniors and children 3-18 $7) is a first-rate primer on the 1889 disaster. It won an Academy Award for best documentary, short subject. The museum also features a large relief map that illustrates the flood's path with lights and sounds and an original "Oklahoma house," which served as temporary housing for people left homeless by the flood.

Tickets to the museum and to the Frank & Sylvia Pasquerilla Heritage Discovery Center, also operated by the Johnstown Area Heritage Association, are $12 for adults and $10 for seniors and students. The combo tickets are good for five days.

Frank & Sylvia Pasquerilla Heritage Discovery Center

The **Heritage Discovery Center** (201 6th Ave., Johnstown, 814/539-1889, www.jaha.org, 10am-5pm Tues.-Sat., noon-5pm Sun. Apr.-Oct., 10am-5pm Wed.-Sat., noon-5pm Sun. Nov.-Mar., adults $9, seniors and children 3-18 $7) occupies a former brewery in the Cambria City section of Johnstown, where thousands of European immigrants settled in the 19th and early 20th centuries. In 1880, 85 percent of the neighborhood's residents were immigrants. Appropriately enough, the center's main exhibit is the interactive *America: Through Immigrant Eyes.* Upon entry, visitors choose a card with a photo of a character—a 12-year-old peasant from Poland, for instance—and follow their character's path from the old country to Johnstown.

The Discovery Center also houses the **Iron & Steel Gallery** and **Johnstown Children's Museum.** The centerpiece of the former is a film that tells the story of the Cambria Iron Company, whose rise and fall ushered Johnstown's. The theater is equipped with infrared heaters to give viewers a sense of the heat in a working steel mill. The children's museum, located on the third floor of the Discovery Center, is geared toward children 3-10.

The 40-Foot Wave

In Hollywood's hands, the story of the Johnstown Flood of 1889 would probably begin like many thrillers: with an idyllic scene. The camera would pan the South Fork Fishing and Hunting Club, a summer retreat for Pittsburgh's wealthiest industrialists and financiers. It would zoom in on the likes of Andrew Carnegie and Henry Clay Frick fishing on the club's private Lake Conemaugh, their wives strolling with parasols, their children sailing. Then the camera would dive beneath the surface to take in the expensive game fish and, finally, the dam holding back the lake. The dam, we'd discover, is in dire need of repair.

A night of torrential rain found the lake swollen on the morning of May 31, 1889. In Johnstown, 14 miles downstream, there was water in the streets. Residents weren't terribly concerned, even as they lugged belongings to the upper stories of their homes and businesses. Johnstown's position in a river valley meant that flooding was a fact of life.

At Lake Conemaugh, club officials rounded up laborers to fortify the dam and relieve pressure from its breast wall. Despite their furious efforts, the dam crumpled shortly after 3pm, unleashing 20 million tons of water. Witnesses would later describe a 40-foot wave of water and debris rushing toward Johnstown. The wave was so powerful that bodies of victims were found as far away as Cincinnati. Some people swept up by the wave were deposited on a massive pile of wreckage that accumulated at the Pennsylvania Railroad Company's stone bridge in Johnstown. About 80 who survived the wild ride perished when the debris caught fire.

In the weeks and months after the disaster, the death toll climbed to 2,209. More than 750 of the victims were never identified because their bodies were so badly damaged. Journalists, photographers, doctors, and relief workers, including American Red Cross founder Clara Barton, rushed to Johnstown. Donations of money, food, clothing, medical supplies, furniture, and even lumber for rebuilding arrived from all over the world. The South Fork Fishing and Hunting Club contributed 1,000 blankets.

Lawsuits against the club proved fruitless—the courts ruled that the flood was an act of God. But its elite members were condemned in the court of public opinion. One newspaper cartoon depicted them sipping champagne on the clubhouse porch as the flood leveled Johnstown. In fact, only a handful of members were on the premises that deadly day. It was spring yet; most of them were still in their city manses. And they would never return.

Combo tickets for the Discovery Center, including the Iron & Steel Gallery and the children's museum, and the Johnstown Flood Museum are $12 for adults and $10 for seniors and students. The tickets are valid for five days.

★ Johnstown Inclined Plane

In the aftermath of the Great Flood, communities sprang up in higher elevations. One of those was Westmont, which sits atop Yoder Hill. The hill, with its 70.9 percent grade, was too steep for a road—so an inclined railway was built to carry people, horses, and wagons to the tony neighborhood 900 feet above the river valley. The **Johnstown Inclined Plane** (upper station 711 Edgehill Dr., Johnstown, 814/536-1816, www.inclinedplane.org, 11am-9pm Sun.-Thurs., 11am-11pm Fri.-Sat. Apr.-Dec., adult fare $5 round-trip, $3 one-way, children 2-12 $3 round-trip, $2 one-way, seniors free) began operating in June 1891 and hauled about a million passengers a year in its heyday. It was both commuter line and lifeline: During the deadly floods of 1936 and 1977, the world's steepest vehicular inclined plane carried people out of the valley to safety.

The lower station is accessible from downtown by a footbridge that crosses Route 56. If driving east on Route 56, pull onto the ramp that leads to the incline and either park there or continue across a bridge that spans the Stonycreek River and drive right onto a cable car. The fare for automobiles is $8 one-way. That fare includes the driver. Motorcycles ride for $6. Bicycles are free with the driver's fare.

There's a visitors center and gift shop up top, where you can learn more about Johnstown's various floods and pick up information about area attractions. An observation deck affords a bird's-eye view of greater Johnstown and insight into the path of the 1889 floodwaters, which crashed into Yoder Hill. Ice cream and other refreshments are sold on the deck during the warmer months.

Cable cars aren't the only way to climb Yoder Hill. The **James Wolfe Sculpture Trail** takes hikers past large steel sculptures made with remnants from local plants.

Grandview Cemetery

Many of the 2,209 victims of the 1889 flood are interred at **Grandview Cemetery** (801 Millcreek Rd., Johnstown, 814/535-2652, www.grandviewjohnstownpa.com, gates open at 7:30am daily, close at dusk May-Oct. and 5pm Nov.-Apr.) on Yoder Hill, a mile south of the inclined plane's upper station. A monument dedicated in 1892 overlooks the Unknown Plot, where 777 unidentified victims are buried.

Johnstown Flood National Memorial

Operated by the National Park Service, the **Johnstown Flood National Memorial** (733 Lake Rd., South Fork, 814/495-4643, www.nps.gov/jofl, 9am-5pm daily, free) marks the site of the infamous South Fork Dam, whose collapse on May 31, 1889, caused the hellish Great Flood. The visitors center features a 35-minute film, shown at 15 minutes past the hour, and exhibits designed to convey the flood's magnitude. In addition to the dam ruins, the Park Service preserves several buildings that were part of the South Fork Fishing and Hunting Club, which owned the dam and the lake it created. In summer, rangers lead tours of the vast clubhouse where Pittsburgh's elite swilled brandy and smoked cigars.

ENTERTAINMENT AND EVENTS

Bars

Tulune's Southside Saloon (36 Bridge St./Rte. 403, Johnstown, 814/536-1001, www.southsidesaloon.com, 4pm-close Tues.-Sat., food under $10) boasts the area's largest selection of imported and craft beers—large enough to fill an eight-page menu—and a strict "no jerks allowed" policy. The kitchen, open until 10pm on weeknights and 11pm Friday and Saturday, dishes up burgers,

Johnstown Inclined Plane

Bavarian soft pretzels, and other beer-friendly grub.

Performing Arts

The **Pasquerilla Performing Arts Center** at the University of Pittsburgh at Johnstown (450 Schoolhouse Rd., Johnstown, 814/269-7200, www.upjarts.pitt.edu) hosts a wide variety of touring acts, including Broadway companies, dance troupes, comedians, and tribute bands. It's home to the **Johnstown Symphony Orchestra** (814/535-6738, www.johnstownsymphony.org), founded in 1929. Homegrown dance and theater groups also take the stage on occasion.

The **Band of Brothers Shakespeare Company** (814/539-9500, www.bandofbrothersshakespeare.org) has raised more than $200,000 for Johnstown's Stackhouse Park, where it has performed every summer since 1991.

Festivals and Events

A throwback to the years when Johnstown teemed with immigrants from Central and Eastern Europe, **PolkaFest** (St. Mary's Byzantine Catholic Church, 411 Power St., Johnstown, 814/536-7993, www.visitjohnstownpa.com/polkafest, weekend after Memorial Day, free) features nationally known polka bands, an outdoor dance floor, and plenty of ethnic eats. Jazz may be an American-born art form, but **Jazz Along the River** (St. Mary's Byzantine Catholic Church, 411 Power St., Johnstown, 814/539-5875, fourth Fri. May-Sept., free) concerts are another opportunity to fill up on kielbasa, pierogies, and haluski. The parish kitchen opens about an hour before the music starts at 6pm.

For four days in June, Johnstown becomes biker heaven. The streets fill with all manner of motorcycles: pimped-out choppers, dirt bikes, drag-racing machines—you name it. **Thunder in the Valley** (814/536-7993, www.visitjohnstownpa.com/thunderinthevalley) welcomes them all. The rally attracted about 3,500 motorcycling enthusiasts in 1998, its first year. Now, more than 200,000 pour into Johnstown and surrounding communities during the fourth weekend in June. The city's hotels burst at the seams; Altoona, Bedford, Ligonier, Indiana, and other towns absorb the overflow. Thunder isn't a leather-clad bacchanalia. It's a family-friendly event that attracts plenty of non-riders. Motorcycle manufacturers show off their latest models. Vendors peddle chaps, helmets, jewelry, and other biker accoutrements. There's also live music, a children's play area, charity rides, stunt shows, and a parade.

The **AmeriServ Flood City Music Festival** (Peoples Natural Gas Park, 90 Johns St., Johnstown, 814/539-1889, www.floodcitymusic.com, first weekend in Aug., single-day ticket $20-30, two-day ticket $40) boasts multiple stages and acts from across the country. If you're planning to stay for both days of the festival, book your overnight lodging well in advance.

Today's **American Legion County Fair** (883 N. Julian St., Ebensburg, 814/472-7491, www.cambriacofair.com, Sept., admission $8), formerly called the Cambria County Fair, is held on the same grounds as the original in 1891. It's a weeklong celebration of rural life, complete with livestock exhibits, amusement rides, tractor and truck pulls, square dancing, and the crowning of a fair queen. Cambria County is the second-largest producer of potatoes in Pennsylvania, which is cause for another annual celebration, **PotatoFest** (downtown Ebensburg, 814/472-8780, www.ebensburgpa.com, last Sat. in Sept., free). Food vendors serve up potato soup, homemade potato chips, sweet potato fries, potato pancakes, potato pizza, and even potato candy.

FOOD

Johnstown eateries eschew pomp in favor of a laid-back vibe. The city likes its sub sandwiches and hot dogs, and local establishments do a fine job with both. Skip Subway and try a torpedo from **Em's Original Sub Shop** (345 Main St., 814/535-5919, 7am-8pm Mon.-Fri., 9am-7pm Sat., 11am-4pm Sun.; 612 Goucher St., 814/255-6421, 6am-9pm daily; 1111 Scalp

Ave., 814/269-3493, 8am-9pm daily, under $10), which has three locations in Johnstown. To look at the menu behind the register is to broadcast your out-of-town-ness. Locals know exactly what they like between their 11 inches of French bread.

As tempting as it is to skip straight to the fried ice cream at **Rey Azteca** (736 Scalp Ave., 814/266-2294, 11am-10pm Mon.-Sat., 11am-9pm Sun., $6-17), the lunch and dinner deals at this low-key Mexican spot are too good to pass up. Midday, get a burrito, a taco, and Spanish rice for $6.

"If it swims, we have it," promises **The Fish Boat** (544 Main St., 814/536-7403, www.thefishboat.com, 10am-5:30pm Mon.-Thurs., 9am-6:30pm Fri., 10am-4pm Sat., $4-16), an otherwise humble seafood market and restaurant. The Fisherman's Delight platter offers a bit of everything: haddock, scallops, clams, shrimp, oysters, and a crab cake, plus your choice of sides.

"Comfort food" and "health conscious" are an improbable duo of restaurant descriptors. The romantic ★ **Back Door Café** (402 Chestnut St., 814/539-5084, www.thebackdoorcafe.com, 4pm-9pm Tues.-Thurs., 4pm-10pm Fri.-Sat., $13-29) proves it's possible with dishes loaded with fresh seasonal ingredients, many of them local. The ever-changing menu always includes a variety of brick oven-baked flatbreads with toppings such as roasted chicken, grilled shrimp, or wild mushrooms handpicked by chef Tom Chulick.

The menu at **Press Bistro** (110 Franklin St., 814/254-4835, www.pressbistro.com, 7:30am-9pm Mon.-Wed., 7:30am-10pm Thurs.-Fri., 10:30am-11pm Sat., 11am-3pm Sun., $10-22) spans the globe, offering everything from baked brie to Thai curry mussels to Mongolian beef. Not enough choices? Add in chicken and waffles, fish-and-chips, and veggie burgers. Owners Jennifer and Jeremy Shearer like to experiment. They host live music on weekends and set up outdoor seating when the weather permits.

Ambience reaches new heights at **Asiago's** (709 Edgehill Dr., 814/266-5071, www.asiagostuscanitalian.com, 11am-9pm Tues.-Thurs., 11am-10pm Fri.-Sat., 11am-8pm Sun., $12-24), located atop the Johnstown Inclined Plane. In addition to fantastic views, the restaurant offers Tuscan Italian cuisine, more than 50 wines, and an intriguing array of martinis.

ACCOMMODATIONS

National chains dominate the lodging scene in downtown Johnstown, but independent establishments can be found in the hills and valleys around it.

Under $100

Once the homestead of Johnstown founder Joseph Schantz, **Schantz Haus** (687 E. Campus Ave., Davidsville, 814/479-2494, www.schantzhaus.com, $65-80) offers two en suite guest rooms and one with a private bathroom in the hallway. It's located on a working dairy farm; guests can try their hand at milking a cow or bottle-feeding a calf. You can expect fresh milk, along with homemade entrées, at the included breakfast. The Swiss-born Schantz, whose surname was anglicized to Johns, is buried on the property along with several generations of descendants.

The ★ **Noon-Collins Inn** (114 E. High St., Ebensburg, 814/472-4311, www.noon-collins.com, $95) is so replete with antique furnishings that it has the feel of a (slightly cluttered) house museum. The Red Room's grand bed with decorative scrollwork once belonged to railroad builder Philip Collins, who lived in the 1834 Federal-style stone mansion more than a century ago. During World War I, the local draft board occupied the parlor. Pittsburgh native Gene Kelly ran a dance studio on the property in the 1930s. Today the historic home has six guest rooms, each with a private bathroom, and modern amenities such as air-conditioning and wireless Internet access. Breakfast is included.

$100-250

The row of rocking chairs on the shaded wraparound porch is the first indication guests are in for relaxing stay at **Cresson House Bed & Breakfast** (417 Park Ave., Cresson, 814/886-5014, www.cressonhouse.com, $120-139), located between Johnstown and Altoona. Each of the five guest rooms comes with Wi-Fi, a flat-screen TV, and a dedicated bathroom, but two bathrooms are in the hallway, not en suite.

The garden-themed **Dillweed Bed & Breakfast** (7453 Rte. 403 S., Dilltown, 814/446-6465, www.dillweedinc.com, $95-125) has four flower-festooned guest rooms that share two bathrooms, plus a suite with a small kitchen and full private bathroom. It's adjacent to the 36-mile Ghost Town Trail, and its two-floor Trailside Shop offers snacks and beverages for weary hikers along with country gifts such as scented candles and homemade soaps.

TRANSPORTATION AND SERVICES

Getting There

Johnstown is about 70 miles east of Pittsburgh, a drive of about 1.5 hours. From Pittsburgh, follow Route 22 east for about an hour, exit at Route 403 south, and follow the road into Johnstown.

Johnstown has an airport, the **John Murtha Johnstown-Cambria County Airport** (JST, 814/536-0002, www.flyjst.com), but you can only fly there from Baltimore-Washington International Thurgood Marshall Airport (BWI) or **Pittsburgh International Airport** (PIT, 412/472-3525, www.flypittsburgh.com). The latter is the nearest major airport to Johnstown.

Amtrak (800/872-7245, www.amtrak.com) provides train service between Johnstown and New York City, Philadelphia, Harrisburg, Pittsburgh, and other cities on its Pennsylvanian line. Johnstown's Amtrak station (47 Walnut St.) is across the Little Conemaugh River from downtown. Local transit provider **CamTran** (814/535-5526, www.camtranbus.com) offers a shuttle (Route 18, $1.60) between the train station and its downtown transit center. But don't rely on it: It only stops at the station once daily on weekdays and Saturdays and not at all on Sundays. The shuttle makes more frequent stops at the Johnstown Flood Museum and Johnstown Inclined Plane.

Greyhound (800/231-2222, www.greyhound.com) offers bus service to Johnstown, discharging passengers at the Amtrak station (47 Walnut St.).

Getting Around

Driving is the easiest way to get around Johnstown and the surrounding area, but it's not the only way. **CamTran** (814/535-5526, www.camtranbus.com) provides bus service in and around the city. The base fare is $1.60 and transfers are 30 cents. One-day passes are available ($4.25 adults, $2.25 students) at the Bus Stop Shop (551 Main St., Johnstown, 814/535-4720, 7am-6pm Mon.-Fri.), a convenience store in CamTran's downtown transit center.

For door-to-door service, call **Greater Johnstown Yellow Cab** (814/535-4584).

Visitor Information

The **Greater Johnstown/Cambria County Convention & Visitors Bureau** (111 Roosevelt Blvd., Johnstown, 814/536-7993, www.visitjohnstownpa.com, 9am-5pm Mon.-Fri.) is a good source of information about area attractions and events.

Altoona and Vicinity

Altoona is a product of the railroad industry. For the first half of the 19th century, what's now Altoona was farmland and wilderness. Its location at the eastern foot of the Allegheny Mountains—a formidable obstacle as railroads moved west across America—made it attractive to the Pennsylvania Railroad. The PRR, or "Pennsy," transformed it into a base camp, and thousands of workers arrived to help design, build, test, and repair trains. By 1945, the Altoona Works had become the world's largest rail shop complex. The area was so important to the nation's transportation infrastructure that it was a Nazi target during World War II.

A railroad museum occupies the 1882 building that housed the Pennsy's testing labs. Some 50 trains a day still snake around the Horseshoe Curve, the railroad's ingenious answer to the problem posed by the mountain range. Steam engines were retired more than 50 years ago, but the soot they produced still necessitates frequent dusting in the city.

SIGHTS

Railroaders Memorial Museum

A life-size replica of a steam locomotive dominates the lobby of the impressive **Railroaders Memorial Museum** (1300 9th Ave., Altoona, 814/946-0834, www.railroadcity.com, 9am-5pm Mon.-Sat., 11am-5pm Sun. May-Oct., 9am-5pm Fri.-Sat., 11am-5pm Sun. Apr. and first half of Nov., adults $11, seniors $10, children 2-11 $9), located in the former Pennsylvania Railroad master mechanics building in downtown Altoona. Three floors of interactive exhibits tell the story of the Pennsy, the enormous task of crossing the Allegheny Mountains, and the rail barons and laborers who made it happen. Regularly shown films help visitors make sense of the engineering marvel that is Horseshoe Curve, which is about 20 minutes away by car. Museum ticket prices include same-day access to the trackside viewing area at the Curve.

★ Horseshoe Curve

How do you solve a problem like the Allegheny Mountains? The answer came from a young

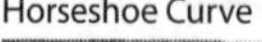
Horseshoe Curve

civil engineer named J. Edgar Thompson, who designed a way for trains to ascend gradually—about 90 feet per mile—along the mountain contour. The **Horseshoe Curve** (1500 Glenwhite Rd., Altoona, 814/946-0834, www.railroadcity.com, 9am-6pm Mon.-Sat., 11am-6pm Sun. Apr.-Oct., 9am-5pm Fri.-Sat., 11am-5pm Sun. first half of Nov., admission $8, combo package that includes admission to Railroaders Memorial Museum available) opened for rail traffic in 1854, revolutionizing east-west transport of people and the raw materials essential to industry. Today the curve is owned by the Norfolk Southern Railway, which hauls everything from ethanol to appliances over the Alleghenies. It's rare for an hour to pass without at least one train making an appearance. You can ride a funicular or climb roughly 200 steps to reach a trackside viewing area, dotted with benches and picnic tables. Turn your back to the tracks for a striking panorama of the mountain landscape, which has changed hardly at all since the curve's earliest days.

Allegheny Portage Railroad National Historic Site

Before the railroads revolutionized travel and trade, canals were America's "highways." To overcome the Allegheny Mountains, Pennsylvania's canal builders designed a railroad system of 10 inclined planes, five on each side of a mountain. Stationary steam engines moved thick ropes that pulled barges up the mountain. Completed in 1834, the Allegheny Portage Railroad cut travel time between Philadelphia and Pittsburgh to three to five days—versus three or more weeks by horse and wagon. It remained in operation until 1854, when the Pennsylvania Railroad completed the Horseshoe Curve, cutting travel time between the two cities to less than a day.

The **Allegheny Portage Railroad National Historic Site** (110 Federal Park Rd., Gallitzin, 814/886-6150, www.nps.gov/alpo, 9am-5pm daily, winter hours vary, free), about 12 miles west of Altoona, features a historic tavern and a replica of an engine house. Exhibits and models tell the story of the ingenious—and dangerous—mode of transport. Deadly accidents were common because the ropes that pulled barges up from Johnstown on the west side of the Alleghenies or Hollidaysburg on the east side were wont to break.

"The Portage" had the first railroad tunnel in the United States. Today the 900-foot **Staple Bend Tunnel** is an outlying part of

Allegheny Portage Railroad National Historic Site

the National Historic Site and can be reached via a two-mile hiking and biking trail.

Other Railroading Sights

One mile from the Allegheny Portage site, **Gallitzin Tunnels Park & Museum** (411 Convent St., Gallitzin, 814/886-8871, www.gallitzin.info, park open dawn-dusk daily year-round, museum open noon-4pm Mon.-Fri. May-Oct., free) features a restored 1942 Pennsylvania Railroad N5C caboose and killer views of trains entering and exiting the 3,605-foot Allegheny Tunnel, built in the early 1850s. A bridge overlooking the tracks has camera ports so photographers can get unobstructed shots.

The **Portage Station Museum** (400 Lee St., Portage, 814/736-9223, www.portagepa.us, noon-4pm Wed.-Sat. May-Dec., free) occupies a restored 1926 railroad depot building about 25 miles southwest of Altoona. A 173-square-foot model train display features area railroad attractions, including the Horseshoe Curve and the depot itself, which was used by the Pennsylvania Railroad until 1954.

Canal Basin Park (101 Canal St., Hollidaysburg, 814/696-4601, www.blairco.org, park open dawn-dusk daily, free) in Hollidaysburg, a quaint county seat just south of Altoona, gives visitors a window into canal culture. Hollidaysburg once had two large water basins connected by a canal lock. Boats were pulled out of the lower basin and onto the Allegheny Portage Railroad. The park features a replica of the lock mechanisms and other displays about the canal system.

The Wall That Heals

The Wall That Heals (James E. Van Zandt VA Medical Center, 2907 Pleasant Valley Blvd., Altoona, 814/940-7759, open year-round, free), a half-scale replica of the Vietnam Veterans Memorial in Washington DC, came to Altoona in 1999 and was supposed to leave after four days. But locals were so reluctant to see it go that they raised enough money to keep it there for good. Located on the grounds of Altoona's VA medical center, the powerful memorial is inscribed with the names of more than 58,000 U.S. service members who were killed or classified as missing during the Vietnam War.

ENTERTAINMENT AND EVENTS

Performing Arts

The grand **Mishler Theatre** (1212 12th Ave., Altoona, 814/944-9434, www.mishlertheatre.org), more than a century old, is home to **Altoona Community Theatre** (814/943-4357, www.altoonacommunitytheatre.com), **Allegheny Ballet Company** (814/941-9944, www.alleghenyballet.org), and the **Altoona Symphony Orchestra** (814/943-2500, www.altoonasymphony.org). It also plays host to touring artists and companies.

Festivals and Events

The **Blair County Arts Festival** (Penn State Altoona, 814/949-2787, www.blaircountyartsfestival.org, mid-May), which benefits Altoona's historic Mishler Theatre, combines a juried fine arts exhibit, a crafts market, a children's village, and oodles of live entertainment.

On select Friday evenings from June through August, regional artists play free **Summer Sounds** concerts along 11th Avenue in downtown Altoona. The Blair County Historical Society hosts free **Summer Concerts on the Lawn** at Baker Mansion (3419 Oak Ln., Altoona, 814/942-3916, www.blairhistory.org) on Sunday afternoons in August.

SPORTS AND RECREATION

Canoe Creek State Park

Not long ago, **Canoe Creek State Park** (205 Canoe Creek Rd., Hollidaysburg, 814/695-6807, www.dcnr.pa.gov/stateparks) was best known for having one of the largest bat colonies in Pennsylvania. Sadly, the disease known as white-nose syndrome has all but wiped out the bat population, making bat-watching a thing of the past. There's still good reason to visit the 961-acre park—several good reasons, actually. Not the least of them is Canoe Lake, which is popular for fishing year-round. The 155-acre lake is stocked with walleye, muskellunge, bass, trout, crappie, and other fish. The lake also offers a sand beach, open 8am to sunset May-September. A boat rental adjacent to the swimming area offers rowboats, paddleboats, kayaks, and canoes.

Twelve miles of hiking trails explore the lakeshore, wetlands, forests, and fields, which provide habitat for more than 200 species of birds and mammals. Biking is limited to a one-mile trail. Cross-country skiing is permitted on all hiking trails.

The park doesn't have a campground, but eight modern cabins are available year-round. The cabins have two bedrooms, a living/dining room, a bathroom, and a kitchen. Reserve online at http://pennsylvaniastateparks.reserveamerica.com or by calling 888/727-2757. A one-week minimum applies during the summer months.

Lower Trail

The 16.5-mile **Lower Trail** (814/832-2400, www.rttcpa.org), which runs along the Frankstown Branch of the Juniata River, has seen all sorts of traffic. Before it was a recreational trail—open for **hiking, biking, horseback riding, cross-country skiing,** and any other nonmotorized activity—much of the Lower was a rail corridor. And before that, it was a towpath for the Pennsylvania Canal. Remnants of the canal era can still be seen along the trail, which is extremely flat. The Lower (pronounced like "flower") has six trailheads, all of which are located at or near former railroad stations and can be reached from Route 22. The westernmost trailhead, near Canoe Creek State Park, is about a quarter mile south of Route 22 and reachable by Flowing Springs Road. Map boxes can be found at each trailhead.

Prince Gallitzin State Park

With its 1,635-acre lake and large campground, **Prince Gallitzin State Park** (966 Marina Rd., Patton, 814/674-1000, www.dcnr.pa.gov/stateparks) is popular with boaters, anglers, and campers. The picturesque park about 30 minutes northwest of Altoona also beckons with many miles of trails for hiking, mountain biking, snowmobiling, and cross-country skiing.

Boats with motors of 20 horsepower or less are permitted on Glendale Lake, the recreational heart of the park. The lake has multiple boat launches, mooring facilities, and marinas. It also has a public beach open from late May to mid-September.

Open from early April to late October, the park's modern campground features a beach of its own, a boat rental, playgrounds, and a camp store. In addition to nearly 400 campsites, the campground has a handful of camping cottages that overlook the lake. For a touch more luxury, book one of 10 modern cabins on the other side of the lake. The two- and three-bedroom cabins are available year-round. Campsites, camping cottages, and cabins can be reserved online at http://pennsylvaniastateparks.reserveamerica.com or by calling 888/727-2757.

FOOD

There's no shortage of national chains in the Altoona area. Thoroughfares are lined with the likes of TGI Friday's, Olive Garden, Red Lobster, and Chili's. Locally owned restaurants are a rarer breed.

Altoona

★ **Tom and Joe's Diner** (1201 13th Ave., 814/943-3423, www.tomandjoes.com, 7am-2pm Mon.-Fri., 7am-1pm Sat., 7am-noon Sun., under $10), across from City Hall in downtown Altoona, was founded in 1933 by brothers named—you guessed it—Tom and Joe. Tom's grandson runs the place today. Like the retro decor (checkered floors, red counter stools, and knotty pine walls), the specials hark back to an era before cholesterol checks. Cap a meal of ham potpie or liver and onions with a malted shake.

Chef-owner Bill Sell put together an

eclectic American menu with an emphasis on seafood for **Bill Sell's Bold** (1413 11th Ave., 814/946-0301, www.billsellsbold.com, 11am-2pm and 4pm-10pm Mon.-Fri., 4pm-10pm Sat., $18-34). The elegant dishes are set atop white tablecloths, but the vibe is still relaxed. Outdoor seating is available in the warmer months.

Marzoni's Brick Oven & Brewing Co. (1830 E. Pleasant Valley Blvd., 814/201-2358, www.marzonis.com, 11am-10pm Sun.-Thurs., 11am-11pm Fri.-Sat., $9-21) sells exactly what its name suggests: pizza cooked in brick-lined ovens and hand-crafted beers. Sandwiches, salads, and meat and seafood selections are also on offer. The beers are brewed at the first location of the Marzoni's mini-chain in the diminutive town of Duncansville, 15 minutes south of Altoona.

Hollidaysburg

Breakfast crepes are reason enough to visit **Allegheny Creamery and Crepes** (505 Allegheny St., 814/696-5055, www.alleghenycreperie.com, 7am-3pm Mon.-Tues., 7am-8pm Wed.-Fri., 8am-8pm Sat., 8am-2pm Sun., under $10) in Hollidaysburg, about seven miles south of Altoona, but you'll also find excellent soups, salads, and panini.

ACCOMMODATIONS

Altoona's lodging scene is dominated by chains. The **Courtyard Altoona** (2 Convention Center Dr., Altoona, 814/312-1800, www.marriott.com) is conveniently connected to the Blair County Convention Center. The **Altoona Grand Hotel** (1 Sheraton Dr., Altoona, 814/946-1631, www.altoonagrandhotel.com) has its own event center, plus three restaurants. Bed-and-breakfasts near the city offer an alternative.

Under $100

Guests are welcome to play the folk instruments, including the extensive collection of mountain dulcimers, on display at the **Allegheny Street Bed & Breakfast** (703 Allegheny St., Hollidaysburg, 814/317-7410, www.alleghenystreet.com, $79-130) in Hollidaysburg, a darling little town just south of Altoona. Five uniquely decorated guest rooms range from a small room with a full-sized bed to the Zebra Suite with two beds, window seats, and a claw-foot tub in the large bathroom.

The Blue Lantern (327 High St., Williamsburg, 814/937-1823, www.thebluelanternbandb.com, $90), about half an hour east of Altoona, is a great choice for outdoor enthusiasts because it's a few blocks from the Lower Trail and a few miles from Canoe Creek State Park. The B&B has three guest rooms and spacious porches overlooking a trout pond.

Nothing says "away from it all" like a dirt lane, so don't be surprised if you feel your worries melting away as you approach **Sunhearth Trails Bed & Breakfast** (204 Sunhearth Ln., Roaring Spring, 814/227-5558, www.sunhearth.org, $80-105). The rural escape less than 30 minutes south of Altoona has four guest rooms, two of which share a bath. Feel free to bring your furry friends; the 5.5-acre property has a fenced area for pets.

$100-250

Location, location, location—and historic flair—make the ★ **Mimosa Courtyard Inn** (418 N. Montgomery St., Hollidaysburg, 814/330-9917, www.mimosainn.com, $129) a fine choice. The mansion, which dates to the 1830s, is half a block from the main drag in Hollidaysburg. Enjoy a country breakfast in the formal dining room before taking a short walk to boutique shops or a short drive to attractions such as the Railroaders Memorial Museum and Canoe Creek State Park. Groups can rent the entire three-bedroom house for $299 per night.

TRANSPORTATION AND SERVICES

Altoona is about 95 miles east of Pittsburgh, a drive of about two hours. From Pittsburgh, take Route 22 east to I-99/Route 220 north.

Exit 33 (17th Street) will put you in the center of town.

You can fly to **Altoona-Blair County Airport** (AOO, 814/793-2027, www.flyaltoona.com), about 20 miles south of Altoona in Martinsburg, from Baltimore-Washington International Thurgood Marshall Airport (BWI) or **Pittsburgh International Airport** (PIT, 412/472-3525, www.flypittsburgh.com). Pittsburgh International Airport is the nearest major airport to Altoona.

Amtrak (800/872-7245, www.amtrak.com) trains and **Greyhound** (800/231-2222, www.greyhound.com) buses serve the **Altoona Transportation Center** (1231 11th Ave.), which is the primary hub for Altoona's public transit provider, **AMTRAN** (814/944-4074, www.amtran.org). Local taxi services include **Blue & White Taxi** (814/941-2711) and **Yellow Cab Co.** (814/944-6105).

For brochures, maps, discount cards, and answers to any and all questions about the area, contact **Explore Altoona** (814/943-4183, www.explorealtoona.com).

State College and Vicinity

State College is home to Pennsylvania State University, better known as Penn State, which was founded in 1855 as a publicly supported agricultural college. In 1875, the school had only 64 undergraduates. In 2016, enrollment at its 24 campuses exceeded 99,000. Almost half of Penn State students are enrolled at the flagship campus, University Park. Their numbers make State College a lively, culturally rich, and commercially robust town.

Penn State long ago expanded its curriculum beyond the agricultural sciences, but farming is still the way of life for many in this region. Farmlands radiate from State College. They're interrupted by mountains and forests and the occasional town, including quaint Boalsburg and Bellefonte. When Penn State's Nittany Lions play football at home, State College and its neighbors swell with fans. If that's when you visit, you'll see why Penn State has been ranked among the nation's biggest party schools. Tranquility awaits most other times of year.

SIGHTS

★ Berkey Creamery

Penn State's **Berkey Creamery** (corner of Bigler and Curtin Rds., University Park, 814/865-7535, www.creamery.psu.edu, 7am-10pm Mon.-Thurs., 7am-11pm Fri., 8am-11pm Sat., 9am-10pm Sun.) isn't your ordinary ice cream joint. People go far out of their way to indulge in fresh ice cream produced by the country's largest and most sophisticated university creamery. How fresh? We're talking four days from cow to cone. The school's own cow herd can't supply enough milk to meet demand, so the creamery relies on local producers. Don't be deterred by the snaking line to the counter. Most patrons know what they like, and there's no agonizing over one scoop or two. There's only one serving size: generous. Quarts and half-gallons are such popular souvenirs that Berkey sells travel bags and dry ice for the road.

The creamery, which occupies the first floor of the Food Science Building, is a laboratory for students in the College of Agricultural Sciences. They learn the dairy business by producing milk, cheeses, yogurt, sour cream, frozen yogurt, and sherbet along with the famous ice cream. Want a taste of life in the ice cream trenches? The university's Ice Cream Short Course covers every aspect of production. It's how Ben and Jerry got their start.

Beaver Stadium

The best way to experience **Beaver Stadium** (University Dr. and Park Ave., University Park), den of the Nittany Lions football team, is to go to a home game. Alas, tickets are so prized that even students have to scramble for

Anatomy of a Mascot

What is a **Nittany Lion** anyway? The question will brand you an outsider in State College, where the Penn State mascot is revered. Here's the lowdown on the region's favorite feline.

Until 1904, Penn State didn't have a mascot. That year, the school's baseball team visited Princeton University, home of the Tigers. When Penn State's Harrison "Joe" Mason was shown a statue of the fearsome mascot, the ballplayer pulled a fast one: He crowed that the Nittany Lion, "fiercest beast of them all," would take down the Tiger. And, indeed, Penn State defeated Princeton that day.

Mason's fabrication had roots in reality. Mountain lions roamed central Pennsylvania when Penn State was founded. A mountain named Nittany was and remains the most prominent natural landmark near campus. Mason put the two together to create a unique symbol of might. A branding whiz couldn't have done it better. Back at Penn State, support for Mason's brainchild was so widespread that the mascot was adopted without so much as a vote.

them. Don't let the lack of a ticket keep you away on game day. Penn State has a tailgating tradition par excellence. Fans with motor homes arrive as early as Thursday to set up camp. On Saturday, the parking lots and fields around Beaver Stadium fill with revelers. There's music. There's food. There's even a good chance you'll find fans (and the occasional scalper) selling extra tickets.

Beaver Stadium is impressive even when empty. With a seating capacity of 106,572, it's the second-largest stadium in the country after Michigan Stadium. Tours that include the Nittany Lions' locker room are offered by the **Penn State All-Sports Museum** (814/865-0044, www.gopsusports.com/museum, 10am-4pm Tues.-Sat., noon-4pm Sun., hours vary in winter and on home game weekends, suggested donation $5, children/students/seniors $3). The 10,000-square-foot museum in the southwest corner of the stadium celebrates the achievements of Penn State athletes and coaches. Its collection includes the 1973 Heisman Trophy of running back John Cappelletti and the 1952 Olympics gold medal of steeplechaser Horace Ashenfelter.

Beaver Stadium, by the way, is named not for the dam-building rodent but for James A. Beaver, a former governor of Pennsylvania and president of the university's board of trustees.

Nittany Lion Shrine

Said to be the most photographed site on campus, the **Nittany Lion Shrine** resides near the Recreation Building at the west end of Curtin Road. Sculptor Heinz Warneke and stonecutter Joseph Garatti coaxed the crouching lion out of a 13-ton block of Indiana limestone. It was dedicated during homecoming weekend in 1942. In 1966, fans of homecoming rival Syracuse University doused the lion with hard-to-remove paint. Penn State students, faculty, and alumni have guarded (read: partied at) the shrine during homecoming weekend ever since.

Boalsburg

On an October day in 1864, three women decorated the graves of fallen Civil War soldiers in a small Boalsburg cemetery. Their respectful gesture would later become an American tradition, giving Boalsburg bragging rights as the birthplace of Memorial Day. Few towns do it up like Boalsburg come the last Monday in May. The village along Business Route 322, just minutes east of State College, hosts a day-long festival that culminates in a ceremony at the same cemetery where the three paid their respects. A life-size statue of the ladies in ground-sweeping skirts stands there today. Boalsburg's reverence for history makes it worth a visit any day of the year. It has three museums, diligently maintained 19th-century homes, and a tavern that opened its doors in 1819. To boot, the quaint village boasts several boutiques worthy of a big city.

Boalsburg was settled in 1808 but called Springfield until 1820, when it was renamed to honor its most distinguished residents, the Boals. The **Boal Mansion Museum** (163 Boal Estate Dr., 814/466-6210, www.boalmuseum.com, 1:30pm-5pm Tues.-Sun. May-Oct., by appointment Nov.-Apr., adults $10, children 7-11 $6) displays the family's many treasures, including original furnishings and military artifacts from the Revolutionary War to World War I. In 1909, a Boal and his French-Spanish wife, a descendant of Christopher Columbus, imported a centuries-old chapel from the Columbus Castle in Spain. The **Columbus Chapel** is preserved in a structure of Pennsylvania stone adjacent to the mansion. It contains an admiral's desk said to have belonged to the explorer himself and religious statues from the 15th century.

The **Boalsburg Heritage Museum** (304 E. Main St., 814/466-3035, www.boalsburgheritagemuseum.org, 2pm-4pm Tues. and Sat. and by appointment, closed mid-Dec.-late Mar., suggested donation adults $3, children $2) is an example of a more modest early home, filled with historical and community artifacts.

The site of the **Pennsylvania Military Museum** (51 Boal Ave., 814/466-6263, www.pamilmuseum.org, 10am-5pm Wed.-Sat. and noon-5pm Sun. mid-Mar.-Nov., adults $6, seniors $5.50, children 3-11 $4) was once part of the Boal estate. In 1916, with war raging in Europe, Theodore Davis Boal organized a horse-mounted machine gun troop on his property. The museum honors them and other Pennsylvania military men and women. It also showcases the tools of war, including the massive gun barrels of a battleship that survived the 1941 Japanese attack on Pearl Harbor. Military service ribbons inspired the cubistic mural on the front facade of the museum.

If you're hungry for more history or just plain hungry, head to **Duffy's Tavern** (113 E. Main St., Boalsburg, 814/466-6241, www.duffystavernpa.com, 11:30am-10pm daily, hours subject to change in winter, $8-33), a watering hole since circa 1819. Boalsburg was a busy stop on a stagecoach route in the early 19th century—busy enough to keep three taverns in business at one point. This one, with its 22-inch stone walls, is believed to have served the gentry.

Nittany Lion Shrine

Bellefonte

The very Victorian town of Bellefonte, 15 miles north of State College, is the seat of Centre County. It owes its (somewhat faded) grandeur to the prosperous and powerful men who called it home in the 19th century: iron and limestone barons, bankers, lawyers, judges, and seven governors. Much of their real estate is lovingly preserved, which makes Bellefonte attractive to architecture and history buffs, romantics, and the tea-and-scone crowd. It's also popular with anglers: Spring Creek, famous for its large trout, meanders through the storybook town. Bellefonte is never more magical than in winter, when homes, businesses, and county buildings are dressed in holiday finery. The annual **Bellefonte Victorian Christmas** (814/355-2917, www.bellefontevictorianchristmas.com, second weekend in Dec.) is a town-wide trip back in time complete with horse-drawn buggy rides, a gingerbread house contest, tours of historic homes, concerts, and, of course, a Victorian tea party.

Start your visit at pretty **Talleyrand Park** along Spring Creek. Bring breadcrumbs for a closer gander at the waterfowl and trout. Talleyrand's 1889 train station is home to the Bellefonte Intervalley Area Chamber of Commerce (320 W. High St., 814/355-2917, www.bellefontechamber.org) and a satellite office of the Central Pennsylvania Convention & Visitors Bureau. You can pick up free maps, information about area attractions, and a Wi-Fi signal.

A former match factory at the edge of Talleyrand Park is now the **American Philatelic Center** (100 Match Factory Place, 814/933-3803, www.stamps.org, 8am-4:30pm Mon.-Fri., free), headquarters for a society of more than 44,000 stamp collectors. Visitors can learn the ABCs of stamp collecting, browse exhibits of stamp collections and stamp-related memorabilia, and learn about Bellefonte's important role in the early days of airmail. Pilots refueled in the town on their way from New York City to Chicago. A monument honors those who lost their lives en route.

Follow High Street east to the very center of town, where the **county courthouse** stands. The 1810 Georgian-style house at 133 North Allegheny Street, two blocks north of the courthouse, was once home to former governor James A. Beaver. Today it's the **Bellefonte Art Museum** (814/355-4280, www.bellefontemuseum.org, noon-4:30pm Fri.-Sun., free).

the town of Bellefonte

For an ivy-clad Victorian gem, continue to the intersection of North Allegheny and Linn Streets. The **Reynolds Mansion** (101 W. Linn St., 814/353-8407, www.reynolds-mansion.com, $129-219) is so fetching that it once graced the cover of a *Select Registry* guidebook to distinguished inns. Built in 1885 by a wealthy businessman, the B&B is a blend of Gothic, Italianate, and Queen Anne styles. You don't have to book a room to explore the ornate interior. Guided tours of the common areas, including a snuggery where men retired after dinner to sip brandy and smoke cigars, are offered 11am-4pm for $5. Call ahead. For more Victorian splendor, continue east on **Linn Street.** The three-block stretch of elegant residences between North Allegheny and Armour Streets includes no fewer than four bed-and-breakfasts.

Show Caves

An all-water limestone cavern 17 miles northeast of State College has been wowing tourists since the 19th century. **Penn's Cave** (222 Penns Cave Rd., Centre Hall, 814/364-1664, www.pennscave.com, open daily Mar.-Nov. and Sat.-Sun. Dec. and Feb., adults $18.50, seniors $17.50, children 2-12 $10.50) is a half-mile wonderland of stalactites and stalagmites, columns and curtains. Tours by motorboat depart on the hour. Joke-cracking guides dole out geology factoids and point out curiously shaped formations (and the occasional beaver). Bring a sweater or jacket even in summer because the temperature inside is a constant 52 degrees. Boats emerge from the tunnel-like cave into the man-made Lake Nitanee, where they linger for wildlife viewing before the return trip.

Ninety-minute **wildlife tours** (adults $21.50, seniors $20.50, children 2-12 $13.50) of the forests and fields around Penn's Cave are offered April-November. The 1,600-acre property is home to longhorn cattle, bison, gray wolves, black bears, and bobcats, among other animals. A cavern and wildlife tour package is available. Penn's Cave also offers 2.5-hour **off-road tours** (adults $90, children 8-12 $50, reservations required) over man-made obstacles, up steep cliffs, and through mountain ravines.

About 30 miles east of State College is the enormous **Woodward Cave** (Woodward Cave Dr., Woodward, 814/349-9800, www.woodwardcave.com, open daily late May-late Aug., Sat.-Sun. late Aug.-mid-Oct. and mid-Apr.-late May, tour adults $12, children 4-12 $6). Its spacious rooms include the 200-foot-long Hall of Statues, which features a 14-foot stalagmite known as the Tower of Babel. Woodward Cave is extra chilly—48 degrees year-round—so dress accordingly for the 50-minute, five-room tour. There's no menagerie here, but there is a campground: The **Woodward Cave Campground** has hot showers, a snack stand, a game room, and other amenities, plus a packed calendar of events including pig roasts and horseshoe tournaments. Rates start at $18.

ENTERTAINMENT AND EVENTS

Nightlife

Bank on a good time and outstanding brews at **Zeno's Pub** (100 W. College Ave., State College, 814/237-4350, www.zenospub.com, 1pm-2am Mon.-Sat.), which *BeerAdvocate* has called one of the top beer bars on the planet.

Don't go to **Bar Bleu** (114 S. Garner St., State College, 814/237-0374, www.dantesinc.com, 5:30pm-2am Mon.-Fri., noon-2am Sat., 4pm-2am Sun.) expecting live jazz or blues. That was several incarnations ago. Today Bar Bleu is a sports bar with 22 flat-screen monitors, 16 draft beers, and 43-ounce "fishbowl" cocktails. It has the ambience of a place that serves 43-ounce cocktails (i.e., this one is for the younger generation). The same restaurant group owns **The Saloon** (101 Hiester St., State College, 814/234-1344, www.dantesinc.com, 8pm-2am daily). It fancies itself an English pub, but its famous "Monkey Boy" drink is a State College original. The concoction of clear alcohols emboldens many a student on karaoke Mondays. Bands make the noise other nights.

Performing Arts

The likes of Carrie Underwood and Keith Urban perform at Penn State's **Bryce Jordan Center** (corner of University Dr. and Curtin Rd., University Park, 814/863-5500, www.bjc.psu.edu), home of Nittany Lions basketball. Word has it that Tim McGraw borrowed a jeep from a Jordan Center employee some years ago to take another performer, Faith Hill, for a spin. Thus began their romance.

Penn State's **Center for the Performing Arts** (corner of Shortlidge and Eisenhower Rds., University Park, 814/863-0255, www.cpa.psu.edu) hosts some 200 events a year. Wynton Marsalis, David Copperfield, and the Martha Graham and Alvin Ailey dance companies have graced its stage. The **Nittany Valley Symphony** (814/231-8224, www.nvs.org) is a regular user.

The State Theatre (130 W. College Ave., State College, 814/272-0606, www.thestatetheatre.org) in downtown State College opened as a cinema in 1938. Today the renovated venue offers movies and more, including musical theater, stand-up comedy, opera, and rock 'n' roll.

Festivals and Events

More than 125,000 people flood downtown State College and the Penn State campus during the **Central Pennsylvania Festival of the Arts** (814/237-3682, www.arts-festival.com, starts Wed. after July 4), a tradition since 1967. Artists and craftspeople from around the country exhibit and peddle their work. Musicians, dancers, and puppeteers entertain. Sand sculptors show off their skills in Central Parklet. There's funnel cake as far as the eye can see and the whole town takes on a festive atmosphere. Admission to some performances requires a $10 button.

You don't have to go home when the exhibits and amusement rides at the **Centre County Grange Fair** (Grange Fairgrounds, Centre Hall, 814/364-9212, www.grangefair.com, late Aug., adults $7, children 11 and under free) close for the night. The week-long farm-centric fete is one of the largest encampment fairs in the country, with more than 2,000 tent and RV sites. Funnel cake for breakfast, anyone?

First Night State College (814/237-3682, www.firstnightstatecollege.com) is an alcohol-free, arts-focused New Year's Eve celebration known for jaw-dropping ice sculptures. Admission to many performances and crafts workshops requires a $10 button.

SPORTS AND RECREATION

Though best known for college football, the State College region offers much more in the way of sports and recreation, including world-class fishing and glider flying.

Mount Nittany

That tree-covered hump on the horizon? It's probably **Mount Nittany** (www.mtnittany.org), and you should definitely hike it. The mountain is part of a ridge separating two valleys; on a clear day, the crest affords postcard-quality views of both. Its name is derived from the Algonquin "nit-a-nee," which means either "single mountain" or "barrier against the wind," depending on whom you ask. Penn State borrowed the mountain's name for its mascot, the Nittany Lion.

Finding the trailhead is tricky. It's at the dead end of Mount Nittany Road, which begins in the quaint village of Lemont. From State College, take South Atherton Street (Business Rte. 322) east to the traffic light at Branch Road. Turn left onto Branch and follow it to Mount Nittany Road. Turn right, drive one mile, and there it is. Take your pick of two blazed loop trails: the 4-mile white trail or 5.5-mile blue trail. Both start out rocky and steep. For a view of campus from 1,940 feet, you needn't go farther than the Mike Lynch Overlook, 0.75 mile up the white trail. You can hike Mount Nittany any time of year, but spring and fall are particularly good for wildlife viewing. Winter's leafless trees make for exceptional valley views. Hunting is permitted, so it's wise to wear orange.

If you're short on time or shy of the climb,

you can take in Mount Nittany from an observation area between Beaver Stadium and the Bryce Jordan Center on campus. There's no charge to use the high-powered binoculars.

Fishing and Paddling

The State College area is known for superb angling. Bellefonte is one of the best fly-fishing towns in the state, with its proximity to Spring Creek, Penns Creek, Spruce Creek, and other premier fly-fishing waters. Spring Creek, which runs through the town on its way to Bald Eagle Creek, is among the best wild trout streams in the East and even has a section called Fisherman's Paradise.

Part outfitter and part B&B, **Riffles and Runs** (217 N. Spring St., Bellefonte, 814/353-8109, www.rifflesandruns.com) offers fly-fishing instruction and guiding along with two guest rooms with a shared bath.

State College has two specialty stores for fly anglers. **Flyfisher's Paradise** (2603 E. College Ave., State College, 814/234-4189, www.flyfishersparadise.com, 10am-6pm Mon.-Fri., 10am-5pm Sat.) has been in business for over 40 years. Walk in on any given day and you're liable to find a pair of staff members with 80 years of fly-fishing experience between them. Pennsylvania mini-chain **TCO Fly Shop** (2030 E. College Ave., State College, 814/689-3654, www.tcoflyfishing.com, 9am-6pm Mon.-Sat., 9am-4pm Sun. mid-June-mid-Apr., 9am-6pm Mon.-Thurs., 8am-6pm Fri.-Sat., 8am-5pm Sun. mid-Apr.-mid-June) offers a website with loads of information about area waters along with a wide selection of products, instruction, and guide services.

You can explore the waterways that so many fish call home by canoe or kayak. **Tussey Mountain Outfitters** (308 W. Linn St., Bellefonte, 814/355-5690, www.tusseymountainoutfitters.com, hours vary by season) rents and sells both. Its paddle pros are happy to provide shuttle services.

Flying

At **Ridge Soaring Glidersport** (3523 S. Eagle Valley Rd., Julian, 814/355-2483, www.eglider.org, glider ride $120-250), you can take flight in an aircraft with no engine. Seriously.

Sky's The Limit Ballooning (814/234-5986, www.paballoonrides.com, flight $200 per person) offers a different way to soar over the State College area. The hot-air balloon lifts off twice a day year-round, barring rain, fog, snow, or strong winds.

Winter Sports

The Alps it's not, but **Tussey Mountain** (341 Bear Meadows Rd., Boalsburg, 814/466-6266, www.tusseymountain.com, lift ticket $26-48, ski/snowboard rental $24-35, snow tubing all-day pass $32) attracts Penn Staters in need of a quick skiing fix. It offers several trails for skiing and snowboarding, plus a snow tubing park. Tussey does its best to stay relevant in warmer months with a zip line, mini-golf course, go-kart track, batting cages, nine-hole golf course, driving range, skate park, fishing pond, and the occasional concert.

FOOD

A town packed with students is by necessity a town packed with eateries. But State College delivers more than typical student grub. There's inventive cuisine among the subs, pizza, and wings. You won't find this volume or variety of restaurants anywhere else in the Alleghenies. College and Beaver Avenues and their cross streets in downtown State College are particularly crowded with dining options.

Breakfast and Brunch

Breakfast served well into the afternoon is the draw at **The Original Waffle Shop** (www.originalwaffleshop.net, 5:30am-3pm Mon.-Sat., 7am-3pm Sun., under $10), which has locations designated **West** (1610 W. College Ave., State College, 814/235-1816) and **North** (1229 N. Atherton St., State College, 814/238-7460). Along with the waffles, the crowds line up for omelets, pancakes, burgers, and sandwiches. Don't worry: The line moves quickly. You'll find similar fare at what some consider an imposter: **The Waffle Shop** (364

E. College Ave., State College, 814/237-9741, 6am-3pm daily, under $10) has a different owner.

Classic American

A onetime stagecoach stop in Boalsburg, **Duffy's Tavern** (113 E. Main St., Boalsburg, 814/466-6241, www.duffystavernpa.com, 11:30am-10pm daily, hours subject to change in winter, $8-33) serves elegant dishes like smoked pork tenderloin with cherries in its dining room and more casual fare in the adjacent tavern. You can't miss **Kelly's Steak and Seafood** (316 Boal Ave., Boalsburg, 814/466-6251, www.kellys-steak.com, 11am-3pm and 4:30pm-9pm Mon.-Thurs., 11am-3pm and 4:30pm-10pm Fri.-Sat., 2pm-9pm Sun., $7-37). There's a giant bovine on its roof. The kitschy touch belies the kitchen's sophistication. Husband-and-wife chefs Sean and Tien Kelly, who met in Seattle, bring a Pacific Northwest sensibility to dishes such as grilled fish tacos and wild Alaskan salmon.

Italian and Pizza

Wood-fired pizza is the star at **Faccia Luna** (1229 S. Atherton St., State College, 814/234-9000, www.faccialuna.com, 11am-11pm Mon.-Sat., noon-10pm Sun., $8-20), which bills itself as an American trattoria. In addition to the excellent pies, salads, sandwiches, and classic pasta dishes round out the menu.

Thai

Cozy Thai Bistro (232 S. Allen St., State College, 814/237-0139, www.cozythaibistro.com, 11am-3pm and 5pm-9pm Mon.-Fri., noon-9pm Sat., $10-18) pairs fresh herbs with imported seasonings for flavorful renditions of Thai favorites like red and green curry, pad Thai, and lemongrass chicken. It's BYOB.

Brewpubs

Beer even finds its way into the food menu at ★ **Otto's Pub & Brewery** (2235 N. Atherton St., State College, 814/867-6886, www.ottospubandbrewery.com, 11am-10pm Sun.-Thurs., 11am-11pm Fri.-Sat., bar open 2 hours later, $8-28), which offers about a dozen brews daily and taps a firkin every Friday. To eat, there's French onion soup with a beer bread crouton, beer-battered pickles, a beer pretzel with beer cheese, beer-infused pizza dough, beer-battered fish tacos, and so on. Herbivores have plenty of options, from vegan chili (made with beer) and crispy tofu wings to a black bean burger (served with beer-battered fries).

Elk Creek Café + Aleworks (100 W. Main St., Millheim, 814/349-8850, www.elkcreekcafe.net, kitchen open 5pm-8pm Tues., 4pm-9pm Wed.-Thurs., 11:30am-3pm and 4pm-9pm Fri.-Sat., 11am-2pm Sun., $8-32) is 20-some miles from State College, but its craft beers, from-scratch cuisine, and music hall bring in the crowds. The proprietors strive for a zero-waste operation, so no need to feel guilty about that plateful of deep-fried drumsticks or hand-cut fries: The fryer oil is made into biodiesel.

Indian

You can order by the dish at **Kaarma** (120 E. Beaver Ave., State College, 814/238-8141, www.fillay.com/kaarma, 11:30am-10pm daily, $9-14) but the lunchtime buffet—just $7.95 during the week and a dollar more on Friday and Saturday—is awfully hard to pass up. Fill your plate to overflowing with butter chicken, lamb vindaloo, saag paneer, naan, and other Indian delights. Vegetarians will leave stuffed. A dinner buffet ($11.95) is available Saturdays.

Vegetarian and Vegan

Local vegans rejoiced when **Café Verve** (115 E. Beaver Ave., State College, 814/308-8873, www.cafevervestatecollege.com, 9am-7pm Mon.-Sat., 10am-5pm Sun., under $10) opened in 2016 with an all-vegan menu of soups, sandwiches, muffins, and pastries. The low-key café also serves breakfast fare, coffee drinks, and smoothies.

Coffee and Sweets

It's no surprise a university town like State College is chock-full o' coffee shops. Students settle in with their laptops and textbooks at **Saint's Café** (123 W. Beaver Ave., State College, 814/238-5707, www.statecollege-coffeeshop.com, 7am-6pm Mon.-Sat., 8am-4:30pm Sun.), which has been serving up coffee and delicious baked goods for almost 20 years. Feeling left out without a book to pore over? **Webster's** (133 E. Beaver Ave., State College, 814/272-1410, www.webstersbooksandcafe.com, 7:30am-8:30pm Mon.-Fri., 8am-6pm Sat.-Sun.) does triple duty as a café, used bookstore, and record shop. Milk for the cappuccinos and lattes is from the town's Meyer Dairy. **Irving's** (110 E. College Ave., State College, 814/231-0604, www.irvingsstatecollege.com, 7am-8pm daily) is best known for its bagels, but what goes better with a bagel than a cup of joe?

ACCOMMODATIONS

The State College area has a wide array of lodging options, from independently owned motels to elegant B&Bs. Downtown chains convenient to Penn State include the **Hyatt Place State College** (219 W. Beaver Ave., State College, 814/862-9808, www.hyatt.com) and the **Days Inn Penn State** (240 S. Pugh St., State College, 814/238-8454, www.wyndhamhotels.com). Rates at any area accommodation tend to skyrocket during Penn State football games, parents weekend, graduation, the Central Pennsylvania Festival of the Arts, and other busy periods. Not surprisingly, you'll get the best rates during school breaks.

Under $100

Get your fill of fresh air at **Bellefonte/State College KOA** (2481 Jacksonville Rd., Bellefonte, 814/355-7912, www.bellefontekoa.com, campsite $30-114, one-room cabin $52-124, deluxe cabin $96-274). The campground four miles northeast of Bellefonte has 18 rental cabins in addition to tent and RV campsites. It also has a swimming pool, a stocked fishing pond, and a snack bar. Summertime freebies include nightly hayrides, Friday night movies, and Sunday morning pancakes.

You don't have to go to the countryside for accommodations in this price range. **The Stevens Motel** (1275 N. Atherton St., State College, 814/238-2438, www.thestevensmotel.com, $48-60) offers clean rooms, courteous service, and proximity to Penn State.

$100-250

The Penn Stater (215 Innovation Blvd., State College, 800/233-7505, www.thepennstater-hotel.psu.edu, $115-250) is one of two hotels operated by the university's Hospitality Services Department. It looks rather like a dormitory from the outside, but you won't find bunk beds or lava lamps in its 300 guest rooms and suites. The Penn Stater knows well the needs of the PowerPoint crowd. Leisure travelers are also welcome.

The graceful **Atherton Hotel** (125 S. Atherton St., State College, 814/231-2100, www.athertonhotel.net, $90-250) will shine your shoes while you sleep—for free—but it's doubtful you'll need the service. A complimentary shuttle virtually ensures scuff-free footwear.

Penn State's picture-perfect ★ **Nittany Lion Inn** (200 W. Park Ave., State College, 800/233-7505, www.nittanylioninn.psu.edu, $135-300) is the only hotel on campus. An inviting facade and lobby bespeak a boutique lodging, but in fact the hotel has 223 guest rooms and suites, not to mention meeting facilities and ballrooms. How it manages to feel so intimate may have something to do with the white-glove service.

Bellefonte is the area's B&B capital. The kingly ★ **Reynolds Mansion** (101 W. Linn St., Bellefonte, 814/353-8407, www.reynoldsmansion.com, $129-219) has eight uniquely decorated guest rooms, from the bright Louisa's Cherub Room, with its ceiling mural, to the dark wood and leather of Colonel's Green Room, which has a king-size bed, a working fireplace, and a large black whirlpool tub.

The Queen, A Victorian Bed & Breakfast (176 E. Linn St., Bellefonte, 814/355-7946, www.thequeenbnb.com, $99-239) is preened to perfection. Victorian clothes and accessories decorate one room, hunting and fishing collectibles another, and vintage toys a third. The Maid's Quarters, an apartment with a full kitchen and views of the garden, sleeps up to four. Rates for weekdays are significantly lower than weekend rates. Owner Nancy Noll also rents out a three-bedroom house ($229-339) on an adjoining property.

TRANSPORTATION AND SERVICES

State College is in Centre County, so named because it's smack-dab in the center of Pennsylvania. It's about 140 miles northeast of Pittsburgh via Route 22 east and I-99 north, 165 miles northwest of Baltimore via I-83 north and Routes 22 and 322 west, and 190 miles northwest of Philadelphia via I-76 west and Routes 22 and 322 west.

University Park Airport (SCE, 814/865-5511, www.universityparkairport.com), just a couple of miles from Beaver Stadium, offers daily flights from Philadelphia, Detroit, Chicago, and Washington Dulles International Airport (IAD) in Virginia. **Greyhound** (800/231-2222, www.greyhound.com) and **Megabus** (877/462-6342, www.megabus.com) offer intercity bus service to State College.

Local bus service is provided by the Centre Area Transportation Authority, or **CATA** (814/238-2282, www.catabus.com). One-way adult cash fare is $2, and transfers are free. Bus drivers don't carry change. CATA provides fare-free transportation around the Penn State campus and between campus and downtown State College.

Local taxi services include **Handy Delivery** (814/355-5555, www.handydelivery.com) and **Nittany Taxi** (814/867-4646, www.nittanyexpress.com).

For information on everything from birdwatching to brewpubs, stop by the headquarters of the **Central Pennsylvania Convention & Visitors Bureau** (800 E. Park Ave., State College, 814/231-1400, www.visitpennstate.org, 7:30am-6pm Mon.-Fri., 9am-6pm Sat.-Sun. Apr.-Nov., 7:30am-5pm Mon.-Fri., 9am-5pm Sat.-Sun. Dec.-Mar.) across from Beaver Stadium.

Atherton Hotel

Raystown Lake Region

At 8,300 acres, Raystown Lake is the largest lake entirely within Pennsylvania. It's a corkscrew of a waterway, 28 miles of zig and zag. The lake has made tourism the second-largest industry after agriculture in Huntingdon County. Raystown attracts about two million visitors a year. The U.S. Army Corps of Engineers, which manages the lake and surrounding land, places no limits on boat size or horsepower, making Raystown a mecca for boating, Jet Skiing, and waterskiing enthusiasts. Thanks to no-wake areas, it's also popular with anglers, bird-watchers, and other connoisseurs of quietude. The island-riddled lake is home to stripers, walleye, musky, crappie, and other game fish. (Bring high-quality tackle. The fish are fighters.) Bald eagles nest in the tree-covered hills that surround the lake.

The federal government and many locals frown on development here. Only about 2 percent of the 118-mile shoreline is developed. There are accommodations aplenty in the hills and valleys surrounding the lake, but it isn't impossible to find waterfront digs, especially if your idea of a good time includes a tent. If the shore isn't close enough, you can stay *on* the lake: Raystown Lake is one of the few places in Pennsylvania where you can rent a houseboat—complete with hot tub.

The "big town" in Raystown country is the small town of **Huntingdon,** located north of the lake along the Juniata River.

★ SEVEN POINTS RECREATION AREA

There's no better place to kick off your "Raycation" than **Seven Points Recreation Area** (Seven Points Rd., Hesston, 814/658-3405, www.nab.usace.army.mil), located in the central region of the 28-mile-long lake. It's the largest developed area at Raystown and one of two hubs of activity (the other is Lake Raystown Resort). The recreation options include boating, swimming, hiking, and camping. Start your visit at the **Raystown Lake Region Visitor Center** (6993 Seven Points Rd., Hesston, 814/658-0060, 9am-5pm daily Memorial Day-Labor Day, 8am-4pm daily early Apr.-Memorial Day and Labor Day-Oct., 8am-4pm Mon.-Fri. Nov.-early Apr.), where you can pick up information about everything from boat launching at Raystown to rock concerts in nearby Huntingdon. The two-story facility also offers exhibits about area history and wildlife, a gift shop, and stunning views of the lake.

Boating

Seven Points is home to one of eight public boat launches at Raystown. It's unique in that it has overflow trailer parking. That makes it a wise choice on summer weekends and holidays, when launches can fill to capacity. There's no fee for parking or boat launching. For more information on boating at Raystown or to check parking status, call the U.S. Army Corps of Engineers at 814/658-3405.

Seven Points is also home to one of two full-service marinas at Raystown. With roughly 950 slips, **Seven Points Marina** (5922 Seven Points Marina Dr., Hesston, 814/658-3074, www.7pointsmarina.com) is one of Pennsylvania's largest marinas. It's one of the few places where you can rent a live-aboard houseboat. Don't think you could live on a boat? You probably haven't seen a boat with a wet bar, sundeck, and hot tub. Check the marina website for photos and descriptions of the rental houseboats, which sleep anywhere from 4 to 10 people. They can be rented from Monday afternoon to Friday morning (four nights) or Friday afternoon to Monday morning (three nights), with prices starting at $945 during peak season (mid-June through August). Off-season discounts are available.

The marina's rental fleet also includes ski,

Steer Clear of the Bears

What do you do if you're boating on Raystown Lake and see a black bear taking a dip? Take a picture, of course. Besides that? Steer clear. Avoid the temptation to speed toward the teddy for a closer look. Bears can grab hold of a boat and come aboard faster than you can say "ahoy." Many of the bears at Raystown Lake were brought there because they did things like pillage trash cans or bird feeders in residential areas, which is to say that they're not shy of humans.

tube, and fishing pontoon boats, which are available by the hour or day. Eight-person pontoon boats, which come with everything you need for waterskiing or tubing, are $100 per hour or $300-325 per day during peak season.

For those who prefer manpower to horsepower, Huntingdon-based **Rothrock Outfitters** (814/643-7226, www.rothrockoutfitters.com) offers rental kayaks and canoes at the marina (10am-6pm Fri.-Mon. and noon-6pm Tues.-Thurs. Memorial Day-Labor Day).

If you'd rather leave the navigating to pros, hop aboard the marina's 75-foot touring boat, the ***Princess.*** Sightseeing cruises are offered select days from late May to mid-October. The two-hour tours cost $12 for adults, $10 for seniors, and $6 for children 4-12. For a schedule of dinner cruises or information on private charters, visit the marina website.

Hiking and Biking

The forests, meadows, and rocky outcrops surrounding Raystown Lake are threaded with more than 65 miles of trail. Seven Points Recreation Area affords opportunities for short nature walks, long mountain bike excursions, and everything in between.

The **Hillside Nature Trail,** a 0.5-mile loop behind the Raystown Lake Region Visitor Center, snakes through songbird habitats and serves up a scrumptious view of Seven Points Marina. The **Old Loggers Trail,** a 4.5-mile loop connecting Seven Points Campground and the primitive Susquehannock Campground, offers moderate hiking. Exhibits along the trail explain how proper forest management improves food and cover for wildlife.

The 33-mile **Allegrippis Trail System** (www.allegrippistrails.com), which attracts mountain bike enthusiasts from as far as Hawaii and Scotland, has two trailheads at Seven Points. Designed for mountain bikers, the network of single-track trails is also beloved by hikers, cross-country skiers, and snowshoers. **Rothrock Outfitters** (814/643-7226, www.rothrockoutfitters.com) offers rental bikes at its Huntingdon location (418 Penn St., Huntingdon, open daily Memorial Day-Labor Day, Tues.-Sat. early Sept.-late May). Rothrock's Seven Points location does not rent out bikes.

Trail maps are available at the Raystown Lake Region Visitor Center or online at www.nab.usace.army.mil.

Swimming

Though swimming is allowed in most parts of Raystown Lake, the U.S. Army Corps of Engineers encourages visitors to use one of two public beaches, which are inspected to ensure safety. Open daily from Memorial Day weekend through Labor Day weekend, **Seven Points Beach** offers an array of amenities, including water trampolines, a playground, showers, flush toilets, and a food concession.

Picnicking

Picnic tables and pedestal charcoal grills can be found near Seven Points Beach (open daily Memorial Day weekend-Labor Day weekend) and in other parts of Seven Points. The good news: There's no fee to use them. The bad news: They're available on a first-come, first-served basis and cannot be reserved. It's best to arrive early, especially on a holiday weekend. If worse comes to worst, you can always find a grassy spot and roll out a picnic blanket.

Seven Points also has several picnic shelters that accommodate as many as 80 people. Shelter reservations are $75 and can be made at www.recreation.gov or by calling 877/444-6777. Unreserved shelters are available on a first-come, first-served basis for no charge.

Camping

With 261 campsites, **Seven Points Campground** is the largest campground in the Raystown region. Reservations are a must during the peak season of Memorial Day weekend through Labor Day weekend and can only be made at www.recreation.gov or by calling 877/444-6777. In the off-season, sites are available on a first-come, first-served basis. Camping fees start at $24 per night. Waterfront sites are the priciest at $36 per night.

LAKE RAYSTOWN RESORT

Along with Seven Points Recreation Area, **Lake Raystown Resort** (3101 Chipmunk Crossing, Entriken, 814/658-3500, www.raystownresort.com) is one of two hubs of activity at Raystown. Located at the southern end of the lake, the family-owned resort offers a wider array of lodging options than Seven Points—from campsites with cable hookups to beachfront bungalows to log cabins perched on cliffs overlooking the lake. You don't have to be a resort guest to enjoy its amenities, which include a 650-slip **marina;** a **mini-golf** course; and a **water park** featuring twisting slides, an inner tube ride, and a spray park with a 500-gallon dumping bucket.

Like Seven Points Marina, Lake Raystown Resort has a **rental boat** fleet that includes live-aboard houseboats. The four-bedroom, two-bath houseboats sleep as many as 10 people and can be rented Monday-Friday or Friday-Monday for $2,200. For $3,600, the boat is yours for an entire week. The rental fleet also includes ski pontoon boats, 15-horsepower fishing boats, and canoes. Pontoon boats, which come with everything you need for waterskiing or tubing, can be rented 8:30am-5pm or 5:30pm-7:30pm for $200-460. Fishing boats are $30 per hour or $150 per day. Canoes go for $10 per hour or $75 per day.

Lake Raystown Resort is home to the ***Proud Mary Showboat,*** used for public cruises from late May through October as well as private events. Ninety-minute sightseeing cruises ($10) are offered at 2:15pm daily until Labor Day and weekends thereafter. Check the resort website for a schedule of breakfast, karaoke, dinner, and late-night cruises.

The resort is also home to **Angry Musky Outfitters** (814/280-1344), a fishing guide service with the motto "Forget Fishing, Let's Go Catching!" Captain Kirk Reynolds, who has been fishing the lake since childhood, offers four-, six-, and eight-hour trips on a boat that accommodates up to six passengers. Charter rates start at $250. On Wednesday mornings, Angry Musky offers a four-hour public fishing trip for $50 per person. Reservations—and fishing licenses—are required.

ENTERTAINMENT AND EVENTS

Festivals and Events

Folk musicians flock to Huntingdon County twice a year: first for **Folk College** (Juniata College, 814/643-6220, www.folkcollege.com, May, registration fee charged) and later for the **Greenwood Furnace Folk Gathering** (Greenwood Furnace State Park, 814/643-6220, www.folkgathering.com, Sept., registration fee charged). Both feature workshops, jam sessions, and concerts.

The **Huntingdon County Fair** (10455 Fairgrounds Access Rd., Huntingdon, 814/643-4452, www.huntingdoncountyfair.com, early Aug.) is an agricultural expo with midway rides, live music, a fair queen contest, and a demolition derby. A museum dedicated to agricultural history, normally open by appointment only, is open throughout the week.

SPORTS AND RECREATION

Raystown Lake isn't the only recreational amenity in these parts. Huntingdon County is chockablock with creeks, parks, forests, hiking trails, and wildlife. It's long been known for world-class fishing. The opening of the Allegrippis Trail System has also made it a mecca for mountain bikers.

Allegrippis Trail System

Designed by the International Mountain Bicycling Association, the 33-mile **Allegrippis Trail System** (www.allegrippistrails.com) attracts **mountain bikers** from far and wide. It's a stacked-loop system consisting of numerous single-track trails, which means that users can customize the length and difficulty of their trip. The trails, which traverse ridges, woods, and the shores of Raystown Lake, also make for excellent **hiking, bird-watching, cross-country skiing,** and **snowshoeing.** A detailed map can be purchased at the Raystown Lake Region Visitor Center (6993 Seven Points Rd., Hesston, 814/658-0060, 9am-5pm daily Memorial Day-Labor Day, 8am-4pm daily early Apr.-Memorial Day and Labor Day-Oct., 8am-4pm Mon.-Fri. Nov.-early Apr.).

There are two main public trailheads: one at the visitors center and another along Baker's Hollow Road near the Susquehannock Campground. To reach the Baker's Hollow trailhead from southbound Route 26 at Route 22, continue south eight miles to the blinking light, and turn left toward Seven Points (marked by sign). Continue 2.7 miles, and turn left onto Baker's Hollow Road. Continue 1.5 miles to the trailhead (marked by sign). There's a third trailhead along Seven Points Road between the Seven Points entrance station and the visitors center, but parking is very limited.

Rothrock Outfitters (418 Penn St., Huntingdon, 814/643-7226, www.rothrockoutfitters.com, 11am-5pm Mon.-Thurs., 11am-6pm Fri., 9am-5pm Sat., 9am-noon Sun. Memorial Day-Labor Day, 11am-5pm Tues.-Thurs., 11am-6pm Fri., 9am-5pm Sat. Labor Day-Memorial Day) offers rental bikes and a whole lot of expertise.

Bird-Watching

Bald eagles are spotted year-round at Raystown Lake—and that's not the only thing that brings birders to the region. In spring, shorebirds are a sure thing at the man-made **Old Crow Wetland** off Route 22 near Hoss's Steak and Sea House (9016 William Penn Hwy./Rte. 22, Huntingdon). More than 150 avian species have been inventoried in **Whipple Dam State Park** (20 miles northeast of Huntingdon off Rte. 26, 814/667-1800, www.dcnr.pa.gov/stateparks).

For guaranteed sightings of golden and bald eagles, owls, and other birds of prey, head to Penn State's **Shaver's Creek Environmental Center** (3400 Discovery Rd., Petersburg, 814/863-2000, www.shaverscreek.org, 10am-5pm daily mid-Feb.-mid-Dec., free). It's home to injured raptors that can't fend for themselves in the wild. The center's annual Birding Cup, held the first weekend in May, challenges teams to identify as many species as possible in a 24-hour period.

Fishing

Raystown Lake. Juniata River. Spruce Creek. Standing Stone Creek. Aughwick Creek. Shavers Creek. Great Trough Creek. The list of waterways goes on and on, and so does the fishing season. Pros have been casting their lines in this region for decades. Hobbyists unfamiliar with the area may wish to hire a guide.

Lake Raystown is well stocked with boat charter services. Sparky Price is the record-shattering angler behind **Trophy Guide Service** (814/627-5231, www.trophyguide.com). The 53-pound striper he pulled out of the lake is the largest the state has seen. Lake Raystown Resort's **Angry Musky Outfitters** (814/280-1344, www.raystownresort.com) has as its motto "Forget Fishing, Let's Go Catching!"

Open since 1986, **Spruce Creek Outfitters** (4910 Spruce Creek Rd., Spruce

Creek, 814/632-3071, www.sprucecreekoutfitters.org, hours vary by season) specializes in fly-fishing on the Little Juniata River, which is thick with wild brown trout.

Hiking

The Raystown region is a hiker's paradise, with trails for every skill level. **Seven Points Recreation Area** (Seven Points Rd., Hesston, 814/658-3405, www.nab.usace.army.mil) is a good starting point for easy or moderate hiking. It's home to the **Hillside Nature Trail,** a 0.5-mile loop through songbird habitats, and trailheads for the 4.5-mile **Old Loggers Trail** and 33-mile **Allegrippis Trail System.** Designed for mountain bikers, the Allegrippis trails are no less appealing to joggers and hikers. Maps of these and other trails are available at the visitors center at Seven Points (6993 Seven Points Rd., Hesston, 814/658-0060, 9am-5pm daily Memorial Day-Labor Day, 8am-4pm daily early Apr.-Memorial Day and Labor Day-Oct., 8am-4pm Mon.-Fri. Nov.-early Apr.).

For serious trekkers, there's the **Terrace Mountain Trail,** which spans the eastern side of Raystown Lake. The 30-mile route has seven access points, so you can tackle it all at once or in segments. Overnight camping with potable water is available at two access points, and primitive camping is permitted at designated spots along the trail. For trail conditions and more information, contact the U.S. Army Corps of Engineers (814/658-3405, www.nab.usace.army.mil).

Twelve miles of trails traverse **Trough Creek State Park** (16362 Little Valley Rd., James Creek, 814/658-3847, www.dcnr.pa.gov/stateparks), a gorge formed as Great Trough Creek cuts through Terrace Mountain and empties into Raystown Lake. Among the wondrous sights: the large boulder known as Balanced Rock because it clings to the edge of a cliff, beautiful Rainbow Falls, mountain laurel blooms in June, rhododendron blooms in July, and the occasional copperhead.

FOOD

Like many recreation areas, Raystown Lake is blessed with homespun eateries that you can walk into water-soaked or mud-splattered and still be greeted with a smile. Burgers, hoagies, pizza, ice cream, and other foods that don't call for utensils are the norm. But exceptions can be found.

Huntingdon

Start your day at **Standing Stone Coffee Company** (1229 Mifflin St., Huntingdon, 814/643-4545, www.standingstonecoffeecompany.com, 7am-8pm Mon.-Thurs., 7am-9pm Fri., 7:30am-9pm Sat., 9am-8pm Sun), which roasts its own java. Pair your drip-brewed or French-pressed coffee with a mini quiche, baked oatmeal, or other breakfast item. Standing Stone has free Wi-Fi and—get this—a self-service laundry.

The husband and wife behind **Boxer's Café** (418 Penn St., Huntingdon, 814/643-5013, 11am-9pm Mon.-Thurs. and Sat., 11am-10pm Fri., under $10) refuel their modified vehicles with oil used in the kitchen's fryers. With wings, Cajun fries, and breaded mushrooms on the menu, there's nary a shortage. Named for the dog breed, not the fighting sport, Boxer's is known for its large selection of import beers and microbrews.

For an upscale dinner, there's ★ **Mimi's** (312 Penn St., Huntingdon, 814/643-7200, www.mimisrestaurant.net, 4:30pm-10pm Mon.-Sat., bar open as late as 2am, $7-29). The restaurant and martini bar offers sandwiches and burgers along with entrées like crab cakes and chicken piccata. Its lengthy cocktail menu takes a while to digest.

There's more than one way to satisfy a sweet tooth during your stay in Raystown country. **Sweethearts Confectionery** (723 Washington St., 814/643-3785, 8am-5pm Mon.-Fri., 8am-1pm Sat.) in downtown Huntingdon specializes in cupcakes. It also carries a wide selection of candies, including nostalgic varieties and Jelly Belly products. Just outside of town along Route 22, **Gardners Candies** (9154 William Penn

Hwy./Rte. 22, 814/643-5302, www.gardnerscandies.com, 10am-8pm Mon.-Sat., noon-5pm Sun.) offers ice cream and a fantastic variety of locally made chocolates. Founded nearby in 1897 by a 16-year-old boy, Gardners is known for its Original Peanut Butter Meltaways.

Vicinity of Huntingdon

Four miles east of Huntingdon along Route 22, **Top's Diner** (12151 William Penn Hwy./Rte. 22, Mill Creek, 814/643-4169, www.topsdiner.net, 6am-8pm Mon.-Thurs., 6am-9pm Fri.-Sat., 7am-8pm Sun., $4-16) is known for its signature burger and daily specials. The decades-old diner also has outdoor seating, so you can have a side of sunshine with your meal.

ACCOMMODATIONS

The Raystown region is notable as one of the few places in Pennsylvania where you can rent a houseboat, but you don't have to venture out onto the water to find a bed.

Under $100

With roughly 2,000 campsites, the Raystown region calls to nature-loving budget travelers. There are several campgrounds on federal property ringing Raystown Lake, including the amenity-rich **Seven Points Campground** (open seasonally, $24-36), the primitive **Susquehannock Campground** (open seasonally, $16-18), and the remote **Nancy's Camp** (open year-round, $12), which is accessible only by boat. You can reserve a site through the federal recreation portal Recreation.gov (877/444-6777, www.recreation.gov). For information on site availability, call the U.S. Army Corps of Engineers ranger station at 814/658-6809.

The waterfront **Lake Raystown Resort** (3101 Chipmunk Crossing, Entriken, 814/658-3500, www.raystownresort.com, campground open seasonally, campsite $35-85) has a variety of lodging options, including more than 200 campsites. Campground amenities include water, electricity, cable hookups, and wireless Internet. But it's the list of resort amenities—mini golf, water park, rental boats, and more—that makes campers come back again and again.

The smaller **Heritage Cove Resort** (1172 River Rd., Saxton, 814/635-3386, www.heritagecoveresort.com, open seasonally, campsite $45-58) has about 200 campsites with water, electricity, sewage hookups, picnic tables, and fire rings. The retreat at the southern end of Raystown Lake also offers two- and three-bedroom cottages starting at $179. Resort amenities include a pool, playground, volleyball court, and camp store. Canoes, kayaks, a pontoon boat, and bicycles are available for rent.

$100-250

★ **The Inn at Solvang** (10611 Standing Stone Rd., Huntingdon, 888/814-3035, www.huntingdonbedandbreakfast.com, $105-145) looks like something out of *Gone with the Wind*. The three-story brick mansion with four massive columns sits at the end of a tree-lined lane off Route 26 about four miles north of Huntingdon. (It's easy to miss the turnoff. Look for an ornate *S* between two white posts.) Gourmet breakfasts are served on fine china, but the atmosphere is far from prim. Guests are welcome to fish on the stream that runs through the property.

The menu of accommodations at **Lake Raystown Resort, Lodge & Conference Center** (3101 Chipmunk Crossing, Entriken, 814/658-3500, www.raystownresort.com) is as diverse as the menu of activities. The lodge ($119-224 during peak season) has 50 guest rooms and two suites, each with a private balcony overlooking the lake. You could also opt for a one-bedroom log cabin ($139-160), a cottage ($155-180) complete with master bedroom and full kitchen, a two-bedroom beachfront bungalow ($1,499 per week during peak season, $139-174 per night in off-season), or a villa ($775-899 per 3-night weekend stay or 4-night weekday stay, $1,400-1,699 per week) nestled in the woods.

For a romantic getaway à la Tarzan and Jane, swing over to **Junglewood** (2553 Timberlake Dr., James Creek, 814/658-3190, www.shybeaverlakeviewest.com, $240-255), perched high above Raystown Lake. The vacation home feels like a treehouse—a treehouse with satellite TV and a large hot tub.

TRANSPORTATION AND SERVICES

Huntingdon, the Raystown region's commercial center, is about 30 miles east of Altoona via Route 22 and 30 miles south of State College via Route 26. If you're flying commercial, you can't get closer than **Altoona-Blair County Airport** (AOO, 814/793-2027, www.flyaltoona.com) or **University Park Airport** (SCE, 814/865-5511, www.universityparkairport.com) in State College. The larger **Harrisburg International Airport** (MDT, 888/235-9442, www.flyhia.com) is about 100 miles east of Huntingdon. **Amtrak** (800/872-7245, www.amtrak.com) provides train service to Huntingdon from New York City, Philadelphia, Harrisburg, Pittsburgh, and other cities on its Pennsylvanian line. Huntingdon's train station (4th and Allegheny Streets) is less than 500 feet from **Rothrock Outfitters** (418 Penn St., 814/643-7226, www.rothrockoutfitters.com), where you can rent a bicycle, and a short walk from **Enterprise Rent-A-Car** (100 S. 4th St., 814/643-5778, www.enterprise.com). There's no bus service in Huntingdon. **Maidens Taxi Service** (814/644-9999) is your best bet if you don't have wheels.

To get to Raystown Lake from Huntingdon, take Route 26 south and watch for brown Lake Access signs.

The hilltop **Raystown Lake Region Visitor Center** (6993 Seven Points Rd., Hesston, 814/658-0060, 9am-5pm daily Memorial Day-Labor Day, 8am-4pm daily early Apr.-Memorial Day and Labor Day-Oct., 8am-4pm Mon.-Fri. Nov.-early Apr.) is a good place to start your "Raycation," as the folks who market the lake like to say. It houses the Huntingdon County Visitors Bureau (814/658-0060, www.raystown.org). You'll find bushels of free brochures, a gift shop, and exhibits on the region's history, geology, and wildlife. A deck affords majestic views of the lake and Seven Points Marina.

Bedford and Vicinity

As British troops carved a wagon road over the Allegheny Mountains in 1758, they stopped to construct fortifications along the way. One of these, Fort Bedford, sat on a bluff overlooking the Raystown Branch of the Juniata River. Bedford homesteads became hot property because the fort provided protection from Indian attacks.

Bedford got even hotter in the 1800s, when word spread of mineral-rich springs with curative powers. People traveled great distances to "take the waters." The luxe Bedford Springs Hotel attracted a bevy of politicians and other upper-echelon types during the 19th and early 20th centuries. Today, thanks to its rebirth and relatively low property costs, the Bedford area is once again gaining popularity as an idyllic retreat for city folk.

SIGHTS

Historic Bedford

Fort Bedford deteriorated in the 1770s, but a museum suggestive of a blockhouse stands near the site. The **Fort Bedford Museum** (110 Fort Bedford Dr., 814/623-8891, www.fortbedfordmuseum.org, 10am-5pm Mon. and Wed.-Sat., 10am-4pm Sun. May-Oct., adults $7, seniors $6, students 6-18 $5) houses a model of the irregularly shaped fort and a variety of military and civilian artifacts. The jewel of its collection is a 1758 flag that hung in the officers' quarters. It was a gift from England's fourth Duke of Bedford, for whom the fort was named.

The **Espy House** (123 East Pitt St.) served as President George Washington's headquarters during the Whiskey Rebellion. Snap a

Washington Slept Here

Farmers in western Pennsylvania didn't take kindly to a federal excise tax imposed on whiskey producers in 1791. They took out their irritation on tax collectors and other government representatives (think tar and feathers). When their bullying turned to outright insurrection in 1794, President George Washington invoked martial law to summon a force of nearly 13,000. He led the militia army as far west as Bedford. While his men camped in open fields, Washington slept in the home of Colonel David Espy—the nicest digs in town. It was the first and only time a U.S. president would command troops in the field.

By the time troops reached the Pittsburgh area, the epicenter of the so-called Whiskey Rebellion, most of the rebels had fled into the hills. The federal government had proven its might. The whiskey tax remained in force until 1801. In 1984, the **Espy House** was named a National Historic Landmark.

few pictures, but don't expect its current occupants to invite you inside. For a warm welcome, try the **Golden Eagle Inn** (131 E. Pitt St., 814/624-0800, www.bedfordpainn.com). Travelers have been stopping here for a bite to eat and a bed to sleep in since the late 1700s. (Bedford's Pitt Street was once part of the Forbes Trail, the route cut by British troops in 1758 and followed by many a stagecoach driver.) The house next door, now used as a commercial property, was built in 1814 for Dr. John Anderson, who saw patients in the front and operated Bedford's first bank in the back. The architect responsible for Dr. Anderson's house built the **Bedford County Courthouse** (200 S. Juliana St.) in the late 1820s. Two self-supported circular stairways lead to a second-floor courtroom bedecked with portraits of judges.

The **Bedford County Visitors Bureau** (131 S. Juliana St., 800/765-3331, www.visitbedfordcounty.com, 9am-5pm Mon.-Sat. and noon-5pm Sun. May-Oct., 9am-5pm Mon.-Fri. Nov.-Apr.) offers free guided tours of downtown's historic sites on Fridays June-October. Tours start at 3:30pm and last about 90 minutes.

Old Bedford Village

A "living history village" two miles north of downtown leaves nothing to the imagination. When **Old Bedford Village** (220 Sawblade Rd., Bedford, 814/623-1156, www.oldbedfordvillage.com, 9am-5pm daily except Wed. Memorial Day-Labor Day, Thurs.-Sun. after Labor Day-Oct., adults $10, seniors $9, students 6-18 $5) isn't staging reenactments of pre-21st-century battles, its costumed artisans are demonstrating coopering, quilting, candle making, and other early American crafts. The village has more than 40 original and reconstructed structures, including a two-story log farmhouse from the 1700s and an octagonal schoolhouse built in 1851.

★ Omni Bedford Springs Resort

Bedford doctor John Anderson wasted no time when Native Americans led him to mineral-rich springs on the southern outskirts of town. In 1796 he bought a 2,200-acre swath of countryside that included the springs. Soon, patients were arriving from near and far to bathe in and drink the reputedly curative waters. At first the savvy doctor housed them in tents. In 1806 he built a hotel with stone quarried from a nearby mountain. The resort grew along with its popularity, opening one of America's first golf courses in 1895 and an indoor pool fed by spring waters a decade later. Musicians serenaded the swimmers from a balcony overlooking the pool. By the time it closed in 1986—timeworn and cash-strapped—the Bedford Springs Hotel had hosted 11 presidents and a long list of captains of industry and celebrities.

Reopened in 2007 after a restoration and expansion to the tune of $120 million, the **Omni Bedford Springs Resort** (2138 Business Rte. 220, Bedford, 814/623-8100, www.omnihotels.com, $200-450) now boasts a 30,000-square-foot spa that uses water from a spring discovered during the makeover. The restored golf course was named the top playable classic course in Pennsylvania by *Golfweek* magazine. Marble flooring surrounds the lavish indoor pool, and private cabanas ring the outdoor pool.

You don't have to be a guest of the resort to enjoy the 18-hole golf course or the **Springs Eternal Spa.** And you don't have to spend an arm and a leg to have a fantastically soothing spa experience. Book any service—from a $20 eyebrow wax to a $185 mud wrap—and you can spend all the time you like sipping tea in the coed lounge, strolling in the adjacent garden, or moving between steam room, hot-water pool, and cold-water pool as part of the spa's signature self-guided bathing ritual.

Dining options include the **1796 Room,** an upscale steak house, and the casual **Frontier Tavern,** where you can wash down a bacon-topped burger with a Pennsylvania microbrew.

Gravity Hill

There's a spot in suburban New Paris, about 15 miles from Bedford, where a car in neutral will roll uphill—or so it's said. From Route 30, drive to the town of Schellsburg, which is about eight miles west of Bedford. At Schellsburg's only traffic light, turn north onto Route 96, drive about four miles, and turn left onto Bethel Hollow Road. Drive about two miles to an intersection with a stop sign for oncoming traffic, and bear right. Within a quarter of a mile, you'll see "GH" spray-painted on the road. Continue past the first "GH" and stop before you reach the second "GH." Put your car in neutral. Take your foot off the brake pedal. Defy gravity.

Wise men say that **Gravity Hill** (800/765-3331, www.gravityhill.com) is an example of an optical illusion, not of supernatural forces. It's a trip either way.

Covered Bridges

Bedford County has 14 covered bridges. Most were built in the 1800s in the Burr-truss style, named for designer Theodore Burr, and are still drivable. A covered-bridge driving tour is available on the website of the **Bedford County Visitors Bureau** (800/765-3331, www.visitbedfordcounty.com). You can also

Omni Bedford Springs Resort

call the visitors bureau and request a free brochure on the bridges.

ENTERTAINMENT AND EVENTS

Festivals and Events

The weeklong **Bedford County Fair** (just west of downtown Bedford on Business Rte. 30/W. Pitt St., 814/623-9011, www.bedfordfair.com, late July) offers the classic county fair lineup: animal exhibitions, live music, midway rides, and a queen competition. Be sure to check out the unusually large **Coffee Pot** at the entrance to the fairgrounds. The 1920s structure was once a lunch stand along the Lincoln Highway, America's first coast-to-coast road. It was moved to its present location in 2003.

The **Bedford Fall Foliage Festival** (814/624-3111, www.bedfordfallfestival.com, first two weekends of Oct., free) brings hundreds of craft vendors and tens of thousands of visitors to Bedford. Live music, an antique car parade, and children's activities are festival staples.

SPORTS AND RECREATION

State Parks

Blue Knob State Park (124 Park Rd., Imler, 814/276-3576, www.dcnr.pa.gov/stateparks) in northwestern Bedford County is home to Blue Knob, Pennsylvania's second-highest mountain after Mount Davis. The mountain makes for breathtaking views and challenging hikes. Mountain biking, horseback riding, snowmobiling, cross-country skiing, hunting, and fishing are all permitted in the park. **Blue Knob All Seasons Resort** (1424 Overland Pass, Claysburg, 800/458-3403, www.blueknob.com, all-day lift ticket $38-62, children and seniors $33-50, all-day ski rental $35, snow tubing $20-25 per 2-hour session) offers skiing, snowboarding, and tubing on land leased from the state. The resort also has an 18-hole golf course.

Boaters may prefer the smaller **Shawnee State Park** (132 State Park Rd., Schellsburg, 814/733-4218, www.dcnr.pa.gov/stateparks) with its 451-acre lake stocked with warmwater game fish. Paddleboats, canoes, and rowboats can be rented during the summer. A swimming beach is open 8am-sunset from late May to mid-September.

the Coffee Pot at the entrance to the Bedford County Fairgrounds

Both parks offer modern campsites starting the second Friday in April. Blue Knob's 50 tent and trailer sites close in late October. Shawnee has almost 300 sites and a camping season that stretches to late December. Reserve online at http://pennsylvaniastateparks.reserveamerica.com or by calling 888/727-2757.

Biking

Cyclists dig Bedford County's lightly traveled roads and scenic vistas. Turn-by-turn directions for about 20 rides, including an easy 12.2-mile loop that takes in four covered bridges, are available at www.visitbedfordcounty.com/biking.

If you don't have wheels, head to **Fat Jimmy's Outfitters** (109 Railroad St., Bedford, 814/624-3415, www.fatjimmys.com, 10am-6pm Mon. and Wed.-Fri., 9am-2pm Sat.). Bicycle rentals start at $30 per day.

Grouseland Tours (467 Robinsonville Rd., Clearville, 814/784-5000, www.grouseland.net), about 25 miles southeast of Bedford, not only rents and sells bicycles but also offers fully supported bike tours. It's known for its tours of the Pike 2 Bike, an abandoned highway turned bike trail.

Boating

Novice paddlers will appreciate the slow-moving Raystown Branch of the Juniata River, which flows through Bedford. Canoe and kayak rentals are $30 per day at **Fat Jimmy's Outfitters** (109 Railroad St., Bedford, 814/624-3415, www.fatjimmys.com, 10am-6pm Mon. and Wed.-Fri., 9am-2pm Sat.).

Horseback Riding

Greenridge Horse Ranch (130 Horse Ranch Rd., Artemas, 814/784-5223, www.greenridgehorseranch.com) promises to have you riding "the cowboy way" in no time. Trail rides start at $50 for a 90-minute trip. Pony rides are $35 per half hour. The ranch is closed from Thanksgiving through December, when deer hunters roam the woods.

FOOD

Downtown Bedford

There are a good number of recommendable eateries in the heart of Bedford. For breakfast or lunch, **The Green Harvest Co.** (110 E. Pitt St., Bedford, 814/623-3465, 7am-4pm Mon.-Sat., under $10) takes the peanut butter and jelly concept to new heights. Try the Apple PB sandwich, made with all-natural peanut butter, apples, bacon, and cheddar, or the Monkey Panini, which swaps in sliced bananas for the apples.

Bird's Nest Farm Café (113 S. Richard St., Bedford, 814/623-6378, 8am-3pm daily, under $10) is another good daytime choice. The salmon-ginger cake sandwich is a hot seller. Owner Michael Stipanovic's pumpkin blondies are reason enough to visit Bedford in the fall.

The **Bedford Tavern** (224 E. Pitt St., Bedford, 814/623-9021, www.bedford-tavern.com, 5pm-9pm Mon.-Wed., 5pm-10pm Thurs.-Sat., bar open later, $17-34) is known for its seafood—from fried oysters to lobster tail—and Friday night "all you care to eat" dinners. The menu in the downstairs sports bar is more casual, with wings, burgers, and fish-and-chips.

The **Golden Eagle Inn** (131 E. Pitt St., 814/624-0800, www.bedfordpainn.com, noon-9pm Tues.-Sat., pub also open 4pm-9pm Mon., $13-28) also offers a choice of upstairs or downstairs dining. Reservations, recommended for the dining room, are not accepted in the livelier pub. The building is historic but the menu is hardly traditional, featuring dishes like General Tso's cauliflower, pasta with short rib ragout, and the Dubliner: a burger topped with corned beef, swiss cheese, and sauerkraut.

Vicinity of Bedford

A few miles west of town, the ★ **Jean Bonnet Tavern** (6048 Lincoln Hwy., Bedford, 814/623-2250, www.jeanbonnettavern.com, 11am-9pm Sun.-Thurs., 11am-10pm Fri.-Sat., bar open later, $8-36) offers hearty American fare and a selection of draft beers that's heavy on Pennsylvania microbrews. If the thick fieldstone walls of the 1760s landmark could talk, they'd tell of farmers meeting in opposition to a federal whiskey tax and the troops sent to quell their insurrection in 1794. Diners can warm up by old hearth fireplaces in winter or catch a breeze on the outdoor dining porch in summer. Weary travelers can lay their heads in one of four guest rooms ($120-140).

ACCOMMODATIONS

Under $100

Clean rooms, low rates, and gracious hosts of Pennsylvania Dutch stock greet guests at **Judy's Motel** (3521 Business Rte. 220, Bedford, 814/623-9118, www.judysmotel.com, $45-55), 1.5 miles south of Pennsylvania Turnpike exit 146.

The full-service **Friendship Village Campground** (348 Friendship Village Rd., Bedford, 814/623-1677, www.friendshipvillagecampground.com, campsite $30-56, cabin $70-145, weekly rates available) has campsites, rustic cabins, and cottages complete with air-conditioning and cable TV. Amenities include two swimming pools, a miniature golf course, and an arcade room. FYI: From Memorial Day to Labor Day, the campground hosts Saturday evening "gospel sings" and Sunday morning church services.

$100-250

In the heart of Bedford, the **Golden Eagle Inn** (131 E. Pitt St., 814/624-0800, www.bedfordpainn.com, $105-175) was erected in 1794 as the first brick building in town. A gourmet breakfast is included. For dinner and drinks, there's a fine-dining restaurant and a casual pub on-site.

The impeccable **Chancellor's House Bed and Breakfast** (341 S. Juliana St., Bedford, 814/624-0374, www.thechancellorshouse.com, $140-170) in Bedford's historic district has three guest rooms with private bathrooms and a wide front porch with rocking chairs. Breakfast is an elegant affair.

An idyllic vacation on a working sheep farm? That's right. Guests aren't asked to lend a hand at **Monsour Sheep Farm** (120 Oppenheimer Rd., Bedford, 814/623-8243, www.monsourvacationhomes.com), which has four vacation homes along with a flock of more than 1,000 ewes. Accommodations range from the two-bedroom Shepherd's Chalet ($150), a renovated granary with a large deck, to a five-bedroom farmhouse ($299) that sleeps as many as 14. A two-night minimum stay is required for three of the homes; the farmhouse requires a three-night stay. Come in May for a chance to bottle-feed a newborn lamb.

Fronted by columns of solid white pine and rows of balconies, the ★ **Omni Bedford Springs Resort** (2138 Business Rte. 220, Bedford, 814/623-8100, www.omnihotels.com, $200-450) offers more than 200 luxuriously appointed guest rooms and a handful of suites. They're divided between a historic building and a modern spa wing. The latter is advisable if you plan to spend much time luxuriating in the fabulous spa, swimming in the indoor or outdoor pools, or exercising in the fitness center. Guests can pass the time fishing on a private lake or stocked trout stream (kids can have the chef cook their fresh catch), hiking or biking 25 miles of trails (knobby walking sticks provided), or playing a game of golf, tennis, bocce ball, or badminton. Roasting marshmallows around the fire pit is an evening tradition. The resort's cooking workshops are also quite popular.

TRANSPORTATION AND SERVICES

Bedford is about 100 miles east of Pittsburgh via the Pennsylvania Turnpike (I-76) and 140 miles northwest of Baltimore and Washington DC via I-70. The east-west Pennsylvania Turnpike (I-76) and Route 30 pass through Bedford County, as does the north-south Route 220/I-99. To reach downtown Bedford from the turnpike, take exit 146 and turn right onto Business Route 220.

There are no commercial flights into Bedford County Airport.

The **Bedford County Visitors Bureau** (131 S. Juliana St., 800/765-3331, www.visitbedfordcounty.com, 9am-5pm Mon.-Sat. and noon-5pm Sun. May-Oct., 9am-5pm Mon.-Fri. Nov.-Apr.) in downtown Bedford has staff to answer questions and brochures devoted to everything from covered bridges to birding hot spots.

Lake Region

Pennsylvania borders the "Fourth Seacoast," as Congress dubbed the Great Lakes in 1970. The five freshwater lakes on the nation's border with Canada are ocean-like in more ways than one.

They offer sandy beaches, sloping dunes, and surfable waves. And they're vast. At more than 4,500 miles, the U.S. Great Lakes shoreline is longer than the East and Gulf Coasts combined.

The northwest corner of the commonwealth abuts Lake Erie, shallowest and warmest of the Great Lakes. Pennsylvania's share of the shoreline is small—less than 80 miles—but of note. Presque Isle, a peninsula attached to the mainland just west of the city of Erie, is a natural wonderland. Just seven miles long, it boasts six distinct ecological zones and an incredible diversity of plants and animals. *Birder's World* magazine named it one of the best places in the country for bird-watching. It's one of the best—if not *the* best—place in Pennsylvania to watch the sun set. And its beaches are hands down the best in the state (not that they have too much competition).

Erie County is a major grape grower, and that means wineries. Erie, its county seat and largest city, is home port to Pennsylvania's official state ship, the Flagship *Niagara*, a faithful reconstruction of the 1813 brig that sealed one of the most important naval victories in American history. Pymatuning Lake, within an hour's drive of Erie, is the only place is in the state where you can feed wildlife. Like Presque Isle, Pymatuning is a magnet for birders. You're likely to spot a bald eagle. Nearby Erie National Wildlife Refuge rounds out the region's bird-watching triple bill.

PLANNING YOUR TIME

Winter is a bad time to visit northwest Pennsylvania. With an average annual snowfall of nearly 90 inches, Erie is one of the 15 snowiest cities in the country. That would be great if the attractions in this corner of the state included ski resorts, but when locals want to hit the slopes, they head to New York's Peek'n Peak. Among the very few reasons to visit in winter is to gaze at the otherworldly ice

Previous: Presque Isle State Park; Flagship *Niagara*. **Above:** Presque Isle Lighthouse.

Look for ★ to find recommended sights, activities, dining, and lodging.

HIGHLIGHTS

★ **Presque Isle State Park:** A National Natural Landmark, this sandy peninsula is sheer bliss for beach lovers and birders (page 298).

★ **Erie Maritime Museum and Flagship *Niagara*:** The museum brings to life the Battle of Lake Erie, a major American victory during the War of 1812. It's doubly interesting when Pennsylvania's official flagship is docked behind it (page 302).

★ **Bayfront District Boat Tours:** Get out on the water with a scenic cruise aboard a paddle wheeler or kid-friendly pirate ship (page 303).

★ **Wine Country:** With its proliferation of wineries, the town of North East is a first-rate day-trip destination, especially during the harvest months of September and October (page 304).

★ **The Spillway:** Toss bread into this heavily visited spot on man-made Pymatuning Lake to see ducks scramble over fish (page 313).

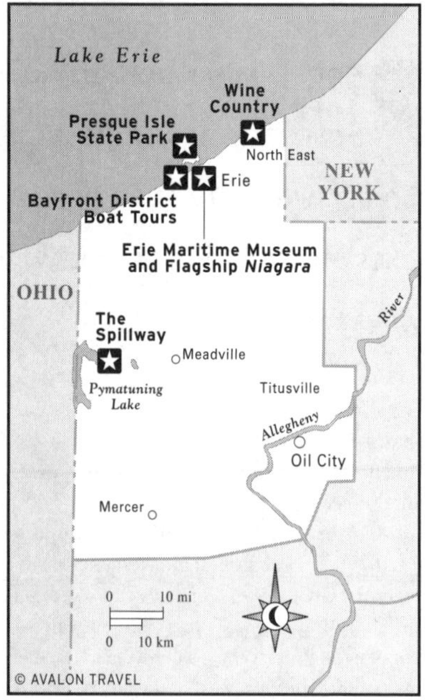

Lake Region

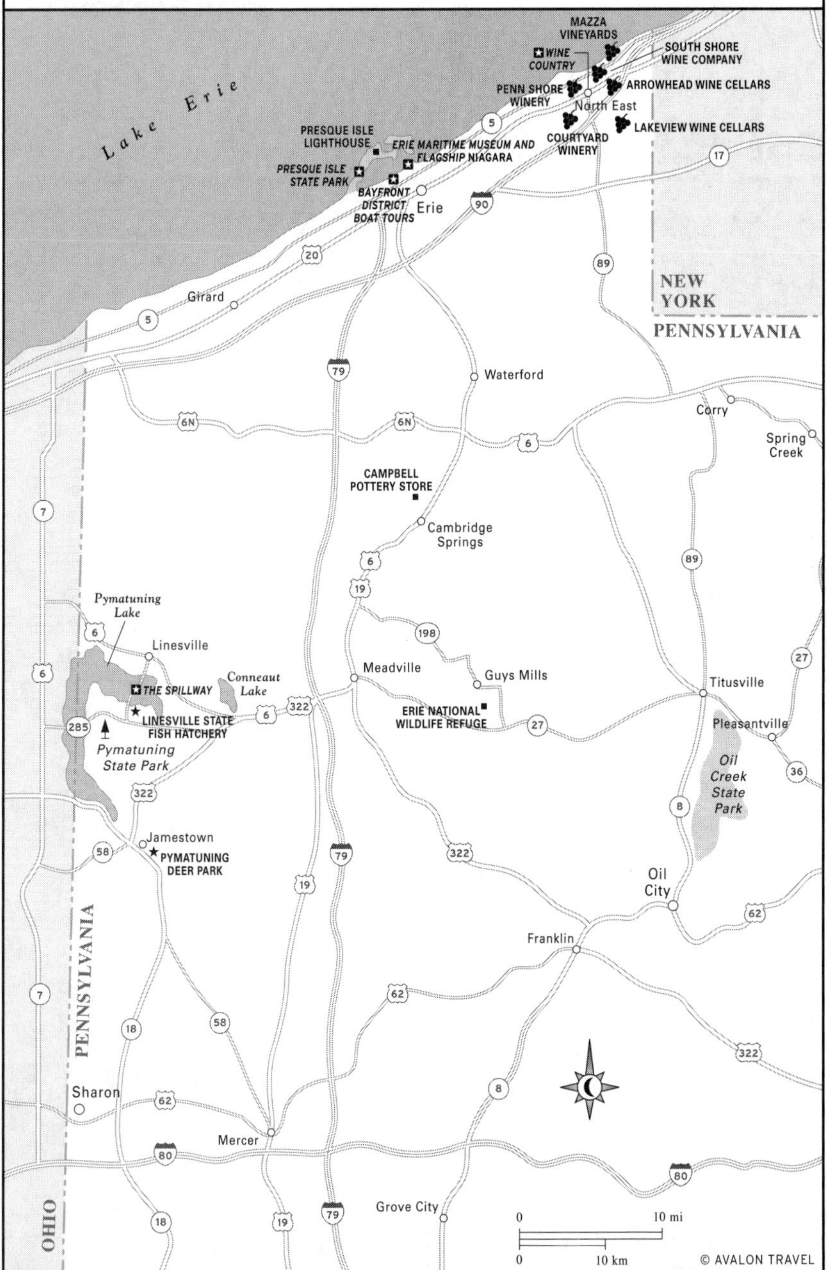

Lake Erie
MAZZA VINEYARDS
SOUTH SHORE WINE COMPANY
WINE COUNTRY
PENN SHORE WINERY
ARROWHEAD WINE CELLARS
North East
LAKEVIEW WINE CELLARS
COURTYARD WINERY
PRESQUE ISLE LIGHTHOUSE
ERIE MARITIME MUSEUM AND FLAGSHIP NIAGARA
PRESQUE ISLE STATE PARK
BAYFRONT DISTRICT BOAT TOURS
Erie
NEW YORK
PENNSYLVANIA
Girard
Waterford
Corry
Spring Creek
CAMPBELL POTTERY STORE
Cambridge Springs
Pymatuning Lake
Linesville
Conneaut Lake
THE SPILLWAY
LINESVILLE STATE FISH HATCHERY
Pymatuning State Park
Meadville
Guys Mills
ERIE NATIONAL WILDLIFE REFUGE
Titusville
Pleasantville
Oil Creek State Park
Jamestown
PYMATUNING DEER PARK
Oil City
Franklin
PENNSYLVANIA
Sharon
Mercer
Grove City
OHIO
0
10 mi
0
10 km
© AVALON TRAVEL

dunes along the shore of Lake Erie. Holing up in a B&B for some R&R is another.

If you're going to visit Presque Isle in summer—the most popular time to visit the beach-lined peninsula—plan well ahead. Accommodations fill quickly. Do the same if your excursion includes wine-tasting during the harvest months of September and October.

Erie and Vicinity

With a population of about 98,000, Erie is Pennsylvania's fourth-largest city after Philadelphia, Pittsburgh, and Allentown. Its relative largeness has much to do with its location on Presque Isle Bay, a natural harbor formed and sheltered by the peninsula for which it's named. Erie was a speck of a town when the United States declared war on Great Britain in 1812. With Canada under British control, the Great Lakes became a theater of war. As one of the few American settlements on Lake Erie and the only one with a good harbor, Erie was a natural staging ground. Virtually overnight, it transformed into a naval shipbuilding center. In August 1813, a fleet of warships left Presque Isle Bay and headed west to meet the enemy. The engagement on September 10 opened with several hours of intense cannon fire and ended with a victory for the Americans. The Battle of Lake Erie marked the first time in history that an entire British naval squadron was defeated and captured.

Erie's reputation as a maritime center was sealed, and Presque Isle Bay quickly became a major stop on the Great Lakes. Completed in 1844, the Erie Extension Canal moved passengers and freight from the port city to the Pittsburgh region. Railroads came to Erie less than a decade later. Its impressive transportation systems made it appealing to industry and by the end of the 19th century the city was renowned for its metalworking factories. Its contribution to the World War I effort included more than 1,400 cannons. In the early 1900s Erie was also regarded as the freshwater fishing capital of the world. At one point in the 1920s, a record 144 commercial fish tugs operated out of the city. The bayfront was crowded with fish-processing houses, icehouses, shipbuilders and chandlers, and restaurants, hotels, and boardinghouses serving the men who worked the fishing fleet. Erie's commercial fishing industry eventually fell victim to overfishing and pollution. By the turn of the 21st century, only one commercial fisherman was still in business. The not-so-crowded bayfront is now home to a museum devoted to Erie's maritime heritage, including its great fishing past. Local waters continue to attract sports and recreational anglers.

Erie remains an industrial city. GE Transportation has its locomotive plant here and tops the list of largest employers. The heyday of lake trade is long past, but Erie's harbor is still in the business of import and export. It's now able to handle the large vessels that carry cargos between the Atlantic Ocean and the Great Lakes via the St. Lawrence Seaway, a system of locks and canals completed in 1959.

★ PRESQUE ISLE STATE PARK

If **Presque Isle** (301 Peninsula Dr., Erie, 814/833-7424, www.dcnr.pa.gov/stateparks) weren't property of the state, the sandy peninsula would almost certainly be crowded with million-dollar vacation homes. It's that stunning. Just seven miles long, the land surrounded by Lake Erie boasts sandy beaches, a 19th-century lighthouse, and a remarkable diversity of plant and animal life. This National Natural Landmark feels more like Southern California than Pennsylvania. (More precisely, in summer it bears some resemblance to SoCal—in-line skaters, kite flyers, and all.

In winter, there's nothing California-ish about it. California doesn't have ice dunes.)

The claw-shaped peninsula juts out from the mainland four miles west of downtown Erie and widens as it stretches northeastward. It forms and protects Presque Isle Bay, the deep harbor that put Erie on the maritime map. The peninsula refuses to stay put. It's been creeping eastward ever since it formed thousands of years ago. Wind and water are forever pushing sand from the peninsula's neck toward its eastern end, known as Gull Point. That's a problem the U.S. Army Corps of Engineers has been battling since the early 1800s. Today the agency's anti-erosion arsenal includes dozens of breakwaters, which are aligned parallel to the beaches and partially block the waves. The Corps also steps in when storms cause breaches in the neck of Presque Isle—French for "almost an island"—and turn it into a bona fide island. It's happened at least four times since 1819.

Presque Isle is reached via Peninsula Drive (Route 832) or by boat. If you're driving, stop at the **Tom Ridge Environmental Center** (301 Peninsula Dr., Erie, 814/833-7424, www.trecpi.org, 10am-6pm daily, free), or TREC for short, to learn about Presque Isle's history and ecosystems and grab a map of the 3,200-acre park. Named for a former Pennsylvania governor who served as the nation's first secretary of homeland security, the airy and eco-friendly facility houses interactive exhibits, a small orientation theater showing a free 15-minute movie, and the **Big Green Screen Theater** (814/838-4123, 45-minute films shown on the hour 11am-5pm daily, adults $7.50, seniors $6, children 3-12 $5.50) with its four-story, 45-foot-wide screen. It also has a café and a shop full of souvenirs, including model sailboats, miniature lighthouses, wind chimes, and beach glass jewelry. Be sure to climb (or take the elevator) to the top of TREC's 75-foot observation tower for views of Lake Erie. You can spot Canada on a clear day.

Presque Isle is strictly a day-use park, so if you're planning to spend the night, you'll have to do it on the mainland. Book accommodations well in advance if visiting in the summer.

Beaches

Plenty of Pennsylvania's interior lakes advertise sandy beaches (that Mother Nature had *nothing* to do with), but none can deliver surf swimming or a water horizon. Lake Erie is so large that Presque Isle beachgoers see nothing but water and sky when they gaze northward. It's almost like being at the ocean. In at least one way, it's better than being at the ocean: There's no risk of being stung by jellyfish. Presque Isle's beaches are open 10am-7:30pm daily. Swimming is allowed only when lifeguards are on duty: noon-7:30pm from Memorial Day weekend to Labor Day, unless otherwise posted.

If you're toting a cooler, take your pick of beaches. If not, you may want to choose Beach 6, Beach 8 (Pettinato Beach), Beach 10 (Budny Beach), or Beach 11, which all have a food and beverage concession. Beach 6 has the added benefit of sand volleyball courts, which attract a lot of teens. Families with small children may prefer Beach 11, a sheltered beach with shallow water, a bathhouse with changing areas, and a playground. Beach 7, also known as Waterworks Beach, is the only other beach with playground equipment. It's notable in that its restrooms and picnic tables and even the water's edge are ADA accessible. If you're looking for a deserted beach, the Mill Road Beaches, a group of adjacent beaches with shaded picnic areas and restrooms, are your best bet for quiet.

Trails

There's no better way to take in Presque Isle than by biking the **Karl Boyes Multipurpose National Recreation Trail,** which makes a 13.5-mile circuit of the park. Named for a late state legislator, the paved trail is popular with in-line skaters and joggers as well as cyclists. No wheels? **Yellow Bike Rental** (814/835-8900, 10am-8pm daily Memorial Day-Labor Day, 10am-6pm Sat.-Sun. May and Sept., weather permitting) offers bicycles, tricycles, in-line skates, and even four-wheeled surreys. It's about 2.5 miles from the park entrance in what's known as the Waterworks Pumphouse area. In winter, part of the Karl Boyes trail is left snow-covered for cross-country skiers.

Maritime history buffs can retrace the steps of lighthouse keepers on the 1.25-mile **Sidewalk Trail.** At its north end is the **Presque Isle Lighthouse.** The brick tower was built in 1873 and raised to 68 feet in the 1890s. Before electric bulbs came into use, keepers climbed to the top every four hours to refill an oil lamp. Today the light is automated, and the attached dwelling, home to nine keepers until 1944, is a residence for park staff. At the south end of the trail is Misery Bay, so named because of the hardships endured by sailors based there during the War of 1812. Lighthouse keepers followed the Sidewalk Trail to their boathouse in the bay when they needed supplies from the mainland. Once a wooden boardwalk, the trail was resurfaced with concrete in 1925.

Hikers can take their pick of about a dozen unpaved trails. Popular with bird lovers, the 1.5-mile **Gull Point Trail** begins at the east end of Beach 10 (Budny Beach) and makes a loop through Gull Point, a resting spot for migrating shorebirds. It's one of the longer trails and requires walking through sand traps. The easier **North Pier Trail** (0.7 mile) follows the shoreline from Beach 11 to North Pier, a popular fishing spot and home to the **North Pier Light,** which has been guiding ships into Erie's harbor since 1858.

Boat Tours

It would be a shame to leave Pennsylvania's Great Lakes port without logging some boat time. Various watercraft can be rented on Presque Isle and in Erie's Bayfront District, but you also have the option to leave the navigating to pros. **Presque Isle Boat Tours** (814/836-0201, www.piboattours.com, adults $16, children 5-12 $9) offers 90-minute voyages aboard the *Lady Kate* on weekends from mid-May through mid-June, daily from mid-June through Labor Day, and on weekends through the remainder of September. The 110-passenger vessel docks near Presque Isle's Perry Monument, a tribute to the sailors who fought under Commodore Oliver Hazard Perry during the War of 1812. Knowledgeable guides describe points of interest, including historic lighthouses and the nature preserve at the eastern end of the isle. Reservations are recommended.

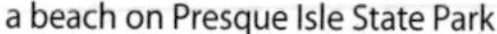

a beach on Presque Isle State Park

Presque Isle's interior lagoons, home to herons, beavers, turtles, and a host of other critters, also beg to be explored by boat. Free pontoon tours are offered Thursday-Sunday from Memorial Day weekend through June and daily from July until early September. Call or check the website of the Tom Ridge Environmental Center (814/833-7424, www.trecpi.org) for a departure schedule. Be sure to preregister for sunset rides, which fill quickly.

Water Sports

Just about anything you can do at the ocean, you can do here, including waterskiing, surfing, windsurfing, paddleboarding, kayaking, fishing, and scuba diving. For boaters, Presque Isle offers four launching areas and a marina with almost 500 slips. All of the boat launches are on the bay side of the peninsula. Vista Launch, closest to the park entrance, is only recommended for small boats and Jet Skis. Niagara and Lagoon Launches can accommodate small- and medium-size watercraft. The four-lane West Pier Launch, located near the marina, is recommended for larger vessels. Open May through October, the marina (814/833-0176) can accommodate boats as long as 42 feet. Slips are highly coveted, so call ahead to determine availability. During the off-season, call the main park office rather than the marina. Beaching of boats along the shoreline is permitted except at the easternmost portion of Gull Point from April through November and within 100 feet of designated swimming areas.

Presque Isle Canoe & Boat Livery (814/838-3938, www.presqueisleboatrental.com, 8am-8pm daily Memorial Day-Labor Day, 10am-5pm Sat.-Sun. Apr. and Oct.), located on Graveyard Pond across from Misery Bay, rents watercraft by the hour. Its inventory includes canoes, kayaks, rowboats, paddleboats, small motorboats, and pontoon boats, plus fish finders and rods and reels.

Famous for its walleye fishing, Lake Erie also yields perch, bass, trout, and steelhead. Presque Isle Bay teems with panfish, muskellunge, northern pike, crappie, and smelt. The peninsula's piers, boat landings, and interior lagoons are popular shore-fishing areas.

Snorkeling is prohibited, but certified scuba divers can swim with the crappies. Divers must register at the ranger station on the bay side of the peninsula, about two miles from the park entrance.

Winter Activities

Presque Isle can be quite a magical place in the dead of winter. Lake ice, wave surge, and freezing spray conspire to create otherworldly ice dunes. Look for them on the lake side of the peninsula. Wintertime activities include ice-skating, ice fishing, iceboating, cross-country skiing, and snowshoeing. A concession in the Waterworks area offers rental skis and snowshoes on weekends from mid-November through March, provided there's snow.

Bird-Watching

Presque Isle is an ecological wonderland. Its birds get the most press. More than 320 species have been spotted on the peninsula, named one of the country's top birding spots by *Birder's World* magazine. Part of the reason for the incredible diversity of birdlife is Presque Isle's location along the Atlantic Flyway, a major bird-migration route. The peninsula is to migrating birds what a turnpike service plaza is to motorists: a place to eat and rest. Shorebirds that migrate from beyond the Arctic Circle to South America and back again "pull over" at Presque Isle in April and September. Waterfowl migration can be observed in March and from late November through December. Come in mid-May or September to commune with warblers.

Shorebirds can be viewed from an observation platform at the edge of the Gull Point Natural Area. The protected area at the east end of the isle is closed to the public from April through November, but the platform can be reached by hiking the Gull Point Trail. For an eyeful of wetland birds, kayak or canoe the interior lagoons. In the hot summer months, morning and early evening are the best times for birding.

The **Presque Isle Audubon Society** (814/860-4091, www.presqueisleaudubon.org), a chapter of the National Audubon Society, offers field trips and workshops throughout the year.

BAYFRONT DISTRICT

Once crowded with shipyards and crisscrossed by railroad tracks, Erie's Bayfront District is slowly transforming into a recreational destination. It's home to the fantastic Erie Maritime Museum, which opened in 1998. Local and intercity buses deliver passengers to a sprawling transportation center, built a few years later, just east of the museum. West of the museum is the $44 million Bayfront Convention Center, which opened in 2007 after seven years in the making. It's connected by a glass-walled pedestrian bridge to the Sheraton Erie Bayfront Hotel, which opened in 2008. Recreational marinas, boat launches, and an amphitheater also dot the evolving waterfront.

Flagship *Niagara*

Bicentennial Tower

First stop for many visitors is the **Bicentennial Tower** (814/455-7557, www.porterie.org/bicentennial, call for hours, adults $4, children 7-12 $2, free first Sun. of each month), which sits on the Dobbins Landing wharf at the foot of State Street, Erie's main drag. Built for the 1995 celebration of the city's 200th birthday, the tower measures 187 feet to the top of its flagpole. Its two observation decks, both reachable by stairs or elevator, afford views of Presque Isle, the natural harbor it forms, and downtown.

★ Erie Maritime Museum and Flagship *Niagara*

America's attempts to seize Canada from the British during the oft-forgotten War of 1812 did not go well. The initial three-pronged offensive was a full-out failure, with Detroit falling to the British in August of 1812. An elaborate attempt to attack Montreal the following year was also unsuccessful. But 1813 wasn't without a bright spot for the United States. On September 10, nine U.S. ships under Commodore Oliver Hazard Perry defeated a British squadron of six vessels on Lake Erie. The victory forced the British to retreat from Detroit and lifted the nation's morale, at least temporarily. (A year later the British would march into Washington DC and torch public buildings, doing serious damage to morale.) The **Erie Maritime Museum** (150 E. Front St., Erie, 814/452-2744, www.flagshipniagara.org, 9am-5pm Mon.-Sat. and noon-5pm Sun. Apr.-Sept., 9am-5pm Mon.-Sat. Oct., 9am-5pm Thurs.-Sat. Nov.-Mar., adults $10, seniors $8, children 3-11 $5) brings to life the dramatic events of the Battle of Lake Erie. One exhibit features a replica of the battered hull of the *Lawrence,* Perry's original flagship. After the 20-gun brig was disabled and most of its crew wounded or killed, Perry transferred to her undamaged sister ship, the *Niagara,* hoisted his battle flag, and sailed to victory.

The Battle of Lake Erie didn't unfold near

Victorian Princess

Erie's shores. It was fought near Put-in-Bay, Ohio. But Erie is rightfully proud of its role in the American victory. Six of the nine U.S. ships that sailed into battle, including the *Niagara,* were built in Erie. If that sounds unremarkable, consider that Erie had roughly 500 residents at the outbreak of the war. It had oak trees but not a single sawmill. Turning the remote town into a warship-building center required the recruitment of shipwrights, blacksmiths, and laborers from other parts. Pittsburgh sent rigging and anchors. Philadelphia contributed canvas for the sails. Cannons arrived from the nation's capital. The fleet was completed in a matter of months.

The museum on Erie's waterfront is home port to the **Flagship *Niagara,*** a reconstruction of Perry's relief flagship. When the square-rigged wooden vessel is in port, museum visitors are treated to guided tours. She sails during the warmer months, visiting other Great Lakes ports. If you're 14 or older, in good health, and crave a taste of the seafarer's life, you can apply to be a live-aboard trainee for a minimum of two weeks. An appetite for spartan conditions is required. Though the present *Niagara,* completed in 1990, has auxiliary propulsion engines and modern navigation equipment, she emulates the original in just about every other way. That means no showers, no hot water, and no privacy. Sailing excursions for those 12 and up of just a few hours are offered when the ship isn't en route to another port. A day sail from the Erie Maritime Museum is $65. Visit the museum website for a training program application or schedule of day sails.

The museum, housed in a former electricity generating plant, isn't solely devoted to the Battle of Lake Erie. Visitors can learn about Erie's lighthouses, its once-booming fishing industry, and its rich shipbuilding heritage

★ Boat Tours

Like Presque Isle, the Bayfront District is a good place to catch a scenic ride on a boat. The ***Victorian Princess*** (1 State St., 814/459-9696, www.victorianprincess.com, sightseeing cruise $20, happy hour cruise $15, meal cruises $30-48), a pretty paddle wheeler that docks beside the Bicentennial Tower, plies the bay from May through October. It offers lunch cruises on Wednesday, Thursday, Friday, and Saturday; a happy hour cruise on Wednesday and Friday; dinner cruises every day but Wednesday; and a brunch cruise on Sunday. A Saturday night moonlight cruise is also available. Reservations are required.

If you're traveling with kids, skip the pretty paddle wheeler for a swashbuckling pirate adventure. The crew of ***Scallywags*** (2 State St., 814/453-2627, www.scallywagspirateadventures.com, cruises several times daily mid-June-Aug., Sat.-Sun. May and Sept., adults $20, children under 2 $10), which you'll be joining as a fellow pirate, sets off from State Street just before Dobbins Landing on the hunt for the thieving Captain Skull. The cruise is very much geared toward kids. Grown-ups can instead opt for one of two 21-plus cruises: The happy hour cruise ($12) is offered Wednesdays and Fridays mid-June through August, while the sunset excursion ($16) is on Thursdays and Saturdays.

Water Sports

The Bayfront District is a popular starting point for boating and fishing expeditions. Boat owners should peruse the website of the Erie-Western Pennsylvania Port Authority (814/455-7557, www.porterie.org) for information on marinas and boat launches on Presque Isle Bay and adjacent waters. The port authority operates the popular **Lampe Marina,** located just outside the entrance to Presque Isle Bay. Lampe has 252 slips that accommodate boats as long as 30 feet, public launch ramps, and 24-hour security. **Perry's Landing Marina** (W. Bayfront Parkway, 814/455-1313), just west of Liberty Park, is also commendable. It has a clubhouse with a heated swimming pool and two-tiered sundeck.

To rent a boat, head to **Port Erie Sports** (Chestnut Street Boathouse, 402 W. Bayfront Parkway, Erie, 814/452-2628, www.porteriesports.com, 8am-sundown weather permitting). The selection includes kayaks, canoes, small motorboats, and Jet Skis. Water skis, tubes, and fishing equipment and bait are also available.

Operating out of Wolverine Park Marina, a transient facility at the corner of State Street and the Bayfront Parkway, **Lake Effect Sailing** (34 State St., 814/434-0600, www.lakeeffectsailing.com, $50 per hour for group of up to 6, 2-hour minimum) offers private charters on a 32-foot cutter named *Namaste* helmed by Captain Ed Garr.

Anglers unfamiliar with Erie's waters can up their big-catch odds by heading out in a party fishing boat. The ***Edward John*** (814/881-7611, www.edwardjohnperchfishing.com), a 52-foot perch-pursuing party boat, departs at 7am and 4pm daily from its slip near the Bicentennial Tower. Each trip is several hours long and costs $35 for adults, $30 for seniors, and $25 for children under 16. It's also possible to reserve the whole boat, which can accommodate as many as 40 passengers.

Other Activities

You don't have to leave dry land to have a good time. The bayfront boasts an 18-hole mini golf course, **Harbor View Miniature Golf** (36 State St., Erie, 814/874-3536, www.harborviewminigolf.com, 4pm-9pm Mon.-Fri., noon-10pm Sat., noon-8pm Sun. May and Sept., 10am-11pm daily Memorial Day weekend-Labor Day, adults $7, seniors and children 3-12 $6). Pack a picnic basket and head to **Liberty Park** in time to watch the sun set. The waterfront park is about a quarter mile west of the Bicentennial Tower and adjacent to Bay Harbor Marina. It has a large children's play area and an outdoor amphitheater that's host to a free summer concert series, **8 Great Tuesdays** (814/455-7557, www.porterie.org).

★ WINE COUNTRY

The massive ice sheet that covered part of the northern United States tens of thousands of years ago left mementos behind, among them the Great Lakes. On the southern shores of Lake Erie, it also left ridges of soil and gravel that proved ideal for grape growing. The Lake Erie grape belt is North America's largest grape-growing region outside of California and the largest Concord grape-growing region in the world.

Concord grapes aren't the only variety cultivated in this prolific region. Recent decades have seen a profusion of small wineries and a good deal of land has been replanted with premium wine grapes. The town of North East, located 15 miles northeast of downtown Erie on the New York border, is home to several wineries. North East embraces its viticulture heritage: Its high school athletes are known as the Grapepickers (their fans are filled with "Picker Pride") and its charming lodgings include the Grape Arbor B&B and Vineyard B&B. The social highlight of the year is the three-day **Wine Country Harvest Festival** (2 locations, 814/725-4262, www.nechamber.org, last full weekend of Sept., wine-tasting day pass $20 in advance, $25 at gate). WineFest traditions include live music, an arts and crafts show, and, of course, grape stomping.

If you catch the winemaking bug, head to **Presque Isle Wine Cellars** (9440 W. Main Rd./Rte. 20, North East, 814/725-1314, www.piwine.com, 9am-5pm Mon.-Fri., 9am-noon Sat., closed Sat. Jan.-Mar.), which sells all manner of equipment and raw materials. And if North East's wineries leave you wanting more, drive east along Lake Erie's shore into New York. You'll find more than a dozen wineries between the border and Silver Creek, New York. Visit the website of **Lake Erie Wine Country** (877/326-6561, www.lakeeriewinecountry.org) for a map and more information.

Mazza Vineyards

Established in 1972 by Italian-born brothers, **Mazza Vineyards** (11815 E. Lake Rd./Rte. 5, North East, 814/725-8695, www.mazzawines.com, 9am-8pm Mon.-Sat. and 11am-4:30pm Sun. July-Aug., 9am-5:30pm Mon.-Sat. and noon-4:30pm Sun. Sept.-June, tasting fee $2-4) has a distinctly Mediterranean look. But don't expect to sample chianti and montepulciano d'abruzzo inside. The Mazza brothers thought the land better suited for Germanic varieties and became known for riesling in the early years. Mazza Vineyards still offers riesling, but today it's better known for sweet, fruity wines made from niagara, concord, and catawba grapes—varieties born in the United States. It's also known as a pioneer of Pennsylvania ice wines. Producing an ice wine can be tricky business. At Mazza, vidal blanc grapes are left on the vine for two or three months after they ripen, getting ever sweeter but losing their looks. When the temperature dips below 15 degrees and the shriveled grapes freeze, they're picked by hand (sometimes in two or three feet of snow) and pressed immediately. The result is a honey-like dessert wine that sells for upwards of $40 a bottle. Mazza also produces fruit wines, made from cherries, raspberries, or apples. Most bottles are under $18, including oak-aged dry reds such as cabernet sauvignon and chambourcin.

South Shore Wine Company

In 2007, the family behind Mazza Vineyards restored and reopened Erie County's first commercial winery, which had fallen victim to Prohibition in the 1920s. The **South Shore Wine Company** (1120 Freeport Rd./Rte. 89, North East, 814/725-1585, www.ss.mazzawines.com, 10am-5:30pm Mon.-Sat. and noon-4:30pm Sun. May-Oct. with

Mazza Vineyards

extended hours Mon.-Sat. in July and Aug., noon-5:30pm Mon.-Fri., 10am-5:30pm Sat., and noon-4:30pm Sun. Nov.-Apr., tasting fee $2-4) features a stone wine cavern built in the 1860s, one of very few of its kind in the United States. Don't pass up a tasting if you've already visited Mazza Vineyards; their wine selections are different. In the warmer months, buy a bottle and enjoy it with a cheese plate, sandwich, or salad in the patio café.

Penn Shore Winery

Penn Shore Winery (10225 E. Lake Rd./Rte. 5, North East, 814/725-8688, www.pennshore.com, 9am-5:30pm Mon.-Thurs., 9am-8pm Fri.-Sat., and 11am-4:30pm Sun. July-Aug., 9am-5:30pm Mon.-Sat. and 11am-4:30pm Sun. Sept.-June, tasting fee $2) snagged one of the first two "limited winery" licenses issued after passage of the Pennsylvania Limited Winery Act of 1968, which allowed grape farms to break into the wine biz, and opened its doors in 1970. It claims the distinction of offering the first Pennsylvania sparkling wine. Tours of the facility are self-guided. Head to the open-air patio to drink in the view of row upon row of grapevines.

Arrowhead Wine Cellars

Nick and Kathy Mobilia opened **Arrowhead Wine Cellars** (12073 E. Main Rd./Rte. 20, North East, 814/725-5509, www.arrowhead-wine.com, 10am-5:30pm Mon.-Sat. and noon-4pm in summer and fall, winter and spring hours vary, tasting fee $2) on their 250-acre fruit farm in 1998, making them relative newcomers to the winemaking scene. But their wines are perennial medalists at the Pennsylvania Farm Show and other competitions. Their peaches, sweet and sour cherries, frozen sour cherries, and freshly pressed grape juice for home winemaking are also held in high esteem and sold seasonally at the farm stand adjacent to the winery.

Courtyard Wineries

Even newer than Arrowhead, **Courtyard Wineries** (10021 W. Main Rd., North East, 814/725-0236, www.courtyardwineries.com, 10am-6pm Mon.-Sat., noon-5pm Sun., tasting fee $3) opened in 2010. The winery has two tasting bars, one for its LaCourette line of dry and semidry wines and another for its Barjo Bons line of sweet and semisweet blends. For a special occasion, reserve a VIP tasting in the barrel room. Led by the winemaker himself, the tasting features a flight of wines paired with chocolates, artisan cheeses, or other foods.

Lakeview Wine Cellars

A retirement dream turned reality for Sam and Becky Best, **Lakeview Wine Cellars** (8440 Singer Rd., North East, 814/725-4440, www.lakeviewwinecellars.com, 11am-5pm Mon., Thurs., and Fri, 10am-5pm Sat., noon-5pm Sun., tasting fee $1) specializes in oak-aged wines. The hilltop winery also serves up spectacular views.

ENTERTAINMENT AND EVENTS

Concert Venues

Elton John, Rod Stewart, and Cher have rocked the **Erie Insurance Arena** (809 French St., Erie, 814/453-7117, www.erieinsurancearena.com), which is home to the city's professional basketball and ice hockey teams.

Boats drop anchor within listening distance when bands perform at the **Highmark Amphitheater at Liberty Park** (W. Bayfront Parkway, 814/455-7557, www.porterie.org). Bring a blanket or chair to listen from dry land; the waterfront venue doesn't have seating. On Tuesdays in July and August, the amphitheater hosts a free concert series, **8 Great Tuesdays** (814/455-7557, www.porterie.org).

Performing Arts

Erie's lavish **Warner Theater** (811 State St., Erie, 814/453-7117, www.eriewarnertheatre.com) was built during the Great Depression. Within months of opening its doors in 1931, the movie palace initiated a vaudeville season, and Bob Hope made an appearance soon thereafter. Today the theater hosts the **Erie Broadway series** (814/452-4857, www.eriebroadwayseries.com) and concerts by touring musicians. It's also home to the **Erie Philharmonic** (814/455-1375, www.eriephil.org), which predates the Warner, and the younger **Lake Erie Ballet** (814/871-4356, www.lakeerieballet.org).

Founded in 1916, the **Erie Playhouse** (13 W. 10th St., Erie, 814/454-2852, www.erieplayhouse.org) is one of the oldest community theaters in the country. Homeless at times in its history, the theater is now ensconced in a 1940s movie house that seats about 420.

The Station Dinner Theatre (4940 Peach St., Erie, 814/864-2022, www.canterburyfeast.com) is best known for *A Canterbury Feast,* a long-running musical comedy set in medieval times. Performers do double duty, serving the victuals while staying in character. The dinner theater also cooks up farces and musical tributes.

Festivals and Events

Thousands of motorcyclists roll into Erie for **Roar on the Shore** (814/833-3200, www.roarontheshore.com, mid-July, free), which kicks off with a celebrity-led bike parade. Past grand marshals have included rocker Bret Michaels, professional daredevil Robbie Knievel, actor Danny Trejo, and 1990s hip-hop sensation Vanilla Ice. Bikers ride en masse through Presque Isle State Park and other parts of Erie County during the five-day bike rally, which raises money for a chosen charity.

Another major event in July is **Discover Presque Isle** (Presque Isle State Park, 814/838-5138, www.discoverpi.com, last weekend of July, free), a celebration of the superb state park and a fund-raiser for the nonprofit organization devoted to making it even better. It has all the fixings of an arts festival, plus sporty activities. Festivalgoers can try their hand at rock climbing, archery, and kayaking; compete in beach volleyball and sand sculpting; and explore the peninsula alongside professional naturalists.

Downtown Erie gets its turn in the spotlight during **Celebrate Erie** (814/870-1234, www.celebrateerie.com, Aug., free). The four-day extravaganza highlights the city's culinary and cultural offerings. Fireworks over the bayfront serve as the grand finale.

Stars of such films as the original *Texas Chain Saw Massacre* and *Dawn of the Dead* turn out for the cleverly named **Eerie Horror Fest** (Warner Theatre, Erie, 814/452-4857, www.eeriehorrorfilmfestival.com, Oct.). Started in 2004, the four-day event is part indie film festival and part fan convention. Horror, science fiction, and suspense films culled from hundreds of submissions are shown on the big screen.

FOOD

Presque Isle

Presque Isle's dining scene consists of concession stands. Beach 6, Beach 8 (Pettinato Beach), Beach 10 (Budny Beach), and Beach 11 all have a food stand. If you're looking for something with a little more character, one of the region's most adored eateries is just outside Presque Isle's entrance. With its red-and-white striped awning, picnic tables, and six-foot hot dog statue, you can't miss **Sara's** (25 Peninsula Dr., Erie, 814/833-1957, www.sarasandsallys.com, 10:30am-9pm daily Apr.-Memorial Day and Labor Day-Sept., 10:30am-10pm daily Memorial Day-Labor Day, $4-8). Its menu, like its decor, pays tribute to 1950s malt shops. Even its prices are on the retro side. The hot dogs are Smith's brand, produced locally by a fourth-generation family business. Save room for soft-serve ice cream: Sara's is famous for its Creamsicle-like "orange vanilla twist."

Bayfront District

There's a small cluster of restaurants at the foot of State Street near the Bicentennial Tower in Erie's Bayfront District, and they have just the recipe for a summer day: outdoor tables, cold drinks, and water views. The most casual of the bunch is ★ **Rum Runners** (133 E. Dobbins Landing, Erie,

Battling Chocolatiers

Pass on dessert when dining out in Erie. Pay the bill, get in the car, and drive straight to **Romolo Chocolates** (1525 W. 8th St., Erie, 814/452-1933, www.romolochocolates.com, 8am-8pm Mon.-Fri., 9am-8pm Sat., 10am-5pm Sun., open until 10pm daily June-Aug.), showplace of master chocolatier Tony Stefanelli. At one end of the building, modeled on an Italian villa, is an airy café. Sink into a couch with a cup of the signature cocoa, made with dark chocolate, cream, and milk. If it's warm outside, order the iced version and have a seat on the patio. The strawberry cocoa—imagine chocolate-covered strawberries in liquid form—is especially delightful. Romolo's Cocoa Café also serves coffee, ice cream, and baked goods made on-site. At the other end of the building is a theater-style chocolate shop, where you can observe the last stages of the candymaking process as you browse shelves lined with truffles, caramels, nougats, and other confections. Between them is a gift shop.

The sweets emporium is named for Stefanelli's Italian-born grandfather, who immigrated to New York City around the turn of the 20th century and learned the candymaking trade. The Great Depression brought sugar rationing and drove many candymakers out of the city. Romolo Stefanelli settled in his wife's hometown of Erie, where he began making candy in the basement of his father-in-law's house. By the mid-1950s the operation had outgrown the basement and the backyard. He opened a store on West 8th Street and shortly after passed the reins to his two sons. The business thrived. Today there are four **Stefanelli's Candies** (www.stefanelliscandies.com) stores in Erie, including the original (2054 W. 8th St., Erie, 814/459-2451, 9am-6pm Mon.-Sat.), and one in Linesville, but there hasn't been a Stefanelli at the helm since the early 1990s. Tony Stefanelli, who studied the art of candymaking under his grandfather, father, and uncle, opened Romolo Chocolates in 1994, shortly after Stefanelli's was sold out of the family.

Erie has a third homegrown chocolatier. Established in 1903, **Pulakos Chocolates** (www.pulakoschocolates.com) has two locations. Its flagship store (2530 Parade St., Erie, 814/452-4026, 10am-4pm Mon.-Fri, 10am-3pm Sat., check the website or call for winter hours) and manufacturing facility are at 26th and Parade Streets in downtown Erie.

Ask a group of locals if they prefer Romolo, Stefanelli's, or Pulakos, and you'll likely get a heated debate. Pulakos has long been known for its chocolate-covered strawberries (far-flung fans pay upwards of $80 to have them overnighted) and Stefanelli's for its "sponge candy," a melt-in-your-mouth confection with an airy, crispy center and a coat of chocolate. But Romolo does a brisk business in both, and the youngest brand on the block may well be the most traditional. "We do things like my grandfather wanted us to," says Tony Stefanelli, whose grandfather introduced sponge candy to Erie. "We use older-style machines. We don't use any kind of enzyme or thinner when we're working with our chocolate. We don't use preservatives." That doesn't mean there's no room for new ideas. "When my father was alive, he would let my kids coat anything they wanted to coat with chocolate," he says. "My daughter was a grape freak, so we coated some red seedless grapes. When I opened Romolo, she was in her early 20s, but that was the first thing she asked for." He made a batch and put some on a tray for customers. The rest, as they say, is history: Today the shop sells upwards of 10 pounds of chocolate-covered grapes a day.

814/455-4292, www.rumrunnerserie.com, 11am-midnight Sun.-Thurs., 11am-2am Fri.-Sat., kitchen closes at 10pm or 11pm, open Apr.-Oct., under $10), named for the bootleggers who braved the unpredictable waters of Lake Erie to bring Canadian booze into Prohibition-era America. Boats can dock right beside its large waterfront patio, which hosts DJs or live bands nightly throughout the summer (weather permitting). Rum Runners isn't much to look at and its fare is nothing fancy, but the bay view and the potent signature drink—a frozen blend of rum, liqueurs, and fruit punch—make the seasonal eatery a favorite among locals and tourists. Its all-seasons sister restaurant, **Rum Runners Cove** (2 State St., Erie, 814/454-7160, www.rumrunnerscove.com, 11am-10pm Mon.-Thurs.,

11am-11pm Fri.-Sat., 11am-9pm Sun., hours vary in off-season, $10-23), has a seafood-heavy menu and a thatch-roofed outdoor bar. Food options are limited to starters, soups, salads, and sandwiches until 4pm, when they expand to include entrées such as Cajun shrimp skewers and Tuscan-style swordfish. The pirate-themed **Smuggler's Wharf** (3 State St., Erie, 814/459-4273, www.smugglerswharfinc.com, 11:30am-10pm Mon.-Thurs., 11:30am-11pm Fri.-Sat., 11:30am-9pm Sun. mid-May-mid-Oct., 11:30am-9pm Wed.-Thurs., 11:30am-10pm Fri-Sat., 11:30am-7pm Sun. mid-Oct-mid-May, $9-24), located between the two Rum Runners, is more similar to the Cove. It has seating indoors and out and plenty of seafood options for dinner. Seafood is on offer during lunch as well, along with deli sandwiches.

The **Bayfront Grille** (55 W. Bay Dr., Erie, 814/454-2005, www.sheraton.com/erie, 6:30am-10pm Sun.-Thurs., 6:30am-11pm Fri.-Sat., $11-36) is the most upscale option in the area but hardly hoity-toity. Part of the Sheraton Erie Bayfront Hotel, it offers something none of the others do: breakfast.

Downtown Erie

State Street, Erie's main drag, has a good number of restaurants and bars. But judging an establishment by the size of the crowd inside could lead you astray. That's because the city has a couple of colleges, and students generally gravitate toward cheap grub and suds. Colm McWilliams came to Erie from Ireland to attend one of those colleges and stayed to open **Molly Brannigans** (506 State St., Erie, 814/453-7800, www.mollybrannigans.com, 11am-11pm Mon.-Wed., 11am-midnight Thurs., 11am-1am Fri., noon-1am Sat., noon-9pm Sun., $8-18), one of the State Street standouts. The Irish pub is furnished from floor to ceiling with items imported from the Emerald Isle, including a bar salvaged from a hotel. A large fireplace lends a cozy feel to the high-ceilinged space. The menu includes burgers, wraps, and other standard American fare, but the big movers here are shepherd's pie and the fish-and-chips platter. Wash it all down with a Guinness combo—a pint consisting of the quintessentially Irish stout and another draft beer.

State Street offers more than pub grub. The upscale **1201 Kitchen** (1201 State St., Erie, 814/464-8989, www.1201restaurant.com, 5pm-9pm Mon.-Thurs., 5pm-10pm Fri.-Sat., $19-31) serves what it calls "contemporary Latin/Asian cuisine," including the best sushi in town. Named for its address, the chic chef-owned restaurant changes its menu every month or so. Kobe beef and scallops almost always make the cut. Reservations are encouraged but not required.

Not every recommendable restaurant in downtown Erie has a State Street address. Less than a mile off the main drag in a residential part of town, **Mi Scuzi** (2641 Myrtle St., 814/454-4533, www.miscuzirestaurant.com, 5pm-9pm Tues.-Thurs., 5pm-10pm Fri.-Sat., 1pm-5pm Sun., $20-38) is a cozy trattoria in what was once a house. The menu is made up of tried-and-true Italian dishes like pasta fagioli soup, linguine carbonara, and veal piccata. For dessert: cannoli, tiramisu, and spumoni. There's a patio for outdoor dining in warmer weather.

Head farther from State Street—to an area without much to beckon tourists—for a meal you're not likely to find anywhere else in this neck of the woods. **Pineapple Eddie Southern Bistro** (1402 W. 10th St., 814/454-0700, www.pineappleeddie.com, 11am-2pm and 4pm-9pm Wed.-Fri., 4pm-9pm Sat., $10-20) serves a fusion of Caribbean and American Southern fare from Haitian-born chef Jean Paul, who owns the eatery with his wife and sister-in-law. The menu ranges from Creole spiced shrimp and *griyo* (Haitian fried pork) to fried chicken with Belgian waffles. There's a kids' menu with the usual suspects like grilled cheese and mini-burgers, plus a smaller portion of the chicken and waffles. Don't skip dessert.

There's no shortage of historical atmosphere at **The Brewerie at Union Station** (123 W. 14th St., Erie, 814/454-2200, www.

brewerie.com, 11:30am-10pm Mon.-Thurs., 11:30am-midnight Fri.-Sat., $8-22), which is housed in Erie's 1927 train station. Its menu is heavy on comfort foods: beer-battered pickles, pulled-pork nachos, fried bologna and grilled cheese sandwiches, and a "Pittsburgher" burger topped with fries, Swiss cheese, and coleslaw. The Brewerie isn't too proud to offer bottled beer from other Pennsylvania microbreweries alongside drafts of its own creation. It hosts live music most Friday and Saturday nights.

ACCOMMODATIONS

Waterfront

Many people who come to Erie when it's best—in summer—want to be near the water. Surprisingly, waterfront accommodations are scarce in this waterfront city. There's no lodging on Presque Isle and just two hotels on Erie's bayfront. A seashore-style vacation requires advance planning.

You'll increase your odds of scoring waterfront digs if you're open to camping. At **Sara's Campground** (50 Peninsula Dr., Erie, 814/833-4560, www.sarascampground.com, $30-34, trailers and RVs $38), a stone's throw from the entrance to Presque Isle State Park, you can pitch a tent on a private beach. But Sara's doesn't accept reservations. Its 100-some campsites are doled out on a first-come, first-served basis, ostensibly because they're worth the gamble.

Lampe Marina Campground (foot of Port Access Rd., Erie, 814/454-5830, www.porterie.org, $32 Sun.-Thurs., $37 weekends and holidays), open May through October, accepts reservations up to six months in advance. Operated by the Erie-Western Pennsylvania Port Authority, the campground near the entrance to Erie's natural harbor has 42 campsites with water and electrical hookups, a dump station, and fantastic views. All sites have picnic tables; some also have fire rings. On one side of the campground is the popular Lampe Marina with its free public boat launch; on the other is a pier popular with anglers and anyone who likes to watch boats go by.

If camping isn't what you had in mind, there's the **Sheraton Erie Bayfront Hotel** (55 W. Bay Dr., Erie, 814/454-2005, www.sheraton.com/erie, $155-250), opened in 2008 near the Bicentennial Tower. It's connected to the Bayfront Convention Center by a water-spanning pedestrian bridge and has all the amenities you'd expect from a hotel that caters to conference-goers, including complimentary Wi-Fi and a business center open round-the-clock. All 200 guest rooms are nonsmoking. Many feature bay or marina views to match the nautical color scheme. Bring a swimsuit for the indoor pool and sunscreen for the adjacent deck. There's one restaurant on-site, the classy but casual Bayfront Grille, and several more close by. The Sheraton's competition is the newer **Courtyard by Marriott Erie Bayfront** (2 Sassafras Pier, 814/636-1005, www.marriott.com, $189-329), opened in 2016. The 192-room hotel also offers free Wi-Fi, direct access to the convention center, and an indoor pool. The Courtyard's edge? An outdoor infinity pool overlooking the lake. On-site eateries include the quick-serve Bistro and the sit-down Shoreline Bar & Grille, which features water views and an outdoor patio.

About 15 minutes east of downtown Erie is an altogether different waterfront option: the family-owned ★ **LakeView on the Lake** (8696 E. Lake Rd./Rte. 5, Erie, 814/899-6948, www.lakeviewerie.com, $149-269). This is the sort of place to bring that stack of books you've been meaning to work your way through. Adirondack chairs dot the charming mini-resort, which sits atop a 120-foot bluff overlooking Lake Erie. Guests can reach the water via a wooden staircase. Many return year after year for the spectacular sunsets and laid-back vibe. LakeView has several types of accommodations, including a six-room motel, one- and two-bedroom cottages, and "Annie's Retreat," a one-bedroom home-away-from-home with a living room, dining room, full kitchen, two bathrooms, and private deck. Amenities include a swimming pool and lawn enough for bocce, badminton, and horseshoes.

Inland Erie

That's it for waterfront accommodations, but there are plenty of places to bed down within a few minutes of Presque Isle State Park and its sandy beaches. The **Glass House Inn** (3202 W. 26th St., Erie, 814/833-7751, www.glasshouseinn.com, $100-150) is a very pleasant motel owned by a very pleasant couple. Its 30 rooms are equipped with refrigerators, microwaves, coffeemakers, and wireless Internet. The small outdoor pool is open for hours after Presque Isle's beaches close for the day.

If romance is on the agenda, consider a bed-and-breakfast in Erie or wine country to its east. With its very reasonable rates, the Queen Anne-style **George Carroll House** (401 Peach St., Erie, 814/504-0845, www.georgecarrollhouse.com, $75-105) in downtown Erie is a great choice. A simple continental breakfast is included. Another good option: **The Spencer House** (519 W. 6th St., Erie, 814/464-0419, www.spencerhousebandb.com, $99-179), a Victorian manse on "Millionaire's Row." Once home to manufacturing, shipping, and banking magnates, the historic district is now home to a good deal of college students. Neither B&B allows children under 12.

Wine Country

Wine lovers should make a base camp in North East, a town known for vineyards and Victorian architecture. The **Grape Arbor Bed & Breakfast** (51 E. Main St., North East, 814/725-0048, www.grapearborbandb.com, $115-200) consists of two side-by-side mansions in the center of town. Built as private homes in the 1830s, they housed a stagecoach tavern, professional offices, and a primary school before their rebirth as a B&B. Grape Arbor's eight guest rooms and suites are traditionally furnished, outfitted with wireless Internet, and named for varieties of grapes grown in the region. The Cabernet Suite comes with a private entrance through a side porch, a built-in gas fireplace, and a two-person whirlpool tub. Also grape-themed, **Vineyard Bed & Breakfast** (10757 Sidehill Rd., North East, 888/725-8998, www.vineyardbb.com, $90-120) offers cheaper, country-style accommodations. Innkeepers Clyde and Judy Burnham have lived in the turn-of-the-20th-century farmhouse since 1953. Breakfast includes their homemade grape juice.

TRANSPORTATION AND SERVICES

Getting There

Erie is in Pennsylvania's northwest corner, about 130 miles north of Pittsburgh via I-79, 100 miles northeast of Cleveland via I-90, and 90 miles southwest of Buffalo, New York, via I-90. If you're coming from Pittsburgh or other points south, you'll arrive via I-79. I-90 is the major east-west thoroughfare, but if you value scenery over speed, follow the coastal Route 5 into town. The **Great Lakes Seaway Trail,** one of the first roads in America to be designated a National Scenic Byway, runs along Route 5 for most of its course in Pennsylvania.

Erie International Airport, Tom Ridge Field (ERI, 814/833-4258, www.erieairport.org) is served by three major airlines offering service from Chicago, Detroit, and Philadelphia. **Amtrak** (800/872-7245, www.amtrak.com) provides train service to the city via its Lake Shore Limited line. Erie's train station (125 W. 14th St.) includes an on-site brewpub. **Greyhound** (800/231-2222, www.greyhound.com) buses pull into the **Intermodal Transportation Center** (208 E. Bayfront Parkway, Erie) in the Bayfront District.

Getting Around

Local bus service is provided by the **Erie Metropolitan Transit Authority** (814/452-3515, www.ride-the-e.com). A good way to get the lay of the land is to hop on the free **BayLiner Trolley,** which runs between the bayfront and downtown's 14th Street every day but Sunday.

You'll find taxis at the airport and the Intermodal Transportation Center. Call **Erie Yellow Cab** (814/461-8294, www.erieyellowcab.com) if you need a lift from elsewhere in the area.

Visitor Information

If you're driving to Erie from New York via I-90 west, look for the Pennsylvania **welcome center** near the state line. It's stocked with brochures about attractions in the region and throughout the state. Personalized travel counseling is available 7am-7pm daily; the restrooms are always open.

If you're driving from Ohio via I-90 east, you can load up on brochures at a rest stop about a mile past the state line. If you're coming from Pittsburgh or other points south via I-79 north, there's a rest stop near Edinboro, Pennsylvania. Erie County's tourism board staffs an information desk inside both rest stops from Memorial Day to Labor Day. Once in Erie, head to the main office of **VisitErie** (208 E. Bayfront Pkwy., Ste. 103, 814/454-1000, www.visiterie.com, 8:30am-5pm Mon.-Fri.) or, better yet, the **Tom Ridge Environmental Center** (301 Peninsula Dr., Erie, 814/833-7424, www.trecpi.org, 10am-6pm daily) for answers to any questions about where to go and how to get there.

Pymatuning and Vicinity

Lake Erie isn't the only body of water luring boaters, anglers, and bird-watchers to Pennsylvania's northwest corner. Less than an hour south of the Great Lake's shoreline is a great lake named Pymatuning. Unlike Lake Erie, a thousands-year-old product of geologic forces, Pymatuning is relatively young and the product of a man-made dam. It's Pennsylvania's largest lake and the centerpiece of one of its largest state parks, Pymatuning State Park. (The lake spills into Ohio, which has a Pymatuning State Park of its own.) Man-made though it is, Pymatuning has long been a destination for ardent observers of the natural world. The state's first migratory waterfowl refuge was established there in 1935, shortly after the dam was constructed. A few years later, Pymatuning became the site of the state's first wildlife education center. From 1968 to 1980, only three pairs of bald eagles were known to nest in Pennsylvania, and all of them were in the Pymatuning area. The raptors can now be found in many areas of the state, but the frequency of sightings at Pymatuning brings birders back again and again. There's something else that brings people back again and again—something delightfully freakish. At Pymatuning, ducks walk on the backs of fish.

Just a few miles east of the state's largest lake is its largest natural lake, Conneaut Lake, which is popular with the speedboating set. East of Conneaut is the city of Meadville, home to a very old market house and the very unusual Johnson-Shaw Stereoscopic Museum. And east of Meadville is the Erie National Wildlife Refuge, a federally managed haven for waterfowl and, like Pymatuning, a paradise for bird-watching enthusiasts.

PYMATUNING STATE PARK

At almost 17,000 acres, **Pymatuning State Park** (2660 Williamsfield Rd., Jamestown, 724/932-3142, www.dcnr.pa.gov/stateparks) is one of the largest of Pennsylvania's 121 state parks. It's home to Pennsylvania's largest lake and has more campsites than any other Pennsylvania state park. It's one of the most visited state parks in Pennsylvania. And it's the only state park where feeding of (certain) wildlife is not seriously frowned upon.

You can rent a boat, take a swim, and stay the night on the south or north shore of Pymatuning Lake. The south shore, near the town of Jamestown, can be reached from Route 322. The north shore, near the town of Linesville, can be reached from Route 6. Head to the north shore for the region's main attraction: a reservoir spillway where feeding of ducks and fish results in the phenomenon that made Linesville famous as the place "Where the Ducks Walk on the Fish."

Pymatuning Lake spills into Ohio, which has its own Pymatuning State Park. For information about recreation on the west shore, call 440/293-6030 or visit the website (http://parks.ohiodnr.gov/pymatuning).

★ The Spillway

Want to see a monkey atop an elephant? Buy a ticket to a circus. Want to see a duck atop a fish? Buy a loaf of bread and head to the Pymatuning spillway, located two miles south of Lineville on Hartstown Road. Each year, hundreds of thousands of people visit the spillway to hurl bread crumbs (or whole loaves) at the fish and waterfowl that congregate there. The fish—big, mean-looking carp—are so thick that they form a writhing carpet on the water's surface. A carp with its sights set on a saltine or slice of Wonder bread will sometimes leap out of the water and somersault over its brethren. To say that ducks walk the carp carpet is a bit of an overstatement. Once in a while, a duck in hot pursuit of baked goods will waddle over a fish or two. It's an odd enough sight to keep many families coming back year after year.

In 2008 state conservation officials tried to put a stop to the decades-old bread-tossing tradition, arguing that the carp were eating too many carbs (or something like that). They proposed visitors could feed the fish with pellets sold at a state-run concession stand. The "let them eat pellets" proclamation incited a public outcry, attracting the attention of state legislators. Attacked like a hot dog bun in the heart of the spillway, the Department of Conservation and Natural Resources backed down. They still stress that only bread or pellets should be thrown to the fish. Keep the popcorn, chips, and cupcakes for yourself.

The bread hurling begins with the spring thaw and continues through late fall. Refreshments, souvenirs, and fish food are available at the spillway concession stand, which is generally open weekends mid-April to Memorial Day, daily through Labor Day, and weekends for the remainder of September.

The road to the spillway takes you past a

ducks at the Pymatuning spillway

large fish hatchery and then Ford Island, a renowned bird-watching site.

Linesville State Fish Hatchery

Anglers and anyone who's owned an aquarium will enjoy a visit to the state-run **fish hatchery** (13300 Hartstown Rd., Linesville, 814/683-4451, www.fishandboat.com, 8am-3:30pm daily, free) about a mile north of the spillway. Built in 1939, the hatchery raises millions of gilled swimmers each year: about a dozen warmwater species as well as trout destined for Lake Erie's tributaries. Its visitors center houses a two-story aquarium filled with walleye, crappie, perch, catfish, bass, and other warmwater fish; a collection of vintage fishing equipment and boat motors; and plenty of mounted trophy fish, including the state-record muskellunge—a 54-pounder pulled from nearby Conneaut Lake in 1924. Kids get a kick out of an interactive exhibit that tests their fish identification skills.

A platform overlooking the hatch house gives visitors a chance to observe workers bringing in adult fish, stripping the eggs out, fertilizing them, and otherwise going about their day. Though fish rearing is a year-round business at Linesville, there's less to see during the coldest months. Sometime in October or early November, hatchery workers drain the 10,000-gallon aquarium, releasing the fish into Pymatuning. Production ponds are also drained. They remain empty until the ice comes off the lake in March or early April.

The hatchery grounds are popular with bird-watchers. Bring binoculars or a spotting scope to scan the skies and trees for bald eagles. Bring a picnic basket if you plan to stay awhile; there are tables and benches on the property but no concession stand.

Boating and Fishing

Pymatuning Lake isn't a destination for adrenaline junkies. A 20-horsepower limit rules out Jet-Skiing, waterskiing, wakeboarding, and the like. (Head to nearby Conneaut Lake if that's what floats your boat.) If you enjoy peace and quiet and pretty scenery, you'll enjoy Pymatuning. Ditto if you enjoy sailing or canoeing.

The lake's Pennsylvania shores are dotted with boat ramps and three public marinas: the 203-slip Jamestown Marina (724/932-3267) on the south shore, the 170-slip Linesville Marina (814/683-4339) on the north shore, and the 184-slip Espyville Marina (724/927-2001) on the east shore. Generally open from late March or early April through October, the marinas rent a variety of watercraft, including motorboats, pontoons, and canoes. Fishing tackle, bait, and snacks are available.

Common species in the warmwater fishery include walleye, muskellunge, crappie, bluegill, and largemouth and smallmouth bass. Anglers can cast anywhere on the lake with a fishing license from either Pennsylvania or Ohio, but shore fishing requires a license from the appropriate state. Popular fishing spots include an 850-foot breakwater at Espyville Marina and a 280-foot fishing pier adjacent to Linesville Marina.

Serious anglers can be found on Pymatuning even in the dead of winter. Iceboating is permitted everywhere on the lake.

Swimming

The state park has several swimming beaches, which are open the weekend before Memorial Day through Labor Day, weather permitting. There's one public beach on the north shore, near Linesville Campground and Marina. The southern/Jamestown end of the park has two public beaches, and Jamestown Campground has its own beach for campers.

Campgrounds and Cabins

The state park has two camping areas: **Jamestown Campground** (716 Williamsfield Rd., Jamestown) on the south shore of Pymatuning Lake and the smaller **Linesville Campground** (3388 W. Erie St. Extension, Linesville) on the north shore. Open mid-April-mid-October, the campgrounds have showers, flush toilets, and a mix of electric and nonelectric campsites.

Both are convenient to swimming, boating, and fishing.

Not a camper? There are **cabins** near both campgrounds. The two- and three-bedroom cabins have a furnished living area, kitchen/dining area, and bathroom. Bring your own linens, towels, cookware, and tableware. There are 20 cabins at the southern/Jamestown end of the park, and they're available year-round. The five cabins at the northern/Linesville end are available from mid-April to late October. Reserve campsites and cabins online at http://pennsylvaniastateparks.reserveamerica.com or by calling 888/727-2757.

CONNEAUT LAKE

Less than 10 minutes from Pymatuning's shores, **Conneaut Lake** is the largest natural lake in Pennsylvania. Let's get this clear: It's not very large. At 934 acres, it's a puddle compared to the 17,088-acre Pymatuning. But the glacial lake near the town that shares its name has a certain appeal. Pymatuning is no deeper than 35 feet, and the state imposes a 20-horsepower limit on the man-made lake. Conneaut is almost 70 feet deep and there's no horsepower limit. So speedboating, water-skiing, Jet-Skiing, and the like—prohibited on Pymatuning—are allowed on Conneaut. You'll need your own watercraft, however. Rentals are hard to come by.

Conneaut Lake Park (12382 Center St., Conneaut Lake, 814/382-5115, www.newconneautlakepark.com, Memorial Day weekend-Labor Day, hours vary, free, single ride $2.50, all-day ride pass $10, all-day water park pass $10, combo pass $18) is an amusement park that traces its history to 1892. The park is best known for its classic Blue Streak coaster, which opened in 1938. In recent years it's become known for financial woes and some lousy luck. Its rides stood idle in 2007 due to a lack of funds. In early 2008 an arson fire destroyed its century-old Dreamland Ballroom, where Perry Como and Doris Day once sang. Just two months later, its old bowling alley collapsed. Another fire in 2013 tore through its restaurant. But the debt-laden park limps on, touting Blue Streak rides and a trip back in time. Splash City, a water park-within-the-park, has a lazy river and waterslides.

MEADVILLE

About 15 minutes from Conneaut Lake and 25 from Pymatuning, the city of Meadville offers a handful of quaint B&Bs and cultural attractions. It's a college town—about 2,000 of its roughly 13,000 residents are students of Allegheny College, a liberal arts institution founded in 1815—and the county seat of Crawford County. (It's also the birthplace of actress Sharon Stone. Years before Hollywood fame, she enjoyed Meadville fame as Miss Crawford County.) The **Meadville Market House** (910 Market St., Meadville, 814/336-2056, 10:30am-6pm Mon., 10am-6pm Tues.-Fri., 9am-4pm Sat. summer, 10am-6pm Mon.-Fri., 8am-4pm Sat. winter), a community gathering spot since 1870, is a good place to start the day. It's home to a greasy spoon known for its breakfasts. It's also a destination for locally made crafts and specialty foods, including baked goods and homemade pasta. During the growing season, farmers sell their produce outside.

The **Baldwin-Reynolds House Museum** (639 Terrace St., Meadville, 814/333-9882, www.baldwinreynolds.org, tours on the hour noon-3pm Wed.-Sun. June-Aug., free) is another of Meadville's cultural attractions. The Greek Revival mansion was built in the 1840s for U.S. Supreme Court Justice Henry Baldwin. He died within a year of moving in, and for a few years his dream home served as a finishing school for girls. In 1847 his widow deeded the property to her nephew, William Reynolds, a young Pittsburgh attorney and graduate of Allegheny College. Reynolds moved his family to Meadville, became one of its most influential businessmen, and served as its first mayor. The house stayed in the Reynolds family until 1963, when it was purchased by the Crawford County Historical Society. Tours take visitors through more than 20 antiques-filled rooms.

A Train Ride Through History

In 1857, a New York native named Edwin Drake arrived in the northwest Pennsylvania town of Titusville with a notion to dig down deep into the earth to collect oil. People thought he was off his rocker. It's not that there wasn't clearly crude oil in these parts: It oozed from the banks and bed of the creek flowing through Titusville, giving the Allegheny River tributary a rainbow sheen and its name, Oil Creek. But no one in Titusville had ever attempted to drill for it. Drake's method was thought ludicrous—until August 1859, when he stuck pay dirt. Drillers and speculators poured into the Oil Creek valley in search of "black gold." By the end of 1860, there were more than 70 producing oil wells in and around Oil Creek. U.S. oil production that year totaled 509,000 barrels, up from about 2,000 barrels the year before. "Drake's folly," as it was first considered, had given birth to the modern oil industry.

There's no better way to experience the Oil Creek valley than aboard a vintage train. The **Oil Creek & Titusville Railroad** (home station 409 S. Perry St., Titusville, 814/676-1733, www.octrr.org, runs weekends June-Oct. and select weekdays July-Aug. and Oct., adults $20, seniors $18, children 2-12 $14) snakes along Oil Creek from Titusville to Rynd Farm Station at the southern tip of Oil Creek State Park, crossing multiple bridges on its 27-mile round-trip journey. Guides regale riders with colorful stories of the oil boom days, when the banks of the creek were thick with derricks. Today they're thick with trees, which is why OC&T tickets are in hot demand in October. Be sure to make a reservation during leaf-peeping season.

Rail fans will find plenty to ooh and aah over on the train. Its most unusual car is a railway post office—the only operating one in the country. RPOs were used on thousands of routes during the salad days of passenger train service. Mail was sorted while in transport to speed up delivery. Today riders can buy and mail postcards on the restored 1927 car, a substation of the Oil City post office.

STAY OVERNIGHT

Sitting on tracks next to the home station is the **Caboose Motel** (814/827-5730, www.octrr.org/caboosemotel.htm, May-Oct., $90). Each of its 21 caboose cars has a king-size bed or two double beds, a heat and air-conditioning unit, and a television. Overnight packages with reduced train fares are available.

GETTING THERE

Titusville lies along Route 8, a north-south route stretching from Erie to Pittsburgh. It's 27 miles east of Meadville via Route 27 east. The drive takes about 40 minutes. From Erie, Titusville is about 45 miles southeast via Routes 19, 97, and 8 south.

Meadville also has a museum devoted to stereoscopy, a parlor pastime in the days before television and Nintendo. The **Johnson-Shaw Stereoscopic Museum** (423 Chestnut St., Meadville, 814/333-4326, www.johnsonshawmuseum.org, 10am-4pm Sat. Apr.-Nov., by appointment 10am-4pm Sun.-Fri., adults $5, seniors and students 6-17 $3, children under 6 free) houses a collection of stereoviews—photographs that appear three-dimensional when viewed through a binocular-like device—made by the Keystone View Company. Founded in Meadville in 1892, the company was the nation's leading manufacturer of stereoviews by the early 20th century.

Another unusual Meadville attraction is the **Greendale Cemetery** (700 Randolph St., Meadville, 814/336-3545, www.greendalecemetery.org). More than 160 years old, the historic, parklike cemetery is enchanting in springtime, when more than 1,500 rhododendrons bloom.

ERIE NATIONAL WILDLIFE REFUGE

About 30 miles east of Pymatuning Lake is another bird-watching mecca. Established in 1959 as a haven for migratory birds, **Erie National Wildlife Refuge** (11296 Wood Duck Ln., Guys Mills, 814/789-3585, www.fws.gov/refuge/erie, headquarters generally 8am-4:30pm Mon.-Fri., call to confirm, outdoor facilities open daily from 30 minutes before sunrise to sunset unless otherwise posted, free) consists of two expanses of federal land. It attracts some 240 species of birds, including waterfowl, bald eagles and other raptors, shorebirds, and marsh birds. A detailed bird brochure is available at the refuge headquarters, located on the larger and more intensely managed tract. The 5,206-acre Sugar Lake Division lies in a narrow valley on the outskirts of Guys Mills, about 10 miles from Meadville. A two-loop trail near the headquarters offers a 1.2- or 1.6-mile jaunt through wetlands, meadows of upland grasses, and mixed forests. In winter it's popular with cross-country skiers and snowshoers. It's possible to spot a variety of birds without stepping foot outside the headquarters. An indoor bird observation area with seating, binoculars, and bird identification materials overlooks feeding stations installed outside. Thanks to microphones placed under the stations, visitors can even listen to the banter of the feasting birds.

The 3,594-acre Seneca Division is about 10 miles north of the Sugar Lake Division, or 4 miles southeast of the town of Cambridge Springs.

Note that hunting is permitted in the refuge. If you're visiting during hunting season, wear blaze orange.

ENTERTAINMENT AND EVENTS

Performing Arts

Opened in 1885, the **Academy Theatre** (275 Chestnut St., Meadville, 814/337-8000, www.theacademytheatre.org) welcomed more than its fair share of traveling troupes thanks to Meadville's location along railroad lines between New York City and Chicago. These days the performers who take its stage are mostly local (and there's no passenger train service to Meadville).

Festivals and Events

More than two dozen hot-air balloons take flight over Meadville every Father's Day weekend. The **Thurston Classic Hot Air Balloon Event** (204 Park Ave., Meadville, 814/336-4000, www.thurstonclassic.com, June, free) pays tribute to Samuel Sylvester Thurston, a Meadville hotel operator who took up ballooning in 1860, and the son who followed in his footsteps. The younger Thurston launched his balloon from the roof of the still-standing Meadville Market House on at least one occasion.

The **Crawford County Fair** (Rte. 77, Meadville, 814/333-7400, www.crawfordcountyfairpa.com, Aug.) is billed as the largest agricultural fair in Pennsylvania. It's got all the hallmarks of an ag fair: lots of livestock, lots of food, live entertainment, amusement rides, truck and tractor pulls, and a pageant. Actress Sharon Stone won the coveted Miss Crawford County crown in 1975.

SHOPPING

Bill Campbell's pottery is sold in some 600 galleries in the United States and Virgin Islands, but opening his own store a few miles from his production facility was a gamble. The big question: Would people come to the country for his elegant, richly colored porcelain? They did. The **Campbell Pottery Store** (25579 Plank Rd., Cambridge Springs, 814/734-8800, www.campbellpotterystore.com, 10am-5pm daily Mar.-Dec.), about 20 minutes north of Meadville and 30 minutes south of Erie, is well worth a detour. There are three floors to explore. The basement level, once a dirt-floored milking area, is now a gallery used for group or solo shows, demos, workshops, and other special events. Exquisite creations in a variety of mediums and price ranges fill the ground level and loft area, where massive hand-hewn beams and other original architectural features compete for the eye's attention. In addition to the largest selection of Campbell pottery in the world, including experimental pieces available nowhere else, you'll find handcrafted soaps, baby goods, decorative items for home and garden, and jewelry.

FOOD

You won't have to scramble over a fish's back to get fed near Pymatuning Lake. **Rebecca's Family Restaurant** (144 W. Erie St., Linesville, 814/683-4484, www.goodfoodlinesville.com, 8am-2pm Sun.-Tues., 8am-8pm Wed.-Thurs., 8am-9pm Fri.-Sat., $7-13) is delightfully cozy with its hand-hewn log furniture, river rock fireplace, and expansive brick wall uncovered during a renovation. The casual eatery in the heart of Linesville is known for phenomenal pies and its "cinnamon roll sundae." Named for the owners' daughter, Rebecca's does everything from eggs to meatloaf sandwiches to steak dinners. Breakfast is served all day.

As the largest town in the area, with a college to boot, Meadville has its share of chain restaurants, sandwich shops, and pizza joints. It's also home to the original **Voodoo Brewery** (215 Arch St., Meadville, 814/337-3676, pub 3pm-8pm Mon.-Wed., 3pm-midnight Thurs.-Fri., noon-midnight Sat., noon-10pm Sun., kitchen 3pm-10pm Thurs.-Sat., noon-8pm Sun., $5-15), which now has four locations in western Pennsylvania (including one in Erie). To go with Voodoo's brews, the kitchen puts out snack foods—pretzels with beer cheese, deep-fried sweet potato balls—plus a short menu of salads, pizzas, sliders, and veggie burgers.

Ten miles north of Meadville and well worth the drive is ★ **Sprague Farm & Brew Works** (22113 Rte. 6/Rte. 19, Venango, 814/398-2885, www.sleepingchainsaw.com, 3pm-9pm Thurs., noon-9pm Fri.-Sat., noon-6pm Sun. summer, winter hours vary, under $10), a brewpub in a refurbished dairy barn. Fresh beer and joviality are the main attractions, but the Brew Works also offers a selection of Pennsylvania wines and a menu that includes soft pretzels, made-in-Erie Smith's hot dogs, sandwiches, and wood-fired pizza. Don't have a designated driver? Rent Sprague's Sleeping Leaf Lodge ($300), a five-bedroom farmhouse within stumbling distance of the pub.

ACCOMMODATIONS

If you're a camper, you won't have trouble finding a place to lay your head near Pymatuning Lake. Pymatuning State Park has hundreds of campsites—more than any other state park in Pennsylvania—and 25 cabins. Should you encounter a No Vacancy sign, take your business to **Pineview Camplands** (15075 Shermansville Rd., Linesville, 814/683-5561, www.pineviewcamplands.com, open late Apr.-mid-Oct., $20-30). It's extremely well situated: Pymatuning 10 minutes away in one direction, and Conneaut Lake 10 minutes away in another.

There are no hotels on Pymatuning's shores. Conneaut Lake had quite a few during its heyday as a resort area in the late 19th and early 20th centuries. **Hotel Conneaut** (12241 Lake St., Conneaut Lake, 814/573-7747, www.thehotelconneaut.com, $55-125) is the lone survivor. Room rates were $1 per day when it opened on the grounds of Conneaut Lake Park, the amusement park on the western shore, in 1903. In 1943 it was struck by lightning, and the resulting blaze led to a major remodeling. The hotel, which shows its age, is open daily during the summer and weekends-only from Labor Day to Memorial Day.

Year-round—and more modern—accommodations can be found in Meadville. The college town has a mix of budget hotels and a few B&Bs. **Mayor Lord's House Bed & Breakfast** (654 Park Ave., Meadville, 814/720-8907, www.mayorlords.com, $110-140) is in the heart of Meadville, just two blocks from Allegheny College. The beautifully restored house was built in the 1920s for a former Meadville mayor. The included breakfast is buffet-style. Not all of the rooms have en suite baths.

TRANSPORTATION AND SERVICES

The town of Linesville, gateway to the northern end of Pymatuning State Park, is an hour southwest of Erie and nearly two hours north of Pittsburgh. From Erie, head south on I-79 for about 35 miles and then west on Route 6, which will take you past Conneaut Lake on your way to Linesville. If you're coming from Pittsburgh, head north on I-79 for about 70 miles, then west on Route 285 to Conneaut Lake. From there, follow Route 6 west into Linesville.

Greyhound (800/231-2222, www.greyhound.com) provides bus service to Meadville, which is 15 miles east of Linesville. Private jets can land at Port Meadville Airport (GKJ), but passenger aircraft can't get any closer than **Erie International Airport, Tom Ridge Field** (ERI, 814/833-4258, www.erieairport.org). It's served by three major airlines offering service from Chicago, Detroit, and Philadelphia.

The **Crawford County Convention and Visitors Bureau** (16709 Conneaut Lake Rd., Meadville, 814/333-1258, www.visitcrawford.org, 8:30am-4:30pm Mon.-Fri.) is a good source of information about the Pymatuning region. It's closed on weekends, but you'll find brochures outside its doors.

Pennsylvania Wilds

To say that north-central Pennsylvania has more trees than people is a colossal understatement. More than 80 percent of the Wilds is forestland.

Almost a third of the region—about two million acres—is public land, open to anyone with an itch to explore. There's room for just about every form of outdoor recreation. Anglers and boaters will find thousands of miles of streams and waterways, including more than 2,000 wild trout streams. Hikers will find trails at every turn. But the region isn't just for rugged types. It's for berry pickers, leaf peepers, and stargazers. It's for anyone with a yen for nature. Pennsylvania's only national forest, the river gorge known as the "Grand Canyon of Pennsylvania," and the largest free-roaming elk herd in the northeastern United States can all be seen without so much as leaving your car.

You may as well turn off your phone when you visit the Pennsylvania Wilds. It won't work in many parts of the vast and lightly populated region.

PLANNING YOUR TIME

The largest region in Pennsylvania is bigger than some states. That means you'll be doing a lot of driving if you want to take in the major sights. Fortunately, the region is made for road trips. Its east-west thoroughfares are Route 6 across the upper half and I-80 across the bottom. The former is a favorite of motorcyclists and other aficionados of the open road. Contact the **PA Route 6 Tourist Association** (877/276-8836, www.paroute6.com) for a free guide to the highway's historic and scenic attractions. If you're visiting the region for just two or three days, take in Kinzua Dam in the Allegheny National Forest and Pine Creek Gorge in Tioga County, traveling Route 6 between the two. If you have more time, head south via Route 15, Route 219, or any number of meandering roads, and pay a visit to Pennsylvania's wild elk herd or the birthplace of Little League Baseball.

Previous: elk-watching in Benezette; Pine Creek Gorgen. **Above:** Gobbler's Knob.

Look for ★ to find recommended sights, activities, dining, and lodging.

HIGHLIGHTS

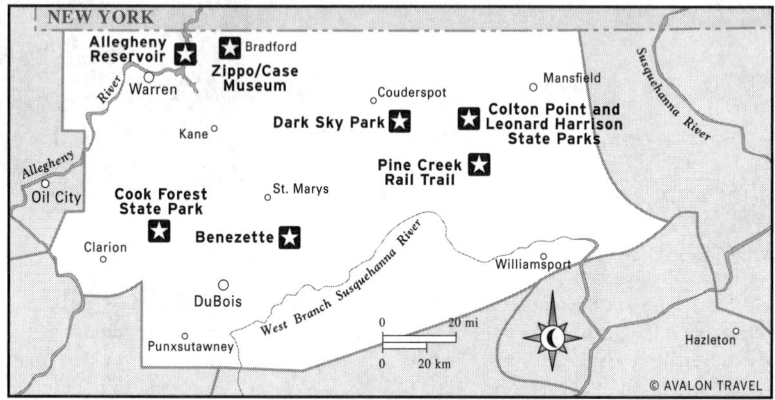

★ **Allegheny Reservoir:** The lake born of a 1960s flood-control project is a stunner whether you're gazing at it from a perch in Pennsylvania's only national forest or racing across it in a motorboat (page 325).

★ **Zippo/Case Museum:** Dedicated to the handsome lighter that has appeared in more movies than John Wayne (who himself carried a Zippo), this museum speaks volumes about American culture (page 327).

★ **Cook Forest State Park:** Wrap your arms around a 350-year-old tree, take a horseback ride, and race a go-kart all in one day. Now that's recreation (page 328).

★ **Colton Point and Leonard Harrison State Parks:** Both afford breathtaking views of the gorge known as Pennsylvania's Grand Canyon (page 336).

★ **Pine Creek Rail Trail:** The 60-mile trail that winds through wondrous Pine Creek Gorge is open to hikers, bikers, snowshoers, skiers, and even covered wagons (page 337).

★ **Dark Sky Park:** Cherry Springs State Park offers some of the best stargazing on the Eastern Seaboard (page 339).

★ **Benezette:** Stay a night in this tiny town to spot the largest herd of free-roaming elk in the Northeast (page 351).

Pennsylvania Wilds

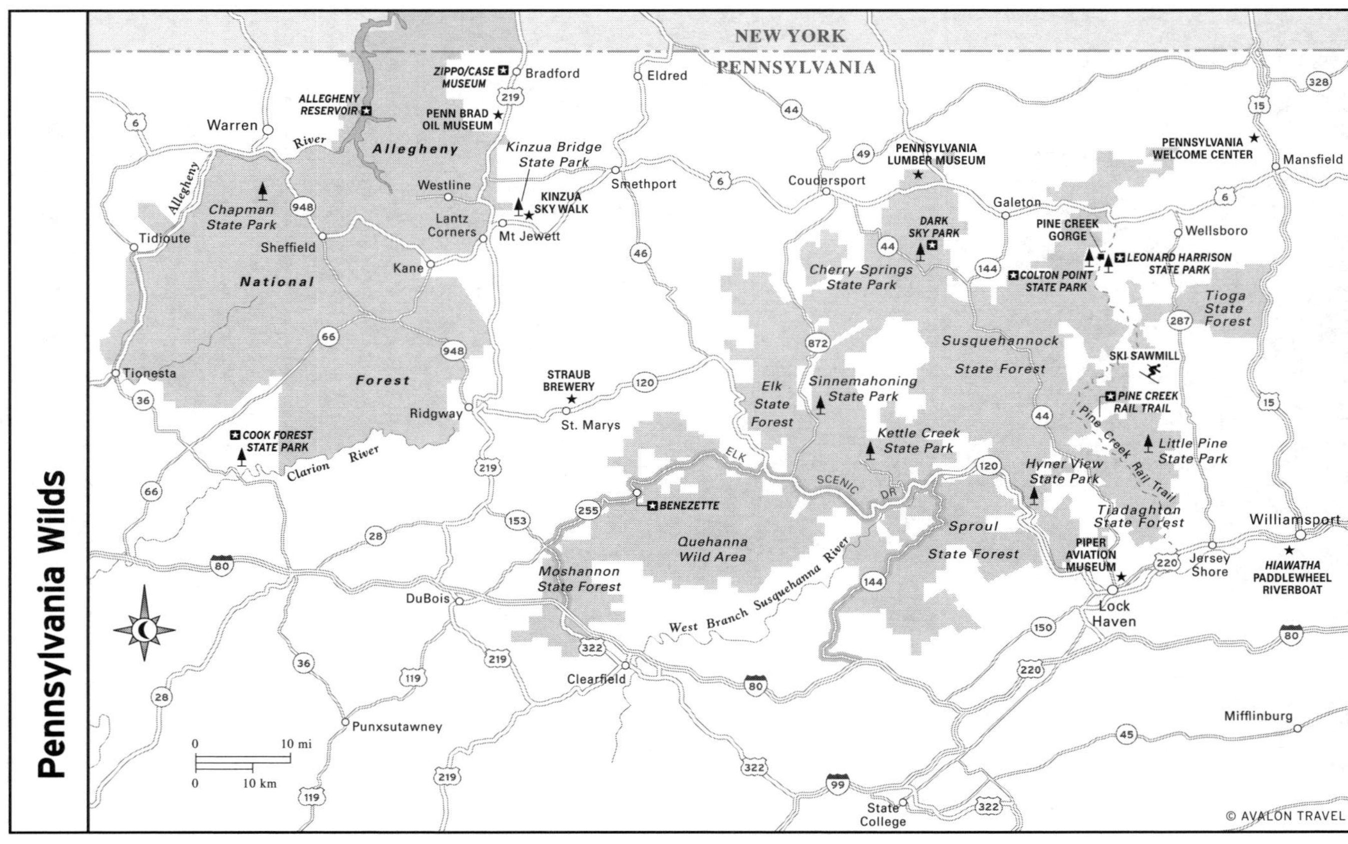

National Forest Region

The river valleys and steep hillsides of Pennsylvania's only national forest are blanketed with black cherry, red maple, and other hardwoods. They didn't always look like this. Two hundred years ago, the woods of northern Pennsylvania were thick with shade-tolerant eastern hemlock and American beech and laced with white pine and oak. When European settlers arrived in the early 1800s, they cut trees to make cabins and barns and to clear land for farming. As the nation grew, so did the demand for timber. Sawmills, tanneries reliant on hemlock bark for turning hides into leather, and railroads sprouted across the state's northern tier. The wood chemical industry, born near the end of the century, provided a market for virtually every accessible tree. By the time the **Allegheny National Forest** (814/723-5150, www.fs.usda.gov/allegheny) was established in 1923, the land was so barren and so prone to wildfires that residents jokingly referred to it as the "Allegheny brush patch."

Worries that the forest would never recover proved unfounded. A new and different forest arose, dominated by sun-loving hardwoods. They make motor touring a popular pastime in the fall, when the hills are ablaze with crimson and gold. (The best leaf peeping is in late September and early October.) In the 1940s, timber harvesting resumed under the strict guidelines of the U.S. Forest Service. It continues to this day, so don't be surprised if you find yourself driving behind a trailer loaded with timber. The biggest change to the national forest came in 1965, with the completion of Kinzua Dam on the Allegheny River. The resultant reservoir is the hub of recreational activity in the forest, which spans more than half a million acres in four counties. The small cities of Warren and Bradford on the forest's fringes offer lodging and dining options, plus cultural attractions including a museum dedicated to Zippo lighters. A few more lodging and dining options dot the towns of Kane, Westline, and Cooksburg.

Allegheny National Forest

"As Long as the Grass Shall Grow"

The construction of Kinzua Dam on the Allegheny River flooded lands that had been promised to the Seneca Nation by President George Washington. Native American folk singer Peter La Farge wrote a song about the plight of the Senecas, which Johnny Cash recorded in 1964. "As Long as the Grass Shall Grow" is the first song on Cash's *Bitter Tears* album.

> ... On the Seneca reservation there is much sadness now
> Washington's treaty has been broken, and there is no hope no how
> All across the Allegheny River, they're throwing up a dam
> It will flood the Indian country, a proud day for Uncle Sam ...
> As long as the moon shall rise
> As long as the rivers flow
> As long as the sun will shine
> As long as the grass shall grow

★ ALLEGHENY RESERVOIR

The construction of Kinzua Dam was not without controversy. It forced the relocation of Pennsylvania's only remaining Native American community and its sacred burial ground, inspiring a federal lawsuit and a song recorded by country legend Johnny Cash. But the U.S. government saw the dam as necessary armament in its war against flooding. The Army Corps of Engineers estimates that Kinzua Dam (pronounced "KIN-zoo") has prevented flood damages in excess of $1.2 billion since its completion in 1965.

The dam created the **Allegheny Reservoir** (814/726-0661, www.corpslakes.us), also known as Kinzua Lake. More than 24 miles long, the lake straddles the Pennsylvania-New York border. In Pennsylvania, it's completely surrounded by the Allegheny National Forest. In New York, it's bordered by Allegany State Park and the Allegany Indian Reservation of the Seneca Nation. (Yep, the spelling varies.) Its largely undeveloped shoreline is dotted with picnic areas, boat launches, and campgrounds.

Kinzua Dam itself is in Warren County, nine miles east of the city of Warren. From Warren, head east on Route 6 for about two miles and turn left (east) on Route 59, which leads to a parking lot at the top of the dam. Check out the giant carp that congregate on one side of the dam and the hydroelectric facilities on the other. Displays at the Army Corps' **Big Bend Visitor Center** (Rte. 59, 814/726-0678, open daily Memorial Day weekend-Labor Day, weekends only Sept.-Oct.), just downstream of the dam, illustrate the hydroelectric process. The outflow area is a popular fishing spot.

Two nearby overlooks offer bird's-eye views of the river valley (and attract rock climbers). Leaving the dam, drive east on Route 59 for about three miles. Just before reaching a bridge that crosses the reservoir, turn right onto Longhouse Scenic Drive (Forest Road 262). Make the first right off Longhouse to reach **Jakes Rock Overlook**. The access road to **Rimrock Overlook,** Forest Road 454, is about three miles farther east on Route 59. Follow the forest road until it ends at a parking lot. A short hike leads to the viewing area atop a large rock face. There are picnic areas at both overlooks.

Between the overlooks is the 250-slip **Kinzua Wolf Run Marina** (Rte. 59, 3 miles east of Kinzua Dam, 814/726-1650, www.kinzuamarina.com, mid-May-mid-Sept.), which rents houseboats, pontoon boats, motorboats, canoes, and kayaks. The entrance to **Kinzua Beach** is across Route 59 from the marina. The beach features a roped-off swimming area, a sandbox, picnic tables and grills, and restrooms.

Camping

You can pitch a tent just about anywhere in the Allegheny National Forest (814/723-5150, www.fs.usda.gov/allegheny), but nothing beats lakeside camping. There are several modern campgrounds on the shores of the Allegheny Reservoir in Pennsylvania. **Willow Bay** is on the eastern shore along Route 346, about 15 miles west of Bradford. It has more than 100 campsites and about a dozen rustic cabins with electricity. Amenities include a concrete boat launch and a large picnic area overlooking the reservoir. Canoes and kayaks are available for rent.

There are two modern campgrounds, **Dewdrop** and **Kiasutha,** along Longhouse Scenic Drive (Forest Road 262) on the western shore of Kinzua Bay, a southern branch of the Allegheny Reservoir. Both have concrete boat launches. The latter also boasts a large swimming beach and picnic area. **Red Bridge** campground, located along Route 321 on the eastern shore of Kinzua Bay, doesn't have a boat launch, beach, or picnic area, but it is adjacent to a popular bank fishing area.

Willow Bay is open year-round. Dewdrop and Kiasutha are open from Memorial Day weekend through Labor Day. Red Bridge is open April to mid-October. Campsite fees are $18-25. The four- and six-person cabins at Willow Bay rent for $55-65 per night. Peak-season reservations can be made through www.recreation.gov or by calling 877/444-6777. Off-season reservations can be made through Allegheny Site Management (814/368-4158, www.alleghenysite.com), a private company that operates recreation facilities in the national forest.

There are also several primitive campgrounds on the shores of the Allegheny Reservoir in Pennsylvania: Handsome Lake, Hooks Brook, Hopewell, Morrison, and Pine Grove. They can only be reached by foot or boat. Campsites are available on a first-come, first-served basis. Visit the website of the Allegheny National Forest or Allegheny Site Management for more information.

The Forest Service prohibits camping on the shores of the reservoir except in these designated areas.

Fishing

The Allegheny Reservoir has produced record-setting walleye, northern pike, and channel catfish. Keep in mind that a Pennsylvania fishing license doesn't fly in New York's share of the reservoir, where jurisdiction is divided between the state and the Seneca Nation. Be sure to have a license from the appropriate agency for the portion of lake you're fishing. Want to maximize your odds of catching a trophy fish? Call Red Childress of **Allegheny Guide Service** (814/688-2309, www.alleghenyguideservice.com). He offers fishing trips on the Allegheny River, Allegheny Reservoir, and Tionesta Lake, an Army Corps project at the southwest corner of the national forest.

WARREN

The city of Warren, just west of the Allegheny Reservoir, boasts a 28-block National Historic District. Ask for a walking tour brochure at the **Warren County Historical Society** (210 4th Ave., 814/723-1795, www.warrenhistory.org, 8:30am-4:30pm Mon.-Fri. year-round). The society's headquarters is itself a historic property: an 1870s Second Empire-style house that's especially enchanting come Christmastime. The tour ends at the **Warren County Courthouse** (204 4th Ave., 8:30am-4:30pm Mon.-Fri.), site of a 1954 courtroom shooting that left a judge dead and captured the nation's attention. You can still find bullet holes in the woodwork.

BRADFORD

The city of Bradford, east of the Allegheny Reservoir on Route 219, was once a small lumber town named Littleton. Its population exploded in the late 1800s with the discovery of a prolific oil field. In 1881, at the height of production, the field produced three-fourths of the world's oil output, and Bradford reigned as the "High-Grade Oil Metropolis of the World."

Bradford is still a hub of oil-related activity. The world's first billion-dollar field is still in business, though on a much smaller scale. Bradford's Minard Run Oil Company, owned by the same family since its establishment in 1875, is still prospecting. American Refining Group's Bradford refinery, established in 1881, is the world's oldest continuously operating crude oil refinery. The McDonald's in downtown Bradford has the usual—Big Macs, McNuggets, fries—and a working oil well in its parking lot. Drilled in the 1870s, the well produces up to three-fourths of a barrel a day.

Downtown Bradford deserves a stroll for its historic architecture and smattering of specialty shops. Start at the **Allegheny National Forest Visitors Bureau** (80 E. Corydon St., Bradford, 800/473-9370, www.visitanf.com, 9am-5pm Mon.-Fri.), where you can grab a map and brochures about area attractions. The visitors bureau is housed in one of Bradford's most impressive buildings, a former post office fronted by six large pillars.

Don't miss **Main Street Mercantile** (45 Main St., Bradford, 814/368-2206, www.bradfordmsm.com, 10am-6pm Mon.-Thurs., 10am-7pm Fri., 10am-6pm Sat., noon-4pm Sun.), a sprawling store with more than 75 vendors. You'll find antiques, local art, alpaca products, pottery, maple syrup, and more.

★ ZIPPO/CASE MUSEUM

The most visited museum in the region isn't dedicated to art or history, but a little bit of both: the Zippo lighter. The Zippo was born in the early 1930s, after Bradford native George G. Blaisdell noticed a friend fumbling with an Austrian-made lighter. Blaisdell decided to make one that was easier to use and handsome to boot. The first lighter he produced is one of hundreds of models and prototypes displayed at the museum within the **Zippo/Case Visitors Center** (1932 Zippo Dr., Bradford, 814/368-1932, www.zippo.com, 9am-5pm Mon.-Sat., 11am-4pm Sun., free). The museum tells the uncommonly compelling story of how a lighter became a cultural icon with more than 1,000 movie, TV, and stage credits under its belt. Its collection includes contemporary artworks created with Zippos and examples of "trench art"—lighters decorated by servicemen during wartime. Knives made by W. R. Case & Sons Cutlery, a subsidiary of Zippo Manufacturing Company since 1993, are also exhibited.

Visitors can watch technicians at work in the Zippo Repair Clinic. The company fixes or replaces any broken Zippo, no matter how mangled, free of charge. (Tours of the factory, elsewhere in Bradford, are not available.) The store adjacent to the museum sells the complete line of Zippo and Case products, including collectors' items not found anywhere else.

PENN BRAD OIL MUSEUM

Located three miles south of Bradford on Route 219, the **Penn Brad Oil Museum** (901 South Ave., Bradford, 814/362-1955, 9am-4pm Mon.-Fri., 9am-2pm Sat., adults $5, seniors $4.50, children under 12 free) takes visitors back to oil boom times. Its large collection of oil field artifacts includes a 72-foot-tall drilling rig. Tours led by oil industry veterans heighten the experience.

KINZUA SKY WALK

When the Kinzua Viaduct was built in 1882, it was the highest and longest railroad bridge in the world. At 301 feet high and 2,053 feet long, the bridge spanning the Kinzua Creek valley was heralded as a work of engineering genius. Originally built of iron, it was reconstructed of steel less than 20 years later to handle heavier trains loaded with coal, timber, and oil. Long after it was outranked by other bridges and discarded by the Erie Railroad in 1959, sightseers packed excursion trains to cross it. A *New York Times* writer described soaring over the valley as "more akin to ballooning than railroading." But after more than a century of service, the man-made marvel was no match for Mother Nature. In July 2003, a tornado ripped 11 of the bridge's 20 towers from their concrete bases, tossing them on the valley floor.

Instead of rebuilding the bridge, the state transformed its remains into an unusual tourist attraction. Built on six surviving towers, the **Kinzua Sky Walk** (Kinzua Bridge State Park, 296 Viaduct Rd., Mount Jewett, 814/778-5467, www.dcnr.pa.gov/stateparks) is a 600-foot walkway ending in an observation deck with a partial glass floor. Those who brave it are rewarded with spectacular views, especially at the height of fall foliage.

Exhibits at the **Kinzua Bridge State Park Visitors Center** (Kinzua Bridge State Park, 296 Viaduct Rd., Mount Jewett, 814/778-5467, www.dcnr.pa.gov/stateparks, closed Sun. in winter) tell the story of the building of the bridge, the tornado that destroyed it, and the creation of the skywalk.

★ COOK FOREST STATE PARK

The Cook Forest literature talks a lot about old trees. No doubt, the trees are something to talk about. Many of the pines and hemlocks in the forest's old-growth areas are about 350 years old. Some are pushing 450. But old-growth timber isn't what brings most people to **Cook Forest State Park** (Rte. 36, Cooksburg, 814/744-8407, www.dcnr.pa.gov/stateparks). The sprawling park just south of Allegheny National Forest offers some of the most scenic hiking and paddling in Pennsylvania. And unlike many wilderness areas, it has spawned a small tourist industry. The area is peppered with rental cabins, canoe liveries, horse rentals, and family fun parks. It's one of those rare places where you can hike to a National Natural Landmark—the old-growth area known as the Forest Cathedral—and race a go-kart in the same day.

If **hiking** is on your agenda, it's best to start at the park office, just right of the main entrance, where you can pick up a park guide and a brochure describing the trails. Several trailheads are a short walk from the office. In addition to 47 miles of hiking trails, the park boasts a 13-mile **biking** route composed of lightly traveled roads and part of a short hiking trail. Biking on all other hiking trails is prohibited. A description of the bike route is available at the park office.

The Clarion River is another of the park's main attractions. It's a beginner river, which means you don't need **paddling** experience—or even a paddle—to take it on. Plenty of visitors forgo canoes and kayaks in favor of an inner tube. Area liveries include **The Pale**

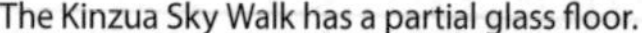
The Kinzua Sky Walk has a partial glass floor.

Whale Canoe Fleet (115 Riverside Dr., Cooksburg, 814/744-8300, www.canoecookforest.com, Apr.-Oct.), which rents canoes, kayaks, single and double tubes, and even floating coolers. The river also provides good **fishing.** Tom's Run, which runs through Cook Forest and joins the Clarion River near the park office, is popular for trout fishing. There's also a fishing pond stocked with trout near the park office. It's reserved for children 12 and under and people with disabilities.

Horseback riding is permitted in parts of the park. Horse rentals are available through **Cook Forest Scenic Trail Ride** (1661 Scott Dr., Clarion, 814/226-5985 May-Oct., 814/856-2081 Nov.-Apr., www.patrailride.com) and **Silver Stallion Stables** (83 Meadow Ln., Cooksburg, 814/927-6636, www.silverstallionstable.com).

There are plenty of places to **spend the night** in and near the park. Open from mid-April to mid-December, the park's Ridge Campground has more than 200 campsites. The park also offers rustic cabins. Some are perched on a hill overlooking the Clarion River. Campsites and cabins can be reserved online at http://pennsylvaniastateparks.reserveamerica.com or by calling 888/727-2757.

The website of the Cook Forest Vacation Bureau (www.cookforest.org) is a good resource on privately owned campgrounds, cabins, and lodging properties in the Cook Forest area. It can also point you to attractions like the **Cook Forest Fun Park** (2952 Rte. 36, Leeper, 814/744-9404, www.cookforestfunpark.com, open mid-Apr.-mid-Nov.), featuring go-karts, bumper boats, miniature golf, and a large waterslide.

ENTERTAINMENT AND EVENTS

Performing Arts

The **Struthers Library Theatre** (302 W. 3rd Ave., Warren, 814/723-7231, www.strutherslibrarytheatre.com) in the heart of Warren's historic district was built in 1883. It's home to the **Warren Players** (www.warrenplayers.com), an amateur theater company organized in 1930, and an annual film series. The **Warren Concert Association** (814/723-6505) organizes a few concerts at the Struthers throughout the year.

The **Bradford Creative & Performing Arts Center** (814/362-2522, www.bcpac.com) presents music, theater, and dance by talented Bradfordians as well as professional artists and troupes from around the country.

The hexagon-shaped **Verna Leith**

a cabin in Cook Forest State Park

Sawmill Theatre at the Cook Forest Sawmill Center for the Arts (140-170 Theatre Ln., Cooksburg, 814/927-6655, www.sawmill.org) hosts performances by area theater groups from May to September.

Festivals and Events

There's no better time to visit the forest region than late September and early October, when the leaves are changing color. And there's no better place to take in the majesty than Kinzua Bridge State Park and its 225-foot-high observation deck. Time your visit to coincide with the **Kinzua Bridge Fall Festival** (814/331-7331, www.kinzuabridgefoundation.com, 3rd weekend of Sept., free), featuring live music, food and craft vendors, and a Bigfoot-calling contest.

Competitions between professional lumberjacks and lumberjills from as far away as New Zealand are a highlight of the **Johnny Appleseed Festival** (www.johnnyappleseedfest.net, Oct., free). Held in the forest town of Sheffield, the three-day affair also features chainsaw carving, an antique tractor pull, wine-tasting, a pie-baking contest, and fireworks.

Perfectly sane people plunge into insanely cold water during **Warren County Winterfest** (814/726-1222, www.warrencountywinterfest.com, Jan., free) at Chapman State Park. In addition to the "polar bear plunge," the weekend festival includes ice fishing and snow-sculpting contests, dogsled races, and sleigh rides.

SPORTS AND RECREATION

The Allegheny Reservoir and Cook Forest State Park are popular hubs of recreation in the national forest region, but they're hardly the whole story. The region is crisscrossed with trails and rivers, peppered with state parks and game lands, and blessed with the sort of scenery that makes driving a pleasure. What follows is a mere sampling of recreation opportunities.

ATV Trails

The national forest has more than 100 miles of trails for all-terrain vehicles and dirt bikes. For directions to trailheads, trail maps and descriptions, condition reports, and other information, visit the forest website (www.fs.usda.gov/allegheny) or call 814/362-4613 or 814/927-6628.

All ATV trails are marked with yellow diamonds. Riding on unmarked routes is a major no-no, as is riding without a permit. Annual permits ($35) are available at a number of locations, including the forest supervisor's office (4 Farm Colony Dr., Warren, 814/723-5150), the Bradford Ranger District office (29 Forest Service Dr., Bradford, 814/362-4613), and the Marienville Ranger District office (131 Smokey Ln., Marienville, 814/927-6628).

If you're new to off-roading or bringing along children, head to **Majestic Trails** (Rte. 46, 9 miles south of Bradford, 814/465-9979, www.majestictrails.com), an ATV park on privately owned property just east of the national forest. Majestic offers guided ATV and dirt bike tours, dirt bike lessons, and kid-friendly trails, along with plenty of challenging terrain for experienced riders. It also offers cabin rentals and "wilderness-style" camping, which translates to no hookups, showers, or potable water.

Biking

Mountain bikers are welcome on ATV trails, though they may prove too rough for most riders. Snowmobile trails, select hiking trails, and gated roads in the national forest (814/723-5150, www.fs.usda.gov/allegheny) are also open to bikers. Road cyclists can pedal through the forest on Route 6. The state-endorsed Bicycle PA Route Y generally follows Route 6 from one end of the state to the other.

Boating

The national forest region is beloved by powerboaters and paddlers alike. The former make waves on the **Allegheny Reservoir** and **Tionesta Lake** (Rte. 36, just south of Tionesta, 814/755-3512, www.corpslakes.us), an Army Corps project on the western fringe of the national forest. The latter are welcome on these lakes but also have their pick of rivers and streams.

The **Allegheny River** below Kinzua Dam sees a good number of professional canoe and kayak races, but it's calm enough for paddling novices. **Allegheny Outfitters** (2101 Pennsylvania Ave. E., Warren, 814/723-1203, www.alleghenyoutfitters.com, Apr.-Oct.) offers rental canoes and kayaks and facilitates paddling trips on the river. Its most popular trip starts at Kinzua Dam and ends seven miles later at the livery.

Tionesta-based **Outback Adventures** (Rte. 62, just south of Tionesta Bridge, 814/755-3658, www.outbackadventurespa.com, Apr.-Oct.) specializes in trips on **Tionesta Creek** as well as the Allegheny River. The creek makes for a magical float in early spring; by June, water levels are generally too low for paddling. Outback Adventures also operates a riverfront campground.

The **Clarion River,** one of the major tributaries of the Allegheny, was once believed to be the most polluted river in Pennsylvania due to acid mine drainage. You wouldn't know it from the recovered section that snakes through Cook Forest State Park and along the southern border of the national forest. There are several liveries in the Cook Forest area, including **The Pale Whale Canoe Fleet** (115 Riverside Dr., Cooksburg, 814/744-8300, www.canoecookforest.com, Apr.-Oct.).

Fishing

The region's lakes, ponds, rivers, and streams are home to many species of fish. Directions to more than two dozen fishing spots are available on the national forest website (www.fs.usda.gov/allegheny). The **Allegheny Reservoir** and **Allegheny River** below Kinzua Dam are particularly popular with anglers because they yield some of the largest freshwater fish in the state. For help getting in on the action, call Red Childress of **Allegheny Guide Service** (814/688-2309, www.alleghenyguideservice.com), who leads fishing trips on the Allegheny River, Allegheny Reservoir, and **Tionesta Lake.**

If you're confident in your skills, consider visiting the region in late September, during the **Pennsylvania State Championship Fishing Tournament** (814/484-3585, www.pascft.org). It's open to anyone with a valid Pennsylvania fishing license, including children as young as three. The tournament has been held in the itty-bitty town of Tidioute,

canoeing on the Clarion River

which sits at a sharp bend in the Allegheny River, for more than 50 years.

Information on fishing licenses and seasons can be found on the website of the Pennsylvania Fish & Boat Commission (814/337-0444, www.fishandboat.com).

Hiking

Hundreds of miles of hiking trails snake through the national forest region.

Trails near the Allegheny Reservoir include the **Morrison Trail,** an 11.4-mile loop that can be broken into two shorter loops. The trailhead parking lot is off Route 59, seven miles east of Kinzua Dam. The trail leads to the primitive Morrison Campground on the shores of the reservoir.

Trails in the southern part of the forest include the 11.2-mile **Buzzard Swamp** system, near the town of Marienville. Buzzard Swamp—a string of 15 man-made ponds—offers some of the best wildlife viewing in the forest, especially during the spring waterfowl migration. From Marienville, follow Lamonaville Road 2.5 miles east to reach the northern trailhead.

The **North Country National Scenic Trail** (616/897-5987, www.northcountrytrail.org), which stretches from New York to North Dakota, traverses the length of the national forest.

Guides to these and other trails are available on the national forest website (www.fs.usda.gov/allegheny) and at Forest Service and tourism promotion offices.

Horseback Riding

Riding is permitted in most parts of the Allegheny National Forest. A number of ranches on its borders supply well-mannered horses. **Hickory Creek Wilderness Ranch** (2516 Economite Rd., Tidioute, 814/484-7520, www.hickorycreekranch.com) offers trail rides, camping, and cabin rentals. In July it offers a chance to see professional bull riders in action at the **Battle on Bull Mountain.**

The 600-acre **Flying W Ranch** (685 Flying W Ranch Rd., Tionesta, 814/463-7663, www.theflyingwranch.com) also offers trail rides, camping, and cabin rentals. Its overnight pack trips, which include a night on the ranch, a night on the trail, and a cook, are a great way for city slickers to sample the cowboy life. In July the ranch hosts the **Allegheny Mountain Championship Rodeo,** featuring steer wrestling, bronco riding, and other man-versus-wild spectacles.

Winter Sports

The Allegheny National Forest has more than 350 miles of groomed snowmobile trails and about 50 miles of trails designated for cross-country skiing. Visit the national forest website (www.fs.usda.gov/allegheny) for trail maps and information on snow conditions.

FOOD

Bradford

True to its name, **Beefeaters** (27 Congress St., Bradford, 814/362-9717, www.thebeefeatersrestaurant.com, 11am-10pm Mon.-Sat., $7-30) specializes in beef. Guests can eye the goods at the "beef bar," where roast after roast is carved into slices for dishes like beef on weck, a sandwich distinguished by its seasoned roll. Chicken, seafood, and pasta dishes are also on offer. The restaurant is housed in a stately building that served as Bradford's library for nine decades.

For breakfast or lunch, you can't beat **John William's European Pastry Shop** (20 Mechanic St., Bradford, 814/362-6637, 6am-4pm Mon.-Fri., 6:30am-3pm Sat.-Sun., under $10). In addition to delectable baked goods, the old-fashioned bakery serves up omelets, panini, croissant sandwiches, salads, and more.

Warren

The ★ **Plaza Restaurant** (328 Pennsylvania Ave. W., Warren, 814/723-5660, 7am-8pm Mon.-Sat., under $10) is "still doing things the hard way," according to its owner, whose Greek-born father opened the diner in 1959. In other words, it still makes just about everything from scratch—from mashed potatoes to heavenly pies. Greek specialties like souvlaki complement standard diner fare. Expect a crowd at breakfast; avoid the noon lunch rush by showing up before or after. Whenever you go, don't skip the cream pie.

St. Louis-style ribs, chargrilled chicken, and half-pound burgers await at **Ribs & Bones** (6452 Jackson Run Rd., Warren, 814/723-8205, 4pm-9pm Tues.-Thurs. and Sun., 4pm-10pm Fri-Sat., $9-25), a local favorite with a jovial pub atmosphere. If you're not in the mood for a half rack and a side of wings, the menu also includes seafood, pasta, and salads.

Westline

The town of Westline is a speckle on forest maps. Find it and you'll be rewarded with fine French cuisine. **The Westline Inn** (15 E. L. Day Dr., Westline, 814/778-5103, www.westlineinn.com, 5:30pm-9pm Tues.-Thurs., 5:30pm-10pm Fri.-Sat., 3pm-7pm Sun., bar open from 3pm Mon.-Thurs., noon Fri.-Sat., 3pm Sun., $15-30) offers escargot, crepes stuffed with seafood, bouillabaisse, and the like. Prefer an American-style burger? Ask for the pub menu. First, though, you have to find the place. From the intersection of Routes 6 and 219, head north on 219 for five miles to a sign pointing left to Westline. Follow the narrow road for three miles.

Kane

You can swirl, sniff, sip, and snack at **Flickerwood Wine Cellars** (309 Flickerwood Rd., Kane, 814/837-7566, www.flickerwood.com, 11am-7pm Mon.-Tues, 11am-9pm Wed.-Thurs., 10am-9pm Fri.-Sat., noon-6pm Sun., $6-9). The family-run winery features a lounge where guests can savor a glass of wine and nibble on bruschetta or cheese, or chow down on food you'd expect to see in a pub: toasted sub sandwiches, individually sized pizzas, fried pickles. Flickerwood's reds, whites, and blushes were originally the creations of Ron Zampogna, who served the red, white, and blue as a Forest Service employee for 36 years. His son, Rick, is the current winemaker.

Cooksburg

Just south of Allegheny National Forest by Cook Forest State Park, **Gateway Lodge Restaurant & Wine Bar** (14870 Rte. 36, Cooksburg, 814/744-8017, www.gatewaylodge.com, 5pm-9pm Mon.-Sat., 8am-2pm Sun., $17-36) promises "a farm to forest dinner experience" to go with its award-winning wine list. Meat-eaters can cut into a locally sourced steak served with campfire potatoes, while vegetarians have options like mushroom-filled crepes and "crab" cakes made out of hearts of palm. Sunday brunch ($20, children under 12 $12) includes an entrée plus a pastry and fruit buffet.

ACCOMMODATIONS

Campgrounds and cabins abound in the national forest region, but it also offers upscale lodging options like the Lodge at Glendorn in Bradford, a member of the exclusive Relais & Châteaux group. Bradford, along with Warren, is also where you'll find the chain hotels. A small number of locally owned inns and bed-and-breakfasts are scattered throughout Kane and other small towns.

Under $100

Kane Manor (230 Clay St., Kane, 814/837-6522, www.kanemanor.com, $59-69) was built in the final years of the 19th century for Elizabeth Kane, widow of the abolitionist and Civil War general for whom the town of Kane is named. Today it's a B&B with 11 guest rooms, period furnishings, Kane family mementos, and an impressive portico overlooking the lush grounds. Two of the guest rooms share a bathroom.

$100-250

Hand-crocheted afghans and homemade baked goods await at **The Inn on Maple Street Bed & Breakfast** (115 E. Maple St., Port Allegany, 814/642-5171, www.theinnonmaplestreet.com, $109-169), one block off

Route 6 in picturesque Port Allegany. **Horton House Bed & Breakfast** (504 Market St., Warren, 814/723-7472, www.hortonhousebb.com, $139) in downtown Warren is named for Isaac Horton, the lumber magnate who built the 7,500-square-foot house (of wood, naturally) in the late 1800s. Guests can play a game of Ping-Pong in the ballroom or soak in the outdoor hot tub year-round.

Built in 1934 at the "gateway" to Cook Forest State Park, ★ **Gateway Lodge** (14870 Rte. 36, Cooksburg, 814/744-8017, www.gatewaylodge.com, rooms $179-199, suites $199-250, cabins $135-300, weekly rates available for cabins) has morphed into the picture of rustic elegance in the hands of Deb Adams, its owner since 2006. It boasts fireside whirlpool tubs, private balconies, an on-site spa, and fabulous food and wine. Gateway's farm-to-table restaurant is open to hotel guests for breakfast, which is included with the rooms and suites. The restaurant opens to the public for dinner and Sunday brunch.

Pull up to ★ **The Lodge at Glendorn** (1000 Glendorn Dr., Bradford, 814/362-6511, www.glendorn.com, rooms from $475, suites from $750, cabins from $850) and a staff member or two will be waiting outside to greet you. Sink into a velvety couch in the all-redwood main lodge and another will offer you a drink. Come dinnertime, a server will produce a menu written that day, incorporating vegetables and herbs from an on-site garden. At night, retire to one of just four guest rooms and suites in the lodge or one of 12 private cabins. You'll feel like you own the place. Indeed, for almost 70 years, Glendorn was a private estate, an idyllic retreat for the oil-rich Dorn family. They opened it to the public in 1995 and it quickly earned a reputation as one of the nation's premier hideaways. The property is so secluded that many area residents don't know what or where it is—all the better for guests like Denzel Washington, who stayed there during filming of 2009's *Unstoppable*. One of only two Orvis-endorsed fly-fishing lodges in Pennsylvania, Glendorn offers 4.5 miles of privately managed trout angling. Other amenities include three trout-filled ponds, a 60-foot pool, tennis courts, a spa, and a vast trail system. Breakfast is included with the room rates; the prix fixe dinner is $105 per person.

TRANSPORTATION AND SERVICES

Getting There and Around

The forest region, like the rest of the Wilds, is

The Lodge at Glendorn

driving country. The national forest is roughly framed by Route 62 on the west and Route 219 on the east. Route 6 wriggles across it. Another east-west road, Route 59, crosses the Allegheny Reservoir, the recreational heart of the forest.

Bradford Regional Airport (BFD), just east of the Allegheny Reservoir, offers daily flights to **Pittsburgh International Airport** (PIT). **DuBois Regional Airport** (DUJ) to the forest's south and **Chautauqua County Airport-Jamestown** (JHW) to its north also offer commercial service. The larger **Erie International Airport** (ERI, 814/833-4258, www.erieairport.org) and **Buffalo Niagara International Airport** (BUF) are within a two-hour drive of the forest.

Visitor Information

The headquarters of the **Allegheny National Forest** (4 Farm Colony Dr., Warren, 814/723-5150, www.fs.usda.gov/allegheny, 8am-4:30pm Mon.-Fri.) is about five miles north of downtown Warren on Route 62. In addition to reams of free literature on forest recreation, you'll find T-shirts, topographical maps, books on plants and birds, and other merchandise. You can also load up on information at the **Bradford Ranger District** office (29 Forest Service Dr., Bradford, 814/362-4613, 8am-4:30pm Mon.-Fri. and 8am-4:30pm Sat. Memorial Day weekend-early Oct., 8am-4:30pm Mon.-Fri. mid-Oct.-late May), responsible for the upper part of the forest, or the **Marienville Ranger District** office (131 Smokey Ln., Marienville, 814/927-6628, 8am-4:30pm Mon.-Fri. and 8am-4:30pm Sat.-Sun. mid-May-mid-Oct., 8am-4:30pm Mon.-Fri. mid-Oct.-mid-May), responsible for the lower part.

The Army Corps of Engineers operates the seasonal **Big Bend Visitor Center** (Rte. 59, 9 miles east of Warren, 814/726-0678, 10am-4pm daily Memorial Day weekend-Labor Day and weekends through Oct.), just downriver of Kinzua Dam. For a daily summary of water conditions, call 814/726-0164.

The national forest stretches across four counties represented by three tourism promotion agencies, each of which can supply a plethora of information about the region. The **Allegheny National Forest Visitors Bureau** (80 E. Corydon St., Bradford, 800/473-9370, www.visitanf.com, 9am-5pm Mon.-Fri.), which represents McKean County, is headquartered in downtown Bradford. The **Warren County Visitors Bureau** (22045 Rte. 6, Warren, 814/726-1222, www.wcvb.net) is about six miles west of downtown Warren. The lower part of the forest lies in Forest and Elk Counties, which are represented by the **PA Great Outdoors Visitors Bureau** (2801 Maplevale Rd., Brookville, 814/849-5197, www.visitpago.com, 8:30am-4:30pm Mon.-Fri.).

Pine Creek Gorge and Vicinity

Often referred to as the "Grand Canyon of Pennsylvania," Pine Creek Gorge deserves an identity all its own. With its thick blanket of trees—the kind that change color—Pine Creek Gorge has no comparison in the arid Southwest. It's Pennsylvania through and through.

The glacially carved gorge starts near the Route 6 village of Ansonia and continues south for 47 miles. Most visitors take in its majesty from one of two state parks near its northern end, where the canyon is about 800 feet deep. Near its southern end, Pine Creek Gorge is as deep as 1,450 feet and a mile wide. That may sound like nothing much compared to the real Grand Canyon, in Arizona, which is as deep as 6,000 feet and 10 miles wide on average. Still, Pine Creek Gorge is "one of the finest examples of a deep gorge in the eastern United States," according to the National Park Service, which has seen them all.

The 60-mile Pine Creek Rail Trail brings hikers, bikers, horseback riders, cross-country skiers, and snowshoers to the region, while the swift waters of Pine Creek call to anglers and paddlers.

★ COLTON POINT AND LEONARD HARRISON STATE PARKS

On the west rim of the gorge, there's Colton Point State Park. On the east, there's Leonard Harrison. The former is accessible from Route 6 at Ansonia, though the road leading to it is easily missed. You'll find Colton Road between a small gas station and the Burnin' Barrel Bar. Follow it for five miles to the state park and its series of scenic overlooks.

The better-groomed Leonard Harrison offers superior views of the canyon (and bathrooms with plumbing). From the town of Wellsboro, follow Route 660 west for 10 miles to the park. You can stop at the **Tioga County Visitors Center** (2053 Rte. 660, Wellsboro, 570/724-0635, www.visitpottertioga.com, 9am-6pm Mon.-Fri., 10am-2pm Sat.) along the way. The state park office at the entrance to **Leonard Harrison** (4797 Rte. 660, Wellsboro, 570/724-3061, www.dcnr.pa.gov/stateparks, park open year-round, office and education center open late Apr.-Oct., call for hours) handles queries about both parks. The main overlook and an environmental interpretive center are 0.25 mile up the road.

Both parks have picnic tables and pavilions, several miles of hiking trails, and seasonal campgrounds. Sites at Colton Point, which has rustic toilets, are first come, first served. The Leonard Harrison campground has modern facilities, including flush toilets and some electrical hookups. Sites can be reserved online at http://pennsylvaniastateparks.reserveamerica.com or by calling 888/727-2757.

Hiking

While short, the steep rim-to-creek trails at Colton Point and Leonard Harrison State Parks can challenge even experienced hikers. The highlight of **Colton Point's Turkey Path,** a three-mile down-and-back trail, is a 70-foot cascading waterfall less than 0.5 mile from the trailhead. **Leonard Harrison's Turkey Path** is two miles down and back, leading to a vista and waterfall before reaching the canyon floor. There's no bridge across Pine Creek, so hikers can't waddle down one Turkey Path and up the other.

a covered wagon tour of Pine Creek Gorge

Pine Creek Gorge

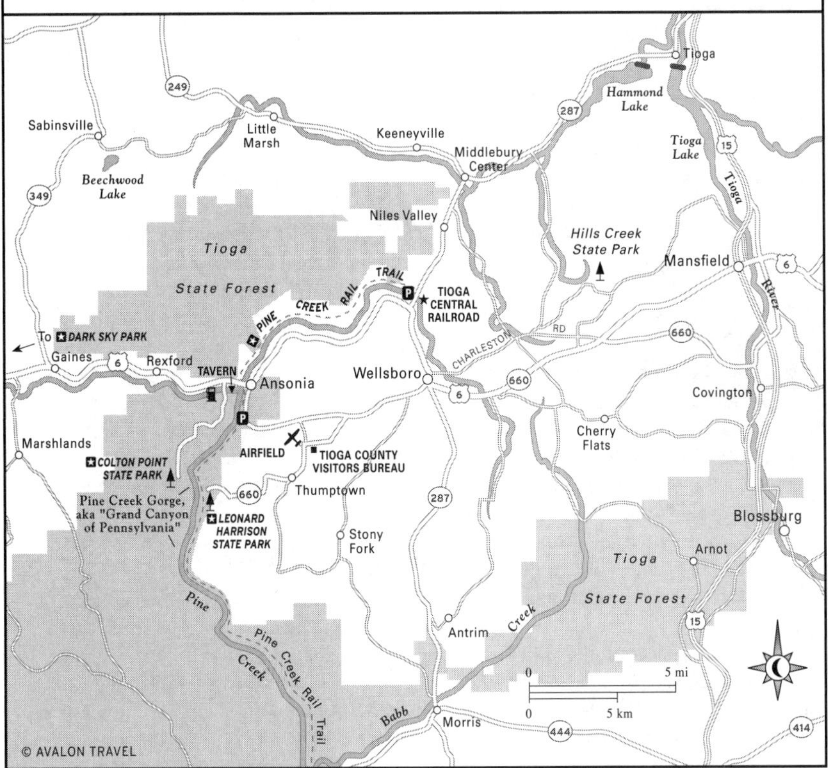

★ PINE CREEK RAIL TRAIL

To traverse the 60-mile Pine Creek Rail Trail is to experience unspoiled wilderness. Dramatic outcrops, gushing waterfalls, and diverse flora greet today's visitor. The woods are home to coyote, deer, wild turkey, and black bear, among other creatures. River otters were reintroduced to the canyon in the 1980s and fishers in the 1990s. Even bald eagles have returned to the area.

Maps of the Pine Creek Rail Trail are available at state park, forestry, and tourism promotion offices. The gently graded gravel path starts at Wellsboro Junction, a defunct railway junction at Routes 6 and 287, about three miles north of downtown Wellsboro. Darling Run, about nine trail miles from Wellsboro Junction, is a popular point of entry for hikers and bikers. It's located along Route 362, 1.5 miles south of Route 6 at Ansonia and about 7 miles west of Wellsboro.

The horseback trailhead is along Marsh Creek Road near the junction of Routes 6 and 362 at Ansonia. Horses are restricted to the dirt access road that runs alongside the trail for nine miles. Thanks to **Ole Covered Wagon Tours** (1538 Marsh Creek Rd., Wellsboro, 570/724-7443, www.olecoveredwagon.com, adults from $25, children 4-11 from $12), even non-equestrians can have a giddy-up experience of the gorge. Pulled by teams of Percheron draft horses, the covered wagons are larger and cushier than the

Conestogas of yore. Call or check the website for departure times. Walk-ins are welcome, but be sure to make a reservation from late September to mid-October, when the gorge is awash with autumn color and demand is highest. Ole Covered Wagon is about 12 miles west of Wellsboro on Route 6. Look for the covered wagon sign at the intersection of Route 6 and Marsh Creek Road.

If you're looking for more than a day trip, you're in luck. There are camping areas on public forestlands and private property along the trail.

DOWNTOWN WELLSBORO

The gateway to the Grand Canyon of Pennsylvania is the exceedingly charming town of Wellsboro, where gaslights burn 24/7. It's small enough to see in one day, and that's exactly why some visitors stay a few. Wellsboro's manicured town square, tree-lined streets, and general absence of hustle and bustle are almost as soothing as a spa getaway.

Let the calming begin at the town square, better known as "the green," across from the county courthouse on Main Street. The fountain statue at its center, *Wynken, Blynken, and Nod,* was inspired by an 1889 lullaby of the same name and depicts three children sailing across the sky in a wooden shoe. The bronze sculpture is a replica of the marble original in Denver. Wellsboro has another Denver connection: Its **Gmeiner Art and Cultural Center** (134 Main St., 570/724-1917, www.gmeinerartscenter.com, 2pm-5pm Wed.-Fri., 11am-5pm Sat.-Sun, free) was a gift of the late Arthur Gmeiner, a Denver entrepreneur and philanthropist who was born not far from Wellsboro. Exhibits change frequently.

Information about local events, attractions, and businesses is available at the **Wellsboro Area Chamber of Commerce** (114 Main St., 570/724-1926, www.wellsboropa.com, 8:30am-4:30pm Mon.-Fri.). You'll find brochures on the porch even when the chamber is closed. Pause in the front yard to meet Wellsboro's oldest resident: a massive elm tree that's been growing since the 1700s.

TIOGA CENTRAL RAILROAD

The passenger trains that once served this region are long gone, but it's still possible to ride the rails. The **Tioga Central Railroad** (Rte. 287 and Muck Rd., 3 miles north of downtown Wellsboro, 570/724-0990, www.tiogacentral.

the Tioga Central Railroad

com) operates excursion and charter trains on a 34-mile railroad extending from Wellsboro to just south of Corning, New York. It offers daytime, sunset, and dinner excursions from Memorial Day weekend to late October.

PENNSYLVANIA LUMBER MUSEUM

It's hard to imagine what north-central Pennsylvania looked like when work, not play, attracted people to its woods. The **Pennsylvania Lumber Museum** (5660 Rte. 6 West, Galeton, 814/435-2652, www.lumbermuseum.org, 9am-5pm Wed.-Sun., adults $8, seniors $7, children 3-11 $5) makes it a little easier. Thousands of artifacts, including a 1912 logging locomotive, tell the story of the state's forest industries. Visitors can tour an operational steam-powered sawmill and a re-created logging camp complete with blacksmith shop, horse barn, and mess hall. From November to March the outdoor exhibits, including the logging camp, are open only when the weather permits.

★ DARK SKY PARK

Thanks to its exceptionally dark night sky, **Cherry Springs State Park** (4639 Cherry Springs Rd., Coudersport, 814/435-5010, www.dcnr.pa.gov/stateparks) is one of the best places on the Eastern Seaboard for stargazing. In 2008, the 82-acre park on Route 44 about 15 miles southeast of Coudersport was designated as the second International Dark Sky Park by the International Dark-Sky Association, an Arizona-based nonprofit that agitates against light pollution.

The park's stargazing field offers a 360-degree view of the sky. If you plan to stay for just a few hours, park at the defunct Cherry Springs Airport and walk to the field. You can drive onto the field if you're staying overnight—but if you arrive after dark, you have to enter the field sans headlights. On a dark-moon weekend, some 200 amateur astronomers and their equipment could be scattered across the field. Observatory shelters and **campsites** ($17-24) can be reserved online at http://pennsylvaniastateparks.reserveamerica.com or by calling 888/727-2757.

The park's location affords an excellent view of the nucleus of the Milky Way. If you can't tell Sagittarius from Scorpius, check the park's schedule of free public stargazing programs. For a personal sky tour, contact local star guru Stash Nawrocki of **Crystal Spheres: Adventures in Stargazing** (814/848-5037, crystalspheres@gmail.com).

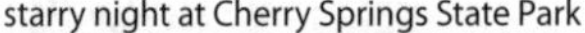
starry night at Cherry Springs State Park

Football, 1890s Style

The world's first night football game was played on September 28, 1892, on a field in Mansfield, Pennsylvania. Electric lights and the game of football were both novelties, so organizers weren't surprised that a crowd of thousands gathered to watch it. The players wore little padding and no helmets, and the lighting was so minimal that it was hard to tell which team had the ball. Before either squad could score, the referee deemed it too dangerous to continue.

A reenactment of the anticlimactic but historic game is the highlight of **Mansfield Heritage Weekend** (Smythe Park, Mansfield, 570/662-3442, www.mansfield.org, late Sept.). Mansfield University students and area residents play by the rules of 1892 in uniforms created 100 years later for a commercial for General Electric, which supplied the lights for the first night game. The game is followed by fireworks, just as it was in 1892. A parade the morning of the game also strives for historical accuracy, which means no motors and a whole lot of horses.

ENTERTAINMENT AND EVENTS

Performing Arts

The art deco **Arcadia Theatre** (50 Main St., Wellsboro, 570/724-4957, www.arcadiawellsboro.com) in downtown Wellsboro was built in 1921 for silent pictures. These days it shows the fruits of Hollywood's labors and art house films on four screens, along with live theater productions.

Wellsboro's **Deane Center for the Performing Arts** (104 Main St., Wellsboro, 570/724-6220, www.deanecenter.com) houses five performance venues, including a black-box theater that seats 190.

Festivals and Events

The blooming of Pennsylvania's state flower is cause for much merrymaking in Wellsboro. The **Pennsylvania State Laurel Festival** (570/724-1926, www.wellsboropa.com) starts the second weekend in June and continues through the third. Events include a crafts fair, live music, footraces, the crowning of the Laurel Queen, and a parade.

The parade of renowned musicians who perform at the **Endless Mountain Music Festival** (570/662-5030, box office 570/787-7800, www.endlessmountain.net, summer) makes it one of Pennsylvania's premier classical music events. The international festival was born in 2006, after a vacation in Wellsboro convinced acclaimed conductor Stephen Gunzenhauser that mountain scenery and world-class music would be a potent combination. The festival features solo recitals, chamber music concerts, and an orchestra of musicians from around the world—conducted, of course, by the maestro who fell in love with the mountains.

The hills are alive with the buzz of chainsaws during the **Woodsmen's Show** (814/435-6855, www.woodsmenshow.com, early Aug.) at Cherry Springs State Park. ESPN watchers may recognize the pro lumberjacks who face off in events like two-man logrolling, ax throwing, and tree felling. Amateurs can also test their skills. Chainsaw artists create masterpieces on-site over the course of the weekend.

The three-day **Hickory Fest** (570/723-1004, www.hickoryfest.com, mid-Aug.) brings the finest in bluegrass and acoustic music to canyon country.

During the first full weekend in December, Main Street in Wellsboro is transformed into an early Victorian marketplace for the **Dickens of a Christmas** holiday celebration. Costumed food and craft vendors, carolers, and street-corner thespians help turn back the clock.

SHOPPING

Wellsboro

The bulk of Wellsboro's shops line Main Street. No national chains here. **Dunham's**

(45 Main St., 570/724-1905, www.dunham-swellsboro.com, open daily), one of the oldest family-owned department stores in the country, has called Wellsboro home since 1905. Wellsboro's answer to Barnes & Noble is **From My Shelf Books** (7 East Ave., 570/724-5793, www.wellsborobookstore.com, open daily), just off Main Street. The ever-changing stock of new and gently used books includes out-of-print treasures.

Adventurers can stock up on brand-name gear and apparel at **Wild Asaph Outfitters** (71 Main St., 570/724-5155, www.wildasaphoutfitters.com, open daily). Its staff is a good source of information about area trails and rock climbing spots. **CS Sports** (81 Main St., 570/724-3858, www.cssports.biz, open daily) sells bicycles, skis, snowboards, and related apparel and equipment. It doubles as a repair shop.

SPORTS AND RECREATION

Biking

Bikers who want a bumpier ride than the Pine Creek Rail Trail provides can find any number of backcountry routes in and around the gorge. The Asaph section of Tioga State Forest, site of the **Laurel Classic Mountain Bike Challenge** (www.bikereg.com, Sept.), boasts a course with quad-busting climbs and creek and log crossings. Longtime biker Bill Yacovissi recommends more than a dozen loops, mostly on unpaved state forest roads, on his Pine Creek Canyon Bike Rides website (www.pinecreekbikerides.com).

Paddling and Fishing

Paddlers can sightsee and fish on Pine Creek, but the window of opportunity is small. With no dams, Pine Creek relies on snowmelt and rainfall for its flow. As spring turns to summer, water levels begin to drop. Paddlers must find other waters—or pray for thunderstorms heavy enough to swell the creek again.

Maps of the Pine Creek Rail Trail indicate creek access areas. The 54-mile state-designated Pine Creek Water Trail begins at the Big Meadows access area at Ansonia. The road leading to it is on the south side of Route 6, opposite a church. Don't put in at Big Meadows if you're looking for a quickie float: The first advisable take-out is 17 miles downstream, at the village of Blackwell. It takes about six hours to get there, though vigorous paddlers can do it much faster and an unhurried angler can take much longer. A few sections approach Class III (difficult) water, so novice paddlers would be wise to hire a guide. **Pine Creek Outfitters** (5142 Rte. 6, Wellsboro, 570/724-3003, www.pinecrk.com, 9am-6pm daily Mar.-Oct.) offers daily raft tours from March to late May. Guided trips may continue into June if water levels allow. The outfitter also rents rafts, canoes, kayaks, and wetsuits, along with bikes for cycling the Pine Creek Rail Trail. Shuttle service and sage advice are available for anyone paddling the creek, biking the rail-trail, or hiking the West Rim Trail.

The upper stretches of Pine Creek and its many tributaries offer some of the finest trout fishing in the Northeast. The lower part of the creek (downstream of Waterville) is better known for warmwater species. Vehicles can access the western riverbank from Ansonia by turning onto Colton Road and then left onto Owasee Road, which traces the creek for about four miles. There are ample pull-offs along Route 414, which hugs the creek from Blackwell to just north of Waterville. **Slate Run Tackle Shop** (Rte. 414, Slate Run, 570/753-8551, www.slaterun.com, open daily) is a full-line Orvis dealer with an impressive inventory (thousand-dollar fly rods included) and an equally impressive acquaintance with local waters. Staff gladly dispense directions to sections of stream and can tag along to provide on-stream instruction.

Hiking

The Pine Creek Rail Trail and the rim-to-creek trails at Colton Point and Leonard Harrison State Parks are popular with day-trippers. Backpackers will find even more to love in canyon country. The 30-mile **West**

Rim Trail traverses the western rim of Pine Creek Gorge, affording spectacular views of the valley. Its northern terminus is on Colton Road one mile south of Route 6 at Ansonia. The southern terminus is on Route 414 at the Rattlesnake Rock access area, two miles south of the village of Blackwell. Contact Tioga State Forest (570/724-2868, www.dcnr.state.pa.us/stateforests) for more information about the trail. It connects with Pennsylvania's longest hiking trail, the **Mid State Trail** (www.hike-mst.org), at Blackwell.

As if that weren't enough, backpackers can reach the 42-mile **Black Forest Trail** from the southern end of the West Rim Trail by following the Pine Creek Rail Trail to Slate Run. The Black Forest trailhead on Slate Run Road can also be reached via Route 414. The very difficult loop trail darts into and out of the gorge several times. Contact Tiadaghton State Forest (570/753-5409, www.dcnr.state.pa.us/stateforests) for information.

Skiing

The Pine Creek Rail Trail and state forestlands offer hundreds of miles of cross-country skiing. Downhill skiers and snowboarders looking for slopes will find them at **Ski Sawmill** (383 Oregon Hill Rd., Morris, 570/353-7521, www.skisawmill.com, all-day lift ticket adults $30-44, children 6-11 $28-41, all-day ski rental $25, snow tubing 1-hour session $10), 18 miles south of Wellsboro. The ski resort has 12 slopes, a terrain park, and a tube slide. It also offers a range of on-site lodging options, all fairly basic.

Snowmobiling

There are hundreds of miles of snowmobile trails on public lands surrounding Pine Creek Gorge. The **PA Grand Canyon Snowmobile Club** (4814 Rte. 6, Wellsboro, 570/724-2888, www.pagrandcanyonsnowmobileclub.com) is a good source of information about trails at the northern end of the gorge. Trails from the clubhouse lead everywhere from the west rim of the canyon to local watering holes.

FOOD

Wellsboro

Ask for the Grand Canyon at **The Native Bagel** (1 Central Ave., 570/724-0900, www.nativebagel.com, 6am-4pm Mon.-Fri., 7am-3pm Sat., 7am-2pm Sun., under $10) and you won't get directions to the Pine Creek Gorge. You'll get a triple-decker sandwich with ham, turkey, bacon, and barbecue sauce. Sandwiches are named for local attractions and made with breads that couldn't be more local: Loaves, bagels, and pastries are made on-site.

The **Wellsboro Diner** (19 Main St., 570/724-3992, 6am-8pm Mon.-Sat., 7am-8pm Sun., $5-15) serves up meatloaf, mashed potatoes, and the like in a deliciously authentic setting. The 1938 Sterling diner car was placed at the corner of Main Street and East Avenue in 1939 and hasn't budged since.

Chicken parm, "beef and reef" (aka surf and turf), and burgers have all stood the test of time, but if you're looking for a white pizza with shrimp and asparagus or grilled portobello on a Portuguese roll, those are also on offer at **Timeless Destination** (77 Main St., 570/724-8499, www.timelessdestination.com, 11am-9pm Mon.-Thurs., 11am-10pm Fri.-Sat., noon-9pm Sun., $9-26). Eat in the dining room or order off the same menu in the more casual lounge.

The building dates back to the 1860s, but the beer is as fresh as can be at restaurant and microbrewery **Wellsboro House** (34 Charleston St., 570/723-4687, www.wellsborohouse.com, 5pm-9pm Mon.-Thurs., noon-9pm Fri.-Sat., $8-25). Owners Chris and Laura Kozuhowski serve a menu of burgers, mussels, shrimp scampi, and chicken parm to go with the house-made brews. Look no further than the menu's South Philly cheesesteak to guess which team the Kozuhowskis root for.

South of Wellsboro

Cedar Run Inn (281 Beulah Land Rd., Cedar Run, 570/353-6241, www.cedarruninnpa.com, dinner only, reservations recommended, $17-26) is home to one of the finest restaurants in the region. Anglers and other outdoor adventurers can wash up at an old marble sink beneath a mounted buck before digging into the house pâté, a medley of clams and herbs baked with parmesan cheese, and chicken in a Frangelico cream sauce. Be sure to call ahead for restaurant hours; they vary throughout the year.

Coudersport

For a sweet treat before stargazing at Cherry Springs State Park, stop by **Cream 'n Sugar** (111 N. Main St., 814/320-0782, www.creamnsugar.net, 8:30am-7:30pm Mon.-Sat., under $10), in the town of Coudersport about 20 minutes from the Dark Sky Park. The café offers coffee and tea drinks, baked goods, candies, and, most importantly, ice cream direct from Penn State's Berkey Creamery in State College.

Fezz's Diner (9 Ice Mine Rd., 814/274-3399, 6am-3pm Mon.-Wed., 6am-7pm Thurs.-Sat., 8am-3pm Sun., $4-13) nails the 1950s diner look inside and out. The food is an All-American lineup of burgers, tuna melts, meatloaf, and breakfast fare like pancakes, waffles, and eggs.

ACCOMMODATIONS

Camping

It doesn't cost a cent to camp on state forestlands within the spectacular Pine Creek Gorge, but it does require a permit. Contact **Tioga State Forest** (570/724-2868, www.dcnr.state.pa.us/forestry) about camping in the Tioga County portion of the gorge and **Tiadaghton State Forest** (570/753-5409, www.dcnr.state.pa.us/forestry) about the lower portion in Lycoming County. The county line is between the villages of Blackwell and Cedar Run, about 20 miles from the northern mouth of the gorge. Some state forest camping areas have amenities like potable water and vault-style bathrooms.

For those who prefer a touch more luxury, there are modern campgrounds and other accommodations on private property in the canyon. You'll find them at Blackwell and points farther south. One such campground is **Pettecote Junction** (400 Beach Rd., Cedar Run, 570/353-7183, www.pettecotejunction.com, campsite $28-40, cabin $100). The proprietors aren't exaggerating when they advertise "direct access": The campground is wedged between Pine Creek and the rail-trail. Not surprisingly, it offers rental canoes, tubes, and bikes. In addition to tent and RV sites, Pettecote Junction has several cabins that sleep four to six people. It also offers "glamping" sites ($80) with a bed, a table and chairs, and even a coffeemaker inside a tent.

Canyon Country Campground (130 Wilson Rd., Wellsboro, 570/724-3818, www.canyoncountrycampground.com, Apr. 15-Oct., campsite $27-43, cabin $57-76) isn't in the gorge but has an enviable location near its eastern rim. A walking trail leads from the campground to Leonard Harrison State Park and its acclaimed overlooks.

Under $100

In downtown Wellsboro, **Canyon Motel** (18 East Ave., Wellsboro, 570/724-1681, www.canyonmotels.com, $75-94) is a step up from the image "motel" usually conjures. Suites have separate sitting rooms and kitchenettes. Select rooms include Jacuzzi tubs built for two. There's room for more in the indoor pool and hot tub.

West of Wellsboro with its own two-acre pond, **Colton Point Motel** (4643 Rte. 6, Wellsboro, 570/724-2155, www.pavisnet.com/coltonpoint, $75-80) offers basic but comfortable and clean accommodations convenient to Pine Creek.

Go rural without roughing it at **Frosty Hollow Bed & Breakfast** (1077 Cherry Springs Rd., Coudersport, 814/274-7419, www.frostyhollowbandb.com, $85-125), 10 minutes from Cherry Springs State Park. Joe and Gail Ayers converted a barn, farmhouse, and small cottage into 10 cozy guest rooms. The barn's Roseberry Loft is perfect for families, with two beds, a pullout sofa, and a full kitchen. The buffet breakfast is a hearty affair with hot entrees, fruit, and homemade baked goods.

$100-250

It's not hard to imagine former guest Groucho Marx striding through the **Penn Wells Hotel** (62 Main St., Wellsboro, 570/724-2111, www.pennwells.com, $75-140, closed Jan.-mid-May). Built in 1869 on the site of Wellsboro's first inn, the hotel pulses with history. Soak in the vibe of bygone days in the lobby or adjacent bar, but stay in one of the more recently renovated rooms if you can. The on-site restaurant is open to the public and particularly hopping during the Friday-night fish fry and Sunday brunch. The Penn Wells Hotel closes from winter through well into spring, but its younger sister, the **Penn Wells Lodge** (4 Main St., Wellsboro, 570/724-3463, www.pennwells.com, $80-195) is open year-round. It boasts larger rooms and an indoor pool.

Laura Lee and Jesse Robinson strive for European elegance at **La Belle Auberge** (129 Main St., Wellsboro, 570/439-7845, www.labelleaubergeinn.com, $119-225), originally established by Laura Lee's grandmother. Four well-decorated guest rooms come with private baths, electric fireplaces, and Wi-Fi. The gourmet breakfast is served buffet-style and taken in the dining room or on the wraparound porch. The Robinsons, who run Emerge Healing Arts & Spa a few blocks away, also set up a spa room at their B&B for massage services.

It's easy to reach the Pine Creek Rail Trail from **Bear Mountain Lodge** (8010 Rte. 6, Wellsboro, 570/724-2428, www.bearmountainbb.com, $149-259). Just walk or bike half a mile down a country road. What's hard is leaving the den of creature comforts. Two of the four guest rooms have private decks complete with hot tubs, and the other two have whirlpool baths. All have natural-gas fireplaces, flat-screen TVs, and queen beds of hickory, white cedar, or black cherry—crafted locally.

TRANSPORTATION AND SERVICES

Getting There

The town of Wellsboro, gateway to Pennsylvania's Grand Canyon, is about 50 miles north of Williamsport. It lies along the east-west Route 6. Leonard Harrison State Park, on the east rim of the canyon, is 10 miles west of Wellsboro via Route 660. Colton Point State Park, on the west rim of the canyon, is five miles south of Route 6 at Ansonia.

The nearest commercial airport is New York's **Elmira Corning Regional Airport** (ELM, 607/739-5621, www.ecairport.com), 55 miles northeast of Wellsboro.

Visitor Information

If you're arriving via Route 15 south, look for the state-run **welcome center** seven miles south of the Pennsylvania-New York line. Personalized travel counseling is available 7am-7pm daily; the restrooms are always open.

The **Tioga County Visitors Center** (2053 Rte. 660, Wellsboro, 570/724-0635, www.visitpottertioga.com, 9am-6pm Mon.-Fri., 10am-2pm Sat.) is conveniently located just a few miles east of the entrance to Leonard Harrison State Park and its glorious views of Pennsylvania's Grand Canyon. The visitors center has loads of information about the gorge and other area attractions. The county seat, Wellsboro, also has an advocate in the **Wellsboro Area Chamber of Commerce** (114 Main St., 570/724-1926, www.wellsboropa.com, 8:30am-4:30pm Mon.-Fri.).

South of Blackwell, Pine Creek and its eponymous rail-trail cross from Tioga County into Lycoming County, represented by the **Lycoming County Visitors Bureau** (102 W. 4th St., Williamsport, 570/327-7700, www.vacationpa.com, 8:30am-6pm Mon.-Fri., 8am-3pm Sat., 11am-3pm Sun.).

Williamsport and Vicinity

The largest city in the Wilds region is the not-so-large city of Williamsport, population roughly 29,000. It's situated on the West Branch of the Susquehanna River. In the latter half of the 19th century, so many logs were floated down tributary streams and captured by a log boom at Williamsport that the city became known as the "Lumber Capital of the World." Its riverfront was crowded with sawmills—more than 30 at the peak of logging activity in Pennsylvania. Its West 4th Street was crowded with the opulent residences of lumber barons. They moved to (literally) greener pastures as the lumbering era waned, but their showplaces still stand on the street known as Millionaires Row. The local high school's sports teams are known as the Williamsport Millionaires.

The city that once claimed to have more millionaires per capita than any place in the world now prides itself on a different distinction: birthplace of Little League Baseball. Every August, 16 teams of preteen ballplayers and tens of thousands of fans converge on the Williamsport area for the Little League Baseball World Series. A museum dedicated to Little League serves as a year-round pilgrimage site for little kids with big dreams.

Lock Haven, home to a state university, is about 30 minutes west of Williamsport.

LITTLE LEAGUE SIGHTS

In 1938, an oil company clerk named Carl Stotz decided to start a baseball program for boys in his hometown of Williamsport. He rounded up neighborhood children and began experimenting with different equipment and field dimensions. By the summer of 1939, Stotz had found sponsors for three teams and a name for his program: Little League. To learn how Williamsport's three-team league grew into the world's largest organized youth sports program, visit the **World of Little League: Peter J. McGovern Museum** (525 Rte. 15 Hwy., South Williamsport, 570/326-3607, www.littleleague.org/museum, 9am-5pm daily, adults $5, seniors $3, children 5-12 $2). The collection includes balls signed by U.S. presidents and professional players, photographs of major leaguers with their Little League teams, and the uniform Williamsport-area native and baseball great Mike "Moose" Mussina wore when he represented local restaurant Johnny Z's as a Little Leaguer.

The museum is part of Little League International's 66-acre complex in the borough of South Williamsport, across the Susquehanna River from Williamsport. It overlooks two stadiums used during the annual **Little League Baseball World Series** (571/326-1921, www.littleleague.org, Aug.). First held in 1947, the World Series wasn't always played in South Williamsport. Before 1959, the action unfolded on a field across the street from Williamsport's minor league ballpark, Bowman Field. The original field, listed in the National Register of Historic Places and now named **Carl E. Stotz Field** (1741 W. 4th St., Williamsport, 570/323-1308, www.leaguelineup.com/originalleagueinc), is still in active use. It's operated by Original League Inc., a youth baseball organization born of a rift between Stotz and Little League International in the 1950s. Surviving members of Little League's original teams gather at the field during World Series week and give tours of the memorabilia-filled clubhouse.

MILLIONAIRES ROW HISTORIC DISTRICT

A drive down West 4th Street in Williamsport belies the wealth that once flowed into the city in the form of tens of millions of logs. The moneyed have moved elsewhere and their erstwhile homes show their age. More than a few house students from the nearby

Pennsylvania College of Technology. But a stop here and there reveals Williamsport's rich history.

First up is the Lycoming County Historical Society's **Thomas T. Taber Museum** (858 W. 4th St., Williamsport, 570/326-3326, www.tabermuseum.org, 9:30am-4pm Tues.-Fri., 11am-4pm Sat., 1pm-4pm Sun., closed Sun. Nov.-Apr., adults $7.50, seniors $6, children $5), a modern building amid the Victorian-style structures of West 4th, aka Millionaires Row. The museum chronicles the history of the region, which didn't start with the arrival of loggers. Visitors can explore a gallery devoted to Native Americans as well as a string of period rooms that illustrate the lifestyles of subsequent inhabitants. The Taber is also home to more than 300 toy trains.

A real train car sits outside the **Peter Herdic Transportation Museum** (810 Nichols Place, Williamsport, 570/601-3455, www.phtm.org, 10am-3pm Tues.-Sat. June-Aug., 10am-3pm Fri.-Sat. Sept.-May, adults $5, seniors $4, children 12 and under $3), a stone's throw from the Taber. Named for Williamsport's most prominent lumber baron and the inventor of a horse-drawn taxi, the museum celebrates transportation achievements as wide-ranging as the birch-bark canoe and the public bus. As the hub of the 19th-century lumber industry and the home of so many millionaires, Williamsport was first in line for transportation innovations. Herdic himself oversaw the construction of a streetcar railway that went into service in 1865.

To learn more about the city's history, take a **Williamsport Trolley Tour** (570/326-2500, www.ridetrolleys.com, June-Aug., adults $5, seniors $4, children under 12 $3). The trolley tours and the Peter Herdic Transportation Museum are operated by River Valley Transit, Williamsport's public transit agency. A ticket to one includes admission to the other. In addition to the transportation museum, trolleys stop at the riverfront Susquehanna State Park, where the *Hiawatha* riverboat docks, and River Valley's 3rd Street parking garage. You can hop on or off at any of the three stops. The tour takes about 1.5 hours.

HIAWATHA PADDLEWHEEL RIVERBOAT

The ***Hiawatha*** (2205 Hiawatha Blvd., Williamsport, 570/326-2500, www.ridehiawatha.com) is a gaily painted excursion boat that cruises the Susquehanna River from May through October. A variety of cruises, including dinner cruises, karaoke cruises, and concert cruises, are offered throughout the season. You can learn about the river and its role in Williamsport's lumber era during a narrated "public cruise" (adults $8.50, seniors $8, children 3-12 $4.50). The hour-long cruise is offered several times a day Tuesday-Sunday from June through Labor Day.

The *Hiawatha* docks in Susquehanna State Park, accessible via the Reach Road exit of Route 220. The park has restroom facilities, riverside picnic tables, and a public boat launch.

PIPER AVIATION MUSEUM

In 1937, a fire destroyed the Bradford, Pennsylvania, factory of aircraft manufacturer William T. Piper. The man who would come to be known as the "Henry Ford of Aviation" relocated to an abandoned silk mill in Lock Haven, a river city about 25 miles west of Williamsport. It was there that his company, Piper Aircraft, produced the legendary J-3 Cub, the low-cost, easy-to-fly airplane that "taught the world to fly." Lock Haven is no longer home to Piper Aviation (new owners consolidated manufacturing in Florida in the 1980s), but it is home to the **Piper Aviation Museum** (1 Piper Way, Lock Haven, 570/748-8283, www.pipermuseum.com, 9am-4pm Mon.-Fri., 10am-4pm Sat., noon-4pm Sun., closed Sun. Dec.-Mar., adults $6, seniors $5, children 7-15 $3). The museum, which occupies a former Piper engineering building, preserves all things Piper, from vintage aircraft to flight journals.

ENTERTAINMENT AND EVENTS

Performing Arts

Williamsport's cultural hub is the **Community Arts Center** (220 W. 4th St., Williamsport, 570/326-2424, www.caclive.com), a 1920s vaudeville theater turned modern performance venue. The acoustically exemplary theater seats just over 2,100 people for concerts, dance performances, plays, comedy acts, and movies. The likes of Jerry Seinfeld, Ray Charles, Barry Manilow, and B. B. King have brought down the house. Local performing arts organizations, including the **Williamsport Symphony Orchestra** (570/322-0227, www.williamsportsymphony.org), also take the stage.

All about local talent, the **Community Theatre League** (100 W. 3rd St., Williamsport, 570/327-1777, www.ctlshows.com) produces about 10 plays a year and hosts concerts that run the gamut from jazz to barbershop. Its intimate theater-in-the-round can be found in Trade and Transit Centre 1, Williamsport's former bus hub.

Founded in 1831, Williamsport's **Repasz Band** (www.repaszband.org) is one of the oldest community bands in the country. It played at Appomattox Court House in Virginia when General Robert E. Lee surrendered to General Ulysses S. Grant. Today the band plays pieces from its lengthy repertoire at free indoor and outdoor concerts throughout the area.

Festivals and Events

Live music, meet-the-artist events, and extended store hours enliven downtown Williamsport on the **First Friday** (570/326-1971, www.williamsport.org) of every month.

The city of Lock Haven (570/893-5900, www.lockhavenpa.gov) sponsors free concerts not once but twice a week from June through August, dishing out classic rock, country, swing, polka, and more. On Friday evenings, bands perform at Triangle Park at Bellefonte Avenue and West Main Street. The Sunday-evening venue is the charming **J. Doyle Corman Amphitheater** at Jay and Water Streets. The amphitheater is built into the levee that guards Lock Haven from flooding by the Susquehanna River, and the stage floats on the water.

Fans of bluegrass and blues look forward to June, when the **Billtown Blues Festival** (Lycoming County Fairgrounds, 300 E. Lycoming St., Hughesville, 570/584-4480, www.billtownblues.org) is held.

SPORTS AND RECREATION

Pine Creek Rail Trail

The southern trailhead of the 60-mile Pine Creek Rail Trail is in the town of Jersey Shore, a 20-minute drive from Williamsport. (The town has no connection to the MTV show, and its connection to New Jersey dates back to the 1800s.) The trail shortly meets Pine Creek and follows it into the deepest section of Pennsylvania's Grand Canyon. It's beloved by hikers, bikers, cross-country skiers, and snowshoers.

Boating

Susquehanna State Park (Arch St., Williamsport, 570/988-5557, www.dcnr.pa.gov/stateparks) in Williamsport has a boat launch that provides access to the Susquehanna River and to a 652-acre impoundment that's deep enough for waterskiing. The park is also home to the *Hiawatha* (570/326-2500, www.ridehiawatha.com), an old-style riverboat offering public cruises from May through October.

Fishing

Pine Creek and Loyalsock Creek, tributaries of the West Branch of the Susquehanna ("Suskie" to local in-the-know anglers), are among the more popular fishing streams in the Williamsport area. The former empties into the West Branch near Jersey Shore, about 15 miles west of Williamsport, and the latter at Montoursville, about 8 miles east of the city.

Fly fishers will find a selection of more than 350 hand-tied flies at **McConnell's Country Store & Fly Shop** (10853 Rte. 44

N., Waterville, 570/753-8241, www.mcconnellscountrystore.com, 6am-8pm Mon.-Thurs., 6am-9pm Fri.-Sat., 7am-7pm Sun., winter hours 6am-6pm Mon.-Thurs., 6am-9pm Fri., 6am-7pm Sat., 7am-6pm Sun.), 12 miles north of Jersey Shore in the village of Waterville, where Little Pine Creek meets the "Big Pine." McConnell's offers guides as well as gear.

Hiking

The 59-mile **Loyalsock Trail** runs roughly parallel to Loyalsock Creek, which empties into the West Branch of the Susquehanna River at Montoursville, east of Williamsport. It's a strenuous trail that rewards hikers with spectacular vistas. The western terminus is on Route 87, about nine miles north of I-180/Route 220 at Montoursville. The Alpine Club of Williamsport (570/322-5878, www.alpineclubofwilliamsport.com), which maintains the trail, sells a detailed guide with full-color maps. The trail also appears on the free public-use map of Loyalsock State Forest (570/946-4049, www.dcnr.state.pa.us/forestry).

Scuba Diving

For the lowdown on local dive sites, plus diving lessons and gear, hunt for **Sunken Treasure Scuba Center** (664 Geiler Hollow Rd., Jersey Shore, 570/398-1458, www.divestsc.com, summer hours noon-9pm Mon. and Fri., 10am-5pm Tues. and Thurs., 9:30am-1pm Sat.).

FOOD

Williamsport

Award-winning microbrews and frequent live entertainment are reason enough to hop to **Bullfrog Brewery** (229 W. 4th St., Williamsport, 570/326-4700, www.bullfrogbrewery.com, 11am-midnight Mon.-Sat., 9am-midnight Sun., $8-28), but the food is also something to croak about. The Bullfrog bakes its focaccia, baguettes, and desserts in-house and buys its beef and produce from local farms. On Sundays it opens early for brunch and serves up free jazz starting at noon. Call or check the website for information about performances throughout the week.

Built in 1854 for Williamsport's most extravagant lumber baron, the ★ **Peter Herdic House** (407 W. 4th St., Williamsport, 570/322-0165, www.herdichouse.com, 5pm-close Wed.-Sat., lunch offered on select days in Dec., $25-31) now serves meals befitting a millionaire. Appetizers include such delicacies as escargot and oysters Rockefeller. Be sure to explore the ornate property before or after your meal. There's a wisteria-covered patio for outdoor dining and a lounge with its own menu of upscale snacks, like bacon-wrapped scallops.

Founded in 1984 as a maker of fine pastas and sauces, **DiSalvo's** (341 E. 4th St., Williamsport, 570/327-1200, www.disalvopasta.com, 5pm-9:30pm Mon.-Tues., 11:30am-2pm and 5pm-9:30pm Wed.-Thurs., 11:30am-2pm and 5pm-10pm Fri., 5pm-10pm Sat., $20-30) now enjoys a reputation as Williamsport's finest Italian restaurant. Offerings range from simple wood-fired pizzas to wood-roasted rack of lamb.

The **Barrel 135 Wine Bar & Bistro** (135 W. 3rd St., Williamsport, 570/322-7131, www.barrel135.com, 11am-10pm Tues.-Thurs., 11am-midnight Fri.-Sat., 10am-2pm Sun., $10-31) is one of the trendier spots in Williamsport, offering sushi and small plates along with soups, salads, sandwiches, and dinner entrées.

Don't let memories of school cafeterias keep you from **Le Jeune Chef** (1 College Ave., Williamsport, 570/320-2433, www.pct.edu/lejeunechef, lunch 11:30am-1:30pm Mon.-Fri., dinner 5:30pm-8pm Wed.-Sat., $13-19) on the Pennsylvania College of Technology campus. The restaurant offers real-world training for students in the college's School of Hospitality and a fine-dining experience for patrons. Call or check the website to see if Le Jeune Chef—French for "the young chef"—is offering an à la carte menu or multicourse meal.

Freshly baked sticky buns make **Mr. Sticky's** (1948 E. 3rd St., Williamsport, 570/567-1166, www.mrstickys.net, 6am-7pm

the historic Genetti Hotel

Mon.-Thurs., 6am-8pm Fri.-Sat., under $10) a good choice for a sweet treat. Phil Poorman and his family opened the restaurant in 2003 after several years of peddling their buns from concession trailers. Now they serve soups, salads, and sandwiches on homemade rolls along with a few varieties of gooey buns.

Lock Haven

It's not much to look at, but the **Old Corner Grill and Bottle Shop** (205 N. Grove St., 570/748-4124, www.theoldcorner.com, 11am-midnight daily, bar closes at 2am, $5-9) is revered for its burgers cooked to order at budget prices. The neighborhood hang also serves soups, salads, sandwiches, wings, ribs, and takeout beer. It only has a few tables; grab a seat at the bar if you're dining in.

Dutch Haven Restaurant (201 E. Bald Eagle St., 570/748-7444, www.dutchhaven-restaurant.com, 11am-8:30pm Wed.-Thurs., 11am-9pm Fri., 5pm-9pm Sat., 9am-2pm Sun., $7-19) is more American than Pennsylvania Dutch (i.e., German), with burgers, chicken sandwiches, and crab cakes. Come Sunday, Dutch Haven puts on a buffet (adults $11, children 6-10 $6) of eggs, pancakes, ham, turkey, homemade sticky buns, and a whole lot more.

ACCOMMODATIONS

Chain hotels far outnumber boutique options in and around Williamsport. Even the historic Genetti Hotel is now a Best Western—though it retains its charm.

$100-250

The ★ **Genetti Hotel** (200 W. 4th St., Williamsport, 570/326-6600, www.genettihotel.com, $85-130) has welcomed the likes of Gene Kelly, Rita Hayworth, and Robert Kennedy since opening in 1922. The Williamsport landmark, now owned by Best Western, offers the comforts and amenities of a modern hotel along with a heaping of historic charm. Amenities include an outdoor pool and an American restaurant. It's as centrally located as it gets, next door to the Community Arts Center.

The **Peter Herdic Inn** (411 W. 4th St., Williamsport, 570/326-0411, www.herdichouse.com, $95-200), a beautifully restored mansion on Williamsport's Millionaires Row, has six guest rooms, including a two-room suite with a whirlpool tub. Expect great things at breakfast, which is included in weekend rates and may be available on weekdays for an extra charge. The innkeepers also own the Peter Herdic House Restaurant, one of the city's finest restaurants, next door.

Each of the 15 guest rooms at **City Hall Grand Hotel** (454 Pine St., Williamsport, 570/447-1010 www.cityhallgrandhotel.com, $109-179) recalls an event or time period in Williamsport history, from the Houdini Room, dedicated to a local appearance by the famed magician, to the Lumber Room. Rooms categorized "traditional" have carpet and soft colors. The industrial-feeling Hulk rooms, designed by a local construction company named Hulk, have furniture made from salvaged materials, wood floors, and open showers. The 1890s building, formerly

Williamsport's city hall, is in the National Register of Historic Places, and it's a popular place to set up shop: Businesses share the building with the hotel.

As remote and tranquil as its name suggests, the **Serene View Farm Bed & Breakfast** (80 Engle Mill Ln., Williamsport, 570/478-2477, www.sereneviewfarm.com, $135-180) sits on 128 acres of critter-filled woodlands and meadows about 20 miles northeast of Williamsport. The 1890s farmhouse has a wraparound porch complete with rocking chairs, a family room with an original working cookstove, and three homey guest rooms.

TRANSPORTATION AND SERVICES

Getting There and Around

Williamsport is about 85 miles north of the state capital of Harrisburg via Route 22 west and Routes 11 and 15 north. American Airlines flies to Philadelphia from **Williamsport Regional Airport** (IPT, www.flyipt.com). **Fullington Trailways** (888/847-2430, www.fullingtontours.com) provides intercity bus service between Williamsport and several cities in Pennsylvania, New Jersey, and New York.

Local bus service is available through **River Valley Transit** (570/326-2500, www.ridervt.com). For door-to-door service, call **Billtown Cab Co.** (570/322-2222).

Visitor Information

You can download a visitors guide to Williamsport and other Lycoming County communities from the website of the **Lycoming County Visitors Bureau** (102 W. 4th St., Williamsport, 570/327-7700, www.vacationpa.com, 8:30am-6pm Mon.-Fri., 8am-3pm Sat., 11am-3pm Sun.), or pop by its headquarters in downtown Williamsport for brochures.

For information about the Piper Aviation Museum and other attractions in Clinton County, Lycoming's neighbor to the west, visit the website of the **Clinton County Economic Partnership** (570/748-5782, www.clintoncountyinfo.com) and browse the Visitor's Bureau section.

Elk Country

Majestic elk once roamed throughout Pennsylvania. But as the human population increased in the mid-1800s, the elk population dwindled. By the end of the century, every last elk had fallen victim to unregulated hunting and habitat loss. Which is why it's no small matter that Pennsylvania is today home to the largest herd of free-roaming elk in the northeastern United States. The animals we see today are descendants of 177 Rocky Mountain elk from Yellowstone National Park and other parts that were released in Pennsylvania between 1913 and 1926. Now almost 1,000 elk make their home in an 835-square-mile range stretching across Elk, Cameron, and Clearfield Counties. The heart of the elk region is the remote village of Benezette, so tiny that elk-viewing visitors outnumber residents at times. The nearest city is St. Marys, a 20-mile drive from Benezette.

The best time to visit is during elk mating season, aka the rut. It starts in September and winds down in October. During the rut, elk country reverberates with the bugling of mature bulls. The piercing, startlingly high-pitched call is an invitation to cows and a challenge to rival bulls. Bulls battle for control of cow harems, locking antlers until the weaker of the two retreats. Much of the action takes place in the open, where it's easier for harem masters to stand guard. Bring binoculars and a camera with ample zoom capabilities; stay well clear of the frays.

In winter, snow and ice make the country

Elk FAQs

WHAT EXACTLY ARE ELK?

The elk is the second-largest member of the deer family in North America. The moose is larger. Good luck finding one of those in Pennsylvania.

HOW DO I DISTINGUISH ELK FROM WHITE-TAILED DEER?

For one thing, white-tailed deer are common throughout the Commonwealth. Free-roaming elk can be found only in a handful of counties in the Wilds region. Elk are much larger than white-tailed deer. A mature male elk, aka a bull, weighs 600-1,000 pounds. His female counterpart, aka a cow, is a relative featherweight at 500-600 pounds. Elk have the barest hint of a tail; white-tailed deer have longer tails with white undersides. Elk have darkish necks; white-tailed deer have a white throat patch. The antlers of bulls sweep backward; those of bucks (male deer) curve forward.

WHY CAN'T BULLS JUST GET ALONG?

Normally they do. For the bulk of the year, bulls roam on their own or in small "bachelor groups." It's not until mating season that they butt heads—literally. Their battles over the females rarely end in serious injury.

CAN I FEED THE ELK?

Absolutely not. In fact, Pennsylvania law prohibits it. Elk that are habituated to humans generally have shorter life spans than elk that steer clear of them. Think poachers. Think car-elk collisions.

HOW CLOSE CAN I COME TO THE ELK?

Elk will let you know how close is too close. When they sense danger, they raise their heads, cock their ears forward, and move stiffly. They sometimes bark to warn their comrades. Or they simply flee. Try not to make the elk flee. It ruins things for other viewers, and it stresses the elk. They're particularly vulnerable in wintertime, when they need every ounce of energy just to survive. And, of course, never do anything to provoke or threaten a 1,000-pound wild animal.

IF ELK ARE SO PRECIOUS, WHY ARE ELK BURGERS ON THE MENU?

That's a bigger question than this guidebook can tackle, but the short answer is the elk on a menu wasn't part of Pennsylvania's free-roaming herd. It was raised on a farm.

roads riskier and some areas inaccessible. The upside: If you find elk, you'll probably find a large number of them. The animals congregate in lower elevations, where they're more likely to find food. A good bet is to travel Route 555, which connects the villages of Weedville and Driftwood and passes through Benezette.

Elk continue to feed near streams in the spring, gradually moving out of the valleys as higher elevations green up. (If you have a mantel just begging for a pair of elk antlers, this is the time to go scavenger hunting. Bulls drop their antlers in late winter or early spring—finders keepers.)

Come summer, when food is plentiful throughout the range, it's unusual to see large groups of elk. The hottest months are the worst for elk viewing because the animals skulk in the relative coolness of dense forest. No matter when you visit, the best times to view elk are the first hour or two of daylight and just before dusk. That's when they're most likely to be grazing on legumes, grasses, and forbs in open fields.

★ BENEZETTE

The capital of elk country is the Route 555 village of Benezette. Elk can often be found near town (and occasionally in town) in large

part because the state and conservationists roll out the green carpet. Area forest openings are planted with alfalfa, clovers, and other food crops irresistible to elk. By attracting elk and other animals to clearings on public land, these buffets also serve human visitors hungry for wildlife sightings.

The **Elk Country Visitor Center** (950 Winslow Hill Rd., Benezette, 814/787-5167, www.experienceelkcountry.com, 8am-8pm daily June-Oct., 9am-5pm Thurs.-Mon. Apr.-May and Nov.-Dec., 9am-5pm Sat.-Sun. Jan.-Mar.), located just north of town off Winslow Hill Road, is a good place to start an elk-spotting adventure. It features exhibits about elk and wildlife conservation, a "4-D" theater (adults $3, children under 5 free) presenting a 22-minute show every half hour, and panoramic windows that look out at elk feeding areas. A series of trails and wildlife viewing areas is accessible from the center.

Continue along Winslow Hill from the visitors center, heading away from Benezette, and you'll soon arrive at two popular elk-viewing areas. The first is **Winslow Hill** (Winslow Hill Rd., 2.2 miles from Route 555 in Benezette). **Dents Run** (Winslow Hill Rd., 3.6 miles from Route 555 in Benezette) is another few minutes up the road. The vantage points overlook fields where many a bull have locked antlers to win the affections of cows. The fields are also visited by white-tailed deer, wild turkeys, foxes, and even bobcats and black bears. Scan the skies for hawks and other birds of prey.

Another premier viewing area, **Hicks Run,** is 12 miles east of Benezette on the north side of Route 555. The blind affords a front-row view of elk and other animals in a wide clearing planted with succulent snacks.

Driving in circles is rather effective as elk spotting goes. Try the following loop: From Benezette, follow Winslow Hill Road for 2.2 miles, turn right to stay on Winslow Hill Road, continue for 0.7 mile, and bear right at Summerson Road. Continue on Summerson to Route 555, and turn right to return to Benezette. Repeat as necessary.

If you spot elk while driving, don't stop in the middle of the road. Find a place to pull off, being careful to avoid shoulders near sharp bends and private driveways. (If you see cars parked along a road, it's safe to assume that elk are nearby.) Keep in mind that people who live in Benezette don't necessarily appreciate the growing wave of ecotourism. Don't go traipsing through private lands

Elk

without permission. And certainly don't honk if you find yourself in traffic.

ELK SCENIC DRIVE

Elk Scenic Drive is a 127-mile route peppered with 23 sites of interest to nature lovers, including the viewing areas near Benezette. It winds through three state forests and three state game lands, starting and ending at points on I-80. From the west, leave I-80 at Penfield exit 111 at Route 153. From the east, take Snow Shoe exit 147 at Route 144. Look for distinctive signage. You can download a map of the route on the website of the Pennsylvania Department of Conservation and Natural Resources (www.dcnr.pa.gov).

All but a few of the sites require diverging from the main route. The journey can take a few hours or a few days, depending on your level of interest in sites such as Kettle Creek State Park, with its 167-acre stocked trout lake. It's not unusual for animals to amble across roads, so drive carefully. Be especially alert when you see an "elk crossing" sign.

GUIDED ELK VIEWING

Spotting elk is never a sure thing, but you can stack the odds by hiring an experienced guide. Few know elk habits better than the husband-and-wife team behind **Hicks Run Outfitters** (814/787-4287, hicksrunoutfitters@yahoo.com). Jeff and Janet Colwell, along with Janet's daughter, Cody Ball, happily lead photographers, hunters, and anyone else seeking a close encounter of the elk kind off the beaten track. Call **PA Elk Range Adventures** (814/486-0305, http://paelkrangeadventures.tripod.com) to explore the range alongside nature photographer and writer and self-described hunting "addict" Phil Burkhouse.

STRAUB BREWERY

Elk aren't the only attraction in these parts. The city of St. Marys, a 20-mile drive from Benezette, is not only Pennsylvania's second-largest city by land area after Philadelphia but also the home of **Straub Brewery** (303 Sorg St., St. Marys, 814/834-2875, www.straubbeer.com). The award-winning brewery, family owned since 1872, has a fiercely loyal following in places where its beers can be found. Try it for yourself, for free: Come between 9am and 4:30pm on a weekday or Saturday (before 1pm Saturdays in winter) to drink from the keg known as the "eternal tap." Tours are also free and open to anyone 12 or older, but you need to reserve in advance. They're conducted 10:30am Tuesday through Friday and 12:30pm Thursday and Friday. The brewery's drive-up store is open 8:30am-8pm Monday-Saturday.

FOOD

When it comes to high-quality grazing, elk have it somewhat better than humans in these parts. Restaurants are few and far between and tend toward pub grub. But the pub grub is rather good in some cases.

Benezette

The **Benezette Hotel** (95 Winslow Hill Rd., 814/787-4240, www.benezettehotel.com, 11am-9pm daily, late-night menu 9pm-midnight daily, $5-20) is so centrally located that it's frequently referenced in directions to elk-viewing areas. It serves everything from pizza and wings to prime rib, along with beer and other beverages. Wrangle a table on the patio and you may spot a live one as you bite into an elk burger (or that might make you avoid the elk burgers altogether).

St. Marys

Gunners (33 S. St. Marys St., 814/834-2161, www.gunnerspa.com, 4pm-10pm Mon.-Sat., bar open until midnight Mon.-Thurs. and 1am Fri.-Sat., $11-28) hits the mark with a cheerful atmosphere and just-right steaks.

ACCOMMODATIONS

Cabins and lodges rented out by their owners through the websites HomeAway, Airbnb, and VRBO are the most plentiful lodging options in these parts, but there are a handful of

The World's Most Famous Groundhog

Groundhog Day in Punxsutawney

The resurrection of Pennsylvania's elk herd is a good story, but it's a different animal that grabs headlines year after year. That would be Punxsutawney Phil, the world's most famous weather forecaster (apologies to Al Roker). His hometown of Punxsutawney is a bit southwest of the elk range and more than a bit enamored of its renowned resident. Six-foot fiberglass effigies of the furry seer are scattered throughout town.

Unless you've been in a burrow for the last few decades, you probably know that Phil comes out of his hole every February 2, aka Groundhog Day, to predict if spring weather is around the bend or still weeks away. You may have seen him portrayed in *Groundhog Day,* the 1993 comedy starring Bill Murray. Maybe you caught him on *Oprah*. But Phil hasn't let the fame go to his head. Most days of the year, you'll find him at his pad in downtown Punxsy, **Phil's Burrow** at Punxsutawney Memorial Library (301 E. Mahoning St., 814/938-5020, www.punxsutawneylibrary.org). He and his groundhog entourage are visible from inside or outside.

The best time to visit, of course, is **Groundhog Day** (814/618-5591, www.groundhog.org). In the dark of night, thousands of people gather at **Gobbler's Knob** (1548 Woodland Ave. Ext.), a clearing just south of town, to await Phil's prognostication. He delivers it at daybreak. (Sadly, Phil himself does not address the crowd. That's left to men in top hats and bow ties who call themselves the Inner Circle.) The annual prediction is occasion for several days of festivities and activities, including the Groundhog Ball.

Punxsutawney also honors its favorite citizen in the summer with the weeklong **Punxsutawney Groundhog Festival** (814/938-2947, www.groundhogfestival.com, week of July 4), featuring free concerts, a craft show, and fireworks. The **Punxsutawney Chamber of Commerce** (102 W. Mahoning St., 814/938-7700, www.punxsutawney.com) hawks all things groundhog, from a fuzzy groundhog golf club cover to the official Groundhog Day Habanero Hot Sauce.

Are Phil's predictive abilities good enough to merit all the fuss? Members of the Inner Circle will tell you he's never wrong. They'll also tell you there's been only one Phil since the Knob tradition began in 1887. You can explore the science and lore of weather forecasting at the kid-centric **Punxsutawney Weather Discovery Center** (201 N. Findley St., 814/938-1000, www.weatherdiscovery.org, 10am-4pm Mon.-Sat. June-Aug., 10am-4pm Mon.-Tues. and Thurs.-Sat. Sept.-Dec. and Apr.-May, 10am-4pm Mon. and Thurs.-Sat. Jan.-Mar., adults $6, children under 2 free).

inns and bed-and-breakfasts in the Benezette area.

The cheery Jerome Powell Suite at the ★ **Towers Victorian Inn** (330 South St., Ridgway, 814/772-7657, www.towersinn.com, $85-149) pays tribute to the lumber baron who built the Italianate mansion in 1865. But the stateliest of guest accommodations is named for town founder Jacob Ridgway. The inn has a two-bedroom carriage house that sleeps as many as seven in addition to six rooms and suites in the main house. Hikers, bikers, and boaters can arrange for drop-off and pick-up service.

The three guest rooms at **Bennett House Bed and Breakfast** (14039 Rte. 555, Benezette, 814/787-4842, www.bennetthousepa.com, $100) are small and plain and the bathrooms shared, but the location is hard to beat. Hicks Run, one of the most prolific elk-viewing areas, is just two miles away.

Location is also a selling point at **Winslow Hill Bed & Breakfast** (2313 Winslow Hill Rd., Benezette, 814/787-4212, www.winslowhillbb.com, $135, cabin $150), next to the Winslow Hill elk-viewing area. The porch is perfect for soaking in the scenery. Five guest rooms each have a private bathroom. The owner also runs the adjacent Schoolhouse, a one-bedroom cabin with a full kitchen and living room.

The third-floor suite at the elegant **Victorian Loft Bed and Breakfast** (216 S. Front St., Clearfield, 814/765-4805, www.pawildsvacation.com, $120-150 double occupancy, children 3-17 additional $10 each), big enough for two or three couples, boasts a whirlpool tub overlooking the West Branch of the Susquehanna River. The second-floor guest room comes with a private balcony. Antique silver and china place settings greet breakfasters in the formal Victorian dining room. Innkeepers Tim and Peggy Durant also offer a one-bedroom pad in downtown Clearfield and a divinely secluded three-bedroom cabin in Moshannon State Forest.

The 10 modern cabins at ★ **Wapiti Woods** (5186 River Rd., Weedville, 814/787-7525, www.wapitiwoods.com, $175, weekly $1,050) boast wood-burning fireplaces, creek-facing porch entryways, and off-the-charts coziness. Five of the knotty pine masterpieces, designated the "romantic cabins," also have two-person whirlpool tubs. The peaceful retreat along the Bennett Branch of Sinnemahoning Creek has its very own wildlife-wooing feed plot.

Located on the same property as the Elk Country Visitor Center, the three-bedroom **Elk Mountain Homestead** (950 Winslow Hill Rd., Benezette, 814/787-5168, www.experienceelkcountry.com, $150-250, $220-$320 Sept.-Dec. and select holiday weekends, rates good for up to 6 people, $50 per night for each additional person) offers sweeping views of fields, woods, and wildlife. Proceeds from the rental of the state-owned farmhouse benefit conservation efforts. The house, which sleeps as many as 12 people, has a fully equipped kitchen, two showers, and a covered viewing platform. Light sleepers should consider shutting their windows in the fall, when bulls bugle all night long. That's an attraction, not a deterrent: Rates go up significantly in the prime elk and leaf peeping months.

Your majesty may enjoy a stay at **MacDarvey Castle** (153 Elk Terrace Dr., Benezette, 814/787-5356, www.macdarveycastle.com, $491 for two adults for two nights, two-night minimum), undoubtedly the most unusual lodging in elk country. Guests can gaze upon grazing elk from 67 windows or from one of the decks, entertain guests in the great hall, or feast in the dining room. You'll be king or queen of the castle whether you rent one bedchamber or all five; it's rented to just one group at a time. Dragon not included—nor are sheets, pillowcases, or towels.

TRANSPORTATION AND SERVICES

The main corridor through elk country is the east-west I-80. Benezette, its unofficial capital, is about 130 miles northeast of Pittsburgh via Route 28 north, I-80 east, and Routes 255 north and 555 east.

The closest airport with commercial service is **DuBois Regional Airport** (DUJ), about 40 miles southwest of Benezette. It's served by Southern Airways, with flights to Pittsburgh and Baltimore.

The **PA Great Outdoors Visitors Bureau** (2801 Maplevale Rd., Brookville, 814/849-5197, www.visitpago.com, 8:30am-4:30pm Mon.-Fri.) is a fount of elk-viewing tips and other information about the region.

Background

The Landscape

If you look at a map of the original 13 American colonies you will see that Pennsylvania is located right in the middle. The "Keystone State" was so named because Pennsylvania is geographically in the center of the arch formed by the other colonies, similar to the keystone that stonemasons put in the middle of an arch to hold the rest of the stones together. Today Pennsylvania is surrounded by the states of New York, New Jersey, Delaware, Maryland, West Virginia, and Ohio. It has a land area of 44,820 square miles, ranking 33rd among the 50 states, and has 1,239 square miles of water surface. Its highest point is at Mount Davis in Somerset County, 3,213 feet above sea level; its lowest point is at sea level, on the banks of the Delaware River outside Philadelphia.

It was for good reason that King Charles II of England in 1681 coined the name Pennsylvania, translated from Latin to mean "Penn's woods." When early Europeans first explored the eastern shores of North America they were awed by the vastness and density of the forest. Trees covered more than 90 percent of Pennsylvania's territory. The region's moderate climate, abundant rainfall, and rich soils gave rise to dense forests with plants and animals unknown to European settlers. A famed natural scientist named John Bartram was traveling up the Susquehanna River in 1743 and found forests so thick that "it seems almost as if the sun had never shown on the ground since the creation." Today, 17 million acres, almost 60 percent of the state, are forestland, and Pennsylvania is the nation's largest producer of hardwood lumber (over a billion board feet per year). The state forest system, comprising 2.2 million acres, is one of the largest public forest ownerships in the eastern United States.

GEOGRAPHY

The variety of natural landscapes in Pennsylvania is the result of millions of years of continents shifting and crashing into one another, creating the state's mountains and valleys. The Appalachian mountain range, which bisects present-day Pennsylvania, was formed some 480 million years ago and marks the first of several mountain-building plate collisions that culminated in the construction of the supercontinent Pangea, with the Appalachians near the center. The Appalachians once stood as tall as the modern-day Himalayas, and they were covered under large glaciations and vast oceans. Weathering and erosion prevailed as Pangea broke apart and the mountains began to wear away. By the end of the Mesozoic era (65 million years ago), the Appalachian Mountains had been eroded to an almost flat plain. It was not until the region was uplifted during the most recent geologic era that the distinctive present topography formed. Broad-topped mountains, called plateaus, include the Allegheny and Pocono ranges of the Appalachian Mountains.

From the Appalachian Mountains, the landscape slopes downward to the east and west, forming rolling hills and lowlands that make up the five major land regions. The largest of these land regions is the Appalachian Plateau, which covers most of western and northern Pennsylvania. This region, which includes the areas south and north of Pittsburgh, holds a big share of the state's natural resources; it was the location of the world's first successful oil well and a source of rich veins of coal. East

Previous: Independence Hall in Philadelphia; Gettysburg National Military Park.

of the Appalachian Plateau is the Appalachian Ridge and Valley, a region of narrow and steep mountain peaks and numerous valleys that resemble parallel arcs if viewed from space. The valleys of Cumberland, Lebanon, and Lehigh compose the Great Appalachian Valley, an area that stretches from the south-central border with Maryland to the eastern border with New Jersey. Farther southeast is the region called the Piedmont Plateau, an area of low hills, ridges, and valleys that has some of the richest farmland in the state and, some say, in the country. Due to the soil conservation techniques practiced by the Amish since the early colonial days, the area has remained agriculturally productive even through the industrial pillaging of the 19th and 20th centuries. The remaining two regions are close to water and the smallest regions of the five—the Atlantic Coastal Plain and the Erie Lowland (or Erie Plain). The Atlantic Coastal Plain covers the extreme southeastern corner of the state while the Erie Lowland covers the extreme northwestern corner.

The River Valleys

Three major river systems in Pennsylvania drain more than 90 percent of the state's land: the Delaware, Susquehanna, and the combined Allegheny, Ohio, and Monongahela Rivers. These river systems were important in the development of the state's transportation systems and industries such as steel and lumber. The Delaware River is the main river of the eastern part of the state and defines Pennsylvania's jagged eastern border. The river separates Pennsylvania from New York and New Jersey as it serpentines through narrow rapids and wide expanses from New York to the Delaware Bay. This is the same river of the famous "Delaware Crossing," an improvised boat crossing undertaken by George Washington's army during the American Revolution on Christmas Day 1776.

Due to its access to the Atlantic Ocean, the Delaware is a major shipping lane that is second only to the Mississippi River in the amount of commerce it carries each year. The Upper Delaware offers some of the finest recreational opportunities in the northeastern United States. In particular, sightseeing, boating, camping, hunting, fishing, hiking, and bird-watching are popular activities in the river area.

Running north to south through the central part of the state is the Susquehanna River, renowned for its fantastic fishing and recreation. Anglers can fish for muskies, walleye, smallmouth bass, panfish, catfish, and carp. The river meanders 444 miles from its origin near Cooperstown, New York, until it empties into the Chesapeake Bay at Havre de Grace, Maryland. In a similar north-to-south manner, the Allegheny River flows down the western portion of the state. This river begins as a spring in a farmer's field off of Route 49, a couple of miles east of the little town of Colesburg and nine miles from Coudersport in the upper Appalachian Mountains of northern Pennsylvania. The Allegheny River joins the Monongahela River in Pittsburgh to form the westward-pointing Ohio River, which eventually flows into the Mississippi.

CLIMATE

Pennsylvania is in the conflict zone between polar air masses from the north and tropical air masses from the south. These air masses create large temperature ranges that Pennsylvanians experience in four distinct seasons. Elevation and geological features can drastically vary the climate. The greatest weather extremes usually occur in the northeastern and north-central part of the state.

Winters usually bring snow to most of the state (more to the mountainous areas), with temperatures ranging from below zero Fahrenheit to the high 30s. The coldest time of the year is usually January, with northern latitudes recording colder temperatures and southeastern locations experiencing milder temperatures. In summer the temperature rarely breaks 100 degrees, yet the humidity is often high, especially in July and August. Evenings during the summer months cool down from their daytime highs, which average in the 80s in July. Spring and autumn are the best times to travel to Pennsylvania: The temperatures are moderate, and the state is covered in greenery in the spring and blanketed in brilliant colors in the autumn. The spring months of March through May see the temperatures slowly ramping up from an average of 40s to 70s, while the autumn months of September through November see the reverse.

The state averages 41 inches of precipitation each year, which helps trees and other plants grow abundantly. The greatest amount of precipitation usually occurs in spring and summer months, while February is the driest month. Thunderstorms, which average between 30 and 35 occurrences per year, are concentrated in the warm months and are responsible for most of the summertime rainfall. Sometimes tropical systems from the south (or their remnants) affect the state by causing flooding rains, especially in the eastern portion of the state. Tornadoes can and do occur, but they usually cause minor damage.

ENVIRONMENTAL ISSUES

When the first Europeans settled in Pennsylvania, the seemingly endless forest had many trees. Early settlers cut down many of these, either for timber or to clear areas for farming.

By 1900, Pennsylvania had lost more than 60 percent of its forests. Its polluted waterways, denuded landscapes, impoverished soils, extinct and disappearing plant and animal life, and foul air motivated new conservation and preservation ethics. Fears of a "timber famine" gave birth to a national conservation movement for the protection and rejuvenation of forests for future use. In the early 20th century, Pennsylvania passed laws to restrict the pollution of its waters and air, protect wildlife, and regulate extraction of natural resources. The state acquired more than four million acres of land and established 20 state forests for timber conservation, plant and wildlife preservation, and recreation. Unfortunately, most of the damage was done and is irreversible: Pennsylvania has lost as many as 156 native plant and animal species in the past 300 years. An additional 351 species have become endangered or threatened. Moreover, 56 percent of Pennsylvania's wetlands have been lost since 1780.

New threats emerged during the 20th century. By 1999, Pennsylvania led the nation in toxic discharges into its surface water, had the worst acid rain problem in the nation, and was the nation's largest importer of municipal waste. The state was second in the number of Superfund toxic waste sites, rate of suburban sprawl, and toxic air emissions from coal mining and processing; third in toxic air emissions from coal, oil, and electrical utilities; and fourth in the release of toxic chemicals from manufacturing. In the town of Centralia, an exposed seam of coal caught fire in 1961, forcing the entire community to flee the area; the underground fire continues to this day and is expected to burn for decades more. No single event drove home the potential costs of industry more than the accident at Three Mile Island, which in 1979 ended the American romance with nuclear energy. Yet the greatest danger to Pennsylvania's remaining wildlife is the risk of habitat destruction by sprawl: the building of parking lots, shopping malls, and houses.

Conservation efforts by the state and private organizations have made great strides in turning back the clock to the pre-European settlement days. Over the last century the Pennsylvania Game Commission has reintroduced beaver from Canada, elk from Wyoming, white-tailed deer from Michigan, cottontail rabbits from Kansas and Missouri, and quail from Mexico. Using the fees paid each year by hunters and fishers, the state has set up hatcheries and nurseries to restock streams and forests with shad, trout, ruffed grouse, pheasant, and other species. River otters, once ubiquitous across Pennsylvania before over-trapping and stream degradation, are thriving after being reintroduced throughout the state starting in the mid-1990s. Likewise, several bird species, such as the osprey, peregrine falcon, and bald eagle, are slowly increasing in population.

Plants and Animals

PLANTS

Pennsylvania is situated in the middle of the transitional zone between the great northern and southern forests of eastern North America. Here the mixed hardwoods of the southern forests (broadleaf oak, hickory, chestnut, and walnut) merge into mixed softwood and hardwood forests of the north (great white pine, hemlock, sugar maple, beech, and birch). The forest that you see today is largely the result of two things: the exploitation of timber at the turn of the 20th century, which devastated the old-growth trees, and 100 years of Mother Nature's forces and mankind's management. Various disturbances such as wind, fire, insects, disease, deer, and human intervention worked together to create the unique conditions for hardwood trees to become established and flourish (over 100 species of native trees and many others introduced from Europe and Asia). Pennsylvania's forests contain more hardwood growing stock than those of any other state, providing raw material for a forest-products industry that earns $5 billion per year while employing 90,000 people.

Located primarily in the north-central part of Pennsylvania are 20 sites that are designated "old-growth" or virgin forests. These forests contain trees that have attained great age (usually 300 to 400 years old) and exhibit characteristic features such as large trunk diameters. Most of the sites are within what is known as the Lumber Heritage Region, the 15 counties from which most of the timber resources were extracted in the 19th and early 20th centuries. Industrialization removed the majority of these trees; those that are left from that era are usually in areas that were inaccessible, such as steep slopes, or accidents of boundary overlaps. Within Cook Forest State Park are nine different old-growth forest areas covering more than 2,200 acres. Every fall, the state's deciduous trees put on a blaze of glory along the highways and country roads, with rich and vibrant hues of red, orange, yellow, and brown.

Spring in Pennsylvania brings abundant rainfall and glorious blooms of native wildflowers and flowering shrubs. Throughout spring, yellow forsythia, azaleas, rhododendrons, trilliums, elderberries, honeysuckles, and mountain laurels bring splashes of color to the state's forests, fields, and roadsides. This colorful display brings thousands of tourists from the Commonwealth and surrounding states each spring. Mountain laurel, the state flower of Pennsylvania, normally begins to bloom late in May, and its pink and white blossoms are in evidence well into June. It is particularly abundant in the mountainous sections of the state, particularly the Laurel Highlands in the south and the Allegheny Mountains in the northeast. The distinctive plant, with its three- to five-inch lustrous, dark green leaves, is used extensively as ornamental shrubbery. Pennsylvania's climate also ensures wild berries such as cranberries, blackberries, thimbleberries, strawberries, and elderberries throughout the early spring and into the fall season. Wild strawberries, noticeable by their smaller size compared to their cultivated cousins, can be seen in early May through June throughout the state. High-bush cranberries grow in northern Pennsylvania and can be recognized by their three-lobed leaves and large seeds.

ANIMALS

The white-tailed deer, the official state animal, is undoubtedly one of the most influential species of wildlife in Pennsylvania. Deer provide value to Pennsylvanians as watchable wildlife, a huntable resource, and a source of venison for countless families. Much of Pennsylvania's rural cultural heritage is closely linked to this species. Around 1900, the Game Commission estimated that only about 500 white-tailed deer remained in the state. The commission began bringing deer from Michigan and Kentucky in 1906 and continued through the 1920s. Seeing a deer in the forest (or in the headlights) is no longer a rare event in much of Pennsylvania, so keep a lookout along roads. Along with deer, the garden variety of forest critters are commonly seen in Pennsylvania, including: wild rabbits, black and gray squirrels, raccoons, foxes, minks, opossums, skunks, and woodchucks. Beavers, once nearly extinct due to over-trapping (prime pelts netted $65 each in colonial times), are now abundant in each county. Less common, but still found around campsites and cabins, are black bears, which are mostly found in the north-central and northeastern counties of the state. Black bear attacks in the eastern United States are rare, though bears dependent on human food can become aggressive when people get between them and food. Rarer still are bobcats, which live in northern mountain habitats.

Between 1913 and 1926, the Pennsylvania Game Commission attempted to restore the state's elk herd by releasing 177 western elk from Wyoming. In 2017, there were about 1,000 elk in Pennsylvania, typically found in southwestern Cameron and southeastern Elk Counties. Elk are much larger than white-tailed deer: Adult males weigh 600-1,000 pounds with a height of about five feet. Males usually sport a set of backward-curving antlers that can have as many as 16 points, while females are somewhat smaller and antlerless. Elk coats can vary from dark brown to reddish, depending on the season, yet a large buff-colored patch covering the rump is its characteristic signature. Elk are best observed at dawn and dusk, in September and October during the mating season, and from a safe distance. They can be very dangerous, especially bulls during the mating season.

Snakes

Most snakes in Pennsylvania are harmless, although there are three native poisonous snake species that inhabit the state (northern copperheads, timber rattlesnakes, and the eastern massasauga rattlesnake). All these venomous snakes possess an indentation or pit on each side of the head between the eye and nostril, a vertically elliptical eye pupil resembling that of a cat, and a single row of scales on the underside of the tail. Reports of venomous snakebites in the state are rare, with bites usually occurring while a person is trying to catch or carelessly handle one of these snakes. All of these species are usually nonaggressive and prefer to avoid confrontation, usually moving away from an approaching human or remaining completely still as a threat passes by.

Birds

Bird-watching, or birding, has become a popular activity in Pennsylvania thanks to the 414 species of birds recorded here. The largest number and species of birds may be found during May, when migration for most long-distance migrants is well under way. In some locations more than 150 species have been recorded in 24 hours; these include flycatchers, wrens, thrushes, and orioles. Birdsong all but ends in August, when the nesting season is usually over for most species. The ruffed grouse, the state bird, is easily recognized by its territorial drumming and the roar of its wings when it takes flight. Distinguishable characteristics include a plump body, feathered legs, and mottled reddish-brown color. Great horned owls, the largest and most widely distributed resident owl in Pennsylvania, are powerful birds of prey that feed on a wide variety of mammals and birds. They are most often detected when vocalizing during the mating and breeding season in fall through winter. A nesting female may sit on eggs through the worst of weather and sometimes is seen covered with snow.

In the Water

With 83,184 miles of streams and rivers and more than 4,000 lakes and ponds, Pennsylvania has no shortage of game fish, including trout, bass, muskie, walleye, steelhead, and panfish. The Susquehanna River and its tributaries feature wild and stocked trout and smallmouth bass. Potter County boasts a huge collection of Class A wild trout streams, while Oil Creek State Park offers excellent fly-fishing for walleye and smallmouth bass. Lake Erie is sometimes called the freshwater fishing capital of the world thanks to its trout, perch, walleye, smallmouth bass, northern pike, and muskie. In recent years, more attention has been given to the threat of nonnative species and the impact these species have on native wildlife within the lake. Nonnative fish (e.g., round goby) and invertebrates such as the zebra mussel or rusty crayfish are found in high densities in the Lake Erie drainage and may be seriously impacting native fauna by eliminating them from their former ranges.

One positive trend in wetland wildlife is the increase in river otters, whose population had drastically declined in the state because of fur trapping and stream degradation. Through a state reintroduction program that started in 1982, more than 150 river otters have been released in Pennsylvanian rivers and streams. Otters were reintroduced in several watersheds across northern Pennsylvania and as far south as the lower Susquehanna River and Youghiogheny River. You might notice a river otter due to its playful antics, particularly its practice of repeatedly sliding down stream banks into the water. Amphibians such as frogs, salamanders, and turtles can also be seen throughout the state. One turtle in particular, the bog turtle, is a 3-4-inch-long species usually found in southeastern and eastern Pennsylvania. Development and selfish collectors who find them irresistibly cute have decimated their population, and as a result they have received federal threatened status. Eastern hellbenders, large and wondrously ugly amphibians, are usually found in the western part of the state and can live to be 30 to 50 years old. They are a superb indicator of the health of the environment; because they prefer clean and clear-flowing rivers and streams, they can provide an early warning of when an ecosystem is in trouble.

History

ANCIENT CIVILIZATION

The first people to live in Pennsylvania were part of the earliest waves of human migration that came during the end of the last ice age (about 30,000 to 10,000 years ago), when lower ocean levels exposed the Bering Land Bridge between Siberia and Alaska. These Paleo-Indians, as archaeologists call them, were a nomadic hunter-gatherer tribe that fashioned tools from stone, bone, and wood in order to hunt mammoths, elk, and moose but did not plant crops or build permanent dwellings. The Meadowcroft Rockshelter, a Paleo-Indian archaeological site 30 miles southwest of Pittsburgh, shows evidence of human occupation possibly as early as 16,000 years ago, meaning it may be the earliest documented site of human occupation in North America. About 13,000 years ago the glaciers in the northeastern and northwestern parts of the state began to recede. During the Archaic Period (8000-1000 BC), as the climate slowly got warmer, Indian hunter-gatherers continued to seek shelter at Meadowcroft, but their technology diversified and they began to hunt deer, elk, bear, and turkey in deciduous forests with a rich understory of berries and other plant foods.

Several sites have yielded arrowheads, stone axes, sinkers for fishing nets, and other Archaic Period artifacts. By the Late Woodland Period (AD 1000-1500), there were two major Indian population centers along the major river systems of the Delaware and the Susquehanna. The northern and southern parts of the Delaware Valley were inhabited by the Lenapes or Delawares. To the west, close to modern-day Lancaster County, the northern Susquehanna Valley was home to Iroquoian-speaking peoples called the Susquehannocks. Numerous tribes, which can't be identified with certainty, inhabited western Pennsylvania before the Europeans arrived but were eliminated by war and disease in the 17th century. The Iroquois Nation, a confederacy of numerous tribes, lived mostly in present-day New York but traveled to present-day northern Pennsylvania to hunt.

EUROPEAN EXPLORATION AND SETTLEMENT

The age of discovery in Europe brought a desire for territorial gains beyond the seas, first by Spain and Portugal and later by England, France, the Netherlands, and Sweden. Captain John Smith, famous for establishing the Jamestown settlement, journeyed from Virginia up the Susquehanna River in 1608, visiting the Susquehannock people. In 1609 Henry Hudson, an Englishman in the Dutch service, sailed the *Half Moon* into Delaware Bay and made contact with the Lenape, thus giving the Dutch a claim to the area. Not until 1640, however, did the Dutch establish their first trading post at Fort Nassau (near present-day New Jersey), which soon developed a fairly prosperous exchange of Dutch items for Indian beaver pelts. Surprisingly, the Swedes were the first to establish a settlement in the Delaware Bay area, called New Sweden, beginning with the expedition of 1637-1638, which established a small colony of Swedes near the current site of Wilmington, Delaware. Governor Johann Printz of New Sweden relocated the capital to Tinicum Island in 1643, which was 20 miles south of present-day Philadelphia. There he directed a rough band of conscripts, army deserters, and debtors to build new blockhouses and log cabins as well as a new fort that aimed four cannons at a Dutch trading station. In the 1640s, Holland and Sweden were at peace, yet competition in the fur trade created ongoing tensions between Printz and his Dutch counterpart, Peter Stuyvesant, governor of New Netherlands. After some skirmishes between the two groups, the settlers lived and worked together peaceably and established an effective legal system that punished crimes via fines rather than imprisonment.

In 1664 King Charles II of England decided to give all the land between Connecticut and Maryland to his brother, James, Duke of York. As a result of this declaration, the Dutch decided to seize the Hudson and Delaware Valleys, in spite of English claims to these regions. During the war that followed, the British captured New Amsterdam, whose name they changed to New York, and English laws and civil government were introduced to the region in 1676. By 1680, Pennsylvania included Swedes (the largest nationality in the region) along with lesser numbers of Dutch, Finnish, German, French, Welsh, and English settlers.

WILLIAM PENN AND THE QUAKERS

During the late 17th century, England was undergoing religious upheaval as Protestants persecuted Catholics, Catholics persecuted Protestants, and both persecuted other religious beliefs. A new Protestant sect called the Religious Society of Friends came in the spotlight due to its rejection of rituals and oaths, its opposition to war, and its simplicity of speech and dress. Outsiders tended to call the followers of this sect Quakers because they were said to quake and tremble when they rose to speak during their religious services. George Fox, the radical preacher credited with founding the Quakers, was decried a heretic, and his followers were widely persecuted and imprisoned. William Penn, a charismatic young aristocrat who frequented the king's court and was trusted by the Duke of York (later known as King James II), embraced Fox's teachings. Despite high social rank, Penn shocked his upper-class associates with his conversion to Quaker beliefs that insisted God valued each individual equally—a drastic change to the British class system. King Charles II of England owed a large sum of money to Penn's late father, who was an admiral in the Royal Navy. Seeking a haven in the New World for persecuted Quakers, Penn asked the king to grant him land in the territory between Lord Baltimore's province of Maryland and the Duke of York's province of New York. With the duke's support, Penn's petition was granted. By giving Penn a colony, the king managed to pay off an outstanding debt and at the same time get rid of a group of people who challenged English laws and the legitimacy of the Anglican Church, the nation's established church. On March 4, 1681, King Charles II of England granted 45,000 square miles of land, an area almost as large as England itself. King Charles named the new colony "Penn's woods" (in Latin, Pennsylvania) in honor of the admiral.

The old manorial system in Europe was breaking down, creating a large class of landless people ready to seek new homes. Wars in southern Germany caused many Germans to migrate to Pennsylvania. The Reformation led to religious ferment and division, not only with Quakers, Puritans, and Catholics from England, but with Pietists, Mennonites, and Lutherans from the Rhineland, Scotch Calvinists via Ireland, Amish from Switzerland, and Huguenots from France. Penn guaranteed the settlers of his new "Holy Experiment" freedom of religious worship, yet Pennsylvania's charter restricted the right to vote and to hold political office only to Protestants. In addition, Penn's Holy Experiment did not extend the protections of his charter to enslaved Africans and African Americans.

CITY OF BROTHERLY LOVE

Penn's first visit to Pennsylvania in 1682 brought 100 prospective colonists, one-third of whom would die after smallpox broke out during the voyage. His ship, the *Welcome,* was the first of a fleet of 23 ships that carried more than 2,000 men, women, and children to Pennsylvania in the next year. The capital (named Philadelphia, or City of Brotherly Love) was established on a sparsely settled peninsula at the confluence of the Schuylkill and Delaware Rivers. The peninsula was also one of the original three counties, along with Bucks and Chester. Rather than occupy the land without consent of the Lenape people, Penn wrote letters and met with Lenape chiefs, asking permission to "enjoy the land with your love and consent."

The capital city of Philadelphia laid claim to most of Penn's attention during his first months. He appointed a surveyor general and immediately directed him to lay out "a greene country town where every house be placed in the middle of the plot, so that there may be ground on each side, for gardens, or orchards or fields and so that it will never be burnt, and always be wholesome." Penn also called for the creation of parks by directing that "four squares be set aside for physical recreation" and that a "ten-acre Center square be reserved for a House of Public Affairs." In addition, he mandated that land for "Publick Houses" be set aside on every block as community gathering places. A city grid pattern was developed that set precedent for future American towns; streets running east-west were to be named after trees, and those running north-south were to be numbered. During his second visit in 1699-1701, Penn lived at a country estate he had built north of Philadelphia on the Delaware River that was known as Pennsbury Manor. Forced to return to England in 1700 to protect his control of the colony from the government and required to remain there because of poor health, Penn spent only five years in Pennsylvania over his two visits. But his colony paved the path for the future of the young American republic by providing a democratic form of government and a legacy of toleration, which can still be seen in the First Amendment's protection of religious liberty. Thanks to its central position in the colonies and its wealth, Philadelphia became the largest and most important city in the colonies by the time of the American Revolution.

EXPANSION AND THE COLONIAL WARS

As immigrants arrived in waves to North America, many were drawn to Pennsylvania by its reputation as "the best poor man's country," since the land was cheap and plentiful, taxes were low, and no state church hounded religious dissenters. The vast majority of these immigrants stepped ashore in the Delaware River ports of Philadelphia or New Castle (in present-day Delaware), yet they did not stay there for long. The quickest way to acquire property and independent livelihood was to move west, into the frontier region of the lower Susquehanna Valley. This westward expansion intruded on Native Americans who had only recently settled in the area, already displaced by expanding colonial populations elsewhere. In diplomatic councils with colonial leaders, these Indians often reminded their counterparts of William Penn's pledge to always deal peacefully and fairly with them; unfortunately, Penn's successors were not so principled. In the Walking Purchase of 1737, the Lenape agreed to give away the amount of land a person could walk in a one day. The colonists cheated by hiring athletes to run in relays, covering much more land than the Lenape thought they were giving away.

In 1753 and 1754, the French sent troops south from their Canadian territory to occupy and claim the Ohio Valley. George Washington failed to persuade the French to leave, and in 1754 they defeated his militia company at Fort Necessity, about 10 miles southeast of present-day Uniontown. Washington's humiliating defeat touched off an international crisis that in North America became known as the French and Indian War, which pitted the British versus French and Indian forces. While this war had many theaters around the globe, much of its blood and treasure were spilled in western Pennsylvania at French forts at Erie (Fort Presque Isle), Waterford (Fort LeBoeuf), Pittsburgh (Fort Duquesne), and Franklin (Fort Machault). In 1755, General Edward Braddock led a British army into the Pennsylvania wilderness to take Fort Duquesne, only to be decimated by French and Indian forces. British might returned in force in 1758 when General John Forbes cut his own route across southern Pennsylvania from Carlisle to the Forks of the Ohio, forcing the French to abandon Fort Duquesne and making possible the construction of Fort Pitt, a fortress designed to cement British supremacy in the region. After the war, the Native Americans were disillusioned with the British, and Ottawa war chief Pontiac sparked a widespread resistance movement known as Pontiac's Rebellion. Pennsylvania, a state known for its peaceful relations, had become a killing ground. Two military campaigns in 1763 and 1764 by Colonel Henry Bouquet brought the hostilities to an end at the Battle of Bushy Run and a subsequent punitive expedition against the Delawares and Shawnee in the Ohio Country. As the 1760s gave way to the Revolutionary Era, the British would find that governing an American empire was more difficult than conquering one.

THE REVOLUTIONARY WAR

The First Continental Congress met in Philadelphia in 1774 to protest commercial restrictions and taxes levied on the colonies. By the time the Second Continental Congress convened in May 1775, the opening salvo of the War for American Independence had already been fired in Massachusetts, and Pennsylvania joined the 12 other colonies in a war against Great Britain for national liberation. During the American Revolution, the Pennsylvania State House—today known as Independence Hall—became the center for the wartime business of the new United States government, except when the British threat caused the capital to be moved successively. While Congress was sitting in York, Pennsylvania (October 1777-June 1778), it approved the Articles of Confederation, the first step toward a national government. The final military victory at Yorktown, Virginia, in 1781 ensured political independence, greater social equality, and more economic freedom.

But at the end of the war, Pennsylvanians, like the rest of American people, still had to determine how to govern themselves and how to adapt to the new, more egalitarian society that was taking shape in the new nation.

By the end of the war, Pennsylvania had won control of the disputed areas in its northeast section and received title to most of the disputed lands in western Pennsylvania, extinguishing all Native American claims to their lands within the state. Pennsylvania became the first state to begin the gradual abolition of slavery; by 1800, all but 55 of Philadelphia's more than 6,400 blacks were free. Philadelphia grew in importance as the nation's financial and cultural center, as well as its temporary capital while Washington DC was being constructed. The city boasted the nation's first museum (1786), first stock exchange (1791), first paved road and turnpike (1792), the largest public building (the State House), and largest market.

INDUSTRIALIZATION AND THE CIVIL WAR

Into the 1790s, large areas of the northern and western parts of the state were undistributed or undeveloped. The state adopted generous land policies and distributed free "Donation Lands" to Revolutionary veterans. The immigrant tide into the state increased as Irish fled the potato famine of the late 1840s and Germans fled the political turbulence of their homeland. In 1820 more than 90 percent of the working population was involved in agriculture, and by 1840 more than 77 percent of the 4.8 million employed persons in Pennsylvania were in agriculture. As agriculture began to decline into the 1860s, there was increased industrialization as Pennsylvania became the leading iron manufacturer in the nation. The state was blessed with iron ore deposits, vast forests that provided charcoal, abundant coal beds that also supplied fuel, limestone used as flux, and streams for water power. By 1861, the factory system became the foundation of the state's industrial greatness. Leather-making, lumbering, shipbuilding, publishing, and tobacco and paper manufacture all prospered throughout the 1800s.

The expression "underground railroad" may have originated in Pennsylvania, where numerous citizens, especially Quakers, aided the escape of slaves to freedom in Canada. During the Civil War, Pennsylvania played an important role in preserving the Union; Confederate forces invaded Pennsylvania three times by way of the Cumberland Valley, a natural highway from Virginia to the North. Pennsylvania's railroad system, iron and steel industry, and agricultural wealth were essential to the economic strength of the Union. In June 1863, General Robert E. Lee turned his 75,000 men northward across the Mason-Dixon Line and into Pennsylvania. Confederate forces captured Carlisle, Pennsylvania, and advanced to within three miles of Harrisburg. In a bitterly fought engagement at Gettysburg, the Union army threw back the Confederate forces in the war's bloodiest battle, marking the major turning point in the struggle to save the Union.

With the end of the war came an era of industrialization led by entrepreneurs who built the mills, mines, and factories of the late 19th century. Businessmen like Henry Clay Frick, Andrew Carnegie, Joseph Wharton, and William Scranton amassed fortunes as the coming of mass-produced steel in the 1870s created a modern industrial society in Pennsylvania. These new mills, mines, and factories created a labor shortage. While most of the state's pre-1861 population was composed of ethnic groups from northern Europe, the later period brought increased numbers of Slavic, Italian, Scandinavian, and Jewish immigrants. Between 1900 and 1910, during the height of this "new immigration," Pennsylvania witnessed the largest population increase of any decade in its history. Several important labor struggles took place in the state, such as the Homestead Steel Strike of 1892, igniting the birth of the modern labor union movement.

THE WORLD WARS

As an industrial state, Pennsylvania followed a predictable course that involved devastating economic slumps and financially invigorating wars throughout the 20th century. Although the state continued to be an industrial powerhouse, its national prominence began to subside as economic development became more widespread into the western and the southern parts of the country. Pennsylvania's resources and manpower were of great value in World War I, as shipyards in Philadelphia and Chester were decisive in maintaining maritime transport. African American migration from the South intensified after 1917, when World War I restricted European immigration, and again during World War II.

The effects of the Great Depression were drastic: 24 percent of the state's workforce was unemployed in 1931, with the rate rising to 37 percent by 1933. Only the production demands of World War II, which began in Europe in 1939, restored vitality to the state's economy. Tagged as the "Arsenal of America," Pennsylvania factories poured out planes, tanks, armored cars, fuel, and guns. A steady stream of war goods flowed over the state's railroads and highways. It's estimated that one out of every seven members of the armed forces in World War II was a Pennsylvanian. In 1940 the commonwealth was the second most populous state, after New York.

Pennsylvania played a key role in the development of major technologies from the late 19th century into the 20th century. George Westinghouse, an American entrepreneur and engineer based in Pittsburgh, invented the railway air brake and was a pioneer in the electrical industry. Westinghouse's electrical distribution system, which used alternating current based on the extensive research by Nikola Tesla, made it possible to provide electricity to the nation's homes and factories. The state became a center for electronics during World War II, when the first computer, ENIAC, was constructed at the University of Pennsylvania in Philadelphia. The first all-motion-picture theater in the world was opened on Smithfield Street in Pittsburgh on June 19, 1905, where the term "nickelodeon" was coined. The first commercial radio broadcast station in the world was KDKA in Pittsburgh, which started daily scheduled broadcasting on November 2, 1920.

CONTEMPORARY TIMES

After World War II the coal, steel, and railroad industries declined considerably in Pennsylvania. Oil and natural gas were by then preferable to coal for heating buildings, while the railroads were losing ground to the growing trucking industry. The state's steel production began to contract in 1963, although the nation's output, stimulated by the Vietnam War, rose to its all-time maximum in 1969 of 141 million tons. The decline in manufacturing jobs has been followed with an increase in education and health services as well as high-tech industry jobs.

Although the state continues to be one of the largest coal-producing states in the nation, a natural gas boom spurred by the Marcellus Shale that covers two-thirds of the state is creating new economic opportunities. Both Philadelphia and Pittsburgh, along with numerous other Pennsylvania cities, are undergoing revitalization efforts to reclaim abandoned or underused industrial and commercial facilities and are trying to reverse the "brain drain" of talented people moving out of the state. Newly constructed sports stadiums, convention centers, and art centers have attracted new businesses, which in turn have brought hotels, restaurants, and housing to previously blighted sections. This transformation is also seen in the landscape, as once-polluted rivers become viable for fishing and recreation and unused railways are converted to trails.

People and Culture

DEMOGRAPHY

Pennsylvania's 2016 population was estimated at 12.78 million, up from 12.70 million in 2010, making it the fifth most populous state in the country. Eighty percent of Pennsylvania's current population growth comes from international immigration, and 20 percent from the excess of births over deaths among residents. The number of people leaving Pennsylvania each year is larger than the number moving here from other states, so domestic migration is not a positive factor in the state's population growth.

Although most of Pennsylvania is rural, about 70 percent of the population lives in urban areas.

Pennsylvania's population has been growing older. The median age increased to 40.7 years in 2015 from 38 years in 2000. An estimated 17.4 percent of the population was 65 or older in 2016.

RACE AND ETHNICITY

According to the 2010 census, the racial composition of the state is about 82 percent white, 12 percent black or African American, and 3 percent Asian. About 7 percent of Pennsylvanians identify as Hispanic or Latino. The percentage of black or African American residents is slightly below the national average of 13 percent, and the percentage of Hispanic or Latino residents is considerably lower than the national average of 16 percent. Philadelphia County has the state's highest concentrations of black or African American and Hispanic or Latino residents. (Black or African American residents represent about 44 percent of the county's population. About 13 percent of residents identify themselves as Hispanic or Latino.)

The largest number of Pennsylvanians identify their ancestry as German, followed by Irish, Italian, English, and Polish. The late 19th and early 20th centuries brought increased numbers of Slavic, Scandinavian, and Jewish immigrants from the eastern Mediterranean and Balkan regions. Many of the new immigrants settled in the east-central and Ohio Valley regions, where coal-mining jobs were plentiful. You can still find ethnic enclaves throughout the state. In 2015, Pennsylvania's foreign-born population was about 800,500, or 6 percent of the total population, which was less than the national average of 13 percent.

RELIGION

According to the Pew Research Center, 73 percent of adults in Pennsylvania identify as Christian. Six percent are Jewish, Muslim, Buddhist, Hindu, or another world religion. Two percent are unaffiliated and 14 percent are categorized as "nothing in particular."

Pennsylvania Germans belonged largely to the Lutheran and Reformed churches, but there were also several smaller sects, such as German Baptist Brethren or "Dunkers," Schwenkfelders, and Moravians, the largest groups of which are the Amish and Mennonites. Lancaster County has the second-largest Amish settlement in the country after Holmes County in Ohio. Other Amish settlements can be found in Mifflin, Indiana, and Lawrence Counties.

LANGUAGE

As in other states in the United States, English is the dominant language in Pennsylvania. The 2000 census shows that 10,583,054 Pennsylvanians—91.6 percent of the population five years old or older—speak only English at home. Two distinctive dialects are noticeable when listening to native Pennsylvanians. One of these is the Midland dialect, which is the foundation for speech across the midwestern and western United States. In the northern counties of the state you hear predominantly the

Northern dialect, which has its origins in upstate New York State. In much of south-central Pennsylvania, descendants of the colonial Palatinate German population retain their speech as Deutsch, often misnamed Pennsylvania Dutch. Travels around the state will show that names of numerous rivers and towns have Native American origins, such as Punxsutawney, Aliquippa, Pocono, Towanda, Susquehanna, and Shamokin.

Essentials

Transportation

AIR

Philadelphia International Airport (PHL, 215/937-6937, www.phl.org), the only major airport serving Pennsylvania's largest city, is by far the busiest airport in the state. More than 30 million passengers pass through it every year. But seasoned travelers will find it quaint in comparison to airports in Atlanta, Chicago, Los Angeles, Miami, and other major cities. It's served by 25 passenger airlines, including low-cost airlines Frontier, JetBlue, Southwest, and Spirit, and it's a primary hub for American Airlines. You'll want to price flights to Philadelphia even if your ultimate destination is Pennsylvania Dutch Country or the Pocono Mountains because your savings could be significant. Smaller airports in the eastern half of the state include **Harrisburg International Airport** (MDT), **Lehigh Valley International Airport** (ABE, 800/359-5842, www.lvia.org) in Allentown, and **Wilkes-Barre/Scranton International Airport** (AVP, 570/602-2000, www.flyavp.com).

Pittsburgh International Airport (PIT, 412/472-3525, www.flypittsburgh.com) is Pennsylvania's second-busiest airport. It's what the Federal Aviation Administration calls a "medium hub," meaning it's rarely a madhouse. It's served by about a dozen passenger airlines, including low-cost airlines Frontier, JetBlue, Southwest, and Spirit. It's a good idea to price flights to Pittsburgh even if you're bound for the Alleghenies or the Lake Region. Smaller airports in the western half of Pennsylvania include **University Park Airport** (SCE) in State College and **Erie International Airport** (ERI, 814/833-4258, www.erieairport.org).

CAR

Pennsylvania is an easy drive from cities including New York, Baltimore, and the U.S. capital of Washington DC. Its major north-south highways are **I-81** in the eastern part of the state and **I-79** in the western part. I-81 enters Pennsylvania from Maryland and passes through or by the cities of Carlisle, Harrisburg, Wilkes-Barre, and Scranton before continuing north into New York State. I-79 enters Pennsylvania from West Virginia, passes by Pittsburgh, and ends in Erie.

Pennsylvania's main east-west highway is the 360-mile **Pennsylvania Turnpike** mainline (I-76/I-70/I-276), which connects the Pittsburgh, Harrisburg, and Philadelphia areas. It's about five hours from Philadelphia to Pittsburgh via the turnpike, which is a toll highway. When you enter the turnpike, you pick up a ticket listing the toll for each exit. Be sure not to misplace the ticket; if you do, you'll have to pay the maximum toll at your exit. You'll save money and a bit of time if you have an E-ZPass transponder. E-ZPass is an electronic toll-collection system used on most tolled roads in the northeastern United States. The transponder allows you to enter the turnpike without stopping for a ticket and exit without stopping to pay. Any tolls you incur will be deducted from your prepaid E-ZPass account. You can sign up for E-ZPass at www.paturnpike.com, by phone at 877/736-6727, at all Pennsylvania Turnpike service plazas, and at select retail locations across the state. As of late 2017, it cost $51.60 cash to drive the length of the mainline westbound versus $37.14 using E-ZPass—a savings of nearly 30 percent. Pennsylvania Turnpike tolls are increased each year. If you don't have an E-ZPass transponder, be sure to have some

Previous: 30th Street Station in Philadelphia; parking sign in Amish Country.

cash in your wallet, and steer clear of lanes marked "E-ZPass Only."

You don't have to exit the turnpike to grab a bite. There are 15 service plazas along the mainline and two more on the turnpike's Northeast Extension (I-476), which connects the Philadelphia, Lehigh Valley, and Scranton/Wilkes-Barre areas. In addition to dining options, plazas offer fuel and restrooms. Many have gift shops and picnic areas. All plazas are open 24 hours.

It is possible to travel across the southern part of Pennsylvania without paying any tolls. **U.S. Route 30** passes through Pittsburgh, the Laurel Highlands, Bedford, Gettysburg, York County, Lancaster County, and Philadelphia on its way from the West Virginia line east to New Jersey.

I-80 is the major east-west roadway across northern Pennsylvania. It doesn't serve any major cities in Pennsylvania. **U.S. Route 6** is the choice for an exceptionally scenic drive across northern Pennsylvania. Visit www.paroute6.com for trip ideas.

In 2010 the American Society of Civil Engineers (ASCE) gave Pennsylvania's roads the grade of D-minus, down from a D four years earlier, warning that "many of the state's roads are at or have exceeded their design capacity." Pennsylvania has some of the oldest highways in the country, and truck traffic on its interstates is more than double the national average. ASCE's Report Card for Pennsylvania's Infrastructure also noted that Pennsylvania has more road miles than nearly any other state that contends with severe winters, which take a heavy toll on pavements. Maintaining the extensive road system is a costly and Sisyphean endeavor.

Traffic can be severely hampered by snow and ice in the coldest months and road construction in the warmer ones. Motorists should take extreme care in winter, especially on steep or winding roads. Heavy snow can render minor roads impassable. Road crews are one of the first signs of spring in Pennsylvania. Where there are crews, there are often road or lane closures, decreased speed limits, and increased police presence.

Safety Laws

Nothing ruins a perfectly good day like a traffic ticket—or worse yet, an accident—so pay close attention to posted speed limits and other traffic signs. It's especially important in areas with road construction. If you're caught speeding or violating other traffic laws in an active work zone, you'll face doubled fines and could lose your license temporarily.

In addition to posted signs, heed the following Pennsylvania safety laws:

- **Cell phones:** Pennsylvania law allows talking on the phone while driving, but texting and emailing are forbidden. The fine for using a mobile device to send or receive messages is $50. Just because it's legal to talk on the phone doesn't mean it's sensible. Use a hands-free device or pull off the road when possible, especially when driving in an unfamiliar area.
- **Seat belts:** Pennsylvania law requires drivers and front-seat passengers to wear a seat belt. Passengers under 18 years old must buckle up even when seated in the back.
- **Child car seats:** Pennsylvania law requires a federally approved child car seat for children under four years old and a booster seat for children four to eight years old.
- **Motorcycle helmets:** Motorcyclists under 21 years old must wear protective headgear. Pennsylvania law allows motorcyclists 21 or older to go without a helmet if they have at least two years of riding experience or have passed a motorcycle safety course approved by the Pennsylvania Department of Transportation or Motorcycle Safety Foundation. The fine for riding without a helmet is $25.

Welcome Centers

State-run welcome centers are located along many major roads into Pennsylvania. Don't pass one up. Welcome centers are stocked with free maps and brochures and staffed by travel specialists. They're generally open 7am-7pm.

From Delaware:

- I-95 north, 0.5 mile north of the PA border

From Maryland:

- I-70 west, 0.5 mile west of the PA border
- I-81 north, 1.5 miles north of the PA border
- I-83 north, 2.5 miles north of the PA border

From New Jersey:

- I-276 west, King of Prussia service plaza of PA Turnpike
- I-78 west, 0.5 mile west of the PA border
- I-80 exit 310, 0.5 mile west of the PA border

From New York:

- I-84 exit 53, 1 mile west of the PA border
- I-81 south, 0.5 mile south of the PA border
- Route 15 south, 7 miles south of the PA border
- I-90 west, 0.5 mile west of the PA border

From Ohio:

- I-80 east, 0.5 mile east of the PA border

From West Virginia:

- I-70 east, 5 miles east of the PA border
- I-79 north, 5 miles north of the PA border

BUS

Greyhound (800/231-2222, www.greyhound.com), the largest intercity bus company in North America, offers service to about 130 locations in Pennsylvania, including Philadelphia, Pittsburgh, Allentown, Altoona, Bethlehem, Erie, Harrisburg, Lancaster, Reading, Scranton, State College, Wilkes-Barre, Williamsport, and York. Traveling by Greyhound is generally more time-consuming than driving because buses make frequent stops, and many trips require transfers. But it is economical, especially if you're traveling alone. As of late 2017, service between Philadelphia and Pittsburgh cost as little as $19 with advance purchase. The trip from Philadelphia to Pittsburgh takes anywhere from 5.75 hours to more than 9 hours, depending on the route as well as the number of stops, layovers, and transfers. Competition from **Megabus** (877/462-6342, www.megabus.com), which offers fares as low as $1, has helped keep prices down (the typical Megabus fare is higher than $1, and there's a $2.50 online booking fee). In Pennsylvania, Megabus provides service to Philadelphia, Pittsburgh, Harrisburg, and State College.

RAIL

Pennsylvania has a rich train heritage—witness the number of tourist railroads, train museums, and rail-trails across the state—but today there's only one choice for passenger service: the National Railroad Passenger Corporation, better known as **Amtrak** (800/872-7245, www.amtrak.com). About a dozen Amtrak routes serve Philadelphia's 30th Street Station, making it one of the busiest intercity passenger rail stations in the country. Rail travel is generally pricier than bus travel, and it's not necessarily faster. The following Amtrak routes include stops in Pennsylvania:

- **Acela Express:** Boston to Washington DC by way of Philadelphia
- **Capitol Limited:** Washington DC to Chicago by way of Pittsburgh
- **Cardinal:** New York to Chicago by way of Philadelphia
- **Carolinian:** New York to Charlotte, North Carolina, by way of Philadelphia
- **Crescent:** New York to New Orleans by way of Philadelphia
- **Keystone:** New York to Harrisburg, with stops including Philadelphia and Lancaster
- **Lake Shore Limited:** New York/Boston to Chicago by way of Erie
- **Northeast Regional:** Boston to points in Virginia by way of Philadelphia

- **Palmetto:** New York to Savannah, Georgia, by way of Philadelphia
- **Pennsylvanian:** New York to Pittsburgh, with stops including Philadelphia, Lancaster, Harrisburg, Altoona, Johnstown, and Latrobe
- **Silver Service:** New York to Miami by way of Philadelphia
- **Vermonter:** northern Vermont to Washington DC by way of Philadelphia

Travel Tips

CONDUCT AND CUSTOMS

Photo Etiquette in Amish Country

It's tempting to take pictures at every turn when visiting Pennsylvania's Amish communities, whose way of dress and way of life are in stark contrast to the mainstream. Exercise self-restraint. Most Amish believe that posing for photographs violates the biblical commandment against graven images. They also see it as a sign of pride—a dirty word in a society that cherishes humility and community. You don't need to agree with their reasons to see the case for restraint. Imagine tourists cruising through your neighborhood, snapping pictures of your house, your vehicles, and your children. Disconcerting, to say the least.

That's not to say that you can't take any photos of their picturesque farmlands, horse-pulled buggies, and one-room schoolhouses. Just be discreet, and don't aim your camera at anyone's face.

Liquor Laws

Pennsylvania's alcohol laws are among the strictest and most befuddling in the country—though they are slowly starting to loosen up.

Vodka, gin, rum, whiskey, and other spirits can only be sold at stores operated by the Pennsylvania Liquor Control Board (PLCB, www.lcb.pa.gov), whose monopoly has made it the largest purchaser of wine and spirits in the United States. PLCB stores also sell wine. The PLCB operates more than 600 locations; its website has a store locator feature. The PLCB chooses which products it sells, and some may find the selection limited. Be aware that some wine and spirits stores are closed on Sunday.

Thirsting for beer? You won't find it in the state-operated stores. Beer can be purchased from licensed bars, restaurants, retailers, and distributors. Distributors generally have better prices but until recently they could only sell by the case or keg. For a six-pack, heading to the nearest bar is usually the most efficient, but not most cost-effective, choice. Some convenience stores (think corner deli, not 7-11) also carry six-packs.

A selection of Pennsylvania supermarkets can now sell beer and wine, but the selections are quite limited.

Per state law, bars and restaurants cannot sell alcohol after 2am. With limited exceptions, it's illegal to bring alcohol into the state. (But between you and me, there's not much chance of getting caught.)

SENIOR TRAVELERS

Pennsylvania has a large elderly population, and senior travelers will find it quite welcoming. Many attractions offer senior discounts, which can be significant. Seniors also enjoy free or discounted public transportation in cities including Philadelphia and Pittsburgh. Discounts aren't necessarily posted, so make a habit of inquiring before paying.

TRAVELERS WITH DISABILITIES

Federal laws protecting the rights of people with disabilities are generally adhered to throughout Pennsylvania, but the historic nature of some attractions makes them inaccessible to wheelchairs. In some parts of Pennsylvania, sidewalks are in such terrible disrepair that they're impassable to wheelchair users. The state and some municipalities have also been slow to install or improve curb ramps at pedestrian intersections.

GAY AND LESBIAN TRAVELERS

Philadelphia, the largest city in Pennsylvania, was one of the first cities in the country to prohibit discrimination based on sexual orientation. It's the site of multiple annual events for the lesbian, gay, bisexual, transgender, and queer (LGBTQ) community, including the largest LGBTQ film festival on the East Coast and one of the largest National Coming Out Day events in the world. Street signs in a busy downtown neighborhood named the Gayborhood sport the colors of the rainbow flag and one intersection is painted with a rainbow crosswalk. The *Philadelphia Gay News* is one of the nation's oldest and most respected LGBTQ newspapers.

In 2017, Philadelphia, Pittsburgh, and Allentown each earned a score of 100 out of 100 on the Human Rights Campaign's Municipal Equality Index, which rates U.S. cities on their inclusivity of LGBTQ people. The town of New Hope in Bucks County, about an hour north of Philadelphia, is also known as a gay-friendly destination. Unfortunately, many parts of Pennsylvania between the cities of Philadelphia and Pittsburgh are not as welcoming.

Health and Safety

MEDICAL SERVICES

Pennsylvania has high-quality health care, but it usually comes at a high price. Visitors from other countries would be wise to purchase international health insurance. Domestic travelers who have health insurance should be aware that some plans will not cover care provided by "out of network" doctors and hospitals.

If you have a medical emergency, dial 911 from any phone. You'll be connected to an operator who can dispatch an ambulance. U.S. law requires hospitals to treat emergency cases regardless of the patient's ability to pay (though patients will be billed for treatment).

EXTREME TEMPERATURES

Pennsylvania can be very hot and humid in summer and very cold in winter. Extremes of temperature are potentially dangerous. Heat-related dangers include heat exhaustion, which is characterized by weakness and dizziness, and heatstroke, which can be deadly. The elderly and those in poor health are particularly vulnerable. The best defense is to drink plenty of water and take it easy. Even healthy young people can suffer heat disorders, often from exercising outside. Seek medical aid if you notice signs of heatstroke, which include lethargy, confusion, and unconsciousness.

In winter, temperatures can dip below 0°F (-18°C). Cold-weather dangers include frostbite, falls on icy sidewalks, and car accidents on icy or snow-covered roads. Protect yourself by dressing appropriately—a coat, hat, gloves, and shoes with good traction are must-haves—and limiting your time outside. If you're going to drive, make sure your vehicle is in good condition and has plenty of gas. Breakdowns are downright scary when the weather is frigid. It's a good idea to invest in all-season tires or winter tires. Clear snow and ice from your vehicle before hitting the road, and drive with caution.

TICKS AND LYME DISEASE

Pennsylvania has one of the highest incidences of Lyme disease in the United States. The disease is transmitted to humans through the bite of infected ticks. Early symptoms include fever, headache, fatigue, and a red rash that resembles a bull's eye. If left untreated, Lyme disease can affect joints, the heart, and the nervous system. The best defense is to reduce your exposure to ticks, which are most active in the warmer months. The U.S. Centers for Disease Control and Prevention advises avoiding wooded and brushy areas; walking in the center of trails; applying an insect repellent with 20-30 percent DEET to clothing and exposed skin; treating clothing and gear with products that contain permethrin; and checking your body, clothing, and gear for ticks. For more information and instructions for tick removal, visit www.cdc.gov/lyme.

Information and Services

MONEY

The U.S. dollar ($) is the only currency accepted in Pennsylvania. Visitors from other countries may be able to purchase U.S. dollars from their bank. Most international airports, including Philadelphia International Airport and Pittsburgh International Airport, have currency exchange counters. Don't wait until you're settled in to exchange currency; exchange companies can be hard to find in U.S. cities. If you have an Automated Teller Machine (ATM) card, you can withdraw U.S. dollars from any ATM in the country. ATMs are ubiquitous in Pennsylvania's larger cities, and you shouldn't have much trouble finding one even in small towns or rural areas. When using an ATM that's not owned by your bank, you may be charged a service fee by both the ATM's bank and your bank.

Credit cards are widely accepted throughout the state. If you're visiting from another country, check with your credit card company about fees for foreign transactions. The U.S. has been slow to convert to EMV cards (cards with chips) from cards with magnetic stripes, but machines that accept chip cards are now common.

CELL PHONES

Cell phone reception is generally strong in urban areas of the state. In rural or mountainous areas, expect some dead zones. Reception is particularly shaky in north-central Pennsylvania. It's a good idea to check your cell phone carrier's coverage in and around areas you plan to visit. You can find coverage maps on most carriers' websites.

Pennsylvania law prohibits texting or emailing while driving.

INTERNET ACCESS

If you want Internet access while traveling, it's best to have a data-enabled mobile device. Internet cafés are virtually unheard of in Pennsylvania, and while wireless networks are numerous, many are password-protected. Hotels and coffee shops are your best bet for finding a public wireless network, though some charge for access. Free wireless access is available at Philadelphia International Airport and Pittsburgh International Airport, on most Greyhound and Megabus trips, and in select Amtrak stations and trains.

MAPS AND TOURIST INFORMATION

Road maps are sold at most gas stations, but if you're not planning to do a lot of driving, they're hardly necessary. Pennsylvania's visitors centers are well stocked with tourist maps, many of which are free. Maps focused on hiking, biking, fishing, boating, or other recreational opportunities are also available at many visitors centers. There are more than a dozen state-run welcome centers near Pennsylvania's borders, and visitors centers operated by local or regional tourism promotion agencies can be found in many popular destinations. In addition to maps, they usually carry a large selection of brochures on area attractions and accommodations. Some offer free wireless Internet access. If you're heading to a national or state park, there's little need to stop at a visitors center en route; you'll find maps on arrival.

Resources

Suggested Reading

HISTORY AND CULTURE

Ellis, Joseph J. *Founding Brothers: The Revolutionary Generation.* Winner of the 2001 Pulitzer Prize for History, this book explores the oft-contentious relationships between America's founding fathers. Read it en route to Philadelphia, where so many of their squabbles played out.

Kraybill, Donald B. *The Amish of Lancaster County.* Donald Kraybill, a professor at Lancaster County's Elizabethtown College and a nationally recognized authority on Anabaptist groups, has authored or edited more than 20 books. This 2008 tome is an easily digestible explanation of the lifestyle of the Lancaster County Amish, complete with full-color photographs.

McCullough, David. *The Johnstown Flood.* First published in 1968, this riveting account of the 1889 flood that killed more than 2,000 people in a Pennsylvania steel town was David McCullough's first book. The Pittsburgh-born historian has since won two Pulitzer Prizes and the Presidential Medal of Freedom.

McIlnay, Dennis P. *The Horseshoe Curve: Sabotage and Subversion in the Railroad City.* This is the gripping story of the Nazi plot to destroy the Pennsylvania Railroad's Horseshoe Curve during World War II. Published in 2007, the book includes eyewitness accounts of the execution of six saboteurs convicted of the failed plot. Author Dennis McIlnay, who lives within a few miles of the targeted section of rail track, delves into the history of the Pennsylvania Railroad and the construction of the curve.

FICTION

Chabon, Michael. *The Mysteries of Pittsburgh* and *Wonder Boys.* Michael Chabon's first two novels are set in Pittsburgh, where the Pulitzer Prize-winning author went to college. The main character in *Wonder Boys* was inspired by one of his professors at the University of Pittsburgh. Both books were adapted into films.

Dillard, Annie. *An American Childhood.* Annie Dillard's enchanting memoir paints a vivid picture of Pittsburgh in the 1950s.

Quick, Matthew. *The Silver Linings Playbook.* Matthew Quick's novel about a man who moves back home while he struggles with mental illness weaves in Philadelphia landmarks and plenty of Philadelphia Eagles lore. Bradley Cooper and Jennifer Lawrence played the main characters in the 2012 movie adaptation.

Shaara, Michael. *The Killer Angels.* Winner of the 1975 Pulitzer Prize for Fiction, this superbly crafted historical novel tells the story of the Battle of Gettysburg. The page-turner was adapted into the 1993 film *Gettysburg,* another excellent treatment of the Civil War's bloodiest battle.

OUTDOORS

Carson, Rachel. *Silent Spring.* Pennsylvania-born biologist and nature writer Rachel Carson has been called the mother of the modern environmental movement—largely because of this 1962 book on the harmful effects of pesticides.

Egan, Timothy. *The Big Burn: Teddy Roosevelt and the Fire that Saved America.* This is the story of a devastating blaze that killed more than 100 firefighters. It's also the story of Gifford Pinchot, America's first forester and one of Pennsylvania's favorite sons.

MAGAZINES

Pennsylvania Heritage. Historians, curators, and archivists contribute to this illustrated magazine, copublished by the Pennsylvania Historical and Museum Commission and the Pennsylvania Heritage Foundation. To receive the quarterly magazine, become a member of the Heritage Foundation at www.paheritage.org or by calling 866/823-6539. Individual issues can be purchased at http://shoppaheritage.com.

Pennsylvania Magazine. Showcasing the state's places, people, and events since 1981, *Pennsylvania Magazine* is published six times a year. Request a free issue or subscribe at www.pa-mag.com or by calling 800/537-2624.

Internet Resources

TRAVEL

Pennsylvania Tourism Office
www.visitpa.com

Pennsylvania's official tourism website provides information on countless attractions, plus trip ideas for those not sure where to start.

HISTORY

Pennsylvania Historical & Museum Commission
www.phmc.pa.gov

The website of Pennsylvania's official history agency is a good starting point for information on the people and events that shaped the commonwealth.

www.explorepahistory.com

WITF, Harrisburg's PBS and NPR affiliate, organizes this website in conjunction with the Pennsylvania Historical and Museum Commission. You could spend days engrossed in the stories behind the 2,000-odd historical markers that dot the state.

CULTURE

Amish Studies
http://groups.etown.edu/amishstudies

This site, maintained by the Young Center for Anabaptist and Pietist Studies at Lancaster County's Elizabethtown College, answers frequently asked questions about the Amish.

OUTDOORS

Pennsylvania Bureau of State Parks
www.dcnr.pa.gov/stateparks

This site provides detailed descriptions of Pennsylvania's state parks, which numbered 121 at last count. The companion reservation site, http://pennsylvaniastateparks.reserveamerica.com, allows you to search for parks by region and amenities such as white-water boating and mountain biking.

National Parks in Pennsylvania
www.nps.gov/pa

About 30 of Pennsylvania's historic sites, scenic trails, and river corridors are part of the national park system. Visit this site for a comprehensive listing.

Pennsylvania Trails
www.explorepatrails.com

Run by the state Department of Conservation and Natural Resources, this site allows outdoorsy types to find and share information on thousands of miles of land and water trails.

Pennsylvania Fish & Boat Commission
www.fishandboat.com

Purchase a fishing license, register a boat, read up on regulations, or submit a request for the state agency's free publications. The site boasts a number of interactive maps designed for anglers and boaters.

Pennsylvania Game Commission
www.pgc.pa.gov

Hunters can find information on seasons, bag limits, and everything else they need to know on the website of Pennsylvania's wildlife management agency.

LODGING

Pennsylvania Campground Owners Association
www.pacamping.com

This trade association represents more than 200 individually owned and operated campgrounds. Search its online directory, download a digital version, or request a free copy of the printed version.

Pennsylvania Association of Bed & Breakfast Inns
www.painns.com

This is a handy directory of bed-and-breakfasts, inns, boutique hotels, and other unique accommodations represented by the PA Association of Bed & Breakfast Inns.

Index

A

B

C

D

E

F

G

H

I

INDEX

J

K

L

M

N

QR

S

T

UVWXYZ

List of Maps

Photo Credits

Title page photo: © F11photo | Dreamstime.com

page 4 © Dave Newman | Dreamstime.com; page 5 © Tupungato | Dreamstime.com; page 6 (top left) © National Aviary / VisitPittsburgh, (top right) © Rachel Vigoda, (bottom) © F11photo | Dreamstime.com; page 7 (top) © Kiya/123rf.com, (bottom left) © Delmas Lehman | Dreamstime.com, (bottom right) © Americanspirit | Dreamstime.com; page 8 © Justin Blasi; page 9 (top) © Harry Collins | Dreamstime.com, (bottom left) © Pennsylvania's Americana Region, (bottom right) © Kenneth Keifer | Dreamstime.com; page 10 © Justin Blasi; page 13 © M.Edlow for Visit Philadelphia; page 14 © Justin Blasi; page 15 © Ekaterina Hashbarger | Dreamstime.com; page 18 © James Dugan/123rf.com; page 21 (top) © B. Krist for Visit Philadelphia, (bottom) © M. Edlow for Visit Philadelphia; page 23 © Visions Of America LLC/123rf.com; page 27 © Justin Blasi; page 28 © M. Fischetti for Visit Philadelphia; page 30 © Justin Blasi; page 31 © Rachel Vigoda; page 33 © R. Kennedy for Visit Philadelphia; page 38 © R. Kennedy for Visit Philadelphia; page 39 © M. Edlow for Visit Philadelphia; page 40 © Zrfphoto | Dreamstime.com; page 41 © M. Edlow for Visit Philadelphia; page 44 © Justin Blasi; page 45 © Justin Blasi; page 47 © R. Kennedy for Visit Philadelphia; page 48 © G. Widman for Visit Philadelphia; page 49 © C. Smyth; page 59 © M. Edlow for Visit Philadelphia; page 62 © Justin Blasi; page 70 © Rachel Vigoda; page 82 © R. Kennedy for Visit Philadephia; page 94 (top) © Destination Gettsyburg, (bottom) © Tanyabird777 | Dreamstime.com; page 95 © Rachel Vigoda; page 100 © Georgesheldon | Dreamstime.com; page 103 © DiscoverLancaster.com; page 105 © Justin Blasi; page 106 © Lei Xu | Dreamstime.com; page 110 © DiscoverLancaster.com; page 112 © DiscoverLancaster.com / Coy Butler; page 118 © DiscoverLancaster.com; page 119 © Rachel Vigoda; page 122 © Pennsylvania's Americana Region; page 124 © Pennsylvania's Americana Region; page 126 © Justin Blasi; page 132 © VisitHersheyHarrisburg.org; page 136 © VisitHersheyHarrisburg.org; page 138 © VisitHersheyHarrisburg.org; page 139 © VisitHersheyHarrisburg.org; page 140 © VisitHersheyHarrisburg.org; page 141 © VisitHersheyHarrisburg.org; page 143 © York County Convention & Visitors Bureau; page 145 © York County Convention & Visitors Bureau; page 146 © Destination Gettsyburg; page 149 © Destination Gettsyburg; page 152 © Destination Gettsyburg; page 153 © Destination Gettsyburg; page 155 © Destination Gettsyburg; page 156 © Destination Gettsyburg; page 158 (top) © Justin Blasi, (bottom) © Jon Bilous | Dreamstime.com; page 159 © Pocono Mountains Visitors Bureau; page 162 © Pocono Mountains Visitors Bureau; page 167 © Pocono Mountains Visitors Bureau; page 170 © Pocono Mountains Visitors Bureau; page 175 © Pocono Mountains Visitors Bureau; page 177 © Pocono Mountains Visitors Bureau; page 178 © Pocono Mountains Visitors Bureau; page 180 © Pocono Mountains Visitors Bureau; page 182 © Pocono Mountains Visitors Bureau; page 183 © Pocono Mountains Visitors Bureau; page 185 © Pocono Mountains Visitors Bureau; page 186 © Cheryl Fleishman | Dreamstime.com; page 189 © Justin Blasi; page 190 © Pocono Mountains Visitors Bureau; page 192 (top) © Visit Pittsburgh, (bottom) © David Reid/Visit Pittsburgh; page 193 © Rachellynn Schoen/Visit Pittsburgh; page 196 © Christian Hinkle | Dreamstime.com; page 200 © Phil Scalia/Visit Pittsburgh; page 201 © Senator John Heinz History Center; page 203 © Justin Blasi; page 204 © Kurt Miller; page 205 © National Aviary/Visit Pittsburgh; page 210 © Carnegie Museum of Art/Visit Pittsburgh; page 211 © Jeff Greenberg/Visit Pittsburgh; page 214 © Dave DiCello; page 222 © Justin Blasi; page 223 © Justin Blasi; page 227 © Justin Blasi; page 231 © LeMont Pittsburgh; page 236 © Justin Blasi; page 237 © Inn on Negley; page 241 © Justin Blasi; page 242 © Christopher Little, courtesy of the Western Pennsylvania Conservancy; page 245 © Laurel Highlands Visitors Bureau; page 251 © Nemacolin Woodlands Resort; page 256 (top) © Visit Penn State, (bottom) © Tupungato | Dreamstime.com; page 257 © Cmoulton | Dreamstime.com; page 262 © Laceduplutheran | Dreamstime.com; page 266 © The Alleghenies ; page 267 © Zrfphoto | Dreamstime.com; page 273 © Visit Penn State; page 274 © Visit Penn State; page 280 © Visit Penn State; page 289 © The Alleghenies ; page 290 © Cmoulton | Dreamstime.com; page 294 (top) © Zrfphoto | Dreamstime.com, (bottom) © Visit Erie; page 295 © Visit Erie; page 300 © Visit Erie; page 302 © Paul Lemke | Dreamstime.com; page 303 © Visit Erie; page 305 © R. Frank / Visit Erie; page 313 © Jennifer Martinek | Dreamstime.com; page 320 (top) © The PA Wilds, (bottom) © Zrfphoto | Dreamstime.com; page 321 © The Punxsutawney Groundhog Club; page 324 © ANF Visitors Bureau; page 328 © ANF Visitors Bureau; page 329 © PA Great Outdoors Visitors Bureau; page 331 © PA Great Outdoors Visitors Bureau; page 334 © Glendorn; page 336 © Visit Potter-Tioga; page 338 © Visit Potter-Tioga; page 339

© Michael Ver Sprill | Dreamstime.com; page 349 © James Kirkikis | Dreamstime.com; page 352 © PA Great Outdoors Visitors Bureau; page 354 © PA Great Outdoors Visitors Bureau; page 357 (top) © J. Fusco for Visit Philadelphia, (bottom) © Borg Enders | Dreamstime.com; page 371 (top) © F11photo | Dreamstime.com, (bottom) © Rachel Vigoda

Acknowledgments

Living in Philadelphia, I'm tucked away in the southeast corner of the giant rectangle that is Pennsylvania. I wouldn't have been able to run around the state making sure all my knowledge and opinions were up to date without the help of several tourism reps, including Kristin Wenger, Joel Cliff, Cara Schneider, Courtney Smyth, Carl Whitehill, Lisa Haggerty, Kelly Shannon, Molly Moore, Rick Dunlap, Jennifer Fleck, Mark Ickes, Andrew Staub, Linda Devlin, Morgan Christopher, Dave Sherman, and Christine Temple.

Thank yous are also in order for the team at Avalon Travel: Nikki Ioakimedes, who brought me on board for this project and answered my many questions; Leah Gordon, who guided me through writing the manuscript and answered even more questions; the very helpful production and graphics coordinators Elizabeth Jang, Krista Anderson, and Suzanne Albertson; and map editor Kat Bennett, who somehow understood all my little notations.

Another dose of gratitude goes to Tasha Vigoda for, among other things, reading my initial proposal for this book and catching my typos.

And thank you to Justin Blasi, for joining me on research trips, taking photos, keeping me calm while I panicked about deadlines, and, as always, doing the grocery shopping.